Konstantinos Kapparis
Prostitution in the Ancient Greek World

Konstantinos Kapparis

Prostitution in the Ancient Greek World

—

DE GRUYTER

ISBN 978-3-11-065898-9
e-ISBN (PDF) 978-3-11-055795-4
e-ISBN (EPUB) 978-3-11-055680-3

Library of Congress Cataloging-in-Publication Data
A CIP catalog record for this book has been applied for at the Library of Congress.

Bibliographic information published by the Deutsche Nationalbibliothek
The Deutsche Nationalbibliothek lists this publication in the Deutsche Nationalbibliografie;
detailed bibliographic data are available on the Internet at http://dnb.dnb.de.

© 2019 Walter de Gruyter GmbH, Berlin/Boston
This volume is text- and page-identical with the hardback published in 2018.
Cover image: Jean-Léon Gérôme, Phryne revealed before the Areopagus,
Hamburger Kunsthalle (© Wikimedia Commons)
Printing and binding: CPI books GmbH, Leck
♾ Printed on acid-free paper
Printed in Germany

www.degruyter.com

Foreword

The seminal study which started this project was completed over the Christmas break of 1987, during my first year as a PhD student in the University of Glasgow, under the supervision of D.M. MacDowell. This early study had limited objectives. My main goal was to provide some background for the numerous issues related to prostitution in the speech *Against Neaira*. My understanding of the subject expanded in subsequent years as I was preparing the commentary on the speech, and by the time that project was completed it had become apparent that a comprehensive study of prostitution in the ancient Greek World was sorely needed. I started collecting materials, primary and secondary literature, and began taking notes for a future study, and this process continued for a number of years in the margins of other projects. When the number of pages with notes exceeded 3000, it seemed that it was time to channel this vast material into a readable account. The challenges have been many, most important of which was the extent to which one could engage the vast literature on the subject, primary and secondary, and still produce a reasonably sized volume. The second major challenge was to decide the timescale. I felt that a comprehensive study was necessary, but a full account of the whole of the ancient world until Christianization would be unrealistic. The solution was to place emphasis on the classical period, from which we have the most important, interesting and remarkable evidence. I dedicated one chapter to the archaic period, and a concluding chapter to the postclassical world and the transition into Christianity, while the core of the study deals with the classical world with frequent references to post-classical sources or historical facts, when these are necessary to complete the picture.

The bulk of the research for this volume was completed in the summer of 2015, with a few important exceptions such as the inclusion of material from the recent book of Edward Cohen. Different aspects of ancient prostitution explored in the pages of this study have received very different levels of scholarly attention. While one could never hope to engage closely with the entire body of secondary literature on gender, masculinity and the legal aspects of male prostitution explored in chapter 4 within the space of this volume, there is hardly any scholarly work on the education of prostitutes explored in chapter 2, and there is only limited research into the economics of ancient prostitution explored in chapter 5, or the relationships of prostitutes with famous men discussed in chapter 3. In this respect the level of engagement with modern studies may at times seem uneven. Nonetheless, the focus of this book has been firmly set upon the vast body of ancient evidence. My primary objective has been to make sense of the testimony of ancient authors and reconstruct the emerging picture as accurately, faithfully, and without prejudice or judgment, as possible.

I am hoping that the final product is sufficiently comprehensive to provide substantial commentary on the primary sources, reflect the tenor of the lively debate on the numerous issues discussed in this volume, and offer a platform for further research and scholarly discussion in the important and yet understudied fields of the history of prostitution, gender studies, women's history, study of masculinity, and the social and legal history of the ancient world as a whole. I also hope that it would provide a reference for better understanding of some difficult social issues which are still heavily debated in our times. Considering that many of our attitudes on issues like prostitution, sexuality, marriage, monogamy, family values, or same, opposite or non-binary sex relations, were formed within the timeframe discussed in this book before becoming an integral part of the cultural heritage of the Western world, a better understanding of the formation of these ideas can be enlightening for the modern debate, as it can challenge assumptions long taken for granted and encourage free and unbiased thinking.

The full list of scholars who have provided valuable input over the years would be too long to include here. I owe many people a large debt of gratitude. However, even the shortest list needs to include Madeleine Henry and Allison Glazebrook for some very productive discussions, and Tim Johnson who shared with me important unpublished work on the *paraklausithyron*. I owe many thanks to colleagues at the University of Florida, and especially our two successive chairs, Victoria Pagan and Mary Ann Eaverly, who made sure that I had the necessary time to complete the project in its final stages, and the faculty of the Center for Greek Studies at the University of Florida, Robert Wagman, Gonda Van Steen, Eleni Bozia, Tom Kostopoulos, Andrew Nichols and Nick Kontaridis for the generous funding of various parts of this project over the years, and their friendship and support. Last but not least, I am very grateful to Ken Silverman for intercepting many errors during proofreading, and the highly professional publishing team of Walter De Gruyter, Serena Pirrotta, Katharina Legutke, Antonia Schrader and Marco Michele Acquafredda for their support during the production of this volume.

Contents

Introduction

The debate on prostitution is as ancient as it is modern. It is one of the most controversial social issues of our times, and has been so for a very long time in history. Rarely can an issue unite natural ideological opposites in the way radical feminists and Christian fundamentalists unite in opposition to prostitution,[1] while few issues can be as divisive as the legalization of prostitution. The controversy is only expected to get more acrimonious as greater mobility, more relaxed sexual mores, and easier access to sex-workers through online networks, combined with increasing social isolation and the break-down of traditional family structures, create fertile grounds for prostitution to flourish in the 21st century in new forms and settings. The history of prostitution is not only about the past, since our current ideological positions rest squarely upon the foundations of arguments and norms developed in the first two centuries of the Christian era, within the wider framework of Greek and Roman individual, family and community values, social paradigms, laws, traditions and customs.

The evidence for prostitution in ancient Greek literature is vast, cuts across time periods, and transgresses the boundaries of genres. The reason for such riches is the central position which prostitution held at the core of ancient Greek life and culture, and the earliest evidence is almost as old as written Greek literature. It goes back to the early days of Greek Lyric, the time of Archilochos of Paros - this irreverent, yet revered figure of Greek letters, who is our earliest source for prostitution in the Aegean. The term πόρνη (*porne*), which would remain the primary term for prostitute in the Greek language all the way to the present day, makes its first appearance in Archilochos. The alternative term "ἑταίρα" (*hetaira*: companion), essentially a euphemism used primarily, but not exclusively, for an upper-end prostitute, does not appear in this sense before the middle of the 5th c.[2]

---

1 For the feminist anti-prostitution stance see for example Barry 1995.
2 Before the time of Herodotos *hetaira* retains its original meaning "friend, companion" (see e.g. Sappho fr. 142 and 160 Lobel - Page; Pindar Py. 3.18 *parthenoi hetairai* "virgin friends"). Herodotos 2.135 is the earliest source speaking about the epaphroditoi hetairai "lovely hetairai" of Naukratis, unambiguously referring to the famous hetairai of the city. Elke Hartmann (2011: 141 and n. 54) astutely observes that the *hetaira* was the woman sitting with the men (*hetairoi*) in the symposion as their dining companion (cf. D.59.24: συνέπινεν καὶ συνεδείπνει ἐναντίον πολλῶν Νέαιρα αὐτῇ ὡς {ἂν} ἑταίρα οὖσα), in contrast to musicians, dancers and other prostitute entertainers. Hartmann is convinced that the term *hetaira* originated in the archaic symposion. This is likely but not provable, since there is not a single attested instance where "ἑταίρα" has this meaning in the archaic Lyric.

DOI 10.1515/9783110557954-000

The distinction between the two terms is not rigid. Contrary to a common misconception, the term *porne* does not refer only to low-end prostitutes but to all prostitutes; all prostitutes are *pornai* in Greek. This is the all-encompassing, generic term throughout the history of the Greek language. Other terms are more specialized, primarily referring to specific types of prostitutes: *hetaira* would refer to an upper-end prostitute, and is often translated in the literature as "hetaira" or "companion"; αὐλητρίς (*auletris*) would refer to a prostitute-flute player; χαμαιτύπη (*chamaitype*) would refer to a low-brow brothel or street prostitute, and so on. The term πόρνη often indicates a low-end prostitute, but only in the absence of a more defining typology (let's say, someone who is not a hetaira, or a flute-player, or a street-walker, but still practices prostitution, would be considered a plain, downright whore at the lowest end of the market). Greek has over 200 words to indicate the broad spectrum of male and female prostitution in all its diversity. A more detailed study of these terms has been published elsewhere; here it is important to stress that the vocabulary of prostitution is a continuum, where terminological distinctions are relative to the intention of the speaker, the form of prostitution practiced, and to stylistic and literary purposes, rather than firm and clearly defined semantic boundaries.[3]

The meanings of these words were never a constant in time either; they kept changing as the historical parameters of ancient prostitution continued to evolve. For example, in later antiquity the term *hetaira* lost its luster and was increasingly used to indicate common prostitutes, as a mere synonym of *porne*. Eventually, in the Byzantine period, its usage drastically declined, as distinctions between luxury *hetairai* and common whores were no longer culturally significant.

The sources and their reliability

We do not have the luxury of firm certainties about the early days of prostitution, as the authenticity of some of the works attributed to Archilochos has come under suspicion. A few references to venal sex in Anacreon, and some scattered words for "prostitute" in the fragments of Hipponax, offer very limited additional information. Sappho, a towering figure in any study of eroticism and sexuality in Greek Lyric, has a much cleaner image than her male predecessors, but we may be missing something important from her work too. Her stinging

---

3 See Kapparis 2011: 222–255. For a summary of the scholarship on the primary terms of prostitution see McClure 2003a: 9–26, and Henry - Glazebrook 2011: 4–8.

attacks on the hetaira Rhodopis are reported by ancient authors, most notably Herodotos and Poseidonios, and yet we can find no trace of them in the fragments of Sappho. This is why some scholars believe that the entire story about the attacks of Sappho on Rhodopis is fictional, while others are prepared to put faith in these reports and accept that Sappho wrote scolding poetry directed at Rhodopis. Also difficult in its interpretation is a fragment from a Pindaric skolion for Xenophon of Corinth, which has often been considered as evidence for the existence of sacred prostitution in the city.[4] The last major name from that era, the poet, lawgiver and statesman, Solon, was credited in later centuries with the establishment of legal prostitution in Athens. His surviving works can provide valuable evidence about his legislative program and its intentions, but say nothing about prostitution. The relevant evidence comes from sources which are at least 200 years later than his time, and for that reason rather questionable.

At the beginning of the classical period Herodotos was the first among our sources to provide substantial information about prostitution in his famous story about Rhodopis, the first hetaira to be known by name in history. Herodotos also offers evidence about a communal effort to build a monument in Lydia which was dedicated to a prostitute, and is a critically important source for the controversy over the existence of sacred prostitution in the Middle East. In recent years the evidence of Herodotos on this matter has been discredited as a misunderstanding of eastern customs. Thucydides, the second major historian of the classical period, has nothing to say about social issues. They were of no interest, and seemingly of no consequence to his perception of the Peloponnesian war as a masculine power-game, although there are a few marginal discussions important for our purposes - like for example his discussion about the Tyrannicides and the undoubtedly fictional hetaira Leaina. The third major name in the historiography of the classical period, Xenophon, is a significant source not only for his discussion of gender and family issues in the *Economics*, but also for his accounts of the dialogue between Socrates and Theodote, and the presence of prostitute entertainers in the classical symposium.

Among the rest of the Greek historians, Timaios and Theopompos have several interesting tales to tell, like for example the one about the lustful lifestyle and the wild parties of the Etruscans. This narrative is crucially important for our understanding of Attic vase iconography and images of prostitution and sexuality in vases painted in the 6th and the first quarter of the 5th c. for the Etruscan market. Ptolemy VIII provides significant details about the mistresses

---

4 fr. 122 Snell; see the discussion in Ch. 1.1.

of his predecessors, the monarchs of Hellenistic Egypt, and the evolution of high-end prostitution into a practice with rather undefined boundaries between the sex-worker and the mistress / concubine, in the third and second century BC. Many more tales of depravity, and stories about prostitutes and their lovers can be found in Greek historiography all the way to the Byzantine period. Among early Byzantine historians Prokopios has important information about prostitution in later antiquity in his tales about Theodora, the wife and empress of Justinian. I am convinced that the entire *Anecdota* is a literary composition bearing more resemblance to Lucian's humorous accounts of historical and literary personalities, than to a historical biography of one of the most powerful emperors ever to sit on the Byzantine throne and his consort. As such it borrows and reshuffles elements from previous literature, some of which is probably lost to us, combining them with contemporary facts, and if read with sufficient caution it can serve as a significant source for both the time of Justinian and previous historical periods. Emperor Constantine VII Porphyrogennetos, who often borrows from lost sources, also contains useful information, and his eye-witness account of the monument of Boidion at Chalcedon is important for the history of this famous landmark.

Attic oratory is an even more substantial source for the history of prostitution in the classical period. Some of the famous speeches like the speech of Apollodoros *Against Neaira* or Aeschines *Against Timarchos* have already been used extensively in modern scholarship as significant sources for social history and the study of gender and sexuality. Notwithstanding the significance of these sources, I have suggested caution, as both speeches are politically motivated, and the high-pitched rhetoric in them should not be mistaken for contemporary Athenian morality. Since I have published independent commentaries on both these speeches explaining in greater detail my views regarding their reliability as historical sources, here I have limited myself to specific points related to the numerous discussions for which these speeches are important sources, while the reader could always refer to these commentaries for a more complete assessment.[5] Several other speeches, like Lysias 3 and 4, are important sources for legal and social aspects of prostitution in the classical period, while some of the fragments of the Attic Orators, as preserved in later rhetoricians and lexicographers (like the poor remains of the famous speech of Hypereides in defense of Phryne, the two speeches *Against Aristagora*, or the prosecution speech against Philonides for his violent assault on the hetaira

---

5 For the speech *Against Neaira* see Kapparis 1999, and for the speech *Against Timarchos* see Wolpert - Kapparis 2011.

Nais) should also be treated as significant sources. Additional scattered references in the Attic Orators, and themes inspired from Attic Oratory in the declamations of later antiquity, offer supplemental materials, and all these sources
have been used with the necessary circumspection.

Attic comedy and its heirs supplement the evidence of the historians with a
wealth of information. Aristophanes, the most extensively preserved Greek
comic poet, offers us glimpses of prostitution as it was practiced in Athens in
the third quarter of the 5th c. The references in Aristophanes are sporadic, compared to New Comedy, partly because of a difference in genre, but also because
the era of the Attic hetaira as we know it from the plays of Menander, Diphilos,
Apollodoros, Plautus and Terence, was still at its infancy in the last quarter of
the 5th c. Aristophanes mentions a few brothels around Attica, names several
prostitutes and prostitute entertainers, and contains one of the earliest explicit
references to male prostitution, with an old woman hiring a youth for sexual
services. *Wealth*, the last of his surviving plays, contains information about
prostitution in Corinth at the beginning of the fourth century, a time when the
Athenian high-end market had not yet recovered from the trauma of the Peloponnesian war and Corinth was the primary hub, where wealthy men from the
whole of Greece arrived for some good time with the city's pricy hetairai. The
poets of Old Comedy reveal rich diversity in the lower end of Athenian prostitution, and without a doubt our understanding of the common prostitute would
have been so much richer if more of Old Comedy had been preserved.

Dramatic changes take place as we move towards Middle Comedy, because
the era of the Attic hetaira has arrived. As Athens is gradually recovering and
through renewed capitalist enterprise regaining its primacy among southern
Greek states, Corinthian hetairai begin to move to Athens, or to travel between
the two cities and serve customers in both places. Their arrival further stimu-
lates the local market and now Athenian women also enter the trade. The works
of Middle Comedy certainly reflect this geographic and cultural shift. Many of
these plays are inspired from the famous hetairai of the time, and a fair number
are named after them. Since we do not have any of the plays in its entirety, it is
impossible to tell how much they actually preserved of the real person after
whom they were named. Nonetheless, even with these limitations, the fragments of Middle Comedy substantially contribute to our understanding of the
Attic hetaira.

New Comedy, in some ways, enhances our understanding of the hetaira,
but there are certain drawbacks. Unlike Middle Comedy, which has been preserved only in fragmentary form, we have several well-preserved plays of New
Comedy by Menander and Roman adaptations of Greek plays by Plautus and

Terence. They tell us much about perceptions of the hetaira in the late classical and early Hellenistic period. However, besides the fictional character of this evidence, one of its major drawbacks is that there is a narrow focus upon the upper-end hetaira. Rarely would New Comedy have an interest in anyone below that golden standard; lower end prostitutes are infrequently mentioned, and even then they are completely marginal to the plots. The other major drawback is that New Comedy is highly stylized, which means that the images of life found in these plays are far less realistic and many a time built around literary topoi, such as the good hetaira, the ruthless hetaira, the cunning hetaira and the pseudo-hetaira. These stereotypical representations of hetairai are repeated from play to play, albeit with some interesting variations, and one has to be very cautious when it comes to a realistic assessment of this information, as the hold of those topoi to historical reality is often tenuous. Moreover, the Latin adaptations need to be read with extra caution as it is not always easy to tell the extent to which they are faithful to the Greek original, and how much of a contemporary Roman element has slipped into their plots. One good example would be the brothel of Ballio in the Pseudolus of Plautus: although the scene might have some elements based on the original play, the event which offers the opportunity to describe the brothel - that is, the birthday of Ballio himself - is a very un-Greek concept, as the Greeks did not celebrate birthdays. Thus the basic premise for the entire scene is Roman, and one wonders how many of the other details in that scene would lead us in the wrong direction, if we were trying to use the brothel of Ballio to reconstruct the realities of brothels in the Greek world.

When the goldmine of Greek Comedy dried up in the Roman period, it continued to feed humorous accounts in antiquarians, philosophers and historiographers for centuries after the extinction of Attic comedy. Authors of later antiquity revisited Attic comedy to find inspiration and information about the famous hetairai of the classical period. The selection and adaptation of this material is very eclectic, but still significant as they had so much more of Attic comedy than we do. For example, what we know about the plays of Middle Comedy dedicated or inspired by hetairai has reached us indirectly through authors of later antiquity such as Athenaios. In particular, the 13th book of the Deipnosophists contains numerous citations from the poets of Old and Middle comedy, and also draws from late classical or early Hellenistic authors like Machon and Lynkeus, both of whom took a great deal of interest in the classical hetaira and the sympotic literature of that period. Thus, we owe to Athenaios whatever little we have from these fascinating authors and most of the comic production of the classical period. Athenaios has also preserved for us numerous extracts from historians and Atthidographers, the bulk of whose work is now lost, as he was searching through the body of ancient historiography for information about the classical hetaira.

The fictional epistolography of later antiquity scavenged the works of Greek Comedy and Historiography just as much, looking for suitable themes which could be developed into epistolary tales. New Comedy, with its mildly amusing plots and soapy stories was naturally more appealing to the epistolographers, but suitable material could be found anywhere, even in sources as unexpected as the medical records of the ancient physicians. Aristainetos for example, utilizes a famous Hippocratic passage about an induced abortion in early pregnancy performed on a prostitute-entertainer, a musician brought to the physician by her mistress who was worried that a pregnancy would devalue her. The epistolographers of later antiquity have reassembled themes and images of prostitution, which would be decidedly out of touch with contemporary moral standards in their world. In the times of Alciphron and Aristainetos, Christianity was asserting its dominance through Ecumenical Councils, while the era of the Attic hetaira and the images of merry symposia, with guests having insightful conversations with hetairai over dinner, or sexy frolicking with the entertainers, was a nostalgic vision of a past long gone. This is probably why the fictional epistolography of later antiquity keeps looking back towards the golden era of the Attic hetaira and a freer more joyous world where beauty, sexuality, jealousy, love, risqué games, partying, dancing and eroticism were celebrated. Among the epistolographers, Alciphron relies more on themes from comedy and historiography, while Aristainetos has a broader range of sources from which he draws inspiration to produce an academic synthesis of disparate elements.

The last epistolographer who draws extensively from the classical tradition is Theophylaktos Simokattes, the well-known 7th century Byzantine historian straddling the boundary between the ancient and the medieval world. While his fictional epistles are reminiscent of some of the nostalgia and themes found in Alciphron and Aristainetos, they also contain some of the dark, humorous cynicism which would sound very familiar to readers of Byzantine texts, but almost alien to those better acquainted with ancient Greek authors. Important information about the transition from pagan liberalism to Christian rigidity with regards to attitudes towards prostitution can be found in Christian authors, but this is not the only kind of information that we can find in the voluminous works of authors like Clement, Origen, Tertullian, Augustine or John Chrysostom. They took a great deal of interest in pagan decadence, and as they wrote abundantly condemning the excesses of the pagan world, they unwittingly preserved for us a wealth of information about ancient prostitutes often drawn from sources now lost to us.

Several other literary genres and individual authors offer additional information about prostitution, but in a less concentrated order. Among these the epigrams of the Greek Anthology sometimes can offer valuable information as they are drawing their themes from sources now lost to us. Composers of epigrams often sought inspiration in authors like Menander and Diphilos, or their descendants, and in this respect they can be used as evidence with a great deal of caution, since they preserve for us not first-hand evidence but rather the memory of lost sources, authors and themes. Philosophy is another source which can provide important evidence but still needs to be used with caution. The authors of the classical period such as Plato, Aristotle, Xenophon, the literature about the Cynics and the Cyrenaics, and perhaps to some degree the Pythagoreans, the Epicurians and the Stoics, can enhance our knowledge and understanding of prostitution in the classical period, but in a rather patchy fashion; and, important as this information may be, we always need to be very alert, because many a time philosophers cited information, sources, materials and customs as it suited their own purposes, and made such evidence subservient to their argument. Information about prostitution can be found almost everywhere in Greek literature. Unexpectedly casual references here and there contain important pieces of evidence, which we do not really have from more concentrated or significant sources, and for this reason I have left no stone unturned while hunting for evidence throughout the body of Greek literature.

Beyond literary sources, inscriptions might help us with a few details, especially the graffiti which praise the beauty of a boy or a girl, some written on walls and some on vase paintings. The extent to which these graffiti can be trusted as historical sources is a highly controversial issue and I am inclined to agree with other studies that their importance as sources for the history of prostitution is rather limited.[6] Vase iconography has been extensively used in the scholarly discussion about prostitution, especially in the past 30 years. A cautious approach is necessary here too, since the interpretation of the surviving images is far from straightforward. Vase iconography is an artistic rather than a photographic representation of the past. Many a time it offers stunning glimpses into the sexual fantasies of the creators and buyers of this art. How much of an image is fantasy, to what extent these images are created to match the tastes of the specific market for which most of the surviving vases were created (in this case, the Etruscan market of the late sixth and early fifth century), and what each individual artist wanted his audience to read into this image are complex topics which do not have easy answers. Confusing sexual fantasy with reality

---

6 See the discussion in Ch. 6.2.

could lead us astray, and this is why it is necessary to place these images in context, to the extent that this is possible since the bulk of literary sources on the subject comes from a later period and may not reflect accurately the social realities of the 6th and early 5th c.

I am not convinced that there is a lot of new evidence to be found in vase iconography not known to us from literary sources. Most of what these images represent we recognize because we have read about it in some author or another, and those elements which are not familiar from literary sources generate more questions instead of offering confident answers. Sometimes, however, vase iconography can offer stunning visual confirmation of elements which we have read in literary sources. Sometimes it can help us interpret literary evidence with more clarity, intrigue us by making surprising suggestions, and compel us to go back to the literary sources for a second reading with a fresh perspective. Therefore it is a useful investigative tool, but moreover, beyond any practical uses it is a glimpse into the past, direct, unaffected by time, and fascinating no matter what it represents or how useful it can be.

Ultimately there is no shortcut and no easy way out. Every piece of information - a literary source, an inscription, an image on a vase, a monument, a house, or some other kind of material evidence from the past - needs to be critically analyzed, collated with other pieces of information, and combined along with everything else, to add to a painstaking reconstruction of the history of prostitution in the ancient Greek world.

Histories of Prostitution in the 19th and 20th century

The first significant study in the modern era was the article of K. Schneider in the *Real Encyclopedie*, published in 1913. Schneider outlined that prostitution in the ancient Greek world was a complex phenomenon with a wide array of types and categories, and was the first to generate much of the terminology still in use. He believed that the boundaries from one category to the next were much more fixed than what is generally accepted today, and some of the rigidity of his definitions can still be traced in modern studies. He also offered the first inventory of hetairai to be compiled in the modern era. After 20 years Paul Brandt, publishing under the pseudonym Hans Licht, discussed in his book *Sexual Life in Ancient Greece* several important aspects of prostitution adding to the account of Schneider.

More research was published at an accelerated pace since the 1970's. Several article collections on women in ancient Greek society, like for example the volumes *Goddesses, Whores, Wives and Slaves: Women in Classical Antiquity* edited by Sarah Pomeroy in 1975, or *Women in Antiquity New Assessments* edited by Richard Hawley 20 years later, touched upon the subject of the female prostitute as the antithesis to the wife. For Eva Keuls this antithesis was central to her argument that men and women had an antagonistic relationship in classical Athens. Keuls in a militant 1980's spirit constructs a model of a split psyche based on a series of antitheses (men vs. women; hetaira vs. wife, sex vs. respectability). This model has largely been abandoned in more recent studies, as more nuanced and precise approaches to these issues have been proposed. Carola Reinsberg's study *Ehe, Hetärentum und Knabenliebe im antiken Griechenland* published in 1984 upheld the sharp contrast between wife and hetaira, and in many ways was a carrier of orthodoxies dominant in the 1980's but surpassed in later years.[7] However, her thorough study of the vase iconography related to prostitution remains valuable. Chronologically and culturally close to the previous studies was the book of Violaine Vanoyeke *La prostitution en Grèce et à Rome*, published in 1990. This modest monograph was heavily criticized for inaccuracies and major misunderstandings,[8] and had almost no impact in subsequent literature.

Much of the literature produced in the 70's, 80's and early 90's viewed the Athenian woman as the passive victim of history, effaced and deprived of all personality, almost of all the joys of living, locked away in dark quarters and only leaving the house on rare occasions. As a result, all female figures who either appear nude in vase iconography or seem to be having some kind of fun, like drinking wine, dancing or singing, were considered to be hetairai, for respectable women, we were told, could never be portrayed as nude in public. A change to his very dark, pessimistic and, one might think, very northern image of the Greek woman, was spearheaded in the 1990's by Sue Blundell, Christine Schnurr-Redford, and several other scholars.[9] An early witness to this reversal is Elke Hartmann's book *Heirat, Hetärentum und Konkubinat im klassischen Athen* published in 1992. Although her account of prostitution does not exceed 80 pages, and it is insufficient for an in-depth analysis of the large volume of ancient evidence, it is nonetheless engaging and thoughtful, and has moved away from some of the excesses common in the literature of the 1980's.

---

7 Reinsberg's book was sharply criticized by Simon Goldhill (*JHS* 112 [1992] 196–198) for lacking in intellectual depth and viewing the images from the vases as photographic representations of the past. True as these criticisms may be, still Reinsberg's discussions of the images remain important.

8 See for example the savage review by F. Picard in *Topoi* 2 (1992) 285–289.

9 Sue Blundell *Women in Classical Athens*; Christine Schnurr-Redford *Frauen im klassischen Athen*.

I accept the more balanced view put forward by these studies that Athenian women were not locked away in dark quarters, that many of them had to go out and work, often forced by circumstances, and that even those who did not need to work because they were enjoying sufficient financial comfort, certainly had a social life outside the house. They were known in their community, they had friends whom they visited, typically during the day when the men of the house most likely would be away, and went on shopping trips with their friends to stores which sold items like jewelry, clothes, household materials, shoes and other feminine apparel. They would also go to temples for private worship, or for public festivals, and there were certain festivals open only to women. Far from being locked up in their homes, Athenian women had plenty of opportunities for social interaction and life in the community, and the ones who needed to work could and did so even if grudgingly. Once we correct this fundamental concept of the Greek woman, then we start seeing in Attic vase iconography female figures in a broad variety of settings, which we no longer need to interpret as images of prostitution. Instrumental for this reappraisal of women's images in vase iconography have been studies by Martin Kilmer, Robert Sutton, Sian Lewis, Ulla Kreilinger and Mary Ann Eaverly.

Important work on the legal aspects of prostitution was done by scholars writing general books on Athenian law, especially Douglas MacDowell, A.R.W. Harrison and Stephen Todd.[10] For the first time the legal aspects and complications of venal sex, especially concerning citizen men offering their services as sex workers, were discussed thoroughly in the broader context of Athenian law and legal procedure, and they initiated a debate which was going to gain strength in subsequent years. The publication of Dover's controversial and influential study on Greek homosexuality in the late 70's shed light upon some topics which until then had been almost considered apocryphal in the modern era. Dover's work was very significant because it started an intensive modern dialogue, but also ominous for the way this debate was going to unfold for the rest of the 20th century. This book substantially influenced Michael Foucault's History of Sexuality. Foucault found faithful followers and fervent proponents and has seriously influenced modern works, like for example the study of Julia Sissa *Sensuality and Sexuality*. On the whole, I consider Foucault's discussions to be insightful, thought-provoking philosophical or intellectual propositions, but not historical studies. Not much later two very influential studies by Jack Winkler and David Halperin contributed to the intensifying discussion on Greek

---

10 MacDowell 1978; Harrison 1968–71.

same sex relations, as well as male prostitution, and in some significant ways linked the ancient discussion to modern sexual politics.

James Davidson's sensational book *Courtesans and Fishcakes* offered the first engaging, modern account of high-end prostitution in the social backdrop of the Greek symposion. Not long after Davidson's book a volume edited by his teacher Oswyn Murray dealt with several important aspects of the symposion. Davidson returned 10 years after his influential first book with a lengthy study on homosexual relations in the ancient world, and tried to address some of the orthodoxies established by the Dover - Foucault - Halperin triad concerning the laws on male citizen prostitutes. One of the sharpest critics of this book, Thomas Hubbard, says:

> Study of Greek same-sex relations since Sir Kenneth Dover's influential *Greek Homosexuality* (London 1978) has been dominated by a hierarchical understanding of the pederastic relations assumed to be normative between older, sexually and emotionally active "lovers" and younger, sexually and emotionally passive "beloveds." Michel Foucault's subsequent *History of Sexuality: Vol. 2, The Use of Pleasure* (New York 1986) was heavily influenced by Dover's collection of evidence and concretized these roles into formalized "sexual protocols." Self-consciously invoking Foucault was David Halperin's *One Hundred Years of Homosexuality* (London 1990), which envisioned phallic penetration as a trope for the asymmetrical political empowerment of adult citizen males over "women, boys, foreigners, and slaves -- all of the persons who do not enjoy the same legal and political rights and privileges that he does" (Halperin, p. 30). This orthodoxy, conditioned by the academic hegemony of feminist theory and contemporary anxieties over child sexual abuse, has begun to be seriously challenged only during the last several years.

Davidson has led the charge against this "academic hegemony" and in my opinion, Hubbard's sharp rebuke, although thoughtful over the details and to some extent fair, does not do justice to the strengths of Davidson's account. This sizeable volume has many intriguing discussions, and does a great service to modern classical scholarship by questioning so many of the "Dover-Foucault-Halperin" assumptions, which had loomed large for more than a quarter of a century.

The presence and functions of prostitutes in the sympotic space have been the subject-matter of several studies published or edited by Laura McClure, including the significant study *Courtesans at Table*, primarily focusing upon Athenaios, and the useful collection of articles *Prostitutes and Courtesans in the Ancient World*, co-edited with Christopher Faraone, which has made a substantial contribution to the exploration of specific aspects of ancient prostitution.[11] The representations of hetairai in New Comedy was the subject of an influential book by Madeleine Henry, while her second book on Aspasia of Miletos contains among others an excellent discussion of the sources of Athenaios. A new collection of papers, edited by Madeleine Henry and Alison Glazebrook, with focus not on the high-end of prostitution, as all previous studies had done so far, but rather on the lower end, the common prostitute and the brothel, was published in 2011. The articles in this collection approach the subject from a different angle and reveal in many ways changing attitudes and a departure from some of the most persistent dogmas of the 80's and 90's. The most recent book on the subject, Edward Cohen's *Athenian Prostitution*, was developed from the author's previous work on sexual contracts and focuses upon economic aspects of Athenian prostitution.

This is only a small, subjective selection of important stops in the long journey towards understanding better the first 1000 years in the history of prostitution. Many more works are cited and engaged throughout the book, some narrowly focusing on specific aspects of prostitution, others providing a more general background. I have tried to consider as much of the potentially limitless bibliography on this subject as possible, but truth be told, many more studies could have been included, and I could have just as easily continued for another 20 years reading, adding and interpreting. But everything has to come to an end; at some point, I had to pick my battles and bring to completion a project as large and complex as this, fully aware of the limitations of time and space, and the potential for omissions, with the modest objective of presenting a readable and comprehensive account of the ancient evidence on prostitution in the ancient Greek world.

---

11 For a thorough discussion of the articles included in the Faraone-McClure volume see the review article of Julia Assante (2007: 117–132).

1 Prostitution in the Archaic Period

1.1 Images of Venal Sexuality in Greek Lyric

The mythical beginnings of prostitution, according to Quintus Ennius, go back to the time when Venus taught the art of prostitution (*artem meretriciam*) to the women of Cyprus so as to have company in her immodesty.[1] In reality, the early history of prostitution in the Ancient Mediterranean is lost in the mist of time, but we can be sure that in an area where sea-travel was widespread in the second millennium BC, and agricultural settlements had grown into cities with market-places already from the late stone age, sex as a commodity should be present well before the time of our historical records. From our earliest written records comes loud and clear the voice of a rebel poet who reacted to the lofty ideals of the epic tradition that had bred many generations before his time.[2] The verses of Archilochos set out to demolish the epic ideology of glory, immortality, wealth and honor, and later centuries remembered him through Pindar's words as the "vitriolic Archilochos".[3] Among the limited number of his fragments which have survived we find a glorification of cowardice in the infamous poem about the shield, a renunciation of wealth and glory in favor of drink and sex, cynical remarks about how pointless bravery can be when in war victory goes to the one who has the better weapons, bragging about drunkenness while on guard, and a whole array of other human flaws.[4] In this anti-heroic world we should not be surprised to find a number of references to prostitution. Archilochos is the first author who offers definite testimony about the existence of organized prostitution in the Greek world as early as the first half of the 7th century. A shockingly explicit reference to oral sex with ejaculation is probably the oldest unambiguous reference to a prostitutional setting in Greek literature:

---

1 Ennius *Varia: Euhermerus sive Sacra Historia* 142–145:
Venus prima artem meretriciam instituit auctorque mulieribus in Cypro fuit, uti vulgo corpore quaestum facerent: quod idcirco imperavit, ne sola praeter alias mulieres inpudica et virorum adpetens videretur. (Venus first established the trade of prostitution, and she was the instigator among the women of Cyprus, so that they could publicly make a profit from their bodies. She set such rules, so as not to be the only immodest woman with a craving for men among the others.)
2 See for example Rankin 1977: 36–56; Anderson 2008: 255–260.
3 Pi. P. 2. 55 ψογερόν Ἀρχίλοχον βαρυλόγοις ἔχθεσιν / πιαινόμενον (the vitriolic Archilochos feeding on heavy-worded hostilities). See also Brown 2006: 36–46; Riu 2012: 249–278; Rankin 1977 passim.
4 See e.g. fr. 2, 3, 4, 5, 19 West. A rich and multifaceted portrait of Archilochos is presented in the volume edited by Katsonopoulou - Petropoulos - Katsarou 2008; see also Rankin 1977.

DOI 10.1515/9783110557954–001

> She was sucking like a man from Thrace or Phrygia drinking beer
> From a pipe; and she was bending over doing her job.[5]

H.D. Rankin interprets this as an allusion to fellatio, and believes that it could be an attack on Neoboule, or alternatively "another preserved vignette of the poet's sordid experience".[6] This short couplet contains everything we would normally associate with the common prostitute: the references to the boorish and incontinent barbarians who in later times would be typically associated with her clientele in literary sources,[7] a graphic image of female lust and oral sex, and an unmistakable description of a sexual position which indicates rough and ready sex. A lengthier reference to prostitution, this one bringing together the infamous pair of the *cinaedus* and the *porne*, is found in a poem of doubtful authenticity attributed to Archilochos:[8]

> The catamite (κίναιδος)[9] and the bad whore (πόρνη) have the same mind:
> Both are very glad to take the coins,
> Getting aroused and penetrated deep,[10]
> Laid and bonked hard,
> Banged and screwed deep,
> Stretched and humped all over the place,
> And no stallion was ever enough to satisfy both of them

---

5 Archil. fr. 42. West. While the first line could be open to other interpretations, the second (κύβδα δ' ἦν πον<εο>μένη) is an unambiguous reference to lewd sexuality, as κύβδα refers to a sexual position where the man stands behind having his partner bending before him and facing away (e.g. Ar *Eq.* 365 and Sch. Ar. Eq. 365 b; Κυβδάσῳ Pl. Com. fr. 204. 17–8).

6 Rankin 1977: 62–66; on Archilochos and the family of Lycambes see Carey 1986: 60–67.

7 See for example the μαστιγίας (someone with scars from a whip) of Machon 16.285–294, or the stereotypical soldier as the client of a prostitute (Ch. 3.4.).

8 Archil. fr. 328 West. It is difficult to decide on the authenticity of this poem. It has a later feel to it as the cultural concepts and the intensity of the hostile references to homosexual and heterosexual prostitution would belong more comfortably to the Hellenistic or the Roman period, but as we know so little about cultural perceptions of prostitution in the 7th c. BC, we cannot build a decisive argument against Archilochean authorship.

9 κίναιδος is a very difficult term to render into English, because its meaning in Greek is far from clear (see Davidson 2007: 59–71; Dover 1978: 75 agrees that the meaning is unclear and roughly identifies κιναιδία with effeminacy) The old-fashioned, vague and derogatory English term "catamite" perhaps comes close, and this is why I have chosen it here.

10 It is impossible to keep the translation very literal at this point, as the poet is throwing in obscene slang indicating some form of intercourse or another. I have used every synonym I could think in English, but I must admit the English expressions pale by comparison to the graphic obscenity of the Greek words: κινούμενοί τε καὶ διατρυπώμενοι / βινούμενοί τε καὶ διεσπεκλωμένοι / γομφούμενοί τε καὶ διασφηνώμενοι / χορδούμενοί τε καὶ κατασποδούμενοι (vv. 3–6).

But they love sucking more and more dick, of every dirty scum
Trying big dicks, thick dicks,
Those that leap forward, and the ones that hide too,
Pulling everything into the deep chasm of the terrifying pit,[11]
Right through the middle and all the way up to the belly button.
So, the lecherous trollop could really go to hell
with her entire clan of wide-ass buggers;
We should only care about the source of the Muses and a proper life,
for we know that this is pleasure and unadulterated joy.

If this passage belongs to Archilochos, it contains the earliest occurrence of the term *porne* in Greek literature. It would also provide certain proof for the presence of social attitudes which are commonly encountered in the literature of the classical period and its heirs, such as the stereotype of the insatiable whore and his/her love of money. The persona of the *kinaidos* is developed further in another poem attributed to Archilochos:

Iron is the only object which Kapys values -
The rest is nonsense to him; unless standing upright a penis
disappears into the recesses of his buttocks;
He is delighted to see his lover,
up to the point that he's having fun getting pierced.
When this ceases, he ditches the old lover
in search of more robust stallions.
Zeus, let them all die and go to hell,
those untrustworthy and loveless hustlers (κινουμένων)[12]

The opening line of the fragment is difficult to interpret. Davidson understands it as a reference to a sword and translates "it is the only kind of steel that Capys cherishes ... it is, for him, no sword worth talking about".[13] However, there is no word meaning "sword" in the original and the syntax, at least in the preserved section of the poem, does not allow us to read it in this manner.[14] To add to the

---

11 The pit as a metaphor for the overused vagina or anus of an immodest person is a standard theme in Greek literature. The Aristophanic χαυνόπρωκτος (*Ach.* 104 and 106) and εὐρύπρωκτος (*Eq.* 1084–1102), as well as λακκόπρωκτος (Poll. 6.127; Hsch. s.v.) come to mind. See also Davidson 2007: 57–59 and 66–70.

12 Archil. fr. 327 West.

13 Davidson 2007: 54.

14 The word which Davidson translates as "sword" is σίδηρος (steel) understanding it as a synecdoche. Davidson's reading of the passage would assume an οὗτος or similar in a lost section before the first line of our fragment, or a partitive genitive (σιδήρου) or some other device alluding to more than one kinds of iron or steel, of which Capys only cherishes an "upstanding penis".

problem, the term which Davidson has translated as "upstanding" (ὀρθοστάδην) is an adverb and alludes to a sexual position,[15] suggesting an interpretation according to which Capys enjoys being penetrated in an upstanding position. This is why we should probably understand the word σίδηρος literally as a reference to iron.

If we accept the latter interpretation, we would then need to answer the question why a lecherous man who enjoys relentless penetration would love iron too. If one were to interpret iron as a form of currency, like the famous iron bars which the Spartans used down to the classical period,[16] then the passage makes very good sense as a reference to a male prostitute. Maria Kostoglou, in a study which discusses iron and steel bars as a form of currency on the Aegean coastline and Thrace, has concluded that between the 9th and the 5th century steel spits were commonly used as currency bars, and were even used in a cultic context as votives to temples.[17] So, according to this reading of the opening line, Kapys (which incidentally sounds like a Thracian name) rejoices in low value currency which he receives in return for sexual favors. This interpretation would also cast the last two lines of the poem into a new light: the speaker brings damnation not upon men who enjoy sex with other men,[18] but upon cheap prostitutes who would do anything for cash.[19] This reading of the poem would also speak for an earlier date, when the use of steel bars as currency was still widespread, and it would support Archilochean authorship.

Several other Archilochean poems can be interpreted as a reference to prostitution, although not with absolute certainty. For example, Douglas Gerber has plausibly interpreted fr. 34 West "there is no way that we will entertain you for

---

15 See for example Hsch. s.v. ὀρθοσταδόν: τὸ ὀρθόν ἀφροδισιάζειν.

16 Plu. *Lyc.* 9,1 "First he (sc. Lycurgus) invalidated all golden and silver coins and ordered that they (sc. the Spartans) were to use only iron currency; and to this he attached a small value, despite is large weight and volume", and ibid. 9.3 "the iron currency was not possible to exchange among the rest of the Greeks, and it did not have any value, as it was perceived to be ridiculous". See also the discussion in Ch. 6.1. on the wealth and iron dedication of the hetaira Rhodopis.

17 Kostoglou 2003: 63–68. Kostoglou also refers to an unpublished Oxford Thesis by P. Haarer, *Obeloi and Iron in Archaic Greece*, Oxford 2001, which I have not seen, for a more detailed discussion on the use of iron bars as currency.

18 Davidson for example seems to understand the passage in this manner when he translates "those who get bounced for pleasure".

19 Compare for example with the detailed argument of Aeschines in 1.136 ff., that fair love (δίκαιος ἔρως) is above blemish, however, the sale of sex is shameful. Just as we read in the speech *Against Timarchos*, it was not the *erôs* that was considered deplorable but the sale of it; see Ch. 4.3.

free" as a reference to prostitution.[20] Whether we are prepared to accept such interpretations or not, and despite any quibbles about the authorship or context of individual fragments, we can safely infer from the works of Archilochos that prostitution was in existence and probably flourishing already in the first half of the 7th century in the coastal cities of the Aegean; the great Parian poet is the first witness in its history whose voice reaches us loud and clear.

Hipponax of Ephesos is a true heir of the tradition of Archilochos, to the extent that sometimes there is confusion about specific works, and even biographical tales - such as the story that both drove their enemies to suicide with their bitter verses. He lived approximately a century after Archilochos, at a time when political unrest and uprisings, which led to the establishment of tyrannies, were commonplace in the Greek world. Perhaps in this respect he differs from Archilochos. Whereas the latter was reacting to a tradition which believed in great universal values, and was trying to replace the Homeric world of gods and heroes with one of flawed human beings, rebellious and full of questions, Hipponax is not interested in these larger issues. His outlook is typically mid-archaic, concentrating mostly on the small, the mundane, the ephemeral viewed from a negative and depressed perspective. As Albin Lesky puts it, Archilochus "views the whole of human existence, or at least the whole of his own life ... But Hipponax asks no questions; his verses express the momentary perception and nothing more."[21] The meagre fragments of Hipponax include several references to prostitution. From Suetonius' collection of the terminology of prostitution we learn that Hipponax introduced several terms for prostitute, which were preserved in later lexicographers.[22] Particularly intriguing is the reference to *mysachnos*, in the masculine.[23] Suetonius attributes the invention of the term *mysachne* (in the feminine) to Archilochos and correctly recognizes that it refers to a prostitute who has sex in the filthy dust, presumably a street-walker.[24] If Hipponax was indeed referring to a male prostitute, it would imply that he borrowed the term from Archilochos, and

---

20 Gerber 1989: 99–103: ἀμισθὶ γάρ σε πάμπαν οὐ διάξομεν. The meaning of διάγω is broad, and its usage at this point may have been intentionally ambiguous.

21 Lesky 1966: 116.

22 Hip. fr. 104.34; 135 West; Suetonius Περὶ βλασφημιῶν καὶ πόθεν ἑκάστη; Kapparis 2011: 222–255.

23 Hip. fr. 105.10 West. Although the gender of μυσαχνός could be feminine, the surviving letters in the surrounding lines give the impression of a masculine gender. West prints the accent over the ultima, while all other editors prefer the stress over the penultima for the feminine and the antepenultima for the masculine. In terms of etymology it is derived from μύσος (filth) and ἄχνη (dust).

24 Archil. fr. 248 West.

changed the gender. More important, this would be one of the earliest references to male prostitution, and the earliest reference to a street-walker in Greek literature.

Anacreon of Teos, a junior contemporary of Hipponax, is another important name associated with the Archilochean tradition. His references to prostitution are more extensive than his predecessors, and for that reason studied to a greater extent in previous scholarship. Moreover, they are not plagued by the same doubts about authenticity which shadow the works attributed to Archilochos. Anacreon is extensively associated with sympotic literature. Scenes which feature drinking parties, games and playful scenarios are prominent in his work, to the extent that an entire collection of drinking poetry from later antiquity, the *Anacreonteia*, was linked to him. A fair number of young boys and women, sometimes mentioned by name, feature in his works in situations which from the perspective of classical Athenian morality would appear compromising. Women mentioned in those poems are commonly thought to be hetairai and references to overt sexuality are usually interpreted as references to prostitution. This assumption is based upon perceptions and stereotypes of women from the literature of the classical period, and should be viewed with skepticism. A number of these passages has been discussed to some length by Leslie Kurke in a study of the origins of prostitution in the archaic lyric.[25]

Anacreon's poem on Artemon has received a considerable amount of attention for its savage critique of a nouveau-rich man, an "upstart parvenu,"[26] with his ostentatious show of wealth and a luxurious lifestyle which was typically associated with oriental effeminacy.[27] William Slater suggested that the poem is not an attack but rather affectionate teasing for being cheap. The traditional view that the poem is an attack for ostentation and bad taste was re-established in two subsequent studies by Malcolm Davies and C. Brown.[28] The second stanza contains a reference which is significant for the study of prostitution in the archaic world. It is just one word, which means "whores by choice" (ἐθελοπόρνοισιν), signifying the existence of free persons in prostitution, who chose this trade on their own volition:

---

25 Kurke 1997: 106–154; for the opposing view see Hammer 2004: 479–512.

26 Davies 1981: 289.

27 fr. 82 Gentili = 388 PMG. See also Kurke 1997:119–131; Brown 1983: 1–15. A typical example of Greek perceptions about unmanly oriental effeminacy is that of Sardanapalus as narrated by Ktesias of Knidos (*FGrH* 688 F 1b).

28 Slater 1978: 185–194; the opposing thesis is advanced by Davies 1981: 288–299 and Brown 1983: 1–15.

That filthy cover of a bad shield, the companion
Of bread-makers and whores by choice, the wicked Artemon,
Making a dishonest living.

The issue of voluntary prostitution may be difficult and polarizing in modern discussions of the topic, but it must be considered a fact of life and an important
parameter in ancient discussions of prostitution as it delineates the difference
between free persons choosing to pursue what appeared to be a profitable line of
work and slaves forced to work in the markets of venal sex with no say over the
matter.[29] The existence of slave prostitution is well attested from the classical period, while the fragment of Philemon talking about Solon's brothels only refers to
slave prostitutes; for some modern scholars, like for example Allison Glazebrook,
this aspect of ancient prostitution is centrally important.[30] The majority of sex
workers in the brothels of the ancient world were slaves, with no control over
their bodies or their fate; the most they could hope for would be that one day an
infatuated lover was going to free them. The Anacreontean passage about Artemon provides valuable evidence about the other side: free-born women and men
who chose to enter prostitution motivated by the desire for higher profits, lured
by projections of glamour abundantly promised by deceitful procurers, or simply
compelled by poverty, frustration and the hopelessness of their daily lives. It also
suggests that free-born sex-workers who chose this path for their own reasons
were already around in the archaic period. Those free-born sex workers might not
have the power or wealth of the famous hetairai of the classical and Hellenistic
world, but certainly they were their predecessors and the alternative to the slave-
whore. Both forms of prostitution were in existence in the archaic world, and in
the classical period they proliferated into something more complex and varied.

---

29 Almost half a century after the sexual revolution of the 1960's and globalization, which have
altered very drastically the trafficking and marketing of prostitution, curiously the parameters
of the modern markets resemble more and more those of ancient Greece. In much of the modern
literature a distinction is made between individuals who enter the market without compulsion,
and sex slaves uprooted and transported very far away into foreign lands, and compelled to offer
their bodies under the fear of immigration laws, dangerous traffickers, threat of violence and
imprisonment, and law-enforcement itself. The main arguments of the modern debate are explored in Matthews 2008: 29–37; Lazos 2002; Barry 1995; Cusick et al. 2003; Doezema 1998;
Ousthoorn 2004, et al. The reader might find much of the literature partisan, but this is a very
controversial issue, which evokes strong responses.
30 Philemon fr. 3. About slave prostitution in the classical period see Dem. 59.18; Is. 6.19–21 al.

The image of the bread-seller as a vile, rough and lowly creature of the agora is well attested in later comic tradition.[31] Thus, this passage of Anacreon adds another important piece to the puzzle: by linking bread-makers and prostitutes in the same breath it conveys an image of the sale of sex for profit which is in sync with the rather dispassionate Aristotelian view of prostitution as nothing more than yet another lowly trade, not suitable for respectable people, but not necessarily carrying any more stigma or moral disapproval than the work of other tradesmen in the market place.[32] His reasoning was that those individuals are exposed to much undignified behavior for a small profit. Undoubtedly a similar theme is running through the Artemon fragment: the disapproval is not so much moral as it is elitist, political and economic. Prostitution is reprehensible because it is an activity linked with the "disembedded economics of the agora", as Leslie Kurke puts it.[33] This principle would be consonant with the perception of prostitution as a home-wrecker, a vice that destroys fortunes, in most of the sources from the classical period.[34] It would also function well as a contrast to the lifestyle of upper class softness and luxury (*habrosyne*), which according to Kurke created the hetaira.[35] In this scheme of things the uncouth nouveau-rich Artemon, who lacks the sophistication and elegance of a genuine aristocrat and yet pretends to be one, used to be the associate of free-born but lowly trades people, like bread-sellers and prostitutes.

There is an additional dimension to Anacreon's bread-sellers, well attested but more difficult to understand in its details, and this may be the reason why it has been ignored in previous scholarship. An entire play of Hermippos was entitled *Bread-sellers* (Ἀρτοπώλιδες). Only a few lines have survived, among which there is a clear reference to prostitution with someone addressing a woman with the words "you rotten sow, everybody's whore".[36] In Aristophanes *Lysistrata* an appeal to the rough tradeswomen of the agora to intervene with physical violence and abuse includes the bread-sellers. What is significant though is that they are

---

31 See e.g. Ar. *Lys.* 458–460; *Ra.* 857–858; Luc. *Demon.* 63; Alciphron 3.24,1.

32 Aristotle in the *Politics* (*Pol.* 1314 b 4) links the work of a *hetaira* to that of foreign workers (ξένοι) and other skilled tradesmen (τεχνῖται), and in the *Nicomachean Ethics* (*EN* 1121 b33) he mentions the work of a pimp as one among those which are unsuitable for free persons (ἀνελεύθερον), together with that of a lender on interest, a petty thief, or a robber.

33 Kurke 1997: 122.

34 See Ch. 5 for a more detailed presentation of this aspect of prostitution. For a quick reference, see the full development of this theme in the opening scenes of Plautus *Truculentus*, especially the introductory monologue of Diniarchus and his exchange with Astaphium.

35 Kurke 1997: 115.

36 Hermippos, fr. 9: ὦ σαπρὰ καὶ πᾶσι πόρνη καὶ κάπραινα.

linked into one comic word with inn-keepers, a profession typically associated with prostitution in many sources.[37] The same association is made in the *Frogs* (112), where places selling bread are mentioned in the same breath with brothels. It may be the case that bread-sellers' shops were one of the outlets of organized prostitution, like inns and taverns. Thomas McGinn, speaking about Pompeian establishments, says "generally speaking, inns, lodging houses, taverns, and restaurants of all kinds were associated with the practice of prostitution, often, though not exclusively, by the staff".[38] The Artemon passage seems to suggest that prostitution was practiced in these outlets in the archaic period, and in this respect it helps us form an image of a very diverse market in full bloom already by the 6th century.

Another passage of Anacreon apparently referring to a prostitute is found in a mutilated papyrus fragment from Oxyrynchus (P.Oxy. 2321 = fr. 60 Gentili). In line 13 we can read the name of a woman called Herotime. The adjective "people-carrier" (λεωφόρε) repeatedly attached to her name implies a common prostitute, and this understanding is corroborated by the testimony of Suetonius and later lexicographers.[39] At first sight this creates a discrepancy with the first two stanzas of the poem, which portray a tender young girl in elevated lyrical language. Eleonora Cavallini sees two different women in the poem, Herotime and her mother, while Gregorio Serrao has considered it a chronicle of Herotime's career in prostitution from tender youth to decline, and Kurke agreed.[40] In this interpretation of the fragment Herotime starts as a teenager with a beautiful face (καλλιπρόσωπη παίδων), grows into a young mare of Aphrodite, a high-end hetaira, and ends up a debased common whore trodden by everyone.

This reading of the poem is based upon assumptions which should not be taken for granted in Anacreon's time, such as a sharp distinction between the hetaira and the common prostitute. These artificially neat distinctions of class and rank were not a clear-cut historical reality in the classical period, and are even less clearly circumscribed in the archaic world. Moreover, this interpretation would undermine the complexity and elegance of the Anacreontean composition, where beauty, grace and universal availability are intermingled. Herotime

---

37 Ar. *Lys.* 458 σκοροδοπανδοκευτριαρτοπώλιδες. For further discussion on establishments that offered sex along with other services see Ch. 5.5. For inns and taverns as establishments of prostitution in the Roman world see McGinn 2004: 15–22, and 182–219.
38 McGinn 2004: 15–16.
39 See Kapparis 2011: 222–255, s.v.
40 Serrao 1968: 36–51; Kurke: 123–127; Cavallini 1988: 213–215.

is exceptional not because she is a former beauty, a washed up "has been" degraded to the place of a common slave, but because instead of carefully guarding her lovely face and stunning beauty, as expected of a delightful young woman, she makes it widely available to a lot of people. The final line, the address to Herotime (λεωφόρε, λεωφόρ' Ἡροτίμη *people-carrier, people-carrier, Herotime*) is typically interpreted as disparaging, but it need not be. A splendid beauty who offers herself to everyone is a worthy subject of Anacreontean poetry, a nuanced character from an era where overt female sexuality did not carry the same negative connotations and did not generate the same anxiety that it did in later centuries.

Much more difficult in its interpretation is fr. 13 Gentili (= 358 PMG). The literature on this small fragment is unusually extensive, as a heated debate has been going on for almost half a century.[41] It is uncertain whether the fragment is complete. In its present form it appears to be making a reference to female homoeroticism with an attractive young woman from Lesbos, associated with Sappho by a later tradition, rejecting the poet's advances and turning her affections towards another woman. This interpretation, however, is not certain, as it depends exclusively upon a pronoun (ἄλλην) with insufficient context.[42] The passage has been taken to refer to a hetaira, but there is nothing in it to indicate venal sex in any form. It reads like a rejection of the old white-haired male lover, in favor of an attractive young woman, and it is meant to express at a primary level the sadness of unrequited love in old age, and at a secondary level to introduce a more

---

41 In alphabetical order see: Campbell 1973: 168–169; Carbone 1993: 71–76; Davidson 1987: 132–137; Davies 1981: 288–299; Gentili 1973: 124–128; Giangrande 1973: 129–133, 1981: 15–18; 1995: 9–12; Marcovic 1983: 372–383; Pace 1996: 81–86; Pelliccia 1991: 30–36; Renehan 1984: 28–32; Rosenmeyer 2004: 163–178; Urios-Aparisi 1993: 51–70; Wigodsky 1962: 109–109; Woodbury 1979: 277–287.

42 The critical line πρὸς δ' ἄλλην τινὰ χάσκει creates ambiguity, since much depends on the interpretation of the pronoun ἄλλην. Scholarly opinions vary widely. Davidson proposed a sexless interpretation, where the young girl is simply playing ball with another girl and is indifferent to the sexual advances of the ageing male who is propositioning her. But in this case one would have a great deal of difficulty in interpreting χάσκει (which, as Gentili correctly argues, can only be interpreted in an erotic context), as well as the rejection of the man with the white hair. Giangrande, on the other hand, in no less than three different articles insisted in an obscene meaning for χάσκει (fellatio), with the agreement of Carbone, and interpreted ἄλλην as a reference to pubic hair. However, κόμη only means hair of the head and χάσκω does not easily imply fellatio in any attested instance (the Suetonian χάσκαξ used as an argument, which is an insult for a man not a woman, might just as easily refer to a loose anus). Most studies accept a homoerotic context, where the young Lesbian girl is attracted (which would be the correct meaning of χάσκει) to her young female companion, and rejects the ageing male who is propositioning her.

complex pattern of sexuality, attraction, love-games and rejection involving an erotic triangle of an ageing male and two young females.

Homoerotic themes appear in a number of other fragments, some specifically referring to a boy called Kleoboulos, and others to an unnamed boy (who could also be Kleoboulos).[43] There is nothing in Anacreontean homoeroticism alluding to any form of bought love. Especially fr. 12, the lengthiest of these passages, is a prayer to Dionysos to make Kleoboulos love the poet.[44] The theme of unrequited love dominates fr. 72, which on account of its connection with Thrace, seemingly a hub for prostitution in the archaic period, and the references to erotic gazes and games could be interpreted in a prostitutional context, but again the evidence for such an interpretation is not compelling. fr. 66b was recognized as a reference to prostitution by several lexicographers, and indeed the term *bassara* (*bassaris* in Anacreon) does have this meaning in Lycophron.[45] However, Lycophron may be the person who subverted *bassara*, a term traditionally referring to the followers of Dionysos, and used it for a prostitute. Anacreon's verse could simply be referring to the erratic gait of a Bacchant in a trance, as it may be indicated by the fact that neither Aristophanes Byzantios nor Suetonius have included it in their collections of the terminology of prostitution, although both were very familiar with the works of Anacreon and had scanned them carefully to collect material.

The two Lesbian poets Alkaios and Sappho have left us fragments of drinking songs, where similar topics of love, desire, disappointment and overt sexuality are explored. A brief fragment of Alkaios offers significant evidence about the development of prostitution on the island of Lesbos in the 6th century:

> Whatever someone gives to a whore
> is like throwing it into to waves of the white sea.[46]

This concept of the prostitute as a trap bringing financial ruin is very common in Attic comedy and its Roman heirs, typically in connection with high-class prostitution, as it would make no sense to represent the cheap, lowly prostitute of the brothel as a money hazard.[47] This passage of Alkaios is the earliest surviving occurrence of the topos, and may indicate the existence of expensive, upper-end prostitution in 6th century Lesbos.

---

43 fr. 12, 14, 15, and 18 Gentili.

44 We can easily draw a parallel with Sappho fr. 1 Page, the prayer to Aphrodite to make her favorite girl love her.

45 Lykophron *Alexandra* 771–2. See also Kapparis 2011: 232.

46 Alkaios fr. 117b Lobel-Page.

47 See e.g. Athen. 13.21–26, and the discussion in Ch. 5.

In the surviving works of the other great Lesbian poet, Sappho, there is not a single allusion to venal sex. The poet, whom a 4th century critic associated with grace (χάρις), beautiful words (καλλιεπής) and sweetness (ἡδεῖα),[48] has left behind verses built with bold and powerful, but also graceful and humanizing images, which enhanced her reputation in antiquity and subsequent centuries. Sordid jokes and explicit references to prostitution would look out of place in Sapphic poetry. This is why it is surprising to read in Herodotos that she used her poetry to attack an Egyptian hetaira named Rhodopis, whom her brother Charaxos had liberated for a lot of money when he went to Naucratis on a business trip.[49] Herodotos refutes the tradition which considered Rhodopis the person for whom the pyramid of Mycerinus had been built, correctly understanding that a great deal of time had passed from the era of the pyramid builders (26th c. BC) to that of Sappho (6th c. BC). The historian was probably reacting to the tradition attested in a fragment of Hekataios, where one of the pyramids had been built as a grave for Rhodopis, because some local magistrates (νομάρχαι), former lovers and very fond of her, built the pyramid in honor of her memory.[50] An additional argument which Herodotos provides is that although Rhodopis was well off, she could not afford to build an entire pyramid. He actually finds her wealth quite modest with calculations based on the story that she sent one tenth of her entire fortune to Delphi as a dedication in the form of numerous iron spits, which he had seen lying on a pile behind the altar of the Chians.[51] Several scholars have suggested that the legend has roots in local Egyptian history, and that later the Greek historicans merged queen Nicotris with the hetaera Rhodopis.[52] However, such a hypothesis would be very difficult to prove as the historicity of Nicotris herself is very much in question.

Strabon preserves a slightly different version of the story arguing that the same woman was called Doricha in Sappho's works, while in Naukratis she was known as Rhodopis.[53] Athenaios believed that Herodotos had confused two different women, a Thracian called Doricha, about whom Sappho speaks in her works, and an Egyptian hetaira called Rhodopis, and fused them into the same person.[54] Pausanias of Attica seems to be following the version of the historian Apollas (or Apellas), the same one that appears in Strabo, where Doricha and

---

48 Demetr. *Eloc.* 148 and 166.
49 Hdt. 2.135; cf. Apellas *FGrH* 266 F 8.
50 Hekataios *FGrH* 264 F 25.
51 See the discussion in Ch. 6.1. on the dedication of Rhodopis to Delphi.
52 See Biffi 1997: 51–60; Stezzini 1955: 177; Walle 1934: 303–312; Zivie-Coche 1972: 115–138
53 Str. 17.1.33.
54 Athen. 13.69.

Rhodope are the same woman with different names in different authors.[55] Madeleine Henry suggests that a woman originally named Doricha could have been renamed Rhodopis ("rosy face") after she took up prostitution.[56] The appearance or absence of Doricha from the story is a generally related to the actual source of the story in Byzantine lexicography and scholarship. Tzetzes, for example, relies exclusively on Herodotos and does not mention Doricha at all, while the lemma of the Suda, although aware of Herodotos, is also drawing from another source where Doricha makes her appearance.[57]

Rhodopis/Doricha, "the first historical female in the Greek record who seems to have been trafficked" (according to Henry[58]), was a legendary figure. A tradition which begins with Herodotos and gets augmented in later antiquity connects her to Aesop.[59] Rhodopis is a character in two Greek novels, a beautiful virgin in Achilles Tatius, and a Thracian woman living in Egypt, only second to Charikleia in good looks, in the *Aethiopica* of Heliodoros.[60] Two later sources attest a Cinderella type story: the exceptionally beautiful Rhodopis was bathing when an eagle snatched her garment and dropped it into the lap of the king. Impressed by the garment and the incident he searched the entire land for the owner, found and married her. Thus, Rhodopis ended up queen of Egypt, and when she died she had a pyramid built to house her grave.[61] There is even a proverb attested which mentions Rhodopis; it reads "everything is the same, even the beautiful Rhodopis". The mainstream interpretation of it was that all mortals have a similar fate, but one source interprets it in a prostitutional setting applying to men who had spent a lot of money on hetairai, foolishly, since all women, including the beautiful Rhodopis, are the same.[62]

On account of this tradition Wilamowitz supplemented the name Doricha in a papyrus fragment of Sappho.[63] Joel Lidov has argued against this restoration on

---

55 Paus. (s.v.). The note of Pausanias is repeated by Photios (s.v.) and Suda (ρ 211) and may have its origins in the version of the historian Apollas *FGrH* 266 F 8.
56 Henry 2011: 14–33.
57 Tz. *Prol.Com.* 1.46; Sud. ρ 210.
58 Henry 2011: 14.
59 Hdt. 2.135; Plu. 400f-401a; Sud. ε 3266; Tz. *Prol.Com.* 1.46–47.
60 Ach.Tat. 8.12.1; Hld. 2.25.1.
61 Str. 17.1.33; Ael. *VH* 13.33. Strabo does not give a name for a king, perhaps with some awareness of the Herodotean note about the great antiquity of the pyramids. Aelian names the king Psametichus (664–610 BC).
62 *Appendix proverbiorum* 4.51; cf. Phryn. *PS* 233; Phot. a 2248; *Lexica Segueriana* α 111; *Paroem.Gr.* 3.43; Sud. α 2897; π 191; ρ 210;
63 15b.11 L-P = P Oxy. 1231 frag. l..1. 11.

the grounds that the tradition which links Sappho to the Doricha/Rhodopis tale is a later invention, probably from 5th century Athens.[64] Lidov traces images of Sappho in Attic comedy, where she is presented as a hetaira and a pimp.[65] *Sappho* is the title of no less than six Attic Comedies by Ameipsias, Amphis, Antiphanes, Ephippos, Timocles and Diphilos. For two of them there is insufficient evidence even to link them to the poet, although it is hard to imagine another famous Sappho who would be the star character in those plays. Diphilos undoubtedly had in mind the poet, as in the only surviving line of the play Archilochos too is featured as a character having one last drink in the end of a symposium. The fragment of Antiphanes is making jokes about gender issues with Sappho being portrayed as the champion of all things female; this play surely has something to do with the poet.[66] The one surviving fragment from the play of Ephippos is an unambiguous reference to parasites and prostitutes:

> When someone in his youth
> Comes to learn how to eat someone else's fish
> And sticks his hands into a dinner to which he hasn't contributed,
> Believe me, he will settle the bill later, during the night.[67]

One can clearly infer that the young man will need to offer sexual favors in exchange for a lavish meal. The passage of Timocles also makes a probable reference to male prostitution, if one considers that the name mentioned in this short fragment was a real Athenian man named Misgolas, an affluent gentleman well known for paying for the services of attractive young male entertainers:

> You do not think that Misgolas is approaching
> Excited by young men at their prime[68]

Sappho's character in Plato's comedy *Phaon* may shed more light on the mystery and suggest an answer to the question of what Sappho was doing in all these plays. Athenaios says that she was portrayed as a hetaira and the brothel-keeper of Phaon. This supports the possibility that she could be portrayed as a hetaira in some of the other plays. The image of Sappho as a hetaira in Attic literature apparently was so ill-fitting with that of the much-loved and revered poet, that a

---

64 Lidov 2002: 203–237.
65 Plato *Phaon* = Athen. 10.58.
66 Antiphanes, fr. 194.
67 Ephippos fr. 20.
68 Timocles fr. 32. For the reputation of Misgolas as a lover of young prostitute boys see the discussion in Ch. 4.5.

later tradition invented another hetaira from Eressos, Sappho's native town, and tried to differentiate between the two women. Aelian says "I hear that another Sappho lived in Lesbos, a hetaira not a poet".[69] When Tatian the Apologist in his savage attack on all Greek women writers mentions Sappho the hetaira in the same sentence with Erinna, Myrtis, Myro of Byzantium and other poets, he undoubtedly refers to the one and only historical Sappho and probably has in mind this long literary tradition which pictured her as a hetaira.[70] How this tradition was created may simply have to do with the fact that Sappho keeps calling her friends "hetairai". Athenaios was aware of the semantic shift at the beginning of the classical period and knew that in Sapphic poetry it is simply a reference to the female friends and companions of the poet.[71] Others might have been less meticulous in their interpretation of these references; deliberately or carelessly they could have perceived them as references to fellow-hetairai. Moreover, Sappho may have been compared to intellectual women from the classical period who had been hetairai, like Aspasia of Miletos, Leontion the Epicurean, or Nikarete the Megarian, and retrospectively fitted into the model of the learned, independent hetaira of the 4th century.

This account seems to strengthen the argument of Lidov that the Doricha/Rhodopis tale was a tradition born in Athens in the 5th century from this comic image of Sappho. What works against Lidov's position is the number of authors who assert with very specific language that Sappho wrote poems attacking Doricha, to the point where the reader is left with the strong impression that they had seen this poetry. Herodotos does not just vaguely suggest that Sappho attacked Doricha, as he might have done if he were reflecting a contemporary tradition untraceable in the works of Sappho. On the contrary, he vividly says that the poet tore her to shreds (πολλὰ κατεκερτόμησέ μιν) in a song (μέλος). Strabo provides more detail saying that Charaxos, the brother of Sappho, was in Naucratis on business carrying Lesbian wine, when he came across Rhodopis. Athenaios adds that Sappho attacked Doricha / Rhodopis through her poetry (διὰ τῆς ποιήσεως), because the latter robbed Charaxos of a lot of money during his stay in Naukratis. The actual wording of Athenaios is intriguing: for "robbed" he uses a very old-fashioned verb (νοσφισαμένην), frequent in early epic, lyric, and

69 Ael. *VH* 12.19.
70 Tatianus *Oratio ad Graecos* 33.1.
71 Athen. 13.108.

tragedy but very rare in prose.[72] Could Athenaios be echoing the actual words of Sappho? Moreover, Athenaios preserves an epigram of Poseidippos about Doricha which would not make any sense at all if poems under the name of Sappho speaking about Doricha had not been preserved down to the third or early second century when Poseidippos wrote:

> Doricha, your bones have long turned to dust,
> And the scent of your hair and perfumed garments has subsided
> With it once you subdued the elegant Charaxos
> And closely together you touched the morning cup.
> But, Sappho's white pages in a lovely song
> Speaking your precious name still remain
> And Naukratis will treasure it
> For as long as ships sail down the Nile to the open seas.[73]

Poseidippos does not make any reference to negative criticism. His Doricha has gained immortality through the songs of Sappho, and although her lovely presence has long turned to dust, her name lives on in the pages of the poet, cherished by the citizens of Naukratis. Poseidippos, it seems, set out to present Doricha/Rhodopis in a positive light, and he suppressed any criticisms in the verses of Sappho, mentioning only that Doricha gained immortality through them. This epigram makes very specific references to songs, words preserved on white writing material and specific mentions of Doricha in those. Equally specific is a reference in Ovid, where in a fictitious letter of Sappho addressed to Phaon it is said that she warned her brother about meretricious love, in vain, for he ignored her advice and ended up destitute.[74] This reference is important too, because, like everything else in the poem is based on well-known Sapphic themes, and would hardly make sense without some famous verses about Charaxos and his hetaira in Sappho's works, familiar to Ovid and his learned readers.

It would be very difficult to discard this evidence. If Sappho wrote scolding poetry, she did nothing different from what some of her illustrious contemporaries like Alkaios, or later lyric poets like Anacreon did, the witty Praxilla, famous for her *skolia*, and even the lofty Pindar. Accepting the tradition that Sappho

---

72 See e.g. Pi. *N.* 6.62; A. *Ch.* 620. The only other instance where Athenaios uses this verb is in 6.20, where he is quoting Poseidonios (*FGrH* 87 F 48). Clearly there he borrowed the verb from the polymath philosopher.
73 Anthologiae Graecae Appendix 77.
74 Ovid *Her.* 15, 67–8: me quoque, quod monui bene multa fideliter, odit; / hoc mihi libertas, hoc pia lingua dedit. (He hates me too, because I faithfully gave him plentiful advice, and this is the reward for my frankness and good counsel).

wrote poetry scolding the hetaira Doricha as genuine and factual, at least as far as the main points are concerned, would widen the scope of Sapphic poetry, and moreover provide us with valuable evidence about the early days of high-class prostitution in the Greek world. Along with the works of Archilochos and Anacreon, it would provide even more support for the theory that Thrace was a hub for prostitution in those early times, and confirm the evidence of Alkaios that upperend prostitution was already in motion around the Greek world, all the way to its fringes and as far away as Naukratis, the one Greek colony in Egypt. It would also confirm that this flourishing port, like the other major harbor city, Corinth, experienced an early rise in high-end prostitution, which lived on down to the time of Athenaios, the most famous son of Naukratis.

The poetry of Pindar would be an unlikely place to find substantial information on prostitution at the borderline between the archaic world and the classical period, and yet in a much-discussed Pindaric *skolion* (fr. 122 Snell) we find important evidence about prostitution in Corinth in the first half of the 5th century. The passage has received a lot of attention because a number of scholars have interpreted it as a reference to sacred prostitution and take it as evidence that this was practiced in Corinth all along, before the time of Pindar and all the way down to the time of Strabo.[75] This is most unlikely: Herodotos, when he discusses what has been widely perceived to be sacred prostitution in Babylon, he uses strong disapproving language for this alien custom (ὁ δὲ δὴ αἴσχιστος τῶν νόμων).[76] How could he have failed to mention such a practice in the heartland of the Greek world? In recent years the substantial work of Stephanie Budin on the subject has discredited the myth of sacred prostitution altogether.[77] The whole issue arises from a single passage of Strabo,[78] while the attempts to associate the *skolion* with the remark of Strabo are based upon misinterpretations of the Pindaric fragment

---

75 See Strabo 8.6.20; Kurke 1996: 49–75; Against the interpretation of the *skolion* as a reference to sacred prostitution see Breitenberger 2007: 132–135; Conzelmann 247–261; Calame 1989: 106–107.

76 Hdt. 1.199.

77 See Budin 2008 and 2006: 77–92. Corinne Bonnet 2009: 71–77 has brought some objections, but the core of Budin's work remains convincing. See also MacLachlan 1992: 145–162.

78 It is important to point out that Strabo wrote centuries after pagan Corinth and its famous hetairai were nothing more than a nostalgic memory. There is no real possibility that he had reliable evidence in his hands. Clearly he is relating a story told about the wealthy Corinth of the past, seemingly invented to explain the proverb "οὐ παντὸς ἀνδρὸς ἐς Κόρινθόν ἐσθ' ὁ πλοῦς." (not every man can sail to Corinth). The mere number of 1000 hetairai living and working in the temple is a suspect impossibility, and the fact that such a distinct practice would go unnoticed by every Greek author who wrote in the Classical and Hellenistic periods beyond reasonable doubt suggests a legend of later antiquity.

and the attached testimony of Athenaios. Kurke believes that the servants of Peitho appearing in the first stanza of the *skolion* are hierodules, which later turn hetairai during the sacrifice and the subsequent party. Breitenberger, however, correctly objects, stating that there is no specific cultic significance to the first two stanzas. The testimony of Athenaios ought to be sufficient to resolve the disagreement: he states that the women mentioned in the poem are hetairai present at the sacrifice and the party.[79]

This is the simplest and easiest explanation of the poem. A celebratory party after the sacrifice in the city of Corinth would inevitably include some hetairai, almost like any other high-spirited party, anywhere in the Greek world. The presence of hetairai to the sacrifices and festivities at the temple of Aphrodite is well attested in a story mentioned first by Theopompos and repeated by Chamaileon and Timaios, according to which the hetairai of the city went to the temple to pray during the Persian wars, and in recognition they were always included in the festivities afterwards.[80] It must have been a strange spectacle for some visitors to Corinth, especially from more conservative communities in the Greek world, to watch the illustrious hetairai of the city present en mass in celebrations at the temple. Yet, if one were to be cynical, such occasions were the perfect recruiting grounds for the hetairai, and Corinth was a place sufficiently open-minded to include those prolific creators of wealth into the festivities.

The presence of hetairai at victory parties is not unique to Corinth but rather a common occurrence as the substantial testimony from an Attic law-court speech confirms. About a hundred years later (in 374/3 BC) hetairai participated in a party to celebrate the Pythian victory of Chabrias in Athens, and, if we were to believe Apollodoros, the entire party disintegrated into a wild sex orgy as the night progressed and the guests became increasingly drunk.[81] Moreover, the party of Xenophon need not be historical and the women taking part in it could be nothing more than a literary theme in a poem inspired by the reputation of Corinth as the city of beautiful, elegant hetairai. Elroy Bundy, perhaps the most influential figure in Pindaric Studies in the 20th century, did not consider Pindaric

---

79 Athen. 13.33. The passage of Athenaios is not easy to interpret as it discusses a custom which involves hetairai. The verb ἀπάγειν (twice) makes it difficult to understand what he means. The easiest interpretation would be to interpret it as "to lead away, to hire", and understand that the believers promised Aphrodite that if their prayer was successful, they were going to hire some hetairai. The hetairai had nothing to do with the temple in any capacity, but came from the numerous upper class brothels around the city. See also the discussion on the inscription in the temple of Aphrodite, supposedly commemorating the prayers of hetairai in Ch. 6 .1.
80 Theopompos *FGrH* 115 F 285 a; Chamaileon fr. 31 Wehrli; Timaios *FGrH* 566 F 10.
81 Dem. 59.33–34, and Kapparis 1999, com. ad loc.

poetry to be historical or biographical in nature, and if we were to accept these lines as a literary motif, then their value as critically important evidence attesting the presence of ritual prostitution in the Greek world would be instantly annihilated.[82] Either way, these lines could not possibly provide reliable evidence on a phenomenon which almost certainly never existed in the Greek world.

Yet the *skolion* provides valuable evidence about prostitution in the early 5th century in a city whose name was identified with glamorous hetairai down to Roman times. It confirms, as we would have suspected, that high-class prostitution was fully developed already in the early 5th century, and integrated into the social life of Corinth. The practice surely goes back to times well before the 5th century, perhaps as far back as the 8th century, when under the Bacchiads the city enjoyed unprecedented prosperity and expansion thanks to its important location and vigorous trade.

The archaic period was an era of change, doubt and experimentation throughout the Greek world.[83] In this fluid and uncertain world, the epic ideal of a heroic honor code seems to have lost its appeal and was aggressively trashed by poets like Archilochos and Hipponax, or subverted more subtly in the pessimism of Hesiod or Mimnermos. The great, sweeping themes of the epic were replaced by the small, the personal, the intimate and the mundane, and although the lifestyle and ideals of the aristocracy still inspired lyric themes, we are left with the impression that the world of the aristocratic symposium was transient. In many parts of Greece this was an era of turmoil, conflicting ideologies and split identities; it was a society in constant, rapid motion. James Davidson, focusing on the sympotic space and the literature which it generated, prefers to view the

---

82 See for example Bundy 1962: 126: "It seems apparent that in this genre the choice involved in composition is mainly a choice of formulae, motives, themes, topics, and set sequences of these that have, by convention, meanings not always easily perceived from the surface denotations of the words themselves."

83 For example: The Athenians underwent vast political changes from monarchy to aristocracy to tyranny to democracy, all in the space of two or three centuries. The Spartans introduced sweeping reforms, which they later attributed to the wise lawgiver Lycurgus, and set the foundations of their hegemony over the Greek world, and a special place in history. In other cities tyrannies rose and fell, states experimented with representative and direct democracy, legal codes and constitutional reforms were introduced, and by the end of this process only two monarchies remained in the Greek world, Sparta and Macedonia, and the former was a monarchy only in name. The Megarian poet Theognis bemoans the loss of the old aristocratic world, its morals, soft lifestyle and honor code, and loathes its replacement by the power of the vulgar majority. Athenian literature, on the other hand, celebrates these changes as the path to enlightenment, resulting in equality of speech (ἰσηγορία), equality of all citizens before the law (ἰσονομία), and power for the people (δημοκρατία).

archaic period as "the flipside of the world of heroic warriors. It is self-consciously off duty, a place for not competing, for not fighting, for hard warriors to allow their bodies to unwind and to take time off from the system. But the symposium brought something else with it, pleasure, and eventually, a market for pleasure, for professional performers, even professional boys, the most beautiful money could buy."[84] Elke Hartmann, following Leslie Kurke, sees the aristocratic symposion as the epicenter of venal sexuality.[85] However, the previous discussion suggests the presence of a more complex and evolved market ranging from upper end Corinthian establishments to the cheap brothels of seaside towns throughout the Aegean.

Whichever way we see it, we are still bound to conclude that archaic Greece proved to be fertile ground for the development of commercial sex, both male and female. The prosperity in a few trading centers such as Corinth, Naukratis and Lesbos favored the evolution of high-class prostitution. Nearby large impoverished populations, in a struggle for survival, were providing in plenty bodies for the pleasure of those who could pay. As there was an increase in contacts with the outside word, sea-travel, and enhanced movement of goods and people, the political and economic circumstances were truly conducive for the explosion of sex markets, while the cultural fluidity and moral relativism of a world in constant motion certainly favored this development. Greek lyric provides sufficient evidence to conclude that prostitution was already in motion in the archaic period and had already branched out to satisfy all purses, tastes and desires, that it was legally recognized and regulated in some places (as the examples of Athens, Corinth and a few other major centers suggest), and that it was set to grow even further and become a distinct and important feature of Greek life and culture in the coming centuries.

1.2 The Brothels of Solon

In Solonian Athens prostitution was predominantly practiced by slave women, captured at war or by women coming from other cities without a family or someone to support them. The picture has not changed much since then, despite the recognition of women's rights and the sexual revolution. Today the industry of sex is flourishing.[86]

---

84 Davidson 2007: 509–510.

85 Hartmann 2002: 135–149.

86 Quote from a speech by Anna Karamanou, Member of European Parliament and Chair of the Committee for Women's Rights and Equal Opportunities, entitled "Without a voice: Supply and

The tradition that Solon was the founder of organized prostitution is deeply embedded in popular wisdom. In conference papers, online publications and even in the delightfully amateurish *History of Prostitution* by W. W. Sanger, M.D.,[87] Solon emerges as the first brothel-keeper in history, frequently commended for his insightful handling of public decency in such a radically effective manner. Scholarly opinion is much more skeptical. Two independent studies, by F.J. Frost and V.J. Rosivach, both reach the same conclusion that it is highly improbable for Solon to have been the founder of organized prostitution.[88] Moreover, the possibility is altogether ignored in most of the authoritative literature on Solon's constitutional and socioeconomic reforms, such as the classic studies of Victor Ehrenberg and W.J. Woodhouse, and more recently the substantial monographs of Ron Owens and Elizabeth Irwin or the hefty collection of essays edited by J.H. Blok and André Lardinois.[89]

The tradition itself may have been consonant with the tendency of 5th and 4th century authors to attribute to Solon almost every statute of the Athenian state and even the foundation of democracy itself. Our oldest source attesting that Solon established brothels all over Athens is the comic poet Philemon (late 4th c.) in his play *Brothers*.[90] Athenaios, Plutarch, and even Eustathios, bishop of Thessalonica, repeat this information with praises for the insight of Solon to provide an acceptable alternative for the desires of young men. According to Athenaios, Nicander of Colophon (2nd c.) believed that Solon had used the revenues from prostitution to build the temple of Aphrodite Pandemos[91]. Eustathios comments that Aphrodite loved the gold brought to her from the wages of the women in the temple (using the disparaging term γύναια for women), and that this is why Aphrodite herself was sometimes called Hetaira.[92]

---

demand of prostitution Services. The industry of sex". The speech was delivered on Saturday, 22 May 2004, at an international conference in Athens organized by the Center for the Support of the Family, an organization operating under the aegis of the Church of Greece. Karamanou was referring to the influx of women into western Europe after the collapse of the iron curtain. Countries like modern Greece where prostitution is legal and tolerated by social norms, and has large transient populations in the form of tourism, naturally were a prime target. Many of the women are being trafficked in conditions which do not differ much from ancient slavery, as they are deprived of basic human rights and living in fear of ruthless procurers, immigration authorities and law enforcement itself. For further discussion see Makei 2013 and Pyclik 2006.

87 Sanger 1937: 43–49.
88 F.J. Frost 2002: 34–46; Rosivach 1995: 2–3.
89 Ehrenberg 1968; Woodhouse 1938; Owens 2010; Blok-Lardinois 2006.
90 Philemon fr. 3; see also the discussion in Ch. 5.4 and 5.5.
91 Philemon, *PCG* fr. 3; Plu. *Sol.* 23; Athen. 13,25; Eust. *Com. Il.* 4.331.
92 Eust. *Com. Il.* 4.331.

The nature of this evidence is such that one might be tempted to dismiss it in its entirety as yet another tale about the quasi-mythical figure of Solon. Frost and Henry effectively expose the problems of the proposition that the Athenian state used revenues from prostitution to erect a temple to Aphrodite (of which there is no material evidence). Frost considers the evidence of Philemon on the brothels of Solon as nothing more than a joke.[93] Indeed, a late 4th century comic poet and a few later references, some of which evidently are based upon the passage of Philemon, hardly constitute solid proof for events that supposedly took place in the early 6th century. However, dismissing this evidence outright would probably be a serious error in this case, since we have very substantial corroborating evidence from more reliable sources, which enhances the credibility of this tradition and to some degree explains how and why Solon established organized prostitution.

Apollodoros in the speech *Against Neaira* quotes a law which defined when charges of adultery could not be brought:

> The law does not allow a man to be treated as an adulterer if caught with one of those women who are established in a brothel or wander around.[94]

This law was also known to Lysias and Plutarch, and attributed to Solon by both authors (as it was by Harpocration and the Byzantine lexicographers).[95] The antiquated language of this document is the surest proof that it was a genuine Solonian law. Scholars unanimously agree on this, and Ruschenbusch has included it in his collection as a genuine law.[96]

The Athenians continued to use an old set of laws dealing with homicide for centuries after their introduction. Historical memory asserted that these laws were introduced by Drakon in 621/0, and were written in blood; the penalty for all offences was death. Among these laws there was one on justified homicide, which exonerated a man who killed someone caught in bed with his wife, mother, sister, daughter or a concubine kept for the birth of free children. This is the oldest

---

93 Frost 2002: 34–46; his main argument is that believing Philemon would be like believing Aristophanes, when he suggests in the Acharnians that the Peloponnesian war was fought over two slave prostitutes belonging to Aspasia, the mistress of Pericles, who were abducted by the Megarians (Ar. *Ach.* 522–537). See also Henry 2011: 14–33.

94 Dem. 59.67; See Kapparis 1999, com. ad loc.

95 Lys. 10.19 with Hillgruber's commentary (1988: 77–78). Plu. *Sol.* 23; Harp. s.v. ἀποπεφασμένως, Sud. α 3475; Phot. α 2604; *EM* s.v. ἀποπεφασμένως; *Anecd. Bek.* s.v. ἀποπεφασμένως.

96 Ruschenbusch 1966: 77; Glazebrook 2005: 35, n. 8.

piece of Athenian legislation known to us which effectively criminalizes adultery,[97] and defines it by naming the categories of women to whom the law applied. Even if this had not been the original purpose of the statute, it stayed firmly in place as the centerpiece of legislation on adultery and other extramarital relationships for centuries. The enduring qualities of the Drakonian legislation were an association with religion, which made Athenian homicide law conservative and not susceptible to frequent changes like other laws, and the admirable simplicity of this legislation in dealing with serious offences in an effective and well-defined manner.[98]

The objectives of the Draconian legislation may have been clear and direct, but undoubtedly the socioeconomic problems which they tried to resolve were still around 25 years later, perhaps exacerbated. The Drakonian law allowing self-help simultaneously created a dramatic potential for abuse in a financially hard-pressed society. Unscrupulous procurers could now entrap customers with false allegations of adultery, and attempt to extract substantial compensation with a legally sanctioned death-threat.[99] I have argued elsewhere that, in order to deal with these problems, Solon introduced several new laws, one of which was to exclude from the power of the adultery laws women who were already practicing some form of prostitution.[100] Steven Johnstone has objected, saying: "there are no prostitutes, no brothels, and not even any sex. Instead, there are men and women consorting in the marketplace — and a lurking possibility of a jealous, violent

---

97 Although the primary concern of the lawgiver probably was the setting where the woman had consented to receive the seducer, we can be certain that the law could also be invoked in a case of rape, if the rapist had been caught in the act; otherwise, an adulterer could always claim to be a rapist and get away with it. The lawgiver did not expect someone catching another man in bed with one of the women of his family to be running an investigation into the motives and intent of the act; he simply allowed that man to exact immediate revenge by means of killing the intruder into his family, without punishment.

98 The Draconian legislation seems to have been a response to increasing socioeconomic problems, caused by the excesses and power abuses of the ruling aristocracy. The primary purpose of the homicide law probably was to curb these abuses by empowering the ordinary person to protect his family. If, for example, an attractive poor woman caught the eye of an aristocrat, before Drakon he could abuse her, seduce her, or both, and there was nothing much that the woman's *kyrios* could do to protect her and the good name of his household. Drakon genuinely empowered that man by bypassing corruptible aristocratic magistrates and placing in his hands powers of life and death upon the intruder. For a thorough discussion of the laws of Drakon see Phillips 2008; Carawan 1998; Gagarin 1981; Stroud 1981.

99 One such case of entrapment is attested from the 4th c. in the speech *Against Neaira* (59.64–71; see also Kapparis 1999: 295–300).

100 Kapparis 1995: 97–122.

husband." Johnstone understands that the law was trying to protect ordinary customers buying goods from women in the market place or visiting women workers in the workshops around the city.[101]

A reading of this law outside the context of prostitution would not be consonant with the way Lysias and Plutarch read it; like Apollodoros, they undoubtedly understood it in a context of prostitution. All three, Apollodoros, Lysias and Plutarch, understand the verb πωλῶνται in the Solonian text as "to wander around," correctly so, because the verb does not acquire the meaning "to sell" before the classical period. In Homer, Hesiod and in archaic lyric it always means "to run up and down, to wander around." [102] From the early 5th century the meaning shifts to "selling" or "being sold." One would imagine that as sales persons were wandering around trying to sell their goods, the verb "to wander" came to mean "to go about with the intent to sell" and then simply "to sell." [103] To my knowledge, the oldest attested case where the verb πωλεῖν has already acquired the meaning "to sell" is in Herodotos (1.196), a century and a half after the Solonian law. This semantic shift prevails in the course of the 5th century, to the extent that an early 4th century audience needed to be lectured by the speaker on the original meaning of this verb.[104]

We are told that the main purpose for the existence of brothels was to ensure the availability of public women who would steer the lust of young men away from respectable women. Considering the non-specific formulation of the Dra-

---

101 Johnstone 2002: 253. His argument is based on the reading of the manuscripts πωλῶσι(ν) τι, which he defends, understanding it as "to sell something." All modern editors of the speech have accepted the emendation of Heraldus πωλῶνται (to wander around) based on πωλοῦνται transmitted by citations of the same statute in Harp. s.v. ἀποπεφασμένως, Lys. 10,19 and Plu. *Sol.* 23, before the corruption which we find in our manuscripts had occurred. There is a possibility that the Solonian text used the archaic/Ionic form πωλεῦνται, which might easier explain the error in our manuscripts. This form appears quite a few times in pre-classical texts (e.g. Hom. *Od.* 17.534, 22.352; A. *Pr.* 645).

102 See Hom. *Il.* 1.490; 5.788; *Od.* 4.384; 4.811; 9.189; Hom. *Hym. Ap.* 170; Hes. *Th.* 781; Hes. fr. 302.5 Merkelbach; Archil. fr. 49.7 West, al.

103 See for example a similar change of meaning in the word "πλανόδιος" in Modern Greek. Initially the πλανόδιος μικροπωλητής would be a traveling salesman, but then the adjective alone (after omission of the noun) shifted from its original meaning "wanderer" and came to mean "salesman". See also the Ps-Herodotian *Vita Homeri* 443: πολλὰ μὲν εἰν ἀγορῆι πωλεύμενα, πολλὰ δ' ἀγυιαῖς (referring to pottery sold in the market place and the streets by wandering salesmen), of uncertain date.

104 Lys. 10.19–20: "Ὅσαι δὲ πεφασμένως πωλοῦνται" .... Πρόσεχε τὸν νοῦν. τὸ μὲν πεφασμένως ἐστὶ φανερῶς, πωλεῖσθαι δὲ βαδίζειν...

konian law, sexual acts with prostitutes without fear of the severe legal consequences and dangers of the adultery laws only became possible under this law of
Solon, which drew the line between activities that constituted *moicheia*, and activities that did not. When such a dispute arose in the mid-4th century, with the
woman's father claiming that she was a respectable woman who had been seduced, and the woman's lover claiming that she was a prostitute, this law was
invoked.[105] The prospect of having to defend his household from public accusations that it operated as a brothel compelled the woman's father to accept private
arbitration and settle out of court.

Frost erroneously believed that only free hetairai are mentioned in the Solonian law which legally recognized prostitution.[106] Seemingly he missed the technical sense of καθῶνται, which down to the classical period was the primary verb
for being established in a brothel.[107] The somewhat euphemistic language of the
Solonian law was referring to two different types of prostitutes, '*eas quae in domo
meretricia prostent et eas quae in viis publicis versentur*', to use the words of a

---

105 The law protecting innocent shoppers and customers of workshops and warehouses from
entrapment under allegations of adultery (with the ultimate objective of extracting compensation) is also quoted by Apollodoros just a few lines above (59.66):

> If anyone wrongfully imprisons a man as an adulterer, the victim may bring an indictment
> before the Thesmothetai that he was wrongfully imprisoned, and if he secures the convic-
> tion of the man who imprisoned him and it is judged that he was the victim of an unjust
> plot, he is to be innocent and the sureties are to be free from liability; but if he is judged to
> be an adulterer, it is laid down that the sureties must hand him over to the successful liti-
> gant, and he is to inflict upon him in the court-room any punishment he wishes, without
> using a knife, as one would with an adulterer.

I have argued elsewhere that this law too was probably Solonian in origin (Kapparis 1995: 113–
116; and 1999: 308–10). If an innocent shopper had been wrongfully entrapped he could invoke
this law in order to escape any obligation for compensation agreed under duress; and, at least in
the classical period, he had the choice to escalate matters further with a private lawsuit for damages (δίκη αἰκείας), or theoretically even a public lawsuit for insolent and outrageous conduct
(γραφὴ ὕβρεως), which could carry the death penalty. Thus, innocent shoppers were very well
protected from scheming or jealous husbands, and surely market forces offered additional protection. An extortion attempt in a shop or workshop under allegations of adultery would rapidly
become public knowledge in a place like archaic or even classical Athens, and this would certainly discourage other customers and prove detrimental for business.
106 Frost 2002: 41–2.
107 E.g. Aesch. 1.74; Is. 6.19.

prominent 19th century scholar.[108] The law refers both to organized and to free-lance prostitution, acknowledges that both were practiced around the city, and attempts to include every form of prostitution practiced at the time. With this law Solon legally recognized prostitution de facto, and defined which women are to be considered prostitutes by the law, and thus exempt from the powers of the adultery laws. The vocabulary of the law does not suggest that Solon invented prostitution as a measure to deal with the desires of young men, as later authors alleged, but rather to regulate an existing situation. This would not be untypical of Solon as a lawgiver: as Victor Ehrenberg puts it "many of his laws did little else than put customary rules under the state's authority".[109]

Moreover, the law drawing a line between respectable women to whom the adultery laws applied, and public bodies not subject to the same rules, was not the only Solonian statute regulating prostitution, sexual morality and family life.[110] Another Solonian law, which scholars have found very puzzling, also refers

---

108 "Those who prostitute themselves in a whore-house, and those who go about the public streets": G. Dindorf, *Demosthenis Orationes*, Oxford 1846, vol. 4, com. on 59.67.

109 Ehrenberg 1968: 74.

110 Plutarch mentions several more Solonian laws regulating sexuality and family life, some of which he finds absurd and ridiculous (ἄτοπος καὶ γελοῖος). Among these he mentions the law on the *epicleros*, with invasive provisions such as the requirement for the husband to have sex with her three times a month, even though Plutarch understands that its purpose was to increase the chances of procreation (Plu. *Sol.* 20 and 23). He finds it strange that a woman given in marriage was only allowed three pieces of clothing and a few pots and pans of small value, although he approves the purpose of it, which he believes was to encourage marriages on a basis of graceful and affectionate devotion (χάριτι καὶ φιλότητι), rather than financial interest. In reality, these provisions probably made good sense in the economically depressed climate of Solonian Athens, but had become obsolete in the classical period, where we hear that the average dowry was between 20 and 30 minae, and that very valuable jewelry and fine clothes were routinely included in it (Schaps 1979: 99; see also Kapparis 1999: 267–69). He also finds the legal provisions on rape totally absurd (πλείστην ἀτοπίαν ἔχειν). He cannot understand how it could be punishable with a mere fine, when adultery was potentially punishable by death: "It defies logic to punish the same offence sometimes with inescapable severity, and sometimes with playful leniency, setting the penalty to a casual fine, unless money around the city was hard to find at that time, and this difficulty made fines a heavy punishment (Plut. *Sol.* 20)." Plutarch's fundamental error in this case was to telescope the Drakonian law on homicide, which allowed the killing of an adulterer caught in the act, with the Solonian laws on sexual offences (See also Glazebrook 2006: 39 and n. 22). By doing so, naturally he could not reconcile the very different purposes of these laws. I have argued elsewhere that the Solonian legislation on adultery did precisely what Plutarch observed: it was intended to provide more lenient alternatives to murder for the kyrios of a woman who caught her with a lover (Kapparis 1995: 97–122 and 1996: 63–77). Under the Drakonian legislation the kyrios of a woman caught committing adultery had a very difficult choice to make: he could either kill the adulterer on the spot and soil his hands with blood - an odious course of

to prostitution, in all likelihood. Plutarch mentions a law which allowed the father or brother of an unchaste woman to sell her. Typically this has been taken to mean that the woman was sold into slavery.[111] However, this traditional interpretation runs into two serious problems. First, the laws of Solon went to great lengths to prohibit slavery for debts and even restored to freedom persons who had already become slaves; how likely is it that at the same time they explicitly sanctioned slavery merely for sexual indiscretions? Second, there is no attested case in the time of Solon or later where a father or brother ever sold a free woman to slavery, which led scholars to believe that by the classical period this law had become obsolete. D.M. MacDowell concludes that "it seems unlikely that Athenian fathers still sold even their naughtiest daughters in the fifth and fourth centuries." [112]

Allison Glazebrook has recently offered a new, more convincing interpretation of this law, which does not create the same problems, and helps solve a difficult puzzle regarding the laws for procurers.[113] She reads the verb πωλεῖν as a reference to prostitution and understands that a father or brother was not allowed to procure a free-born woman, unless she had already been unchaste. Such an interpretation would be in line with the other Solonian laws forbidding the procurement of a free-born boy, under heavy penalties. This particular clause in Plutarch comes in the end of a passage, which also discusses the Solonian laws on adultery, rape, and procuring of a free person, except recognized prostitutes. Undoubtedly in his mind all these passages were connected and the law forbidding the sale of one's daughter or sister comes as a natural extension to the passage

---

action for most people even if the law was prepared to forgive them for this - or let the adulterer walk free. Neither alternative would seem satisfactory for the majority of Athenians. Solon, by permitting the humiliation of the adulterer – a quite substantial punishment considering how seriously the Athenians took torture of free persons and physical abuse – offered the kyrios a kind of satisfaction which he might find sufficiently appealing to abstain from murder in order to seek redress for the insult inflicted upon his household, honor and masculinity. This would be consistent with Solon's main objective to end the feuds and establish the rule of law. To be fair, this provision, despite corroboration by several other reliable sources (e.g. Lys. 1.22–23), has generated just as much disbelief among modern scholars, and a long debate in the international bibliography. See the discussion in Gernet 1955: 51–9; MacDowell 1978: 125; Harris 1990: 370–377; Carey 1995: 407–417; Ogden 1996: 146–150 and 1997: 25–41; Kapparis 1999: 305–6; Omitowoju 2002.

111 Plu. *Sol.* 23: ἔτι δ' οὔτε θυγατέρας πωλεῖν οὔτ' ἀδελφὰς δίδωσι, πλὴν ἂν μὴ λάβῃ παρθένον ἀνδρὶ συγγεγενημένην. For the discussion and previous bibliography see Glazebrook 2005: 33–34; Just 1989: 70.
112 MacDowell 1978: 80 and 125
113 Glazebrook 2006: 33–53.

referring to procurers. Glazebrook's elegant solution suggests that the procurement of a free, respectable woman was forbidden, unless she was unsuitable for marriage because she had already had sexual relations outside marriage.

Aeschines in the speech Against Timarchos erroneously claims that male prostitution was thoroughly regulated by Drakon and Solon.[114] The orator devotes one fifth of his speech to a discussion of legal documents which were allegedly instituted by those ancient lawgivers in order to regulate the conduct of all male citizens from boyhood to adulthood. But this was never the Athenian way. In reality, the laws concerning the orderly conduct of children and their protection from adult predatory behavior are dated by MacDowell to the late 5th or early 4th century, probably correctly,[115] while the laws banning male prostitutes from certain offices and from speaking in the Assembly do not make sense in the archaic state, as they are based upon the assumption of a fully-developed democratic constitution, and were also introduced in the late 5th or early 4th century. A probably Solonian law forbidding a slave to fall in love with a free boy or pursue him under penalty of 50 lashes is reported by Aeschines, which might have some implications if the free boy was practicing prostitution.[116] However, in practical terms the impact of this law upon the markets of prostitution would have been negligible as Athenian slaves would not have been able to afford free boys, even if they wanted to pursue them, and this is probably why we never hear of this law again.

The Solonian laws on procuring, as reported by Aeschines are contradictory: first, there is a law penalizing the procurement of a free boy, and, as a penalty or part of the penalty, it frees the boy from the legal obligation to provide for his father in his old age.[117] Arguably this law has a similar underlying philosophy to the prohibition of the procurement of a free woman by her family (see the discus-

---

114 See Aesch. 1.6–36; see also the discussion in Fisher's commentary ad loc. and MacDowell 1976: 26–31.
115 MacDowell 2000: 17; see the discussion in Ch. 5.1. and 5.2.
116 See Aesch. 1.139 and MacDowell 2000: 19.
117 Aesch. 1.13. The wording of Aeschines (Καὶ ἴσα τὰ ἐπιτίμια ἑκατέρῳ πεποίηκε, καὶ μὴ ἐπάναγκες εἶναι τῷ παιδὶ ἡβήσαντι τρέφειν τὸν πατέρα μηδὲ οἴκησιν παρέχειν, ὃς ἂν ἐκμισθωθῇ ἑταιρεῖν· ἀποθανόντα δὲ θαπτέτω καὶ τἆλλα ποιείτω τὰ νομιζόμενα) does not make clear whether there was an additional penalty, like a fine, as in the case of the procurement of a free-born woman. καί after πεποίηκε seems to suggest that there was a fine in addition to the release of the boy from the obligation to look after the father in his old age, but this is not explicitly mentioned in the part of the law which Aeschines appears to be quoting. See also MacDowell 2000: 17–18 and the discussion in Ch. 4.1.

sion above). In the case of procuring a woman the penalty for the father or guardian was probably a fine of 20 drachmas, while in the case of a boy, possibly in addition to a fine, the penalty was deferred until a father or guardian reached a helpless old age.[118] In both cases the law removes from the father or guardian the authority to procure a child, but the legal procedures and the penalties lack the intimidating precision of classical statutes, which in itself supports the conclusion that they were genuinely Solonian. Whether these laws remained valid in the classical period is complicated by the fact that procurers were not penalized for practicing their trade, and also by the citation of another law on procurement by Aeschines, this one carrying the death penalty.[119] Clearly it is difficult to take this evidence at face value. The bigger picture seems to be that Solon introduced laws intended to stop the exploitation of free-born children of both sexes by unscrupulous family members, guardians or outside procurers. However, these laws were re-defined, ignored or forgotten altogether in the classical period, when the markets of sex exploded along with the prosperity and rising importance of Athens as a trading and imperial city, and this is why, whatever their original purpose, their validity and objectives in the classical period need to be re-examined within the political climate, legal philosophy, cultural norms and socioeconomic circumstances of the time (see the discussion in Ch. 4.1. and 4.2.).

The picture which emerges is that Solon's laws on family life and sexual morality were instrumental for the legal definition, recognition and regulation of prostitution, but that they neither created a sex market nor introduced prostitution to Athens; Solon simply tried to deal with an existing situation in a sensible and measured manner. Madeleine Henry in a significant study discussing the origins of prostitution in the Greek world relates the principal ideologies and dynamics of it to the trafficking of women in earlier times as shown in the epic tradition.[120] Henry argues that in the epic world women are often viewed as trophies, as rewards for the male conquerors. Winning women was like a currency: the more one could carry away, the braver and more valorous he was considered. Henry's thesis rightly suggests that the development of organized and free-lance prostitution in the archaic polis was a rather gradual process, and not the work

---

118 I understand that Glazebrook's reading of the law about a father selling his daughter refers to prostitution (Plu. *Sol.* 23; Glazebrook 2006: 33–53.), and that the penalty for the father or guardian of the woman would be the same as that for any other procurer, set at 20 drachmas in Plutarch (*Sol.* 23).

119 Aesch. 1.14 and 184: Καὶ τὰς προαγωγοὺς γράφεσθαι κελεύει, κἂν ἁλῶσι, θανάτῳ ζημιοῦν.

120 Henry 2011: 14–33. Some of her references to the trafficking of women in Homer include *Il.* 1.29–31; 1.161–162; 2.689–690; 18.338–341; 9.260–290; *Od.* 16.108–109; 20.318–319; 22.37 and 313–314).

of a single man or a specific piece of legislation, as some Athenocentric sources of questionable authority suggest.

Not far from Athens, wealthy Corinth had reached a high level of development very early in Greek history. Already in the 8th century it was a prosperous and flourishing commercial center with an almost un-Greek taste for luxury, frequented by merchants, traders and sailors able and willing to spend. These conditions were very conducive for the proliferation of prostitution, and one would be justified to think that the legendary hetairai of Corinth, and the sex tourism which they generated, had been around for centuries before high end prostitution reached Athens. Other references in non-Athenian poets from the archaic period, such as Archilochos, Hipponax or Alkaios (see previous section), also suggest that prostitution was already widespread all around the Greek world at the time of Solon. We should be in no doubt that market forces and conducive ideologies allowed prostitution to take hold and flourish in the archaic Greek world.

In pre-Solonian Athens most of the wealth and all political power were in the hands of the *eupatridai*, the aristocracy which had ruled the city for a long time. This ruling elite had the power to drive free-born farmers to slavery for unpaid debts, and was not accountable to anyone but itself. We can imagine that rape and abuse of free women of the lower classes were not rare, and we can interpret the Drakonian self-help law mentioned above as an attempt to offer some protection against the excesses of the aristocracy. We can also reasonably assume that poorer women, whose husbands, fathers or male protectors had lost their property, ability to sustain their household and maybe even freedom, were driven by desperation into the grip of unscrupulous procurers, or into the streets, trying to sell sexual favors in order to secure the means of survival for themselves and their families. Plutarch's reference to a Solonian law forbidding the sale of women for the purposes of prostitution suggests that this was a serious problem which the lawgiver considered necessary to address, and furthermore may imply that not infrequently the families themselves procured daughters or sold them into prostitution in order to make a living. The link between prostitution and deprived communities is strong and ubiquitous, and pre-Solonian Athens was no exception.[121] It was a community with large populations below the poverty line, and a

---

121 See for example Finnegan 2007; Zimmermann 1996; Khan et al (2010: 365–383), investigating the causes of prostitution in Pakistan, have reached the following conclusion: "Content analysis of data resulted in identification of one main theme: 'Poverty of opportunity forcing women into prostitution.' The identified driving forces behind women resorting to sell sex were poverty, materialism, and the desire to move up in society. They continued to sell sex due to poverty of opportunity and influencing social factors."

ruling class willing to take advantage of its power and affluence. These circumstances favored the development of low class prostitution centered around cheap
brothels, in the streets of Kerameikos and the harbor of Piraeus. Just as the Solonian law implies, prostitution both in organized establishments and in the streets
had already developed along these lines before his time.

Like most human civilizations, the Athenians were fond of *aitia*, foundation
myths, and legendary figures who single-handedly changed the course of history.
Although Athenian authors understood well the contribution of the true founders
of democracy, in particular Kleisthenes and Ephialtes, oral tradition still linked
the foundation of democracy to Theseus, and sometimes to Solon, as it attributed
the start of agriculture to the instruction of Demeter. In this context, the tale that
prostitution was the brainchild of the "founding father" of the Athenian constitution should come as no surprise to us, as it was consonant with Athenian custom. However, when it comes to facts we are bound to consider the stories about
Solon's brothels to be fundamentally incompatible with his aspirations. For a
lawgiver who set out to regenerate the Athenian economy and society, and to im-
prove the conditions of the lower classes, it would be odd to sanction and perpet-
uate the exploitation of the poor through state-run brothels.[122] More to the point,
Solon's reforms were legislative, not executive: he created a law code, a set of
measures to stimulate economic growth, deal with some of the social problems,
introduce some political reform and promote harmony. He did not take over the
functions of magistrates, did not build or manage public projects, and did not
take over the state like a tyrant.

As Victor Ehrenberg puts it, Solon "founded the state of justice. He made the
people its executant, and secured the personal freedom as well as the political
responsibility of every citizen ... He was the first deliberately to proclaim 'freedom
under the law'".[123] One would need to dismiss the part of the story which suggests
that Solon erected and managed brothels as an invention of later centuries intended to rationalize his contribution to the institution of organized prostitution.
His contribution is to be found in his legislative work, and it proved long-lasting,
like the rest of his statutes regulating sexuality and family life. Solon formally
recognized prostitution as an activity that was taking place in a variety of forms
around the city, set the boundaries between women who were to be treated as

---

122 State-run brothels like those found in medieval France and other parts of Europe, are not
attested anywhere in the ancient world, at any point in history; prostitution always remained a
private enterprise in the Greek city states and the kingdoms and empires that followed. See Rossiaud 1988: 3–10 and 198–199.
123 Ehrenberg 1968: 74.

prostitutes and women who were respectable members of a family, disallowed the application of the adultery laws upon women who practiced prostitution, and, by penalizing their procurement, tried to protect respectable women and boys from unscrupulous family members who might want to exploit them. Thus, the Solonian legislation concerning prostitutes set the stage for the explosion of organized and free-lance prostitution in the classical period. As the city grew in prosperity and power, the humble brothels and cheap street prostitution of the Solonian era gave way to more up-market establishments and top of the range hetairai, like those who in the time of Solon could be found in wealthy Corinth.

2 The Making of the Classical Prostitute

2.1 A Hetaira's Education

The comic poet Philemon jokes that the fee in some brothels was as little as one obol (1/6 drachma), while according to Athenaios the retired hetaira Gnathaina charged a rich old foreigner 1000 drachmas for a single night with her daughter Gnathainion.[1] Even making allowances for comic exaggeration, one wonders why a night with a hetaira was supposed to be 6000 times more expensive that an encounter with some other prostitute. Surely looks and age had something to do with it, but there is no evidence to suggest that all the slave girls in the brothels of the ancient world were ugly or old, and chances are that such establishments catered for a variety of tastes with a range of ages, types and looks to satisfy every purse and appetite. It had to be more than looks or sex. Personality, style, reputation, social skills, the ability to form emotional bonds and captivate their lovers, or to put it more cynically, manipulate customers into believing that their company was worth the expense, are some of the secret weapons in the arsenal of the ancient hetairai attested in our sources. Numerous references to the training, education, expected behavior and encounters of high-end hetairai with male clients, especially in comedy, epistolography and sympotic literature, ironically suggest that the customer paid so much more for their time, conversation, companionship and emotional attachment than they did for sex.[2] He paid, in order to be made to feel important, someone worth the affections of a stunning-looking girl or boy, who was staring adoringly into his eyes, in this make-believe scenario. When Ischomachos in Xenophon's *Economics* describes the training of his new wife for her duties as the household mistress,[3] he does not include advice on how

---

1 Philem. fr. 3; Athen. 13.44. We are told that Gnathaina was so confident that the 90 years old satrap will be happy to pay this much for a night with her daughter that she asked him to pay only half of it in advance and the other half in the end.

2 While paradoxically all these qualities are typically associated with family life, there is one fundamental difference, as outlined in court by the well-known American actor Charlie Sheen during the Heidi Fleiss trial: "I do not pay them for sex, I pay them to leave". Despite the ubiquitous motif of the man being slave to his mistress (as developed for example in the opening monologue of Diniarchus in Plautus *Truculentus*, or the *paraklausithyron* literature; see Ch. 5.5.), the man was in control and could choose to leave the relationship at will, with no consequences, while a Greek man could not easily do this with his family.

3 X. *Oec.* 7.1 ff: The wife of Ischomachos needed to learn how to manage the household, take charge of the processing and storage of raw materials and agricultural resources, keep tabs on the assets of the household, manage and oversee the servants, and even look after their well-

DOI 10.1515/9783110557954-002

to be a gracious hostess, refine her social skills, become more erudite or learn specific marketable and transferable skills. These would not be considered useful for a married woman, but it is precisely the kind of instruction offered to a hetaira in another passage of Xenophon. The famous account from the *Memorabilia* where Socrates instructs the hetaira Theodote how to search for customers, using images and metaphors from hare hunting, has received some scholarly attention primarily because of the difficulty to understand its purpose and function in the context of the *Memorabilia*.[4] Stefan Tilg, arguing against Armand Delatte, suggests that the character of Theodote in the *Memorabilia* is modelled on Aspasia and that the ultimate goal of Socrates was to criticize Pericles through his mistress, but he nonetheless believes that the information presented here can be useful for our understanding of a hetaira's education.[5]

---

being, and in general make sure that the household runs well. As part of this training she would learn how to cook, clean, weave, saw, spin and process the wool, and perhaps the basics of reading, writing, and healthcare.

4 X. *Mem.* 3.11: The details of this lengthy and complex discussion on the functionality of this passage in its context should not concern us at this point, as our main purpose is to assess this narrative as a historical source of some significance. See the discussion in Delatte 1933; Goldhill 1998: 105–124; Tilg 2004: 193–206. For the basics of hare hunting and further bibliography see Kapparis 1997: 154–156.

5 X. *Mem.* 3.11. (Translation by E. C. Marchant. *Xenophon in Seven Volumes*, Harvard University Press, Cambridge, MA; William Heinemann, Ltd., London. 1923):

[THEODOTE] "Then can I adapt this plan for the pursuit of friends?"
[SOCRATES] "Of course you can, if for the hound you substitute an agent who will track and find rich men with an eye for beauty, and will then contrive to chase them into your nets."
[TH.] "Nets! What nets have I got?"
[SO.] "One, surely, that clips close enough to your body! And inside it you have a soul that teaches you what glance will please, what words delight, and tells you that your business is to give a warm welcome to an eager suitor, but to slam the door upon a coxcomb; yes, and when a friend has fallen sick, to show your anxiety by visiting him; and when he has had a stroke of good fortune, to congratulate him eagerly; and if he is eager in his suit, to put yourself at his service heart and soul. As for loving, you know how to do that, I am sure, both tenderly and truly; and I know that you convince your friends that their company is pleasing to you I know, not by words but by deeds."
[TH.] "Upon my word," said Theodote, "I don't contrive one of these things."
[SO.] "Nevertheless," he continued, "it is very important that your behavior to a man should be both natural and correct. For assuredly you can neither catch a friend nor keep him by violence; it is kindness and sweetness that catch the creature and hold him fast."
[TH.] "True," she said.
[SO.] "First, then, you must ask such favors of your suitors as they will grant without a moment's hesitation; and next you must repay their favors in the same coin; for in this way

There is nothing overtly sexual in the dialogue between Socrates and Theodote. As Tilg puts it, the entire discussion is pervaded by "sinnlicher und sokratisch-geistiger Erotik".[6] This eroticism does not go beyond circumstantial references to the ἴυγξ (love-wheel), love filters and magic in the end of the dialogue; otherwise everything remains very respectable, employing the language of friendship (φιλία) and benefaction (εὐεργεσία) to describe the relationship of Theodote with men who craved her company. Even in the places describing the beauty of The-odote, her physical appeal is never degraded below the level of an art-work or a source of inspiration for painters. However, the reader is under no illusion that she is a hetaira, earning her very affluent lifestyle through prostitution. She dresses and acts like a hetaira, but only to the extent that she allows her "friends" access into her house and private life, and graciously shares with them her exceptional beauty. The customary behaviors attributed to hetairai, like shameless greed, deception, entrapment and duplicity are absent, and in a strange twist Socrates is actually trying to instruct her in these skills so that she can maximize her clientele and profits. In a sense Socrates and Theodote are alike: both rely on the affection and benefactions of their friends, and both possess a sought-after commodity, which they are willing to share. But while Socrates is endowed with clarity Theodote cannot even see what is expedient for her, and this is why she needs his instruction.

Socrates suggests that Theodote ought to cast a net like a hunter trying to catch hare, or like a spider trapping insects. He also suggests that she should have someone looking out for potential "friends" and bringing them to her, in other words, a procurer, only Socrates would not use such distasteful language and this is why he employs another metaphor from hare-hunting. Then he proceeds with instruction on how she could make herself appealing to lovers. A seductive

---

they will prove most sincerely your friends, most constant in their affection and most generous. And they will appreciate your favours most highly if you wait till they ask for them. The sweetest meats, you see, if served before they are wanted, seem sour, and to those who have had enough they are positively nauseating; but even poor fare is very welcome when offered to a hungry man." [14]

[TH.] "And how can I make them hunger for my fare?"

[SO.] "Why, in the first place, you must not offer it to them when they have had enough, nor prompt them until they have thrown off the surfeit and are beginning to want more; then, when they feel the want, you must prompt them by behaving as a model of propriety, by a show of reluctance to yield, and by holding back until they are as keen as can be; for then the same gifts are much more to the recipient than when they are offered before they are desired."

6 "sensuous and Socratic, spiritual eroticism"; Tilg 2004: 193.

glance, a kind word, a warm welcome for a keen lover, a firm attitude towards a lazy, soft man, and a kind, generous and affectionate disposition would create an aura of reverence and go a long way towards attracting and consolidating relationships. In order to keep the lovers keen one should not offer too much of herself, but should wait until she is asked, and even then coyly hold back for as long as possible, so that the desire of her company grows to the point that her friend is prepared to offer rich rewards. At that point she could repay the favor by faithfully offering herself, and this could be the beginning of a lasting and beneficial friendship. Socrates is constructing an image of the ideal hetaira, someone who has perfected the technique of obtaining, satisfying and keeping lovers interested, and forming deep and lasting bonds with rich rewards, both material and spiritual. Euphemisms aside, the practical value of this advice is evident. Skills such as the ability to appear gentle, generous, trustworthy and coy have always been considered paramount feminine virtues, conducive for erotic relations and likely to enchant a potential suitor.

The first non-fictional reference to the education of hetairai comes from the speech of Apollodoros *Against Neaira*, where the proper training of young slave girls to become gracious hetairai is presented as a *sine qua non* for a career at the upper end of the job market.[7] This passage is very significant as it assumes that beauty alone could never be enough. The promising good looks of Nikarete's girls were the necessary foundation upon which good training could build, under the expert guidance of someone who understood well the market and its needs. An aura of domesticity, brought about by the pretense that the girls had been brought up in a "family", apparently enhanced their appeal, even though the customers must have been well aware that this was only a veneer.

In the *Kampylion* of Eubulos, a contemporary of Apollodoros, we encounter advice on good table manners specifically aimed at hetairai. Stuffing one's face with mouthfuls of leek, a killer of sexual desire because of its distinct smell and

---

7 D. 59.18: "Nicarete, a freedwoman of Charisius of Elis, and wife of his cook Hippias, acquired seven little girls from a very young age. She was skilled in discerning the potential for beauty in very young children and knew how to bring them up and train them meticulously, since she was an expert in this trade and made her livelihood out of it."

instant bad breath potential,[8] or grabbing greedily large chunks of meat[9] is not enticing, and very likely would put someone off. A woman who wants to appear attractive should be careful with her manners, nibbling on food with tact and discretion.[10] In the *Isostation* of Alexis, another contemporary of Apollodoros, we find substantial information on the kind of training involved in a hetaira's education and intended to enhance her appearance (ὄψεις) and manners (τρόπους).[11] Of course, the ultimate objective was profit and ripping off their customers (τὸ κέρδος καὶ τὸ συλᾶν τοὺς πέλας). The passage alludes to a form of apprenticeship which allowed the "beginners in the trade" (πρωτοπείρους τῆς τέχνης) to learn some of its secrets from more seasoned workers. The actual use of the word *techne* is significant, because it portrays prostitution as a craft like medicine, sculpture or rhetoric, with a specific set of skills that need to be carefully learned. The areas of learning included dress and make up, and also sessions about smiling or at least pretending to smile, even if one did not happen to be of a cheerful disposition. The advice offered in such a case was to keep a stick of mint between one's teeth until a habit forms conveying the appearance of a smile.

Further evidence of training for the beginners in the trade can be found scattered in a number of sources and includes a broad variety of topics. A well-known Hippocratic passage attests that women in prostitution knew how to induce relatively safe abortions very early in the pregnancy, as soon as they became aware

---

8 Modern science agrees that allium-containing foods like onions, leeks, and garlic create bad breath instantly, because they contain thiols (organosulphur compounds which smell like garlic). Once they are digested they release a strong smell from the skin, urine and lungs. The nutritional benefits of the humble leek notwithstanding, it has been the bane of lovers, and the ancient comic tradition has picked on it. See for example a passage from the *Sleep* of Alexis (fr. 242):

δια ταῦθ' ὁ πόρνος οὗτος οὐδὲ τῶν πράσων
ἑκάστοτ' ἐπιδειπνεῖ μεθ' ἡμῶν· τοῦτο δ' ἦν,
ἵνα μή τι λυπήσειε τὸν ἐραστὴν φιλῶν.

That's why this man-whore would not always eat leek with us.
This was the reason: he did not want to annoy his lover,
when he kissed him.

9 This would be unattractive, as it would imply poverty and deprivation.
10 Eub. fr. 42. This by contrast would imply success. She has plenty at home and is accustomed to good food, and this is why she does not need to assault the meat platter; she only samples food for good company.
11 Alexis fr. 98.

of it.[12] He actually implies that their knowledge was superior to that of other women, and even to that of doctors, and was handed down from one generation to another as a secret of the trade. Since there is no emotional tone of approval or disapproval attached to this statement in the Hippocratic text, we can accept its testimony at face value and assume that some skill in effecting the termination of unwanted pregnancies for women making a living with their bodies was passed on from one generation to the next.

From the 4th century advice on how to conquer and keep a lover, how to behave in social circles and even how to please a lover in bed, is more systematically presented in a number of manuals, some of which are attributed to hetairai of the time. Several of them had to do with etiquette at symposia and dinners, and savoir vivre. Athenaios attests that Gnathaina's *Sympotic Rules* manual (*Σισσυτικός Νόμος*), with instructions for diners at her house, was modeled on similar manuals published by philosophers to serve as ground-rules in their association with their students.[13] Such manuals were probably not confined to manners and good society, but involved all kinds of advice on public and private pleasures, like the famous book of Archestratos entitled *Gastronomy* (*Γαστρονομία*), which was offering plentiful advice on gourmet food, and met the disapproval of Chrysippos for including an abundance of useless information.[14]

Chrysippos was equally critical of another work, even more famous that the *Gastronomy* of Archestratos, and in this instance he was not alone in his disapproval of the provocative erotica manual of Philainis of Samos. Her work was sufficiently famous by the end of the 4th century to attract the criticism of Klearchos of Soli, while Timaios of Tauromenion called her, along with a certain Botrys,[15] "the writers of shame" (ἀναισχυντογράφοι).[16] Similar criticism is piled up by several Christian authors, such as Justin or Tatian the apologist in his critique of

---

12 Hip. *Carn.* 19; see also Kapparis 2002: 107–113.
13 Athen. 13.48; Arist. fr. 4.26 Rose; D.L. 5.26, where one book entitled *Νόμοι Σισσυτικοί* is included in the list of works of Aristotle, (Proclus *in R.* 1.8). Aristotle, Xenokrates and Speusippos seemingly had written such manuals (Σισσυτικοί or Συμποτικοί Νόμοι), and Gnathaina playfully adapted them for prostitutes. We cannot be sure whether this manual was to be taken seriously, or it was nothing more than a humorous parody by a hetaira renowned for her sharp wit.
14 Chrysippos fr. 5 and 6 von Arnim; Athen. 1.7, 2.47, 3.44, 77, 7.42, 113, 8,13.
15 His name means "grape", probably a pseudonym for a writer of sympotic literature.
16 The earliest reference to the Erotica of Philainis may be in Aristotle (Arist. *Div.Somn.* 464 b 2), but the text is problematic at this point.

Greek women for choosing to be writers instead of minding domestic virtue.[17] Several sources, some more reliable than others, state that Philainis was a hetaira, and we have no reason to doubt this information. The earliest is a fragment of Poseidonios attesting that she was one of the erudite hetairai who frequented the Gardens of Epicurus.[18] We also have the weighty testimony of the learned scholiast of Lucian, and two significant sources in fictional literature - a passage from Menander's Συναριστῶσαι where Philainis appears in the company of other recognizable names of 4th century hetairai, and an epigram of her junior contemporary and compatriot Asclepiades of Samos.[19] Considering the nature of her book in addition to this evidence, we should be in no doubt that Philainis had been a hetaira, and that her manual was to some degree distilled from her own experience, but the few fragments which we now have suggest that it went far beyond that.

A lucky find among the papyri of Oxyrinchus (POxy 2891), first published by E. Lobel, then improved and discussed in some detail by Kyriakos Tsantsanoglou,[20] has preserved a few, precious lines from the famous work. The following translation is based upon the improved version of Tsantsanoglou:

> This is what Philainis of Samos, the daughter of Ocymenes, wrote for those who want to live their lives with a sense of history and systematically … from her own experiences …
> On Seduction Techniques (Περὶ πειρασμῶν)
>
> Someone intent on seduction should arrive without cosmetics and rugged-looking, so that he does not give the woman the impression that he is up to something. … in mind …treat the one as if she were equal to the gods, the ugly one as if she were lovely, tell the old woman that she is like Rea. …
> On Kisses (Περὶ φιλημάτων)

There are several more references to the contents of the manual of Philainis in other authors. The part of the work which seems to have caught the public imagination was the Greek "Kama-Sutra," the section which offered advice on sexual positions. Clement, in a sarcastic remark, says that Philainis mentioned extensively sexual positions like they were the labors of Herakles. An epigram of Asclepiades, who undoubtedly was aware of the work, makes a double entendre

---

17 Klearchos fr. 63,1 Wehrli; Timaios *FGrH* 566 f 35 b; Chrysippos fr. 5 and 6 von Arnim; Justin *Apologia Secunda* 15.3; Tatian *Oratio ad Graecos* 34.3
18 Poseidonios fr. 290a 500 Theiler.
19 Sch. Luc. 49.28 Rabe; Menander fr. 190 Austin; Asklepiades *AG* 5.162.
20 Tsantsanoglou 1973: 183–195. Further improvements on the text have been proposed by Wolfgang Luppe in two articles (1974 and 1998).

about a horse (κέλης) race between Plangon and Philainis.[21] The fragment of Chrysippos criticizing the manual of Philainis mentions sexual movements and positions (κινήσεων καὶ σχημάτων). Timaios vilifies Demochares, the cousin of Demosthenes, accusing him of prostitution, and saying that he had engaged with the upper part of his body in more sexual positions than those described by Botrys and Philainis. The pseudo-Lucianic *Amores* reveals that transsexualism was included in the manual of Philainis. Suda is aware of an entire tradition of works on sexual positions, the mythical founder of which was Astyanassa, the maid of Helen of Sparta. Where this myth comes from is uncertain; it first appears in Hesychios (s.v.), and then in Photios and Suda. However, while Hesychios and Photios simply relate the myth, Suda links it to the manuals of Botrys, Philainis and Elephantine, thus creating a line of tradition which relates the origins of such manuals to Helen herself.[22]

Two epigrams, one by Aischrion of Samos, and one by Dioscorides, are trying to clean up the reputation of Philainis by denying that she was the author of such filth, and Tsantsanoglou is prepared to accept their testimony and consider the manual a pseudepigraphon, written under the pseudonym Philainis.[23] But this does not make sense on several levels. First of all, if Philainis had been a hetaira prominent enough to lend her name to a manual of erotica, why should her name need cleaning in the first place? Then, how can two fictional sources, like these epigrams, amount to sufficient evidence against the signature of the author in the actual extant text of the manual and numerous, specific and historical references to this famous work in other ancient authors, explicitly and without a doubt attributing it to Philainis, the 4th century hetaira? The language, essentially a proto-koine with sparse Ionic forms, just as one would have expected of a work composed in Samos in the second half of the 4th century, also supports the authorship of Philainis. Even Tsantsanoglou admits that a forgery produced in Athens would probably have been written in pure Ionic dialect.[24] Overall, the few surviving lines from the manual of Philainis have a natural flow, and an untidiness and inconsistency in the use of the dialects which should be expected of a period

---

21 The joke is based upon the double meaning of the word κέλης, which typically means "race-horse," but in Greek slang it also refers to the sexual position "doggy-style".

22 Clem.Al. *Protr.* 4.61.2; cf. Sch. Clem. Al. *Protr.* 314.29; Asclepiades *AG* 5.202; Chrysippos fr. 5 von Arnim; Timaios *FGrH* 566 f 35 b; Polybios (12.13) rejects the comment of Timaios as nothing more that slander; Ps.Lucian *Amores* 28; Suda α 4261; Phot. *Bibl.* 190.149 α 26–29.

23 Aischrion *AG* 7.345; *AG* 7.450; cf. Tsantsanoglou 1973: 183–195.

24 Compare and contrast, for example, the works attributed to Pythagorean women (see Ch. 3.2.). They are written in what appears at first to be pure Doric Greek, but abundantly bear the unmistakable marks of Hellenistic forgeries.

when major shifts were about to lead to convergence into the Koine. Moreover, the reference to Polycrates in the epigram of Aischrion is very problematic. Is Aischrion, a Samian himself, trying to white-wash the bad reputation of his compatriot Philainis by ascribing the provocative work to an Athenian man who has the name of the most famous Samian in history? This has got to be a joke.

Ultimately the primary objection of Tsantsanoglou has rather to do with modern sensibilities than any reliable evidence against the authorship of Philainis. He finds it hard to comprehend that a woman in the 4th century would have written such a work. This should not be considered sufficient reason to reject the authorship of Philainis. There is no doubt that she was a real person and a hetaira, and such a work should not be so unexpected of a sophisticated and educated woman of the time. Philainis would not be the only woman of letters to write a manual, however daring or provocative, and her work is not some kind of unique oddity. It seems to be the most famous representative of a rich tradition of manuals on how to win and keep a lover and how to enjoy the finer things in life, including sex, sumptuous dinners and good company. This tradition, which later antiquity referred all the way back to the most famous beauty in the ancient world, Helen of Sparta herself, included some names which are unfamiliar to us, like Pythonikos of Athens, Niko of Samos (or Leukas?), Kallistrate of Lesbos, Botrys and Phainarete, as well as some names and works which are more familiar, like the manual of Archestratos on gourmet eating, the *Sympotic Rules* of Gnathaina, or the Pseudo-Lucianic *Amores*. At the top of our list we might want to place Ovid's *Ars Amatoria*. While Ovid's work is refined and less explicit than some of the manuals of his predecessors,[25] he is certainly the heir of a long and popular tradition that educated many generations in the pleasures of love and the art of living with urbanity and style, and his *Ars Amatoria* can be safely placed within the broader context of the Graeco-Roman didactic tradition.[26] Such manuals would be valuable aids in a hetaira's education, and this is why we should not be surprised to hear that some of them were actually written by erudite hetairai. In Lucian's *Dialogues of Hetairai* we find additional materials on a hetaira's training, which certainly draw from the classical comic tradition. Dialogue 8 is a lesson on how to manipulate a lover's jealousy in order to squeeze more money out

---

25 See for example the important study of Roy Gibson (2007), who, contrary to much of the earlier literature that considered the *Ars Amatoria* to be racy, has argued that in fact it was advocating restraint and moderation. Certainly, compared to what we hear about the manual of Philainis, Ovid's work is tame and urbanite.
26 See for example, Binnicker 1967; Gibson 2007; Kueppers 1981: 2507–2551; Volk 2006: 235–251; Schniebs 2001: 49–76 Solodow 1977: 106–127.

of him.[27] The more experienced hetaira Ampelis, who admits that she has been practicing the trade for 20 years, is giving a lesson to the naïve 18 years old Chrysis.[28] Another passage of Lucian provides more specific advice about a hetaira's education. The widow Krobyle is offering thorough instruction to her daughter Korinna on how to be a good hetaera, on the day after her naïve daughter lost her virginity to a handsome lad who paid her a mina.[29] As the conversation progresses it becomes clear that Korinna did not initially make the association between money for sex and prostitution, and reacts with apprehension when she finally realizes what she was becoming. Korinna and Krobyle appear to be the last surviving members of an impoverished, working class Athenian family living in Piraeus. What follows is the instruction of Korinna on how to become a good hetaira:

> KROBYLE: First she takes good care of her appearance, then she is polite and pleasant with everyone, not giggling with everything, like you do, but smiling nicely and seductively, then behaving gracefully and not deceitfully when someone comes to her house or she goes to someone's place, never directly approaching a man first. If she is paid to attend a dinner party, she does not get drunk – for it is ridiculous and men dislike such women – nor does she fill up with delicacies in a vulgar manner, but barely touches it with the tips of her fingers, and puts it in her mouth quietly not stuffing it into both sides of her mouth, and she is drinking gently, not guzzling greedily but in a paced manner.
> KORINNA: Even if she happens to be thirsty, mother?
> KROBYLE: Especially then, Korinna. And she does not talk more than she should, nor mock anyone present, but only has eyes for the man who hired her, and for those reasons they

---

27 Luc. *DMeretr.* 8; for an idea about the tradition from which this dialogue is drawing see the opening scenes of Plautus *Asinaria*, and *Truculentus* in its entirety.

28 Ampelis relates a story where one of her own lovers was mistreating her until she rejected him and took another lover. After a few weeks of wrangling, the jealous man came back willing to spend much more on the fickle mistress. Ampelis advises her young friend to be secretly pleased if her lover is giving her a good beating amid jealous tantrums, because a guilt trip is an excellent way to make him spend a lot more than he intended. As with the passage of Alexis mentioned above, the ultimate goal was to extract more money from the lover, no matter how far one would need to go in order to accomplish this.

29 This sum of money is suspiciously high even for a young virgin (see Ch. 5.4.). We are told that Korinna in a single night made half of what the entire workshop of her father was worth. While the breadwinner father was alive the family prospered, and in a real Athenian household like this one Korinna would have been brought up to become someone's wife when she reached adolescence. However, the death of the father and the prolonged poverty which followed changed things for her: now she was viewed as an asset by her ruthless mother, who confesses that she was only providing for her daughter with the hope that she would become a hetaira when she reaches her peak.

love her. When bed-time comes, she should not do anything shameless or careless, but everything she does has a single purpose, how to seduce him and make him her lover; everyone is praising her for these things. If you learn these, we will be fortunate too.[30]

Kate Gilhuly in a lengthy study of this dialogue connects the construction of Korinna's education with male elite attitudes in Homer and Plato and the "discourse of self-control," and she concludes that "Krobyle tries to teach her daughter to be no-one".[31] Gilhuly is aware of the comic roots of this account but does not fully explore this path, one might think because the comic connection would not be consonant with her argument. On the other hand, she ignores the obvious connection of this text with the Socratic education of Theodote in the *Memorabilia*. The polite conversation, the seductive eyes, the cautious and tactful conduct, and more important, the advice to hold out for as long as possible and not give in to a lover's lust from the beginning, the suggestion that one should treat the current lover with courtesy and devotion, and the singleness of purpose when it comes to the goals of a skilled hetaira, are all topics common in both texts, which easily leads to the conclusion that Lucian had in mind the *Memorabilia*. However Lucian's account contains elements not found in Xenophon, and for the most part these can be traced to the fragments of Alexis and Euboulos mentioned above. Far from unexpected, this recasting of elements from philosophy and comedy to produce an original, intelligent, and often highly entertaining result is typical of Lucian, and one of the reasons for his lasting appeal.

Gilhuly's main argument, that teaching a hetaira good table manners and etiquette amounts to effacing her, makes no sense in this context. Krobyle's advice focuses upon easily recognizable turnoffs and "don'ts" when it comes to sexual desire. Slobbishness, filth, misery, silliness, giggles, bad table manners, or lack of basic social skills are distinctly unattractive qualities in erotic affairs, and moreover, for a woman to be too forward and predatory has been considered unappealing in most human societies. Krobyle advises Korinna to avoid such negative triggers, to study the necessary etiquette for social occasions, to be pleasant to everyone, and smile seductively without being too forward, if she wants to project an enticing image to potential lovers.[32] Hetairai had a reputation for being deceitful and manipulative, and this is another important "don't" for Krobyle.

---

30 Luc. *DMeretr.* 6.3

31 Gilhuly 2007: 78.

32 This part of Lucian's account has been partly influenced by Alexis (fr. 98), who mentions numerous tricks to make a hetaira look physically attractive, and also persistent exercises to give the appearance of a smile, even if she is not of a cheerful disposition.

One needs to be skilled in her handling of potential lovers and avoid obvious deceit, and should refrain from direct monetary transactions with the men, as this destroys the love-affair illusion; this task should be left to an agent like a pimp or servant.[33]

The part of Krobyle's advice on good table manners is probably influenced by Euboulos. Considering the importance of making a good impression in symposia, where hetairai could meet potential lovers, this part of the instruction would be of paramount practical significance. We are told that men find a drunken woman unattractive, and would not be impressed by someone noisily and greedily stuffing both sides of her mouth with delicacies, and then drowning the food with copious amounts of alcohol. Drooling over food and guzzling down drinks were strong enough stereotypes to generate many jokes in Attic comedy, while on the other hand, proper dinning etiquette has been an almost universal subject of instruction in good manners throughout history.[34]

In her final statement Krobyle reveals the source of her wisdom. She confesses that she has done her own market research in order to find out what is the secret of their neighbor Lyra, who has been a very successful hetaira. She has taken notes of the items for which Lyra was widely praised by lovers, and this information has formed the core of her instruction. If Korinna wishes to be as successful as Lyra she must do what Lyra does. Krobyle's lesson is presented as instruction based on practical experience of what works and what does not, and for

---

33 See for example the hilarious epigram from the *Greek Anthology* (5.101) where a slave girl is negotiating the price for her mistress in the street. The potential client does not approach directly the mistress, who is walking ahead with airs and graces. He asks the slave girl, who refuses when she hears how much the client is prepared to offer. One wonders to what extent the text of Lucian at this point is a reflection of a male wish that a proper hetaira ought to be less deceitful and double-faced. On the other hand, the harsh reality from a hetaira's point of view is given succinctly by the hetaira Bacchis in her conversation with Antiphila, the young bride of her lover (Terence *Heauton Timorumenos* 388–391):

> quippe forma inpulsi nostra nos amatores colunt;
> haec ubi immutata est, illi suom animum alio conferunt:
> nisi si prospectum interea aliquid est, desertae vivimus.

> The lovers are doting on us, compelled by our looks
> when these are gone, they transfer their devotion to someone else,
> and unless we have made some provisions, we live in destitution.

34 Quietly nibbling and drinking in moderation imply that one is not starving in poverty, and does not need to go to the dinner party to enjoy good food.

the most part it sounds like mainstream, common-sense advice on what can be a turn on or a turn off in a high stakes sexual game, where success brings great financial rewards, and failure brings poverty and ridicule.

In Dialogue 7 the mother who is advising the eighteen years old beginner hetaira Mousarion suggests that she should learn from her peers who know how to be hetairai (ἐκεῖναι γὰρ ἴσασιν ἑταιρίζειν). Mousarion's career has not been successful since she met her current lover Chaireas, an affluent Athenian boy, still a handsome teenager himself. The infatuated Mousarion ends up giving him two valuable necklaces, instead of accepting gifts. Her mother is instructing her to learn how to behave like a hetaira, for she will be very disappointed when Chaireas marries some citizen woman with a large dowry. In this comic reversal of the traditional theme, the infatuated hetaira is actually the one who gives, and her pretty boy lover with elusive tactics and vague promises is the one taking from her. Mousarion certainly needs instruction on how to be a hetaira.[35]

The account of Prokopios on the young days of Theodora, before her meteoric rise to power, contains information on her training as a prostitute in the sex entertainment industry of late antiquity. His account is of interest for the history of prostitution in the classical period as it contains echoes from classical literature; however, it needs to be treated with caution, since these elements are mixed with the realities of the early medieval world, and it is difficult to separate fact from fiction.[36] Theodora's training seems to be gradual, like an apprenticeship; we are told that she was learning all along from her older sister, her mother and her own experiences in an environment which is described as blatantly unsuitable for the upbringing of respectable girls, but ideal for the induction of hetairai into the

---

35 In a fictional reshuffling of the theme by Aristainetos (1.14) it is the older sister, a hetaira herself, who functions as the educator for her younger sibling on how to become a hetaera.

36 I am convinced that the *Anecdota* is closer to skilled storytelling with a shock value, as cultivated by Lucian or Suetonius, than to the Greek historiographic tradition, of which Prokopios is a true heir in his Histories. There are several unmistakable loans from Against Neaira, as for example, in *Anecd.* 9.18 ff., and, furthermore, echoes from other classical sources, which may suggest that the primary purpose of the *Anecdota* was literary rather than historical. As with Lucian, a mix of literary themes and contemporary real life elements probably lies at the core of the narrative of Prokopios, and, while the wild stories about the emperor and empress of Byzantium are probably fancy tales for the most part, the elements of which they are composed can still be valuable as witnesses to the historical realities of prostitution in the ancient and early medieval world. However, this is a subject meriting an independent study, as it is too large and complex to be discussed here. See also Spatharas 2012: 846–858.

trade.[37] We can confidently conclude that this part of the narrative reflects the experiences of many hetairai in the ancient world. Then, Prokopios tells us that before she reached her prime she was already sexually active, having anal intercourse indiscriminately with slaves,[38] and that she even worked in a brothel offering anal sex to her clients. Unlikely as this story may sound, it may be an accurate reflection of actual practice, as it appears to be an effective strategy for profiteering from immature girls without deflowering and devaluing them, or risking a premature pregnancy, but there is no solid evidence to verify this, unless we take the roundabout phrase of Apollodoros, that Neaira was still too young to be a hetaira but was already working with her body, to mean that she was offering anal sex to her clients.[39]

When Theodora reaches her prime she is put on stage as a hetaira entertainer,[40] and from this point onwards the narrative of Prokopios contains a fair amount of visible contradictions. On one hand, he tells us that she was not trained in anything: she could not sing, or play an instrument, and was just a plain hetaira (πεζή ἑταίρα) with her body as her sole marketable commodity, but on the other hand, he goes on to extol her skills as a lewd entertainer capable of setting the theater ablaze with her steamy and witty performances. We are told that she was very funny (ἀστεία διαφερόντως) and adept at poking fun (σκώπτρια). One would think that Prokopios had the witty, funny and erudite hetairai of Machon or Athenaios in mind at this point, like Gnathaina or Mania, but this would be a backhanded compliment as he goes on to describe in scintillating detail her obscenities in word and act.

The comment of Prokopios that Theodora had no additional skills is meant to be an insult, but in reality a *peze hetaira* at her prime was the most pricy type of prostitute (see Ch. 6). His Theodora is described as a prominent hetaira at her prime, but at the same time she behaves like a low-class stripper/entertainer/common whore available to everyone frequenting the obscene shows of later antiquity, which still bore the name "theater" but had so little in common

---

37 This aspect of the story may have been inspired by the narrative of *Against Neaira*, where the young Neaira, probably around 12 at the time, was following around Metaneira, who was at her prime (D. 59.20–22).
38 This again may be an echo from *Against Neaira* (33–4), where Apollodoros alleges that a drunken Neaira slept with guests and even some of the slaves at the dinner party of Chabrias.
39 D. 59.22. Elsewhere (possibly in 108: see Kapparis 1999: 402–404) Apollodoros does say that Neaira offered her clients sex "from three holes" (ἀπὸ τριῶν τρυπημάτων), meaning vaginal, anal and oral.
40 By the time of Prokopios the term "hetaira" is rather loosely used for any kind of prostitute.

with the classical theater.[41] All good advice mentioned above on how to become a successful hetaira seems to have completely missed the Procopian Theodora; in fact she stands at the antipodes doing exactly everything that she should not be doing, breaking every rule in the handbook of savoir vivre, and reaching lows which would embarrass even the lowest of the common prostitutes. These contradictions and inconsistencies challenge the historicity of this account and probably are the end-result of very diverse influences from literary sources, such as Attic Oratory and Comedy, but subverted and realigned to a unified purpose - namely, to portray Theodora as the most depraved whore ever.

There is some evidence to suggest that hetairai occasionally received higher education in the philosophical schools of the ancient world. Nikarete of Megara, a woman of noble birth, was a student of the Megarian philosopher Stilpon, according to Athenaios, who praises her thirst for learning. Athenaios also quotes a fragment of Hippias the Sophist about an educated Milesian woman called Thargelia, who took 14 husbands.[42] Another famous Milesian woman, Aspasia, the life-long partner or Pericles, was renowned for her wit, education, and conversations with Socrates and other men of intellect, but was also reviled in comedy as a prostitute and a pimp. Both traditions co-existed for a long time and created a fascinating ambiguity in the perceptions of this exceptional woman in later centuries.[43] Similar two-sided traditions coexist about other highly educated women linked with famous philosophers. If we believe Athenaios and Diogenes Laertios, Leontion, the lover of Epicurus, continued prostitution while she had started studying philosophy with Epicurus. Apparently, she slept with everyone in the Gardens, and had sex with Epicurus even in public view.[44] A hetaira named Leontion was also linked to the poet Hermesianax, a senior contemporary of Epicurus. If it is the same woman, then she sounds like a cultivated and unconventional individual with interests in literature and philosophy, which she pursued at the side of the most distinguished men of letters in her time.[45]

Learning with a distinguished philosopher, poet or rhetorician could be expensive and limited to a small number of people who could gain access to the

---

41 About the disintegration of theater into lewd entertainment closely connected with prostitution in the Roman period and later antiquity see Duncan 2006: 252–273.

42 Athen. 13.89 = *FGrH* 6 F 3.

43 See Henry 1995: 66–67 regarding her wit, and Ch. 3.1. about the two traditions on Aspasia.

44 Athenaios and Diogenes Laertios seem to be quoting a letter of Epicurus to Leontion, now lost: Epic. Epist. fr. 47 = Athen. 13.53 and 13.70. See also D.L. 10.7; Theon *Progymn.* 112; Alciphr. 4.17 al.

45 For further discussion on the relationships of hetairai with famous philosophers see Ch. 3.2.

inner circle, and even more difficult for women, since many schools did not accept them in their midst. More broadly accessible avenues to an education were offered in the symposion and the theater, and there is plentiful evidence suggesting that the hetairai benefited from both.[46] One could hardly imagine a symposion without hetairai engaging in stimulating banter with the symposiasts, citing poetry or sometimes even singing the immortal verses of Sappho and other poets from the golden age of Greek Lyric. Machon and Athenaios have many stories to tell about the legendary exchanges between Diphilos and Gnathaina, or king Demetrios and Lamia, and they depict Mania quoting Sophocles in a response to king Demetrios, Lais quoting Euripides to Euripides, Glykera quoting Agathon, and so on.[47] Beyond casual conversations, there is an entire tradition that Glykera was assisting Menander with his plays (see Ch. 3.3.), and another one which turned the poet Sappho into a hetaira (see Ch. 1.1.). Whether these specific traditions or events were historically accurate or not is not important; the fact remains that hetairai were presented in the Greek literary tradition as literate, erudite women capable of making their own substantial contribution to Greek letters and holding their own in witty and humorous conversations with some of the most distinguished men of letters in their time.

The majority of hetairai were not interested in scholastic accomplishment or specialized learning of any kind. What they needed most was some general instruction which improved their social skills, enhanced their dexterity with customer care, and gave them the background to casually quote high poetry, to spice up a dull conversation or put a badly-behaved client in his place. The spaces which offered this kind of education, the symposion and the theater, were both open to a hetaira, and the education they provided, enhanced with the guidance of a more experienced sex worker, may have been enough for many. However, for those who wanted more, an opportunity to pursue scholastic accomplishment for its own sake was there, which was not open to any other woman. Consequently, this form of education might have a special appeal to some precisely because it was a rare gift, an unobtainable luxury typically denied to other women. However, for the most part, the scattered pieces of available evidence on a hetaira's education suggest a certain functionality and specificity of purpose. A hetaira

---

46 For the symposion and the theater as avenues of higher education, and further bibliography on Greek higher education as a whole, see Joyal et al. 2008 (with an excellent collection of source materials); Sommerstein –Atherton 1996; Poulakos – Depew 2004. See also Ch. 3.3. for the connection of hetairai with the theater.

47 See Athen. 13.39; Machon fr. 4 = Athen. 6.43; Athen.13.42 = S. *El.* 2; Machon fr. 18.420 = Athen. 13.45 = E. *Med.* 1346; Athen. 13.46 = Agathon fr. 14 Nauck. See also McClure 2003a.

was taught ways to make herself appealing, charming, a catch, or an insidious honey-trap, depending on the perspective. Not infrequently, however, it seems that these goals were exceeded and a good education with all its inherent rewards for the individual became a goal worth pursuing in its own right.

2.2 Beauty and Aesthetics

Those who desire someone care about beauty, not good character. Love does not promise good morals (σωφροσύνη), but tempts the licentious eye with the beauty of the body.[48]

Whereas so much discussion has been dedicated to the elevated aesthetic ideals of the Greeks, as these are reflected in literary masterpieces, like Plato's *Phaidros* or the *Symposion*, or in the sculptures of Polykleitos and Praxiteles,[49] the literature referring to the famous prostitutes of the ancient world takes a less idealistic view, one based on raw attraction, erotic games, easy access, a language of overt and unashamed sexuality and adulation for the pleasures of the flesh. This is a world far removed from the idealized construction of the beauty of high-born women like Kallirhoe or Anthia in the Greek novel, or the attractive modesty of virtuous, citizen-born but misunderstood pseudo-hetairai in New Comedy.[50] The Greek prostitute is intentionally sexual, ready to please her partner, and not required to be submissive or virtuous; nor is her good character all that important, so long as she knows how to put on a convincing act of coyness, affection and modesty in order to make the game more interesting and maximize her profits.[51]

---

48 Theophylaktos *Epist.* 66; In this fictional letter by the prominent Byzantine historian and intellectual a hetaira ominously named Peitho (persuasion) writes to an infatuated lover named Hippolytos, who professes to be in love with her character, that sexual attraction is all about looks.
49 See for example: White 1989: 149–157; Montserrat 1998; Bett 2010: 130–152; Crowther. 1985: 285–291; Delivorrias 1995: 200–217; Ferber 2010: 51–76; Hawley 1998: 37–54; Held 2009:155–167; Hyland 2008; Kosman 2010: 341–357; Lear 2006: 96–123; Massey 2006; Nehamas 2007: 97–135; Obdrzalek 2010: 415–444; Schenk 1992.
50 A fair number of studies discusses the construction of feminine beauty, often in relation to the evolution of the character of the heroine in the Greek novel: See Schmeling 2005: 36–49; De Temmerman 2007: 235–52; Haynes 2001: 73–92 al. For a study of beauty in Plato's Symposium see e.g. White 1989: 149–157. For a discussion of the aesthetics of prostitution see McClure 2003a 107–136. For a more interdisciplinary approach of the aesthetics of prostitution across cultures see the useful collection of Feldman – Gordon (2006), including an article by James Davidson on the Greek hetaira (pp. 29–51).
51 This commentary on the prostitute's body is almost completely unaffected by the literature on physiognomy, a pseudo-scientific fad which reached its peak in the 2nd c. AD. Physiognomic

Thus, the following discussion needs to focus on the sexually charged aesthetics of prostitution.

Several sources suggest that girls and boys were chosen and pushed down the path of prostitution from a very young age because of promising looks.[52] These children could be slaves bought specifically for this purpose, or less often children brought up to become prostitutes by their families or guardians. In the narrative of *Against Neaira*, the freedwoman Nikarete bought seven little girls over the years, brought them up and taught them how to become hetairai, and made a handsome living from their work.[53] For most of the women mentioned in the list of Apollodoros there is external evidence from comedy suggesting that they were truly notorious in their heyday, and supporting his observation that Nikarete had a very keen eye for potential and promising looks.[54] The other major source on

---

studies were around already in the 5th c. BC, but the most substantial body of this work was produced in later antiquity, starting with the *Physiognomica* attributed to Aristotle (3rd c. BC), and followed by the *Physiognomica* of Polemon (2nd c. AD), Adamantios (4th c. AD) and an anonymous Latin handbook (4th c. AD). For the literature see Evans 1969: 6–17. Physiognomics sought to correlate specific features and body types with certain behaviors. E.C. Evans has studied ancient physiognomics in considerable detail, and her findings confirm that very little from this entire body of literature would be relevant for the study of the aesthetics and construction of beauty in a prostitutional setting (Evans 1935: 96–108; 1969: 5–101). One would imagine that philosophical and pseudo-scientific discussions on the correlation between body types and features is one thing, looks for the enjoyment of which one is induced to pay good money is another. In the cynically down-to-earth world of prostitution, neither theoretical perceptions on what constitutes an attractive look, nor its possible correlation to a good character matter very much. What matters is whether the customer is inspired and sexually aroused by what he (and sometimes she) sees, and this sometimes may not be conventionally attractive, youthful or ideally beautiful, although it often is. Ultimately it is in the eye of the beholder.

52 To pay 20 or 30 minae for a fully-grown hetaira would have been an expensive and pointless investment, because she would be past her peak before one could turn a good profit. A child might be a better investment, even if uncertain: it would be cheap to buy, as for years in the future it would generate no income and consume resources in the form of sustenance and an education. However, the patient procurer stood to make a great deal of profit when this child reached her or his peak and the infatuated lovers started flocking in prepared to meet whatever excessive demands the master or mistress was making. This is why it seems that the practice of acquiring small children with promising looks and bringing them up to become prostitutes was firmly established.

53 D. 59.18–20. I have argued elsewhere (Kapparis 1999: com. ad loc.) that the girls were not all of the same age, and that they were bought one or two at a time, so that when one of Nikarete's girls went past her prime or was freed by an infatuated lover, another was in line to take her place.

54 See Kapparis 1999: com. ad loc.

prostitution from the classical period, the speech *Against Timarchos*, also suggests that the good looks of Timarchos facilitated his induction into prostitution.
If we were to believe Aeschines (and we have very good reasons not to),[55] the man
with whom Timarchos had his first affair, the aristocratic and wealthy Misgolas,
was attracted to the youth's firm body (εὔσαρκον ὄντα καὶ νέον).[56] Further down
we are told that the prominent Athenian politician Hegesandros was instantly
love-struck as soon as he set his eyes on the handsome young man. Timarchos
was by now probably in his twenties and already forging his political career (57).
However, when Aeschines comments on the appearance of the middle-aged
Timarchos, he says that his body looked disgusting (αἰσχρόν) from the drink and
bad lifestyle (26).

Athenaios relates a story from an unidentified source about Apelles the
painter who saw the young Lais carrying water and invited her to join him to a
party, taken by her beauty. When his fellow-partygoers mocked him for bringing
a virgin to the party he replied that he was looking forward to his future pleasure
in less than 3 years.[57] Athenagoras the 2nd c. apologist considers beauty a necessary condition for boys to take up prostitution:

> Those who set up the market for prostitution and created the indecent establishments for
> young people, for the purposes of every decadent pleasure, did not spare the males. Men
> on men are performing terrible acts, those who have more attractive and shapely bodies,
> abusing and disgracing them and the beauty created by God (for beauty is not automatically
> made on earth, but it is sent by the hand and the mind of God).[58]

Athenagoras clearly refers to boys established in brothels and compelled to cater
for a male clientele. Timaios, in his unlikely portrait of the tyrant Agathocles,
states that at the prime of his youth he offered himself as a common whore to
everyone who wanted his behind, and was totally impudent and had three testicles. Naturally the sober-minded Polybios, while quoting Timaios, dismisses this
information.[59] The Scholiast of Aristophanes, although uncertain which Antimachos was mentioned in the *Clouds*, thinks that the person mentioned was

---

55 See the discussion in Ch. 4.1. and 4.2.
56 Aeschines is misrepresenting the relationship between Misgolas and Timarchos as one based
on money, where the older man has taken in the beautiful youth and is keeping him as his lover.
If anything, Timarchos was the older man. See the discussion in Ch. 4.2. and 4.
57 Athen. 13.54. The story is almost certainly an invention of later antiquity trying to connect
the famous painter with the most fabulous hetaira of his time; it places the upbringing of Lais in
Athens contrary to what is known about her life from almost every other source (see Appendix).
58 Athenagoras *Legatio sive Supplicatio pro Christianis* 34.1.
59 Timaeus *FGrH* 566 F 124b; Plb. 12.15.

maybe a story-teller (perhaps he means the poet Antimachos of Kolophon), who was unjustly slandered as a male prostitute simply because of his exceedingly good looks.[60] Similar stories surrounding famous and ordinary men and women who genuinely or allegedly offered their youth for profit very often have these underlying themes: beauty, looks, physical attraction, brutal desire, mindless infatuation, and a disregard for loftier principles.

Many a time, such references are specific to certain body parts. The most complete portrait of a hetaira's ideal beauty is the description of Lais in one of the fictional letters of Aristainetos:

> If I could describe sufficiently with words her erotic charms, the cheeks are white with rosy spots imitating the natural charm of the rose, her thin lips are gently divided and redder than her cheeks, the eyebrows black, and their black is pure, while the space between the brows divides them symmetrically. Her nose is straight and as thin as her lips, the eyes are large and clear, shining with pure light. Their black part, the pupils, are very black, and the white part around them, the eyeballs, are very, very white, and each part looks better through this intense contrast with its neighboring part. One could pay tribute to the Graces who have taken residence there. The hair is naturally curled similar to a hyacinth flower, as Homer says, and the hands of Aphrodite herself are arranging it. Her neck is white and symmetrical compared to the face, and even without jewelry it has confidence in its own beauty, but usually wears a necklace with precious stones on which the name of the beauty is written, and the placement of the stones is creating the letters. Her stature is tall and her shape is beautiful and well-built with harmonious distribution of the limbs. Dressed she has a very beautiful face, and undressed she looks as if she were all face. Her walk is gentle, like a cypress or a palm tree moving slowly, because beauty is lofty. But these plants are moved by the gentle breeze of the westerly wind, while she is gently shaken by the breezes of the Erotes. This is how the top painters have represented her. When someone needs to paint Helen or the Graces, or the queen of the Graces herself, they look at the picture of Lais, as an exceptional example of beauty, and from there they copy on their paintings the divine appearance. I almost forgot to mention that her breasts like quinces are pushing violently against her garment. The limbs of Lais are as symmetrical and tender, as the soft bending of her bones when someone embraces her. Because of their softness they are almost squeezed along with her flesh, and yield to the erotic embraces. When she speaks, wow, how many sirens in her speech, how talkative her tongue. Lais has definitely put on the girdle of the Graces, and smiles very seductively. This is why not even Blame himself could find something to blame on my beautiful woman, who is basking in such wealth of charms.[61]

Almost a millennium separates the lifetime of Lais from the time of Aristainetos (5th c. AD), which raises the question how one could possibly have any faith in his

---

60 Sch. Ar. *Nub.* 1022.
61 Aristaenet. 1.1.

account. But with Aristainetos, as with authors like Plutarch, Lucian, or Photios, who had read vast amounts of literature now lost to us, one cannot afford to be dismissive. Aristainetos alludes to works of art which were inspired by Lais, and he may well be describing one of them, or more. Another possibility is that he has collected scattered references to the appearance of Lais in sources now lost to us, like the plays of Kephisodoros and Epikrates both entitled *Antilais*, or the lost speech of Lysias *To Lais*. A third alternative may be that Aristainetos has created the ideal Greek beauty by combining an array of features typically considered attractive. Whether this portrait matches the historical Lais or not cannot be proved or disproved on the existing evidence, and is not important. What matters for our purposes is that Aristainetos has provided us with a compilation of features which would constitute an unblemished beauty and has imagined for us how the most famous hetaira of the ancient world should look.

The eyes, which so distinctly adorn the splendid face of the Aristainetan Lais, feature quite prominently as the route of desire in ancient Greek literature.[62] The Aeschylean fiery eye (φλέγων ὀφθαλμός) of a woman who has experienced a man, as opposed to that of a virgin,[63] or the honest gaze of Antiphanes, which invariably betrays wine and love even if those afflicted deny it with words,[64] are such examples of the poetic language of desire as expressed through the eyes. The Corinthian hetaira in the *Corinthiastes* of Philetairos has a melting and soft gaze (ὡς τακερὸν καὶ μαλακὸν τὸ βλέμμα), which he finds a sufficient explanation of the reason why there is no monument of a wife anywhere in the Greek world but plenty of monuments dedicated to hetairai.[65] In an epigram of Asclepiades the lightning bolt shooting out of the eyes of Nikarete has burned Kleophon at her doorstep.[66] In a comic reversal of the motif, in the *Wealth* of Aristophanes the young man who is selling sexual favors to a lustful and inept old woman keeps telling her that she has a soft and charming gaze, in order to exploit her.[67]

A shameless (ἀναιδές) gaze, raised neck, constant movement of the eyebrows and a swaggering gait are definite signs of a wanton soul, in the opinion of Chrysippos.[68] The transgender *kinaidos* of Lucian has a wandering gaze

---

62 For the eye as an erotic feature in Greek culture see Wohl 2012: 45–60; Cairns 2005: 123–155; Davies 1980: 255–7; Degener 1998; Goldhill 2001: 154–194; Walker 1992: 132–148.
63 Aesch. fr. 242 Radt.
64 Antiphanes fr. 238.
65 This is not entirely true: see the discussion in Ch. 6.1.
66 *AG* 5.153.
67 Ar. *Plu.* 1022–1024.
68 Chrysippos fr. 592 von Arnim.

(διασεσαλευμένον) and the head resting seductively over the shoulders.[69] In another work of Lucian the effeminate character is described as someone with a feminine gaze (γυναικεῖον),[70] while the reformed hetaira of Aristainetos has the soft (προσηνές) gaze of a respectable woman. It goes without saying that these are stereotypes, some from a certain time and place, others more timeless, but nonetheless ripe for exploitation in the hands of an author trying to communicate a certain cultural image to his readers, as well as in the hands of an experienced sex worker, when she/he needed to play a role to attract and manipulate a client.

Hair was another distinct feature with the potential to attract or repel a lover from the early days of Greek lyric: The famous verses of Alcman about the shining hair of Hagesichora, or the grey hair of the old man which repels the young girl in Anacreon, readily come to mind.[71] The blond hair of a boy is the centerpiece of a tender epigram of Asclepiades with a paraklausithyron motif from the 3rd c. BC. The lover prays that the drops of his tears falling from the garlands hanging over the door will wet the hair of the boy when he opens it.[72] In Lucian Eros advises Zeus that, if he wants to have lovers, he should not look stern and throw thunderbolts; instead, he should arrange his hair nicely with a headband, and look soft and smooth.[73] By contrast, the reformed hetaira of Aristainetos keeps her hair simply braided. Untidy hair is a sign of sorrow for a hetaira in one of the epigrams of the *Greek Anthology*.[74] A fair amount of epigrams revolve around a prostitute lover's hair, some in praise and others to tease a formerly haughty hetaira with vengeful disdain, as for example one by Kallimachos where the graying hair will remind the hetaira Konopion (the Mosquito) how badly she has treated her lover, when she will no longer be desirable and men will not be spending the night at her doorstep.[75]

The beauty of the face has also inspired poets from the time of Greek Lyric, with some splendid examples like the "silver faced" Hagesichora of Alcman, or

---

69 Luc. *Merc.* 33

70 By contrast, a man's man is described as someone strong, with a lot of sun on his body and a masculine gaze (ἀρρενωπὸς τὸ βλέμμα) walking decisively as if he owns the road.

71 Alcman fr. 1.51–54; Anacr. fr. 13. For the Greek obsession with hair see the useful dissertation of Preston Massey (2007, especially chapters 6–8). Although I disagree with Massey's thesis that the veil was an essential accessory of Greek married women, and I am more in favor of a variety of veiling practices, based on local custom, fashion, season and individual preference, his work contains a wealth of information on Greek aesthetics and discussions of beauty.

72 *AG* 5.145.

73 Luc. *DDeor.* 6.2

74 Aristaenet. 1.19; *AG* 5.130.

75 *AG* 5.23.

the lovely face of Anactoria in Sappho, while the comic poet Antiphanes was joking in his *Flute-player* that Menelaos went to war with Troy for the sake of a pretty
face.[76] The first reference to the face in relation to a prostitute is in the famous
Anacreontean poem on Herotime, the "lovely-faced" (καλλιπρόσωπη).[77] Then
there is a fair number of further references in Greek Comedy. In Aristophanes several of the female characters who were at least modeled on hetairai, if not actually
played by hetairai, such as Diallage in the *Acharnians* and Theoria in *Peace*, are
praised for their beautiful face.[78] Anaxandrides comments on the adorable face of
Anteia, and the even lovelier one of Theolyte, while Machon praises the stunningly pretty face of the Athenian hetaira Melitta, the so-called Mania, especially
in combination with her small stature which created an unusually attractive overall effect.[79]

Athenaios transmits a fair number of stories from various authors involving
hetairai with fabulously beautiful faces, like one from Ptolemy VIII Euergetes
about Bilistiche, the lover of Ptolemy II Philadelphos, who had the most attractive
face of all other woman of her time, or the joke of Antiphanes about Nannion,
that she was called "proskenion" (forestage) because she had a very presentable
face, and was bedecked in jewelry, but she was horribly ugly when she took off
her clothes.[80] More such stories have been included in the fictional letters of Aristainetos, like the story about the hetaira Leimone who had a very pretty face, but
unlike Nannion the rest of her body was so stunning that naked she looked almost faceless, or the story about the exciting face of Melissarion (a character
based on a well-known Hippocratic passage describing an induced abortion performed on a musician).[81] The face is also an important concept in a number of
epigrams from the Greek Anthology praising the beauty of respectable women[82]
and hetairai alike.[83] Several epigrams have a satirical twist, like one by Rufinus
where a motherly figure, maybe a pimp, is advising a woman just beaten up by
her lover, when he caught her with someone else, to stop crying or she will spoil

76 E.g. Alcman 1.55; Sappho fr. 16.18; Antiphanes fr. 50.
77 Anacreon fr. 60 Gentili; see also Ch. 1.1.
78 Ar. *Ach.* 990; *Pax* 524.
79 Anaxandrides fr. 9; Machon fr. 14.199.
80 Athen. 13.37 and 51. Ptolemy Euergetes *FGrH* 234 f 4; Antiphanes fr. 50.
81 Aristaen. *Epist.* 1.3.33; 1.19 and Hip. *Sem.* 13.
82 See for example the tender poem of Nossis about the bright face of a baby (*AG* 6.353), or the praise of the beauty of virtuous Kassia (7.695).
83 As, for example in 5.153, where the face of Nikarete is struck by desire.

her pretty face.[84] The beautiful face of a boy frequently figures in sources too, typically in a more idealized context of tender love, rather than venal sex.[85] Interesting is letter 1.11 of Aristainetos, where the maid is essentially "pimping" (μαστροπεύουσα) to her mistress a youth with a beautiful face just growing a beard, a confident but not arrogant gaze and a colorful girly garment. Aristainetos is thus constructing an image of that soft, well-trimmed youth so reviled by many authors from Aristophanes to the Christian theologians of the second millennium as the stereotypical image of a male prostitute. Although adultery rather than prostitution is the main theme here, the quintessentially immodest youth, who is tending his appearance because he is up to no good, is a stereotype shared by both settings.

References to sexually charged parts as a focal point of overt eroticism go back to Archilochos, who said that even an old man would fall in love with perfumed hair and breasts.[86] The theme of scented breasts also appears in Alkaios and in Anacreon with reference to a boy's chest (probably Eros). Athenaios explains the cus-

---

84 Rufinus *AG* 5.43

85 E.g. Pindar fr. 123, where the face of Xenocles of Tenedos is beaming rays of light. Amphis (fr. 15) in his Dithyrambos cynically joked that a man who claimed to be in love only with the character of a boy and not his pretty face would be like someone who persistently pursued rich people but did not want their money. A more obscure joke of Hermippos (fr. 57) also seems to refer to the soft face of a boy. In a tender image from Aristainetos the hetaira Glykera, who is taken by the beauty of a boy, first admires the back of his neck, then touches his face and secretly kisses her own hand that came in contact with the boy's skin, while in another letter a virgin girl is in love with a youth who is as beautiful as a painting of Achilles (Aristaen. *Epist.* 1.22, 2.5; see also 2.6 describing the loveable face of a youth called Phormion). A fair number of sources attest that the face appears even lovelier if it reflects modesty and youthful embarrassment when it is the object of someone's affections, as, for example, the boy of Anacreon with the virginal look, or boys, girls and "busty" women in a well-known fragment of Lykophronides (fr. 1 Page):

> Neither a boy's, nor a golden virgin's,
> Nor a deep-bossomed woman's
> Face is beautiful, if it is not modest -
> For modesty sows flowers

See also Anacr. fr. 15 Page; *AG* 5.67; Aristaen. *Epist.* 1.15 and 1.16; and the rich collection of quotations in Athenaios 13.16 ff. When prostitutes tried to imitate this effect of innocent modesty on their face they added on top of the psimython some type of rouge, and one of these products, an extract from a kind of thorn, was even called παιδέρως "puppy-love" (See e.g. Alexis fr. 103; Dsc. *Eup.* 1.160, 218 al.).

86 Archil. fr. 48.5–6 West.

tom of applying perfumes to the chest not only as an act of vanity, but as conducive to good health too, since the soul was perceived to reside inside the chest.[87]
The famous breasts of Lais, which according to Athenaios inspired even the jealousy of Phryne, are mentioned several times in the literature of later antiquity,
most notably in the vivid image of Aristainetos that they pushed against her cloak
like quinces (κυδωνιῶντες). In another one of his letters the breasts of Leimone
resemble apples.[88] Similar comparisons of breasts either with quinces or with apples are much older than the time of Aristainetos and go back to the poets of Old
Comedy such as Kantharos and Krates.[89] Dikaiopolis in the Acharnians when he
feels the breasts of Diallage exclaims: "Wow, Wow! The breasts, how hard like
quinces, kiss me softly, darlings".[90]

The fabulous behinds of the Corinthian hetairai, available only to the
wealthy, are at the center of a joke in Aristophanes *Wealth*, while in *Peace* we are
told that Theoria has just bathed and she has a very pretty posterior, the cakes
are baked and the only thing missing is a penis.[91] Machon tells a story involving
the hetaira Mania and king Demetrios: he wanted her bottom, but she told him
she needed a favor first, before she would let him have his way.[92] The fiction of
later antiquity also has a few stories to tell involving the bottoms of famous hetairai. Alciphron is particularly fond of the theme of sexually charged beauty contests where groups of hetairai come together, undress, and compete with each
other to establish who has the better parts. In one of these contests the backside
of Plangon is so beautiful that even Pan would leap onto her, while the competition between Thryallis and Myrrhine as to who has the smoother behind is going
to be a close call.[93] The same theme, a beauty contest among three hetairai imitating the mythological contest among the three goddesses, appears in an epigram from the Greek Anthology.[94] This ultimate male fantasy, where the girls
(and sometimes boys) get together, strip naked and provocatively compare their

---

87 Alc. fr. 362 Lobel-Page; Anacr. fr. 18 Page; Athen. 15.36.
88 See Athen. 13.54; Aristaen. Epist. 1.1, 1.3.
89 Kantharos fr. 6; Krates fr. 43.
90 Ar. *Ach.* 1198–1200
91 Ar. *Plu.* 150–152; Pax 868–870
92 See the full text of the joke in App. ii.
93 E.g. Alciphr. 4.13, 4.14.
94 *AG* 5.36; it is noteworthy that in the famous contest in Lucian's *Judgement of the Goddesses*,
which has probably influenced masterpieces like the paintings of Ruben and Hendrick van
Balen, Aphrodite appears dressed and acting like a hetaira, Hera like a housewife, and Athena
like the plain virgin girl.

most attractive erotic parts, is a recurring theme in Greek literature, especially in a mythological context as Richard Hawley has demonstrated.[95]

References to the exquisite behinds of boys are equally common. For example, Euboulos in his *Antiope* immortalized the chunky behind of Kallistratos, whom he regarded highly among male prostitutes (κόλλοπα), while the famous behind of a certain Menekrates, adorned by the Graces themselves, is the theme of an epigram of Rhianos.[96] The thighs of women and boys (μηροί), as a prelude to the more secretive parts (μυχοί), are also mentioned with excitement,[97] like, for example, the "precious" thighs of Rhodope, which have been immortalized in an epigram of the Greek Anthology.[98] The list can be endless, and suggests a very concrete, physical, even if sometimes metaphorical, language of the human body in Greek literature as a whole, and very much in the vocabulary of prostitution. The discourse on body parts underlines a fundamentally physical perception of relationships between prostitutes and clients and suggests that despite the rhetoric of love and devotion these contacts were for the most part based on raw attraction and the ability of the prostitute to excite and maintain a lover's sexual interest.

An epigram of Philodemos urges the reader to excuse the un-Greek manners of Flora of Osci. What if she cannot sing the lyrics of Sappho? With a body and face like hers, who cares about culture:

> Ah, the leg, Ah, the calf, Ah – I'm dying, and rightly so-
> The thighs, Ah, the buttocks, Ah, the pubes, Ah, the ass,
> The shoulders, Ah, the breasts, Ah, the slender neck,
> Ah, the hands, Ah – I am going mad – the eyes,
> Ah, such an elegant movement, Ah, the superb kisses
> Ah, - kill me – the voice.
> Even if Flora is from Osci, and does not sing Sappho,
> Perseus too fell in love with the Indian Andromeda.[99]

It's all about looks, we are told, and many references to exotic, barbarian beauties working in the sex industry of the Graeco-Roman world would confirm that culture and education were only supplementary to enticing looks. Famous beauties like Phryne, Lais, Glykera or Pythionike had monuments erected in their name, and the most famous sculptors and painters of their time were looking up to them

95 Hawley 1998: 37–54.
96 Euboulos fr. 10; Rhianos fr. 69
97 E.g. Ar. *Ec.* 902, *Nub.* 973, *Lys.* 552; Eub. fr. 127;
98 *AG* 5.36.
99 *AG* 5.132.

for inspiration in their representations of divine figures (See Ch. 4.1.). Young men professed to be in love with hetairai, spent time chasing them, competed with other men for their favors, became jealous and composed poetry for their loved ones (See Ch. 3.3.). But it wasn't about character or good morals; it was about the eyes, the face, the hair, the buttocks, the breasts, the thighs, the soft skin, the lovely voice, the whole array of physical characteristics which defined beauty, and raw attraction. Personality, manners and culture mattered a lot in so far as they enhanced someone's looks, creating an effect or illusion of modesty, innocence, urbanity or elegance, which a customer might value - but, let's say, Phryne or Lais would not have been who they were without their exceptional looks. Men might marry for good character or a large dowry, and the wife could look like a turtle (χελώνη), in the words of the hetaira Leaina,[100] but when they hired pleasure, whether the object of one's desire was a boy or a girl, an enticing appearance was at the top of the list.

2.3 Cosmetics, Clothing and Fake Beauty

Artificial beauty enhancements in the form of clothing, jewelry and cosmetics have been a very ancient skill. From time immemorial women, and to a lesser degree men, have used a wide variety of methods to retain and prolong youth. The ever-growing literature, especially from later antiquity, suggests that a vast array of cosmetics was widely used by kings, queens, and noble Roman matrons as much as they were used by lowly whores in the brothels of the ancient world. Many of these cosmetics consisted of plant extracts, some were from basic chemicals or rocks, like chalk or alum, and many contained animal products like fats or organic compounds. The inventiveness of the ancient cosmetic industry was prolific and a fair amount of these substances, like oil extracts and natural dyes, are still in use by the cosmetic industry. It is outside the purposes of this study to enter the details of this large topic, or provide a full catalogue of cosmetic substances; the reader could turn to more authoritative accounts on this subject.[101] Our purpose here is to explore how cosmetics were used to construct the image of the male or female prostitute, and how their employment is viewed as part of the ancient debate on the ethics of prostitution.

---

100 Alciphr. 4.12.
101 See for example: Grillet 1975; Dayagi-Mendels 1989; Garland 1995: 105–122; Alden 1999: 68–73. Ambrosio 2001; Richlin 1995: 185–213; Rosati 1985; Wyke 1994: 134–51; Croom 2002; Saiko 2005; Olson 2008, and 2009: 291–310; Glazebrook 2009: 233–248; Stewart 2007.

Galen recognized cosmetic treatment as a legitimate part of medicine, so long as it was used to preserve one's natural looks, or to repair damage caused by disease or trauma.[102] He disapproved of vanity cosmetics and considered these to be part of hairdressing.[103] We are unaccustomed to seeing Galen yielding to someone else's authority without contest, but he does so in the case of Kriton, whose work he considers to be the best, most comprehensive, and most popular manual on cosmetics. Kriton's collection seems to be building on previous collections by Herakleides of Taras (3rd-2nd c. BC), Kleopatra (1st c. BC - 1st c. AD) and Archigenes (early 2nd c. AD); Kleopatra seemingly had the most authoritative information on hair-loss and Archigenes on hair dyes. Galen attests that since all three predecessors of Kriton (2nd c. AD) were doctors, their manuals were largely composed with medicinal uses in mind, but admits that a fair amount of their material was used for cosmetics.[104] The work of Kriton summarized and enhanced previous knowledge in the field, and it seems to be the standard manual in the time of Galen, in fact so widespread that the latter takes it for granted that every physician has easy access to it and does not bother to repeat the information included in it, but simply makes references to this valuable work.

Galen offers a summary of the topics in Kriton's manual arranged in four books, each consisting of several chapters. The first book included discussions on hair dyes and enhancements, face cosmetics and oral hygiene, mouth-washes and dental health. The second book discussed body and skin conditions and

---

102 A similar divide between reconstructive and plastic (aesthetic) surgery can be observed in modern clinical practice.

103 Galen *De compositione medicamentorum secundum locos libri x*, 12.434–5 Kühn: [How the cosmetic part of medicine is different from hairdressing]: "The purpose of hairdressing (κομμωτικόν) is artificial beauty, while the cosmetic part of medicine (ἰατρική) preserves everything natural in the body, and in this manner natural beauty comes with it, as in the case when the eye-lashes and the hair from one's head fall. This hair not only contributes to beauty, but first and foremost to the health of those parts of the body, as has been demonstrated in the study *On the Use of the Parts*. Is it necessary to say that mentagra, itch, and leprosy are not natural? However, making the skin lighter with chemicals or more pink, or the hair on one's head curly or red, or dark, or making it grow to a great length, like women do, this and that are the works of the hairdressing evil, not of the art of medicine. However, from time to time, because they have something in common, royal women or the kings themselves demand from us some of the services of hairdressing, and it is not possible to refuse by attempting to explain that hairdressing is different from cosmetic medicine."

104 Galen is prepared to forgive Archigenes, because he was a royal physician, and had to give in to the demands of the royal women for beauty treatments, and he is even softer on Kriton, because he was an imperial physician (probably to Trajan). Since Galen himself served as imperial physician for years (under Marcus Aurelius, Commodus and Septimius Severus), he understood the constraints which a physician working for royalty was under.

flaws, purgatives, perfumes, and a vast array of plant extracts and oils used by the cosmetic industry. The third book was dealing with common hair, scalp and facial conditions, and the fourth with dermatological and enterological complaints, and cracked heels. Galen praises Kriton's information on this wide array of medical conditions and considers his work valuable for such problems. However, he admits that Kriton had added a great deal of information on cosmetics, the sole purpose of which was to generate "fake, not real, beauty" (νόθον κάλλος οὐκ ἀληθινόν), such as perfumes, aromatic oils, room and air fresheners, sweet-smelling dyes, and even medicine to delay the growth of a girl's breasts and a boy's testicles for as long as possible. The modern reader is left with some regret that Kriton's manual on ancient cosmetics did not survive.

Galen was aware of a sharp increase in cosmetic products and studies in imperial Rome, which he attributes to the vanity (τρυφή) of his contemporary women. He believed that Herakleides (3rd -2nd c. BC) had lived at a simpler time, and that a large body of literature on medicinal cosmetics had been added in subsequent centuries, which Kriton incorporated in his work.[105] As far as we can tell from the extant corpus of medical literature, this is broadly correct. Hippocratic medicine was aware of cosmetic products, especially ceruse (ψιμύθιον), which was sometimes used in prescriptions, but there is no dedicated study until Herakleides, when favorable conditions for the development of the cosmetics industry emerged in the cosmopolitan urban centers of the Hellenistic world. The image we obtain from non-medical sources concurs: references to cosmetics are sporadic in classical literature,[106] but become much more frequent and focused from the Hellenistic period. In Roman times cosmetics are not only deemed important as a medical and pharmacological subject, but are also considered to be suitable material for poetry in Ovid's didactic work *Medicamina Faciei Feminae* and in the third book of his *Ars Amatoria*. Ovid, like Galen, asserts that extensive use of cosmetics was a sign of his time, while in simpler times of the past beauty enhancers were not necessary. It didn't matter if Andromache or Tecmessa did not wear cosmetics; the husband of the first was a rough soldier, while Ajax was wearing seven bovine skins for clothing.[107] In the words of the poet, *simplicitas rudis ante fuit: nunc aurea Roma est.*[108] In the golden Rome of Ovid the cultivation of beauty was imperative and needed to be perfected with elegance and discretion. Unlike

---

105 Galen 12.445–446.
106 See for example the references in Aristophanes *Lysistrata*, and Xenophon's *Economics* discussed below.
107 Ov. *A. A.* 3.109–112.
108 Ov. *A. A.* 3.113: "Then there was a rough simplicity; now it is the golden Rome."

Galen's critical attitude to vanity the Ovidian model suggests that, like everything else, beauty flourishes if it is cultivated and carefully nurtured.[109]

One would expect that prostitutes would be prime customers of the fashion and cosmetics industry, and there is plenty of evidence from later antiquity to suggest that this was the case. Lucian's Aphrodite in the *Judgment of the Goddesses* (10) appears dressed like a hetaira with make-up and colorful outfits, to the dismay of her competitors who feel that she has an unfair advantage with such trappings and demand that, for the sake of fairness, she must compete naked. Lucian's joke about young Charmides, who professed to be madly in love with the hetaira Philemation, but changed his mind as soon as he heard that she was 45 years old and horribly ugly without her make-up and cosmetics, tells the whole story.[110] Maximos of Tyre, in a similar spirit, suggests that a hetaira's beauty is a mere deception, not natural (αὐτοφυής) but "plastered on" (ἐπίχριστος), and the same concept is reflected in the 3rd letter of Theopylaktos where cosmetics are tantamount to cheating.[111]

For women and men who earned a living with their bodies beauty products would be necessary tools of the trade. This is why it is all the more surprising to find that the debate on cosmetics and clothing in the classical period focuses primarily on married women, and it is only in later times that it shifts towards the prostitute. Jewelry and clothes were often calculated in the dowry which a woman brought with her to her husband's house, [112] could be liquidated for cash

---

109 Patricia Watson and Francesca Cioccoloni have argued that the *Medicamina Faciei Feminae* was a subversive work, an ironic polemic against Augustan propaganda advocating the values of *austeritas* and *pudor*. (Watson 2001: 457–471; Cioccoloni 2006: 97–107. See also Binnicker 1967; Churchill, L. J. 1985; Gibson 1998: 295–312 and 2007; Kueppers 1981: 2507–2551; Volk 2006: 235–251; Schniebs 2001: 49–76 Solodow 1977: 106–127; Myerowitz Levine 1981: 30–56; Nikolaidis 1994: 97–103, and the discussion in Ch. 2.1.). Watson also views the work as a parody of serious didactic poetry, and "the poetic challenge of turning into verse highly intractable technical material" (Watson 2001: 471). Typically the work has been interpreted as an inferior composition within Latin didactic poetry. However, Watson and Cioccoloni are probably right that more credit is due, especially if it is read, along with the *Ars Amatoria*, as an erudite, playful and nuanced heir to an ancient tradition of erotic manuals going back to the late classical period (see the discussion in Ch. 2.1.). In line with this tradition, the advice in both Ovidian works extends beyond cosmetic materials to include instructions on hairdressing, mannerisms, and the right conduct in order to appear attractive.

110 Luc. *DMeretr.* 11. A translation of this passage is provided in Appendix II

111 Max. Tyr. 37.4 f.

112 If the speaker in the Demosthenic speech *Against Spudias* (27–28) is telling the truth, both daughters of a well-off Athenian family took with them expensive clothing and jewelry to their husbands' houses, which was not even calculated in the dowry, but on top of that one of the daughters was promised a house, while the other chose to receive pricy jewelry and clothing

or used as collateral for a loan, if necessary, and in time passed on to the next generation as part of the family fortune.[113] However, the everlasting appeal of jewelry and fine materials extended beyond basic economics. Jewelry and clothes were a matter of status, and could incite envy, as in the case of the concubine of Olympiodoros, an ex-hetaira; her conspicuous and pricy outfits elicited jealousy from his sister and nieces.[114] Women who had been caught committing adultery could be stripped off their jewelry and clothes with impunity if seen in a public temple. Aeschines interprets the intent of this law as *atimia*, namely stripping the woman of her status as a dignified citizen.[115] Moreover, presents of jewelry, clothes and servants were perceived as personal gifts to the woman, to own and pass on to someone else as she pleased, and as such they might be considered a personal favor.[116] A reference to jewelry, clothing and cosmetics in Aristophanes *Lysistrata* concerns all women.[117] In a play where the plot demands the absence of prostitutes, all women are presented as inept victims of fashion and the cosmetic industry. A similar joke is told by Euboulos in the *Wreath Sellers* (Στεφανοπώλιδες):

But, by Zeus, not plastered with rouge,
Nor like you do when you dye your cheeks
With mulberry juice. And if you go out in the summer,
Two black streams are pouring down from your eyes,
And the sweat from your cheeks leaves a red furrow
On your neck, and any hair

---

instead, valued at 10 minae, a sum equal to years of wages for a manual laborer, and roughly equal to the estimated value of the family home. See also D. 27.10 where clothing, jewelry, furniture, and drinking cups (probably made of gold or silver), were part of the dowry of Kleoboule, the mother of Demosthenes; Is. 2.9; 8.8 al.
113 See e.g. Is. 2.9, 8.3; Ar. *Ec.* 446–8; Lys. 12.19; D. 27.10.
114 D. 48.55.
115 D. 59.87; Aesch. 1.183; cf. Kapparis 1999: com. ad loc.
116 D. 59.35 and 46.
117 Ar. *Lys.* 42–8: *Kal.* And what kind of wise or illustrious deed
Could women accomplish? We are sitting all day dolled up
Wearing make-up and saffron dresses
And Cimmerian tunics and fancy shoes!
Lys. Precisely this is where I can see the source of our salvation,
In the saffron dresses, and the perfumes, and the fancy shoes,
And the rouge, and the see-through gowns.

> That touches your face, looks as if it has turned grey,
> For it is dipped in ceruse.[118]

Athenaios, who quotes the passage, introduces this fragment as following: "our lawful wives are not the way Eubulos makes them out to be in the *Wreath Sellers*."[119] Richard Hunter, on the basis of a note by E. Fraenkel, dismisses this testimony of Athenaios, arguing that the speaker is addressing one or more hetairai, and not respectable women.[120] The rejection of the testimony of Athenaios relies upon other references in Attic Old Comedy where hetairai are criticised for their make-up excesses.[121] However, the existence of such parallels alone does not amount to a sufficiently strong reason for the dismissal of the testimony of Athenaios, who had probably read the entire play, after all. Even though hetairai might be fond of cosmetics, they were not the only ones to use them, and, if anything, because they were more skilled in their application they could probably avoid the mishaps ridiculed by Euboulos. Mulberry juice to make one's cheeks look rosy would be nasty, and an excess of whitening powder in the hot Greek summer could, indeed, create a grey mess. No self-respecting hetaira would be quite so careless with her appearance. A closer look into this passage seems to corroborate the understanding of Athenaios that this was referring to amateurs, married women who used cheap, readily available garden materials as cosmetics, with disastrous results.

If we are to understand this passage as an attack on the clumsiness and excesses of married women with cosmetics, the identity of the person who is addressing them is important for the overall interpretation of this passage but impossible to answer with any certainty. A minor emendation in the opening line could make it possible to understand that the speaker is a man and that the entire passage is a male versus female confrontation: a man is addressing a woman or a group of women and is chastising them for their excesses.[122] An alternative interpretation,

---

118 Euboulos fr. 97 (= fr. 98 Hunter)

119 Ath. 13.6: αἱ δὲ γαμεταὶ ἡμῶν γυναῖκες οὔκ εἰσι τοιαῦται οἵας Εὔβουλός φησιν ἐν Στεφανοπώλισιν

120 Hunter 1983: com. ad loc: "gametai gynaikes in Ath.'s introduction to this fragment is of no relevance to its interpretation".

121 The best-known passage criticizing hetairai for their make-up excesses would be Alexis fr. 98 (fr. 103 Arnott). For further information and relevant literature see Hunter 1983: 192–3, Arnott 1996: 273–283.

122 I am convinced that περιπεπλασμένοι instead of περιπεπλασμέναι is a viable possibility, especially since the speaker is swearing "by Zeus", a male deity, which in accordance with another Aristophanic passage (*Ec.* 155–162), could be taken as a further indication that it is a man. This

based on the feminine gender of the transmitted text, would suggest that hetairai are confronting married women and making fun of them for their clumsiness with cosmetics. It is impossible to decide on the current data which interpretation is the correct one.

The use of cosmetics by married women sometimes is accompanied by suspicion of mischief. One can recall the angry reaction of Ischomachos in Xenophon's *Economics* (10.2.2), when he returns home to find his 15 years old wife waiting for him plastered with make-up. Her husband describes the scene as following: "One day I saw her covered with plenty of make-up, so as to look paler than she actually was, and a lot of rouge, so as to look more red, and wearing high heels, so as to look taller." Ischomachos was outraged and urged her to keep her natural appearance, avoiding such excesses in the future. His perfect wife, of course, obeyed.[123] The reason for his angry reaction (apart from the rather strange sight of a 15–year-old with layers of make-up and high heels) is probably better explained in relation to a fragment of Hypereides, which reveals suspicion for a respectable woman using make-up.[124] This passage implies that society would not disapprove of a married woman wearing make-up and cosmetics in order to appeal to her husband. However, a woman could come under suspicion for wearing it for the wrong reasons, like for example the alleged adulteress wife of Euphiletos in Lysias *On the murder of Eratosthenes*,[125] who was suspected by her husband, when he noticed traces of make up on her face, while she was still in mourning

---

is not a foolproof criterion, as in *Lys.* 55 Kalonike says μὰ Δί', and in *Ec.* 550 ff. Praxagora and Blepyros exchange sentences containing the expression μὰ Δί' after it is revealed that the city will be run by women in future, here perhaps with intended effect. In the passage of Euboulos the subject changes after ψιμυθίοις, and ὑμεῖς (namely 'you, the women') emphatically indicates this change where it occurs, which may support the possibility that the speaker is male.

123 The overall interpretation of the narrative in the 7th chapter of Xenophon's *Economics*, where Ischomachos is advising his young wife how to become the perfect Athenian wife, has divided scholarly opinion. While some have viewed the advice of Ischomachos as benign and well-intentioned (e.g. Scaife 1994: 225–232), for others it is a failure juxtaposed to the ethically superior Socratic advice (e.g. Nee 2009: 246–270; MacKenzie 1985: 95–6), an attempt to eliminate the difference between the public and the private by instructing the woman to think like a man (Murnaghan 1988: 9–22; Gini 1992: 483–486), or an attempt by Xenophon to clear the name of Chrysilla (the wife of Ischomachos, and later Kallias) which was marred by scandal in later years (Harvey 1984: 68–70). For a more general discussion see also the always useful commentary of Pomeroy (1994), the recent discussion in Lu 2015: 203–220, and the short account of Tsouyopoulos 1994: 41–49.

124 Hyp. Ἀπαράσημα fr. 10 Blass: "It is right for a woman to adorn herself for her husband as she may please, but when she is going out, one must be wary that this is not for her husband but for other men."

125 Lys. 1.14.

for her brother. The same topic appears more expanded, with specific references to make up practises, in the work *Feminine Harmony* attributed to the Pythagorian Periktione:

> Human opinion coupled with ignorance is drawn to empty and superfluous things. This is why <the good woman> will not wear gold, nor any stone from India or any other place. She will not make her hair into complex patterns, nor will she rub on herself ointments with Arabian scent. She will not apply make-up or rouge on her face, nor pencil around her eyes or eyebrows. She will not dye grey hair, nor wash herself all the time, because the woman who seeks such things is seeking an admirer for her feminine indiscretions. [126]

From the 4th century onwards, as literary sources focus more closely on the famous hetairai of the classical period, references to their fondness of cosmetics, jewelry and make up multiply, and from that period we have the most extensive account on the cosmetic trappings of hetairai, found in Alexis *Isostasion*:

> First with an eye on profit and ripping off the customers
> Every accessory is put into use by them, and they manufacture
> Traps for everyone. If they ever do well,
> They take under their wing new hetairai, beginners in the trade,
> And immediately give them a makeover, so that they will no longer
> Be the same in looks or manners;
> One happens to be small; cork is sewn into the shoes
> One is too tall; she wears thin sandals
> And walks out bending the head over the shoulders.
> This takes off some of the height. Someone has no hips:
> She will sew fake ones underneath, so that anyone who sees them
> Will praise her fine ass. Someone has a fat belly;
> There are artificial breasts at their disposal, like those used by comedians:
> They place them upright, shifting everything forward like poles
> And disguising the flabby belly.
> Someone has red eyebrows; they paint over them with soot.
> If she happens to be dark-skinned, she will plaster her face with white led.
> If she is very pale, she applies rouge;
> Some part of her body is beautiful; this she shows naked.
> She has nice teeth; well, it is necessary to laugh,
> So that those present can see how elegant her mouth is.
> And if it is not in her disposition to laugh, she spends the day indoors,
> Like the things the cooks have when they sell
> Goats' heads, holding between her lips a stick of mint
> So that with time she will get the hang of it,

---

[126] Periktione fr. 143.21–27 Thesleff. I have argued that the letters attributed to Pythagorean women are forgeries from later antiquity: see Ch. 3.2.

Whether she likes it or not.
Through such devices they construct the impression of good looks.[127]

A fragment of Aristophanes from his lost second *Thesmophoriazousai* lists more of such beauty trappings.[128] There seems to be no particular logic to the list. All kinds of items related to beauty and routine feminine toiletry are heaped together:

[Speaker A] Razor, mirror, scissors, wax, soap
frontal wig, neckband, headbands, snood,
rouge, tanning lotion, skin whitener,
perfume, pumice, chest band, ring
scarf, blush, necklaces, eye-pencils,
fancy dress, hellebore, hair-net,
girdle, shawl, little luxuries, bordered robe, long gown,
tunic, ornament, coat, hairdressing tool -
[Speaker B] You are forgetting to mention the most important.
[Speaker A] Which ones?
[Speaker B] Earrings, set with precious stones, earpieces, neckpieces, dangly earrings,
bracelets, buckles, ribbons, necklaces, chains,
seal rings, chains, rings, poultices,
head ornaments, breast-band, dildos, Sardian stones
low necklaces, twisted earrings, and so much more;
trying to name them all would be endless.

The association of such excesses with hetairai is attested by many other sources. Hair dyeing, according to Galen, was thoroughly explored by Kriton in his study on cosmetics, and clearly the ancient world had the knowledge to alter hair color in any direction, for the most part using plant extracts such as henna and indigo dye.[129] Galen only relates Kriton's advice on how to disguise white hair, or dye it blond, no doubt because these two would be the most popular hair treatments, one to make a person look younger,[130] and the other to appeal to the fascination with blond hair among predominantly dark-haired peoples like the Greeks and the Romans.[131] However, just a few lines above Galen makes a passing reference

---

127 Alexis fr. 98.
128 My translations of some of these items are approximate, as they would only correspond roughly to items which the modern reader can easier identify.
129 Galen 12.434–5 Kühn; see also the discussion above and Cartwright-Jones 2006.
130 Like, for example, Lysikrates in Aristophanes *Ec.* (736–737), who dyes his hair black obviously because it is naturally greying.
131 For the fascination of the Greeks and Romans with blond hair see the discussion below.

to almost every treatment which one would expect to find in a modern hair-dresser's shop, such as turning one's hair to blond, dark, red or curly, whatever the customer wanted.

Hairstyles could be considered as the telltale signs of an inappropriate life-style already in the classical period.[132] A note of Suda referring to an Aristophanic passage suggests that there was a particular hairstyle for men called moichos "the seducer", which was indecent and a favorite of whorish (κιναιδώδεις) men.[133] A short fragment of Kratinos, which mentions lint as an attire for a head full of indecency, might be the earliest reference to a specific type of head-gear which was fashionable among prostitutes, and it is possible that he echoes a verse of Archilochos.[134] Several sources suggest that for men a neatly arranged and trimmed hair is a sign of effeminacy, while the opposite, namely wild, long hair and a beard are a sign of masculinity.[135] Hairdressing does not enjoy a good rep-utation among classical authors because it is seen as an exercise in vanity by peo-ple with suspect intentions. Plato reflects these views in Gorgias:

> Hairdressing is a wrongdoer, deceitful and ignoble and slavish, deceiving with fashion and dyes and smoothness and outfits, to generate fake beauty detracting from the natural.[136]

Similar views we encounter in other authors, most prominently in Galen in his critique of hairdressing as the evil counterpart of cosmetic medicine, and in the early Christian theologians.[137] Clement is particularly suspicious of women who dye their hair blond: he suggests that they do so in secret during the day, and this is how they are not discovered in the dim light of the oil-lamp, for their drunk partner does not notice that the golden shades on their hair are not natural. He then quotes Menander's lines saying that a decent woman should not dye her hair

---

132 For hair-styles in their cultural context see Ehrhardt 1971: 14–19; Matthews 1996: 37–39; Bartman 2001: 1–25; May 2005: 275–289; Stephens 2008: 110–132.
133 Sud. μ 1360; cf. Ar. *Ach.* 848-9.
134 Crat. fr. 1. The reference comes from a play entitled *Archilochoi*, which is a parody of Arhilo-chos and his contemporaries, and thus the reference to lint as indecent headgear might be an echo of an Archilochean line, taking us back to the early days of prostitution in the Greek world.
135 E.g. Pseudo-Lucian *Cynicus* 14, where the ultra-masculine Theseus is walking around na-ked, with a long beard and long, wild hair; Luc. *Bacch.* 2, where the super-effeminate Bacchus, among others, is wearing a tiara on his well-kempt hair, and Luc. *DDeor.* 22.1, where Hera is teasing Zeus that he should be ashamed of his son Bacchus, the way he dresses and keeps his hair, smoother than the maenads who accompany him. It seems that some gender-based stereo-types related to hairstyles are timeless.
136 Pl. *Grg.* 465b.
137 Gal. 12.434 Kühn; Philostr. *Dial.* 1.22;

blond.[138] For Tertullian the question of dying one's hair blond goes beyond aesthetics and becomes one of ethnicity. Using saffron to give the hair a yellowish shade suggests to him that a woman does not like to be a dark-haired Roman but would rather prefer to be a barbarian born in Gaul or Germany where blond hair was prevalent; this he finds astonishing and advises Christian women not to put on their head such impurities.[139] He then asks:

> Why is no rest allowed to your hair, which must now be bound, now loosed, now cultivated, and now thinned out? Some are anxious to force their hair into curls, some to let it hang loose and flying, not with good simplicity: beside which, you affix I know not what enormities of subtle and textile perukes; now, after the manner of a helmet of undressed hide, as it were a sheath for the head and a covering for the crown; now, a mass (drawn) backward toward the neck.[140]

This description of hairstyles, as well as the testimony of Aristophanes, who mentions a fair number of hairdressing tools in the above mentioned list of cosmetic devices, and that of Galen, who mentions hair dyes and other treatments, some medicinal and intended to help a healthy hair growth, and some purely cosmetic, suggest that hairdressing was such an important part of the ancient cosmetic industry that sometimes the primary term for it (κομμωτική) encompassed all forms of cosmetics and not only hairstyling.[141]

Facial make up is the most commonly attested kind of cosmetic. The passage of Alexis quoted above suggests that depending on skin color and type a wide variety of plant extracts and chemicals, some of them quite toxic, were extensively used. The most frequent forms of make-up were those which made the skin appear paler. Considering that Mediterranean women tend to tan easily under the strong summer sun, we can believe our sources that such substances were very popular. A pale skin was an indication of wealth and modesty,[142] and thus a mat-

---

138 Clem.Al. *Paed.* 3.2.6.1
139 Tert. *Cult.Fem.* 2.6.
140 Tert. *Cult.Fem.* 2.7. Translation S. Thelwall (1869).
141 Galen, for example, when he criticizes hairdressing he means not only hairstyling, but a wide array of cosmetic devices.
142 Poorer women spent more time outdoors working or performing tasks which rich women did not need to perform, such as going to the market-place and performing household and maybe farming chores. Their skin would show more the ravages of sun and hardship, and if some form of powder or liquid could make it look paler, like that of aristocratic women who spent much of their time in sheltered spaces, that substance would be in high demand. Xenophon (*Oec.* 7.22–3) offers a teleological explanation: τὴν φύσιν, φάναι, εὐθὺς παρεσκεύασεν ὁ θεός, ὡς ἐμοὶ δοκεῖ, τὴν μὲν τῆς γυναικὸς ἐπὶ τὰ ἔνδον ἔργα καὶ ἐπιμελήματα, <τὴν δὲ τοῦ ἀνδρὸς ἐπὶ τὰ ἔξω>.

ter of culture and an artistic ideal, as Mary Ann Eaverly has convincingly demonstrated in her excellent monograph on the subject.[143] The most common compound used to make the skin appear paler was white lead (ψιμύθιον), a poisonous substance widely used for dyes, paints and cosmetics until recently, and also as a contraceptive, according to Aristotle.[144] Theophrastos describes in detail the method of its extraction from lead by means of corrosion: lead bars were left in acid for ten days, and each day the top layer was scraped off. Traces of the substance have been found in pyxides.[145] One of its most famous derivatives, the Venetian ceruse, was highly prized as a cosmetic in the Elizabethan era and immortalized in the pale faces of portraits from that period. A passage of Xenophanes (6th/5th c. BC) suggests that its use was already widespread in the archaic period as a way of making the skin look paler.[146] It was often used in combination with blush applied to the cheeks on top of the psimython to convey an impression of health and modesty.[147] The most common form of blush was derived from alcanet root (*anchusa tinctoria*), often used as a red dye. In Attic Greek it was called enchousa, but in science it is known by its Koine version as anchousa.[148] Xenophon's testimony in the *Economics* (10.2) makes clear that enchousa could be used on top of the white lead compound to add a healthier look to a face already whitened with psimython, which otherwise might look sickly pale, like the face of Dracula in modern fantasy cinema. We can get an idea of the final result through Elizabethan portraits or the images of aristocrats in the paintings of Thomas Gainsborough, where the visibly whitened faces have an unnatural-looking spot of rouge over the cheeks, added almost like an afterthought over the ceruse. Euboulos in the afore-mentioned passage mentions mulberry juice (συκάμινον) as an agent to add redness to the cheeks, no doubt a cheaper alter-

---

A woman's body was built for indoors, and the ravages of the sun would be unnatural for her, while they were natural for a man.

143 Eaverly 2013; see also Thomas 2002: 1–16.

144 See Sear 1936: 314–317. For the use of ψιμύθιον as a contraceptive see Arist. *HA* 583 a 22–4,

145 Thphr. *Lap.* 56; Sear 1936: 314–317, Glazebrook 2009: 234.

146 Xenophanes, *Testimonia* 28.978a D-K.

147 E.g. X. *Oec.* 10.2; Ar. *Ec.* 929.

148 E.g. Thphr. *HP.* 7.8.3. Several occurrences of the form *anchousa* can be found in the Hippocratic Corpus, such as in *Ulc.* 17 and *Nat. Mul.* 32, probably because the works in question were not written in Attica. See also Andrews 1951: 165–166.

native readily available in the garden in summer months but not as classy as professional grade enchousa.[149] Somewhere in between in terms of price and prestige stood orchil, the dye obtained from seaweed (φῦκος).

Eye-liners as a routine part of feminine make-up are attested by Alexis, who mentions soot (ἄσβολος) as the main compound, and also by Euboulos.[150] Soot would be readily available as a residual element in chimneys, from where Dioscorides recommends that it should be collected.[151] In some sources eyeliner is primarily associated with prostitutes.[152] Then as now a heavily made up face with excessively emphasized eye-lines might appear meretricious, but it would be erroneous to go to the other extreme and assume that only hetairai used eye-liners, as A. Glazebrook does on the basis of the omission of eye-liners from the toiletry of the wife of Ischomachos.[153] The evidence of Euboulos above refers to wives, and one would imagine that the difference between a respectable and a meretricious make up would be one of quantity and style rather than use or absence of any single compound. The same conclusion can be drawn from the relentless criticism of women's cosmetics by Clement.[154]

As the two Aristophanic passages mentioned above and Alexis suggest, clothing and jewelry were also perceived to be important in a hetaira's lifestyle. Although, it seems, no particular garment or outfit can be exclusively associated

---

149 Glazebrook 2009: 234 n. 4 understands that mulberry juice was applied as lipstick, and quotes Euboulos as evidence. However, Euboulos clearly says that the mulberry juice was applied on the jaws (γνάθους) on top of the psimythion.

150 Alexis fr. 98; Euboulos fr. 97 (= fr. 98 Hunter).

151 Diosc. *Eup.* 2.126.3. Soot is a known carcinogen, but like ceruse, the ancient world was unaware of its ill-effects.

152 For example, according to Plutarch (*Alc.* 39), Alcibiades just before his death dreamt that the hetaira Timandra, who was with him in his last days, was holding his head in her lap and applying psimythion and eyeliner. The dream turned out to be a bad omen. The fact that Timandra was applying the make-up and eyeliner on his face points towards an association of make-up and eyeliners with hetairai. Philo (*De aeternitate mundi* 57) indeed says that eyeliners are the tool of ugly hetairai who try to disguise themselves with false beauty, since they are short of true decorum (κόσμος). He is using *kosmos* with ambiguity to refer to physical as well as inner beauty and decorum.

153 Glazebrook 2009: 236–7.

154 Clem.Al. *Paed.* 3.2.4–5: Clement is not exclusively referring to prostitutes, but to all women who use cosmetics, and is trying to persuade them to adopt a way of life which places emphasis on spiritual rather than physical beauty. He mentions a fair number of cosmetic devices, such as face creams, eyeliners, hair dyes, jewelry and gold, and compares the women who use them to Egyptian temples, very luxurious outside and surprisingly strange and poor inside, harboring crocodiles and snakes venerated like gods. In this analogy women who adorn themselves on the outside are like inept monkeys or dangerous snakes on the inside.

with prostitutes, more expensive garments, brighter colors and patterns which would make one stand out were high on their list. In particular, flowery dresses (ἄνθινα), purple (πορφυρᾶ) and gold (χρυσία) are often encountered in the sources as a hetaira's attire. This association appears to be so strong that it generated a story repeated several times in the sources, but set in a different location and context in each case. In Greek Italy of the 7th century the famous lawgiver Zaleukos allegedly prohibited women from wearing gold and fancy clothes unless they were prostitutes, and men from wearing rings and Milesian-type tunics unless they were prostitutes or adulterers. The reliability of the story is highly suspect, as it probably comes from a much later time, but nonetheless the tale highlights the perception of cosmetics and certain types of clothing as a hetaira's plaything. A similar tale is found in the historian Phylarchos, only here the setting is Syracuse: the law forbade women to wear gold, flowery dresses and gowns with purple borders, and men to wear elaborately woven garments. Refusal to conform would be taken as evidence of prostitution or intent to commit adultery.[155] Clement places the prohibition in Sparta, and in this version only hetairai are allowed to wear flowery dresses and gold, while decent women need to be educated to avoid the love of adornment (φιλοκοσμία).[156]

Perhaps somewhat more believable is a similar tale about the Pythagoreans, as told by Iamblichos. Wearing gold is included among many other prohibitions of luxuries, such as eating anything that has a soul, or tasty and expensive delicacies. The followers were advised to give away the delicacies to the servants, in order to learn good discipline, while golden jewelry was only to be worn by hetairai, and, in that case, only to teach respectable women the value of modesty.[157] These stories are most likely fictitious, but such prohibitions would not be unheard-of, and some are attested in inscriptions, in particular sacred documents including rules regulating entry to certain sanctuaries.[158] The association of flowery dresses, luxury outfits dyed in purple, gold and cosmetics with prostitutes

---

155 Phylarchos *FGrH* 81 F 45 = Athen. 12.20.

156 Clem.Al. *Paed.* 2.10.105.2. This story is probably a creation of later antiquity, an attempt to reinvent and apply to Spartan women the same famous austerity which Xenophon describes in relation to the dress codes of Spartan boys and men (X. *Lac.* 2.1–4; 7.3).

157 Iambl. *VP* 31.187

158 For example, an inscription from the temple of Despoina at Lykosoura in Arcadia (3rd c. BC) prohibits gold, purple, flowery or black dresses, shoes or rings. Any of these items brought by a believer needs to be dedicated to the temple (*IG* v². 514. 3–9). An inscription from Delos prohibits entry to a drunk person or someone wearing a flowery dress (*IG* xi 4.1300). One would think that such items were sometimes perceived as offensive to the divine because they were luxury products associated with excess and debauchery.

and the lifestyle of debauchery was firmly established in popular culture, and on account of it cosmetics and artificial beauty enhancers received a lot of bad publicity among early Christian writers and theologians.

From our perspective, this obsession of Christian theologians with luxury items has proved beneficial, as their accounts abound with detailed information on substances, materials, techniques and literature related to the lifestyle of ostentation, which they were so determined to eliminate.[159] To give one small example, Clement, in his criticism of meretricious dresses made of fine materials, woven and dyed in elaborate patterns, offers a very exact description of the method of silk production and the manner silk dresses would be worn by women in his time. Of course he firmly disapproves of such a fine material, which, he says, is a very thin veil accentuating and revealing rather than concealing the shame of the body.[160] He also provides information on dyes, listing among others one made from unripe grapes, green, pink and red dyes, materials dyed with sea products, like purple, cloth with animal designs, perfumed saffron dresses, ostentatious dresses made with animal skins or exhibiting the signs of the zodiac, precious stones like the diaphanous Sardian, and so on. In the end of his long list Clement quotes Aristophanes *Lysistrata*,[161] asking what kind of virtuous deed (φρόνιμον) women could ever accomplish by wearing flowery and saffron dresses and make up.

Among dyes, Clement singles out the Tyrian purple as the ultimate symbol of luxury, because, he says, treacherous women and womanly men use it to dye fine Jewish or Cilician linen in order to groan with pleasure in their excesses.[162] Tertullian's stern disapproval of the use of purple and other dyes derived from living beings rests upon the interesting argument that one should not misuse and abuse God's creatures for inappropriate purposes.[163] This rare extract from a sea organism was an item of luxury used by royalty, statesmen and the very wealthy throughout the ancient world, and in Byzantium purple was the exclusive privilege of the imperial family. It seems that in this most Christian of all empires, the stern warnings of the early Church Fathers had fallen on deaf ears. Even a single ribbon dyed in purple would be costly, and this is why for a high class hetaira a purple dress, or even one with a purple border, would be a matter of status,

---

159 On Christian theologians and their views on cosmetics, clothing and beauty products see Daniel-Hughes 2010; Hartney 2002: 243–258; Upson-Saia 2011; Edwards 1993.
160 Clem.Al. *Paed.* 2.10.107.
161 See the discussion above on *Lysistrata*.
162 Clem. Al. *Paed.* 2.10.115.2. See also Athen. 13.52, where it is said that ugly hetairai are dressed in expensive linen by pimps.
163 Tert. *Cult. Fem.* 2.8; see also Daniel-Hughes 143–168.

wealth and success, and a very desirable item. Such dresses are mentioned in an alleged law of Syracuse prohibiting respectable women to wear them, and limiting them to hetairai, and also in the inscription from Lykosoura which bans them from the temple of Despoina (see above). Xenophon lists purple as one of the items typically associated with the luxurious lifestyle of the Medes, but also as a sign of power, wealth and prestige, and this perception is widely attested in other classical sources, as M. Reinhold has convincingly demonstrated.[164] Lucian describes purple as an attire for prostitutes:

> The hetairai, especially the uglier ones, make the whole of their dress from purple and cover their neck in gold, trying to seduce with luxury and compensate for their lack of beauty with superficial tricks. They believe that their arm will shine brighter with the gold and their ill-shaped foot will go unnoticed in golden sandals, or that the face itself will appear more attractive if seen next to the most shining object. This is what they do, but the prudent woman only uses a modest and necessary amount of golden jewelry, and would not be embarrassed to show off her natural beauty, even when she is totally naked.[165]

This passage is significant because it provides support for the thesis that the difference between a hetaira and a respectable woman was one of quantity and style. What would make a hetaira stand out was the excess and immodesty in her appearance, which Clement considers to be intentionally evil tricks with the intent to deceive.[166]

In an image very familiar to western culture, the notorious Whore of Babylon in John's *Revelation* (17.4) is presented wearing purple and scarlet and decked with gold, precious stones and pearls, and holding a golden cup. What generates the sense of meretricious lack of modesty in this image is not the precious materials themselves but their excess into an extravagant combination that popular imagination typically identified with a prostitute.[167] Artemidoros in his interpretations of dreams paradoxically sees the stereotypical prostitute as a woman established in a brothel and yet wearing purple. When debating clothes he says that a flowery and colorful dress in a dream is a good omen for all women and especially hetairai or rich women, while monochromatic materials are a good omen for everyone.[168] Lucian's Lyra the daughter of Daphnis, a seasoned hetaira who was dressed in rags before she reached her prime, was seen in beautiful flowery

---

164 X. *Cyr.* 1.3.2, 2.4.6, 8.3.3, 8.3.13 al.; Reinhold 1970; see also Forstenpointner 2007: 201–214.
165 Luc. *Dom.* 7
166 Clem.Al. *Paed.* 2.10 bis.104.1
167 See Glancy 2011: 551–569
168 Artemid. *Onir.* 4.42.6; 2.3.83

dresses (εὐανθεῖς) once she became wealthy, while the young Corinna is promised even more luxurious purple dresses (ἀλουργεῖς) if she becomes a successful
hetaira, like Lyra. Lucian's passage suggests a hierarchy, with purple dresses oc-
cupying the top position of luxury outfits, while fine cloth with flowery patterns
comes a close second in the preferences of hetairai. Pollux (4.120) attests that the
association of purple with prostitution was celebrated on the comic stage where
female pimps or mothers of hetairai were typically presented with a purple ribbon
round their head, while male pimps would be wearing a dyed tunic and flowery
wrap, and holding a straight stick called ἄρεσκος. He also mentions an expression for "a through and through golden hetaira" (διάχρυσος ἑταίρα), which he
interprets as a hetaira who wears a lot of gold on her head, and a similar expression for a hetaira who wears splendid tiaras (διάμιτρος ἑταίρα).[169]

Some of this jewelry was famous throughout antiquity, like the legendary
necklace (ὅρμος) of Bacchis, which inspired a moving story of jealousy, desire
and unselfishness.[170] Clement offers a long list of precious materials, jewelry and
chains which he considers an inappropriate exhibition of wealth and one recalling the mythical bonds in which Aphrodite was bound, while she was caught
committing adultery. He relates an episode where Apelles the painter seeing that
one of his students had painted Helen decked in gold told him "Boy, since you
could not paint her beautiful you painted her rich." [171] A more irate Tertullian
finds it detestable that women would adorn themselves with putrid parts of animals and fish, like the pearl.[172] The connection between purple and golden jewelry as the typical luxury attire of hetairai is easily noticeable, and one can add
more stories such as the one about the hetaira Nannion (aka Aix, "the goat"), who
sometimes was called Proskenion (Forestage) because she had a very presentable
face and used to wear a lot of gold, but when she undressed apparently she was
terribly ugly.[173] The opposite is suggested by a passage of Libanios where the gold
enhances the beauty of a hetaira and as a result the infatuated lover is gasping.[174]

---

169 Pollux 4.153.
170 Menetor *Hist.* fr. 1: A young man who was a lover of Bacchis fell in love with Plangon of
Miletos. She tried to discourage his advances by challenging him with an impossible task,
namely to bring her the famous necklace of Bacchis, and then she would accept him as her lover.
The young man pleaded passionately with Bacchis, and she gave in and unselfishly offered her
necklace. A slightly embarrassed Plangon returned the necklace, but accepted the young man
as her lover and shared his affections with Bacchis thereafter.
171 Clem.Al. *Paed.* 2.12.125.3
172 Tert. *Cult.Fem.* 1.6; 2.12.
173 Athen. 13.51.
174 Lib. *Decl.* 32.1.32.

Gold, like purple, was not a symbol of indecent lifestyle in itself as a passage of Klearchos clearly suggests, in which virtuous and modest women are the ones wearing it, as opposed to young virgins who do not.[175] It only became indecent if worn excessively and in a certain way that suggested immodest, oriental-style luxury.

Gold has been seen as an enviable symbol of wealth, status and prestige throughout history, and there is plenty of evidence suggesting that it was seen as a symbol of status and success among hetairai.[176] In a passage from the speech Against Olympiodoros the speaker complains that his wife and daughters were very jealous of the spectacular outings of the hetaira-concubine of Olympiodoros, in splendid garments and golden jewelry.[177] Envy for golden jewelry is also expressed by Krobyle, as she is trying to convince her daughter Korinna to take up prostitution, in Lucian.[178] A hetaira's love of golden jewelry is a standard literary topos and has inspired a wordplay, a fictitious scenario involving a play on words, first encountered in Hermogenes, and subsequently in several other rhetoricians and lexicographers.[179] A hetaira could not live without her gold and other little luxuries, according to one of the fictional letters of Alciphron (4.9.1). Petale replies to a persistent but stingy lover that she cannot be fed with tears; she needs gold, clothes, make up and servants, and someone to take care of household expenses. The topos of the golden hetaira is also encountered in the novel, in particular in Xenophon's *Ephesiaca*.[180] The association of luxury, artifi-

---

175 Klearchos fr. 23 Wehrli.

176 There are many collections of Greek jewelry still surviving in museums around the world; see for example: Ogden – Williams 1994 and Davidson – Hoffman 1965.

177 D. 48.55. The wife of the speaker was the sister of Olympiodoros and was claiming – probably illegally – a significant inheritance which had passed to his possession.

178 Luc. *DMeretr.* 6.2: Krobyle dangles in front of her daughter all the nice things that their acquaintance, the daughter of Daphnis, has had ever since she got into prostitution, like gold, flowery dresses and four servants.

179 Hermog. *Stat.* 2.108–115, and Chapter 12 passim. Allegedly there was a law stating that if a hetaira wears gold, it must be confiscated. When someone who understood that the hetaira herself is to be confiscated tried to hale her to slavery she defended herself by arguing that the law ordered the confiscation of the jewelry, not herself.

180 Xenophon's *Ephesiaca* 5.7 ff.: the virtuous and noble heroine Anthia is captured by pirates and sold to a pimp to become a common prostitute. He thinks that he will make great profit by auctioning her virginity. The beautiful Anthia is dressed in splendid clothes and gold and led to the brothel. There in some kind of auction many volunteer to pay a high price for her. In an attempt to preserve her virtue, she fakes an epileptic fit, which discourages potential customers and induces her pimp to give her away. Her husband, the handsome Abrakomes, has an equally

cial beauty and debauchery with the orient was deeply embedded in Greek literature and thought ever since the Ionians came in contact with the Persian empire in the 6ᵗʰ century. A story of the orient, as told by Ktesias of Knidos, the 4ᵗʰ century historian and royal physician to Artaxerxes II, suggests that hetairai and cosmetics were typical features of the lifestyle of oriental excess, as the Greeks imagined it, even before the formation of the Persian empire. The quasi-mythical Assyrian king Sardanapallos was said to have employed the cosmetics which hetairai used in his lifestyle of effeminate luxury:

> He was living with the concubines, wearing purple and the softest of spun wool, and a woman's outfit, while the face and the entire body had become softer than any tender woman through the use of white lead and the other tricks of the hetairai.[181]

Tales about the early hetairai told by later authors establish associations with a lifestyle of luxury, splendid outfits and perfumes. In a Cinderella-like story in Herodotus, the fine garment of the first hetaira to be mentioned by name, the Graeco-Egyptian Rhodopis, was snatched by an eagle and dropped into the lap of the king of Egypt, who then searched for its owner, found her and made her his queen.[182] An entry of Suda (o 51) associates the grave of Lais with the smell of saffron.[183] There are several more references to prostitutes and perfume in the *Greek Anthology*, like the sweet-smelling skin of Demo and the doorstep of Demarion drenched in perfume, all with connotations of luxury and pleasure.[184]

The association of prostitution with perfumes is widely attested in Aristophanes and other comic poets. Perfumes, along with prostitutes, entertainers, delicacies and garlands are the necessary components of any party or celebration, and Trygaios in Aristophanes *Peace* admits that perfume signifies peaceful, civilized pleasure away from military service.[185] Athenaios provides an extensive selection of passages discussing perfumes and garlands as the necessary items for

---

difficult time fending off the unwelcome advances of a pirate, saying that he won't turn from a man to a *porne* (in the feminine) and lie under him.

181 Ktesias, *FGrH* 688 F 1b.

182 See also the epigram of Posidonius, where we read that the scent of her sweet perfumes no longer lingers around the grave of Rhodopis; all that is left of her is the immortal verses of Sappho about her (see the discussion in Ch. 1.1.).

183 Suda o 51. For an enchanting, even if historically questionable account of the use of saffron in the cosmetic industry of the ancient world, see Willard 2001.

184 *AG* 5.197 and 198.

185 See e.g. Ar. *Ach.* 1089–1093; *Pax.* 525–6; Eupolis, fr. 176; Amphis fr. 9; Nikostratos fr. 27; Apollodoros fr. 5.22. and the discussion in Ch. 5.4. Athenaios (15.1–33) provides numerous quotations from literature regarding the use of garlands in symposia. Perfumes are a mark of the

a symposium, and also very specific information about perfumes used in his time or attested in previous literature, which is outside our purposes to discuss in detail here.[186] Several comic passages are open to interpretation as to whether the joke refers to effeminacy, mischief or prostitution.[187] Sometimes, however, the references to prostitution are unmistakable, as in a very exaggerated passage of the comic poet Apollodoros, where a group of Athenian knights are going to Corinth for a ten day long revelry (κῶμος), an activity typically associated with hetairai, with a per diem allocation of garlands and perfume. A fragment from an unidentified comic poet which translates "they were chewing mastich-gum and smelling perfume" is also an unmistakable reference to male prostitution, as the existence of a term meaning "mastich-chewer" (σχινότρωξ) to indicate a male prostitute is well attested by the lexicographers.[188]

The most extensive account of excesses with perfumes and their associations with prostitution, both male and female, can be found in Clement *Paidagogos*.[189] Clement quotes from previous literature, and has assembled an impressive collection of substances and practices related to the use of perfumes in the imperial era. He mentions several types of perfumes, such as the brenthian, the metallic, the royal and the plangonian, which were obviously composite blends, and quotes Simonides on unguents, incense and perfume derived from hazelwort (βάκκαρι). Several plant extracts used as unguents and perfumes are also mentioned, like lily, rose, nard, myrrh and cinnamon, coming in various forms such as liquid, dry, unguent, oil or incense. Women in his mind were the main culprits who perfumed everything, even the chamber-pots, and corrupted and softened men with such luxuries. Clement draws a distinction between pleasant perfumes which have healing powers and can be used for medicinal purposes, and those with an indecent erotic quality which cause arousal and lead to inappropriate

---

luxurious city lifestyle, as opposed to the country smells of Strepsiades in Aristophanes *Clouds* (51), and frequently a sign of effeminate conduct, as in the *Thesmophoriazousai* (253–4), where the garment which Agathon offers to Mnesilochos has a scent of saffron and, according to the latter, the sweet smell of foreskin (ποσθίου), implying that Agathon was wearing the fine cloak and the perfumes to entice men.

186 Athen. 15.33. See also Stewart 2007; Dayagi-Mendels 1989.

187 E.g. Ar. fr. 305; Eupolis, fr. 176; Nikostratos fr. 27, and fr. 34. Adultery is implied on many occasions, as for example in the exchange between Blepyros and Praxagora in Aristophanes *Ecclesiazousai* (523–6), where she challenges him to smell her as proof that she is not wearing perfume, and thus could not be suspected of adultery. A bemused Blepyros replies "What then? Can a woman not get screwed without perfume"? "Not me, dear" she replies.

188 Cratin. fr. 327; Suet. 3; Luc. *Lex.* 12; Sch. Luc. 46,12 Rabe al.

189 Clem.Al. *Paed.* 2.8.61 ff.

pleasures with loose women. A couple of centuries later Cyril the Theologian took it beyond the level of philosophical instruction and represented smells and perfumes as demons trying to hale the soul to hell.[190]

Shoes and all kinds of footwear also become the target of Clement's relentless critique of meretricious excesses. While he accepts the need for footwear, especially for women who should never show their bare feet in public, he draws a clear distinction between what would constitute unacceptable excesses and what would be deemed as appropriate and modest. He certainly disapproves of sandals with golden flowers on them, and says that such items are often worn by prostitutes, who sometimes engrave messages for potential lovers at the bottom of their shoes. Clement also disapproves of shoes with spiral nails, golden leaves, precious stones, high heels, and footwear from exotic locations. The reason for his disapproval is that such footwear is associated with luxury and debauchery, as many other sources suggest - like, for example, Lucian's *Dialogues of Hetairai*, where a man offers his lover sandals with a golden leaf from Patara.[191] Clement approves simple footwear for women, preferably white, but maybe treated with some kind of shoe polish if someone is planning to walk on dirt roads. For men he praises barefoot walking, but is also prepared to approve some kind of plain sandal with a strap like the one which Jesus was wearing when he went to be baptized.[192]

Tertullian's take on cosmetics can be summarized in the phrase "Quod nascitur opus Dei est. Ergo quod infingitur diaboli negotium est."[193] In his mind God's creation is perfect and does not need any enhancements. Anything that tries to enhance the natural beauty of creation is bound to detract from it and thus is the work of the Devil. Clement shares this philosophy but places greater emphasis on inner beauty, which cannot be enhanced with fake cosmetics, but only through a virtuous lifestyle. He is convinced that cosmetic devices are the tools of the trade for women who have lost all sense of shame and are set to profit from these devices:

> Hairnets and the varied and curious patterns of these hairnets, the myriad of hairstyles, the splendidly wrought mirrors, which they use to apply their make-up and hunt down those who are infatuated by appearances like mindless children, all these are the works of women who have long ago lost the ability to blush. If one were to call these women prostitutes he

---

190 Cyril *De Exitu Animi* 77.1076.1.
191 Luc.*DMeretr.* 14.2; E.g. Krates fr. 17, Kratinos fr. 105, Antiphanes fr. 188. D.S. 5.46.2;
192 Ev. *Marc.* 1.7; Ev. *Luc.* 3.16; Ev. *Jo.* 1.27.
193 "Whatever is born is the work of God. However, what is applied on top is the Devil's invention": Tert. *Cult.Fem.* 2.5.4.

would not be really mistaken, since they have turned their faces (πρόσωπα) into masks (προσωπεῖα).[194]

Whereas Tertullian considers all women to be weak and prone to evil, and his advice to abstain from such unnatural practices as cosmetics is intended for all, Clement is more selective in his criticisms. He is prepared to accept that some women are decent and virtuous (σώφρονες), while some are so shameless that one would rightly call them "whores." Thus he forges a deliberate link between prostitution and the cult of cosmetics, and this link dominates his extensive, thorough and very vocal criticism of all such materials and devices. His conclusion is that virtuous women do not need to use such trappings, but whores do. For us his account represents an important historical document, not only because it is a rich source of relevant information, but also because it summarizes previous relevant literature and offers an insight into the reasons why early Christian theologians were so vocal in their condemnation of cosmetics.[195]

Both Clement and Tertullian are particularly vocal in their condemnation of cosmetics for men. Tertullian's account suggests that male toiletry could be elaborate too, even if somewhat more discreet than the feminine:

> To cut the beard too sharply; to pluck it out here and there; to shave round about (the mouth); to arrange the hair, and disguise its hoariness by dyes; to remove all the incipient down all over the body; to fix (each particular hair) in its place with (some) womanly pigment; to smooth all the rest of the body by the aid of some rough powder or other: then, further, to take every opportunity for consulting the mirror; to gaze anxiously into it.[196]

---

194 Clem.Al. *Paed.* 3.2.11.2–3
195 Several humorous epigrams from the Greek Anthology make fun of cosmetic excesses not on moral but on aesthetic grounds, like the one which lists a number of cosmetic substances that someone bought, like false hair, teeth, honey, and orchil, and concludes "you could have bought a new face for all this money" (*AG* 11.310). Another epigram by Lucillius (*AG* 11.408) is even more entertaining:

> You dye your hair, but you will never dye away your old age,
> Nor can you stretch the wrinkles out of your cheeks;
> Stop plastering white lead all over your face,
> For you will end up with a mask, not a face.
> Nothing matters anymore. Why are you going mad?
> Rouge and make up will not turn Hecuba into Helen.

196 Tert. *Cult.Fem.* 2.8. Translation S. Thelwall (1969). See also Daniel-Hughes 143–198.

Clement has a much longer list of male cosmetic treats, which he considers whorish (πορνικάς) and the actions either of adulterers (μοιχοί) or womanly male prostitutes (ἀνδρόγυνοι), and generally of men who use such cosmetic devices to pursue illicit and inappropriate sexual acts.[197] Among others he mentions womanly and whorish haircuts, bright tunics, shaving and depilation, hair dyes either turning grey hair to black to look younger or to blond, and effeminate hairstyling (διακτενισμοὺς θηλυδριώδεις).[198] What is a sign of effeminacy in his mind is to artificially change one's natural color and appearance. He attests to the existence of an entire flourishing industry which offers cosmetic services for men like waxing, shaving, depilation in many different ways, and personal toiletry. Women routinely removed undesirable hair using wax or singeing it with an oil lamp as a large number of passages suggests, which Martin Kilmer has discussed in a comprehensive article.[199] However, precisely for that reason depilation was perceived as an act which feminized a man, and was appropriate for effeminate men or male prostitutes.[200] Clement finds that the men of his time are taking undue liberties with dress too, wearing soft materials, dyed in bright colors, and wrapping them around their bodies like men who had had their testicles crushed (κατεαγότων), prancing around the women's quarters like "amphibious and lustful beasts."[201] He wonders how anyone in their right mind could choose to look like a prostitute, and expresses sympathy for slave boys working in brothels who are forced against their will to use cosmetics with a view to immoral earnings for their pimps. This perception of meticulous grooming as unmanly is almost as old as our oldest sources.[202]

---

197 Clem.Al. *Paed.* 3.3.15.1.
198 Clement finds nothing inherently effeminate in long or blond hair, recalling that some barbarians, like the Celts, Scythians and Germans, may be blond and keep their hair long, but they are menacing and fierce warriors, and praiseworthy for their preference of a simpler lifestyle (λιτότης).
199 See e.g. Ar. *Ec.* 12–13 and Kilmer 1982: 104–112.
200 See Kapparis 1996: 63–77. See also Alciphron 3.20, where we find a detailed description of the service in a barber's shop.
201 ἀμφιβίων καὶ λάγνων θηρίων: Clem.Al. *Paed.* 3.3.18.1. Clement (*Paed.* 3.3.18.1 and 3.3.19.2) invokes contemporary medical theory which considered the male body to be dry and hot, as opposed to the female which is wet and cold, and argues that hairy beings are dryer and hotter than hairless ones, and this is why anything male, anything with testicles intact and anything perfect, is hairy, while anything female, anything of which the testicles have been removed, or anything imperfect, would be hairless.
202 The famous lines of Archilochos where the vainglorious general (fr. 114 West) pays too much attention to his hair and trimmed beard offer one of the oldest pieces of evidence suggesting that too much grooming detracts from a man. Another fragment of Archilochos, which is paraphrased

Several stories attributed to fourth century philosophers express stern disapproval for male grooming and associate it directly with prostitution. In one of these Diogenes the Cynic saw someone with a trimmed beard, perfumed and dressed in smooth outfits riding a horse, and said "I was wondering before what an ἱππόπορνος was; now I know." [203] Lucian describes the typical male prostitute as someone with a shaved face, still trying to look like a teenage boy even though he is considerably older.[204] According to Lucian's description, a man whom he calls *kinaidos* (a difficult term which may or may not refer to a male prostitute, but definitely refers to effeminacy and a lifestyle of excess) was clean shaven with waxed legs, orchil and eyeliner, a seductive look and bending his neck. The nickname which he had adopted was Chelidonion, a hetaira's name (see Appendix I), and may be suggesting a transvestite prostitute.[205] The cynic philosopher of Pseudo-Lucian argues that wet and smooth flesh is suitable for women, while the beard adorns a man's face like a horse's or a lion's mane. Similar opinions can be found in many other places in the literature of later antiquity, all pointing to the

---

by Aristophanes, suggests that a shaved behind is a sign of unmanliness (fr. 187 West; Ar. *Ach.* 119). Aristophanes repeatedly makes fun of clean-shaven, hairless men with a soft, pale skin, which is interpreted as a sign of effeminacy: e.g. Ar. *Th.* 191–2, 218–9, 1043–6, *Ec.* 60 ff. In the Persian history of Ktesias (*FGrH* 688 F 1) Sardanapallos, that archetypal figure of oriental effeminacy and softness, is sitting among the concubines with his face whitened with ceruse, wearing women's clothes, skin all softened and wearing eyeliner, when Arbakes the Mede steps in and sees him (see also the narrative of Nikolaos of Damascus fr. 10 about Artaios). Then Arbakes is convinced that Sardanapallos is not enough of a man to run the empire and decides to topple him. Theopompos (*FGrH* 115 F 204), although he considers waxing and shaving one's body hair to make the skin smooth to be a sign of barbaric effeminacy and luxury, acknowledges that it is a common habit in the Greek world too, and confirms for us that the shops which took care of men's grooming, as described by Clement, were already in operation in the 4th century BC. Theopompos uses *ergasterion*, the same word as Clement, for these shops, which could be used for any kind of workshop, but also for a brothel. He also considers shaving and making one's skin feel smooth to be a sign of effeminacy, when he is talking about the companions of Philip (*FGrH* 115 F 225b). The comic poet Alexis (fr. 266) indignantly asks "what has your hair ever done to you, for gods' sake? It has only made you look like a man." Chrysippos (28, fr. 2 von Arnim) tells several stories of cities like Rhodes and Byzantium where shaving or having a barber were forbidden, but nonetheless everyone ignored or bypassed the laws and shaved. He also confirms that the habit of shaving the beard became widespread from the time of Alexander, whom he considers responsible for the trend.

203 Chrysippos 28, fr. 2 von Arnim. The joke of Diogenes is based on a word play. Hippopornos meant "arch-whore", but in this case one should understand the two components separately: hippos = horse + pornos = whore, for a whore riding a horse.

204 Luc. *Tim.* 22.

205 See Davidson 1997: 167–182 and Winkler 1990: 45–54; see also Luc. *Rh.Pr.* 11, for a more detailed description of what an effeminate man would look like.

same conclusion, that it is unmanly to shave or pluck one's hair, as this kind of smoothness makes a man look like a woman, and is an activity suitable for prostitutes.[206] This stereotype generated a rhetorical exercise in Hermogenes, the subject of which was how to prosecute and defend a young man accused of prostitution because he used cosmetics.[207]

Time and place are certainly important factors in the entire debate. Cosmetics, personal toiletry, jewelry and fancy outfits for women and men were part of a comfortable, civilized living in the archaic and classical period, but most of the available evidence comes from later times because there was a gradual proliferation of such materials. As we move from the classical period towards the Hellenistic Kingdoms and the Roman empire, greater availability of exotic materials, increasing affluence, at least among ruling elites, and changed socio-political circumstances generated an ever-increasing demand for exotic perfumes, clothes, jewelry and beauty products, and made vanity an integral part of social status, more than ever before in the Graeco-Roman world.

From the early days of prostitution both men and women tried to enhance their natural looks with artificial means and respond to the desires of their customers, the fashion trends of the time, and the underlying cultural stereotypes which favored a certain look. As it often happens, exotic features were in high demand. Blond hair, a rarity among Mediterranean peoples, was considered to be a symbol of innocence and beauty, and hair-dyes, like saffron or combinations of henna with other plant-dyes, met this need. Grey hair, a sign of ageing, was coated either with dark or blond dyes to make a person look younger. A pale face, a sign of a leisurely lifestyle away from the strong sun in the fields or the market place, which only well-off women could afford, was generated by applying white lead. Rosy cheeks, a sign of good health and modesty, could be created with extracts from the madder plant, mulberry juice or orchil.[208] Eyeliners from substances like soot, which we now identify as carcinogens, were used to enhance the erotic gaze. Chewing mastich was the closest one could get to oral hygiene and a specific term was especially coined for male prostitutes who were chewing mastich to keep their breath fresh for intimate kisses (σχινότρωξ "mastich-chewer").[209] The neck was often covered with golden jewelry, pearls and precious

---

206 Pseudo-Lucian *Cynicus* 14.
207 Hermog. *Stat.* 1.36, 3.112 ff.
208 Alexis fr. 98.18; Duris *FGrH* 76 F 27, Diosc. *Mat.Med.* 3.17.1, Eup. 1.160.4; Alciphr. 4.6.4 al. A recent study of the chemical composition of Graeco-Roman blushing powder found that the principal compound was a product of the madder root, which contains substances like purpurine (Van Elslande- Guérineau 2008:1873–1879).
209 See e.g. Suetonius Περὶ Βλασφημιῶν 3. Luc. *Lex.* 12

stones, and so were the arms and the fingers. Tyrian purple, or cheaper substitutes such as orchil and plant extracts, were used to dye and decorate artfully woven linen. Silk made its appearance in the imperial era, only to be criticized as an indecent material which allowed too much of the outline of the body to be seen, but this did not stop the demand, and for the next two millennia the cultivation and trade of this precious commodity would proliferate to gigantic proportions throughout Europe and the Near East. Surely there has to be some irony in the story that the men whom Justinian sent to China to steal eggs of the silkworm and bring them back to Europe were monks. Sandals decorated with golden threads and precious stones, golden or silver chains for the neck, arms and feet, hairnets, elaborate pins and unusual hairstyles, removal of excess hair for both men and women, face and body creams and unguents, perfumes, and skin-softeners; the list is endless. Anything which remotely presented the possibility that it might enhance someone's appearance was put into good use. The consequences of ageing for a prostitute are outlined with some exaggeration in an epigram of Martial, where a Gallic woman begins by charging twenty thousand at her peak, and she cannot even take a lover for free only two years later.[210] Thus cosmetics were not only an issue of beauty or excess, but very much a matter of necessity, status, wealth, influence and success, and this is why not even the most vocal criticism of early Christian theologians ever succeeded in eliminating, or even substantially reducing, their use in the Christian era.

---

210 Martial 10.75.

3 The Prostitute and her Client

3.1 Prostitutes and Famous Men

An affair with a prostitute can end a political career and bring embarrassment and shame on any public figure in our times, but there was a time in history when any man of standing ought to be associated with some famous hetaira. Popular imagination generated elaborate stories linking the most prominent men of the ancient world to trophy women, who could be won over only by the rich and famous. Like the epic heroes of the past who won queens and princesses as spoils of war,[1] the prominent men of classical and Hellenistic Greece were matched with prize women. These relationships are almost invariably literary constructs and assume a deeper degree of compatibility, common interests and passions. Where decency required that high-born women and lawful wives remain shadowy figures away from the public eye, their role as consorts to prominent men was usurped by hetairai, who acted as companions, friends and partners, and shared public life, parties and social events with their lovers in ways that a lawful wife would never be permitted to do. In later antiquity history was revised and the past was rewritten in order to couple the famous men of the past with a trophy girlfriend, and where no historical evidence existed to suggest even remotely the presence of such an iconic figure in the life of a famous man, it could always be invented.

This reinvention of the past would extend as far back as the archaic period and beyond, into the sphere of myth.[2] The famous incident which in the minds of classical Athenians signaled the fall of the Peisistratids was rewritten in later antiquity to involve a hetaira. The noble tale of homosexual love and honor, as told by Thucydides, is refashioned into a story of endurance and self-sacrifice centered around the hetaira Leaina.[3] In this version of the story, which is told by Plutarch, Pausanias and Athenaios,[4] Leaina[5] was a mistress of Harmodios or

---

1 See e.g. Hom. *Il.* 1.110–188; E. *Hec.* 98–106; *Tro.* 28–44.
2 Mythological figures such as Circe and the Sirens were sometimes seen as metaphors for hetairai, as for example in Ar. *Plu.* 302–315.
3 Th. 6.54–60; Plin. *NH* 7.87; Plu. 505 E; Athen. 13.70; Clem. Al. *Str.* 4.19.120. Clement actually considers Leaina to be an example of pagan virtue for her courage to stand up to the tyrants, although she was tortured.
4 Plu. 505 D-E; Paus. 1.23.2; Athen.13.70.
5 Leaina literally means "lioness" and was also the name of several prominent hetairai in the classical period: see Appendix I s.v.

DOI 10.1515/9783110557954–003

Aristogeiton, and was tortured by Hippias for information, but she rather chose to bite her tongue, literally, than betray any information. Out of gratitude the Athenians dedicated a statue of a lioness standing at the gates of the Acropolis, which had no tongue. Pausanias confirms the existence of the statue, which stood next to a statue of Aphrodite. The whole story sounds like an aition, a legend invented in later centuries, after the tongue of the statue had been damaged, to explain its absence. Plutarch, however, was convinced that the statue was made from the beginning with this defect, because the artist was trying to convey a symbolism of silence and resilience, combined with the spirited and ferocious nature of the animal.

In the classical version of the story, as we read it in Thucydides, there is no hetaira involved, as Harmodios and Aristogeiton are lovers, and the one who is tortured to death and tricks Hippias to kill him before he is forced to divulge any information is Aristogeiton.[6] This version was unmistakably reflected in the famous pair of statues of the tyrannicides which stood in the Agora. In a Roman copy of the famous sculpture from the museum of Naples the face of Aristogeiton is bearded, while the face of Harmodios is beardless, in accordance with the ubiquitous artistic convention of the *erastes – eromenos* pair.[7] According to Victoria Wohl "Harmodios and Aristogeiton were lovers, as well as tyrant-slayers, and their love provided the model for a democratic eros that defined the Athenian citizen as socially autonomous and sexually dominant."[8] Wohl's thesis that the sexual relationship between the two men was an integral part of the legend is significant; with this part lost, the second sophistic version is downgraded to a simpler tale of courage and defiance. In this version the entire story has acquired a heterosexual spin, and a brave hetaira is invented to take the place of Aristogeiton in the torture chamber.[9] This story is a revision of the tradi-

---

6 Thuc. 6.56–59; Arist. *Ath. Pol.* 18; Rhodes 1981: 229–233. Charles Fornara (1968: 400–424) is skeptical about the traditional tale on the grounds that the love affair between Harmodios and Aristogeiton is not mentioned before Thucydides and later sources do not mention it. The argument is truly frail, because Thucydides is altogether our oldest source on this tale, while its omission in some of the later authors probably reflects their choices, not historical fact. See also Wohl 1999: 349–385; Meyer 2008: 13–34; Monoson 2000: 42–51.

7 For further information on the Tyrannicides sculpture see Shefton 1960: 173–179.

8 Wohl 1999: 351. Although part of Wohl's account rests upon the Dover-Foucault model of Athenian same-sex relations, a model which in my opinion is untenable in its broad strokes (see the discussion in Ch. 4.2), I very much agree with her main thesis that the discourse of politics and sexuality is central to the story, and that this important component disintegrates in the second sophistic version.

9 One wonders whether this version has in mind the tale of Tacitus (*Ann.* 15.51–57) about the courage of Epicharis before Nero during the Pisonian conspiracy.

tional tale in order to explain the bronze lioness with the missing tongue, and probably also to gloss over the uncomfortable feeling of later antiquity audiences over the homosexual relationship of those two most glorious heroes from the Athenian past.

The introduction of high class prostitution to Athens is attributed to Themistocles, the man who perhaps more than anyone else should be credited with the creation of the Athenian empire. Idomeneus tells a story where Themistocles led into the city a chariot with four hetairai through the middle of the Kerameikos, at a time when many people were present, and provides their names: Lamia, Skione, Satyra and Nannion.[10] Although the whole affair sounds completely fictional, the time-frame which it suggests for the introduction of high class prostitution into Athens is probably close to the historical facts: from the time of Themistocles Athens became rich and open enough to support a market for upper-end hetairai. Athenaios regrets the ambiguity in the language of Idomeneus, which does not allow him to decide whether Themistocles led the four women on a chariot or they were yoked to the chariot themselves.[11]

Amphicrates the sophist (1st c. BC) and Plutarch relate that Themistocles himself was the son of a Thracian hetaira named Habrotonon.[12] This sounds suspiciously similar to a story preserved by Athenaios about Timotheos, the well-known 4th century general and politician, who reportedly was the son of a

---

10 The name of Lamia is easily recognizable from the numerous tales about the affairs of king Demetrios I, Poliorketes (early 3rd c.). Skione was indeed a 5th century hetaira since she is mentioned in the speech of Lysias *To Lais* as someone who had given up prostitution some time ago, but most likely she flourished in the end and not the beginning of the 5th century. Satyra is an unknown figure, while there are several hetairai named Nannion. One of them, the mother of Korone, with a bit of a stretch could be placed in the late 5th century. Clearly the names on the list come from later times, the late 5th century at the very earliest, and as such they do not in any way enhance our understanding of this tale. For further details see Appendix I, under the relevant names.

11 Idomeneus *FGrH* 338 F 4. = Athen. 12.45 and 13.37.

12 Plu. 753 D and *Them.* 1; Amphikrates fr. 1, Müller. The work of Amphicrates *On Illustrious Men* (Περὶ ἀνδρῶν ἐνδόξων) was obviously written in verse, as the quote about the maternity of Themistocles is preserved by Athenaios in the form of an elegiac couplet, reading as following: Ἀβρότονον Θρήισσα γυνὴ γένος, ἀλλὰ τεκέσθαι / τὸν μέγαν Ἕλλησιν φασὶ Θεμιστοκλέα (13.37: Habrotonon a woman of Thracian blood, but they say that she bore / for the Greeks the great Themistocles). D.M. Lewis (1983: 245) has interpreted Plutarch (753 D) as a reference to the Thrasian origin of Habrotonon, and argues that the phrase ἐξ Ἀγορᾶς (a town in the Chersonese) was reinterpreted to mean "from the market-place", and thus disreputable. However, in the light of the discussion above, there are considerably older sources attesting this tradition that Habrotonon was a hetaira, which makes it unlikely that a misinterpretation of Plutarch's wording generated this tradition.

very modest Thracian hetaira.[13] Other sources also consider Themistocles illegitimate, but provide different details. His father Neokles remains a fixed point, but his mother's identity varies. Phanias of Eressos (4th c.) also believes that she was not Greek, but thinks that her name was Euterpe and that she was Carian; Neanthes (3rd c.), agrees with Phanias and adds that she was from Halikarnassos.[14] Neither Phanias nor Neanthes mention anything about her being a hetaira. Amphicrates and Plutarch are considerably later, and taking into account that, in addition to the similarities with the story about the mother of Timotheos (another suspect story), Habrotonon is a hetaira's name very familiar to us from the comic tradition,[15] it is very likely that this version of the story was fabricated using elements from familiar literary themes. The implications about the legitimacy of Themistocles which these sources introduce, and Plutarch augments in the opening chapter of his biography of Themistocles, have no historical value either, as they are based upon a concept of legitimacy which did not exist in the time of Themistocles. Many prominent Athenian citizens in his time were the sons of non-Athenian mothers, and it was not until after 451, when a law of Pericles demanded that a citizen needed to be born of two Athenian parents, that the offspring of mixed marriages were deemed illegitimate.[16]

---

13 Athen. 13.38. Even if his mother had been a foreign hetaira Timotheos would have been a citizen because at the time of his birth, during the Peloponnesian war, the Periclean citizenship law was not in effect. Both Timotheos and his father Konon were prominent figures in Athenian politics and there is plenty of contemporary evidence about both men. Timotheos features heavily in Xenophon *Hellenica* and Isocrates *On the Antidosis*, and he is the subject of intense polemic in the speech of Apollodoros *Against Timotheos* (D.49). Still, nowhere in these sources we find any reference to an alien hetaira or any hint about his alleged mixed origin. This is why the reliability of the information of Athenaios is suspect.

14 Phanias (or Phainias: both forms are attested), fr. 23 Wehrli;

15 E.g. a main character in Menander's *Epitrepontes*.

16 Arist. *Ath.* 26,4, *Pol.* 1275 b 31, 1278 a 34; Plu. *Per.* 37. The literature on the subject is vast and the debate on the actual causes and intent of the law remains open-ended. However, this is a subject beyond the purposes of this study. Broadly speaking, I subscribe to the traditional view, which accepts the testimony of the *Athenaion Politeia* that there were too many citizens to allow the smooth function of Athenian institutions designed with a smaller population in mind, and to this I have added that immigration anxieties, which often go hand in hand with imperial power, have dictated this law. However, I am prepared to accept that in its details the picture is more complex and perhaps there are aspects to it which we do not fully comprehend. In this instance, I am convinced that children of mixed unions (μητρόξενοι) were not instantly equated with illegitimate children (νόθοι) after the introduction the Periclean law; it took some time before these two groups came to be identified as one and the same. For further discussion on the Periclean law see Rhodes 1981: 331–5; Patterson 1981, passim; Walters 1983: 314–36;

Ancient historians and biographers of Pericles love to tell the story of how fate turned the tables against him and forced him to appear tearful before the assembly to beg for the legitimization of the younger Pericles, his son from his life-long companion, Aspasia of Miletos, whom he had excluded from citizenship with his own law. During the war Pericles lost his two legitimate sons from his first wife, Paralos and Xanthippos, and surely many other Athenian families had suffered similar losses. According to Daniel Ogden, the anecdote about his plea to the assembly may be a colorful reflection of the legislative steps taken to reverse his previous citizenship law in the light of the changed realities in Athenian life during the war, and to allow for illegitimately born children to be enfranchised and legitimized as heirs.[17] The relationship of Pericles and Aspasia has attracted much attention in ancient scholarship. Some saw Aspasia as a typical hetaira, seductive and destructive, a bad influence responsible for grave political mistakes, like the Samian war and the Megarian Decree. Others saw her as a wise woman, a positive influence and an intellectual equal with whom Pericles, Socrates and other prominent men of Golden Age Athens could have fruitful and stimulating conversations.[18] The various traditions sometimes emphasized and sometimes de-emphasized her sexual history, as it suited their purposes, and the same woman can be portrayed here as a shameless whore and a pimp and there as a very respectable figure - let's say, as one of the few women from the pagan past who were suitable role models for young Christian women.

Madeleine Henry, who has presented the relevant evidence and studied these contradictions in a thorough monograph, concludes that the ancient evidence is too confusing to reach firm conclusions about the historical Aspasia and whether she was at some point of her life a hetaira or not. Henry argues:

> To continue to construct Aspasia as a powerful prostitute, and to not read the ancient
> sources critically and historicize them as necessary, is to nativize two beliefs: first, that an
> intellectual woman's importance and influence are ultimately traceable to her manipula-

---

Raaflaub 2004: 15–6, 217; Morris 1996: 19–48; Ober 1989: 81; Ogden 1996: passim; Kapparis 2005: 72–6; Blok: 141–170.

17 Plu. *Per.* 37; Ogden 1996: 70–77; Blok: 141–170.

18 Among Aspasia's contemporaries the main sources are Cratin. fr. 259; Ar. *Ach.* 523–9; X. *Mem.* 2.6.36, *Oec.* 3.14; Pl. *Mx.* 235 e ff., and the fragments of Aeschines Socraticus. Among later sources the most significant are Plu. *Per.* passim; Luc. *Gall.* 19 ff., *Im.* 17–20; Athen. 5.61 ff. See also Appendix I s.v. A detailed presentation of this evidence is outside the purposes of this study; the interested reader should consult Henry's excellent monograph on the subject, and also Loraux 1993: 123–154; Trivigno 2009: 29–58; Heitsch 2009: 229–236; Reinsberg 1989: 80–85.

tion of her own sexuality, and second, that intellectual women do not act autonomously, but rather upon and through men."[19]

Both issues which Henry raises affect not only Aspasia, but all the women presented as companions of famous men in this chapter, and should be examined more closely. As far as Aspasia is concerned, one is bound to agree that the facts surrounding her life have been so deeply steeped in the various mythologies that it is not possible to determine with certainty whether her contemporary Aristophanes was making an obnoxious and offensive joke when he called her a whore and a pimp, or whether he expected a former hetaira to take it with good humor and laugh with him next time they met in some intellectual gathering.

It must be noted that the references to her past as a hetaira and a pimp are persistent, and consistent with both the fact that, unlike other respectable women of her time, Aspasia is openly mentioned in the sources by her first name (even in sources which speak of her with admiration and affection), and, second, that several of these sources are contemporary (e.g. Kratinos and Aristophanes), and as such not easy to dismiss, especially considering that personal slurs by name directed at women who had not been prostitutes are very rare in comedy. It truly seems to be the case that calling a respectable woman a "whore" was never considered to be funny, not even in the irreverent world of Old Comedy. On balance, it is possible that Aspasia was targeted simply because she chose to make herself a target by pushing the established standards of contemporary gender roles, but it is more likely that she had been at least for part of her life a sex-worker, before she became the concubine of the most powerful man in Athens. Charles H. Kahn sums up the case as following: "As Pericles' semi-legal wife, Aspasia was the most famous woman in Athens, and the butt of a thousand jokes, above all in comedy. Her image is, on the one hand, that of the hetaira, and on the other hand, that of the dominating female who has Pericles under her thumb."[20]

Aspasia's far-reaching impact as a feminine role model already in her own century is attested by an interesting episode about the mistress of Cyrus the Younger, second son of Darius II and contender for the throne of Persia. While Achaemenid princes customarily were not counted among the clientele of hetairai, as they had at their disposal entire harems of concubines, from time to time

---

19 Henry 1995: 74.
20 Kahn 1994: 95.

we do hear of a Persian nobleman seeking the company of a Greek hetaira.[21] This charismatic prince was unusual in so many ways, cosmopolitan and quite fond of the ways of the Hellenes, and capable of charming representatives from every corner of the Greek world and signing them up to serve his cause. Perhaps this is why we are not surprised to find this exceptional Persian being treated by the Greek historians like an honorary Greek. Inevitably a hetaira was attached to him, but beyond this point the two versions of the story diverge.

In the version preserved by Athenaios the woman whom the prince favored was Milto of Phocaea, a hetaira of stunning beauty and wisdom who followed him on the campaign to seize the Persian throne from his elder brother Arta-xerxes II. Cyrus renamed her Aspasia, but Athenaios does not say why; Plutarch does, when he presents his own side of the story. In this version Milto of Pho-caea, the daughter of Hermotimos, was not a hetaira but the favorite concubine of Cyrus whom he renamed Aspasia, after the renowned and wise Milesian woman, the concubine of Pericles. Plutarch goes on to say that after the death of Cyrus she was taken to the king, and eventually acquired great influence in the harem of Artaxerxes II. The two versions are not as incompatible as they may seem at first. A free-born Greek hetaira becoming a lover of the son of the Great King, and then joining his entourage as his favorite concubine sounds like a plausible scenario, and probably a good settlement for her declining years. This pattern of the hetaira-concubine attached to a powerful prince becomes increas-ingly common in the Hellenistic monarchies.[22]

Among the successors of Pericles, the most capable, and reportedly the most dissolute, was Alcibiades. [23] In the words of Victoria Wohl, "The beloved of Socrates, the lover of the demos, a man of almost irresistible charm, Alcibiades is one of the most explicitly sexualized figures in fifth-century politics."[24] This dark horse of 5th century Athenian politics was reputed to have had many en-counters with pricy hetairai. In an episode narrated in the speech *Against Alci-biades*, attributed to Andocides but probably composed at a much later date, Hipparete, the wife of Alcibiades and daughter of Hipponikos, the richest man

---

21 See for example the episode in Machon (17.333 ff. = Athen. 13.44) involving Gnathainion, the daughter of Gnathaina, and a 90–year-old satrap willing to pay 1000 drachmas for one night.

22 Plu. *Per.* 24; Athen. 13.37.

23 And. 4.14; about Alcibiades, his larger than life personality and his influence upon the politics and intellectual life of his time, there is a very substantial amount of studies. See for example, Rhodes 2011; Scott 2000; Pradeau - Marbœuf 1999; Forde 1989; Gribble 1999; Verde-gem 2010; Ellis 1989.

24 Wohl 1999: 352.

in Athens, took great offence as he kept bringing hetairai into the family home and went to the archon to register a divorce. Alcibiades dragged her back to the house through the market place, with complete disregard for her high birth and even the fact that she came with the largest dowry ever in the whole of the Greek world. The reliability of this source is suspect, but the author may be citing an incident which he read in a classical work now lost to us. Ultimately, this kind of behavior would not be at odds with what we hear about the unbridled sexuality of Alcibiades from other sources.[25] Considering the volume and content of these references it may seem astonishing at first that not a single hetaira attached to him is mentioned by name in any contemporary source from the 5th or even 4th century, but it is very telling of how the literature on hetairai evolved in later antiquity. While in the literature of the classical period the numerous women besieging Alcibiades, respectable and not so respectable, are nameless satellites spinning around the charismatic man, in later literature they acquire names, personalities and interact with him at a deeper level.

There may be one exception to this observation, if we trust Athenaios that his information on the affair of Alcibiades with the hetaira Medontis of Abydos actually comes from a lost speech of Lysias. Athenaios mentions this affair in two different places suggesting that it was an arrangement which lasted for many years.[26] In another place he quotes Antisthenes saying that Alcibiades was a very immoral man and slept with his mother, sister and daughter like the Persians do.[27] Antisthenes might be referring to the alleged relationship of Alcibiades and his male lover Axiochos with the hetaira Medontis, from which a daughter was born. When the daughter became of age both men had sex with the daughter too, Alcibiades claiming that she was the daugher of Axiochos, and Axiochos saying that she was the daughter of Alcibiades. However, unless

---

25 For example, Eupolis in the *Flatterers* (fr. 171) alludes to adultery with married women, while Pherecrates (fr. 164; see also González Almenara, 2005: 587–94) is moving in the same direction when he jokes "although Alcibiades is not a man, it seems, he is the man of all women right now". The Platonic Alcibiades, as portrayed primarily in the *Symposium*, *Protagoras* and the Pseudo-Platonic *Alcibiades I*, is a highly eroticized figure too, one who is desired by men and women alike, "a repository for democratic fantasies", and devotes much of his time and energies in the quest of eros at a physical and intellectual level (Wohl 1999: 373; see also Scott 2000: 25–37; Gordon 2003: 11–30 al.). Xenophon is even less coy: in the *Memorabilia* (1.2.12, 24) Alcibiades is referred to as "the most unrestrained and arrogant man ever" (πάντων ἀκρατέστατός τε καὶ ὑβριστικώτατος), and as someone "hunted by many respectable women for his good looks" (διὰ μὲν τὸ κάλλος ὑπὸ πολλῶν καὶ σεμνῶν γυναικῶν θηρώμενος).
26 Lys. fr. 8 Carey; Athen. 13.34; 12.48.
27 Athen. 5.63; Antisthenes *Decl.* fr. 29a.

one were to understand that the entire affair was conducted through short visits of the two men over many years, the timescale is impossible, because Alcibiades only spent the last few years of his life at the Hellespond. While the threesome of the two men with Medontis may contain an element of truth, an extended timescale which could accommodate the relations with the daughter too seems to be an invention intended to magnify the sordidness of this affair and the immorality of its main protagonist. M. Vickers has suggested that the inspiration for the incest story may ultimately be the play of Euripides' *Hippolytos*, where Phaedra is pursuing an affair with her stepson.[28]

Another threesome, this time involving Alcibiades and two women, Damasandra and Theodote, is attested by Athenaios.[29] The former supposedly was the mother of Lais the Younger and buried Alcibiades in Melissa, a town in Phrygia, after his assassination. Athenaios attests that he (or his unknown source) had seen the grave as restored by Hadrian, with a statue of Alcibiades added on top of it. Probably this Damasandra is the same woman as Timandra, whom at least one later tradition believed to be the mother of the famous Lais of Corinth, not Lais the Younger.[30] Among the fragments of Hypereides we find a few from a speech delivered in a trial involving Timandra. The prosecutor, like Apollodoros in the speech *Against Neaira*, considered it beneficial for his case to drag into the court-room her past life as a hetaira, making distasteful references to items which one would expect to find in a hetaira's house like dildos, mattresses and items for personal hygiene. Timandra, according to Plutarch, was accompanying Alcibiades in his final days and picked up his body for burial, and, in an act which seems apt for the pan-sexual womanizer, covered it with her own meretricious garments. Plutarch describes a dream which Alcibiades had shortly before his death: he saw that he was resting his head on Timandra's lap and she was applying make-up and eyeliner on his face. The scene has captured the imagination of later artists. In the painting of Michele de Napoli representing the death of Alcibiades, Timandra wearing a low cleavage dress is standing on his back stretching protectively her right hand over the shoulder of Alcibiades, and with her left hand is trying to stop the assassin.

We are told that Alcibiades had it all: fabulous looks, sexual magnetism, intuition, intellectual rigor that few of his contemporaries could match, wealth and fame, and a powerful sex-appeal which was often perceived as depravity. His magnetism has inspired many artists through time. From the Roman Alcibi-

---

28 Vickers 2000: 7–17.
29 Athen. 13.34.
30 Athen. 12.48; Sch. Ar. *Plu.* 179; See also Appendix I s.v.

ades of the Naples museum partying in the middle of a group of hetairai, to
Jean-Léon Gérome's painting of Socrates seeking Alcibiades in the brothel of
Aspasia, Jean-Baptiste Regnault's Socrates tearing Alcibiades away from Pleasure, or Félix Auvray's Alcibiades with a group of hetairai, the theme of Alcibiades surrounded by women just as beautiful and immodest as he was has been
pervasive. For all his considerable military and political accomplishments Alcibiades has been trapped into a stereotype, the Platonic image of the bad boy,
turning up drunk at the Symposium and ready for a party with intellectual conversation, more drink, pretty boys and loose women.

A junior contemporary of Alcibiades but almost his diametric opposite in
terms of reputation was Isocrates, a man considered by Athenaios to be very
respectable (αἰδημονέστατος), in the same breath where he mentions a long-
term affair with the hetaira Lagiska. His successful school of rhetoric brought
him substantial wealth,[31] which enabled him to woo the affections of the hetaira
Lagiska while still at her prime as his exclusive concubine. Strattis, a contemporary comedian makes an obscene joke about Lagiska and Isocrates in his play
Atalante, which provides important evidence for the historicity of the affair.[32] In
the middle of the 3rd c. Hermippos in his biography of Isocrates provides more
detail adding that the affair was a long-term relationship, and that Isocrates had
a daughter from Lagiska.[33] Plutarch attests that when this child died, Isocrates
married Plathane, the former wife of Hippias of Elis, and adopted her youngest
son Aphareus as his son. He does not tell us what happened to Lagiska and
many of the details in this part of Plutarch's narrative are difficult,[34] which may

---

31 Isocrates was born in a wealthy family, but it was his work as a teacher of rhetoric that
made him a very rich man. Pliny (*NH* 7.110), no doubt with much exaggeration, reports that he
sold a single speech for 20 talents. Even if this tale is not accurate, the spirit of it, suggesting
that Isocrates was a successful logographer, a good teacher and an excellent entrepreneur, is
not in dispute.

32 Strattis fr. 3: a discussion about the precise meaning of the fragment can be found in Miles
2009: 133–135. Miles cautiously suggests that the central term συκάζουσαν, which she translates as "fig-squeezing," is a reference to masturbation; however, this is far from certain, as the
primary meaning of the term is "fig-picking," and it could simply be a reference to food, or a
double entendre, the full the meaning of which is lost to us. The precise title of the play is also
in question, as three different forms Ἀταλάντη, Ἀταλάνται, and Ἀτάλαντος, appear in different
sources.

33 The significance of Hermippos as a biographical source is explored in detail by Bollansée
1999.

34 For example, marriage to an alien woman, and adoption of an alien boy were illegal in the
4th century. If Plathane had been married to Hippias of Elis, she could not have been Athenian
herself, and their children would definitely be alien.

suggest that his sources for the marriage of Isocrates to the wife of Hippias were of questionable authority.[35] More securely attested in the speech *Against Neaira* is an affair of Lysias with the hetaira Metaneira (D.59.21–3).

The other major figure among the Attic orators, whose name has been associated with the defense of the ideal of the city-state, was also reputed to be an eager lover of boys and women alike. Demosthenes, like Alcibiades, was rich, powerful, smart and, it seems, just as dissolute. Athenaios drawing from various sources provides this summary of the sexual escapades of the prominent statesman:

> It is said that Demosthenes the orator had children from a hetaira. During the speech *On the Gold* he brought the children to court,[36] to arouse pity, but without their mother, even though it was customary for defendants to bring their wives too. He did this because he was embarrassed and wanted to avoid criticism. The orator was dissolute with love affairs, as Idomeneus attests. When Demosthenes fell in love with Aristarchos,[37] a young man, the latter got drank and for his sake attacked Nikodemos and blinded him. It is said that he spent a lot on food, young men and women. This is why his secretary once said "What could anyone say about Demosthenes? Whatever he earned through the entire year, one woman in a single night could carry it all away." It is said that he took into his house a

---

35 See Strattis fr. 3 = Athen. 13.26; Hermippos fr. 65 Wehrli = Athen. 13.62; Plu. 839 B-C; Phot. *Bibl.* 260 488 a. A 4th c. inscription from Keos (*IG* xii 5.542 a 42) which preserves the name Ἀφαρεὺς Ἰσοκράτους is not an authoritative source as most of the name is a reconstruction.
36 D. fr. 4. Tur. This appears to be a reference to the Harpalos affair, when Demosthenes was accused of receiving bribes, and convicted to pay a very hefty fine. See Eder 2000: 201–215.
37 The mysterious affair with Aristarchos and the murder of Nikodemos are mentioned in several contemporary speeches by Demosthenes himself, Aeschines and Deinarchos, which probably were the sources of Idomeneus, as Graig Cooper has suggested (1995: 308). In fact, Cooper believed that Aeschines alone was the source of Idomeneus, but since the other speeches were equally well known in antiquity, it is possible that Idomeneus was aware of these too. The gruesome murder and mutilation of Nikodemos (his eyes were gouged out and his tongue was cut) must have caused sensation in Athens. Rumors were circulating that Demosthenes was behind it, because Nikodemos had accused him of desertion from the army in Euboia. However, Aristarchos was charged with the murder, and as he was obviously guilty, he chose to leave before the verdict of the court was pronounced and spend the rest of his life in exile. It really seems that he was a disturbed (ἡμιμανής: Aesch. 1.171) young man, who killed the person that threatened his lover. Aeschines speaks of him sympathetically, while he is bringing some serious allegations against Demosthenes. He sees Demosthenes as the architect of the murder, and argues that he preyed on the naïve youth and his mother because he was after the large inheritance of Aristarchos. He took Aristarchos as a pupil and a lover and, when the youth had to choose exile over a very probable "guilty" verdict for homicide, Demosthenes reportedly deprived him of three talents which were set aside for his maintenance in exile. The affair with Aristarchos may have had financial motives, as Aeschines suggests, but it was not a typical prostitutional setting.

teenage boy named Knosion, even though he had a wife, and she was so indignant that she ended up sharing a bed with the boy. [38]

The affair with Knosion is suspicious considering the boy's youth and the fact that he lived in the same house with Demosthenes, and, if some hostile sources are right, even had relations with the wife of Demosthenes. Aeschines and Idomeneus are adamant that Demosthenes was aware of the affair of the youth with his wife, and in fact that he allowed it.[39] Hypereides suggests a very close friendship between the young man and Demosthenes, one which someone might have with a long-term lover. No source explicitly states that Knosion was paid to be with the orator, and it is possible that the relationship was nothing more than a close friendship, or a real-life love triangle, without any exchange of money. However, the description of the affair is strange, and given the preference of the orator for attractive youths, and his financial capacity and spending habits, it is difficult to shake off suspicions of a relationship at least partially based on financial considerations.

A third boy named Aristion, son of Aristoboulos the pharmacist, of Plataia is associated with Demosthenes by contemporary hostile sources. Aeschines in the speech *Against Ktesiphon* alleges that the relationship of Demosthenes with the youth was very suspect and in all likelihood improper, as he lived in the house of the orator for a long time. Aeschines pretends not to know in what capacity but unambiguously implies that the youth was offering his exceptionally good looks for money. Then, Aeschines tells us, Demosthenes used the boy to get close to Alexander and plead for the king's forgiveness and reconciliation.[40] Alexander, while he typically considered male prostitutes beneath him and the royal dignity of his office,[41] in this case unaware of the youth's background received him with favor. Diyllos, seemingly drawing from the speech of Hypereides *Against Demosthenes*, suggests that the youth may have been Samian instead,[42] and says that the boy was sent to Hephaistion, and not directly to

---

38 Athen. 13.62–63; Idomeneus *FGrH* 338 F 12; cf. Aesch. 1.170–2, 2.148; D.21.104–122; Din. 1.30, 47; Fisher 2001: 315–18; MacDowell 1990: 328–30.

39 Aesch. 2. 149; Idomeneus *FGrH* 338 F 12.

40 Aesch. 3.162; Diyllos *FGrH* 73 F 2; Harp. s.v. Ἀριστίων.

41 See the discussion below.

42 Both the Plataians and the Samians received Athenian citizenship in the years of the Peloponnesian war, which makes the information relevant because in either case Aristion would be a citizen, and for a citizen boy to move into the house of a stranger for a long time, and without an apparent reason, would be a sure sign of an improper relationship based on financial benefits. See also the discussion on Lysias 3 where Theodotos, another Plataian boy, is the object of

Alexander. The details may be disputable, but it seems that both sources agree on the close relationship between the boy and Demosthenes, and its financial implications. Harpocration is less vocal about the prostitutional dimension, and uses wording which might be interpreted as an indication of a respectable, long-term love affair between the orator and the youth.

Finally, Demosthenes is associated in later literature with Lais, but the evidence comes from later sources and is highly suspect on several grounds.[43] The most significant difficulty with this association would be the chronology. Lais would have been in her sixties or seventies by the time Demosthenes was an adult, and the only way that we can overcome this difficulty would be to assume that these stories were referring to one of the younger copycats of the famous hetaira. It is much more likely, however, that these stories were generated by the homophobia of later antiquity. Scholars of the second sophistic, shocked by the unsavory love-affairs of the venerable orator with young boys, sought to sanctify his memory and rehabilitate him with acceptable heterosexual stereotypes by inventing an impossible courtship with the most famous hetaira of the ancient world.

The man whom Demosthenes was trying to defend from a seemingly unjust charge of prostitution, the prominent politician Timarchos, was himself associated with several female hetairai and male prostitutes. Like Alcibiades, Timarchos had fabulous looks, wealth, a good family background, education, intelligence and influence, and moreover, a very open-minded attitude to sexuality. Aeschines alleges that several of his associations with other men were in a context of prostitution, but this is probably untrue. He tries to suggest that a young Timarchos offered his body for money to the wealthy older gentleman Misgolas, a man well known in the city for his exclusively homosexual proclivities, but he is obviously misrepresenting this affair, as Timarchos was probably older than him (see the discussion in Ch. 4.2.). The short-lived affair between the two well-off young citizen men, if it ever existed, does not fit the profile of a relationship based on money. The relationship with Hegesandros is also misrepresented as a younger/older affair based on money, when in reality the two men were probably rowdy friends and political allies,[44] and both loved parties and the good

---

contention between the speaker and Simon that lands them before the Areopagos with battery charges.

43 Athen. 13.54; Aulus Gellius *Noctes Atticae* 1.8.5–6; Sch. Ar. Plu. 149 D.

44 Both men were at least in their thirties in 361 when they met, both were members of the socioeconomic elite, and both were involved in politics. Their relationship was never unequal in terms of age or financial ability, and this undermines the claim of Aeschines that the young and attractive Timarchos was the toy-boy of the dissolute, older Hegesandros.

lifestyle and spent generously on hetairai, dinners, gambling and symposia. One of these hetairai was Philoxene, and we are told that Timarchos in a short period of time spent the very substantial sum of 20 minae on her, which he had obtained from a bribe.[45] A modern reader trying to understand these relationships through compartmentalized concepts of human sexuality might be at a loss trying to classify the sexual orientation of men like Alcibiades or Timarchos. Suffice to say that their contemporaries found nothing unusual or strange in their whimsical affairs with boys, men and women, but had much to criticize in their lack of self-control, extravagance and haughtiness.

The third prominent member of the anti-Macedonian party, the wealthy and elegant orator and politician Hypereides, was reported to be the patron and lover of several famous hetairai, whom he set free and kept in his various houses around Attica.[46] In his primary house in Athens he kept the extravagant (πολυτελεστάτην) Myrrhine. It seems that his legitimate wife was already dead when this happened, but his adult son had strong objections. Hypereides cast him out of the house in order to take in Myrrhine. We are told that he kept Aristagora, another famous hetaira, in a house in Piraeus. If this is affair is historical,[47] then the relationship must have broken down at some point because among the fragments of Hypereides we have the scant remains of two speeches *Against Aristagora*. She was accused of failing to comply with immigration rules by not taking a citizen as her sponsor, as the law required of all aliens residing in Attica (ἀπροστασίου).[48] The themes of the speech traceable in the fragments are expectedly citizenship, immigration and prostitution.[49] The third woman in the list, Phila, who was established in his house in Eleusis and eventually, when sexual attraction had passed, became his housekeeper, is included in a list of women who belonged to the pimp Nikarete in the speech *Against Neaira*, only there she is a slave girl who was brought up in Corinth before being liberated.[50] Here she is a free-born woman from Thebes. There is a good possibility that Idomeneus was mistaken about her origin because he himself attests that Phila was a slave, whom Hypereides bought for a lot of money and set free. The most famous encounter of Hypereides with a hetaira is his affair with Phryne. He

---

45 Aesch. 1.42, 75, 115.

46 Athen. 13.58 = Idomeneus *FGrH* 338 F 14.

47 The relationship could conceivably be a literary fiction on the basis of the speeches *Against Aristagora*, but in this instance there are some faint indications that it could be historical. See the discussion in Ch. 4.4.

48 For the γραφὴ ἀπροστασίου as a legal procedure see Kapparis 2005: 106–110.

49 For a more detailed discussion of this case see the discussion in Ch. 4.4.

50 D. 59.18–20.

undertook her defense when she was prosecuted by Euthias for impiety, and secured her acquittal with a brilliant speech which was widely admired by ancient rhetoricians (see the discussion on the trial in Ch. 5.4.).

The end of the polis and the subsequent age of empires brought about a new type of leading man, one that was not bound by the constraints of democratic constitutions. In the Hellenistic monarchies the various potentates were often above the law, and in the position to satisfy their whims and desires without regard for the feelings of the common person. Several had a whole entourage of hetairai, upon whom they lavished gifts and favors while they were alive, and splendid monuments after their death, and, unlike the leading men of the classical period, they did not have to account for their extravagances. In the twilight of the classical world a series of scandals rocked the Greek political landscape centered around Harpalos, the treasurer of Alexander the Great, a man with grandiose ambitions and the vast resources of the Persian treasury to fund his plans. While Alexander was absent in the depths of Asia Harpalos was left behind in Ecbatana in charge of the treasury, as he was unfit for military duty because of a congenital disability. There Harpalos acted very much like an oriental despot living with extravagance, and he invited the hetaira Pythionike to join him from Athens. Plutarch attests that they had a daughter together, who was later brought to Athens by Harpalos, when he fled there, and she was looked after by Phocion and his family after the demise of her father. The information of Pausanias that Harpalos actually married Pythionike is probably inaccurate, as it is not confirmed by any contemporary source. Pythionike died prematurely and this led a grieving Harpalos to an extravagant display of mourning. He erected in honor of her memory two splendid monuments, one in Babylon and one in Athens, at a huge expense of more than 200 talents, if we believe Theompompos.[51] The ultimate excess was to build a temple of Aphrodide Pythionike, thus transgressing the boundary from showy extravagance to hybris.[52]

After the death of Pythionike Harpalos invited Glykera to join him in Tarsus, where he demanded from people to prostrate before her like a queen, ordered that if anyone wished to offer him a wreath, they should also offer one to Glykera, and with distinct lack of good judgment erected a bronze statue of Glykera next to one of himself and that of Alexander. The main source for these allegations is a suspect fragment of Theopompos in epistolary format addressed

---

51 Theopompos *FGrH* 115 f 253. See also Dikaiarchos fr. 29 Wehrli, Pausanias 1.37.5; Plu. *Phoc.* 21–22.

52 On the monuments of Harpalos in honor of his hetairai see the discussion in Ch. 6.1.

to Alexander, which concludes with the comment that the honors bestowed upon this whore (πόρνη) should have been reserved only for Alexander's mother and his queen (about the monuments see the discussion in Ch. 6.1.).[53]

Alexander himself has been associated with several hetairai, even though our sources show a degree of awareness concerning his diverse sexual preferences and his affairs with men and boys.[54] Athenaios in the midst of several tales over Alexander's drinking issues retells a story about his reluctance to have sex with women, and attributes it to his excessive consumption of alcohol.[55] In this story the exquisitely beautiful Thessalian hetaira Kallixeina was hired by Olympias, with the blessings of Philip, because, we are told, both were worried about their son's ability to perform with a woman.[56] Although Kallixeina reclined next to him very often, and his mother repeatedly encouraged him to have sex with the beauty, the young Alexander showed no interest in her. When Eustathios, bishop of Thessalonica (12th c.) retells the story, Alexander's possible homosexual tendencies were so inconceivable to him that he

---

53 Theopompos *FGrH* 115 f 254a-b; DS 17.108.6.

54 The sources are Hieronymos fr. 38 Wehrli; Athen. 10.45; Eust. *Com. Od.* 1.409. For an entertaining review of the available evidence see Davidson 2007: 462–4. Daniel Ogden (2007: 75–108 and 2011, especially chapters 6–9) is skeptical about the reliability of our sources, as well as modern concepts of sexuality being applied to Alexander's affairs, and would rather believe that Alexander's sexual relations conform with the pattern of other Macedonian kings. Ogden may be right to think that Alexander would not have perceived his own sexuality as different from that of his predecessors. He understood his duty to continue the dynasty, and used marriage as a means of establishing alliances, while his affairs with men were not unusual, stigmatized or perceived as a deviation from the norm in the ancient Greek world. However, at the same time it must be noted that the sexuality of no other Macedonian king was a subject for debate in the ancient world, and Alexander's affairs with men and boys have received an unparalleled level of attention in our sources. Ancient authors do not simply make passing references to the relationships of Alexander with Hephaistion, Bagoas and other men, as they might do with other historical personalities; they offer significant accounts which leave the reader with the impression that something was different in Alexander's case, and that his preference for men and boys was not casual. Beyond this point nothing can be conclusively proven and nothing needs to be proven, as the ancient world would not have perceived homosexual relations as qualitatively different from heterosexual relations, but rather as alternate and non-permanent variations within the continuum of human sexuality.

55 There is an apparent logical inconsistency which Athenaios seems to have missed: the story involving Kallixeina is placed at the time when Alexander was a healthy teenage boy, not in his latter years when habitual drunkenness and exhaustion might have influenced his sexual appetites.

56 Thessalian women had a reputation for libidinousness and dark skills, like magic (see Ch. 5.4.).

stretches the meaning of γύννις (womanish), the word employed by Athenaios whom he acknowledges as his source, to mean "impotent".[57] Without a doubt both Athenaios and Eustathios understood that Alexander could not get an erection with Kallixeina. It is remarkable that all these sources are trying to find alternative explanations to Alexander's reluctance to have sex with a woman, including far-fetched tales of impotence of a healthy teenage boy, but outright reject the obvious explanation and refuse to believe that it might have something to do with the possibility that he was not attracted to women.

A second hetaira in the entourage of Alexander, the Athenian Thais, was one of the women following the army to the heartland of Persia and, at least according to some of Alexander's historians, the person who first threw the torch to burn the palace of Xerxes in retribution for the burning of Athens in 480.[58] According to Plutarch, she was the companion of Ptolemy (later Ptolemy I Soter), while Athenaios (probably drawing from Ptolemy VIII) adds that Ptolemy I actually married her after the death of Alexander and had three children with her, two sons named Leontiskos and Lagos (after the father of Ptolemy), and a daughter called Eirene.[59]

Several attempts to bribe Alexander with prostitute boys seem to have failed, not least because they were conducted with astounding indiscretion, as James Davidson has rightly pointed out. In the middle of many stories about the famous restraint of Alexander (ἐγκράτεια) Plutarch mentions a couple of episodes which suggest that the preferences of the king for pretty boys were widely known. In the first of these, a pimp from southern Italy named Theodoros approached Philoxenos, one of the admirals of Alexander, with a business proposition. He owned two very beautiful boys and wanted to sell them to Alexander, so he was asking whether the king was interested. Philoxenos passed on the request to Alexander. The king was furious wondering how could Philoxenos disrespect him with such a vile request. In his response he first chastised the

---

57 Eust. *Com. Od.* 1.409. Eustathios is well aware of the full semantic field of the term and acknowledges that the primary meaning is λάγνος (generally "lecherous", but here a man who sleeps with men), while additional meanings can include someone nervous or "cowardly" with women, or someone with a flaccid penis (δι' ἀτονίαν), which he goes on to explain in no uncertain terms as the "inability to have an erection" (διὰ τὸ μὴ ἔχειν ἐντείνειν τὸν καυλόν).

58 For sources and more discussion of the practice see Ch. 3.4. While it is hard to reach definite conclusions regarding the events and motives behind the burning of the most splendid building of the Achaemenids, and the role of Thais and the other hetairai to it, one must confess that the story about the Athenian hetaira avenging the burning of Athens is too convenient, and thus too suspect, on many different levels.

59 Plu. *Alex.* 38.2; Athen. 13.37; Alciphr. 4.19.

admiral and then told him to send the pimp and his cargo to hell. He was equally curt with his extravagant courtier Hagnon, who proposed once to buy
Krobylos for him as a present, a boy from Corinth renowned for his beauty. The
boy without a doubt would be sufficiently costly to be deemed worthy of a king.
Alexander refused angrily.[60] Assuming that there is some truth in these stories,
the king conceivably was annoyed with his men because they considered the
bought love of male prostitutes worthy of him. This libidinous reputation might
befit some of the Diadochi, like Demetrios Poliorketes or Ptolemy II Philadelphos, but not Alexander, for he was as much a shrewd politician and capable
diplomat, ever aware of his public persona, as he was a brilliant strategist and
general. His famous ἐγκράτεια was no doubt a carefully cultivated image spin-
doctored to inspire loyalty and admiration, and he was not going to sacrifice
this for some sordid pleasure with a rent-boy.

An episode mentioned by Aeschines (and also by Hypereides according to
Diyllos and Harpocration) underlines the potential dangers of exploiting the
king's fondness of boys.[61] We are told that Demosthenes used a citizen youth
named Aristion, who seemingly had been one of his own prostitute-lovers, to
convey secret messages of reconciliation to Alexander. Aeschines considers this
very devious and inappropriate, especially since he is convinced that Alexander
was deceived into accepting the boy, while he was kept in the dark about the
colorful past of the youth. It is almost impossible to think that a man as disci-
plined and perceptive as Alexander would be unaware of the dangers of manipulation by dark interests and their agents, when he decisively refused the company and favors of youths willing to sell their good looks and charms to the
highest bidder.

One of Alexander's successors became famous in the literature of later antiquity
precisely for indulging in the sordid and abusive kind of behaviors which his

---

60 Plu. *Alex.* 22. Davidson refers to reports about Alexander's harem of handsome slaves. As
his predecessor, Darius III, possessed a harem of beautiful women sent to him as a gift from all
over the empire, Alexander was supposed to be surrounded by many beautiful boys (Plu. *Alex.*
22; Davidson 2007: 462–4). There is absolutely no evidence to support this, and a direct comparison of the harems of the Persians with Greek practices and customs would be dangerous. It
is one thing to have a well-known fondness for pretty boys, but it is a very different thing to
collect "harems" of beautiful boys, free and slaves. The former is something to which any
Greek man could freely admit without sacrificing any of his moral integrity, while the latter
would be a sign of oriental excess, which would appear very distasteful to Greek eyes, in the
manner that Alcibiades' circle of hetairai was heavily criticized in almost every single source
which mentions it.
61 For sources and further discussion see n. 54.

glorious predecessor carefully avoided. Demetrios I, Poliorketes acquired a reputation for dissolute morals and reckless disregard for social convention largely because of his excesses in his private life. He was associated with several prominent hetairai. The best attested of his love-affairs seems to be a long-term relationship with the capricious Lamia. Plutarch mentions that Demetrios first met her when she was captured with other hetairai on one of the ships of Ptolemy at the battle of Salamis (306 BC), during which he annihilated the naval power of Ptolemaic Egypt. It appears as if it was love at first sight despite the fact that Lamia was already past her prime. Machon preserves several of her witty comments and responses while Athenaios adds that she was very sharp, which might explain how she captivated Demetrios and held a privileged position among the many women of his household.[62]

Lamia had started her career as a flute-player, before she became a highly paid hetaira in her prime.[63] Even in the years when she was with Demetrios, she continued from time to time to entertain dinner guests playing the flute. Her banquets were legendary, and many a time directly supported through voluntary (or not so voluntary) contributions by rich people seeking favor with Demetrios (see also Appendix s.v.). Several anecdotes suggest that she dealt with his affairs with other women with biting humor and awareness of the limitations of her power over him (see also Appendix II for some of her witty remarks).[64] Polemon mentions a daughter of Lamia and Demetrios named Phila.[65] Unless Polemon has mixed up his information, to call a daughter from his favorite hetaira by the name of his lawful wife Phila[66] must have been insensitive even for Demetrios. He had reluctantly married Phila, even though they had a large age difference. He was still very young while she was considerably older, but this was a dynastic marriage in the classic sense, and Demetrios sought sexual and emotional fulfillment elsewhere by taking many more wives and a host of hetairai, and on top of that he had many affairs with respectable women. The irony of

---

62 See Plu. *Demetr.* 16: At that time she was past her prime, and Demetrios was much younger than she was when she took him as a lover. She captivated and kept him with her charm, so that he would be her lover alone (ἐραστήν), even though he might be lusting after other women (ἐρώμενον).

63 Plu. *Demetr.* 16: ὕστερον δὲ καὶ τοῖς ἐρωτικοῖς λαμπρὰ γενομένη.

64 E.g. Machon fr. 12 = Athen. 13.39.

65 Polemon fr. 14 = Athen. 13.39.

66 Plutarch (Plu. *Demetr.* 14) attests that Phila was the most senior among the wives of Demetrios, as she was the daughter of Antipater and former wife of Krateros; she was also the mother of his son and heir Antigonus II Gonatas.

his dissatisfaction with an older wife, while he was lavishing much affection and wealth upon an older mistress, was not missed by ancient commentators:

> It was astonishing that, while he was annoyed at first because his wife Phila was past her prime, he fell in love with Lamia and formed a long-term relationship with her even though she was already in her declining years. Then Demo, the so-called Mania, when Lamia was playing the flute at a dinner party and Demetrios asked Demo "how did you find Lamia?", she replied "old." Later on when the delicacies were served and he told her "You see how many treats Lamia has prepared for me?", she answered "my mother is going to get you even more, if you are willing to sleep with her." [67]

Even his father Antigonos once joked that his son was in love with Lamia (meaning the mythological monster used by parents to scare children into obedience), while Demochares of Soli called Demetrios "The Myth," because he had his own monster, his Lamia. Lara O' Sullivan has traced some of these jokes to the comic stage of Athens.[68] Some of the excesses of Demetrios and his mistress, such as taking residence on the Acropolis in the temple of the virgin goddess (which shocked even Clement of Alexandria), as well as the extravagant flattery from those who wanted to be in the good graces of Demetrios, scandalized and offended many people. [69] Lamia also built several public buildings of her own in Sikyon, no doubt under the auspices of Demetrios, and in order to secure personal notoriety and her own place in history.[70]

Demochares mentions one other hetaira of Demetrios who was honored with a sanctuary, his second favorite after Lamia, and it is this woman, Leaina, who earns the stern disapproval of St. Gregory Nazianzenos for having a temple dedicated to her.[71] Athenaios informs us that Leaina was Athenian, but Suda says that she was Corinthian.[72] The entry of Suda is unreliable, since it also considers as Corinthian Lais who was born in Hykkara, Sinope who was from the Black Sea, and even Rhodopis the Thracian (sic: Ῥοδῶπις Θρακική). The name

---

67 Plu. *Demetr.* 27.

68 Plu. *Demetr.* 19; see Appendix s.v. See also O' Sullivan 2009: 53–79, esp. 69.

69 For example, we are told that the Athenians (and possibly the Thebans) erected temples in honor of the favorite courtiers and hetairai of Demetrios, like sanctuaries of Lamia Aphrodite and Leaina Aphrodite. See the discussion in Ch. 6.1. Demochares, who is providing most of the information about these sanctuaries, comments that this disgraceful and lowly form of flattery actually annoyed and saddened Demetrios himself (Polemon fr. 15 = Athen. 6.62; Demochares *FGrH* 75 F. 1 = Athen. 6.62).

70 Polemon fr. 14–5 Müller = Athen. 6.62, 13.38. For Lamia's monuments see the discussion in Ch. 6.1.

71 Gregory Nazianzenos *Carmina Moralia* 743.3.

72 Athen. 13.38; Sud. ε 3266.

Leaina was linked to the mythology surrounding the tyrannicides, Harmodios and Aristogeiton by a later tradition, which may have had in mind this famous Leaina (see above pp. 101–4). In addition, a hetaira named Leaina appears as a fictional character in two later works. In Lucian's *Dialogues of the Hetairai* a rather naïve young girl named Leaina is drawn into an awkward sexual encounter with Megilla, a wealthy and rather butch woman from Lesbos, in one of the few scenes openly dramatizing lesbian sexuality in the surviving classical literature. In one of Alciphron's fictional letters a hetaira named Leaina features as a former lover with a biting tongue mocking her boyfriend Philodemos for the ugliness of his wife.[73] Several other hetairai of Demetrios are also mentioned by name in Plutarch, but attract less attention.[74]

Patrick Wheatley has argued that Lamia was a bad influence on Demetrios. He maintains that the excesses of the capricious hetaira fostered in the king behaviors which contributed to some of the bad publicity he has received.[75] However, blaming Lamia for the faults and ill-judged actions of Demetrios amounts to blaming the symptom for the disease. Lamia and the other hetairai, concubines, adulterous affairs and improper relationships of Demetrios were the satellites, and often victims, of a greedy and powerful man who knew no boundaries to his authority and no constraints to his public or private conduct. To say that an immoral older woman led him astray would absolve Demetrios from his own flaws in an inexcusably superficial manner. Demetrios chose to be surrounded by a harem of modest and immodest women not because Lamia made him, but because unlike any other Greek leader of the past, he simply could.

Most of our sources are later, and may well be drawing from a comic tradition. This is why it is rather difficult to ascertain whether these episodes are true, but ultimately the accuracy of the details is less important. The zest of it is more significant: Demetrios styled a new role for the Greek hetaira, one which resembled more the concubine in an oriental harem and less the free-spirited hetaira of the classical symposion. In the socioeconomic context of the classical polis no man was big enough, rich enough, or powerful enough to monopolize the affections of entire harems of hetairai/concubines. Lais might be offering herself to Diogenes for free, but no man was rich enough to possess her exclu-

---

73 Luc. *DMeretr*. 5; Alciphr. 4.12; Gilhuly 2006: 274–291.
74 Plu. *Demetr*. 24 and 27. Demo also appears in another place in a conversation with Demetrios, while Chrysis and Antikyra are only casually mentioned, although both are known from other sources (see Appendix s.v.).
75 Wheatley 2003: 30–36.

sively, and the same applies to Phryne or Sinope. At least the free-born among them had a degree of financial and social independence which no respectable woman could ever hope to achieve.[76] They possessed property, sometimes quite a lot of it, which they spent on ostentatious parties, clothes and jewelry, took or abandoned lovers on a whim, had the freedom to move around as they pleased, and had no constraints of modesty or purpose when it came to their own betterment through a good education, but could take it or leave it. At least a few chose a path of enlightenment through study with prominent philosophers, poets and intellectuals.[77] As a result, the term "concubine" rarely overlaps with the term "hetaira" in the classical period, and in fact most of the time they were mutually exclusive. A hetaira was by definition available, a concubine was not. While, for example, Neaira was still a practicing hetaira she had a string of affairs with different men, but belonged to no one. When she meets Stephanos, who promises to protect and look after her, and becomes his concubine, she gives up prostitution. The boundaries are not air-tight but this distinction is broadly observed in the classical period.

Demetrios is an early example of a trend which eventually was going to eradicate the hetaira as a socially relevant model under the Diadochi. In many ways Demetrios does not resemble Alcibiades in his dissolute lifestyle, but rather the womanizing Xerxes in the Herodotean tales of seduction inside and outside the harem.[78] He is surrounded by women whom he feels the need to seduce with gifts and favors, while at the same time his hetairai, at least the main ones, are exclusive concubines available to no other man. It seems that from this point on a promising career path for a hetaira opened in the Hellenistic courts. For those few who had the looks and charisma, the highest prize would be to become the exclusive concubine of a rich and powerful prince, or at least an influential courtier. To do that the Hellenistic hetaira would have to sacrifice some of the freedom which had made the classical hetaira such an icon. To a large extent, this is the reason why the hetaira fades away in later antiquity, as the boundaries with the concubine become fainter, and the hetaira is degraded from an independent iconic figure to one rich and powerful man's inferior paramour.[79]

The leader whom Demetrios Poliorketes displaced in Athens (307 BC) was Demetrios Phalereus, a man reportedly as dissolute and extravagant as his name-

---

76 See also Sullivan 2009: 53–79; Henry 1995, especially chapter 4; McClure 2003.
77 See Ch. 2.1., and Ch. 3.3–4.
78 E.g. Hdt. 9.109–112;
79 The main study of the Hellenistic hetaira/concubine is Ogden 1999.

sake. Demetrios Phalereus, as a protégé of Cassander, became the strong man after the death of Phocion in 317 and remained the effective leader of an oligarchic regime in the city for a decade. During that time he acquired much wealth and power, and became famous for his excesses.[80] A detectable tendency towards transvestism is attested by Duris and Diyllos. We are told that Demetrios wanted to be called Lambito, after the Samian hetaira who was his lover at the time, and sometimes he was called Charitoblepharos (literally: "Charming eyes").[81] Another Demetrios, member of the same family and descendant of Demetrios Phalereus, impressed Antigonos with his plain-talk defense before the Areopagos Council, after charges of a dissolute lifestyle, unsuitable for a member of this ancient body:

> Demetrios, the descendant of Demetrios Phalereus reached such levels of profligacy that, according to Hegesandros, he was keeping Aristagora, the Corinthian hetaira, as his lover, and was living luxuriously. When the members of the Areopagos called on him and asked him to live a more appropriate lifestyle he responded. "But I am living appropriately right

---

[80] Karystios fr. 358 Müller = Athen. 12.60. Karystios of Pergamon reports that Demetrios Phalereus started as a poor man, but when he came to power he hired Moschion, the best cook in town, and that man was able to buy three apartment blocks in two years only by selling the left-overs from the table of Demetrios. Karystios also mentions that it was so important and so difficult to be near Demetrios that all pretty boys in town frequented the place where he took his walks hoping to catch his eye. Duris confirms and augments this very un-Athenian image of excess and debauchery:

> And Demetrius Phalereus, as Duris says in the sixteenth volume of his *Histories*, being possessed of a revenue of twelve hundred talents a year, and spending a small portion of it on his soldiers, and on the necessary expenses of the state, squandered all the rest of it on gratifying his innate love of debauchery, having splendid banquets every day, and a great number of guests to feast with him. And in the prodigality of his expense in his entertainment, he outdid even the Macedonians, and, at the same time, in elegance, he surpassed the Cyprians and Phoenicians. And perfumes were sprinkled over the ground, and many of the floors in the men's apartments were inlaid with flowers, and were exquisitely wrought in other ways by the artists. There were also secret meetings with women, and other scenes more shameful still. And Demetrius, who gave laws to others, and who regulated the lives of others, exhibited in his own life an utter contempt of all law. He also paid great attention to his personal appearance, and dyed the hair of his head with a yellow color, and anointed his face with rouge, and smeared himself over with other unguents also; for he was anxious to appear agreeable and beautiful in the eyes of all whom he met. (Duris *FGrH* 76 F 10 = Athen. 12.60. Translation by C.D. Yonge (1854).

[81] Diyllos *FGrH* 73 F 4 = Athen. 13.65; DL 7.76.6 (acknowledging the *Symposiaka* of Didymos as his source), Sud. δ 429. χαριτοβλέφαρος is a feminine attribute.

now. I have the most beautiful hetaira, and I do no harm to anyone, I drink wine from Chios, and I have everything else in sufficient quantities, spending my own income for it. Unlike some of you, I do not accept bribes nor do I live in adultery," and he mentioned by name some members doing such things. When Antigonos the king heard this he made him a thesmothetes. During the Panathenaia, when he was a cavalry commander, he set up a scaffold for Aristagora next to the pillars of Hermes, only taller than them. In Eleusis during the mysteries he set up a throne for her next to the Anaktoron, saying that if anyone tried to stop him they would regret it.[82]

Like his predecessor and Demetrios Poliorketes, the younger Demetrios shows the kind of disrespect for traditional religious institutions that would have landed him into enormous trouble during the classical period; people had been executed for a lot less in Athens. It was a sign of the times that not only Hellenistic royalty but also men who had their backing could show off by committing hybris against ancient religious rituals and sanctuaries with impunity. Affording one's hetairai such dubious honors was as much a sign of power and prestige for the woman herself as it was for her man. This is why for the authors of later antiquity to attach a famous hetaira to a powerful man of the past, and relate tales of debauchery, insolence and public misconduct, signified that the man was powerful enough to step outside the boundaries of the ordinary. What made men like the three Demetrioi desirable and "sexy" was their power to trample upon convention, popular morality, the law, or traditional institutions, just because they could, and to do so merely for the sake of a whore enhanced and accentuated that power-profile. The paradox which Duris points out in the leadership of Demetrios Phalereus accurately describes this changed political landscape: the man who set the laws was the one that transgressed them, and the man who regulated the lives of others lived a life completely unregulated (n. 80). In this political landscape the whims of the capricious mistress were the law, and divine honors afforded to her hardly raised an eyebrow.

Not all tales involving hetairai and famous men are sordid accounts of debauchery and power games. Some are noble tales of fidelity and devotion, like the incident narrated by Appian where Antiochos Eusebes (the Pious) was saved by a hetaira who loved him.[83] Another oriental royal, Philetairos of Pergamon,

---

82 Hegesandros fr. 8 Müller = Athen. 4.64.

83 Appian *Syr.* 366. Appian offers three versions of the reason why he was nick-named 'The Pious". The first, probably the official one, was that he was thus called because when his nephew Seleukos tried to have him killed he was spared because of his piety. The second version is that a hetaira who had fallen in love with him saved his life. The third version, which Appian approves, is that the Syrians started calling him "the Pious" just for laughs when he married Selene (the moon), like his father had done before him. What Appian does not say but

the founder of the Attalid dynasty, was the son Attalos and his lover (ἐρωμένη), the Paphlagonian flute player Boa.

While such tales in the Greek tradition are rather a rare exception, by contrast, Roman strong men are almost always paired with a "good", submissive hetaira, a χρηστή ἑταίρα in Greek sources. This may have to do first with a difference in the general perception of the past between the two civilizations. While the Greeks liked their heroes imperfect, flawed, dominated by their whims and passions, and still somehow rising above their shortcomings to accomplish great feats, the Romans preferred theirs more pure, single-minded, august, and devoted to duty. Sometimes the relationship between the meretrix and the strong man is not even sexual, as in the case of Acca Larentia, who according to one tradition was a former hetaira and brought up Romulus and Remus. We first encounter this version in Dionysius Halicarnasseus, who reinterprets the traditional Roman myth of the She-Wolf, on the basis of the double meaning of the word *lupa*, which apart from the animal also indicated a low class prostitute.[84] This meaning is well attested in Roman authors over a long span of time.[85] Dionysios suggests that Larentia, who was living with the shepherd Faustulus, was entrusted with the upbringing of Romulus and Remus, but because she had been a prostitute, she was called "lupa." That was confused in later centuries with the literal meaning of the word, and the myth of the She-Wolf was invented to explain this confusion. The anecdote of Dionysius is repeated by Plutarch and several later authors.[86] Servius in his commentaries on the Aeneid believes that the myth had been deliberately misinterpreted to hide the fact that Romulus and Remus were brought up by a prostitute:

> The story that they were brought up by a she-wolf (*lupa*) is a fictional tale intended to hide the shame of the founders of the Roman nation. And it is nicely done too, because we also call the hetairai "wolves" (*lupas*), hence the term *lupanaria* for brothels, and moreover because it is well known that this animal is under the protection of Mars.[87]

---

may be inferred is that someone who relied upon a hetaira lover to be saved could not be much of a man nor pious in the traditional sense of the word, and this is why the term could only be applied ironically in this case.

84 As T. McGinn (2004: 8) states: "Such terminology emphasizes the rapacious, predatory, and greedy nature of the prostitute as a type, and, at the same time, denies her humanity."

85 Plaut. *Epid.* 403; Cat. 99.10; Cic. *Mil.* 55; Mart. 1.34.8; Aug. *Civ. Dei* 18.21; Adams 1983: 333–335

86 D.H. 1.84.4; Plu. *Rom.* 4.4; Zonaras *Epit.Hist.* 2.88; Eust. *Com. Od.* 2.275. 323.

87 Servius *Com. Verg. Aen.* 1.273

The relationship of Sulla with the hetaira Nikopolis fits into this pattern of the Roman statesman and the *chreste hetaira*. Plutarch, in a rather unsympathetic note, remarks that Sulla set out to seduce her using his youthful looks and charm, while in reality he was after her inheritance. Indeed when she died, she left him her substantial property, which combined with the inheritance of Sulla from his stepmother was sufficient to fund his political ambitions at the start of his career. Plutarch in his study *On the Fortune of the Romans* comments that good fortune elevated Sulla from the embraces of Nikopolis to heights above the triumphs of Marius, to multiple consulships and ultimately to the dictatorship.[88] This pattern of a love-affair, where the hetaira appears to be the victim of a young, handsome seducer going after her money, is rather unusual in Greek sources,[89] and yet, it is consistently the dominant pattern in the portrayal of pre-imperial Roman statesmen and their hetairai. None of the men are said to be seduced or defeated by the women; they benefit from the relationship in concrete ways, the women are presented as "good" or at least co-operative, and the relationship is presented as virtually asexual. There is an underlying misogyny in these tales, with the submissive mistress existing only to serve the needs of her masculine lover, who is never swayed by passion and always retains rational control over her and the entire relationship.

The relationship of Pompey with the fabulously attractive Flora of Osci fits perfectly within this pattern. The great statesman is presented by Plutarch as a magnet for women, and Flora among others is invoked as a witness to his appeal. An epigram of her contemporary Philodemos is speaking about her beauty, while Plutarch tells us that in her peak she was so famous and exquisite that Cecilius Metellus placed her painting in the temple of the Dioscuri, when he was decorating it with statues and frescoes. Her affair with Pompey seems to have lasted a while; Plutarch lets us understand that for that time she was his exclusive concubine. One might guess that she was hoping to remain with him once she was past her prime. Instead Pompey passed her on to one of his trusted men. The way Plutarch tells the story is that Geminius was very infatuated with her, but she refused his advances. Geminius secured Pompey's permission to sleep with her, but after that Pompey never touched Flora again. Rather unexpectedly for a hetaira, Flora was heart-broken, fell ill and many years later as an old woman she was still reminiscing about her time with Pompey.[90] The cynical

---

88 Plu. *Sul.* 2; *De fortuna Romanorum* 318 c.
89 Unusual as it may be, this pattern is not unheard of: see e.g. Ar. *Plu.* 959–1096; Lys. fr.1 Carey.
90 *AG* 5.132; Plu. *Pomp.* 2 and 53.

reader might think that Pompey approved his friend's request because he was tired of her and wanted to pass her on to someone else, and along with that the responsibility of having to support her, since she would no longer be his concubine. Far from a historic love affair, this seems to have been a cruel reality tale, with the ageing hetaira being left out in the cold by a tired lover. Pompey, like other Roman males, is presented as a strong man completely in control of his passions, and capable of cutting off the seductive hetaira at a time of his choosing. In this narrative Flora assumes the role of the *chreste hetaira*, faithful and devoted to her lover, like a jilted wife, heartbroken and crushed. No doubt the masculine image of Pompey was meant to be the primary beneficiary from this sad tale.

Aside from cultural differences between Greeks and Romans, the fact that Roman statesmen are portrayed as immune to the charms of seductive hetairai, whom they use and discard when they are done, may have something to do with the fact that most of the texts pairing hetairai with famous men were composed in the Roman period, and perhaps have been colored by contemporary cultural norms. The dissolute Greeks incapable of resisting beauty and dominated by their desires, as opposed to the august Romans in complete control of their emotions and never yielding to loose women, are cultural stereotypes of the imperial era, from where most of the collections preserving tales of hetairai with the statesmen of the past have originated, such as the works of Athenaios, Plutarch and Quintus Curtius. Not surprisingly they rewrite the past under the influence of Roman rather than classical or Hellenistic Greek perceptions of the hetaira and her lovers.

3.2 The Hetaira, the Philosopher and the Hetaira-Philosopher

Greek philosophers dominated the intellectual landscape of the ancient world, perhaps even more than dramatists or historians, with an astounding diversity of ideas, beliefs, philosophical quests, methods, but also lifestyles, morals and social norms, which they advocated and according to which they aspired to live. The earlier philosophers, whom we call pre-Socratics, were for the most part concerned with issues of cosmic significance. They tried to understand the universe, its rules, origins and purpose, the nature of the divine and the fundamental principles of all things. Their interest in the more mundane, the everyday life of the average human, and the fears, hopes, expectations, morals and belief systems of ordinary people was minimal at best and almost invariably indirect. Perhaps this is why those lofty figures from the remote past, like Thales, Anaximander, Heraclitus or Anaximenes, were left undisturbed in the literature of later antiquity. However, from the moment when philosophy acquired an interest in human affairs, and sought to explore and regulate morals, lifestyles, laws and political systems, the hetaira entered the picture as the companion, lover, admirer, student, or sometimes antagonist and enemy of the philosopher.

Arguably the first among the Greek philosophers to explore the application of philosophical theory and principle to morality and human lifestyles was Pythagoras.[91] His followers were not just interested in mathematics or philosophical principles but also in the prospect that the harmony and perfection of mathematical models can be applied to human societies through rigid sets of rules and stringent moral standards. Not surprisingly perhaps, later authors in a scoptic mood had a lot to tell about hetairai and the Pythagoreans. In the hilarious saga of Lucian *The Rooster* the cockerel of Mikyllos turns out to be the latest reincarnation of Pythagoras. The rooster-philosopher (ἀλεκτρυών φιλόσοφος) confesses that in one of his previous reincarnations he was Aspasia, the hetaira, mistress of Pericles. Mikyllos teases him about the various womanly tasks which he/she had to perform, but the rooster-philosopher refuses to answer the question whether he preferred to be a man or to be penetrated by Pericles.

The Pythagoreans seemingly took an interest in the morals of prostitution, sometimes light-heartedly as in the saying that only time can judge the favor of fortune, like that of a hetaira. On other occasions, however, we are told that the Pythagoreans were intolerant of prostitutes, as in the story found in Iamblichos that Pythagoras ordered only hetairai to wear gold, because he wanted to revile the value of the precious metal and suggest that it is unsuitable for respectable women. In the Pythagorean saying "a hetaira should not imitate a wife, and friendship should not imitate flattery," the side of prostitution criticized is the superficial nature of the relationship between lover and hetaira, while the wife in this model represents stability and emotional depth.[92] In the saying "it is

91 For the Pythagoreans and the teachings of a Pythagorean lifestyle see Riedweg 2005; Kahn 2001; Von Albrecht, et al. 2002; García González 2009: 115–134; Lambropoulou 1995: 122–134; Nails 1989: 291–297.
92 The theme is fully developed along the same lines in Terence *Heauton Timorumenos* 381 ff. in the dialogue between the wife Antiphila and the hetaira Bacchis. This model departs from the typically classical view of the wife as the burden, the detractor of a man's enjoyment in life and a necessary evil (whereas the prostitute brings joy and relief from the vicissitudes of life). This model matches more closely the paradigm which evolved in the imperial era, and was inherited by early Christianity, where the wife represents continuity, propriety and safety, while the prostitute represents immorality, deceit and ultimately sin before God. See also the discussion in Ch. 4.1.12. This is one of many indications that the texts attributed to Pythagorean women cannot possibly be dated to the archaic, or early classical period, before the hetaira had

shameful to prefer a hetaira to one's mother, and pleasure to virtue" the wife represents virtue while the fleeting pleasure of the hetaira is viewed as a vice, which should bring shame. On the other hand, the sagacious phrase "looking down on someone brings wealth to hetairai and poverty to politicians" is not concerned with morals; it is simply an observation about social interactions.[93]

This array of themes is explored in greater detail in several works, mostly in epistolary form, attributed to Pythagorean women like Theano, Periktyone, Phintys, Aisara and Myia. Letters, fragments of essays and even larger compositions have survived under the name of these women, but beyond reasonable doubt they are forgeries from later antiquity as the language and dialectic form cannot be from the sixth or fifth century southern Italy, where the Pythagorean school was centered.[94] These works on the "ethics of the household", in the words of Debra Nails,[95] are suspiciously male-oriented with advice for women to be obedient wives, win over the husband through their virtue and good character, refrain from arguments as they are a losing battle, avoid antagonizing their husband's mistresses for they are shameless and have no virtue to lose, and forgive his indiscretions with prostitutes on the grounds that his infatuation with these immoral women will soon be over and he will eagerly return to his wife in the end. We will not find in these artless forgeries the woman's perspective that we were looking for. Far from being rare and precious documents of the feminine voice from that period, they are dry and graceless academic creations from the Hellenistic era full of moralistic banalities. Although there is no compelling reason to doubt the historicity of those pioneering women and their contribution to Pythagorean philosophy, sadly none of the works which have come to us under their name can be authentic.[96]

Plato is probably incorrectly paired with the hetaira Archeanassa of Colophon in a late tradition found in Athenaios and Diogenes Laertios, which seems

---

even taken her place as an iconic figure in Greek letters, and in all probability come from a much later time, possibly as late as the second sophistic.

93 *Sententiae Pythagoricae* 4, 57, 161, 178.

94 Some of the writings, like those attributed to Theano, are in the Hellenistic Koine, others like those of Phintys or Myia are in a Pseudo-Doric form, which unsuccessfully tries to mask its true Koine features. Even more challenging, and certainly beyond the purposes of this study, would be an attempt to reconcile these documents with the primary tenets of Pythagorean philosophy and the socio-cultural context of Magna Graecia in late archaic period.

95 Nails 1989: 291–297.

96 For an anthology of texts in English translation, basic bibliography and brief discussions of the authors and their works see Plant 2004: 68–86. See also García González 2009: 115–134 on Theano; Huizenga 2010; Lambropoulou 1995: 122–134; Nails 1989: 291–297.

to be stemming from an epigram of Asklepiades of Samos praising the beauty of Archeanassa. However, its connection with Plato eludes us.[97] On the other hand, the association of Aristotle with the hetaira Herpyllis is much better attested and certainly historical. Hermippos mentions that Aristotle made provisions for the care of Herpyllis in his will, and this is confirmed in an actual text of the will of Aristotle as transmitted by Diogenes Laertios.[98] Aristotle had a legitimate daughter named Pythias, after her mother, the lawful wife of the philosopher and adoptive daughter of Aristotle's friend Hermeias Aterneus. After the death of his wife he took Herpyllis as his concubine and she bore him a son, whom he named Nikomachos after his father (consonant with the time-old Greek tradition of naming children after their grandparents). In the absence of a natural legitimate son he adopted the son of his older sister Arimneste and left him in charge in his will. Nicanor was to marry Pythias, take control of the considerable estate of Aristotle, and look after Herpyllis and Nikomachos. In the words of A. Lesky, Aristotle took care of his family and also other members of his household "with parental kindness." Lefkowitz and Fant along the same lines say "the provisions for his substantial estate reflect Aristotle's notions of women's limitations, but at the same time show his affection for them and concern for their welfare."[99] The provisions pertinent to Herpyllis read as following:

> The guardians and Nicanor, with consideration of me and Herpyllis, who has been good to me, should also take care of the other matters, and if she wishes to marry, they should give her to someone worthy of me. In addition to the other gifts, which she has received previously, they should give her a talent of silver from the estate, and three female slaves, if she wishes, and the female slave that she has at present, and the slave Pyrrhaeus. (14) And if she wishes to live in Chalcis, she is to have the guest-cottage by the garden. If she wishes to live at Stageira, she is to have my father's house. Whichever of the two she chooses, the executors are to equip it with furniture, which seems to them appropriate and meets the approval of Herpyllis.[100]

In a society where it was the responsibility of the *kyrios* to look after the women of his household, it was not unusual for a dying man to make arrangements for the future of his wife or other women under his care, sometimes by arranging

---

97 Athen. 13.56; DL 3.31; Asklepiades *AG* 7.217. Despite the assertion of both sources that the epigram refers to Plato and was even composed by him, his name is not mentioned in it, and there is nothing to connect Plato to Archeanassa. The entire affair may be based on a mistaken assumption.
98 Hermippos fr. 46 Wehrli = Athen. 13.56.
99 Lesky 1966: 552; Lefkowitz-Fant 2005: 59–60.
100 DL 5.13–14; The text of the will is preserved in its entirety in DL 5.11–16.

another marriage and offering a dowry.[101] Aristotle's dowry to Herpyllis, in the event she decided to get married in future, was as high as that of a citizen woman from a very affluent household, and undoubtedly reflected his desire for Herpyllis to be well looked after and financially secure after his death. It is noteworthy that Herpyllis did not receive lesser treatment than a lawful wife; in fact many would have been envious of the dowry and material comfort bestowed upon the former hetaira. Moreover, it is remarkable that the philosopher's affection for his concubine did not compete with his affection for Pythias, his dead wife, whose remains he wanted moved so that they would be buried together with his and stay physically united for eternity.

A contemporary and student of Plato, the philosopher Xenokrates earned a lot of praise but also took a lot of flak in the literature of later antiquity for his austerity and stern morals. While Diogenes Laertios speaks of his dull and serious nature he narrates a story about an alleged seduction attempt by a famous hetaira. Phryne wanted to prove that Xenokrates would not be able to resist her. So, one day she ran into his house pretending that she was chased by someone. He offered her shelter, and even shared his only bed with her, but refrained from sexual relations. She commented that she did not sleep with a man (ἄνδρα) but with a statue (ἀνδριάντα). Without a doubt the story is a fabrication.[102] In fact, Diogenes Laertios himself expresses doubt and wonders whether an alternative story, where the pupils of Xenokrates placed Lais in his bed in order to test him, is the true one. No doubt this is a fabrication too. More alarming is the comment of Diogenes Laertios that Xenokrates had such restraint (ἐγκρατής) that he often inflicted burns and cuts upon his genitalia, supposedly in order to restrain his sexual urges. Paradoxically though, with such masochistic tenden-

---

101 For example, two very well known cases from classical Athens are the arrangements of Demosthenes the elder for his wife Kleoboule and his two children, Demothenes the orator and his sister (D. 27.4–7), and the will of Diodotos in Lysias *Against Diogeiton* (32.4–7). Kleoboule, the mother of Demosthenes was endowed with 80 minae by her husband, when she had brought in 50. This difference of 30 minae is the equivalent of an average dowry in 4th century Athens. What Demosthenes the elder did was to offer his wife the dowry she brought in plus one more dowry on top of that. This very large dowry should make her a very desirable bride, except that Kleoboule was not interested in taking another husband and preferred widowhood. Likewise Diodotos offered his wife a huge dowry of 1 talent plus the furnishings of the house (which, considering the affluence of the family would probably be quite valuable themselves), if he happened to die in the campaign.

102 This tale is reminiscent of another story told by Diogenes (4.10) to describe the kind and humane nature of Xenokrates: a bird chased by a hawk had run into his lap; he hid the bird and when the danger had passed he set it free. The bird was sheltered by the virtuous philosopher in the same way that the hetaira was.

cies thinly disguised as virtue, Xenokrates came to represent not what is sexually unbridled and experimental, but its mirror opposite, namely the restrained
and respectable.[103] So much so, that another story was generated, told by Plutarch and repeated by the scholiast of Hesiod, according to which a hetaira
refused to perform indecorous acts (δρᾶσαι τι ἄσχημον) with her lover under the
image of Xenokrates, deterred by his modesty.[104]

The affair of Lais with Aristippos of Cyrene, another contemporary of Plato,
student of Socrates and founder of the Cyrenaic School, is well attested in a
number of sources. Hermesianax is the oldest witness to the affair, but the text
as quoted in Athenaios is corrupted and difficult to understand.[105] Pleasure was
the central tenet of Cyrenaic philosophy, and its attainment on a daily basis the
one and only goal in life. The Cyrenaics argued that past pleasure was gone and
future pleasure is uncertain, so all that matters is the present moment and living
it in the most enjoyable way.[106] Xenophon in the *Symposion* engages Aristippos
in a conversation with Socrates on pleasure and restraint, which Kristian Urstad
sees as a pivotal debate about reason, emotion and freedom.[107] It is not difficult
to believe our sources when they repeatedly emphasize the hedonistic and dissolute lifestyle of Aristippos, even if we do not agree with their interpretation of
his tenets.[108] The affair with Lais seems to have been a long-term arrangement
on a recurring basis. According to Athenaios, every year Aristippos hired Lais
for two months during the festival of Poseidonia in Aegina for a very substantial
fee.[109] Noel Robertson understands that by the time of Athenaios the festival had
been extended from its traditional 16 day period to two months, but this need
not be the case.[110] The time that Aristippos spent with Lais did not have to coin-
cide with the exact dates of the festival but could spread around it. Some

103 DL 4.7; cf. Val. Max. 3.15–19.

104 Plu. fr. 85 Sandbach; Sch. Hes. Op. 706.

105 Hermesianax 7.95–98 = Athen. 13.71.95–8. Especially the nonsensical ουδαμενον makes
the last line impossible to understand; the previous lines seem to suggest that Aristippos fell in
love with Lais, and forsook all other women.

106 For the Cyrenaic school and their beliefs on pleasure see: Onfray 2002; Johnson 2009:
204–222; Warren 2009: 249–281; Hourcade 2008: 215–233; Lampe 2007; O'Keefe 2002: 395–416;
Zilioli 2012; Sedley 2002: 159–174.

107 X. *Mem.* 2.1 ff.; Urstad 2008: 41–55 and 2009: 1–22; Mann 1996: 97–119.

108 E.g. DL 2.65–104.

109 Athen. 13.55

110 Robertson 1984: 11–13; for the festival of Poseidonia and its appeal among hetairai and
people looking for a party see also Plu. 301 E-F.

sources attest the affair without reference to time or place, while Diogenes Laertios mentions two dialogues attributed to Aristippos and addressed to Lais.

According to several anecdotes in circulation Aristippos was teased about this affair because he spent so much money on Lais when Diogenes the Cynic enjoyed her favors for free. On a rare occasion in our sources where Diogenes is totally outmaneuvered and lost for words, Aristippos is having a conversation with him. Diogenes is teasing him that he should either become a Cynic like himself and have Lais for free, or quit her. Aristippos then asks him whether he would stay in a house where others had lived or sail in a boat that others had used, and when Diogenes replies that he would Aristippos says that it is equally reasonable to have sex with a woman whom many others had used. In another anecdote one of his servants was chastising him that he was spending too much money on Lais when Diogenes slept with her for free; he replied that he was paying Lais in order to enjoy her, not to stop others from having fun with her. Another saying of his reported in several sources was "I possess Lais; I am not possessed by her". [111] While the historical accuracy of these anecdotes and sayings is questionable, the affair itself is well attested and probably true. It is even harder to verify the historical accuracy of other anecdotes, like the one where Aristippos took some of his students to a brothel. When one of his younger students blushed with embarrassment as they were entering, Aristippos told him that it is not hard to get in but to come out.[112] As it is the case with many such anecdotes related to the famous men and women of the Greco-Roman world, we have to resign to uncertainty and skepticism.

The philosopher whose name came to be identified with *hedone* even more so than Aristippos was Epicurus. The precise definition of this concept as well as its relation to the works of the Epicureans are matters of scholarly debate beyond the purposes of this study.[113] However, regardless of philosophical definitions, other Greek authors often understood the Epicurean ἡδονή in the traditional sense as physical pleasure and no doubt this semantic openness gave rise

---

111 ἔχω καὶ οὐκ ἔχομαι, Athen. 12.63, 13.54–55; Plu. 750 D-E; Clem. Al. *Str.* 20.118.2; DL 2.84–85; Cic. *Fam.* 9.26.2. The famous saying is echoed by Horace (*Epist.* 1.1.18–9): nunc in Aristippi furtim praecepta relabor / et mihi res, non me rebus subiungere conor. "Now I secretly return to the advice of Aristippos, and I try to keep things under my control, not to be controlled by them". See also Guzzo 1957: 31–38.

112 DL 2.69.

113 The literature is vast; see Gordon 2012; Mitsis 1988; Glidden 1981: 177–197; Porter 2003: 205–227; Nikolsky 2001: 440–465; Annas 2003: 75–90; Depew 1981; Warren 2001:135–179, and 2011: 278–293; Nussbaum 1991: 677–687; O'Connor 1989: 165–186; Shaw 2007; Arenson 2009; Long 1985: 283–324.

to several tales about Epicurus and his lifestyle of depravity. Pamela Gordon in a significant study of Epicureanism concludes that the association of women with the Garden comes from a hostile tradition, and recommends skepticism.[114] We should not be quick to believe stories of debauchery like the one told by Athenaios that the hetaira Leontion was having sex with everyone on the grounds of the school of Epicurus, and with Epicurus himself even in public, nor should we readily accept as fact the image of an obese Epicurus surrounded by hetairai and living a lifestyle of extreme depravity, like a Greek Sardanapal-los.[115] On the other hand, we should not try to whitewash the lifestyle of the Epicureans, so as to make it more palatable to modern sensibilities. Although many of the details of the bond between Epicurus and Leontion may be fabri-cated in anti-Epicurean sources, their personal and professional relationship is well attested. It appears that the famous hetaira gave up prostitution, joined the school and became the disciple and concubine of Epicurus. The order in which these events happened is difficult to determine. We do not know whether the relationship started as a love affair or a professional encounter, but most ac-counts agree that Leontion was both the disciple and the lover of Epicurus, recipient of several letters and often mentioned in the works of the philoso-pher.[116]

In some accounts Leontion is only one of the hetairai who were part of the lifestyle of pleasure in the Gardens and were shared among the men of the school, along with Hedeia, Mammarion, Erotion and Nikidion, Philainis and Boidion.[117] Hermarchos, the successor of Epicurus with inside knowledge of the affairs of the school confirms that Leontion had sex with all the men in the Gar-dens of Epicurus, and his testimony is not easy to dismiss.[118] Elsewhere, Her-marchos offers a more refined account of the love-affairs inside the Gardens. Demetria was his own lover, Nikidion was the lover of Idomeneus, Mammarion was the lover of Leonteus (a married man, simultaneously husband of the Epi-curean Themista of Lampsakos), while Polyainos was the lover of Pythokles,

---

114 Gordon 2012;

115 Athen. 7.11, 13.53; D.L. 10.7; Posidon. fr. 290a.495–506 Theiler.

116 Hermarchos fr. 41; Theon *Progymn.* 112.1 ff. Spengel; Athen. 13.53, 64, Alciphr. 4.17; D.L. 10.23

117 Poseidonios fr. 290a.495–506; Plu. 1089 C, 1097 D; DL 10.7.

118 Hermarchos fr. 41; Poseidonios fr. 290a.495–506; Plu. 1089 C, 1097 D; Athen. 13.53. The "Gardens", a privately owned villa with large, secluded gardens, located outside the walls to the northwest of the city, provided the physical location of the Epicurean school, and became synonymous with it the way the Academy became synonymous with Platonism.

whom Epicurus himself desired because of his exquisite looks.[119] Diogenes explicitly says that Leontion was the concubine of Epicurus (παλλακή), although in that unusual circle this assertion should not be taken as evidence that she was expected to be faithful to Epicurus or that she was out of the reach of his pupils and companions.[120] Moreover, Diogenes himself alludes to a ménage a trois involving Leontion, Epicurus and his pupil and life-long friend Metrodoros.[121] It is difficult to decide what to believe and what not to believe, and probably ancient authors too could not tell the difference between rumors and what actually was going on in this exclusive circle. The famous affair inspired their contemporary Aristeides of Thebes; his painting of Leontion is mentioned by Pliny, and became part of a popular mythology which has left its mark in our sources.[122]

In the light of this evidence, the fictional letter of Alciphron where a young Leontion is supposedly writing to Lamia, the mistress of Demetrios Poliorketes, is rather surprising. Leontion is in love with the man who took her virginity, and has been pursuing her since then, a handsome youth called Timarchos, while the 80–year-old Epicurus is jealous and keeping a vigilant eye on her, suspecting that she is planning to run away to her young lover. It seems as if all these tales about the unusual morals of the Garden, where men shared women without apparent jealousy and women held their own as students and willing participants rather than reluctant sex objects, motivated Alciphron to go in the opposite direction and compose a letter more consonant with the comic tradition, where the ridiculous figure of the 80–year-old jealous lover is cuckolded by the young couple.[123]

As a scholar Leontion is often mentioned in Epicurean scripts and at least one substantial study of hers is attested by two Roman authors. She composed a response to Theophrastos which ignited the indignation of Cicero:

> Even an insignificant hetaira (meretricula), dared to compose a response to Theophrastos, it must be said with some elegance in the Attic idiom, but such was the license (licentiae) in the gardens of Epicurus![124]

---

119 Hermarchos fr. 3; DL 10.5.
120 DL. 10.23
121 DL 10.6
122 Pliny *NH* 35.99.
123 Alciphr. 4.17.
124 Cic. *N.D.* 1.93. Cicero held Theophrastos in the highest esteem and considered him the most pleasing (dulcis) of all Greek orators (see e.g. *Brutus* 37).

Pliny is equally amazed by the effrontery of a woman to write against such an eloquent man as Theophrastos.[125] She was not the only woman student of Epicurus, as chances are that some of the other hetairai who frequented the gardens were also interested in the teachings of the Epicureans. However, it is not safe to assume that all women who studied philosophy with Epicurus were hetairai. For example, Diogenes Laertios mentions a married woman, Themista the wife of Leonteus of Lampsakos, who named their son Epicurus, after the philosopher.[126] Cicero makes a caustic remark about the attention Themista had received in the works of Epicurus:

> I have never heard Lycurgus, Solon, Miltiades, Themistokles or Epameinondas being mentioned in the school of Epicurus... Did he have nothing better to do than talk about Themista in so many volumes? But this is the way of the Greeks; although we have philosophy and all higher disciplines from them, there are some things which we do not find palatable, but they do.[127]

The Epicurean was not the only school which welcomed women in its ranks. The Megarian school founded by the gracious and urbane Stilpon, a contemporary of Epicurus and teacher of Zenon the founder of Stoicism, was also a place of higher learning for women including several hetairai.[128] According to Diogenes Laertios, Stilpon was married and had a daughter, and at the same time he had a long-term relationship with a student of his, the hetaira Nikarete. Athenaios praises the learning of Nikarete and adds that she was a Megarian herself from a good family, while her contemporary Asclepiades extols her beauty in one of his epigrams.[129] There is no good reason to doubt the historicity of this affair, but we should be much more skeptical about a supposedly adversarial exchange between Stilpon and Glykera at a dinner party, as it has all the signs of a fabricated witticism. According to the biographer Satyros, an author prone

---

125 Pliny *NH*, Praefatio 29

126 D.L. 10.5 and 25–6. The expression of Diogenes "he was writing to many other hetairai too" (καὶ ἄλλαις δὲ πολλαῖς ἑταίραις γράφειν), may imply that Themista had been a hetaira before her marriage to Leonteus, but aside from this vague hint there is no other evidence of such activity. If Diogenes indeed had in mind that Themista had been hetaira, he might think so because she was a woman of letters, as others had thought that Sappho too was a hetaira for the same reason (see Ch. 1.1.).

127 Cic. *Fin.* 2.67–8.

128 How well-defined the Megarian school was, as a separate entity with clear philosophical tenets, is a complex question beyond our purposes; see Cambiano 1977: 25–53, and also Fine 2011: 993–1034; Kyrkos 1980: 346–362; Wheeler 1983: 287–295.

129 DL. 2.114; Athen. 13.70; *AG* 5.153.

to sensationalism, Stilpon was chastising the hetaira Glykera that she is corrupting the young. She replied that he also corrupted everyone he encountered by teaching them useless arguments, and in this respect the victims of a philosopher and those of a hetaira suffer the same fate.[130]

Greek imagination in later centuries created an unlikely pair: the most costly hetaira of the classical world locked in a passionate love affair with the most penniless man in history. Lais, who commanded massive salaries from her clients and even gets a personal mention in the *Wealth* of Aristophanes for her greed, supposedly had a long-term affair with Diogenes of Sinope, "the Dog" (κύων), one of the most prominent names of Cynic philosophy, and famous for his complete renunciation of material possessions.[131] The affair is not mentioned in any classical source; in fact it is not mentioned anywhere before the Christian era, when we first encounter in the pseudo-Clementine *Homiliae* an elusive reference to public sex between Diogenes and Lais (since Diogenes reportedly lived in a large burial urn in the marketplace of Corinth). Centuries later Theodoretos takes for granted that Diogenes was having sex with hetairai (without mentioning Lais) in public view.[132]

The narrative of the love-affair between Diogenes and Lais must have been fully developed by the time of Lucian, who takes it one step further in the fantasy land of the Elysian Field: there in a happy afterlife Diogenes finally has done the right thing and married her, loosened up his rigid morals and taken on some bad habits, of which he was so critical while he was alive, like heavy drinking and rowdy behavior.[133] Athenaios mentions the affair a couple of times. In the lengthiest of these references he contrasts Aristippos, who spent a fortune on Lais, with Diogenes who had sex with her for free. In this spirit the Scholiast of Aristophanes, commenting on the joke about the greed of Lais, reaches the conclusion that Lais was truly in love with Diogenes, since she offered herself to him for free, while she pretended to love rich men, like the ugly and morose Philonides of Melite in Aristophanes *Wealth*. A different conclusion is reached by Theophylaktos: there it is Diogenes who is in love with Lais, and even the tenacious and incorruptible philosopher has finally become the slave of a woman.[134] Pausanias in his description of Corinth mentions the grave of Diogenes

---

130 Satyros fr.19 Müller = Athen. 13.46; Tronson 1984: 117–118 (with previous bibliography regarding the controversy on the date and works of Satyros).
131 About the Cynics and their philosophy see Kalouche 2003:181–194; Krueger 1996: 222–239.
132 Clem.Rom *Homiliae* 5.18.3; Theodoretos *Graecarum affectionum curatio* 12.48.
133 Luc. *VH* 2.18
134 Theophylaktos *Epist.* 60.

right before he mentions the burial monument of Lais, alluding to an eternal union that transcends death. The rhetorical construction of this affair in the sources, as well as their nature and timescale, should leave us little doubt that the entire relationship was an invention of later antiquity with no historical foundation.[135]

The literature of later antiquity created an antithetical relationship between the prostitute and the philosopher which is entirely absent in the literature of the classical period. While Socrates debates with Theodote in Xenophon's *Memorabilia*, advises her and appears curious and inquisitive rather than critical of the hetaira,[136] in later literature the hetaira and the philosopher appear as polar opposites, with the one cancelling out the work and influence of the other. Despite the fact that several schools included hetairai in their inner circle as scholars and students of their teachings, the only school which considered prostitution to be an acceptable way of life and openly declared that it is not shameful either to be in the company of a hetaira or to earn a living from prostitution were the Stoics.[137] The Epicureans and the Cyrenaics, as far as we know, did not theorize on the positives and negatives of prostitution, yet they receive fierce criticism for including prostitutes in their inner circle and for openly having relations with them.[138] Pythagorean criticisms of prostitution, as these can be read in the correspondence attributed to some of the Pythagorean women, most prominently Theano, cannot be trusted as the nature of these sources is highly suspect.

In Lucian's parody of Pythagorianism *The Rooster*, Mikyllos is amazed to find out that his rooster is a re-incarnation of Pythagoras first, and of Aspasia after that. Mikyllos exclaims with astonishment: "What a transformation, from a philosopher to a hetaira." The contrast could not be sharper, if we can judge from numerous references in other sources. In the *Dialogues of Hetairai*, Drosis is complaining that she lost one of her lovers, a young man, when his father decided to entrust his education to the care of a stern philosopher.[139] In the dialogue the hetaira and the philosopher are in competition over the young man's mind and future. The philosopher represents virtue (ἀρετή), while the hetaira represents pleasure (ἡδονή), and the young man must choose between the two,

---

135 See Ar. *Plu.* 179; Luc. *VH* 2.18; Paus. 2.2.4–5; Athen. 13.54–55; Sch. Ar. *Plu.* 179; Theophylaktos *Epist.* 60.

136 X. *Mem.* 3.11 (see also Ch. 5.5.).

137 Sextus Empiricus *Pyrrhoniae hypotyposes* 3.201.

138 E.g. Posidonius fr. 290a Theiler; Plu. 750 D-E, 1089 C, 1097 D; Athen. 12.63, 13.54–55; Clem. Al. *Str.* 20.118.2; DL 2.84–85, 10.7.

139 Luc. *Gall.* 20, *DMeretr.* 10.3.

as Herakles was expected to do in the myth of Prodikos narrated in Xenophon's *Memorabilia*.[140] While the contrast between the hard life of virtue and the easy life of pleasure is a traditional theme, in later antiquity it acquires a new twist with the philosopher representing virtue, the hetaira representing pleasure, and philosophy providing a cure for the ills which hetairai and the lifestyle of ill pleasure bring into the world.

Diodoros of Sicily presents an unflattering portrait of the young Scipio: he was dull and not a worthy heir and protector of his family's heritage, until his father hired Polybios of Megalopolis, the historian, to teach him philosophy. Such was the change that philosophy brought upon the young Scipio that he declared war on all passions and pleasures and within five years he made discipline and modesty universally respected again. In the same spirit Plutarch suggests that philosophy is a cure for social ills such as spending large sums of money to haughty hetairai, excessive eating, gambling, drunkenness, carousing and adultery. Dio Chrysostom takes a slightly different approach when he considers prostitutes and flute players to be a distraction from virtue (but he does not say that they are positively harmful), while philosophy is conducive because its followers will not be willing to engage into harmful behaviors such as sloth, drunkenness or overeating. Likewise, Poseidonios in his scathing attack on Epicurus demands that, like a new Sardanapallos, Epicurus should go away with his hetairai and leave philosophy to manlier men, for it is a discipline befitting men like Heracles, not effeminate ones (κιναίδους) and their pleasures. Galen enlists male and female prostitution among professions which are the opposite of noble professions like philosophy, geometry, arithmetic, medicine or philology. Origen thought that the entire Jewish nation must be a nation of philosophers (φιλοσοφοῦν), because no whores or rent-boys (θηλυδρίαι) were tolerated to be seen anywhere.[141]

However, the contrast between the hetaira and the philosopher is not always as clear-cut. Dio Chrysostom admits that some philosophers are not much different from prostitutes in their love of money or personal aggrandizement. In the aforementioned passage of Satyros, which contains a fictional dialogue between Stilpon and Glykera, the damage which the philosopher causes is the same as the damage which the hetaira inflicts. This point of view supposedly

---

140 X. *Mem.* 2.1.21–34. In this myth Virtue is contrasted to a woman dressed like a hetaira, and representing the lifestyle of pleasure and comfort; her name is Bliss (εὐδαιμονία) or, as her enemies call her, Vice (κακία).
141 DS 31.26–27; Plu. 5 B-C; D. Chr. 70.9–10; Posidon. 290 a 495–506 Theiler (= Cleom. 166–168); Gal. 4.10–5.8 Kühn; Origenes *Cels.* 4.31.

represents the hetaira's response to the philosopher's accusations that she is corrupting the young. Likewise seen from the hetaira's point of view in Lucian's *Dialogues of Hetairai* the teachings of the philosopher Aristainetos are quite useless and have ulterior motives: Drosis is convinced that Aristainetos only pretends to teach the young Kleinias philosophy, while in reality he is looking for an opportunity to seduce the handsome youth. This is why the plan which Drosis concocts, with the help of her friend Chelidonion, is to expose the philosopher/seducer by inscribing anonymously on the wall in Kerameikos "Aristainetos is corrupting Kleinias." [142] In Athenaios we find a warning against philosophers who are worshipers of an "unnatural Aphrodite", followed by a comment of the hetaira Glykera (as reported by Klearchos of Soli), that boys only look desirable for as long as they look like women. The purpose of this rather odd and uninvited comment appears to be to explain the meaning of the "unnatural Aphrodite" mentioned above.

Sometimes crossing over the boundaries between the hetaira and the philosopher can be a sign of exceptional virtue, as in the case of the Epicurean Leontion who, according to the rhetorician Theon, overcame the misfortune of prostitution (ἀτύχημα) by taking up philosophy.[143] For the moralists of later antiquity moving away from prostitution towards philosophy and the life of virtue which it promised was a move in the right direction. This polarization between the hetaira and the philosopher becomes more emphatic as intensely negative attitudes towards prostitution crystallize in the Roman period, and the prostitute is no longer seen merely as a bad influence, a money-trap, or a rival to the virtuous wife, but also as a social evil and a danger to society which needs to be purged through philosophy.

3.3 The Prostitute and the Poet

The early days of prostitution have left traces in Greek lyric poetry, from which scholars have tried to reconstruct the culture of the archaic symposion and the role of the prostitute in that space. Considering the cultural importance of the symposion in archaic literature, and how much this literature was loved, sung and quoted in later centuries, it is not surprising to find several of those favorite poets paired with hetairai in later times, and the most famous woman poet,

---

142 D.Chr. 32.20; Luc. *DMeretr.* 10.4.
143 Theon *Progymnasmata* 112.

Sappho, actually turned into a hetaira.[144] Since several centuries had passed from the peak of Greek Lyric it is unlikely that later authors had reliable biographical sources from which to draw elements for such stories. Instead, they used references in the works of earlier poets to make up love-affairs and it did not matter how preposterously unrealistic some of these were, so long as they made good reading. Athenaios is well aware of the fictional nature of such affairs, as for example the one between Sappho and Anacreon, but he nevertheless quotes extensively his main source for these, the *Leontion* of Hermesianax, a work written in the late 4th century. Hermesianax of Colophon wrote a long elegiac poem in 3 books, which he dedicated to the hetaira Leontion, and in it he has included many, mostly fictional love connections between famous poets and real or mythological figures. Athenaios adds a commentary reflecting skepticism over the veracity of the tales mentioned in it.[145] The second major source of Athenaios, at least regarding the earlier poets, is the *Erotica* of Klearchos of Soli, a rich collection of themes related to love.

Hermesianax borrows from the Hesiodean Eoiae and other such catalogues of famous mythological women, but subverts these references by placing them in a meretricious context and turning some of those real or imaginary women of the past into hetairai and lovers of the poets who mention them in their works.[146] He thus makes Homer a lover of Penelope and Hesiod a lover of Eoia. In this context the story that Mimnermos was in love with the flute-player Nanno, and dedicated to her a collection of poems, is suspect. An epigram of Poseidippos speaking about the love of Mimnermos and Nanno is obviously based on Hermesianax.[147] Strabon and subsequently Athenaios and Stobaios mention a collection of poems by Mimnermos entitled Nanno and actually quote from it, but considering the nature of this evidence it is unlikely that this was the original

---

144 See Ch. 1.1.

145 Athen. 13.71.

146 The first catalogue of famous mythological women appears in the *nekyia* of the Odyssey (11.225–330), followed by Hesiodean Eoiae, a catalogue of worthy women of the past almost certainly augmented by later additions. The collection took its title from the formula which always introduces a new person ἢ οἵη ("or such as." E.g fr. 58, 59, 181 Merkelbach, al.). An example of this formula can be found in the opening lines of Hesiod's *Shield of Herakles*. Hermesianax is probably joking when he turns a title based on a formulaic phrase into a person, a woman from Ascra and lover of Hesiod. The difficult questions of transmission and interpretation which the fragments of Hermesianax raise, as well as their place in the broader context of late classical and Hellenistic poetry are matters which cannot be discussed here. See Asquith 2005: 266–286; Bing 1993: 619–631; Caspers 2006: 21–42; Gärtner 2012: 77–103.

147 *AG* 12.168.

title of the collection, and it is difficult to believe that Mimnermos had a flute-player lover named Nanno.[148] Several hetairai are known in the classical period under the name of Nanno (or affectionately Nannion or Nannarion; see Appendix I s.v.), and one of the four fictional hetairai whom Themistokles supposedly yoked to a chariot when he introduced prostitution to Athens was also named Nannion (see Ch. 3.1.). Against this background even a casual reference to a woman named Nanno somewhere in the collection of Mimnermos could have been enough to generate this entire affair and the story about the dedication and title of the collection.[149]

Antimachos of Kolophon, the next poet mentioned by Hermesianax, allegedly had a love affair with a woman called Lyde, and when she died he filled an entire book with sad verses. Plutarch, however, says that the poem was written for the unnamed dead wife of Antimachos, not a mistress, and contained stories of unhappy love from myths. The elegiac poem of Antimachos entitled *Lyde* was well known throughout antiquity, several fragments of it have survived and Photios was aware of an epitome by Agatharchides.[150] It seems likely that Hermesianax is making up the love affair of Antimachos with a hetaira Lyde on the basis of this poem, and that the title of the poem is unrelated to some Lydian hetaira. The scant fragments of this work allow us a very limited understanding of the work and its author. An epigram of Asklepiades composed half a century after the *Leontion* of Hermesianax praises Lyde for being more famous than any Athenian woman thanks to Antimachos.[151] Klearchos mentions another Lyde, whom he positively identifies as a hetaira, and adds that she was the muse of the poet Lamynthios who dedicated a poem to her under the title Λυδή.[152]

Sophocles is next in the list of Hermesianax, and he supposedly had an affair with a woman called Theoris. According to Athenaios, Sophocles fell in love with her when he was already an old man, and he supposedly even included her

---

148 Str. 14.1.3–4; Athen. 11.39, 13.70; Stob. 3.11.12, 4.38.3.

149 Such casual references to women under this name can be found in several classical authors, none of which is related to prostitution. For example, there is a reference to the lovely hair of a woman called Nanno in the *Partheneion* of Alcman (1.70), a poem set in archaic Sparta, or a very prosaic reference to Nanno the wife of Gorgippos from Thasos, who died from gynecological complications, in the Hippocratic *Epidemics* (6.8.32).

150 The scant fragments of *Lyde* have been brought together in the edition of B. Wyss *Antimachi Colophonii reliquiae*, Berlin: Weidmann. For the epitome see Phot. *Bibl.* 213.

151 See Hermesianax fr. 7.41–6; Plu. 106 B-C; Klearchos fr. 34 Wehrli; Poseidippos *AG* 12.168; Asklepiades *AG* 9.63; Fuchs 1970: 179.

152 Klearchos fr. 34 Wehrli = Athen. 13.70.

in one of his lyrics when he wrote "Theoris is a friend". [153] However, the word *theoris* also means "sacred ship", so the fragment might not be speaking about a person at all. The entire story about a hetaira lover named Theoris conceivably was generated by the possibly intentional misreading of the Sophoclean line. The mention of a son named Ariston, whose mother was Theoris of Sikyon does not offer any support to the reliability of the information regarding Theoris, because both of our sources, the *Vita Sophoclis* and the Scholiast on the Frogs of Aristophanes are late and secondary, and could have easily been derived from this tradition which makes Theoris one of his mistresses.[154] According to Hegesandros, Sophocles was even older when he met Archippe and forged a relationship with her until the end of his long life at the age of 90. Archippe was left heir to his estate, and cynical people were saying that his property was her primary motivation. Smikrines, her previous lover, when asked how Archippe was doing, replied, "she is sitting on the grave, like owls do." [155]

What is particularly interesting in these stories is that Sophocles always has one foot in the grave. First, they seem to contradict a tale from Plato's *Republic*, where the ageing Sophocles admitted that he had lost his sex drive but considered himself fortunate to be free of the tyranny of such a rabid and savage master.[156] Then they remind us of a familiar story from several Roman period Greek and Latin authors, according to which the old Sophocles was sued by his son for mental incompetence, because he was squandering the family's wealth.[157] This last piece of information would seem to offer some support for the information that Sophocles left Archippe the heir to his estate. From a legal standpoint Sophocles would not have been able to make a will leaving his property to Archippe because Athenian law prohibited men who had legitimate sons to dispose their property through a will; the property by law was equally divided among their sons.[158] Moreover, even in the absence of legitimate heirs a will done under the undue influence of a woman was expressly invalid in Athenian law.[159] But even before his death, if a man in his late eighties was having an affair with a hetaira, this conceivably could have triggered litigation by his sons

---

153 Sophocles fr. 765 Radt: φίλη γὰρ ἡ Θεωρίς; Athen. 13.61.
154 *Vita Sophoclis* 48; Sch. Ar. Ra. 78.
155 Hegesandros fr. 27 Müller = Athen. 13.61.
156 Pl. *R.* 329 b; Plu. 525 A, 788 E; Athen. 12.2; Philostr. *VA* 1.13; Cic. *Sen.* 47. A very useful collection of sources on the life of Sophocles, with translations and some notes, can be found online prepared by W. B. Tyrrell 2006.
157 Plu. 785 A; Cic. *Sen.* 22; Apuleius *Apol.* 37; Luc. *Macr.* 24; *Vita Sophoclis* 13.
158 D. 46.12;
159 D. 46.14; 56.5–7; Hypereides *In Athenogenem* 4 and 11.

to declare him mentally incompetent, since he would be squandering on her money which they were expecting to inherit in the not too distant future. In several of the versions of the story Sophocles got off the hook by reciting to the jurors some of the lyrics of his last play *Oedipus Coloneus*, which proved that he was lucid and still capable of composing glorious poetry.

All things considered, it is not inconceivable that there was a kernel of truth behind these stories, but it would be very difficult to extract it. The references to extreme old age (almost 90) add an aura of disbelief, not because it should be difficult to accept that a very old man was prepared to spend lavishly for the company of a beautiful woman, but because these references seem very stylized and conveniently reminiscent of literary themes. Here were read in Plato that the ageing poet was glad to be free of the bonds of a strong sex drive, and there we find the same topic inverted in stories about his sexual prowess at an extreme old age. Then we hear about litigation from his sons intended to prevent him from spending their inheritance on hetairai, which sounds like a reversal of the traditional theme of the father trying to prevent his sons from spending wildly on prostitutes. These recognizable themes do not appear to be accidental and probably reduce the likelihood that any of these stories is historically accurate, at least in the form that they have been transmitted to us.

Several more stories involving Sophocles and boys were in circulation.[160] In one of them Isocrates admonished Sophocles to restrain not only his hands, but also his eyes from a beautiful boy the latter was chasing.[161] In another one narrated by Hieronymos of Rhodes, Sophocles took a handsome rent-boy outside the walls of the city to have sex with him. As he undressed, he placed his cloak on the ground, so that they could lie on it, while the boy placed his cloak on a bush nearby. In the end the boy snatched the fancy cloak of Sophocles and ran, leaving him with his cheap garment. As he was returning to the city Sophocles came across Euripides, who teased him that he himself had used the same boy in the past, but he had never stolen from him. Sophocles responded with an epigram reminiscent of the familiar myth of the Sun and the Northern Wind saying "It was the sun, Euripides, that made me feel hot and got me to strip

---

160 Athenaios (13.81) assures us that Sophocles was a lover of boys (φιλομεῖραξ), as much as Euripides was a lover of women (φιλογύνης). Whether we should take this seriously, or consider it yet another paradoxical reversal of the main theme of the Aristophanic *Thesmophoriazousai*, where Euripides is the arch-misogynist, remains questionable.

161 Plu. 838 F – 839 A; the story is repeated with a Roman spin to it by Valerius Maximus 4.3.1, and Stobaios 3.17.18. The dates would challenge the veracity of this tale: born in 436 Isocrates would be a young man when Sophocles was in his eighties, and probably not capable of energetically pursuing young boys.

naked, while the freezing wind touched you when you were kissing a hetaira".[162] Athenaios preserves a lengthy quotation from the *Travels* of Ion about the funny, spirited and very civilized manner of Sophocles, when he teased a boy serving him wine in a party. The furthest the poet goes in this story is a kiss, and the tale concludes with a remark that Sophocles was charismatic in his words and actions and overall a decent man.[163]

These tales are almost certainly fabrications, as they put together and reshuffle traditional myths and themes. This is interesting per se, especially if we compare it with the omission of the story of Hieronymos in the 1854 translation of C.D. Yonge. The image of one of the most revered names in Greek letters having sordid sex with a rent-boy, who turns out to be a thief, was too much for the translator and he decided to omit the entire episode without warning. However, the juxtaposition of this omission with the opinion of Ion on Sophocles, that he was a decent man and very civilized in his manners, suggests some profound differences in cultural perceptions. Whereas the 19th century would find these encounters with rent boys shameful and inappropriate, the contemporaries of Sophocles neither found them reproachable, nor embarrassing. This was good-humored material for an intellectual party, and there was nothing morally reprehensible in the fondness of a younger Sophocles for boys or an elderly Sophocles for the companionship of beautiful hetairai. These stories were not coming from hostile sources, but from intellectuals and scholars who were very fond of Sophocles and great admirers of his art, skill and civility. The fact that it would be inconceivable in our times to invent a sexual affair between a literary figure and a rent-boy, in order to enhance and honor his memory and reputation, is indicative of how deeply attitudes have changed.

Several comedians too reportedly had love affairs with notorious hetairai. Philemon, according to Athenaios, was the one who coined the phrase χρηστή ἑταίρα (the good hetaira), when he was in love with one, but Menander responded in one of his plays that none of them was good.[164] Menander allegedly had a celebrated affair with the hetaira Glykera. Although this affair has become something of a scholarly orthodoxy the evidence in support of its existence is slim. The first reference to it is in Athenaios, but this alleged affair came to occupy a central position in the biographical tradition of Menander thanks to two fictional letters of Alciphron, one from Menander to Glykera, and one contain-

---

162 Babrius 1.18; Hieronymos fr. 35 Wehrli = Athen. 13.82.
163 Ion *FGrH* 392 F 6 = Athen. 13.81.
164 Philemon, fr. 198; Antiphanes fr. 282; Athen. 13.66; for the stereotype of the *chreste hetaira* in comedy see Henry 1985.

ing her response.[165] The historicity of the affair between Menander and Glykera was first questioned by Alfred Körte, who pointed out the weakness of the evidence. His skepticism was accepted by two later studies by Ioannis Konstantakos and M. A. Schepers, the editor of Alciphron.[166]

Konstantakos is prepared to put more faith in the relationship between Diphilos and Gnathaina.[167] Unlike the evidence on the affair between Menander and Glykera, which is at least half a millennium later than their lifetime, the evidence for the relationship between Diphilos and Gnathaina comes from contemporary, or almost contemporary sources, like Lynkeus of Samos, Machon and possibly Euboulos.[168] This suggests that even if the details of the stories are made up, the love-affair probably was factual. Several sharp exchanges between Diphilos and Gnathaina are reported: the adept hetaira and the famous comedian are locked in a competition of wit. The hetaira usually has the upper hand. In one of the stories, told by Lynkeus, Diphilos misbehaved badly in the theater and was lifted out and dropped at Gnathaina's. When he asked her to wash his feet she replied "but why, dear, did you not get here air-lifted"? The reporting of such an exchange in a private setting ought to be fictional, but the backdrop of the story, written by an author who was their junior contemporary, does not make sense unless the love-affair between the poet and the hetaira was a well-known fact in contemporary Athens. In another obscure tale found in Machon, Diphilos acts like a protective husband when Gnathaina sits on the

---

165 Athen. 13.49, 66; Alciphr. 4.18.19. In general terms, although the letters of Alciphron may contain valid historical information, it is literature in epistolary form – a genre which was quite popular in later antiquity – and as such no more relevant for the purposes of the modern historian than the novel or the plays from the tragic stage of Athens.

166 Körte 1919: 87–93; Schepers 1926: 258–262; Konstantakos 2006: 150–158. The dates have partly contributed to this skepticism: Glykera reached her floruit around 330, when she had a notorious affair with Harpalos (see Ch. 3.1.); Menander, however, was born in 342/1, and thus still a boy when the famous hetaira was at her prime. We should accept the chronological argument with caution. If Glykera was in her early 20's in 330, when she became the mistress of Harpalos, she was only 10 years older than Menander. The long-term relationship of Demetrios Poliorketes with Lamia, with a similar age difference, suggests that such relationships, even if untypical, were not unheard of. Nonetheless, two very late sources with a tendency to make up stories offer no safe grounds for the historicity of an affair which could have been generated merely out of the fact that Glykera was the name of the main character in the *Perikeiromene*, one of Menander's most beloved plays.

167 Konstantakos 2006: 150–158.

168 Lynkeus in Athen. 13.46; Machon 14.211–217 = Athen. 13.41, 16.258–284 = Athen. 13.43. Athenaios (9.13) quoting Euboulos mentions a dinner at Gnathaina's just a few lines after he has mentioned Diphilos. One would be tempted to think that the unknown speaker who had bread at Gnathaina's is Diphilos.

mattress where Mania was sitting, who was claiming to be suffering from a bladder stone (seemingly a reference to incontinence).[169]

The best known of the exchanges between Gnathaina and Diphilos is given by Machon in two different versions, a short one of only three lines, and a much longer version following immediately afterwards. In the longer version Diphilos turns up ready for a party and brings all the necessary accessories, such as garlands, perfumes, delicacies, even a cook and a flute-player. Meanwhile, Gnathaina has received some gifts from another lover, which include snow, a rare commodity, very difficult to transport from the mountain tops in the hot Greek summer and used to cool down drinks. She does not want him to see these gifts and quickly throws the snow into the bowl with the wine. Diphilos amazed by the coolness of his drink makes an ambiguous remark: "Your pit is very cool Gnathaina," referring to the wine pot and at the same time making an obscene joke about her sexual frigidity.[170] She replies in kind: "it is because we put the prologues of your plays in there." H. Akbar Khan considers the possibility that the derogatory remark was a criticism of the artistic merits of the Diphilan prologues, but concludes that most likely this was a tit for tat response to his criticism: he called her a frigid hetaira and she called him a soulless poet.[171]

The relationship of Diphilos with Gnathaina may have been real, but later centuries were only interested in one very specific side of it: how an ingenious poet and a witty hetaira were interacting with each other. Thus the relationship is taken out of the private sphere into the public, into the sympotic space and the theater, and this is why it is interesting enough to make it into the chronicles of Lynkeus or the tales of Machon. This applies to all relationships between poets and hetairai. Whether real or fictional these relationships were remarkable because they shed some light into the work and legacy of the prominent man involved, and explained some features of his heritage. This is why the poets involved, with the notable exception of the contemporary Diphilos, are golden names from the past, authors whose work was loved and avidly read in the times of Hermesianax and Machon, and continued to be read all the way down to the times of Athenaios and Alkiphron half a millennium later. In this respect, these stories about poets and hetairai transcend the personal and the mundane and become forms of literary criticism, *aitia* which later centuries used to ex-

---

169 About possible interpretations of this difficult passage see Gow 1965: com. ad loc.

170 The Greek word for "pit" is λάκκος, a term often appearing in a sexual context. In the shorter version the word is angeion "vessel". In either case the sexual meaning is unmistakable (see Gow 1965: com. ad loc.).

171 Khan 1967: 273–278.

plain the temperament and character of the works of these poets, or specific passages which they loved and wanted to understand more deeply.

3.4 The Prostitute and the Soldier

> But none of them ever saw another hetaira;
> They were jerking off for ten years
> and had a wretched campaign.
> They took a single city, but when they left
> Their assholes were gigantic[172]

The 4th century comedian Euboulos wonders how the Greeks ever managed for ten years without a woman in sight during the Trojan War: they must have been masturbating a lot and having sex with each other, he jokes. This passage implies that by the time of Euboulos (first half of the 4th c.) things had changed and armies had easier access to prostitutes, and this is significant as there are no reports of prostitutes in the regular entourage of armies before the end of the 5th century.[173] The omission especially in Herodotos is striking; he mentions the women who were accompanying Xerxes' army as concubines[174] and cooks, the eunuchs, animals, transport animals, even the dogs, but no prostitutes.[175] There is probably a good explanation for this omission in Herodotos and Thucydides. Before the turn of the 4th c. the armies of the Greeks were typically composed of citizen soldiers, partly providing for themselves, and partly receiving basic sustenance by their city for the duration of the campaign. They did not view the army as a career, or as the means to accumulate wealth.[176] Citizen armies went out on campaigns for limited periods of time, usually during the summer, and then returned home to get on with their lives. This form of warfare started to change at the turn of the century. Although citizen armies would continue to

---

172 Euboulos fr. 118.

173 However, Madeleine Henry has pointed out that women's trafficking in the epic as spoils for the victor should be interpreted as the opening act for the development of prostitution in the Greek world. See the discussion in Ch. 1.1.

174 We should be in no doubt that only the rich, noble officers would be taking along their concubines, not the regular soldier.

175 See Hdt. 7.187.2.

176 However, there are reports of 5th century corrupt officials who benefited from conquest, bribery and plundering. On the corruption and bribery of officials in the Athenian Democracy see: MacDowell 1983: 57–78; Hashiba 2006 52: 62–80; Conover 2010, esp. 81–125; Strauss 1985: 67–74; Harvey 1985: 76–117; Taylor 2001: 53–66, and 2001b 48: 154–172.

exist, a new, readily available and often more effective type of soldier came into existence.[177] The professional soldier of the later classical period, the Hellenistic world and the Roman times was paid to fight and spent much more of his life in the army. The Roman soldier, for a certain period, was not even allowed to enter into lawful marriage for the duration of his service.[178]

The mercenary soldier features for the first time in the expedition of Cyrus the Younger to seize the throne from his elder brother Artaxerxes II, known among the Greek historians as the campaign of the Ten Thousand. Vast resources were used to fund the armies of rebellion during a long campaign into the heartland of Persia, and it is probably not a coincidence to find that for the first time prostitutes were included in the regular entourage of the army. Cyrus himself took Aspasia of Phocaea with him, while Xenophon attests twice that prostitutes were following the army. We are told that a sizeable contingent of hetairai was following along as the army came under attack in the Armenian mountains on its way back from the battlefield of Cunaxa.[179] Then as the Greeks were crossing the coastline of the Black sea they ran into a savage people who openly wanted to have sex with the hetairai following the army.[180] It seems that the generosity of Cyrus, and subsequently the resources of Asia, funded outlets to the sexual needs of this large mercenary army, and set a precedent to a relationship between the prostitute and the mercenary soldier which was to become a topos in the fictional literature of later antiquity.

References to prostitutes following generals and armies on campaign occasionally appear all the way to the Roman period. Theopompos claimed that the Athenian general Chares was living in luxury and every time he went on a campaign he was carrying with him hetairai, flute-players and singers, and spent on them most of the spoils.[181] Naturally Theopompos disapproves of these oriental excesses, and considers them to be hybris adding that the only reason why the Athenians did not punish Chares was because they were collectively corrupted

---

177 The literature on the professional soldier in the Graeco-Roman world is voluminous. See for example: Trundle 2004 and 1999: 28–38; Miller 1984: 153–160; McKechnie 1994: 297–305; Krasilnikoff 1993: 77–95 and 1992: 23–26; Goldsworthy 1996; Keppie 1984; Gabba 1976: 1–19; MacDonnel 2006.

178 Phang 2001: 13 ff. The ban of legitimate marriage while in active service was instituted by Augustus and remained valid until 197 AD, when Septimius Severus reversed it. This ban certainly did not include illegitimate unions with concubines or relationships with prostitutes.

179 X. *An.* 4.3.20

180 X. *An.* 5.4.33

181 Theopompos *FGrH* 115 f 213. For Chares, his large personality and his eccentric policies see Moysey 1985: 221–227; Salmond 1996: 43–53.

by luxury. Theopompos earns the stern disapproval of Polybios for his account of the companions of Philip, whom he considers not male companions (ἑταῖροι), but female prostitutes (ἑταῖραι).[182] He argues that each one of them was surrounded by several male prostitutes, and then offered himself to the other companions "to be used for the same purpose". Theopompos concludes that although they were "killers of men" (ἀνδροφόνοι), in earnest they were "whores of men" (ἀνδρόπορνοι).

One more piece of evidence from the Hellenistic period may suggest that the image of prostitutes following the army was rather typical of that era. Alexis of Samos speaking about the temple of Aphrodite at Samos says that it was built by hetairai who followed the army of Pericles during the Samian war (440–439 BC) and prostituted themselves to collect the funds for the building project. Although this evidence is not reliable for the time of Pericles, it is significant for the time of Alexis: the fact that this story ever came into existence suggests that the image of hetairai following armies was a familiar sight in the 2nd c. BC. Around the same time prostitutes were a common feature in Roman army camps too, as attested by Appian. Scipio banned such practices during his famous reforms, as he was trying to instill stern discipline.[183]

One can understand the attractions of an entire professional army for the prostitutes and their procurers. In the words of Philostratos, hetairai are attracted "to those who carry sarisas and swords, because they give readily".[184] Where

---

182 Plb. 8.11.5–13 = Theopompos *FGrH* 115 F 225a. Theopompos is making a joke about the semantic shift of the adjective from "friend" in the masculine, to "friend" in the feminine, which after the 5th century came to mean "companion", "escort."

183 Appian (*Hisp.* 366–367:) says about Scipio: "He set out for the army camp in Iberia with a few men, because he heard that it was full of laziness, disobedience and luxury, and knew that he would never defeat the enemy before he deals firmly with his own side. As soon as he arrived he expelled all the merchants, the prostitutes, the oracles and the priests, whom the soldiers were using continuously in a state of fear because of their misadventures. He forbade them to carry anything superfluous in the future." Valerius Maximus mentions two thousand prostitutes following the Roman army, and Werner Krenkel on the basis of this evidence suggested that the army was routinely followed by droves of prostitutes; Sara Phang is skeptical and does not consider this evidence sufficient to reach such conclusions (Valerius Maximus 2.7.1; Krenkel 1988: 1291–7; Phang 2001: 247 and n. 76.). She is also rightly skeptical about the suggestion that the Roman army was running brothels for the benefit of its soldiers (Phang 2001: 248 and n. 81.). See also Walters 1997: 109–114.

184 Philostr. *Dial.* 1.23.4. See also the fascinating discussions and important cultural parallels in Lynn – John 2008 for early modern Europe; Cheng 2011 about prostitute entertainers for the American army during the Korean war; Makepeace 2012: 65–83 and 2011: 413–430 for World War I; Hicks 1997 and Tanaka 2002, for the forced prostitution of Japanese women, to cater for Japanese soldiers during World War II, and American soldiers during the post-war occupation.

there was an army there was prostitution, but one would think that more often than not the market was locally based, offering services to a passing or temporarily stationed army and profiting greatly from such events. And yet, in addition to that, the existing evidence tantalizingly suggests that after the beginning of the 4th c. prostitutes often followed armies on far away campaigns, and the reason why we do not hear more often about them could be that no one considered this feature of army life remarkable enough to mention it without a specific reason.[185] One famous historical incident may support this interpretation of the evidence: some of Alexander's historians mention that hetairai were following the army all the way from Greece and played a leading role during the burning of the palace of Persepolis. Kleitarchos, Diodoros of Sicily, Plutarch and Curtius maintain that the entire idea came from the Athenian hetaira Thais, and as the men and the hetairai who drank with them were inebriated, Thais threw the first torch. Arrian on the other hand does not mention any prostitutes in his version of the incident, or any prostitutes at all in the army of Alexander, even though undoubtedly some were present.[186]

Several other passages mention hetairai following the campaign of Alexander over long distances. Plutarch speaks of a Greek woman named Antigona, who had been captured and enslaved by the Persians, then recaptured by Alexander's troops, and subsequently offered her services first to Philotas as his lover, and then to Alexander as a spy for Philotas. He also makes a passing reference to the presence of many common prostitutes (τῶν συνήθων) following the army. In the same place Plutarch mentions another woman called Telesippa, this time a free person, lover of Antigenes, one of Alexander's seasoned warriors. When Telesippa was just about to leave and go back to Greece, Antigenes pretended to be wounded in order to be able to follow her. When Alexander found out, he was actually moved by the love-story and suggested that they should try to persuade the woman to stay with promises and money.[187]

Apart from cases of omission, inconsistent practice may also account for the fact that only occasionally we hear about such an entourage: it seems that it was up to the general to allow prostitutes to follow, as the case of Scipio suggests, and it might also have to do with the particular circumstances of a certain

---

185 It may be noteworthy that in all instances when we hear about prostitutes in the army it is because an incident happened involving them.
186 Athen. 13.37; D.S. 17.72.2; Curtius 5.7.3–8; Plu. *Alex.* 38. Arrian, on the other hand, sees the burning of the palace as a deliberate act of retribution and propaganda and does not mention Thais (4.10–14).
187 Plu. 339 D-F

campaign. A rapid deployment of troops as a response to an imminent threat would not be the place for a contingent of prostitutes; practical difficulties aside, there would be no large profits to be shared in the end of such a campaign, and the danger from incursions with the enemy would be significant. On the other hand, slow moving campaigns into faraway lands with promises of great riches, like the campaign of Cyrus against the Great King, or that of Alexander into the heartlands of Persia, might act like a magnet for hetairai willing to follow around their lovers, undoubtedly with a view to significant profit.

In New Comedy and the fictional literature of later antiquity the soldier is a stock character. P. G. McC. Brown, in a study of the stereotypical character of the soldier in New Comedy, points out that he is usually an outsider, a foreign mercenary, moving from place to place.[188] W. Thomas MacCary has counted eleven soldier characters in the plays of Menander. Seven of them are named, and their names always remind the audience of their soldiery qualities.[189] In Plautus three soldier characters play an important role. In *Miles Gloriosus*, the pompous Pyrgopolynices is the perfect caricature of the braggart soldier. Equally pompous and aggressive but with some redeeming qualities is Therapontigonus in *Curculio*, while Stratippocles in *Epidicus* is a citizen, and not the typical soldier character in some aspects. These characters are routinely associated with hetairai, true or pseudohetairai,[190] often exhibiting a violent streak towards these women,[191] and some of them have redeeming qualities leading to a happy resolution of the plot. Sometimes the play ends in marriage between the soldier and the pseudohetaira, as between Polemon and Glykera in *Perikeiromene*, or Thrasonides and Krateia in *Misoumenos*; sometimes the unpalatable soldier is removed with some skillful device to make way for the young lovers to marry, as in *Curculio*, and sometimes he is duped and loses the girl, as it happens to the disagreeable and buffoonish Pyrgopolynices in *Miles Gloriosus*.[192] The question why the soldier is often presented as the stereotypical lover of the hetaira in

---

188 P. G. McC. Brown 2004: 1–16.
189 MacCary 1972: 279–298. One play of Menander is named after a soldier (*Thrasyleon*) and another one has the main soldier character as an alternative title (*Misoumenos* or *Thrasonides*). Four more are characters identifiable by name in known plays: Polemon (*Perikeiromene*), Bias (*Kolax*), Stratophanes (*Sikyonios*) and Kleostratos (*Aspis*). Thrason seems to be a soldier character in an unknown play, while the names of four more cannot be determined.
190 The Pseudo-hetaira is a woman of citizen birth, reluctantly forced by circumstances to act as a hetaira. At some point in the plot, her true identity becomes apparent and then she can enter into lawful marriage.
191 See Ch. 5.4.
192 See also Leach 1979: 185–209, and Popov 2008.

New Comedy surely has something to do with dramatic factors: the vainglori-ous, stupid, pompous, arrogant, angry and aggressive character of the soldier has much more dramatic potential than, let's say, the stingy farmer or the fickle sailor. But surely there is a grain of truth in it: in the Hellenistic world the sex-ually hungry male, with no firm family ties and large sums of disposable in-come, would be the prime target of prostitutes and pimps, and the most likely person to seek the fleeting embrace of a paid companion.

The soldier also features as a stock character in several of Lucian's *Dia-logues of Hetairai*. The first dialogue between Thais and Glykera is about a sol-dier who used to be the lover of Glykera, but then was seduced by Gorgona, surely through witchcraft! Jealousy and competition among hetairai are else-where attested in the literature of later antiquity, but here the object of desire that sparks such a bitter contest is an alien soldier, no doubt because they can rip him off (τρυγῶσιν).[193] Dialogue 9 between Pannychis and her maid Dorkas is more explicit about the appeal of the soldier-lover Polemon: Dorkas relates to her mistress the wealth which the soldier brought with him: gold, clothes, es-corts, an elephant, and countless money; even his servant Parmenon was wear-ing a huge colorful ring on his small finger. An excited but also fearful Pannych-is is trying to work out a scheme to keep her current lover Philostratos, a well-off merchant who had been very generous to her, and at the same time reconnect with the wealthy soldier. Finally the treacherous hetaira is caught red-handed, and both lovers in a show-down of male ego enter into a comically grandiose exchange of threats imitating a battle incursion. In Dialogue 13 the naïve, young girl Hymnis is genuinely scared by the fictitious war stories of a soldier lover, and in 15 the aggressive soldier assaults his rival.

Curiously there is no reference to soldiers in later works influenced by the tradition of New Comedy, like the *Greek Anthology*, Aristainetos or Theophylak-tos, and there is only one brief reference in the *Letters of Parasites* of Alci-phron,[194] where the austere soldier explains his views that all hetairai should be common and available to everyone who wanted to sleep with them, in the same manner that jugs in a bath house are available for everyone's use. It seems as if the stock character of the soldier lover surrounded by hetairai fell out of favor in the late empire. The reasons for this change are not clear but may have to do with the shifting role of the soldier as a power broker who put emperors on the throne and took them down at will. By the looks of it, the old stereotype of the buffoonish soldier no longer seemed relevant or funny, while the Christian sol-

---

193 τρυγῶσιν is an interesting choice of word; literally it means "to pick grapes".
194 Alciphron 3.22.

dier of Constantine's army is not the same character as the rootless mercenary drunkard of the Republican era.

The link between the prostitute and the soldier is as old as the presence of prostitution. The evidence suggests that this relationship underwent changes as the role and circumstances of both the soldier and the prostitute evolved. The soldier of the Homeric epic is the heroic conqueror who takes what he wants, and when he conquers cities women are part of the spoils. As this model evolves in the more personal and less heroic world of archaic lyric, the drunk, mercenary soldier of Archilochos is more concerned with loose women and pleasure than heroic deeds and valor (Ch. 1.1.). His women are not noble captives given to him as a prize, but cheap, lowly slaves whom he pays for a quick encounter. The development of hoplite warfare in the archaic and early classical period, where the citizen soldier dutifully defends his city and family with short-term campaigns usually during the summer, is not a world where the prostitute plays a prominent role. However, this changes from the early 4th century, when mercenary warfare gradually replaces the citizen-armies of Greek cities. The new breed of soldier is often rootless, aggressive, enriched with the spoils of war and willing to spend lavishly on women and boys. This character dominates New Comedy and is often associated with the hetaira. As the ancient world was drawing to a close, the romantic affairs of soldiers and prostitutes no longer seemed to be suitable material for fiction. In the new world order, where hagiography became the primary form of fictional literature, soldiers were either the villains who tortured saints, or sometimes saints and martyrs of the new faith themselves, while the vilified prostitute of late antiquity and medieval Christianity no longer resembled the legendary hetairai of the Greek world.

4 The Prostitute and the Law

4.1 Laws and Concepts Regulating Male and Female Prostitution

4.1.1 The legal status of prostitution in the Greek world and beyond

1a. Ps-Clem. _Recogn._ 10.9.19: There is a law among the Seres that no one should kill, or practice prostitution, or steal or pay homage to idols, and in that entire massive country there is nowhere to be seen any temple, whorish woman, or any woman called an adulteress, or a thief haled to a trial, or a murderer or murdered victim.

1b. _Deuteronomy_ 23.17: There is to be no whore among the daughters of Israel, and no man-whore among the sons of Israel.

1c. Philo _De Josepho_ 43: We the descendants of the Jews have excellent customs and laws. Everywhere else it is permitted after their 14th year of age to use with great insolence prostitutes and all kinds of lowly whores and women who earn a living with their bodies. Among us, however, it is not even permissible for a hetaira to be alive, but the death penalty has been established for a woman who practices prostitution. We do not go with any other woman before lawful intercourse, but we enter into marriage pure with pure virgins, because we prefer its purpose to be not pleasure but the sowing of legitimate children.

1d. Origen _Cels._ 4.31: What a marvelous constitution for an entire nation, where not a single catamite was anywhere to be seen. It is also wonderful that the kindling of young men, the hetairai, were exterminated from the whole nation ... and one could see an entire nation exercising wisdom (φιλοσοφοῦν).

1e. Dio Chrysostom 14.14: Do you believe that one should engage in those activities which are not forbidden by written laws, but nonetheless are perceived among people to be shameful and inappropriate, like tax-collecting and pimping?

There is no single and consistent definition of prostitution in Athenian Law, as Maria Nowak has rightly observed, but rather incremental hints and circumstantial specifications in a number of statutes and other literary sources.[1] It is understandable that no legal definition of prostitution was necessary when its practice was never illegal in the Greek world. Greek authors mentioned the criminalization of prostitution in foreign cultures with amazement and some-

---

1 Nowak 2010: 183–197. For a summary of attitudes to prostitution in modern legal systems see Barry 1995: 220–249. However, Barry's account, although informative, is biased towards one side of the argument and strongly advocates actions aimed at the abolition of prostitution.

DOI 10.1515/9783110557954-004

times admiration. It is doubtful how much true information they had about the ancient Chinese.[2] Even at the height of the Roman empire when trade with all corners of the known world was flourishing, it is difficult to imagine that the average Greek or Roman had extensive knowledge of the internal structures and laws of a land so large and so remote. It appears that much of what they believed about the Chinese was legendary material and travelers' tales rather than factual information, although from time to time it might contain a kernel of truth.[3] In this context the statement that there was no prostitution in ancient China is part of the Graeco-Roman mythology about this distant land and no more reliable than the belief that the Chinese lived for 300 years and had no gods or religion.[4] In reality prostitution in ancient China was practiced legally since the 7th c. BC, was a social practice ever present in Chinese history, and remains so even after criminalization in the Mao years.[5]

The information about Jewish law found in authors who wrote in Greek should be more reliable, not least because several of them were Jewish, and the contact between the two cultures was extensive. It appears that prostitution was illegal in Jewish law, and the penalty could be death, but this did not result in the complete absence of prostitutes and brothels from the whole of Judaea, as numerous references to prostitution in Jewish sources suggest.[6] Prostitution was certainly present in ancient Israel and widespread all over neighboring lands throughout the Near East. Philo and Christian authors present an idealized version, where the prohibition of prostitution in Jewish law amounts to complete

---

2 The Greeks called the Chinese Σῆρες (e.g. Str. 11.11.1; 15.1.20), namely "the silk people," and the two cultures came in contact in the later Hellenistic or Roman period, when the trade of silk with the east was established. For a history of sexuality in ancient Chinese culture see Ruan 2013 and Golden 2002.

3 Str. 15.1.34 and 37; Luc. *Macr.* 5. For example, it was a widespread tale that the Chinese lived for more than two hundred years and sometimes closer to three hundred. The Greeks attributed this to the intentionally lean (λιτόβιον) and healthy diet (ὑγιεινόν), even though the land provided everything in plenty (ἀφθονία ἁπάντων). Lucian (*Macr.* 5) adds that they were all "water-drinkers" meaning that they did not drink alcohol.

4 Cels. 7.62.

5 For an accessible comparison between Chinese and Greek civilizations see Zhou 2010.

6 There are, for example, 41 references to prostitution in Philo and no less than 237 in the New Testament, many of them very clearly indicating that prostitution was very much a fact of life in Judaea as it was in other parts of the Roman empire (e.g. *Ev. Matt.* 21.31 and 32; *Apoc.* 17.5, the famous image of the great whore of Babylon modeled on a stereotypical 1st c. hetaira; Philo 1.302 al.). See also *Acta Thomae* 5, where the flute-player in a drinking party is a Jewish woman.

absence of it in real life. However, prohibition never had any such effect in any society, and ancient Israel was no exception.[7]

These references to China and Judaea, regardless of their accuracy, are nonetheless significant: they prove that in the entire Greek world there was not a single city-state, not a single town or village, not even a remote corner where prostitution was illegal. If there had been even a single case, the authors of later antiquity, who are literally scraping the bottom of the barrel to find evidence of prohibitions of prostitution in other cultures, would never fail to mention any such law in the Greek world itself.[8] The weakness of the evidence about places where prostitution was supposedly outlawed beyond reasonable doubt proves that almost everywhere in the ancient world, and certainly without exception among the Greeks, prostitution was legal and widespread.

Additional confirmation of the legality of prostitution throughout the Greek world can be found in a number of references to binding contracts between prostitutes and clients. Several sources speak of such contracts, which outlined the rights and obligations of each side, the amount of compensation and the length of time that the prostitute needed to spend with the customer. The evidence is reliable, as it includes several unambiguous references in Attic law-court speeches and additional references in New Comedy and the lexicographers, and has been discussed in some detail by Edward Cohen.[9] Sex under contract was excellent material for comedians, and they may have overemphasized the frequency and importance of such arrangements, while the evidence outside comedy is not plentiful.[10] Aeschines makes clear that the contracts were not a legal requirement or prerequisite for services, and it seems most people did not enter into some kind of formal agreement prior to having relations with a prostitute.[11] However, considering that large amounts of money were often invested on fickle men or women, it is not surprising that some clients wanted extra safety in the form of a binding agreement, either oral or written, but al-

---

7 For further discussion on ancient Judea and the surrounding regions see Bird 2006: 40–58; Roth 2006: 21–39; Budin 2006: 77–94; Van den Toorn 1989: 193–205.

8 There is also good reason to believe that prostitution was perfectly legal in every other land and peoples with whom the Greeks kept long-term economic and cultural ties, like the Persians, the Egyptians, the Scythians and so on, because if the Greeks had knowledge of any prohibitions among those peoples we would know about it too.

9 E.g. Lys. 3.22; Aesch. 1. 160, 165; Poll. 8.140. Plautus *As.* 746–809, al.; Cohen 2000: 113–148, 2006: 95–124, and his recent 2015 book, especially pp. 97–114.

10 The parody of such a contract in Plautus *As.* 746–809 is a clear example of how comedians could exploit this subject.

11 Aesch. 1.160.

ways in the presence of witnesses who could verify it in case of dispute. These arrangements only make sense if prostitution was legal and it was possible for the prostitute or the client to seek legal redress in those instances where the other side had violated the terms of the agreement. Significantly, when procurement of prostitutes was outlawed by Novella 14 of Justinian, all such contracts were explicitly invalidated. The law also clarified that persons who had served as witnesses or sureties for such contracts were not to be liable.[12]

4.1.2 Laws on Procurement

2a. Aesch. 1.13 [Athens]: The law explicitly says that, if a father, or brother, or uncle, or guardian, or any other person with legal authority, procures a boy, there will be no prosecution against the boy himself, but against the person who hired him and the one who hired him out: against the former, because he hired him, against the latter, he says, because he hired him out. The penalty he [i.e. Solon] made equal for both, and it is not obligatory for the boy who had been hired out as a prostitute to maintain his father or provide a dwelling for him once he reaches adulthood; however, when the father dies, he must bury him and perform the rest of the traditional rites.

2b. Aesch. 1.14 [Athens]: What other law did he establish to guard our children? The one on procuring, whereby he established the greatest penalties if someone procures a free boy or woman.

2c. Aesch. 1.184 [Athens]: He also orders public prosecutions against procuresses and procurers, and if they are convicted, he orders the death penalty, because those who have a desire to engage in shameful acts may be hesitant and ashamed to have encounters with each other, but the procurers, by hiring out their own shamelessness, allow the affair to reach the stage of trial and negotiation.

MacDowell noticed that these laws are "hardly consistent," and concluded that "the truth may be rather that in this matter, as in many others, the Athenians simply made two overlapping laws at different times without noticing the discrepancy."[13] Indeed, if it was illegal for a father to procure a boy, which of the two would happen to him? Would it be sufficient for his son not to look after his father in his old age as 2a suggests, or should he be sentenced to death as 2b and 2c indicate? Then how is it possible that the parent or guardian, who had the most say in procuring an under-age boy, could get away without consequences unless he lived to a very old age and came to be dependent upon his

---

12 Just. *Nov.* 14.107–108
13 MacDowell 2000: 18.

son for his maintenance, while his accomplishes, who needed the father's con-sent and arguably were less responsible, faced the death penalty for the same offence? And since 2a mentions only boys does this mean that two different standards existed and free-born girls, who might be more vulnerable, could be procured without any consequences? If this was the case, then this law would be inconsistent with 2c, where it says that all procurers and procuresses were subject to the death penalty. And if such serious penalties were in place for procurers of free persons, prostitution would not have been able to flourish and expand the way it did, out in the open as a prominent feature of the social and cultural life of the city; rather, it would have been a secretive, underground activity for those prepared to take the risk and engage in an offence which car-ried a capital sentence. Moreover, even under the strict rules of Justinian's code, where Novella 14 (6th c. AD) declared the intent of the law to eradicate pimping from all Roman (sc. Byzantine) territories, breaking the law did not carry a sen-tence as severe as this. How likely is it that a more severe law existed in the classical period, even though there is no trace of it in any other source?

As a matter of fact, the large number of brothel-keepers, pimps and other facilitators of all kinds in the circles of venal sex all over Attica, and in other parts of the Greek world, beyond reasonable doubt confirms that procuring someone, slave or free, boy or girl, man or woman, citizen or alien, was not illegal in the classical period. In a previous publication I have argued that Aes-chines is quoting statutes that he attributes to Solon and presents as valid laws of the Athenian state, even though they were probably obsolete for more than a century before his time.[14] This appears to be the case here too. 2a appears to be a paraphrase of an authentic Solonean statute, if we can judge by the fact that it mentioned an undefined penalty equal for both the father or guardian who procured a boy and the person who hired him.[15] This penalty was probably a fine, maybe significant in the time of Solon, but meaningless in the time of Aes-chines.[16] Even the part which was still meaningful, namely, the provision that a son who had been procured by his father had no obligation to look after him in

---

14 Kapparis 1998: 255–259.
15 Leão and Rhodes (2015: 46–7) are prepared to accept these laws as Solonean, and also accept Plutarch's information (fr. 30a) that the fine for procuring was twenty drachmas. While I agree that the texts are probably Solonean, I have little faith in monetary figures attributed to Solon by later sources. Most likely such figures, even when they come from reliable classical sources, reflect the practices of later centuries, and have been retroactively attributed to Solon.
16 If, for example, the penalty in the Solonean law was a fine, it would have no significance in the 4th century in terms of monetary value.

his old age,[17] was probably nothing more than a theoretical possibility, as there is no known instance where someone invoked this law in order to refuse his old father sustenance.[18]

The other statute, which seems to be one and the same (paraphrased partially in 2b and from a different angle in 2c), was obsolete, as the open existence of many brothels around Attica run by pimps, and also references to a fair number of Athenians and free non-Athenians procuring boys and girls without fear of the law, prove.[19] This law makes sense as part of the Solonean laws protecting free persons from exploitation in an economically depressed climate. However, the socio-economic climate of the classical period was very different. Athenian families did not face servitude for debts, while economic opportunities around the city allowed even poor Athenians to make a living without the need to turn to prostitution. On the other hand, the market of prostitution was large and diverse, ranging from cheap brothels to the most expensive hetairai. Pimps were running those brothels, they were the persons to talk to when someone needed entertainers for a party, and were the handlers of expensive hetairai. In this historical setting the criminalization of procuring makes no sense, and there is not a single scrap of evidence to suggest that pimps lived in fear of a law which if enforced could cost them their lives. The reason is that by the time prostitution had proliferated into an economic and cultural force in classical Athens, the old Solonean statute which threatened pimps with death had been long forgotten and fallen into disuse.

4.1.3 *Hybris* and prostitution

3. Aesch. 1.15 [Athens]: And what else? The one [i.e., law] on *hybris*, which covers all together in one clause all such actions. In this law it is written explicitly that if someone be-

---

17 On this issue see the discussion in *Leão* 2011: 457–72.

18 In a fictional case mentioned by Synesios (*Ep.* 3) which probably has in mind the Aeschinian narrative, a lawyer (ῥήτωρ) son of a hetaira argues that the law exonerates him from looking after his mother.

19 Diphilos fr. 2 is probably referring to the father and pimp of five girls with a mythological reference to Proitos and his daughers; many more instances can be found in the literature of later antiquity. For example, Gnathaina was the procuress of her own daughter Gnathainion, and Korone the procuress of her daughter Kallistion "the Sow." In Lucian *Dialogues of Hetairai* Philina was procured by her mother (3), Korinna by her mother Krobyle (6), and Mousarion by her mother too. Pollux attests that female pimps and mothers of hetairai were wearing a purple ribbon on their head, one would think because the mothers of hetairai were often their pimps (Poll. 4.120; cf. 4.151).

haves abusively towards a boy (and the man who hires him certainly treats him abusively), or a man or woman, free or slave, or commits an illegal act against their person, a
prosecution for abusive behavior is to be commenced and the punishment can be whatever is deemed necessary for him to suffer or pay.

Aeschines here paraphrases the law of *hybris* and links it to sexual offences.[20]
The tenet that *hybris* could be used for prosecutions of rape has been extensively discussed in the international bibliography ever since Edward Harris first
proposed it in the 1980's, despite substantial objections by Christopher Carey
and Rosanna Omitowotzu in more recent times, and it has played an important
part in the thesis of David Cohen "that the overall legal framework indicates
underlying tensions and anxieties about sexual intercourse between males." [21]
Cohen sees in the law of *hybris* a possible way to enforce statutory rape regulations for the seduction or rape of boys too young to be sexually active (but he
does not define any specific age limit).[22]

I am inclined to follow MacDowell's more reserved view that a *hybris* prosecution was a long shot for any offence, and even more so for sexual offences, as
it was not an appropriate procedure against ordinary crime. A *graphe hybreos*
should be brought when the ultimate objective was to punish the attitude and
intention of the criminal, not the crime itself. In this respect it was a generic
procedure which had to do more with the appropriate conduct of a free person
among other free persons. As it was an *agon timetos*, namely a procedure where
the court would decide the penalty in a second ballot, if the first had produced a
"guilty" verdict, potentially it could carry very severe penalties. However, there
was significant risk for the prosecutor too, for if he failed to secure 1/5 of the
votes, he was liable to a large fine of 1000 drachmas, and one could imagine
that in a trial where proof needed to be produced not so much about facts or
events as about intentions and attitudes, the possibility of failing to persuade at
least one fifth of the jury would probably be considerably higher than in other,
more concrete prosecutions.

There is no known instance of a *graphe hybreos* ever being used for a sexual
offence, and altogether the evidence for actual *hybris* prosecutions, for any
reason or offense at all, is very slim. We cannot even name with certainty a sin-

---

20 Aeschines feels that it is necessary to explain how this law can be applied to such offences
(mainly rape), because that would not be self-evident to his audience, since *hybris* had to do
with motives and attitudes rather than any specific crime.
21 Cohen 1987: 187; see also Carey 1995: 407–417 and Omitowoju 2002.
22 About the possibility of legislation on statutory rape, and whether the Athenians had any
concept of consent and sexual maturity at a certain age, see the discussion in Ch. 4.2.

gle individual who was ever tried under a *graphe hybreos* for any kind of transgression or offense.[23] Despite much noise in the literature about its uses for sexual offenses, the available evidence firmly endorses MacDowell's skepticism about the viability of *hybris* prosecutions as a whole. If one were to place the apparent lack of prosecutions through a graphe hybreos side by side with the very high number of references to *hybris* as an attitude or behavioral pattern throughout the classical period, enough to form the basis of a monograph by Nick Fisher and articles by Douglas MacDowell, Douglas Cairns and others, it looks less and less likely that prosecutions for *hybris* went on and that we do not hear about them.[24] This is a central cultural concept for classical Athens, and it is unlikely that no Athenian source would mention such cases if they ever ended up in court and resulted in severe penalties for those who had exhibited *hybris*. In this case the silence in our sources is probably significant.

It appears that a *hybris* prosecution was mostly a theoretical possibility, something which the law allowed for persons who had the wrong attitude to-

---

23 In the extant body of Attic Oratory there are three cases of a *graphe hybreos* mentioned, but probably none of them reached the courts. Apollodoros mentions that he launched a graphe hybreôs against Phormion (D. 45.4), when the latter married his mother Archippe in the early 360's. This action of Apollodoros is strange and only makes sense as a negotiating tactic intended to extract more money from his father's estate. Archippe was given in marriage to Phormion in accordance with the will of Pasion, her late husband and father of Apollodoros. As Pasion had two legitimate sons, the will had no legal validity and ought to be seen as nothing more than a private wish-list settling the family affairs after his death. Apollodoros had the option to ignore the will, take his mother home and assume the guardianship of his under-age brother Pasikles, and no one could have done a single thing to stop him. Instead he launched a *hybris* prosecution against Phormion, who at the time was not even a citizen. His intention without a doubt was to intimidate him and make the entire family agree to a larger financial settlement for Apollodoros. Once this happened and the financial affairs of the family were arranged, Apollodoros dropped the lawsuit. The second case comes from a speech of Isaios (8.40–1), and again we are explicitly told that this case had not gone to trial. A third case in a fragment from the speech of Hypereides *Against Dorotheos* (fr. 97 Jensen) most likely never went to court either, because we are only told that Hipponikos prosecuted the poet Autokles, because the latter had punched him in the jaw, but we are not told anything about a trial or punishment. A few more cases which seem to be actual *hybris* prosecutions consist of nothing more than titles of speeches which have not survived, and considering that the titles were typically given by later grammarians, they need not be actual cases of a *graphe hybreôs*; they could be different procedures where *hybris* was peripheral to the actual case but extensively mentioned, as for example in the speech *Against Meidias*. These titles are Deinarchos *Against Proxenos, Apology of hybris for Epichares*; Lysias *Against Callias, To Sostratos*; Ps-Lysias *Against Diocles*.

24 Cairns 1996: 1–32; Fisher 2005: 67–89 and 1992; MacDowell 1976: 14–31.

wards the rules of civilized society, but which in practice was risky, difficult to prove and unnecessary as Athenian law provided specific and often less dangerous options for the prosecution of specific crimes. Aeschines quotes this law in a desperate attempt to find relevant statutes in support of his argument that Athenian law actually cared about the sexual morals of the citizens. The mere fact that he has to scrape the bottom of the barrel and that almost every law he can find does not endorse sexual protectionism or interventionism in the Athenian legal system, rather proves the opposite, namely that Aeschines is forcing disparate and scattered legal provisions under an artificial umbrella that serves his argument, because he cannot find a law which decidedly aims at regulating the sex lives of his fellow citizens.

4.1.4 The laws barring male prostitutes from speaking in the Assembly

4a. Aesch. 1.19–20 [Athens]: If any Athenian, he [i.e. Solon] says, works as a prostitute, he cannot be appointed as one of the nine archons (I believe because this is a crowned office), nor assume any priesthood (because his body is not clean), nor become a public advocate, nor serve as a magistrate either at home or abroad, appointed by lot or elected; he is not to serve as a herald or an ambassador (and he is not to judge those who have served as ambassadors, or engage in sycophantic activities for money), nor can he voice his opinion either in the Council or in the Assembly, not even if he is a highly accomplished speaker. If someone disobeys these laws, the lawgiver has established a *graphe* for prostitution and the most severe penalties.

4b. Aesch. 1.28–30 [Athens]: Who did he consider unsuitable for speaking? Those who have lived inappropriately; he does not allow these men to address the assembly. Where does he say so? 'Scrutiny," he says, "of the Speakers: if someone is addressing the Assembly, while he is beating his father or mother, or he does not provide for them or offer them accommodation," he does not allow this man to speak, by Zeus, rightly so in my opinion. ... After this whom did he bar from speaking? "The man", he says, "who has not taken part in the military campaigns assigned to him, or has dropped his shield," correctly so. ... Then, whom does he address after that? "A man who has been a male prostitute," he says, "or has sold his body," because he believed that a man who has sold his own body to be abused would easily sell the common affairs of the city. Then whom does he mention? "If he has squandered his parental estate," he says, "or his inheritance," because he believed that a man who has mismanaged his own estate would dispose of the goods of the state in a similar fashion. The lawgiver did not believe that it was possible for the same man to be bad in his private life, but good in public. Moreover, the lawgiver did not think that a man should step on the roster, having taken care of his speech, but not his own life.

4c. D. 22.24 [Athens]: Men who have led a life like his are forbidden by the laws to make even a legal proposal, and if we prove that he [i.e. Androtion] has not only made an illegal proposal but has also led an illegal life, then is it not proper to cite this law which determines his illegal status?

According to K.J. Dover, the earliest evidence about the existence of a law penalizing prostitutes involved in politics is found in the *Knights* of Aristophanes, where Paphlagon boasts that he stopped those who enjoy passive sex (κινουμένους) from becoming politicians by disfranchising (ἐξαλείψας) Gryttos.[25] This interpretation of the Aristophanic passage is very problematic, as there is no other instance where the verb ἐξαλείφω means "to disfranchise".[26] This and other inaccuracies in the language, such as the reference to passive sex rather than prostitution,[27] could signify that the passage does not refer to the law on prostitute politicians at all, but to something entirely different, perhaps an incident involving an alien man and a rather standard joke about politicians who enjoy passive sex, which eludes us.[28]

Some light may be shed by a fragment of Eupolis, which mentions someone who was introduced to the phratry "only yesterday", he could barely speak Attic Greek, and he was from the lowest social strata, the "do nothings" and the whores, but was still a practicing politician.[29] One wonders whether Eupolis

---

25 Ar. *Eq.* 876–80; Dover 1978: 34; See also Lanni 2010: 56. Lanni's argument rests upon Dover.

26 As a legal term it usually refers to the forgiveness or disappearance of public debt. In the speech of Isaios, *Against Euphiletos* (12, cf. D. 25.73; 58.51), it denotes the removal of a man who was thought to be of alien descent from the deme register. The term also refers to the permanent exclusion of people from the register during periods of oligarchic regimes (e.g. Isoc. 18.16; X. *Hel.* 2.3. 51–54). However, on no occasion has it been used as a synonym of ἀτιμῶ, to indicate the loss of someone's citizen rights as a penalty for an offense. ἀτιμία was the penalty imposed upon prostitutes involved in politics (4b above), not complete removal (ἐξάλειψις) from the register of citizens. The difference in legal terms is significant. The children of someone who suffered ἀτιμία as a penalty for an offence would still be citizens, as Athenian law punished individuals for their transgressions, not entire families. However, the descendants of someone who had been expunged from the register of citizens as a non-Athenian (ἐξάλειψις) would not retain any citizen rights, as they were not Athenian themselves. We would need to assume loose phraseology and inaccurate usage of ἐξαλείφω instead of ἀτιμῶ, if this incident were to be understood as a reference to the *hetairesis* law.

27 We must always keep in mind that the actual language of the law (4a ἑταιρήσῃ, and 4b «ἢ πεπορνευμένος», φησίν, «ἢ ἡταιρηκώς») referred to sex in exchange for money, not to any specific sexual position or the actual gender of the participants.

28 The laws, as quoted in Aeschines say nothing about passive sex, but only refer to prostitution regardless of sexual preference.

29 Eupolis, IFF 8.1–4: ωσ φησ παν ..ει ...ε]ι κᾰξιοι δημηγορεῖν,
χθὲς δὲ καὶ πρῴην παρ' ἡμῖν φρατέρων επιι[
κοὐδ' ἂν ἡττίκιζεν, εἰ μὴ τοὺς φίλους ηἰσχύν[ετο,

could be referring to the same man, Gryttos, whom Kleon removed from the register of citizens (ἐξαλείφειν, here correctly used), perhaps through a *graphe xenias*. All things considered, the passage of the *Knights* seems too problematic and too difficult to interpret to take it as evidence about the existence of the *hetairesis* law in the 5th c. D.M. MacDowell, with his impressive credentials in both Aristophanic studies and Athenian law, does not mention the passage of the *Knights*, and this ominous silence probably means that he did not consider it to be a reference to the law on prostitute politicians.

A second potential source for the early days of this law may be Andocides *On the Mysteries*, where the orator is subverting an accusation by his prosecutors that he belonged to an aristocratic group (ἑταιρεία) and turning it into an accusation of prostitution (ἑταίρησις). Andocides accuses Epichares of having been a common whore, despite his ugly looks, a sycophant and a servant of the Thirty. Andocides wonders with indignation how Epichares dares accuse others when the laws did not even grant him the right to defend himself. This has often been interpreted as a reference to the law on prostitutes in politics; however, this interpretation is not inevitable. Andocides suggests that Epichares should have been observing all restrictions of total *atimia*. As explained below, the law on the scrutiny of the orators imposed some restrictions upon persons who had been prostitutes and wanted to be involved in politics, but did not stop prostitutes from defending themselves in court. This rather significant discrepancy may suggest a reading of the text of Andocides from a different angle. The *atimia* which Epichares hypothetically deserved could be due to his unsavory deals with the Thirty, his sycophantic activities, and so many other alleged unpatriotic actions in his record. In any case, the argument is rhetorical, since Epichares was never disfranchised, and given his solid democratic credentials these accusations seem unfounded.[30]

The most significant source for the law on prostitutes practicing politics outside the text of Aeschines is to be found in the speech of Demosthenes *Against Androtion*.[31] This rather thorough account of the laws on prostitute politicians has not received the attention it deserves, although it probably was an important source for the narrative of Aeschines. Demosthenes provides a very

---

τῶν ἀπραγμόνων γε πόρνων κοὐχὶ τῶν σεμνῶν [τις ὢν
The reference to πόρνοι here clearly has nothing to do with *the hetairesis law*; it is an insult intended to reduce someone to the lowest social strata, like Anacreon's Artemon and his ragtag bunch of misfits (see Ch. 1.1.).
30 See And. 1.95 and 100, and MacDowell 1962 com. ad loc.
31 D. 22.21–32. See also Miner – De Brauw 301–313, about Androtion's alleged prostitution contract. For Androtion as a politician the classic study is Harding 1976: 186–200.

different commentary on the purposes of this law, and his account is more reliable than the narrative of Aeschines for two important reasons: first, it seems to be the original commentary on these laws from which Aeschines heavily borrowed to build his case against Timarchos about a decade later, and second, it does not contain quite so many moral platitudes. Demosthenes recognized two different laws, as Aeschines does, one which could be initiated through a γραφὴ ἑταιρήσεως submitted to the Thesmothetai with the risk of 1000 drachmas for the unsuccessful prosecutor who failed to secure 1/5 of the votes, like any other public lawsuit (22.21), and an additional procedure which could be initiated through a denunciation to the Thesmothetai (ἐπαγγελία: 22.29) and was part of the law on the scrutiny of the speakers (δοκιμασία ῥητόρων) in the Assembly. Aeschines mentions the term *epangelia* several times and confirms that this was the procedure which he followed for the prosecution of Timarchos.[32]

The rationale behind these laws is summarized by Demosthenes as following: the lawgiver (Solon) did not want to introduce a very punitive law against citizen prostitutes, for if he wanted to do so he had many severe penalties to choose from. The prohibition from speaking is not particularly punitive because most Athenians entitled to speak in the Assembly do not exercise this right, anyway (τοῖς πολλοῖς ὑμῶν ἐξὸν λέγειν οὐ λέγετε). This comment of Demosthenes is particularly significant, because it goes a long way towards settling the dispute of how many restrictions were actually imposed upon citizen prostitutes. Demosthenes, like Aeschines, clearly says at this point that they were only banned from speaking in the Assembly; he does not say that they were disfranchised, or banned from other activities forbidden to disfranchised citizens.[33] The lawgiver introduced this measure because he did not consider it safe

---

32 E.g. Aesch. 1.64: "until he (sc. Aristophon) threatened to bring before the people the same kind of *epangelia* against him (sc. Hegesandros), as the one which I have brought against Timarchos"; see also 81 "when I brought this *epangelia* against Timarchos"

33 D. 22.30–31: ἑώρα γὰρ (sc. ὁ Σόλων) ἐκεῖνο, ὅτι τοῖς πολλοῖς ὑμῶν ἐξὸν λέγειν οὐ λέγετε, ὥστε τοῦτ' οὐδὲν ἡγεῖτο βαρύ, καὶ πόλλ' ἂν εἶχεν, εἴ γε κολάζειν ἐβούλετο τούτους, χαλεπώτερα θεῖναι. ἀλλ' οὐ τοῦτ' ἐσπούδασεν, ἀλλὰ ταῦτ' ἀπεῖπεν ὑπὲρ ὑμῶν καὶ τῆς πολιτείας. ᾔδει γάρ, ᾔδει τοῖς αἰσχρῶς βεβιωκόσιν ἁπασῶν οὖσαν ἐναντιωτάτην πολιτείαν ἐν ᾗ πᾶσιν ἔξεστι λέγειν τἀκείνων ὀνείδη. ἔστι δ' αὕτη τίς; δημοκρατία. Demosthenes mentions that Androtion should not be entering the temples, since he was a whore (pornos), and thus not permitted to enter. However, this comment is made much later in the speech in relation to a dedication of Androtion to a temple, and not as part of the laws on prostitutes in politics. As it stands this reference would suggest that a *pornos* was subject to the restrictions of total *atimia*, but of course this is a totally hypothetical scenario since Androtion did enter the temples and was never confronted over that. Moreover, the fact that this restriction is not mentioned in the same place where Demothenes provides a thorough account of the laws on prostitutes in poli-

for the democratic constitution to allow male prostitutes to advise the Assembly. Unlike an oligarchy, where vile men are rendered powerless because they cannot criticize the authorities, in a democracy everyone can speak their mind, and vile men have the capacity to destroy the democratic constitution altogether or subvert it, and offer such advice to the citizenry that the entire state becomes like them. Thus, as a precaution intended to prevent the demos from making mistakes, the lawgiver did not allow prostitutes to address the Assembly. It is interesting that, unlike the moral banalities of Aeschines, Demosthenes chooses an interpretation for these laws which is very "masculine," pragmatic and rooted in public life, all about politics and what makes good sense for the city and the democratic constitution. His interpretation corroborates E. Cohen's understanding of the *hetairesis* and *epangelia* laws as an attempt to prevent further corruption in public life, and not as some sort of moral imperative, as Aeschines would have us believe.[34] References to the private sphere, inappropriate innuendos, titillating scandals and sleazy stories of sexual depravity to which Aeschines has accustomed us, are completely absent from the Demosthenic interpretation.

The speech *Against Androtion* is one of the earliest public forensic speeches in the *Corpus Demosthenicum*, delivered in 454/3, that is, almost a decade before the speech *Against Timarchos*.[35] Despite the substantial differences in the justification of the laws between Demosthenes and Aeschines, there are some striking

---

tics strongly suggests that this was an interpretation of the orator and part of his rhetoric, but not part of the laws mentioned earlier. Some scholars (see the discussion in MacDowell 2005: 79–87 and the response of Gagliardi 2005: 89–97) have understood the ban as a disfranchisement (ἀτιμία), but if the law already imposed ἀτιμία before someone was prosecuted, then what would be the incentive for not breaking the law? In a hypothetical scenario, a male prostitute who wanted to become an ambassador might as well ignore the restriction and get on with it as his chances of being prosecuted were statistically negligible (only one known prosecution ever under the *dokimasia* law). Moreover, even if he happened to be prosecuted and convicted he would suffer no additional penalty than he would have suffered if he had voluntarily obeyed these laws. This does not make sense; the penalty for disobeying had to be more severe, and the only reasonable course of action is to accept the evidence at face value. The law banned only speaking in the Assembly and serving in public office; it did not forbid any of the other privileges of citizenship, like attendance of the assembly, voting, access to the justice system, or entering the temples and the market place. However, the penalty of total ἀτιμία for those who did not observe the hetairesis and *dokimasia* laws would result in the loss of these important privileges.

34 Cohen 2015: 69–96

35 Edward Harris (1985: 376–380.) has argued that the speech *Against Timarchos* was delivered in the late summer of 346. This date is broadly accepted.

similarities in the presentation of the legal provisions, which may not be accidental. While it is possible that Aeschines had heard the famous orator speak in that trial, we must also consider the prospect that copies of the speech *Against Androtion* were in circulation at the time of the prosecution of Timarchos, which Aeschines could have used to inform himself of the legal possibilities. The tantalizing prospect that Demosthenes might have been inadvertently responsible for the ruin of his political ally Timarchos by drawing the attention of Aeschines to the legal process of *epangelia* could be yet another bitter irony in the remarkable politics of those perturbed times.

Two more pieces of evidence from later sources supplement the picture which we obtain from the classical sources. Pollux mentions male prostitution (ἡταιρηκότες) as one of the reasons which disqualified the leaders of the demos (δημαγωγοί), and adds that they ought to be disfranchised (ἀτίμους) and refrain from speaking (μὴ λέγειν). Suda states that a person who had been a male prostitute and seen within the boundaries of the Agora was liable to an *endeixis*, but this is probably inaccurate. The author of Suda is referring to persons who had been disfranchised either as a result of debts or a court-decision and extends this ban to persons who had been prostitutes or spoke ill of the dead. But, as we have seen, the processes for such prosecutions are clearly outlined in the narrative of both Demosthenes and Aeschines, and *endeixis*, a serious procedure which potentially carried the death penalty, does not feature in their accounts.[36]

Both 4a and 4b have been quoted and discussed extensively in the wider context of attitudes towards homosexuality in classical Athens. However, as MacDowell and Davidson have rightly stressed, neither of these laws has anything to do with homosexuality; they refer to prostitution alone and proving guilt would require evidence of payment for sexual favors.[37] Even in a case as preposterously misleading as the prosecution of Timarchos, Aeschines is obligated to devote approximately one third of his speech to proving something that probably did not happen at all, namely that Timarchos was compensated for his services as a prostitute. This payment may not have always been in cash, but sometimes in the form of maintenance, gifts, a luxurious lifestyle, parties and good food, as such forms of compensation would not be unusual in the circles of upper class prostitution.

Both laws seem to be dealing with the same offence. They penalize a male prostitute who was active in politics. However, the scope of these laws, the procedure and possibly the penalties are different, which suggests that they were

---

36 Poll. 8.45; Sud. ε 1170 (s.v. ἔνδειξις).
37 MacDowell 2000: 21–22; Davidson 2001: 20–28.

introduced at different times for different purposes. 4a seems to be the primary law and imposes restrictions upon someone who had practiced prostitution.[38] He could not take a leading role in the political life of the city by speaking in the Assembly, propose decrees or laws, or serve as a magistrate or ambassador. However, unlike disfranchised citizens a prostitute could participate in the assembly, speak in court, serve as a juror and enter the temples, and most important, could beget full citizens, as these restrictions were specific to his trade, and were not inherited by his descendants. The terminology is significant, as it is nowhere stated that male prostitutes suffered any form of *atimia*. Even though these restrictions in effect amounted to partial disfranchisement, the term *atimia* did not apply as they had not been convicted of any crime, and so long as they observed these restrictions they were free to do as they pleased in every other area of life.

Conviction carried "the most severe penalties," according to the narrative of Aeschines. This was interpreted by the forger of the document later inserted into the narrative of Aeschines as a reference to the death penalty, and he has composed the document to say so.[39] The narrative of the forger seems to have misled most scholars, who take it for granted that the death penalty could be imposed upon active or former prostitutes for failing to observe the restrictions outlined by this law.[40] However, this is undoubtedly a misunderstanding. The phrase "the most severe penalties" could mean anything at all, not necessarily the death penalty. In fact, Aeschines uses the phrase five times in the speech *Against Timarchos*, but in none of these cases is it likely at all that the death penalty would be imposed.[41] MacDowell acknowledges that "these sweeping statements are misleading summaries of the laws which he has quoted," and even though he seems prepared to believe that death was the penalty for *hetairesis*, still he acknowledges that, as far as we can tell, no person was ever faced the death penalty for such offences in classical Athens.[42]

---

38 MacDowell 2000: 21–27.

39 Aesch. 1.20 τὰ μέγιστα ἐπιτίμια has been changed to θανάτω ζημιούσθω by the forger of the document in 1.21. In a forthcoming article I argue that this document, along with the other documents of the speech *Against Timarchos* and the ones of Demosthenes *On the Crown*, was composed by someone with a schoolboy's understanding of Athenian history and legal procedure, quite possibly a student in a second sophistic school of rhetoric.

40 e.g. Harrison 1968: 37; Dover 1978: 27, MacDowell 1978: 126 and 2000: 21–24.

41 Aesch. 1.14 (procurement), 20 (*hetairesis*), 72 twice (for both the client and the prostitute himself), 90 (for the client who gives evidence about the act, who most certainly could not be put to death).

42 MacDowell 2000: 27.

The other law (4b) was not so much new legislation as it was an assembly of rules bringing together under one umbrella several existing provisions, and making it illegal for any person who aspired to take a leading role in the political life of the city to violate any and all of these provisions. There were certainly laws penalizing failure to join the army or fleeing from the battlefield, and these had been in place from time immemorial.[43] There were also laws, possibly from the time of Solon, forbidding the maltreatment of one's parents.[44] By the time of the introduction of 4b there was also a law forbidding prostitutes to become politicians (4a: γραφὴ ἑταιρήσεως). The new law (4b) brought together all these provisions into one piece of legislation regulating the suitability of the leaders of the city.[45] Thus 4b came into effect at some point in the 4th century, putting under the same heading a number of existing provisions with the intention of providing some safeguards intended to ensure that the city would not be led by unsuitable persons. Cowards, parent-abusers, whores and wastrels were now warned to stay away from politics and public office.

The legal procedure for 4a was γραφὴ ἑταιρήσεως, a standard public procedure submitted to the Thesmothetai and carrying the serious risk of a 1000 drachmas fine for a prosecutor who did not succeed in securing 1/5 of the jury votes. The legal procedure for 4b was ἐπαγγελία (denunciation) to the Thesmothetai. Most likely there was no difference in the risk-factor between an *epangelia* and a *graphe hetaireseos*,[46] but the latter may have been harder to

---

43 Athenian law recognized several offences related to military service, such as *astrateia* (failure to join a campaign), *lipotaxion* (abandoning one's rank), *ripsaspia* (casting away one's shield and running), and set disfranchisement as the penalty for all of them (MacDowell 1978: 159–161).

44 Κακώσεως γονέων (literally: mistreatment of parents): MacDowell 1978: 92.

45 Since it was not illegal to squander one's inheritance, although it would be considered shameful and foolish, the new law was breaking new ground in this respect. One can understand why a person who had squandered his own inheritance would be thought an unsuitable leader in a state which was always worrying about corruption and bribery among its supposedly unpaid magistrates, perhaps with good reason.

46 The sources do not explicitly verify that ἐπαγγελία carried the same risk, and Demosthenes mentions this procedure quite apart from the regular γραφὴ ἑταιρήσεως and the risks which the latter carried. However, the reality of the situation is that, as far as we know, except Timarchos no other Athenian was ever prosecuted with an *epangelia*, which would be improbable if the procedure had been risk-free. Common sense suggests that the state would not have wanted to encourage frivolous prosecutions of the politicians in the Assembly with *epangelia*, as this would have created an explosive potential for abuse in the hands of people who were always looking for the faintest excuse to attack their opponents. Only private lawsuits (δίκαι) were relatively risk free (and even then, the loser had to pay the *prytaneia*, a modest fee or 3 or 30 drachmas, depending on the sum in dispute). All public lawsuits, regardless of their form,

prove as one would need to present substantial proof about acts taking place in private. Perhaps the challenge of providing adequate proof in a *graphe hetaireseos* might be the reason why it remained a theoretical possibility, and as far as we know, no Athenian was ever prosecuted with this procedure. On the other hand, it was typical in a *dokimasia* trial to speak about the entire life and conduct of a person, which in the case of Timarchos provided Aeschines with the opportunity he needed to smear the character of his opponent with all kinds of unproven accusations, rumors, innuendos and tales, and to suggest that Timarchos was a bad citizen and thus not a suitable person to serve as an advisor of the People.[47]

Both Demosthenes and Aeschines (with the latter perhaps following the former), attribute these laws to Solon, but it is unlikely that either of them had been introduced in the early 6th century. First, a single lawgiver would not need to introduce two different laws for the same offence. Demosthenes tries to deal with this difficulty by saying that Solon often allowed different paths for the prosecution of the same offence, because not all citizens had the same abilities in speaking and the same confidence in their powers as litigators.[48] In reality, the existence of two laws for the same offence usually had to do with the different times and circumstances in which these laws had been introduced. In this case, both laws assume advanced political concepts and procedures of the radical democracy which would make no sense in Solonean Athens. Thus, their introduction must be placed at a much later date, when the procedures of the radical democracy, including the scrutiny of magistrates in a certain format,[49] were well in place.

Adriaan Lanni has argued that these laws were introduced around the middle of the 5th century, but this is very unlikely.[50] According to the existing evidence,

---

carried a risk of 1000 drachmas. Only on rare occasions was the state prepared to forego this risk, as, for example, in an *eisangelia* (reporting) for the maltreatment of an *epikleros* or an orphan, in which case the state was prepared to wave the risk in order to encourage citizens to come forth and report abuse of persons in a particularly vulnerable position.

47 About the δοκιμασία and its functions in Athenian public life see Lys. 16, 26, 31 and Weißenberger 1986, esp. p. 14–23; MacDowell 1978: 167–169; Adeleye 1983: 295–306; Hashiba 1988: 23–32 and 1997: 1–10; Efstathiou 2014: 231–54; MacDowell 2005: 79–97; Todd 2010: 73–108.

48 D. 22.25–28. This comment of Demosthenes implies legal procedures of the radical democracy, such as trial by jury and the citizen himself speaking before one's peers, which would not make sense in the time of Solon.

49 Aesch. 1.28–30.

50 Lanni 2010: 55

the term ἑταίρησις, which clearly appeared in the wording of both legal provisions, as quoted by Aeschines and suggested by Demosthenes too,[51] cannot be dated back to the middle of the 5th century. The earliest appearance of the term ἑταίρα is in Herodotos, referring to Rhodopis,[52] while derivatives like the verb ἑταιρεῖν are not encountered before the early 4th c.[53] The term *hetairesis* is attested for the first time in the speech *Against Androtion*.[54] This is why it seems most unlikely that the Athenians could have used such a term in a legal document in the middle of the 5th c. Moreover, as stated above (p. 162) the two alleged references to this law before the middle of the 4th c. are highly problematic and entirely unreliable. Therefore, the certain *terminus post quem* for the existence of this law is the reference in the speech *Against Androtion* (D. 22.21–32), delivered in 354/3, but the law must have been in existence for quite a few years, as its effective incorporation into the δοκιμασία τῶν ῥητόρων suggests. Most likely it was introduced in the 380's or 370's, when upper end prostitution proliferated in the city to such an extent that it became an attractive career option for citizen men and women.

The *dokimasia* law cannot be dated to the middle of the 5th c. either, because there is no trace of the process of *dokimasia* for any public official of the Athenian state in the 5th century.[55] As far as I know, the earliest definite reference to the *dokimasia* of magistrates (of the archons in this case) is in Xenophon's *Memorabilia*, composed in the 360's.[56] We first hear about the *dokimasia* of the speakers in the Assembly, as stated in 4b, in the middle of the 4th century in the speech *Against Androtion*, which probably suggests that the entire process on the scrutiny of the speakers in the Assembly was introduced at some point in the first half of the 4th century, but after the introduction of the *hetairesis* law and probably not long before this speech was composed. When the law on the *dokimasia*

---

51 Aesch. 1.19 and 29; D. 22.21.
52 See the discussion in the Introduction and in Ch. 1.1.
53 E.g. Lys. 3.24 τὸν ἑταιρήσοντα, 14.41 ἡταιρήκασιν
54 D. 22.21
55 Magistrates may have been vetted before the 4th century, but δοκιμασία as we know it, as a set legal procedure for all entering magistrates, features nowhere in the sources before the early 4th c., which may suggest that it was not streamlined and crystalized into law before the great reform of the processes of the Athenian Democracy in 403 and subsequent years.
56 X. *Mem.* 2.2.13. The only form of *dokimasia* attested in the 5th and early 4th century is that of young adults registering as citizens (e.g. Ar. *V.* 578; Is. 9.29) or cavalry men (as in the *dokimasia* speeches of Lysias). One wonders whether the *dokimasiai* of magistrates were introduced in the 4th c. on the model of this more traditional procedure. I hesitate to include the reference to the ἀποδοκιμασία of a general in Lys. 13.10, as the term in the negative may be used loosely and not in a strictly technical sense.

of the speakers was introduced it probably took into account existing legislation on prostitutes, along with other existing laws forbidding the ill-treatment of one's parents and failure to meet the obligations of military service, and added a provision about the squandering of one's inheritance.

All four provisions now enshrined into the new law were to function as a single stern warning intended to keep unsuitable men away from leadership positions, and those who did not heed it were facing complete and permanent disfranchisement.

The *dokimasia* law is in line with *dokimasia* procedures for all public officials of Athens. It is reasonable to assume that at some point it was seen as essential for the most influential persons in the city, namely the politicians who proposed laws and decrees in the Assembly, and provided direction for domestic and foreign policy, to be observing some minimal standards of conduct. While all other officials were scrutinized during their entry to office, and similar questions were asked during their scrutiny, speakers in the Assembly could not be scrutinized in the same way, but still ought to be subject to some form of *dokimasia*. As a workable practical solution, the law on *dokimasia* of the speakers was introduced to deter persons who did not meet minimal standards of civic responsibility, honesty and integrity from assuming important leadership roles. The city was trying to protect itself and its institutions through this law; it certainly was not concerned with the private lives or its citizens, nor intended to castigate their sexual morals and preferences in the bedroom.

4.1.5 Prostitutes and inheritance law

5a. D. 46.14 [Athens]: Any citizen, with the exception of those who had been adopted when Solon entered upon his office, and had thereby become unable either to renounce or to claim an inheritance, shall have the right to dispose of his own property by will as he shall see fit, if he have no male children lawfully born, unless his mind be impaired by one of these things, lunacy or old age or drugs or disease, or unless he be under the influence of a woman, or under constraint or deprived of his liberty.[57]

5b. D. 48.56 [Athens]: To use the language of the lawgiver Solon, he is out of his mind as no other man ever was, falling under the spell of a woman who is a whore. And, of course, Solon has established that everything done under the influence of a woman, especially one of this sort, is to be invalid.

---

57 Loeb translation by A.T. Murray. The same law is quoted with minor variations by Hypereides (5.8) and Plutarch (265 E; *Sol.* 21.4)

5a is probably an authentic quotation of a Solonean law, as several other partial quotations of it confirm, establishing the legal conditions under which a man could leave a will and outlining the circumstances under which someone's will could be invalidated. These include making a will under duress, or in a mentally unfit state either from natural causes, such as disease or old age, or under the influence of drugs, or under undue influence including erotic infatuation. Most of these conditions we would find enshrined in modern legal systems too. Even though our laws would be gender neutral, they still would invalidate a will made under coercion or improper influence. This particular law, as 5b indicates, could be narrowly interpreted as especially applicable to prostitutes, even though the law did not specify that the woman needed to be a prostitute. A passage from the speech of Hypereides, *Against Athenogenes*, clearly states that the law applied to undue influence by any woman, including someone's wife, but adds that it would be of particular significance if the woman was a hetaira.[58]

In practical terms this particular law could be invoked to invalidate the will of a man leaving all or part of his property to a hetaira, with the argument that a prostitute always exerts undue influence upon a besotted lover. Especially if someone had decided to disinherit natural heirs such as legitimate offspring or one's brothers or sisters, in favor of a hetaira or concubine, a challenge of the will should be expected.[59] This does not mean that men were not allowed to leave money, property or valuables to hetairai or concubines, as there are many examples of such arrangements. It means that one would be wise to give priority to heirs with a stronger legal claim, and make his wishes known to his family while still alive, before bestowing part of his belongings to a hetaira or concubine.[60] The will of Aristotle (see Ch. 3.2.) is an excellent example of such a balanced approach; the philosopher was mindful to take care of all his loved ones.

---

58 Hyp. 5.8.

59 We would be on safe grounds to think that, if there was a legitimate son and heir, he would not even need to bring a legal challenge against his father's will, as any such document would have no legal validity in the first place. The law clearly forbade men who had legitimate sons to bequeath their property to someone else through a will (5a). His son and heir would take possession of the property immediately after his father's death, and no one would even try to stop him.

60 In a balanced arrangement such as this one it would not be in anyone's best interests to contest the will on grounds of insanity, coercion or undue influence, as the party who contested it would be taking a risk. If the will were overturned then the court would decide who had the best claim on the entire fortune, usually through a *diadikasia*, and this feat was not as predictable as one might think in a society which mistrusted written documents and did not keep consistent archives of births, deaths and family lines.

Although Aristotle was very generous towards his concubine, the former hetaira Herpyllis, he also took care of the rest of his family, including his legitimate daughter and his illegitimate son, making sure that everyone was left with a substantial bequest and no one would have good reason to risk a court challenge. The absence of a direct, legitimate male heir in this case probably allowed greater freedom for the philosopher to dispose of his property as he saw fit, and necessitated these arrangements.

In an incident narrated by Aristophanes Byzantios in his study on the Athenian hetairai, the childless doctor Nikostratos, seemingly a metic in Athens, was able to leave all of his belongings to his lover, the hetaira Antikyra.[61] However, it seems that she had miscalculated the extent of his wealth, and instead of being left a fortune, as she probably expected, all she inherited was a very large quantity of hellebore (surely a joke about her hometown). By contrast, the hetaira Archippe faced litigation from the family of Sophocles, which resulted in the annulment of his will, if we believe Hegesandros and several stories from the Roman period.[62] Hegesandros says that Archippe was hanging around a very old Sophocles like an owl hovering over the grave, and her intention was to inherit him.[63] She succeeded in her quest; Sophocles wrote a will leaving her his entire, very substantial, fortune. However, Sophocles by law did not have the right to leave a will, since he had legitimate sons, and even if he had decided to denounce and disinherit his sons (ἀποκηρύττειν), that will could still be overturned since his sons would argue that he was mentally incapacitated by old age and wrote the will under the undue influence of a hetaira. Indeed, some later authors attest litigation between the author and his sons, who were trying to prove that he was mentally incompetent.[64] If there is any truth at all in these tales it could suggest legal action to invalidate the will while the poet was still alive, or in some versions of the story a lawsuit to declare him unfit to manage his property, altogether.

Athenian law wanted the property to stay within the *oikos*, and this is why it would be almost impossible for a man to bypass succession by legitimate sons. In that case, if he wanted to provide for his concubine or a favorite lover, he would probably need to make sure that the money went to them while he was

61 Ar. Byz. fr. 5.2.2. Nauck = Athen. 13.51. The town of Antikyra on the northern coast of the Corinthian gulf, after which the famous hetaira was nick-named, was the largest producer of hellebore in Greece. The joke is that Antikyra did not need any more hellebore.
62 For the sources and further discussion see Ch. 3.1.
63 Hegesandros fr. 27 Müller = Athen. 13.62.
64 Plu. 785 A; Cic. *Sen.* 22; Apu. *Apol.* 37; Luc. *Marc.* 24; *Vita Sophoclis* 13.

alive. Real estate could not be transferred to non-Athenians, and since most hetairai in Athens were alien residents they were automatically disqualified from owning real estate.[65] Therefore such transfers would typically take the form of money, jewelry, furniture or other valuables. Similar arrangements would need to be put into effect if a man had only legitimate daughters. If they were already married with children at the time of their father's death, they inherited him directly, but if they did not have children, they became epikleroi, and again, they were fully entitled to their father's property, and any claim by a hetaira through a will would definitely be rejected in court in favor of the claim of the legitimate daughters. If there were no legitimate children, a man had more freedom to make other arrangements and include a concubine or a hetaira, along with other relatives. However, even in this case, leaving one's entire fortune to a hetaira very likely would have triggered a legal contest by lateral relatives, and the law invalidating a will made under undue influence could have been invoked.

4.1.6 The law regulating the hiring of entertainers

> 6. Arist. *Ath. Pol.* 5 76 0.2: Ten astynomoi are appointed by lot. Five of them serve in Piraeus and five in the city, and they make sure that the flute-players, the singers and the cithara-players are not hired for more than two drachmas, and if more than one client wishes to hire the same woman, they draw lots and hire her to the winner.[66]

Pseudo-Zonaras (s.v. διάγραμμα) suggests that the agoranomoi were in charge of the hiring of prostitutes, but he has probably confused them with the astynomoi. Rhodes is probably right to think that the list of the *Athenaion Politeia* is incomplete and should also include dancers.[67] He also seems to think that these were entertainers "for casual hire by the not-so-rich." Indeed, these were entertainers to be hired for the evening and no doubt the two drachmas maximum fee did not include additional sexual favors, but only the entertainment for the symposion.[68] Athenaios, quoting Persaios, attests that it was cus-

---

65 See for example the will of Aristotle, where Herpyllis may have a house in Chalkis, or, if she prefers, the philosopher's parental home at Stageira, but no house in Attica, as this would not be permissible for an alien.

66 For a more detailed discussion of this statute see Ch. 5.4.

67 Rhodes 1981: 574.

68 For example, in the *Symposium* of Xenophon (2.1) the Syracusan owner of a flute player, a dancer and a beautiful cithara boy, who could also dance, is making a lot of extra cash, no

tomary in symposia to auction flute-players, which certainly would be extra and would be paid by the person who was going to have sex with the entertainer-turned-prostitute, not by the host of the party.[69] This fragment of Persaios also throws some light upon the reasons why the state felt obligated to regulate the price and hiring of entertainers. The episode mentioned there ends up in a brawl, as a similar episode does in the *Wasps* of Aristophanes. The competitive spirit and macho display of men under the influence of alcohol fostered violence, while the demand for good entertainers could create the ideal conditions for the exploitation of party-hosts, who might be blackmailed into paying much more than they intended. Since a party without entertainment would be too dull for the taste of most people, hosts could be arm-twisted into paying a lot more the last minute, if the market had been left to its own devices. Even though we might find it strange that, of all things, the Athenian state chose to regulate the prices and hiring of entertainers, there were compelling practical reasons for this, as the state was trying to prevent violence and the exploitation of customers.

4.1.7 The taxation of prostitution

7a. Aesch. 1.119: He wonders whether you recall that every year the Council auctions the prostitutional tax (πορνικόν τέλος); and those who buy the rights to this tax collection do not guess, but know exactly who is doing this sort of work.

7b. Aesch. 1.120: He (sc. Demosthenes) is going to ask in which brothel he (sc. Timarchos) was ever established and whether any tax collector ever collected from him the prostitutional tax.

7c. D. 22.56: On top of that, as if he could do whatever he wanted, he (sc. Androtion) seized the goods of Sinope and Phanostrate, who indeed are prostitutes, but did not owe any tax.

Athens was not the only place which taxed the earnings of prostitution, but here we find sufficient information to understand how the system worked.[70] The procedure was rather typical for state taxes: once a year the Council auctioned the right to collect this tax to the highest bidder. The successful bidder paid the

---

doubt in addition to the two drachmas for each entertainer that he had received from the host of the party.

69 Persaios fr. 451 von Arnim = Athen. 13.86. A more detailed discussion can be found in Ch. 5.3.

70 For the taxation of prostitutes in Rome see Phang 2001: 248; McGinn 2004: 76–77.

public treasury in advance, and then had one year to collect the tax from those who owed it, surely with a very handsome profit.[71] 7b suggests that brothels certainly had to pay this tax, and they were the easy part of the tax-collector's job, as they were readily identifiable establishments with organized finances. Things might get more complicated when it came to freelance prostitutes, who might be working discreetly from less visible establishments, and definitely became very complicated when it came to high class hetairai, who, like the Xenophontean Theodote, might not even call themselves prostitutes, and payments in the form of pricy "gifts" could be interpreted as tokens of "friendship," not as taxable earnings. 7a implicitly acknowledges these difficulties when it says that those who bought this particular tax knew exactly who had to pay and who did not. It goes without saying that precise knowledge of the sex-workers around the city was very important because making a mistake and trying to exact this kind of tax from non-prostitutes would cause grave offence.

As with the *metoikion*, the tax levied upon all alien residents in Athens, payment of the *pornikon telos* amounted to implicit acknowledgement that one belonged to that group (7b). Prostitutes who paid the tax for the first time very likely were included in some kind of list and would be required to make payments by subsequent collectors in the coming years, until it could be demonstrated that they had given up prostitution.[72] Failure to pay the tax, as 7c suggests, could result in the seizure of one's goods.[73] McGinn, speaking about the case of Rome, questions whether taxation amounted to implicit recognition of the legality of prostitution. In Athens there is no such dilemma as prostitution was always permissible by law, and taxing its rather substantial profits would seem the logical thing to do.[74]

---

71 This particular tax no doubt came with special perks, as one can imagine that prostitutes and brothel owners would offer favors in exchange for lower payments. See also the discussion in Ch. 5.3.

72 For example someone who had permanently left a brothel (ἀνίστασθαι), or become someone's wife or concubine, or closed down an entire establishment should be removed from the tax register.

73 The irregular procedures followed by Androtion at this point (7c) are confusing and we cannot tell for sure whether the tax-collectors automatically had the right to seize a debtor's goods, or they had to go to court first and obtain an injunction allowing them to do so (δίκη ἐξούλης).

74 McGinn 2004: 76.

4.1.8 Indecency in public spaces

> 8. Hypereides fr. 14 Jensen (= Harp. s.v. ὅτι χιλίας): Women misbehaving in the streets were fined one thousand drachmas.

There is no trace of such a law anywhere else but we do not have any reason to reject the information of Harpocration. He attests that the law was mentioned in the second speech of Hypereides *Against Aristagora*, and provides tpuhe testimony of the comic poet Krobylos that it had been introduced by Philippides. Prostitutes are not specifically mentioned in this passage; in theory the law applied to all women. However, since it appears to be referring to public indecency, it is fair to say that prostitutes having sex with clients in public places were the primary concern of the lawgiver. A fine of 1000 drachmas is very steep and beyond the means of most independent working women, which confirms that the lawgiver had in mind prostitutes capable of paying from their earnings.[75] A fine of this size signaled the firm determination of the law to ban indecent acts in back alleys and public areas.

4.1.9 The legal status of the children of prostitutes

> 9a. Heraclid. Pont. fr. 146 Wehrli (= Plu. *Sol.* 22): And this was an even stricter one (i.e. among the laws of Solon) stating that those born of a hetaira were not obliged to provide for their fathers, as Herakleides of Pontus has said. For a man who looked down on marriage and took a woman for pleasure and not for the purposes of childbirth, does not deserve a reward and can impose no demands upon those children, whose mere existence he has made shameful.

> 9b. Arist. *Ath. Pol.* 26.3: In the archonship of Antidotos [451], with a proposal of Pericles, they (sc. the Athenian People) decided that only those born of two citizens are to be citizens.

Strictly speaking Herakleides was right: it was true that illegitimate sons of prostitutes did not have to provide for their fathers, even though the law did not exactly say so. The law, still valid in the 4th century, stated that only legitimate sons, natural or adopted, could inherit their father. In their absence, legitimate daughters, natural or adopted, became heiresses, and in the absence of legitimate children the lateral relatives (e.g. brothers or sisters of the deceased) in-

---

75 It is also noteworthy that women were not typically punished by a fine, which suggests that the lawgiver did not have in mind ordinary women, but acts of public indecency by prostitutes.

herited his property. Illegitimate children had no claim to their father's estate, but the father could make arrangements for their well-being inter vivos.[76] The law did not single out children from a hetaira; all children born outside marriage (νόθοι), and after 451 for those periods when the Periclean citizenship law was in force all children of mixed unions (μητρόξενοι), would be deemed illegitimate (8b). In practical terms, many of those children would be from hetaira-concubines, or unplanned children from hetairai with whom the father might have had a relatively short-lived affair.[77]

These children had no rights to their father's estate, while the father might not even want to acknowledge or recognize children born from casual affairs. Since these children had no inheritance rights, and for most of the classical period no right to citizenship either, it would be only fair if they did not have any financial obligations towards their father either. This applied to all illegitimate children, not only to those born of hetairai. However, on the rare occasion when a hetaira happened to be Athenian and the infatuated lover decided to marry her legally through *engye*, as it often happens in the plots of New Comedy,[78] then the children of the union would be legitimate heirs to their father, and thus legally bound to provide for their parents in their old age, regardless of the fact that their mother had been a prostitute. Herakleides and Plutarch have narrowed down the scope of this law to one specific instance, namely the case where the mother was an alien hetaira, and interpreted it to suit their purposes.

---

76 MacDowell 1978: 92–101.

77 Several times in the Attic orators illegitimate offspring are identified as children from hetairai. For example, in Is. 4.10 Chariades attempts to fraudulently legitimize a son from a hetaira, and an illegitimate child from a hetaira features in D. 54.26 side by side with Konon's legitimate sons. The best-known case is the speech *Against Neaira*, where the prosecutor on numerous occasions states that the children of Stephanos from his concubine, the former hetaira Neaira, should not be considered legitimate. However, Stephanos argues that the children were from another woman, his first wife who was Athenian, and thus they were legitimate.

78 For example, the wife of Pyrrhos in Is. 3 was beyond reasonable doubt an Athenian hetaira, whom Pyrrhos at some point married through *engye*. Her citizen status is sometimes disputed in the literature, but the fact that witnesses were able to testify on the *engye*, and her daughter Phile initially fended off a claim to her inheritance brought by a relative who was arguing that she was the daughter of a hetaira and thus illegitimate, strongly suggest that the wife of Pyrrhos was an Athenian woman, albeit with unconventional morals.

4.1.10 Athenian Law forbidding citizens to marry aliens

10. D. 59.16: If an alien man lives in marriage with a citizen woman, by any means or device, any Athenian who has the right can bring a prosecution against him to the Thesmothetai. If he is convicted, he and his property are to be sold, and one third of the sale is to be given to the successful prosecutor. The same applies if an alien woman lives in marriage with a citizen man, and the man living in marriage with the convicted alien woman is to owe a fine of one thousand drachmas.

There was never a law in Athens, or as far as we know anywhere else in the Greek world before the imperial era, prohibiting the marriage between a citizen and a prostitute, as such. Unlike Rome, where the *Lex Iulia de Maritandis Ordinibus* forbade marriage between prostitutes and freeborn persons (and was repealed by Justinian so that he could marry Theodora, according to Prokopios),[79] in the Greek world prostitution did not automatically disqualify a man or woman from marriage with a citizen. However, other restrictions might apply, which limited such possibilities. The most important barriers would be social, not legal, as most men would find the prospect of marrying a common woman unfathomable. For those infatuated men who were prepared to ignore social convention the law still placed some formidable obstacles. In Athens aliens could not legally marry citizens, as this law quoted by Apollodoros in the speech *Against Neaira* confirms. Considering that most hetairai living in Athens were alien women, they would be directly affected by its provisions, and it is a possible scenario that the law was introduced in the first quarter of the 4th c. in order to make sure that alien prostitutes and their brood stay well away from the citizen body. Geoffrey Bakewell has recently argued that the law also reflected the anxieties of Athenian men who had marriageable daughters. With so many attractive metic women in the city, this law was seen as a means of controlling the desires of Athenian bachelors, and ensured that when they decided to marry only properly born citizen women would be eligible brides.[80]

Both, the obstacles to prostitutes marrying citizens and also instances where these obstacles were bypassed are well-attested in the sources. In fictional literature the classic example is Glykera in Menander's *Perikeiromene*. At the beginning of the play, while she is believed to be a free alien of low birth, we find her living in the house of Polemon as his concubine, and we realize that she had been a hetaira before that. Later on, when it is revealed that she was of citizen stock exposed while she was an infant, she becomes Polemon's lawful

---

79 Procopios *Anecd.* 9.51; see McGinn 1998: 70–10; and section 4.1.16 below.
80 Bakewell 2008: 97–109.

wife, which is the happy ending that the audience would wish for this good-natured and unjustly mistreated mistress.[81] The theme of the good citizen hetaira, can be traced back to middle comedy. In Antiphanes' *Hydria* a man falls in love with a citizen hetaira, forced into prostitution by circumstances, as she was poor and had no one to look after her. However, the audience is informed that she was a woman of good character and very virtuous.[82] Several other "good" hetairai in New Comedy and its Roman adaptations also turn out to be citizen women, and after the revelation they can become lawful wives, like Glycerium in Menander's *Andria* and its Latin adaptation by Terence, Palaestra in Plautus *Rudens*, or Silenium in *Cistelaria*.[83]

The heirs of New Comedy continue the same theme. Lucian returns to it in one of the *Dialogues of Hetairai*. Myrtion feels very insecure thinking that her lover Pamphilos is getting married to a citizen woman, while she herself is eight months pregnant with his child. He retorts that this is untrue and that if he wanted to take a lawful wife, he would have chosen his cousin, who was from a good and affluent home.[84] This dialogue assumes that there is a legal obstacle preventing Pamphilos from marrying Myrtion, his true lover and mother of his child, and outlines what his options would be if he wanted a lawful wife. The best Myrtion can hope for is a lover who is willing to help with the financial expenses for her child. In Alciphron we find the former hetaira Philoumene, who has recently been married, putting her husband to sleep and then joining her friends and fellow hetairai for a sacrifice and a mischievous party.[85]

Outside fictional literature the boundaries between hetaira and wife are rarely crossed, but even in real life we hear from time to time that a hetaira has become someone's wife. The woman married to Pyrrhos in Is. 3 is probably a former hetaira of citizen birth, who married one of her rich clients through proper

---

81 See also Konstan 1987: 122–139. Konstan offers a convoluted account of the legal status of Glykera, but otherwise provides some useful information on the transition from hetaira to wife. The legal status of Glykera and her relationship with Polemon are quite clear. A concubine's partner was her legal kyrios, as he could represent her interests in public life and had the authority to discipline her within limits for as long as she lived in his house. However, a free concubine (*pallake*) always had the choice to walk out, as Glykera does. Once she turns out to be a citizen, she can be a *gamete*, a lawful wife.

82 Antiphanes fr. 210.

83 The classic study for the character of the *chreste hetaira* in New Comedy is Henry 1985.

84 Luc. *DMeretr.* 2.

85 Alciphron 4.14. This passage has an artificial ring to it, and while it might be perfectly in place in later antiquity fiction, it probably stretches any link to historical reality to breaking point.

engye conducted between her husband and her brother. Plangon in the two speeches *To Boiotos* may have been a former hetaira of citizen birth, and the speaker refers to her by her first name several times.[86] We are told that the Thracian wife of the general Konon and mother of his son Timotheos was also a hetaira, whom he married at a time when the Periclean law had fallen in disuse during the Peloponnesian war, but that then she became the modest and respectable wife of the prominent general. A similar tale was related by some authors of later antiquity about Themistocles (see the discussion in Ch. 3.1.).[87] Eumachos says that Hieronymos, the Sicilian tyrant, took a common prostitute from a brothel named Pytho and made her his queen.[88] Finally, Procopios in an unforgettably glossy narrative relates how emperor Justinian married a stripper and a common whore and elevated her to the throne as his consort.[89]

The historical evidence about prostitutes turning into wives is not abundant and all put together suggests that crossing over the boundary was a rare exception. Under normal circumstances the dividing line was clearly marked.[90] The speech *Against Neaira* offers a much-discussed description of the roles of the hetaira, the concubine and the wife.[91] Apollodoros says that hetairai are for pleasure and wives for household keeping and legitimate children. Even though, like all generalizations, this statement is not to be taken literally as a universal rule, what Apollodoros says reasonably describes social expectations.[92] Pseudo-Plutarch says that a hetaira or a concubine would be very un-

---

86 D. 39 and 40. Citizen women were not mentioned by their first name in public places like the law courts, unless the speaker intended to treat them disrespectfully. See also the discussion in the Index s.v.

87 For the alleged prostitute mothers of Timotheos and Themistocles see the discussion in Ch. 3.1.

88 Eumachos *FGrH* 178 F 1 = Athen. 13.37.

89 Procopios *Anecd.* 9.

90 The point should not be pushed to extremes, as it was in the literature of the 1980's, where the wife was often presented as the polar opposite of the hetaira (e.g. Pomeroy 1975; Keuls 1975, and 1983: 23–40; Reinsberg 1989). Not all women in Athens where either prostitutes or wives, nor all prostitutes were the same, and frankly, not all wives were the same either, considering large inequalities in wealth and social status. To separate all women into wives and prostitutes would amount to turning the rich, colorful tapestry of women's lives in classical Athens into a blurry black and white image, and this is why more nuanced approaches have been adopted since the 1990s.

91 For the discussion see Kapparis 1999: 422–424.

92 In a similar spirit, Amphis in his play *Athamas* (fr. 1) suggests that the wife, because she has legal rights, she can be abusive towards her husband in his own house, while the hetaira, because she has no rights knows that unless she is good to her man he is going to move on to someone else.

suitable for having glorious children (ἐνδόξων τέκνων).[93] Plutarch in the *Conjugalia Praecepta* suggests that the wife should be grateful because the hetaira simply saves her from drunken, shameless behavior, which would have been directed at her if the husband did not have the option to redirect it towards the prostitute.[94] Further down it is suggested that a man cannot have sex with his wife in the same way as he would have sex with a hetaira.[95] The same spirit governs two fictional letters from later antiquity attributed to the Pythagorean Theano, where the wife is advised to be patient and when the husband has had enough of vile sex, drink and other vices with the hetaira he is going to come home.[96] Aeschines in the speech Against Timarchos says that male prostitutes are easily recognizable from their shamelessness (ἀναίδεια), insolence (θράσος), and their lifestyle choices (ἐπιτηδεύματα).[97]

This is only a small selection of statements separating wives from other groups, but the meaning coming through is clear. The distinction was not only legal, but also social and operational, and in this respect it remained strong throughout antiquity even though in later times the moral pitch changed. The beleaguered wife of classical literature, the source of all of man's troubles and sufferings in comedy, but also more serious genres like tragedy, oratory, philosophy and lyric poetry, became a noble symbol of family life, decency, respectability and all that is good in a man's life in later antiquity, to some degree under Roman influence, and this tradition certainly passed into early Christianity. In a proportionate reversal, the classical hetaira, the joy of a man's life, the woman who offered him relief, affection, attention and pleasure, however fleeting and insincere, became the source of all evils, the destruction of home and country, a man's ruin and a peril for his immortal soul in the moralizing world of later antiquity.

4.1.11 A law of Cyprus

11. D.Chr. 64.2 [Cyprus]: Likewise in Cyprus Demonassa was a woman politician and lawgiver. She set three laws for the Cypriots. The woman who has committed adultery is to have her head shorn and become a prostitute. Demonassa's own daughter committed adultery and had her hair cut and was turned into a prostitute according to the law.

---

93 Ps.-Plu. 1 B.
94 Plu. 140 B.
95 Plu. 142 C.
96 Theano, Letter to Euridice (p. 197 Thesleff) and to Nikostrate (p. 199–200 Thesleff).
97 Aesch. 1.189.

Dio Chrysostom tells this story as a classic tale of self-inflicted unhappiness caused by rigid morals. Demonassa is the writer of her own fate, and despite her wisdom she cannot see that her own heavy-handed actions are destroying her own family. It is unlikely that there is any historical truth in this tale. The only parallel is a story of Megasthenes that the Indians have the right to turn their wives into prostitutes if they are disobedient. This suggests that in reality prostitution as a legal penalty for adultery or any other offense was not imposed anywhere in the Greek world.[98]

4.1.12 Dress rules for prostitutes

12a. Phylarchos *FGrH* 81 F 45 (= Athen. 12.20): Phylarchos in the 25th book of his *Histories* says that there was a law among the Syracusans that women were not to wear gold or flowery clothes, nor dresses with purple borders, unless they admitted that they were common prostitutes.

12b. Clem. Al. *Paed.* 2.10.105: I admire the old city of the Lacedaemonians because it permitted only hetairai to wear flowery dresses and gold, removing the love of cosmetics from respectable women by allowing only hetairai to use them.

The cultural context and implications of these passages are discussed in greater detail in Ch. 2.3.; here it will be sufficient to consider briefly the possibility that in some parts of the Greek world there were laws about dress, which distinguished prostitutes from other persons. Clearly there were sacred laws in some temples which forbade entry to persons wearing ostentatious outfits, as the cases of the temples at Lykosoura and Delos confirm, where entry was prohibited to those wearing flowery clothes.[99] Whether such regulations ever became secular laws of any Greek state is uncertain. All the evidence, that there were actual laws which singled out prostitutes from the clothing that they were allowed or compelled to wear, is late and too inconsistent to be taken seriously, and it may well be the case that local customs and fashion outfits among sexworkers were mistaken for laws. In our times ostentatious and meretricious outfits are not uncommon among sex workers, as part of the paraphernalia of attraction through a certain image, and excessive make up, now as in the past, has been considered "slutty," but no law imposes these outfits like some kind of uniform upon sex workers. In the absence of serious evidence to the contrary, it

---

98 Megasthenes *FGrH* 715 F. 32.
99 *IG* V 2. 514. 3–9; *IG* XI 4.1300; cf Ch. 2.3.

is reasonable to conclude that a few sources have mistaken for laws colorful displays of fashion among sex workers, and made up stories around their ostentatious outfits.

4.1.13 The judgment of Bocchoris

13. Plu. *Demetr.* 27.11: Lamia is also mentioned in the so-called response to the judgment of Bocchoris. While someone in love with the hetaira Thonis in Egypt was being dunned, he had a dream that he slept with her and his desire ceased. Thonis sued him for her fee. Bocchoris, when he heard the case, ruled that the man ought to bring the sum which she was claiming in a vessel and move the vessel here and there with his hand, while the hetaira should take hold of the shadow, because a dream is the shadow of reality. Lamia did not believe that this judgment was fair, because it was the dream that released the young man from his desire, not the shadow of the desire for money.

Hekataios says that the reign of Bocchoris followed that of Amasis (middle of the 7th century), while according to George Synkellos, Bocchoris died in the year 764 after 12 years in power.[100] Either way the historicity of this incident is very doubtful, but apparently it was mentioned as a legal precedent that payment can only be rendered for actual services, and this is why it upset the haughty Lamia. Some evidence from Galen confirms that the tale about the judgment of Bocchoris was quite widespread. He does not mention Bocchoris, but relates a story about Diogenes the Cynic in urgent need of ejaculating, because his regular abstinence (ἐγκράτεια) had accumulated too much sperm, which was causing him pain (ὄχλησις). He called for a prostitute, but as she was late he masturbated and was relieved. When she arrived he sent her away with the comment "the hand came first in singing the wedding song."[101] The basic elements of the story are the same as in Plutarch but the differences are even more significant, as they suggest that this tale was sufficiently widespread to have variations to its main theme. It stands to reason that some legal regulation would be required stating that payment could only be demanded for services rendered, not for mere pursuits or fantasies, and this tale might have provided such regulation by establishing a legal precedent ascribed to a wise king of the past. Even if its historicity was very questionable, the effect of it could still be significant as it

---

100 Synkellos (*Ecloga Chronographica* 216) actually gives the year as 4744 from the creation of the world (5508 in the Byzantine calendar); Hekataios *FGrH* 264 F 25.864.
101 Gal. 8.419.

would discourage sex workers from demanding payment for anything else except actual intercourse, or other specific services agreed in advance.

4.1.14 A fake law in Hermogenes

> 14. Hermog. *Stat.* 2.93–4, Rabe (cf. Valerius Aspines 369.22 Spengel; Syrianus Sch. Hermog. 4.259–60 Walz; Anon. in Hermog. 14.220 Rabe): ... like, if the law says that someone born of a hetaira must not speak in public, someone tries to prevent the son of a male prostitute from speaking in public.

This is one of the pseudo-laws in Hermogenes, in all likelihood modeled on the speech *Against Timarchos*. If anything, the actual source which provided the inspiration for Hermogenes proves that this is a made-up declamatory law, because it is clear in that speech that only male prostitutes were disqualified from advising the assembly, and that this disqualification was personal, not hereditary. On the other hand, in Athens, sons of citizens from prostitutes were full citizens if born before 451, when the Periclean citizenship law was introduced (8b), and between 430 and 403, when this law had fallen in disuse; however, they would be considered as nothoi, and thus disqualified from citizenship for the periods when the Periclean law was in force.

4.1.15 The law forbidding naming prostitutes after four-year festivals

> 15. Athen. 13.51 (= Polemon fr. 3a; cf. Herm. *Inv.* 1.2.47–8 Rabe; Syrianus Sch. ad Hermog. 4.188 Walz): Hypereides in the speech *Against Patrokles* mentions a flute-player named Nemeas. Polemon in the study on the dedications of the Acropolis cites a decree according to which it was forbidden in Athens to give the names of Four-Year festivals to a slave, a libertine, a whore or a flute-player. It is amazing how this name was given to the flute-player.

If Polemon had truly seen evidence of a law forbidding the names of respectable religious festivals like the Olympian, Pythian and Great Panathenaic games celebrated every four years, to be assumed by prostitutes, then beyond reasonable doubt this law was not fully observed. Athenaios, while quoting Polemon, mentions a flute player named Nemeas, and wonders how this could have happened.[102] In fact, there is a number of well-known hetairai drawing their names from Four-Year religious festivals like Olympia of Laconia, the mother of the philosopher Bion Borysthenites, Pythias, and the prominent hetaira Pythionike, the lover of Harpalos. If such a law existed, it would be unenforceable under normal circumstances, because a child was named only days after birth. If a girl had been given the name Olympia after birth, and she became a hetaira when she came of age, how could this law be enforced? It would only make sense if the law was introduced to stop pimps from giving the names of the great religious festivals to hetairai as nicknames, later in life, and even then it would be difficult to prove anything, especially since most prostitutes were not local girls known to the community since childhood, and one could not easily verify what their family name was. On balance, it is not unlikely that such a law existed in the books, but its effectiveness and enforcement in real life was bound to be very limited.[103]

4.1.16 Roman laws regulating marriage with prostitutes

16. *Lex Iulia et Papia: Tituli ex corpore Ulpiani, Tituli 13*: On the unmarried man, childless man, and unmarried man with children.

1. By the *lex Iulia*, senators and their sons are indeed forbidden to marry freedwomen and those who themselves or whose father or mother have been actors or actresses, likewise, a woman making money with her body.

2. Moreover, all other freeborn men are forbidden to marry a procuress and a woman manumitted by a male or female pimp and a woman caught in the act of adultery and her who has been an actress: Mauricianus adds also a woman condemned by the Senate.[104]

---

102 In a lapse of memory Athenaios seems to have forgotten that the Nemean games were celebrated every two years, and thus they would not be covered by the provisions of this decree.

103 On the naming of hetairai see McClure 2003a: 59–78.

104 Tituli 13: *De caelibe orbo et solitario patre.*

1. Lege Iulia prohibentur uxores ducere senatores quidem liberique eorum libertinas et quae ipsae quarumve pater materve artem ludicram fecerit, item corpore quaestum facientem.

2. Ceteri autem ingenui prohibentur ducere lenam et a lenone lenave manumissam et in adulterio deprehensam et iudicio publico damnatam et quae artem ludicram fecerit: adicit Mauricianus et a senatu damnatam.

Citation from McGinn 1998: 91.

This is the primary Roman law prohibiting the marriage between sex-workers and members of the patrician class, and was introduced under Augustus in 18 AD. The problems with the transmission of this law, as well as its content and intentions are discussed by Thomas McGinn, and are outside the purposes of this study, as the impact of this law upon the Greek East before the 3rd c. of the Christian era would be negligible. Even in Rome itself, the actual impact of the law should be small, as prostitutes or pimps did not make likely wives or husbands of Roman citizens, and marriages between citizens and prostitutes hardly ever happened outside the world of New Comedy in East or West, regardless of legal provisions. The *Lex Iulia et Pappia* enshrined into law the long-going practice of marginalizing sex workers, and potentially became an issue in the Greek east only after the *Constitutio Antoniana*, which awarded Roman citizenship to all the inhabitants of the empire in 212 AD. The most famous instance where this law stood as an obstacle to an upper-class Roman is that of Emperor Justinian in the narrative of the *Anecdota* of Prokopios.[105] We are told that he was not allowed to marry Theodora because she had been a prostitute, and that his solution was to repeal the 500 year-old law and marry her, nonetheless. The historical accuracy of this narrative is questionable, but even if the details of the narrative are literary figments, the fact that Prokopios can invoke this law no doubt should be interpreted as evidence that with Christianization and further marginalization of sex-workers from respectable society, the *Lex Iulia et Papia* acquired new momentum and probably new significance in the late empire.

4.2 Male Prostitution, Politics and Homosexual Desire

The study of K.J. Dover *Greek Homosexuality* has dominated the debate on Greek same sex relations, as well as male prostitution, since its publication in the late seventies, and has influenced significantly the pioneering works of Michael Foucault, David Halperin and Jack Winkler in the 1980's and early 1990's. The model of Dover, where an older man as the pursuer (ἐραστής), and a younger man as the pursued (ἐρώμενος) were involved in an unequal relationship, to some degree sexual but under a veneer of friendship (φιλία), and any sexual favors ought to be granted to the dominant older man reluctantly and after persistent requests, has defined perceptions of Greek same sex relations in the past

---

105 Procopius *Anecd.* 9.51; see McGinn 1998: 70–104.

30 years.[106] It was not until the new millennium that a few hesitant voices of dissent were raised.[107] The first study which brought serious objections to the Dover/Foucault model was a little-known doctoral dissertation by Gregory Nall in 2001. On the basis of multidisciplinary and cross-cultural approaches Nall argues that the Dover/Foucault model by lumping all Greek same-sex relationships into a single pattern is fundamentally simplistic, and fails to explore such relationships in all their complexity.[108] Nall in the process points out some of the major methodological errors in Dover's approach, like the misuse and misinterpretation of Attic vase iconography, and the systematic inattention to significant details.

Around the same time a lengthy article by James Davidson was very critical of the emphasis which Dover's model placed upon penetration and the supposed anxieties about it, as well as the sharply defined roles of active and passive, dominant and subordinate, penetrator and penetrated in the definition of same sex relationships. Davidson also provides an interesting discussion on the background of this model, and tries to make sense of it in the context of 1960's and 70's misconceptions about same-sex relationships. In subsequent years Davidson would become the most vocal critic of the Dover/Foucault model, most notably in his large 2007 volume, where he promises a radical re-appraisal

---

106 A good example of the mesmerizing effect which the Dover/Foucault model has had can be found in the 1987 article by David Cohen and the response by Clifford Hindley (1991). Cohen writes in the opening lines (p. 3): "Recent scholarship has succeeded in greatly advancing our understanding of 'Greek homosexuality.' Kenneth Dover and Michel Foucault have argued that the modern dichotomization of sexuality 'as heterosexuality/homosexuality' does not apply to the ancient world, and they have shown how distinctions between active and passive roles in male sexuality defined the contours of the permissible and impermissible in pederastic courtship and other forms of homoerotic behaviour." Clifford Hindley in his response, despite his strenuous objections to the main thesis of Cohen, seems to be treating Dover with the same reverence (e.g. p. 180 "Here, I must state that I find Sir Kenneth Dover's arguments for this distinction compelling," and again p. 181: "I must refer to Dover, who persuasively argues..." and again further down "In support of Dover's exposition..."). It is noteworthy that Hindley fundamentally (and persuasively) disagrees with a key perception in Dover's edifice, the one which suggests that the *eromenos* assumed the feminine role and this is why the Athenians had some anxiety towards same-sex relationships.

107 It is noteworthy that despite the widespread consensus, Eva Cantarella (1992) took a more restrained and sensible approach, and was prepared to accept that the anxieties about penetration had been exaggerated in Dover's model, and that sex did not bring dishonor.

108 For example, Dover's model could not account for pre-adolescent experimentation, or the profound emotional man-to-man attraction (*androphilia*), which extends well beyond sexual roles and in our times would form the basis of a successful same-sex marriage.

of Greek homosexuality. Although Davidson faced sharp criticism,[109] and the Dover/Foucault model still holds an important place in discussions of Greek same-sex relations, some of the luster has faded and increasingly more and more aspects of Dover's views on the subject are coming under scrutiny and adverse criticism.

Dover's entire edifice is based upon two pillars: the speech *Against Timarchos*, and the interpretation of some erotica from Attic vases. The latter I discuss in greater detail in Chapter 6; here I will focus upon the testimony of the speech *Against Timarchos*, assess its reliability and discuss how the law on prostitutes participating actively in politics has fallen prey to the rhetorical manipulation of Aeschines, and has become part of a distorted and misconstrued discussion of Athenian sexual morality.[110] First and foremost, it is an almost universal assumption that Aeschines won this trial because the jury was convinced by his endless barrage of moralistic platitudes. Consequently, some scholars were led to believe that there was a conservative turn in Athenain public opinion, and this this is why the jury accepted the moralistic statements of Aeschines: it must have been because the jury shared his views and values and this is the reason why they sided with him.[111]

This assumption is very unsafe. In a major political trial such as this one the verdict expectedly had much to do with the politics of the time. A comparison with other major political trials from those turbulent years would certainly confirm this. Apollodoros, for example, carried the Assembly with him in his attempt to secure more funds for the campaign against Philip in the summer of

---

109 Most notably by Thomas Hubbard (H-Histsex, February 2009) and Beert Verstraete (*BMCR*, September 2009); see also the response of Davidson in *BMCR*, November 2009.

110 The speech *Against Timarchos* holds a central position in any debate on Greek homosexuality, along with a couple of dialogues of Plato, especially the *Symposion* and *Phaidros*, and a few seriously overstated and misinterpreted jokes of Aristophanes. Much as I would prefer not to turn this account into a discussion on Greek homosexuality, it is impossible to disentangle it from the debate on the laws of prostitution in the secondary literature. This is why it is necessary to clarify a number of widely accepted and repeated statements and assumptions, such as the nature and reliability of the most central of the sources, the speech *Against Timarchos*, or the significance of vase iconography as a source for Athenian social history (which is discussed in more detail in Ch. 6). These two are the main poles around which Dover's theory on Greek homosexual relations has coalesced. It is my contention that these sources are profoundly misleading, each in its own way, and that a complete overhaul of the Dover-Foucault edifice on Greek homosexuality is urgently needed. However, this is a topic much larger than the purposes of this chapter, and this is why here I have tried to focus on male prostitution as tightly as possible.

111 Wallace 1997: 151–166; Lanni 2010: 45–67.

348 BC, when Olynthos was under siege and the Athenians were panicking, but that same proposal was defeated in court through a *graphe paranomon* in less than a year, when the negotiations for the peace of Philocrates were under way, and the Athenians were now in favor of an accommodation with Philip.[112] Timarchos went up against the same political climate in the summer of 346, when this trial came to court. In that year the Pro-Macedonian party, of which Aeschines was a prominent member, was riding high, while the opponents of Philip in Athens were losing the argument for war.[113] Timarchos had the political climate overwhelmingly against him in 346, and this is probably the real reason why he lost this trial. In the light of this, the outcome of this case cannot furnish support for the view that Aeschines expressed the moral majority, or the milieu of Athenian public opinion for much of what he says in this speech.

The second widespread assumption which must be rejected is that Aeschines was knowledgeable, and thus a reliable source on the laws which he quotes and the interpretation of these laws. David Cohen, who is prepared to take the word of Aeschines about these laws, writes:

> In short, the range, variety and overlapping of the Athenian statutes seem to reflect a society which was attempting over a period of time to cope with persistent patterns of behaviour which were felt to jeopardize the well-being of the city. The mechanisms of the public law were deployed to deter and punish such conduct and to protect free boys. Protection from their fathers or relatives who might hire them out, protection from their schoolmasters, protection from seducers, protection from themselves: such legislation reflects strong underlying tensions about homoerotic behaviour.[114]

The main difficulty of Cohen's approach was to reconcile what he believed to be the normative effect of these laws with the actual practices of the Athenians, and this he evaded by resorting to an inconsistent application of this normative intent. Lanni would run into the same difficulty when pushing the same model to its extremes she argued for a widespread normative effect of these laws al-

---

112 D. 59.3–12; Kapparis 1999: com. ad loc. For the date of the trial see Harris 1975: 376–380.
113 One wonders what the outcome of this case would have been if it had reached the courts a few years later, in the 330's, when a disillusioned Athenian public had watched the warnings of Demosthenes about domination from the north come true, and the pro-Macedonian party had been utterly discredited. Let us remember that, for example, in 330 Aeschines lost the case against Ktesiphon so badly that he was disfranchised, even though he was technically correct and had the law on his side, while 70 years earlier a not-so-innocent Andocides walked free from the trial for impiety, because the Athenians were in a mood for forgiveness and reconciliation after 30 years of bloodshed in the Peloponnesian war.
114 Cohen 1987: 9–10.

ready in adolescence.[115] However, in reality it is evident that the Athenians never really acted as this legislative "master plan" would have wanted them to act. They continued to have same-sex relationships, and continued to celebrate them in their literature and art.

The orators often distort facts, present things from a certain standpoint, or make one possible interpretation sound like a universal truth. In this particular instance three things are obvious. First, Aeschines is quoting a number of diverse laws, introduced in different periods and for very different purposes, and is trying to tie them with this particular charge. This does not mean that the ordinary Athenian would have made the same connections in daily life, or indeed that such connections could be reasonably made without purposeful manipulation. Second, on a couple of occasions, as suggested above, he has misrepresented several of these laws. Third, Aeschines is misquoting several obsolete statues as current laws of the Athenian state, although in truth they had not been observed for centuries.

The laws of Solon had survived in the classical period inscribed in boustrophedon script, and the *axones* which contained them were set in an open place where anyone could read them.[116] It stands to reason that some of the laws from the ancient and revered code had been surpassed by historical developments and were no longer relevant or used in 4th century Athens.[117] Aeschines was not concerned with such fine points. He went to the *axones*, found provisions suitable for his argument and presented them in court as active and valid laws of the Athenian state in his time, even though some of them, like for example most of the laws on procurement,[118] had not been invoked for hundreds of years, and no one thought that the activities which they prohibited were illegal anymore in 4th century Athens. Moreover, these provisions were presented as part of a "master plan" by the lawgiver to control homosexual relations, and modern scholars

---

115 Lanni 2010: 45–67.

116 Euphorion in his work *Apollodoros*, apparently mentioned this according to a number of sources (e.g. Anaximenes *FGrH* 72 F 13; Harp. s.v. ὁ κάτωθι νόμος). See also Leão-Rhodes 2016: 1–9, Ruschenbusch 1966 and the review by N.G.L. Hammond (1968: 36–38), who presents the evidence with a brief and concise critique. Leão and Rhodes imagine the *axones* as "revolving wooden beams of square section, set vertically" (p. 5), so that they could accommodate more economically than a wall a large amount of text.

117 For example, the law quoted by Isaios (10.10), according to which a woman could not own property more than one medimnos of barley, although in theory still a valid law of the Athenian state, in reality was not observed, as the presence of women wealthy in their own right like Phryne and Sinope proves.

118 See the discussion in Ch. 4.1., for each of these laws.

have frequently read a deep-seated anxiety about morals in his presentation of this "master plan". Cohen, for example, in the above-mentioned study fully accepts this concept of the "master plan", as does Dover, Patzer and others, without even considering the possibility that no one before Aeschines had ever thought that these disparate and scattered statutes were part of a single piece of legislation.

As discussed above (Ch. 4.1.2), the laws on procurement were genuinely Solonean but introduced for very different reasons. Their primary objective was not to regulate sexual morality, but to protect under-age free boys and girls from exploitation by desperate family members or unscrupulous procurers, as part of the Solonean legislation intended to offer relief to the poorest Athenians. These laws had become dead letter by the time of Aeschines, as the unhindered activity of countless procurers around the city confirms. The laws on seduction and adultery, again, were not a single piece of legislation but separate laws introduced over a long period of time by different persons, as I have argued elsewhere.[119] The laws regulating the operation of schools would probably be little known to most Athenians in their full details, but Aeschines knew them very precisely because his father Atrometos was a schoolteacher. As Nick Fisher has convincingly suggested, it is unlikely that these laws were part of the Solonean legislation; they rather seem to be safety rules and regulations on the operation of schools[120] in effect at the time of Aeschines.[121] The law on *hetairesis* could not have been introduced before the last quarter of the fifth century, and there is a strong likelihood that it actually was a 4th century law, while the law on the *dokimasia* of the speakers in the Assembly probably needs to be dated to the second quarter of the 4th century.[122] Far from being pieces of a "master plan" introduced by a single person and intended to regulate the morals of the Athenians, these laws where introduced by many different people over three centu-

---

119 Kapparis 1995: 97–122.

120 Aeschines, for example, sees an intent to stop sexual acts in the regulation that schools cannot be open before sunrise or after sunset. There is no need to understand that this rule had anything to do with sexual acts. It is a common sense rule, the objective of which was to make sure that children were safely back home before dark.

121 Fisher 2001, 129–133. This conclusion can be easily reached on grounds of language and content. Unlike genuine Solonean laws, no archaic terminology or language can be traced in them, no archaic procedures can be detected, which would seem out of place in the classical period, and above all because they assume institutions like the gymnasium, athletic competitions and musical competitions which we could not imagine as part of the curriculum in the ordinary schools of impoverished Solonean Athens.

122 See the discussion in Ch. 4.1.

ries to serve very different purposes, and there was never a time in Athenian history when all of these scattered laws were valid simultaneously, as Aeschines wanted his audience to believe.

This realization is very significant for the overall picture that we obtain regarding male prostitution in 4th century Athens, as this hodgepodge of valid and obsolete laws from a time period which extends over a quarter of the millennium, by many different people and for different objectives, cannot provide a valid narrative about the alleged anxieties of the Athenians on male sexual morality. We must see the Aeschinean rhetoric for what it was: an isolated and determined attempt to generate a narrative according to which the Athenian state deeply cared about the sexual morality of its citizens from birth to death, simply because such a narrative would be expedient as a means of persuasion in this particular case. In reality, the Athenian democracy never did such a thing, and there is overwhelming evidence to the contrary. The laws of the state stayed away from the private morals of its citizens, so long as their actions did not interfere with important issues of public life like the integrity and suitability of public officials, or the continuation of the citizen stock through legitimately formed families.

When considering the prosecution of Timarchos and the evidence on Athenian morality drawn from it, we are faced with a stark reality: it was a unique event with no precedent and no follow up. No man ever before or after was prosecuted under either of the two laws on prostitutes practicing politics (4a and 4b).[123] Demosthenes confirms this, when he states post eventum that the trial of Timarchos was a stunning and unexpected victory for his opponent and the entire event was a bizarre affair, the like of which had never been seen in Athenian public life, and an exercise in disbelief (ἄνω ἀλλὰ δῆτ' ἄνω ποταμῶν ἐκείνῃ τῇ ἡμέρᾳ πάντες οἱ περὶ πορνείας ἐρρύησαν λόγοι.).[124] It is highly unlikely that the grammarians and rhetoricians of later antiquity, who were so fascinated by the charges of male prostitution brought against Timarchos, would have missed another public case of this kind. This was a freakish incident, a bizarre case, which benefitted from the political climate to score an unexpected victory in court, and decidedly not the expression of mainstream Athenian morality.

---

123 See the discussion in pp. 163–173.
124 D.19 282–287. This is a proverbial expression which in the long history of the Greek language up to the present day has always been used to indicate something very unexpected and unexplainable, like the rivers flowing upwards.

Another issue which seems to have plagued the debate ever since its emergence in the 1980's is the loose definition of the term "pederasty" with reference to the sexual practices of the Greeks. This term, laden with heavy connotations from modern legal and social concerns, has been indiscriminately applied to any relationship involving two Athenian males. Perhaps indicative of how touchy the whole issue may be for modern sensibilities was Davidson's heavily criticized attempt to establish that Greek same sex relations were limited to persons above 18 years of age.[125] The *Athenaion Politeia* specifically confirms that in legal language the Athenians would use the word παῖς (child) in contrast to ἀνήρ (man), to highlight the difference between someone who had been scrutinized and registered with a deme as a citizen (ἀνήρ) and a youth who had not yet undergone the process, or tried to do so but was turned away because he did not appear to have reached his 18th year, and was relegated back to the children (παῖδες) until he reached the right age.[126] However, beyond this legally significant boundary, no attempt has been made so far to draw any kind of distinction between prepubescent children still at school and in need of protection from predatory adults, and sexually grown and active teenagers as old as 17 or 18, one would think partly because modern sensibilities concerning the sexual maturity of teenagers would make such a discussion uncomfortable, and partly because it is generally believed that there is no evidence outlining an age of consent, which would make sex with children below this level statutory rape. David Cohen has asked the question whether the Athenians had an age of consent, and correctly noted the lack of uniformity in the sexual practices of the Greek cities. Cohen, however, was unable to answer conclusively whether there was an age of consent. His suggestion that a *graphe hybreos* might be used to prosecute statutory rape was criticized by Clifford Hindley, and there is absolutely no evidence to support it.[127]

Cohen was certainly asking the right question, as there is a very substantial amount of evidence to suggest that the Athenians had a concept of passage into sexual maturity, and this concept was legally defined too, as the laws on marriage and the *epikleros* (heiress), and a few additional passages suggest. First,

---

125 This view is a core tenet of Davidson's 2007 book, and has been universally rejected. For criticism see Hubbard (H-Histsex, February 2009), Verstraete (*BMCR*, September 2009), al.

126 See Arist. *Ath. Pol.* 42–3.

127 Cohen 1987: 3–21 (especially the series of critically important questions in page 6); Hindley 1991: 167–183 (reply to Cohen); Cohen 1991: 184–194 (reply to Hindley). In addition to the lack of evidence this suggestion runs into the difficulty with *graphe hybreos* outlined above, namely that no one was ever brought to court through this procedure, for any crime and in any context, as far as we know.

the law stated that an *epikleros* should be given in marriage at 14, and her husband ought to have sex with her at least twice a month, to increase the chances
of procreation and repopulation of the oikos. Then, it was customary, if the
marriage contract (ἐγγύη) or the adjudication of an *epikleros* to her future husband (ἐπιδικασία) had been conducted when the woman was younger than 14,
not to complete the process and conduct the marriage ceremony, followed by
the subsequent move into the house of the husband and consummation of the
marriage, until the woman reached that age.[128] Third, the *koureotis*, an offering
at the Apatouria before the phratry which signified that a child had reached
adolescence, happened around a child's 14th year.[129] Fourth, Philo, in his praise
of the customs of the Jews, who did not allow sex before marriage for both men
and women, points out that the rest of the world allows 14 years olds to do as
they please.[130] Finally Xenophon, in his account of the wisdom of Lycurgus for a
life-long endeavor in virtue, states that the rest of the Greeks abandon their
children once they reach adolescence to do as they wish, and they receive no
more schooling.[131]

This evidence firmly suggests a point around the 14th year of age when
someone was thought to be old enough for sexual activity and free to consent to
sexual relations either in a heterosexual or a homosexual context. Females after
this point could become someone's wife and share a home and a bed with him.
Males, on the other hand, would not be able to marry yet, at least not before
registration εἰς ἄνδρας (among the men), and probably not until much later,
when they had the means and maturity to sustain a family. However, they
would be able to form relationships with other young or older men, start attend-
ing symposia with older friends and lovers, lose their virginity to a woman often
paid by an older lover, and eventually, if and when they had the means, start

---

128 For example, the sister of Demosthenes was given in marriage to Demophon when she
was only five (D.27.5). The husband took immediate possession of the very large dowry of 2
talents which came with the girl, but of course she was not expected to move in with him and
commence sexual relations before she was 14. The marriage was never consummated because
Demophon did not honor the contract.
129 Pol. 8.107 and Phot. γ 26: at the same time when girls were ready to be given in marriage
and the *gamelia* (marriage offering) was offered on their behalf, the *koureion* was offered for
boys. However, practice probably varied from phratry to phratry; it seems that some phratries
might allow the ritual to be performed at an earlier age (ten in Pl. *Ti.* 29b).
130 Philo *De Josepho* 43: (passage 1c in Ch. 4.1.1.).: ἐξαιρέτοις ἔθεσι καὶ νομίμοις χρώμεθα
ἡμεῖς οἱ Ἑβραίων ἀπόγονοι. τοῖς ἄλλοις ἐφεῖται μετὰ τὴν τεσσαρεσκαιδεκάτην ἡλικίαν πόρναις
καὶ χαμαιτύπαις καὶ ταῖς ὅσαι μισθαρνοῦσιν ἐπὶ τοῖς σώμασι μετὰ πολλῆς ἀδείας χρῆσθαι, παρ'
ἡμῖν δὲ οὐδ' ἑταίρα ζῆν ἔξεστιν.
131 X. *Lac.* 3.1

chasing hetairai, or have sex with domestic slaves or the cheaply available women in the brothels and streets around Attica. With all these options open, one's tastes and sexual preferences would determine the nature of these relationships, but all were considered part of the privilege and experience of being an Athenian male.

There should be no doubt that the Athenians understood and recognized this passage into sexual autonomy, even if grudgingly, like modern parents do. In this respect they did exactly what modern legal systems do, namely they were prepared to acknowledge the sexual autonomy of teenagers once their bodies reach a certain level of development. The average age of consent in our times is very similar to that of the Athenians. It is set at 14 for about a quarter of the world's population, while the worldwide average is around 15 or 16 with limits as low as 12 in some places.[132] The customs of the Athenians were by no means unusual in this respect. In this context, it would be reasonable to assume that boys and girls who entered into prostitution did so not long after the age of 14, and had a few precious years to make the most of their tender youth. Women might be able to have a longer run than boys, as their appearance did not change as dramatically when they reached adulthood in their late teens or early twenties.

This realization should cast new light upon Aeschines' presentation on the laws governing schools, athletic competitions and the modest conduct of children, and their supposed connection to male prostitution. Athenian parents were as protective of their young as modern parents are, and this is why they had attendants to take the children to school and keep an eye on them, and a whole set of rules and regulations related to the operations of schools which were intended to enhance the safety of the children. Thus, the answer to the question of what the laws about the protection of children too young to have sexual relations have to do with the laws on prostitutes practicing politics ought to be "nothing at all." The inclusion of these laws in the speech Against Timarchos is for rhetorical effect, and this is why they are not mentioned at all as relevant in any of the other sources on the laws regulating prostitution, like, for example, the all-important passages in the speech *Against Androtion*, the prob-

---

132 Modern legal systems set the age of consent usually around 16. Among different US states it fluctuates between 14 and 18, with 16 been the most common. A slightly lower age of consent is generally the rule among European countries: 14 is not uncommon (e.g. Italy, Estonia, Bulgaria, Albania), and in some places it is set even lower (e.g. 13 in Spain). 14 is also the age of consent in China. Throughout the world it fluctuates between 12 and 21 (online data: http://www.avert.org/age-of-consent.htm).

able model of the Aeschinian legal narrative. Aeschines by reminding the Athenians the great lengths to which they go to protect their children suggests that if they failed to do so, their children would become prostitutes, like Timarchos. In a similar argument Apollodoros suggested in the speech *Against Neaira* that unless they punish the former hetaira their unmarried daughters will be taking up prostitution, and the more frivolous of their wives will be taking lovers. This scaremongering does not have any inherent reasoning or basis upon reality, but might have been effective as a means of persuasion of a large audience acting on instinct. In reality, the Athenians, like any parent, could tell the difference between sexually active teenagers who could consent to sexual relations, and prepubescent children that needed to be protected.

Related to this issue is a rather uneasy and distorted presentation of Greek same-sex relations in some of the literature as ideally asexual, or stopping short of penetration at the very most. On the basis of some erotic representations in vase paintings, where lovers are presented with a flaccid penis while being penetrated - no doubt an indication that they were not supposed to enjoy themselves, according to Dover - and the misreading of a few literary sources, such as some Aristophanic jokes and the high-pitched rhetoric of Aeschines in *Against Timarchos*, Dover reached some absurd conclusions, which essentially removed any form of love, pleasure or self-respect from Greek homosexual relations. In this bizarre universe there are two kinds of males, the *erastai*, namely older men with pederastic instincts going to great lengths to secure the favor of young boys (*eromenoi*) who were supposed to seek the intellectual gifts of the older man, but repel his sexual advances.[133] Ideally they should refuse any kind of sex altogether, but if the *erastes* persisted they might just give in unwillingly to

---

133 The terminology as well as the basic concepts of the pursuer and the pursued, the gift-giving, and the ceaseless games of request, refusal and "catch me if you can" are based upon the famous speech of Pausanias in Plato's *Symposion* (180 c – 185 c), of which Dover published a commentary in the Cambridge "green and yellow" series only two years after his book on Greek Homosexuality. It is noteworthy that the term ἐρώμενος (*eromenos*), which has prevailed in modern literature along with the concept of the "passive" and subordinate lover, is virtually absent in classical authors outside the works of Plato and his circle (e.g. Aristotle and Xenophon). Thucydides, for example, does not use the term *eromenos* at all, as he narrates the famous incident of the tyrannicides. He simply says that Aristogeiton became the lover (*erastes*) of Harmodios (6.54: ἐραστὴς ὢν εἶχεν αὐτόν), while the super-masculine Harmodios could never be fitted into this passive/subordinate model. This evidence may astoundingly suggest that, along with the term which we have adopted from the colorful Platonic vocabulary, we may have inadvertently adopted the entire concept of the pursued/subordinate/passive lover.

some intercrural sex, or maybe a bit more but only very reluctantly, and so long as they did not enjoy it.[134]

The absurd concept of intercrural sex initially developed by Dover on the basis of a few vase paintings and scarce references to the term διαμηρίζειν has found an unexpected amount of support.[135] It is astonishing that such weak and unsafe evidence has been considered sufficient to declare intercrural sex to be universal practice and the ideal form of Greek homosexual love. At the same time it is noteworthy that the only instance in which "taking apart the thighs " (διαμηρίζειν) appears in classical Greek literature it refers to heterosexual sex, and may simply imply intercourse in the missionary position.[136] Several references in a male-to-male context come from authors of later antiquity, and even in those instances "taking the thights apart" does not inevitably indicate intercrural intercourse.[137] These scant and problematic references suggest that intercrural contact on occasion might have been one possible hypotonic and somewhat unsatisfactory avenue of sexual gratification, but it certainly would not have been worth a long pursuit, lavish gifts, and the fuss which ancient sources make over same sex relations. If anything, Athenian men were never that desperate for sex, having a large and diverse prostitutional market at their disposal, and slaves to satisfy their whims. Moreover, if intercrural sex had been this universal and morally superior practice in homosexual love, the one associated with the Uranian Aphrodite, as Kenneth Dover, Harald Patzer and others have suggested, we should have expected to hear a lot more about it in classical sources. This forced interpretation of such scanty evidence is fueled by modern taboos about anal intercourse, domination, penetration and shame, which the ancient world obviously did not share.

Harald Patzer took this point even further in his 1982 study *Die griechische Knabenliebe*; he was convinced that there could be no anal intercourse at all

---

134 I am prepared to give some credence to Davidson's impression that Dover's perception of same-sex relations has been colored from the bonding of teenage boys in single-sex English boarding schools in the middle of the twentieth century. A guilt-ridden game of domination, with an older boy pursuing a younger one, and the younger being obliged to refuse, lest he might appear to be eager, seemingly was a common expression of overflowing teenage sexuality, and many a time had nothing to do with desire, but much to do with power. This model does not fit well into the Greek reality, because the power component is far less significant.

135 Dover 1978: 100–109; Halperin 88–112.

136 Ar. *Av.* 1254, where Pisthetairos is threatening to give Iris a demonstration of how stiff his penis can get despite his old age.

137 Some of these references are reported as quotes from classical authors like Zenon and Kleanthes: Zenon fr. 250–252 von Arnim = S.E. M. 190; Kleanthes fr. 613 von Arnim = D.L. 7.172.

because that would devalue and compromise the future citizens of Athens.[138] He believed that the Greek homosexual experience was some form of very ritualistic and sanitized form of pederasty, which could not include distasteful practices such as anal or oral sex. Only intercrural intercourse would be respectable enough to be included in the menu. There is no question that this concept of "devaluation" reflects modern stereotypes, not Athenian attitudes on sex, as Davidson has very convincingly demonstrated.[139] Only a culture which typically perceives same sex relationships as inferior, and the mechanics of man- to-man sex as demeaning and compromising, would view the same sex affairs of the Athenians as improper and unsuitable for the future citizens of the first democracy.

Mark Golden pushing the point to extremes has argued that the passive lover was placed in a position not much different from that of a mere slave, unwillingly serving the lustful desires of the active partner, in the manner that a slave would do his master's bidding.[140] The paradox of equating masculine upper class boys, hotly pursued by adoring lovers, with lowly slaves somehow does not seem to cause any concern in this strange mix of 20th century fetishes and outdated sexual politics. However, Greek culture was different from ours in one significant aspect: it viewed the mechanics of man-to-man sex as somewhat different but not inferior to those of man-to-woman sex, and this is simply why it did not need to have the same anxieties about "compromising" the virtue of young men. A society where sex between two men was not inferior to heterosexual intercourse, but simply a matter of preference, which could readily shift or steadfastly remain unchanged without sparking a sexual identity crisis either way, would not be anxious about who has been penetrating whom and how often, and countless sources suggest that the Greek city states did not burden themselves with such worries.

Thomas Hubbard[141] rejects the widely accepted thesis, propagated by several influential names such as Foucault, Dover and Halperin, that the Greeks had no perception of homosexuality as a cultural construct.[142] On the basis of an admittedly weak article by John Thorp, Hubbard argues that the Athenians had as much anxiety about homosexuality as modern societies do.[143] Shortly after-

---

138 Patzer 1982; See also the lengthy review of Patzer by Halperin 1986: 34–45.
139 Davidson 2007: 119–145; 2001: 3–51; Golden 1984: 308–324.
140 Golden 1984: 308–324.
141 Hubbard 1998: 48–78.
142 Foucault 1986; Halperin 1990, part 1; Dover 1978: 84–90; Winkler 1990: 45–70 al.
143 Thorp 1992: 54–65.

wards Giulia Sissa reiterated this position in opposition to the support which Michael Foucault had lent to the view that homosexuality as an anthropological and cultural construct does not exist before the 19th century.[144] Sissa's argument was that the ancients conceived homosexuality as an identity. However, the only passages which conceivably could lend some credibility to this argument are references to caricatures, literary constructs in comedy, like Agathon, or Kleisthenes (who, by the way, had a wife), or in oratory, like Timarchos (who also spent a fortune on female hetairai, was not a prostitute, and his love-life probably differed from that of other Athenians only in its excesses), or Misgolas, whose portrait in both *Against Timarchos* and Attic Comedy is too stereotypical to lend support to such a significant matter.

It would be very remarkable if the Greeks, who have a term for everything, would not have a single word meaning "homosexual," if they were driven by anxieties about sexual identities. Terminology defines the way we think, [145] and we can actually observe that Greek eventually generated derogatory terms for men who had sex with men in later antiquity, when same-sex intercourse started being viewed as unproductive, and eventually, a vice, a sin, an inferior form of sexual activity, and something which needed to be differentiated and separated from necessary, and consequently virtuous, procreational heterosexual intercourse. The precise meaning of terms like ἀρσενοκοίτης (literally: a man

---

144 Sissa 1999: 147–168. It is noteworthy that Foucault has been influential in Sissa's work, as a whole. Here are some of Foucault's statements, which make the point to which Sissa was objecting: p. 18: "In 19th century texts that is a stereotypical portrait of the homosexual or invert: not only his mannerisms, his bearing, the way he gets dolled up, his coquetry, but also his special expressions, his anatomy, the feminine morphology of his whole body, are regularly included in this disparaging description. The image leads both to the theme of role reversal and to the principle of a natural stigma attached to this offense against nature." p. 187: "The Greeks did not see love for one's own sex and love for the other sex as opposites, as two exclusive choices, two radically different types of behavior. The dividing lines did not follow that kind of boundary. What distinguished a moderate, self-possessed man from one given to pleasures was from the viewpoint of ethics much more important than what differentiated, among themselves, the categories of pleasures that invited the greatest devotion." P. 188 "Were the Greeks bisexual, then? Yes, if we mean by this that a Greek could, simultaneously or in turn, be enamored of a boy or a girl; that a married man could have paidika; that it was common for a male to change to a preference for women after 'boy-loving' inclinations in his youth. But if we wish to turn our attention to the way in which they conceived of this dual practice, we need to take note of the fact that they did not recognize two kinds of 'desire,' two different or competing 'drives,' each claiming a share of men's hearts or appetites. ... To their way of thinking what made it possible to desire a man or a woman was simply the appetite that nature had implanted in man's heart for 'beautiful' human beings, whatever their sex might be."
145 See Kapparis 2011: 222–255

who lies with men) or θηλυδρίας (a girly man), which begin to be used from the 1st c. AD, is very difficult to pin down. For example, ἀρσενοκοίτης appears twice in the letters of Paul in both instances in conjunction with πόρνος (male prostitute), and it has been reasonably argued that it means "male prostitute".[146] One thing is certain: than neither of these terms, nor any other word ever used by the Greeks, even in later antiquity, comfortably corresponds to the modern term "homosexual", as an individual with a distinct, permanent and inalienable sexual and cultural identity. The reason why the Greeks never employed such a term must be because they never constructed this identity.[147] On the other hand, since they had a very clear, even if complicated, concept of male prostitution, they created more than 100 terms over the centuries to denote its multiple facets, and when it came to the laws on prostitutes in politics, they could see very clearly the dividing line between relationships based on desire, love, attraction and affection, and those based on money, profit, leeching and parasitic living.[148] In this instance their choice of words tells the story and explains why Foucault and Halperin's view of "homosexuality" as a modern cultural concept is broadly correct.

Much of the debate on male homosexuality and the laws of prostitution is built upon the argument that such practices were limited to a small group of upper class elite men. This argument is widespread in modern scholarship, it is central in the work of Thomas Hubbard and Giulia Sissa, and traceable back to the studies of Jack Winkler and David Halperin in the 1980's and early 1990's. Winkler writes:

> It cannot be said too strongly or too frequently that the selection of booktexts now available to us does not represent Greek society as a whole. The social and editorial conventions

---

146 ἀρσενοκοίτης: *1 Ep. Cor.* 6.9; *1 Ep. Ti.* 1.10. θηλυδρίας: Arist. *Pr.* 879 b 21 (attempting to describe some form of bizarre intersexuality); D.H. 7.2.4. See also the discussion in Petersen 1986: 187–191; Wright 1984: 125–153, and 1987: 396–398; Kapparis 2011: 222–255. Thereafer, the term appears many times in Christian authors, mostly in the form of repetition of the Pauline passages, and always with a hostile tone, until the 8th century. After that it becomes rather rare and irrevocably drops out of the language at some point in the Comnenian period (12th c.) with the decline of patristic literature. Modern Greek never reclaimed this odd term, but has used Greek stems to generate a term based on the western neologism "homosexual" (ὁμοφυλόφιλος).
147 Eva Cantarella (1992) in her sensible account of same sex relations in the Graeco-Roman world has tried to use the more inclusive term "bisexuality," but in the light of this discussion, this term would be inadequate too. To the Greeks all sexual activity was a continuum of possibilities, different tastes and preferences.
148 See Kapparis 2011: 222–255.

within which most public speaking and published writing took place tended to give voice to a select group of adult male citizens and to mute the others: female, adolescent, demotic, metic.[149]

Consequently Winkler tries to move away from the high literature of the period, like philosophy, which in his mind represents the elite, and focus on more low-brow texts, like dream interpretation manuals, which may preserve a more wholesome view of popular morality. This methodological approach has merit, but Winkler curiously failed to see the most obvious point in his own approach, namely that homosexual love appears to be an elitist practice only because certain of our sources are elitist. Once we move away from the Platonic circle, the practice does not seem to be quite so elitist. For example, Thucydides makes the comment that Aristogeiton was an ordinary citizen (ἀνὴρ τῶν ἀστῶν, μέσος πολίτης), and not a member of some aristocratic elite, when he succeeded in attracting the affections of Harmodios, who was very handsome (γενομένου δὲ Ἁρμοδίου ὥρᾳ ἡλικίας λαμπροῦ), and from a good enough family to be deemed worthy of pursuit by Hipparchos, the tyrant of the city.

Comedy, which routinely offers us glimpses into the lives of the ordinary Athenians, portrays a very different and much less elitist picture from the literature of the Socratic/Platonic circle. A significant passage from the *Knights* makes the point that boys often form relationships with low class men, because they fall in love, and they prefer these lovers to more worthy, upper-class men (καλούς τε κἀγαθούς):

> You are like boys who have fallen in love;
> You do not want more upper-class men
> But offer yourself to lamp-sellers, and cobblers
> And shoe-makers and tanners.[150]

The passage unambiguously suggests that same-sex affairs, pursuit and erotic games were not the exclusive privilege, or exclusive vice, as some of the literature has implied, of the upper classes, but a possibility for every Athenian. The same conclusion can be inferred from the narrative of Aeschines about the affair of Timarchos with Pittalakos.[151] Even if this affair is completely fictional, the fact that Aeschines could claim before an Athenian jury that it was real can only mean that a low-class libertine could conceivably have a male lover. Later in the

---

149 Winkler 1990: 19; see also Halperin 1990: 88–112.
150 Ar. *Eq.* 737–740.
151 Aesch. 1.54–69.

speech, when Aeschines is providing lists of worthy and unworthy lovers, boys and men, his criterion for separating the two groups is neither class nor money, but moral worthiness. Even if we were to consider this a mere cliché, again the fact that he can plausibly include it in his rhetorical strategy needs to be taken as an indication that same-sex love affairs between lower-class men were neither frowned upon, nor unusual in any respect. Then, didn't Aristophanes himself, so often quoted as a source of rather homophobic expressions, say in the *Wealth* that only whorish boys ask for money?

> Ka. They say that boys do this act
> Not as a favor (χάριν) to lovers, but for the money.
> Chr. Not the decent ones, but the whores;
> For decent boys do not ask for money.[152]

Pausanias in the *Symposium*, Aeschines himself in the argumentation of the speech *Against Timarchos* and a myriad of other sources draw clear distinctions between a boy's affection for a worthy lover in a relationship based on *charis*, a concept well explained by James Davidson, Alan Shapiro and Elke Hartmann, and on the other hand one based on expensive gifts and financial transactions of some sort or other.[153] This literature has been cynically interpreted as a façade, an excuse of the dissolute upper classes to engage in their vices. Such cynicism is unnecessary and historically inaccurate. If, on other hand, we accept the substantial testimony of several classical authors that the *dikaios eros* was not based on money or class, but on virtue and character, every respectable citizen should be in the position to pursue a love affair with a youth or man, regardless of his financial muscle. We should not we find it difficult to believe that men of modest means could attract and foster the love of respectable men or boys through their good character, physical appearance and attractive personality. And even if we decided to be cynical and reject all the evidence from classical authors talking about the purity of love between two males as a façade to justify sexual relations that were frowned upon, we still cannot limit same-sex relations to an elite practice as the presence of numerous boys in the brothels of the city, most likely accessible at a modest price, proves that poor men too might enjoy physical contact with other males.

---

152 Ar. *Plu.* 153–156.
153 The relevant evidence is thoroughly presented by Davidson 2001: 20–28. On the concept of *charis* as a foundation of the *dikaios eros* (fair love) see Davidson 2007: 37–75; Shapiro 1981: 133–143; Hartmann 2002: 169–172 al.

With so many references to homosexual relations in all settings, social classes and geographical regions throughout antiquity, enough to make homosexual love known as the "Greek Love" in the literature of modern times, it is highly unlikely that the *dokimasia* and *hetairesis* laws had or were intended to have any kind of restraining normative effect upon homosexual relations among the Athenians. The Periclean saying in the Funeral Oration comes to mind, where Athenian attitudes to private life and personal gratification are explained:

> We are not angry with our neighbor if he does something for pleasure, nor do we look annoyed, which is not injurious per se, but it is unpleasant. In our private lives we conduct ourselves without anger.[154]

Robert Wallace correctly acknowledges the significance of this passage, while he rightly explains that the Athenians generally did not legislate on private acts which did not infringe upon other men's families. However, he still considers homosexual relations to be linked to an elite who did not want controls on their more licentious practices.[155] It is very telling for the Athenian moral compass that in this monumental defense of the way of life in the first democracy, of which Pericles is the mouthpiece, respect for private life holds such a prominent place. Trying to stop one's neighbor from having fun is un-Athenian and undemocratic. This is what the "others" are doing, and such a thing could only happen in secretive and authoritarian societies, run by fear and conspiracy, like Sparta. In Athens people are free to live and enjoy their lives, in an open and relaxed environment where neighbors let each other do as they please so long as they observe their obligations to their neighbors and the common good, and they do so with self-restraint and moderation.

Adriaan Lanni accepts that the laws on prostitute politicians were intended for an elite, but she believes that their impact was widespread and had affected many more people than the "elites." [156] Lanni has argued that the laws described in Aeschines had a normative effect, and discouraged young boys from engaging in homosexual relations. She erroneously dates the *dokimasia* and *hetairesis* laws to the middle of the 5th century and argues that after that point all same sex pursuits were curbed, and not only those based on a financial exchange. In reality these were probably 4th century laws with no normative effect, and no

---

154 Th. 2.37.
155 Wallace 1997: 151–-66. The article of Wallace makes an important contribution at the point where he outlines the attitude of the Athenians to private life, but somehow, in an unexpected twist of logic he views this as licentious behavior of the upper classes, not tolerance.
156 Lanni 2010: 45–67.

such intention either.[157] There is absolutely no evidence to suggest that these laws ever had any kind of impact in Athenian public or private live, and we should not be surprised by this. The prosecution of Timarchos under the *dokimasia* law was not a routine case; it was an unparalleled event which only makes sense as a political move within the vicious and complex network of maneuvers and negotiating tactics surrounding the peace of Philocrates.

These laws were relevant to a tiny demographic, the ἀπράγμονες, πόρνοι κοὐχὶ τῶν σεμνῶν of Eupolis.[158] The number of Athenian citizens who reportedly had practiced prostitution can be counted on the fingers of one hand; there are only five confirmed cases known to us (and the word "confirmed" is used liberally).[159] These men were Diophantos the orphan, Kephisodoros the so-called (καλούμενον) son of Molon, Mnesitheos the so-called son of the cook (τὸν τοῦ μαγείρου καλούμενον), Aristion, who was sent to Alexander,[160] and Theodotos the Plataian.[161] All of these men were low-class from poor backgrounds, and it is highly unlikely that any of them ever had political ambitions. If they represent the typical male citizen prostitute, and we have every reason to believe that they do, then the number of confirmed prostitutes who had an eye on a political career comes down to zero. This is why it is much easier to believe that these laws, far from having a widespread normative effect and functioning as a powerful deterrent for scores of Athenians, had little practical significance as the demographic which they could potentially affect was negligible.

I am convinced that the two laws banning prostitutes from politics and public office, along with persons who had wasted their inheritance, parent-abusers, draft-dodgers, cowards and deserters, were seen as protective measures from corruption and bad decisions in public life, as Demosthenes suggests in *Against Androtion*. D. M. MacDowell agreed with this explanation: "I suppose that these activities were considered to be signs that a man had weak

---

157 I have argued that both laws probably should be dated to the 4th c. See the discussion in Ch. 4.1.
158 Eupolis IFF 8.4: "the good-for-nothing, whores, and not respectable people"
159 Four of them are known from Aeschines, who may not be the most reliable source in this case, but the absence of evidence to the contrary allows us to accept his testimony, even if it is with reservations.
160 See Ch. 3.1.
161 Aesch. 1.158; 3.162; Diyllos FGrH 73 F 2; Harp. s.v. Aristion and Lys. 3. We must exclude from the count men like Timarchos, Epichares, Androtion or Knossion, the friend of Demosthenes, who were slandered by their political opponents, with no serious evidence to substantiate the allegations. In the absence of corroborating evidence we must treat such references with extreme skepticism.

judgement or a poor moral character, so that any advice which he gave to his fellow-citizens was likely to be unreliable or immoral."[162] Edward Cohen in his latest book convincingly presenting classical Athens as a diverse society and prostitution as a practice that cut through social class, has provided an interesting interpretation of the laws trying to limit prostitution among the leaders of the city as the result of economic anxieties. He argues that conservative Athenian circles did not wish the leaders of the city to be profiting from lowly professions, and probably there is a fair amount of truth in this argument, too. A man profiteering from dirty jobs is not a suitable leader, as the *Knights* of Aristophanes so strenuously suggests. Cohen is probably right when arguing that, at least among the more conservative citizens of Athens, a male prostitute or pimp was as unsuitable a leader for the demos as the legendary "sausage-seller" of the play, because, regardless of morals, they made their living from humble professions and infused the political life of the city with a pervasive unworthiness and lowly self-interest.[163]

These laws also had to do with procedural and ritual correctness in the performance of public duty, especially in the case of the nine archons. Aeshines actually says so much when he reminds the jury that some of these offices included religious and performing duties (στεφανηφόρος ἡ ἀρχή), and it is precisely the performance of these duties that made the exclusion of prostitutes and other social undesirables imperative. This conclusion is strengthened by the fact that the actual demographic of citizen prostitutes targeted by these laws was so negligible that one wonders why laws excluding them were needed at all. It only makes sense if the objective was the correct performance of the rituals and duties of magistrates, priests and ambassadors, in which case the number of individuals targeted was irrelevant, as a single unsuitable person would have been sufficient to offend the gods and violate ritual correctness.[164] The law was trying to prevent this from happening with a blanket ban of all unsuitable persons regardless of numbers or practical considerations. Such a law would be perfectly within the spirit of other Athenian provisions motivated by religious or ritual observance, like for example the ban of disabled citizens from the office of

---

162 MacDowell 2005: 81.

163 Cohen 2000: 113–148; 2003: 214–36; 2005: 39–62; 2007: 201–24.

164 See for example the fuss which the Areopagos council made, when they learned that the wife of the *archon basileus* had been married before, even though she was expected by law to be on her first marriage (D.59.80–87, and Kapparis 1999, ad loc.). A practically insignificant issue was treated like a major infraction, and only the pledge of the *archon basileus* to divorce his wife satisfied the Council.

the nine archons, or the ban of first generation naturalized citizens from hereditary priesthoods, or from becoming one of the nine archons.[165]

In this long and not always objective debate which started in the 1970's it has been widely assumed that Aeschines represents the milieu of Athenian morality, which was far less favorable to same sex love affairs than elitist literary sources, like for example the Platonic dialogues, would have us believe. Curiously the obvious weaknesses of Aeschines as a source, his amateurish approach to legal matters, the complete lack of evidence in the form of witnesses or documents for almost every single one of his assertions about the morals of Timarchos, and his high-pitched rhetoric, intended to compensate for this lack of evidence, have been understated. Scholars often rest comfortably upon the fact that he won this trial and he must therefore express the morality of the average Athenian. The possibility that the outcome of this trial may have nothing to do with the moral banalities of Aeschines and everything to do with the messy politics surrounding the peace of Philocrates has been largely overlooked. Moreover, the 25 sections (or 1/8 of the entire speech), which Aeschines has devoted to drawing an unmistakably clear line between respectable homoerotic affairs (δίκαιον ἔρωτα) and prostitutional relations, have been sidelined or interpreted as a concession to those jurors with pederastic preferences.[166] However, 1/8 of the entire speech cannot be a mere concession as it is too long and too important to be brushed aside, while the entire concept of *dikaios eros*, where two lovers of the same sex develop a rich, lasting and constructive relationship which goes far beyond physical contact, is not only important for Aeschines but also a dominant theme in Greek literature over a long span of time, as William Armstrong Percy III has amply demonstrated.[167] The inclusion of the lengthiest account in Greek literature interpreting the mythical friendship between Achilles and Patroclus as a respectable and deeply felt love-affair which transcended death, and Aeschines' own admission that he is keen on love affairs with boys and had many of those himself, have been understated in the debate, because these themes do not fit into the dominant interpretation of Aeschines as a source riddled with anxieties over Athenian sexual morality.

The line which Aeschines, Pausanias in Plato, and Aristophanes draw between youths of good character who would take a lover because of attraction, admiration and love, but never for money, is often treated as superficial rhetoric, but it need not be; this line is very clearly defined. Male prostitutes might

---

165 See Kapparis 1995: 359–378.
166 Aesch. 1.136–160.
167 William A, Percy III 2006: 13–62.

pretend to be "companions" or "friends" or "lovers" of their clients, but no one would miss the difference between these affairs and relationships based on genuine love, affection and admiration.

The *hetairesis* and *dokimasia* laws make no mention of homosexual relations, the mechanics of man to man sex, penetration, anal intercourse, domination, submission, gender role reversals or any of the 20th century mythology on the subject. The laws in fact have no interest whatsoever in the sexual acts or the mechanisms of love-making between consenting lovers. They are only concerned with a single matter, and this is whether money or other financial rewards had been exchanged, and even then only if the person who offered his body for money was trying to play a leading role in the politics of the city. Certainly the matter in question is not the sexual preferences or favorite positions of the participants during intercourse, but the sale of one's body for money. One wonders how many of us would be willing to vote into political office a man or woman who has openly been a prostitute, and we should not find it puzzling if most Athenians had some difficulty with that too. The Romans certainly found it unacceptable, and so did most cultures in history.

Michael Foucault insightfully wrote: "The Greeks did not see love for one's own sex and love for the other sex as opposites, as two exclusive choices, two radically different types of behavior. The dividing lines did not follow that kind of boundary. What distinguished a moderate, self-possessed man from one given to pleasures was from the viewpoint of ethics much more important than what differentiated, among themselves, the categories of pleasures that invited the greatest devotion." Moderation and self-control are key concepts in the 2005 study of Stephen Roismann exploring perceptions of masculinity in the Attic Orators.[168] Roismann rightly argues that youthful indiscretions might be forgiven, but an adult male citizen needed to be able to demonstrate self-control. Aeschines goes to great lengths to describe with colorful images the excesses of Timarchos, especially in the alleged affair with Hegesandros. He needed to do so, because if he had simply said that the two of them had the occasional party and shared good food and the company of a hetaira, he would score no points; this is what young citizen men did. Aeschines needed to demonstrate that what the two men were doing was immoderate, out of control and excessive, and this he does to the full extent. Although lack of control would not in any way constitute proof of guilt in this case, it would be an effective mechanism for generating prejudice against the defendant. A man who was so immoderate and out of control could conceivably commit undignified acts on his body.

---

168 See Roismann 2005.

The accounts of both Demosthenes in the speech *Against Androtion* and Aeschines in *Against Timarchos* make clear that the Athenians did not object to someone who had been a prostitute coming to the Assembly or voting; things became complicated only if that person sought leading positions in politics. The two laws dealing with prostitutes in politics are irrelevant for our understanding of homosexuality in the ancient Greek world, as they have nothing to do with sexuality, morality, desire, sexual positions and preferences, private acts or private life as a whole. These two laws are very much concerned with the public life of the city, honesty, integrity while advising the city or exercising public office, and respectability when representing the city as ambassador in foreign lands, all qualities incompatible with the popular perception of a prostitute's lowly lifestyle. This is not hard to understand, and there is nothing particularly strange or problematic in the desire of the Athenian state to have persons with integrity, good character, honesty, and respectability advising the people and holding the public offices of the state.

4.3 Violence and Abuse

In Byzantine iconography the image of the prostitute in hell, tortured and physically abused with hot rods in the genital regions, forks and other instruments of pain is a standard topic. This somber and highly spiritual art form of the Byzantines, which usually focused on more elevated topics, allowed representations of indecent torture, so long as these were images of hell and punishments directed at the prostitute. One of the most heavily debated issues in the modern bibliography on prostitution is the extent and forms of violence inflicted by clients, pimps, law-enforcement organizations and individuals against women and men in prostitution.[169] Farley and Barkan, after interviewing 130 men, women and transgender people working as prostitutes in the San Fransisco area found that 82% were physically assaulted as adults in prostitution. Kathleen Barry reports a similar figure of 78% from the Council for Prostitution Alternatives, adding that 48% were raped by pimps an average of 16 times a year.[170] A British study led by S. Church came up with very similar numbers for street prostitution (81%), but considerably smaller numbers for prostitutes working

---

169 See Matthews 2008: 45–48, with references to previous bibliography; Baldwin 1992; Brents – Hausbeck 2005; Church et al. 2001; Farley 2003, and Farley – Barkan 1998; Lazos 2002; Lowman – Fraser 1995.
170 Barry 1995: 36.

indoors (48 %). Only 34% of the assaults were reported to the police. The same study found considerable deviations from one city to another, and concluded that a street prostitute in Glasgow was six times more likely to be assaulted than a prostitute working indoors in Edinburgh.[171] A study of legalized prostitution in Nevada yielded similar results concluding that the scrutiny and regulations in legal brothels afforded additional protection and reduced the risks of violence.[172]

This evidence is significant for the study of ancient prostitution, because one wonders how much of the actual violence is reported in our sources. As a matter of fact, most reports of violence in classical authors concern brothels or private houses of well-known prostitutes. If the findings in modern studies could be applied, even very roughly, to the ancient reality, one would think that the level of violence reported in our sources is only a fraction of that which reached the courts or was reported in some form or another, and that would represent a tiny fraction of the actual violence in the brothels of the ancient world, which in turn would be a significantly smaller percentage compared to the violence against street prostitutes. Slave prostitutes had no direct recourse to the law and their only protection from pimps and traffickers was the fact that broken bones and bruises do not look attractive. On the whole, what we find in our sources might only be the tip of the iceberg, but even so, reports of verbal abuse, stalking, physical violence, drunken brawls, abductions, fights, sometimes ending up in vicious and protracted litigation, deceit, rape, child-abuse, torture, and even self-directed violence leading to suicide can be found scattered in the literature of the ancient world.

Several Attic law court speeches have been preserved where prostitution features prominently, and these provide important information about violence against sex-workers. One of the earliest attested court-cases for sexual violence against a prostitute is the trial of Philonides for rape or sexual assault of the hetaira Nais. The facts of the case remain elusive since we only have a few fragments from the prosecution speech, attributed to Lysias.[173] Harpocration doubted the authenticity of the speech, but the issue is unimportant for our attempt to understand the facts of the case, because even if it was not written by Lysias it certainly comes from the same time period. The infamous love affair between the accused and the hetaira Nais may also be mentioned in a passage from Aristophanes *Wealth*, where very plausibly Harpocration, followed by Athenaios and Suda, wanted to change the reading of the manuscripts from "Lais" to

---

171 Church et al. 2001: 524–525.
172 Brents – Hausbeck 2005: 270–295.
173 Lys. fr. 140 Carey.

"Nais." [174] Nais is also mentioned in the speech of Lysias, *Against Medon on the False Testimony*,[175] the *Gerytades* of Aristophanes, and as a toothless, old woman in the *Huntress* of Philaiteros.[176] According to Athenaios, Nais was also the subject-matter of an encomium by Alcidamas of Elea.[177] All this evidence firmly places her floruit in the early 4th century. The reputation of Philonides as a rich man spending lavishly on hetairai seemingly survived for centuries and may have provided the inspiration for the fictional character of Philonides in one of the letters of Aristainetos, the recipient of a letter from the hetaira Chelidonion confessing her undying love.[178] If one considers the fact that Aristainetos draws from classical sources, Philonides and his love affairs with prostitutes may have been even more famous than our extant sources suggest.

Philonides should probably be identified with Philonides of Melite, the father of Onetor, who had served as one of the guardians of Demosthenes. Breitenbach argues that he was born around 420 and died in 366, during the arrangement of his daughter's marriage to Aphobos.[179] Philonides often was the object of comic scorn for his excesses and lavish life style. He is mocked for being large in size, stupid and ill-bred, and at the same time lecherous and extravagant. Aristophanes in the *Wealth* compares him and his companions with dung-eating pigs, in a parody of the famous scene from the Odyssey where Circe has transformed the companions of Odysseys into pigs.[180] The setting of the

---

174 Harp. s.v. Nais; Ar. *Plu.* 179 ἐρᾷ δὲ Ναῖς (Λαῒς codd.) οὐ διὰ σὲ Φιλωνίδου; Athen. 13.62; Sud. v 16.

175 This evidence is problematic for a number of reasons. First, there are several speeches entitled *Against Medon*, one for false testimony attributed to Lysias (fr. 100 Carey), one attributed to Demosthenes (fr. 7 Baiter – Sauppe), and one to Isaios (fr. 29 Thalheim). These could be different speeches, but there is a good possibility that there was some confusion about the attribution of the same speech among later antiquity grammarians and lexicographers. Moreover, Harpocration s.v. Ἀντίκυρα, seems to suggest that it was the hetaira Antikyra (who in his mind is to be identified with Nais) who was mentioned in the Lysianic speech *Against Medon*. However, I argue (see note s.v. Antikyra) that the two women are different and lived fifty years apart, and that a mistake of Aristophanes Byzantios conflating the two women into one person in his work *On the Hetairai of Athens* is probably responsible for the confusion of Harpocration. The woman mentioned in the Lysianic speech *Against Medon* must have been Nais.

176 Athen. 13.62, Philaiteros, fr. 9.7.

177 Athen. 13.62.

178 Aristaen. 2.13. Of course, a reader with good grounding in classical literature, who might know that Philonides was unattractive and uncouth, would see in her confession a cynical attempt to extract more money.

179 Breitenbach 1908: 29; D. 30.4, 7, 33.

180 Ar. *Plu.* 302–315.

parody is Corinth and Circe acts like a Corinthian hetaira. The allusion is that Philonides and his companions went to some Corinthian brothel and acted like pigs with their excesses. Several comedians make jokes about his large size. Plato the comedian in *Laios* and Theopompos in the *Aphrodisia* wonder how Philonides, being as large as a donkey, could have come out of a woman, and Philyllios calls him the son of a camel. Nicochares in *Galateia* mocks his lack of refinement and culture. His riches and extravagance are well attested, and outside comedy we get confirmation of his wealth in the extraordinarily high dowry of 80 minae which he gave to his daughter when she married Aphobos.[181] Only the daughters of the richest Athenians were offered dowries of this magnitude, and only the richest among the Greeks could afford his level of spending on expensive Corinthian and Athenian hetairai.

The actual case against Philonides is something of a mystery, which Christopher Carey succinctly summarizes as following:

> "Philonidem virgini epiclero ... aliquid per vim abstulisse" putat Sauppe. fr. 301 non obstante aeque possis Philonidem virginem vel feminam violasse.

> Sauppe thinks that "Philonides has taken something by force ... from a virgin *epikleros*". Except for fr. 301, you could just as easily think that Philonides has violated a girl or a woman.[182]

Carey is right; there is no compelling reason to interpret the case as Sauppe understood it. Sauppe took a reference to maltreatment of orphans and *epikleroi* (heiresses), as cited by Harpocration,[183] to be central for this case, but for all we know it could be only peripheral to the core case against Philonides. The rest of the fragments rather suggest a case of rape or sexual assault. Fragment 299 Carey, in particular, strongly advocates this interpretation of the primary charge, and preserves the only direct quote from the speech:

> There is a woman, a hetaira named Nais, whose protector is Archias, Hymenaios is her friend, and Philonides claims that he is in love with her.

If Harpocration is right when he reads "Nais" instead of "Lais" in the verse from Aristophanes *Wealth* "Isn't Nais in love with Philonides because of you (i.e. Wealth)?",[184] then the relationship between Nais and Philonides was a well-

---

181 Pl. Com. fr. 65; Theopompos fr. 5–6; Nicochar. fr. 4; Philyll. fr. 22; D. 27.56.
182 Carey 2007: 472.
183 Harp. s.v. κακώσεως.
184 Ar. *Plu.* 179: ἐρᾷ δὲ Λαῖς οὐ διὰ σὲ Φιλωνίδου; [Ναῖς Harp.]

known and ongoing affair around 390, which turned sour and resulted in sexual assault. The term for this particular lawsuit (δίκη βιαίων) seems too broad but it is quite consistent with the perception of rape as a crime of violence in Athenian law. There is clear and substantial evidence linking the *dike biaion* to rape or sexual assault, but not limiting it to these offenses. In a surprisingly post-modern legal concept, rape, sexual assault, violence and the act of taking something desirable by force are folded together into a single offence, of which violence (*biaion*) is the predominant feature. In this definition the emphasis is not upon unwanted sexual acts but upon the violence used by the perpetrator to extract by force what he wanted from the victim. In this respect, it is not limited to sexual acts, but could also include objects or valuables taken by force. Harpocration defines the process as following:

> *Biaion*: the name of a lawsuit brought against those who did anything at all by force; the convicted man pays to the public treasury an equal amount as he does to the successful prosecutor. Demosthenes *Against Meidias*. There are also some speeches for *biaion* among those attributed to Lysias. It is clear that this particular lawsuit, and its name, applied not only to the corruption of virgins (φθορὰ παρθένων), but also to other offenses.

The *Lexicon Rhetoricum Cantabrigiense* and the Scholiast of Plato expand this definition to include free boys.[185] The specifics of the accusations against Philonides are obscure. Like the abusive sailor of Herodas in the brothel of Battaros, Philonides may have been accused of bursting into the residence of Nais, assaulting or raping her, or trying to hale her away. Any of these behaviors would provide sufficient grounds for a biaion prosecution. The case against Philonides may be providing us with the only non-fictional account of a case of rape or sexual assault against a prostitute ever reaching the courts, but as so many important details elude us, we are left with more questions than answers.

Two more speeches concerning charges of violence around prostitutes have been preserved side by side in the corpus of Lysias (3 and 4).[186] Both are cases of deliberate wounding (τραῦμα ἐκ προνοίας), following fighting over prostitutes, one male (Lyias 3: *To Simon*), the other female (Lysias 4, response to an unknown prosecutor by an unknown defendant). Athenian law dealt firmly with violence among citizens and imposed severe penalties when violent incidents landed the parties involved to court, which is understandable in a state that relied mostly upon individual citizens to enforce its laws. Without a strong po-

---

185 Harp. s.v. βιαίων; Sch. Pl. R. 464 e; *Lex. Rhet. Cant.* s.v. βιαίων; cf. also D. 37.33, Pl. *Lg.* 914e; Omitowoju 2002; MacDowell 1978:
186 For a thorough discussion of both speeches see the discussion in Todd 2007: 275–383.

lice presence around the city to keep order, the primary way of controlling civic violence was by means of firm laws and vigorous processes intended to curb it before it even began, and making sure that no citizen would take violence in the streets lightly or treat it casually. Werner Riess has recently argued that the actual court-cases were expressions of violence, the violence itself, settling scores in a less bloodthirsty manner than physical violence.[187] Cases of deliberate wounding were treated as one step below manslaughter, with a trial before the formidable Areopagos Council and exile as the fixed penalty for a convicted defendant. It is noteworthy that this penalty was heavier than the penalty for the murder of a slave or alien (which could be a mere fine), and provides a clear indication about attitudes to violence in the Athenian legal system.[188]

The litigants in both these cases are responding to charges of deliberate wounding as a result of quarrels over prostitutes, but follow very different strategies. The speaker in Lysias 3 treats quite respectfully the boy who was the reason for the fighting, and tries to reverse the charges and present his opponent as abusive and violent towards him, the boy in question, and everyone else. He begins his narrative from the time that he himself and Simon fell in love with a Plataian boy named Theodotos. The fact that the youth was Plataian, and therefore an Athenian citizen, is emphasized in order to explain why the two men considered it sufficiently dignified to pursue a long-term relationship with him. This was not some kind of lowly slave-boy, but a proper citizen youth, maybe from a poor family but no doubt of exceptional looks. The rivalry between the speaker and Simon over the youth began shortly before the battle of Coronea (394 BC). The speaker implies that Theodotos preferred him because his strategy of attraction was to be generous, while his opponent tried to force Theodotos to do his bidding, and when the latter naturally resisted, things turned nasty. The opponent, however, was telling a very different story: Simon claimed that he

---

187 The background of this interesting debate on violence is not a topic which can be adequately discussed here; the reader may find enlightening the recent book of Werner Riess (2012) with rich bibliography and accounts of previous literature.

188 Whether classical Athens was a society which discouraged violence has caused some controversy: see Herman 2006 for the discussion and previous bibliography. At least from a legal point of view the facts are not controversial: the penalties for violence were very stiff, and a drunken brawl could cost someone very dearly, as much as exile, or even the death penalty if the victim died from subsequent infections, internal bleeding or other causes which could be linked to the assault. Attacking someone was a very risky option from a legal point of view, and Gagarin (in Bertrand 2005: 365–376) has correctly pointed out that in Attic law-court speeches violence is always condemned and never seen as legitimate. See also an important passage in D. 54.18–19; Fisher 1998: 68–97 and 2005: 67–89; Parca 2002: 283–296.

had a contract with Theodotos, and had paid him 300 drachmas (22), a very respectable sum in times of economic difficulty in the aftermath of the Peloponnesian war and naturally expected him to stay with him for a while.[189] Our speaker denies this on the grounds that Simon had self-appraised his property to 250 drachmas. How was it possible, our speaker asks, for Simon to pay his prostitute (τὸν ἑταιρήσοντα) more than his entire property was worth? The implication is that either Simon lied about his wealth and tried to hide it, or lied about the contract, or perhaps both, and whatever the case he cannot be an honest and trustworthy man.

This entire scenario so far sounds like a familiar case of rivalry in love, like the ones found everywhere in New Comedy and its heirs.[190] However, from this point the quarrel took a sinister turn. Simon one night broke into the house of the speaker in order to catch him dining with Theodotos. By mistake he landed in the women's quarters where the widowed sister of the speaker was staying with her daughters. He says they were so steeped in modesty that they felt embarrassed even in the presence of close male relatives. This breach of the inner space of the oikos was highly inappropriate, not to mention illegal. Simon was pulled out by his own friends and people who happened to be present. He located the speaker and tried to hit him, but he could not as he was overpowered. Then he went and stood on the other side of the street and started throwing stones, one of which hit Aristokritos, one of his own friends, and tore his forehead. The speaker says at this point that he did not want to proceed with litigation because he felt embarrassed, and instead decided to leave the city for a while, taking Theodotos with him and hoping that Simon would forget about him.

Upon their return Simon found out that Theodotos was at the house of Lysimachos, a friend of the speaker. This seems to have been an unfortunate choice of a venue because the house which Simon was renting was right next door. Simon summoned his gang of friends, they kept watch and continued to drink until the speaker left the house with Theodotos. The gang leaped on them and in the fight which ensued Theodotos dropped his cloak and ran away naked, while the speaker ran in a different direction. The gang caught up with Theodotos in a fuller's shop where he had sought refuge, and dragged him away. The fuller and others tried to help but got beaten up. When the speaker found out where they were he appeared alone - so he says - and tried to remove

---

189 See the discussion in Ch. 5.3. on prostitution contracts.
190 E.g. like the caricature rivalry between Phaedria and the soldier in Terence's *Eunuchus*, or the rival youths (μειρακίων ἀντεραστῶν) mentioned in Men. *Sam.* 26.

Theodotos. The gang attacked him, and a fight ensued between Simon and his gang on the one side, and the speaker and Theodotos assisted by passers-by on the other. The speaker claims that by the end everyone had cuts and bruises on their head.

Simon, however, told a very different story. He claimed that the speaker turned up in his house with a gang of his own and in the fight which ensued he struck him on the head and left him bleeding. Considering that it would be pointless, if not suicidal, for the speaker to go alone into the den of Simon's gang, perhaps we need to be skeptical about the details of the story as given to us. The orator is probably massaging the facts to suit his purposes, understating his own aggression towards Simon. After this climax it seems the quarrel came to an end, and some of the men involved apologized to each other for their behavior. Four years went by without trouble. In the meantime Simon attacked Laches, one of the taxiarchs, while on campaign during the Corinthian war, and was prosecuted for this. Quite possibly the speaker would like to tell the Areopagos Council much more about this incident, as it would be a damaging character reference for Simon, but he was not allowed by the strict rules of this kind of trial, which required that litigants do not speak outside the subject (46). The vengefulness of Simon was reaffirmed and he decided to renew hostilities four years later, when he sensed that the speaker was in a weak position, because he had lost money during a property exchange (*antidosis*).[191]

Regardless of the rights and wrongs of the case, Theodotos found himself in the middle of this violent row. He was dragged through the streets, at some point had to drop his cloak and run for his life, was beaten on several occasions, ended up with bruises and cuts on his head, and we are told repeatedly that he was not in the position to defend himself adequately, probably because he was too young, most likely still in his teens. However, in the final round at the house of Lambon, it seems that he threw a few punches and gave as good as he got (18), fighting against Simon's gang at the side of the speaker. The speaker repeatedly states that the beatings and humiliations the boy received at the hands of Simon and his gang amounted to *hybris*, and were against the laws.[192]

---

191 A person who was asked to perform one of the expensive liturgies in the city (e.g. fund a chorus or equip a war ship), could try to pass it on to a richer citizen by challenging him to an antidosis. The citizen challenged had to either undertake the liturgy, or agree to a property exchange with the challenger. In reality, of course, such proceedings were never straight forward and often resulted in bitter property disputes and complex legal battles. See MacDowell 1978: 162–164.
192 Lys. 3.17 ὑβρισθέντα τὸν νεανίσκον; 26 ἐτόλμα ὑβρίζειν τὸ μειράκιον; 5 ὑβρίζων καὶ παρανομῶν; 17 ἄνομος καὶ βίαιος

The beating of Theodotos was certainly illegal, as he was a Plataian and thus an Athenian citizen, and not even the magistrates or the Eleven, the police of Athens, had the right to hit a free person. Only slaves could be hit legally, either by their master or with his/her permission. That the beating of a citizen could be interpreted as *hybris* and carry severe penalties is repeatedly stated in the prosecution of Meidias for punching Demosthenes in the theater (D. 21), and elsewhere.[193] And yet, the violence against Theodotos does not generate any form of litigation, nor, for all the protestations of our speaker, is it even vaguely implied that Simon was ever in danger of legal consequences for this. The reason why is probably that, as is often the case with violence against prostitutes in our times, rarely were such cases reported and hardly ever they reached the courts; payment seemingly bought a considerable degree of immunity from the legal consequences of physical abuse.[194] There was no shortage of legal deterrents in Athenian law, but the strong sense of shame that would be attached to such litigation (3 and 9: αἰσχυνόμενος), and the general trouble, expense and dangers of legal action limited the potential for this kind of lawsuit.

Stephen Todd rightly considers the rich narrative and the portrayal of the characters to be crucial for Lysias' strategy in this speech. Todd says: "The speaker's character is not flawless, but as often in Lysias the flaw is venial, and serves to render his character more credible, in this case through the studied embarrassment with which he treats his relationship with Theodotos." [195] One must agree that the character portrayal of the speaker is masterful. A violent man, aggressive enough to get into a prolonged fight and seriously injure Simon, who was many years his younger, and sufficiently dishonest to steal someone else's lover, no doubt by offering a lot more money, is presented as a kindly older gentleman, caring for young Theodotos and trying to protect him from the abusive behavior of his opponent, and amiably roguish, still in pursuit of youthful beauty. Michael Gagarin has correctly emphasized the careful language used by the speaker in his attempt to present himself as the victim in self-defense, and not the perpetrator of violence.[196]

Lys. 4 is less skillful, less urbane, and also less straightforward, as it is probably not Lysianic and it is the second speech of the defendant, and as such it lucks a coherent narrative of the events, which probably had been provided in

---

193 See: Fisher: 1992; MacDowell 1976: 14–31 and 1990: 13–23, 262–9.
194 S. Church et al. (2001: 524–525) found that although 81 % of prostitutes had been victims of violence only 34 % had reported it to the police.
195 Todd 2007: 284.
196 Gagarin 2005: 365–376.

the missing first speech.[197] It is less than half the size of Lysias 3, although it was also a defense speech for the same type of lawsuit, namely deliberate wounding, no doubt because it is the second, shorter speech of the set. The basics of the case can be reconstructed from arguments which the defense is offering in response to specific accusations of the prosecution. The prosecutor and the defendant at some point agreed to share a woman. The defendant says that she was initially a slave who belonged to him, and after an *antidosis*,[198] they came to an agreement that the prosecutor would pay him half the value of the woman and share her. We are told that the prosecutor failed to produce the payment, but still kept the woman for himself and maintained that she was free. The speaker asserts that he would be happy to allow his opponent to keep the woman, if the latter came up with the agreed payment.

The prosecutor told a very different story. He was saying that the woman was free in the first place (which counters the defendant's claim that he was her initial owner, and that she was part of an antidosis agreement). It is not unlikely that the two men simply had bought a slave-prostitute for themselves, each paying half the money, and agreed to free her at the time of the purchase, as it often happened with upper-end prostitutes. Sex with a slave perhaps did not seem as gratifying, while with a free woman there was always the illusion of choice, namely that she stayed with her lover because she chose him, and not because she had to. However, the loser in love, our defendant, did not respect this agreement and still maintained that she was a slave, as Phrynion did not acknowledge the freedom of Neaira when he had lost her, even though he had

---

197 For a summary of alternative explanations for the missing narrative see Todd 2007: 349–351.

198 An *antidosis* involved a property exchange, and was triggered when a citizen charged with one of the liturgies did not wish to perform it. The only way of getting out of the obligation was to challenge a citizen richer than him to take over. If the latter disagreed, he could propose a property exchange. In the 4th c. such exchanges were only partial, and disputes often focused on specific property items (see Apostolakis 2006: 93–112; and 2009). In this case the prosecutor had challenged the defendant to an *antidosis*, mainly because, we are told, he had set his eyes upon the woman in question and wanted to possess her. The defendant accepted and they agreed to a partial exchange of property, but the woman was to remain under joined ownership, and to this effect the prosecutor ought to pay the defendant a sum equal to half of her value, which the former failed to do, but still enjoyed the woman's favors for quite a while. This whole account seems suspicious and raises many questions, like, for example, why the defendant allowed the woman to spend any time with the prosecutor if the latter had not paid.

personally agreed to the contract of her manumission with her former masters, on her behalf. [199]

Although the speaker disparagingly calls her a *porne*,[200] we can easily extrapolate that she was a very costly hetaira intended to be a long-term companion, whose favors the two men would share. Such arrangements were not uncommon, considering that the average cost of a high-class hetaira was between 20 and 30 minae, namely equal to the value of a dowry, or a very fancy house in a desirable area of the city.[201] Sometimes they could stay amicable, like the arrangement between the two masters of Neaira, Eukrates and Timanoridas,[202] but when male ego and posturing took over there was always an explosive potential for trouble. The narrative of Apollodoros provides vivid details about the fight between Phrynion and Stephanos, which began with the abduction of Neaira by a gang led by Phrynion, followed by litigation about her freedom and also accusations of theft, and ended with an almost unrealistic reconciliation on condition that she had to be shared between the two men until they changed their minds, even though the arbitrators accepted that she was a free person and mistress of her own fate (ἐλευθέραν εἶναι καὶ αὐτὴν αὑτῆς κυρίαν).[203] This strange ruling was designed to satisfy the male ego which had started the quarrel in the first place by making concessions to both parties at the expense of the former prostitute, even though Phrynion had no legal claim on her.[204]

Lysias 4 appears to be generated by the same kind of posturing. What started as a seemingly amicable arrangement between the two men, escalated into a serious quarrel before the Areopagos and might have ultimately cost the defendant his home, as the penalty for deliberate wounding was permanent exile. We are not informed about the details of the arrangement and how it was derailed, but the speaker hints more than once (e.g. 8 and 9) that an emotional bond had developed between his opponent and the woman. This led to fighting and at some point, it seems, a decision was made to settle their differences through private arbitration. However, the main point of contention, namely the girl, had not been settled. The prosecutor claims that she was freed, like Neaira

---

199 D. 59.38–40. Phrynion treated Neaira as a slave and haled her away through an unlawful abduction when he was informed that she had returned to Athens, even though he was present, and the main agent of her manumission from her previous masters. The subsequent arbitration acknowledged her freedom.

200 Lys. 4.9 and 19.

201 See D. 59.29–32 and 46–47; Kapparis 1999:227–228.

202 D. 59. 29–32.

203 D. 59. 33–48.

204 For a more detailed discussion of this quarrel see Kapparis 1999: commentary ad loc.

was when her masters decided to move on, and that she chose to stay with him as a free woman. The defendant denies that he consented to the decision to free her and still treats her like a slave, as one can imagine Phrynion would have done, when he was claiming that Neaira belonged to him. The defendant maintains that he would be happy to let his opponent have the woman, so long as he is paid his share of the her value, which no doubt would be a very substantial sum. This is probably deliberate strategy, as it weakens the accusation that he was a sore loser, an angry lover (8: δύσερως) who attacked his opponent because of jealousy. The prosecutor disagrees and claims that the whole quarrel escalated exactly because the defendant could not accept defeat and let the woman go, to the point where he turned up uninvited at the prosecutor's house and struck him with a potsherd. The prosecutor claims that he ended up with a black eye and had to be carried on a stretcher. Obviously there were plenty of witnesses to this, and this is why the strategy of the defendant is not to deny it, but rather to undermine the accusation, suggesting that his opponent was simply pretending to be seriously wounded when in reality all he had was a few superficial bruises, as one would expect from a fight over a whore.

The main points of difference between the prosecution and the defense are summarized in the form of five questions which the speaker was going to ask the woman under torture, if his opponent allowed him to take and torture her for evidence. First, he was going to ask whether the woman was commonly owned, or exclusively owned by his opponent. The second question is an extension of this point. The opponent obviously was claiming that he had paid all the money for the woman while our speaker argues that he had paid half of it. The third point has to do with the previous arbitration, which supposedly settled their differences. The speaker claims that they were no longer enemies, which would mean that he no longer had a motive to attack his opponent, while the prosecutor, it seems, claimed that they were still enemies and that the defendant attacked him because he could not put their past differences to rest. The fourth question is about the incident which landed them in court. The prosecutor claimed that the defendant turned up uninvited to cause trouble and assaulted him, while the defendant argues that he was invited to the house of his opponent for a party,[205] and thus the fight was not premeditated but something that happened in the heat of the moment. The final question is intended to show that the opponent started the violence, and far from being the victim of a pre-

---

205 Cf. D. 59.48, where Phrynion and Stephanos had parties in each other's houses after their reconciliation for the brief period that they were sharing Neaira's company, according to the terms of the arbitration ruling.

meditated assault, he was the perpetrator and instigator of the entire violent episode.

The speaker says that was going to ask the woman these questions under torture, if his opponent gave permission. This is a classic litigation trick: many a time speakers in Athenian courts said that they had asked their opponent to hand over a slave who had valuable information to be tortured for evidence until the torturer was satisfied that the slave was telling the truth. Expectedly the torturer would continue until he heard what served his case, and the opponent knew that. This is why permission was almost never granted, and there is no known case of such a process ever being completed. The only purpose served by this challenge was to provide some excuse or justification for missing evidence. The litigant could maintain that he could not provide more evidence, because his opponent was obstructing the proceedings by not granting permission for the torture of a slave. Understandably this trick was very often used when there was no evidence. Its employment by our speaker should be taken as an indication that he had no witnesses confirming any part of the story which he wanted the woman to confirm under torture. This means, probably he had no witnesses confirming that a contract was made according to which the woman was to be a common slave between him and the speaker, or that he paid half the money for her. This would be very strange considering that the sale of the woman could not have happened many years before this trial, as she was still attractive enough to be pursued by both men. It is also very significant from a legal point of view, because it would be impossible to claim any compensation for the woman without witnesses confirming the existence of a contract and shared ownership. It might be harder to ascertain that he had actually been invited to the dinner party, as the person who should know that was the host of the party, namely his opponent. However, it sounds very suspicious if he could not present a single witness confirming that he was the victim and not the instigator of the assault, as he claims, when the incident happened during a party and while other people were present, to be entertained by boys and flute-players (8).

Considering the weaknesses of the defendant's case, it seems that he was motivated by passion for a woman on whom he had no legal claim, perhaps a former lover, and assaulted the woman's current lover. Whether the assault was deliberate or just the result of hot-headed posturing, is hard to tell, but nonetheless could prove very costly for our speaker. From his point of view, the woman was just a whore, not worthy of his love or attention, nothing more than a commodity worth a certain amount of money. Whether he meant this or it was just a defense strategy is hard to tell with absolute certainty. He says that if she really meant anything to him, he could have tried to drag her away by force (5), after disabling her lover. One wonders whether during the incident which led to the charges of deliberate wounding the defendant did just that: he forcibly tried to steal the woman away, but failed.

The parallels of this account with the narrative of Apollodoros in the speech Against Neaira are significant, especially concerning the stereotypical δύσερως, the angry lover Phrynion, son of Demon, of Paiania.[206] Apollodoros does not have anything to gain by portraying him as abusive, but nonetheless makes several references to the angry and violent temperament of the man (e.g. 38 σοβαρόν καὶ ὀλίγωρον), and explains in detail how badly he treated Neaira when she was his lover. Phrynion initially helped Neaira gain her freedom from her Corinthian masters, and then took her to Athens with him as his lover. There, we are told, he was showing off to his friends, making public demonstrations of the power he had over the fabulously beautiful hetaira. He even had sex with her in a party, in public view of everyone and while the guests were watching, and overall he treated her abusively. She could take no more and decided to flee and take her chances as a self-employed hetaira in Megara in the middle of the war which was going to bring about the battle of Leuctra and the demise of Spartan power (371 BC). Financially this was a rather imprudent move and left her struggling to get by, and for this reason she was keen to return to Athens. When she met Stephanos, she was willing to follow him there, despite her fear of Phrynion.

Although physical violence against her person is never mentioned explicitly, the threat of violence is certainly in the air (37), and Neaira experiences it firsthand soon after her arrival in Athens, when she is abducted by a gang led by Phrynion from the house of Stephanos and treated like a slave until Stephanos legally removes her to freedom. In the vivid account of Apollodoros the former hetaira, who it should be noted is a free person by this stage, although in the center of the quarrel does not influence seriously the fighting and posturing of the two men, inside and outside the legal system. As in Lysias 4, the fact that she has already chosen one of the two men as her lover neither ends the quarrel nor stops the loser from pursuing her by means which by all legal definitions constitute violations against her person, freedom and dignity. The final settlement, that the two men were to share Neaira for as long as they saw fit, although in some ways insightful and obviously effective in ending the feud, was certainly unorthodox and designed to satisfy the male ego, but did not take into account Neaira's feelings. Although the ruling recognized previous proceedings

---

206 See D. 59.30–48, and Kapparis 1999: com. ad loc.; R. Omitowoju, in Deacy-Pierce 1996: 1–24.

which had granted Neaira her freedom, in the same breath it treated her like a luxury product, a commodity to be shared by the two men at their discretion, and not as a person with the unalienable right to choose the man with whom she was about to share her life.

A substantial amount of violence and abuse is hinted the speech *Against Timarchos* too. The orator repeatedly states that Timarchos chose to commit outrage on his own body and allowed other men to treat him abusively (ὕβρις: 29, 55, 87, 188 al.), and reports several violent incidents involving him.[207] However, unlike the powerless women in Lysias 4 and Apollodoros, or the immature boy of Lysias 3, Timarchos is the abuser and perpetrator of aggression. Aeschines mentions several instances as testimony to his violent nature, such as the merciless whipping of his former lover, the libertine Pittalakos, which led to a very embarrassing public incident and subsequent litigation (59–62).[208] The pattern of behavior is very different in this case. The prostitute is not the hapless victim, but the inciter and perpetrator, the one who is haughty and arrogant, and assaults others for fun or vengeance. This unusual theme of the violent and aggressively self-assertive prostitute is not encountered anywhere else in Greek literature, and its uniqueness probably has to do with the specific circumstances of this trial. A prominent politician, a man of fabulous looks in his youth, and of certain wealth and standing, and no doubt sometimes haughty and assertive, was accused of prostitution probably unjustly. This incongruity in his portrayal is probably the result of lies and deceptive tactics from the prosecution. Timarchos may have been aggressive, assertive, violent, and arrogant, but he was not a prostitute.

Outside law-court speeches numerous references to violence, aggression, or threats of aggression against hetairai can be found in New Comedy and its heirs. Frustrated lovers from all walks of life, young, old, rich or poor could find themselves in the middle of violent brawls or commit acts of aggression. Threats are frequent, either directed at the rival lover, as Stephanos threatens that Phrynion will shed tears if he lays so much as a finger on Neaira, or against the prostitute herself, as in Lucian's Dialogue 7, where a young hetaira is debating with her procurer mother the merits of various lovers, and reports that her current one

---

207 Nick Fisher (2005: 67–89) discussing the concept of *hybris* in the rhetorical strategy of Aeschines correctly concludes that the goal here was to present the *hybris* of Timarchos, his abusive behavior towards himself and others, as a fundamental threat to the democratic constitution itself.
208 About this incident see Fantham 1986: 50–51; Fisher 2001: 194–204.

has threatened to slaughter both her and a new lover she was considering. Her more pragmatic mother does not seem fazed by these threats:

> "How many others have uttered such threats? You are not going to be without a lover, and live a proper lifestyle as if you were not a hetaira, but a priestess of Demeter Thesmophoros." [209]

Soldier lovers are typically associated with menacing language and behavior in comic literature. In Menander's *Samia*, for example, the incensed Demeas uses very threatening language:

> The woman is a lowly whore, a horror. But so what?
> She is not going to take the upper hand. Demeas, now,
> You've got to be a man. Forget your desire, stop being in love,
> And hide the accident, if possible, for the sake of your son,
> But kick that pretty head of the Samian out of the house
> To go to hell. [210]

And yet, when Demeas gets to the point of actually asking Chrysis to leave (380 ff.), there is no violence, but only a dry request and a warning about the life that she will be facing trying to make a living as a free-lance hetaira. [211] When a tearful Chrysis explains to the neighbor Nikeratos what Demeas did, he exclaims: "By Poseidon and the gods, he (sc. Demeas) will shed tears because he is an evil man." [212] In Plautus Curculio *Therapontigonus*, a caricature of the angry soldier character in New Comedy, [213] yells on stage:

> I am not burning incensed with controllable wrath
> But with the same one that I feel when I raze cities to the ground. [214]

This kind of grandiose posturing and boasting forms a central theme in Plautus *Miles Gloriosus*, and is exploited with great comic results by Lucian in one of his *Dialogues of Hetairai* (13). Leontichos, the stereotypical braggart soldier, nar-

---

209 Luc. *DMeretr.* 7.4. Demeter Thesmophoros was typically associated with respectable married women.
210 Men. *Sam.* 348–354.
211 The warning is comical as Chrysis will be better off if all the "bad" things which Demeas threatens happen to her.
212 Men. *Sam.* 326–328.
213 See e.g. Menander *Misoumenos*, Plautus *Miles Gloriosus*, *Curculio*, Terence *Eunuchus*; Brown 2004: 1–16; MacCury 1972: 279–298.
214 Plautus *Curculio* 533–534.

rates with very graphic details how he killed enemies at war and how he was carrying the head of a slain Paphlagonian on his spear with the blood dripping all over him. The hetaira Hymnis, a naïve young girl, who confesses that she could not even bear to watch a chicken being slaughtered, runs away thinking that she will be haunted by the ghosts of the soldier's victims. It turns out that it was all made up by the soldier who wanted to make himself sound more macho and appealing. Like the Plautine Pyrgopolynices Lucian's Leontichos is wildly exaggerating his war-record in order to make himself attractive to women, naturally with the opposite result.

Dialogue 9 provides a more blasé reaction to such threats of violence from a rival soldier. Pannychis took the well-off sailor Philostratos as a lover in the absence of her soldier lover Polemon. The latter returns from war loaded with riches, and Pannychis does not want to dismiss him, but she does not want to dismiss Philostratos either. The whole rivalry culminates in a comically angry exchange between the two men. Polemon imitating battle formation orders his slave to summon the archers and block the passage, placing the foot-soldiers in the middle and more archers and peltasts on the sides. His rival engages him in the following exchange:

> Phil. You are blabbering and trying to scare us, like we are babies, you mercenary. You haven't even killed a rooster any more than you have seen war. You were standing guard on a little wall, pretending to be some sort of a captain, and I am doing you a favor to give you even this.
> Pol. You will soon find out, when you see us approaching for battle in our shiny armor.
> Phil. Then get into formation and come. Myself and Tibeios here, since he is my only follower, will pelt you with stones and pottery shards and scatter you, and you won't even know where to turn.[215]

Sometimes, however, the angry soldier-lover actually turns violent fueled by antagonistic jealousy and alcohol, and will do more than just use empty threats and intimidating language. The primary plot in Menander's *Perikeiromene* ("The shorn girl") is centered around an act of violence, which, as Elaine Fantham points out, the protagonist herself calls '*hybris*' (723: ὑβριζέτω). [216] Polemon suspects his lover Glycera, and in a jealous fit he shears her hair. This act of aggression sparks a series of events which eventually lead to forgiveness for the aggressor and a happy ending.[217] G. Arnott has drawn attention to a painting

---

215 Luc. *DMeretr.* 9. 5.
216 Fantham 1986: 51,
217 For a succinct presentation of the plot and the main themes related to prostitution in *Perikeiromene* see Henry 1985: 73–84. For the cultural perceptions surrounding Polemon's

from a 2nd c. A.D. house in Ephesos depicting a soldier and a woman covering her head with a cloak to hide her hair, which he perceives as a representation of the scene of *Perikeiromene* immediately after the assault of Polemon on Glykera's hair.[218] W. T. MacCary in an extensive study of the soldier as a character in Menandrian Comedy concludes: "Of Menander's plays involving soldiers, the five best preserved present the soldier in a sympathetic manner: Polemon in the *Perikeiromene*, Thrasonides in the *Misoumenos*, Stratophanes in the *Sikyonios*, Kleostratos in the *Aspis* (and perhaps the unnamed soldier of the *Karchedonios*) all love free-born girls, they are redeemed by this love from the violence to which are susceptible, and in the end they are rewarded with marriage."[219]

Lucian's treatment of the violent soldier is much less redeeming. In Dialogue 15 Kochlis, a tearful flute-player returning from a party holding her broken flute in her hands meets a friend of hers, another prostitute, and relates to her what happened. A hetaira named Krokale demanded the impossibly high sum of two talents from her lover, a soldier ominously called Deinomachos ("terrible in battle"), if he wanted her exclusively. Expectedly he refused, then she took another lover, a farmer from Megara, and locked the soldier out. The soldier turned up at her house with a gang, tore down the gates and burst into the house. Krokale managed to run away to the house of a neighbor hetaira. The soldier struck the flute-player, broke her flute and told her to get lost (ἐκφθείρου), and aided by a fellow soldier gave the farmer such a beating that blood was coming out of his nose and his whole face was swollen; the flute-player doubted that he was going to survive. The farmer finally got up and went to find some citizen friends of his, to ask for their help to bring the soldier to justice, and the flute player was going to report all this to her master so that he can go after the soldier too. Although this account is fictional, such squabbles certainly were not uncommon in the brothels of the ancient world. It is interesting that even in fictional accounts such as this one, the courts seem to be the expected conclusion of a jealous assault. The evils of soldier lovers are summarized by Kochlis as following:

---

aggression see Fortenbaugh 1974: 430–443. There are parallels between Polemon and Thrasonides, a soldier character in *Misoumenos*, but Thrasonides in a reversal of the themes encountered in *Perikeiromene* is the undeserving victim of contempt by his lover Krateia, because she incorrectly believes that he has killed her brother.

218 Arnott 1988: 11–15.
219 MacCary 1972: 297.

This is what you get to enjoy from those soldier lovers: beatings and trials. They brag about being leaders and captains of thousands, but when it comes to giving something, "Wait," they say "for the salary, when I get paid, and I will do everything you ask." Let all those braggarts get lost. I am doing the right thing not to go near them, at all. I'd rather have a fisherman or a sailor or a farmer, just as good with flattery, but a simple man and very generous. Those who shake crests and tell war-stories are just noise, Parthenis.[220]

A different point of view is offered in Dialogue 8. Two hetairai are debating the merits of violent lovers; one is a veteran who has practiced prostitution for twenty years, the other is an eighteen years old starter, who has suffered violence in the hands of a short-tempered lover. Her more experienced friend relates an incident where a lover incensed into a jealous frenzy ended up paying her a much higher fee. Jealousy is presented as a good thing, because it yields higher rewards, even if the side-effect is a certain amount of violence. The enamored soldier is the stereotypical perpetrator of violence in the fictional literature of late classical and post-classical literature, but not in 5th or early 4th century literature for the simple reason that the mercenary foreign soldier, does not become a familiar character before the middle of the 4th century. After that point this new breed of the young, aggressive male with plenty of money, obtained from looting and salaries of war, and willing to spend it on hetairai, drink, parties and parasites, as exemplified in Plautus *Miles Gloriosus*, is a ubiquitous feature of life all the way into the Roman period and beyond.

A drunken sailor, in every respect just as stereotypical as the soldier of New Comedy, is the aggressor in the second mime of Herodas (*Pornoboskos*). The island of Kos forms the backdrop, but the law invoked by the pimp Battaros is that of Charondas, the famous lawgiver of Catane. The setting of the mime is a trial, where the procurer is suing the Carian sailor Thales for damages. He alleges that Thales fell in love with Myrtale, one of the girls of Battaros, but did not want to pay for her, even though his boat was worth a whole five talents (an impossible sum, and certainly a wild exaggeration). The procurer bemoans his own extreme poverty (without a doubt another wild exaggeration), and describes the events which landed them in court. In a drunken rage Thales broke down the door, stormed the brothel and assaulted some of the girls, including Myrtale. To prove this point Battaros presents the girls in court, and asks them to remove their clothing and show the jury the cuts and bruises in their private parts, while he titillatingly comments how smooth and beautiful these parts would be looking if they had not been assaulted by Thales. He pleads with the jurors not to decide the case on the basis of their loathing for him, the vile pro-

---

220 Luc. *DMeretr.* 15.3.

curer, son and grandson of procurers, but to vote in favor of all hard-working foreigners in the city and punish the abusive sailor, showing him that his behavior is not acceptable on the island of Kos. In the end, in a surprising move mimicking similar challenges in the Attic Orators, Battaros offers himself to be tortured for evidence if his opponent wishes to do so. The problem of Battaros is not the assault, but the fact that the sailor did not want to pay for the girl, and the lawsuit is not so much about the violence as it is about the damages. The implication is that if Thales had been willing to compensate the pimp, he could have bought immunity from the charges of assault too, and done as he pleased with the girl.

Several epigrams composed by Paulos Silentiarios in the time of Justinian (6th c. AD) describe various forms of violence against women in an erotic context. In his works love is always violent, like fire, mania inspired by Dionysos, or rabies.[221] One of the epigrams describes an actual beating of a hetaira by her lover, who confesses that he grabbed her by the hair and pulled with such force that some of it came off. Then expectedly he was banned from her company, which he thinks is a punishment harsher than getting killed with a sword.[222] A more disturbing form of violence is presented in an epigram where a hetaira is being raped while she is asleep by a lover she had rejected many times before:

> In the evening the lovely Menekratis was lying in deep sleep
> With her arm wrapped over her head.
> I dared to climb on her bed. As I was gladly
> Half-way through crossing the path of Kypris,
> The girl woke up from her sleep, and with her white arms
> She was pulling every single hair from my head.
> While she was still resisting we completed the rest of love's work,
> Then full of tears she said this:
> "You bastard, you did to me what you wanted, that for which many times
> I pushed away a lot of gold in your palm;
> Now you will embrace someone else right away
> Because men like you are the servants of a greedy Kypris." [223]

There are several interesting facts about this epigram. First, and as far as I know, this is the only attested instance where the rape of a prostitute is explicitly described, and not just inferred or alluded, in the entire corpus of Greek literature. Considering how frequent and lucid references to rape are in Greek My-

---

221 E.g. *AG* 5. 266, 279, 281, 288; 16.57.
222 *AG* 5.248.
223 *AG* 5.275.

thology and Drama, and how often details of such incidents are described in order to shock, intrigue, evoke strong emotions and entertain audiences, especially in New Comedy, it is astonishing that one of the most vulnerable groups of the population would be completely left out of the picture. Several studies of rape scenes in New Comedy confirm that the women raped are always respectable, and discuss the possibility that sexual violence against women in myth and drama paradoxically protects their respectability by making them unwilling participants in premarital or extramarital sex; willing participation would have compromised them in the eyes of the reader or the audience, as it would amount to immoral and socially unacceptable behavior. In the plots of New Comedy, rape functions as an important plot device, setting in motion a series of events which will lead to the marriage of young lovers, the legitimization of offspring until then thought to be illegitimate, the recognition and restoration of citizen women who had been stolen from their families and forced into prostitution to their original status of respectability and a happy ending for all. The question whether in this highly stylized, conventional and moralizing world the audience is expected to accept rape as a mere mishap is more difficult to answer and outside the purposes of this study.[224]

It might be astounding at first, with all these hetairai and other prostitutes parading through the comic stage in almost every single play, that no true hetaira or other prostitute, male or female, is ever presented as the victim of rape. The reason probably is that the rape of a prostitute or hetaira would be inconsequential and thus not convenient as a plot device. How would it surprise or upset the audience, or even merely cause sensation if a prostitute were forced to have sex, or why would it matter, if illegitimate children were produced from the rape of prostitutes? Such things were not uncommon in the numerous brothels of the late classical and Hellenistic world, and this kind of triviality would not be deemed worthy of literary or artistic representation. In tune with the previous observation that only respectable women are the victims of sexual violence in New Comedy, several of the women whom Henry calls pseudohetairai,[225] namely women of citizen birth unlawfully and unwillingly dragged into prostitution, are potential victims of sexual violence. Several of them have become long term companions (hetairai) or concubines against their will, forced by their captors into this situation, like Philocomasium in Plautus' *Miles Glorio-*

---

224 See Rosivach 1998: 13–50 and 146–148; Deacy 1997: 43–64; Pierce 1997: 163–184; Lape 2001: 79–119; Harris 2004: 71–83; Doblhofer 1994; Fantham 1975: 44–74; Scafuro 1997: 246–254.
225 E.g. Henry 1985:102

sus, or unwillingly brought up to become hetairai, like Krateia in Menander's *Misoumenos*, who ends up becoming the lawful wife of her lover Thrasonides when her true identity is revealed, or Silenium in Plautus *Cistellaria* half-heartedly groomed to be a hetaira by the her foster-mother, the hetaira Melaenis, but ending up married to her one and only lover Alcesimarchus, after the discovery of her true identity.

The most extensive of such references can be found in Plautus' *Rudens*, which is based on an Attic play of Diphilos. The pimp Labrax is chasing two girls named Palaestra and Ampelisca who, he claims, belong to him. The girls are desperately trying to escape his control. One of them, Palaestra, is Athenian-born and was taken away from her family at the age of three. The girls take refuge in a temple of Venus. The pimp then tries to seize them; they run to the altar as suppliants and he tries to tear them away by force. This abominable form of violence in the temple is demonstrative of the vile character of the pimp, and results in the intervention of a neighbor, the Athenian Daemones. He orders two strong slaves to restrict Labrax and keep him away from the girls. The slaves are guarding the pimp, toying with him and challenging him to lay a finger on them (706–780); his inability even to touch them under threat of a severe beating is a fitting comic reversal of the theme of the violent pimp hitting women under his control, with the aggressor becoming the victim. Later in the play Plesidippus, the lover of Palaestra, intervenes and drags Labrax tied like a wild animal to the magistrate for punishment. In Athenian legal procedure we would recognize this as an *apagoge*, the appropriate procedure for an *andrapodistes*, someone caught trying to enslave a citizen. The penalty if he confessed, as Labrax very openly has done here, was summary execution. If he did not confess, he was imprisoned until his trial, and if found guilty, then he was executed.[226]

This is an interesting turn of events: the rule of law, a concept which the Greeks identified with civilization itself, is applied even to this vile procurer who had enslaved citizen-women and forced them to prostitution. Violence and direct retribution befitted slaves and barbarians; civilized people abhorred it and relied on the law to punish the criminal.[227] It is hard to tell how much in the play is Plautus and how much is Diphilos, but the reference to *vis* as violence exercised by the pimp on the women is probably a Roman concept (681–683). Using rather intriguing phraseology Palaestra prays that violence may not prevail on her, or else she might be compelled to use violence against herself, which she would have done already had it not been for her timid female nature

---

226 See MacDowell 1978: 80 and 148.
227 See Riess 2012 for this interpretation of violence and the law.

(685–686). *Vis* in Latin combines both the concept of violence (Greek βία) and the arrogant contempt for its victims (Greek ὕβρις), and as such it is well suited to personify the violence of the procurer.

The themes of love, competition, jealousy and violence surrounding hetairai and other prostitutes are exploited in the literature of later antiquity along the lines which are familiar to us from New Comedy and its heirs. An epigram of Agathias (6th c. AD) actually jokes about its dependency on Menander. It makes a reference to the *Perikeiromene*, only here the new Polemon (ὁπλότερος Πολέμων) cuts the hair of Rhodanthe. The epigram ends with a word play consisting of Menandrian titles, like the *Misoumenos* ("the hated one"), the *Dyskolos* ("the grouch"), and the *Perikeiromene* ("the shorn girl").[228] The soldier theme takes a new twist, reminiscent of the Platonic utopia, in one of the fictional letters of Alciphron, where an austere and simple-minded soldier believes that hetairai ought to be common:

> He [i.e. the soldier] said that household tasks and a respectable life are fitting for married heiresses, but the hetairai ought to be openly common and to sleep with everyone who wanted them. As in the baths we use the jugs in common, even though they seem to belong to one person, we should use those women who have enlisted to this lifestyle in the same manner.[229]

In a brief fictional letter by the Byzantine scholar and historian Theophylaktos (7th c.) a hetaira is admonishing a lame lover to take a few blows for her sake:

> Those who desire consider even abuse to be sweet, and often take pride in the beatings and the black eyes. If you can't take the heat, you will not be able to pick a rose either, being afraid of the thorn.[230]

The theme that young people wouldn't mind a beating for the sake of a beautiful hetaira, and that no special significance should be attached by society or the legal system to such quarrels, is stated in the speech against Konon.[231] There the speaker reports comments which allegedly his opponent had made in an attempt to diminish his responsibility over the heavy beating of Ariston. The theme of a certain degree of forgiveness towards young people who might get into a brawl over a hetaira is accompanied by strong condemnation of such behavior at an older age in one of the *Declamations* of Libanios:

---

228 *AG* 5.218.
229 Alc. 3.22.
230 Theophylaktos, *Epist.* 48.
231 D. 54.14.

> If an old man is caught drunk, misbehaving and fighting over a hetaira, giving and receiv-
> ing blows, does this not make the charges worse, because he needs to have wisdom and
> although his age makes wisdom easy, he still acts outside his age and commits the crimes
> of the young?[232]

The theme may be drawn from the third tetralogy of Antiphon, and possibly
even the *Characters* of Theophrastos, where the Late Learner (ὀψιμαθής) acts in
manner that is unsuitable for his age, and does things which would be rather
typical for a young man; he gets into a fight over a hetaira and ends up in
court.[233]

Images of symposiasts fighting under the influence of alcohol are present both
in literature and in vase iconography, and we should be in no doubt that from
time to time drunk guests could get violent while competing with each other
over potential lovers, hetairai or prostitute entertainers. The most famous parody of a party escalating into extreme violence is Lucian's *Symposium*, but there
the guests end up giving each other black eyes, broken limbs and bruises not
over women or boys or but over philosophical questions. Less "erudite" are the
fellow guests of Philocleon in Aristophanes *Wasps*, when they realize that he
has stolen the flute-player in the end of the night, with a promise to set her free
if she gives in to his sexual advances, and they are chasing him and threatening
a lawsuit.[234] A fragment of Persaios gives us an image of how drunken guests
competing in an auction of the entertainers in the end of the night came to
blows when they did not win the bid.[235] Vase iconography abounds in images of
drunken symposiasts fighting, vomiting, losing their balance or simply drop-
ping on the floor,[236] and sometimes women identified by their apparel as entertainers or prostitutes are in the middle of the quarrel. An excellent example of
the motif is a cup from the Hermitage museum, where a group of drunken symposiasts are fighting, it seems over a flute-player, and the woman is caught up
in the middle of it, just like Lucian's flute player mentioned above.[237]

Sadomasochism, namely consensual violence for sexual gratification, is a
difficult topic when the exchange of money is involved, as in this case the term

---

232 Lib. *Decl.* 10.1.18
233 Thphr. 27.9.
234 Ar. *V.* 1332–1381
235 Persaios fr. 451 von Arnim.
236 One great example of a wild symposium portrayed in various phases with some of the
guests peacefully entertaining themselves, some fighting, and some drunken and falling is
4704 = Karlsruhe, Badisches Landesmuseum: 70.395.
237 203327 = ARV [2] (1963): 325.77 = St. Petersburg, State Hermitage Museum: 2110.

"consensual" is not straight-forward, especially when a pimp has made an agreement and the prostitute has simply to choose between the violence inflicted by the customer or the greater violence to be inflicted by the procurer, if he/she refuses to comply. The definition of sexual violence itself is not straight-forward either, as some might consider violence any kind of pain inflicted during sex, while for others some violence spices up things. Pain, at least an agreed amount of it, fits perfectly well with the sexual preferences of many people and a historian of sexuality needs to accept it without judgment as part of human bonding rituals. These issues are complex and the present study is not the place to discuss them in great detail. For our purposes the term "consensual" should be employed for any form of sexual activity agreed beforehand between the client and the prostitute or an agent of his/hers for a fee, usually higher than the standard, so long as both parties adhere to the agreed terms. In literature there are only a few casual references to sadomasochistic sexual practices involving prostitutes, such as the famous *enkrateia* of the philosospher Xenokrates who inflicted burns and cuts on his genitalia and refused to have sex with Phryne (or Lais), or the infamous and strange incident in the speech *Against Timarchos*, where Timarchos, who allegedly had been used by the libertine Pittalakos as a prostitute and had suffered many indignities in his hands, together with his new lover Hegesandros tied up Pittalakos naked and kept hitting him until the neighbors heard his cries.[238] Most of the evidence about sadomasochistic sexual practices comes from vase iconography, and as such it is open to different interpretations. Whether the sadomasochistic sexual images in vase iconography are a true reflection of Athenian life, or pornographic representations of sexual fantasies is a matter difficult to decide conclusively, as Martin Kilmer has demonstrated.[239]

Kilmer stresses that some of these scenes involve mythical creatures such as satyrs or maenads, while others would be impossible in the real world, like the ones involving huge dildos, and must therefore be treated as images of sexual fantasy.[240] Other scenes are more realistic, and could conceivably be images of real life. The most common image typically interpreted as sadomasochistic is that of the sandal used either during foreplay, as for example in the image of a

---

238 D.L. 4.7;

239 Kilmer 1993: 103–132 and 199–215.

240 For example, in ARV [2], 79. n. 1 = Magnoncourt 34 (now lost) women are playing with dildos of such size that they would impale a real person, if used to their full potential. This is the rather routine giant dildo theme in pornography, and should be assigned to sexual fantasy rather than any representation of reality.

woman stimulating with a sandal her partner-to-be leaning over her,[241] or during intercourse as an instrument of sexual pleasure. For example, there is no doubt that this is the intended meaning of a 6th c. pelike portraying a young man beating a youth with a sandal. The youth is sexually aroused and turns his face towards his lover. The semi-erect penis of the youth and the gesture leave us in no doubt that this is an image of consensual gratification involving some pain.[242]

The content of a cup from Paris portraying an orgy may be prostitutional, because one might argue that the ancient viewer could not possibly conceive the women involved in it as respectable, but we should not rush to moralizing conclusions of this kind as erotic triangles are well attested in literary sources. For example, a threesome involving a very respectable Athenian man, Demosthenes the orator, his very respectable wife and a citizen youth named Knossion, is mentioned in the sources (see Ch. 3.1.). What happened behind the closed doors of Athenian homes need not be very different from what happens behind closed doors in our times, and threesomes are neither uncommon nor extraordinary as a sexual pattern in humans. On the contrary, as a modern study by Arno Karsten suggests, people who engage in threesomes are often middle class, and mainstream in most aspects of their lives.[243] Whether a prostitute or not, in this image a woman is performing oral sex on a young man while an older man is penetrating her and lifts a sandal to spank her bottom. The woman's expression is one of pleasure; no doubt we are expected to understand that she loves it all.[244] Perhaps not so thrilled should be the woman in another threesome scene, this time pulled by the hair by an excited youth towards his erect penis and grabbed from her behind by an older man, and yet her expression is again one of pleasure or at least resigned consent. This image is typically interpreted as prostitutional because of a wineskin underneath her body, and a drunk man kneeling with a skyphos on the inside of the cup.[245]

Other sex objects used to inflict pleasurable pain during sex include sex implements like dildos, some unrealistically large.[246] The pain inflicted by such

241 ARV [2] 113, 1626 = Berlin 3251, Florence I B49.
242 200073 = ARV [2], 15/11 = Rome, Mus. Naz. Etrusco di Villa Giulia: 121109; Kilmer 1993: 104–5.
243 Karsten 1988, passim.
244 20069 = ARV[2] (1963), 86/(α), 1578/16 = Paris, Musee du Louvre: G13.
245 203338 = ARV[2] (1963), 326/86 bis, 1706 = Luzern, Market, Ars Antiqua: XXXX0.3338.
246 See Kilmer 1993: 98–102; 201129 = ARV[2] (1963), 135/(a), 1628, 1700 = Paris, Musee du Louvre: S1378; 310515 = Beazley Attic Black-Figure Vase-Painters (1956): 157. 86 = Boston, Museum of Fine Arts, 10.651; ARV [2] 1593 = Berlin F 2272; Cerveteri, ex M. Abanatone 561 (un-

objects needs to be interpreted as pleasurable, as part of the sexual fantasy in all masturbation scenes, while in other erotic scenes involving dildos the imagery typically suggests pleasure, and thus they should be viewed as consensual instruments of pleasure. Other images involving violent sexuality also do not suggest compulsion any more than what is permitted by the sexual game. For example, an older woman is pulled by two men in a cup full of images of a wild sex party and serious drunkenness. An older man is holding her buttock with his right arm. A sexually excited younger man is pulling her hair from the front, but the woman seems content to play along hovering over a wine skin.[247] Kilmer considers pulling a sexual partner towards an erect penis to be an image of sexual violence. A more striking example of what appears to be a forced fellatio can be found on a cup from the Louvre, where there are two scenes portraying fellatio. In one of them a woman is being penetrated by an older man and simultaneously she is fellating a younger man. In the other scene a man seems to be forcing a woman to fellate his exceedingly large penis using his left arm to lock her head in place, while he is holding his penis with his right arm.[248] It would be impossible to determine whether these images are to be understood as representations of unwanted advances which prostitutes are willy-nilly compelled to perform in order to satisfy paying customers, or simply male fantasies of rough sex. Equally ambiguous is another image from Athens, where a naked man with an erection tries to embrace a naked woman and she seems to be trying to flee but her right arm is still wrapped around the waist of the man. Whether this is to be understood as attempted rape or simply a "come and get me" kind of sex game is simply a matter of interpretation, but considering the couple's embrace the latter is more likely. But this is really as bad as it gets in ancient representations of sexual violence. When compared to representations of sadomasochistic sexuality in modern pornography, with leather, whips, metal, inventive instruments of pain and staggering images of domination or humiliation, which as Kilmer notes are most prevalent in North America,[249] images of sexual violence on Attic vase paintings appear very tame. The furthest they go is the use of sandals for spanking someone's bottom, or large toys and some rough sex. Even in

---

published according to Kilmer), where a woman happily is holding two absolutely enormous dildos, et al.

247 Kilmer 1993: 35 -6; 203338 = ARV [2] 326.86BIS, 1706 = Basel, Antikenmuseum und Sammlung Ludwig: BS440

248 200694 = ARV[2] (1963), 86/(α), 1578/16. = Paris, Musee du Louvre: G13.

249 Kilmer 1993: 199 - 215.

their most extreme they cannot be read as blatant images of rape as there is not a single image which we are compelled to interpret as non-consensual.

Whether this rather mild portrayal of SM sexuality is a true reflection of Athenian sexual mores is not easy to tell for sure, but we must admit that there is no surprise in these images. The explosive mix of prudery, sexual repression and religious conservatism, combined with constant images of power, violence and humiliation dominating modern North American culture, would be somewhat alien to the ancient Athenians. They did not have a culture which considered sex dirty or inherently immoral, they did not use abundantly sexual vocabulary in daily bunter and invective, they did not "bugger" or "screw" their enemies, and their experience of violence was real and bloody through life-threatening engagements in the battlefield. As a result, they did not make the same cultural associations which lead to the garish and simultaneously cartoonish images of modern SM pornography. Although, some people, as in every other society in history, enjoyed their sex rougher, this mix of sex and violence, of pain and pleasure, ought to be far less intense and far less demonstrative, just as the vase iconography suggests.

Non-consensual sexual violence, for which English uses the blanket term "rape," is more nuanced in Greek terminology, and in the words of E.M. Harris, "when one uses the word 'rape' when analyzing the ancient sources, one might be imposing an anachronistic concept on the evidence, a concept that may prove to be an obstacle to our understanding of ancient attitudes". Harris, taking into account recent scholarship, has successfully illustrated that sexual violence was not seen as a single offence but a range of different crimes and transgressions, some of which could be treated with leniency while others were perceived as more serious offences.[250] The core thesis of Harris that adultery was not perceived as a more serious offence than rape, as stated in an article in 1990,[251] has not found wide acceptance in the international bibliography, due to overwhelming evidence against it.[252] However, his thesis that the Greeks chose more nuanced approaches to sexual violence is now widely accepted.

Three of the terms used to describe sexual violence appear more often in our sources. Words derived from the verb φθείρω or its compounds (e.g. διαφθείρω) emphasize the corruption of a person's chastity; after the rape this

---

250 Harris 2004: 41–83.
251 Harris 1990: 370–377.
252 See for example the substantial objections of C. Carey 1995: 407–417; Kapparis 1999: 305–6; R. Omitowoju 2002: 72–91, al.

person is compromised.[253] As Vincent Rosivach eloquently puts it, "even though the woman is no way responsible, the condition of having been raped nonetheless imposes a defect upon her (sc. her loss of virginity), which makes her a less than suitable mate for anyone other than her rapist." [254] Terms derived from βία (force) emphasize the force exerted upon the victim, while terms derived from ὕβρις (outrage) project the abusive and arrogant attitude of the rapist.[255] *Hybris* is also used as a euphemism to indirectly imply rape, without providing details or being specifically explicit about a difficult subject. This terminological richness complicates the study of rape in classical sources from the point of view of modern definitions and legal practice. If one were to understand rape as φθορά, namely as a process which damages a chaste woman, this definition would not apply to prostitutes.

The understanding of rape as βιασμός (namely a forced imposition upon someone's body) is nowhere reported in the sources in relation to prostitution, although one might guess that it did happen as a regular occurrence in the brothels of the ancient world. Their typically slave-inhabitants would not even have a legal right to refuse sexual intercourse, as the right to their bodies belonged to their owner, who could grant permission to the customer upon payment of the fee, regardless of the feelings of the prostitute him/herself. According to the law, accepting the fee amounted to absolution of the customer from accusations of adultery with female prostitutes.[256] The question whether it also amounted to explicit consent, if not from the prostitute then from the person who mattered in legal terms, that is his/her owner or kyrios, and thus absolved the customer from potential accusations of rape, is more complicated. The customer reasonably expected that once he paid the fee he would receive sexual gratification in return, and the pimp understood that once he/she accepted payment he/she consented on behalf of the prostitute. Undoubtedly there were boundaries to the level of control and access allowed to the customer. For example, forcing the prostitute to perform acts that could cause injury naturally would not be tolerated, because this would affect her/his marketability with future customers and eventually cost the brothel money, as Herodas 2 suggests.

---

253 E.g. D.H. 13.10.2; Acus. *FGrH* 392 F 1a2; Eratosth. *Cat.* 1.2.
254 Rosivach 1998:14
255 For βιάζειν see e.g. Ar. *Lys.* 226; for references and discussion of rape/*hybris* see Omitowoju 1997: 1–24; for a more general discussion of *hybris* see MacDowell 1976; Fisher 1992; Cairns 1996.
256 See D. 59.67 and the discussion in Ch. 1.2.

Moreover, one would think that certain sexual acts which might require a higher fee would not be on the table, at least not before the customer paid for them.

Hybris as a whole is much more difficult to define within the Athenian penal
system. It was not a specific offence as such but rather an attitude, a behavioral
pattern fit for a barbarian king like Xerxes (and he got punished for it), but certainly not befitting the citizens of the Athenian Democracy or the *homoioi*
(equals) of Sparta. D.M. MacDowell has rightly concluded that *hybris* was very
difficult to prove in a court setting, as it has to do with intentions and attitudes
rather than specific violations of the law. Nick Fisher agreed that it was an offence too difficult to prove, and in the case of rape or sexual offences, a *hybris*
prosecution could be counter-indicated, as it would bring more shame to the
family, and still might be unsuccessful.[257] Edward Harris has objected to this on
the basis of the evidence of the *Old Oligarch*, which enlists *hybris* prosecutions
as one of the reasons why the Athenian court system was clogged with a multitude of lawsuits.[258] However, this is a highly unrealistic text, which makes many
preposterous accusations, and on its own cannot be seriously taken as evidence
of a multitude of *hybris* lawsuits. MacDowell and Fisher are right: we do not
have definite evidence of a single *hybris* prosecution despite frequent allegations of *hybris* in the entire body of the Attic Orators in relation to a wide variety
of lawsuits, disputes over prostitutes included.[259]

Susan Lape draws attention to one prosecution which resulted in the death
penalty for Themistios of Aphidna, an Athenian citizen who committed outrage
(ὕβρισεν) against a Rhodian flute-player during the Eleusinean Mysteries, suggesting the possibility that this was a prosecution for rape using the *hybris*
law.[260] However, this passing reference by no means constitutes definite proof
either of rape or a *hybris* prosecution for rape. The crucial verb ὕβρισεν in context could mean that Themistios raped the flute-player during the festival, but
then again, it could simply mean that his behavior was disrespectful, like a
physical assault, a beating, or even just a verbal humiliation during the festivities in public view of the believers (as it is the case with references to *hybris* in
the speech *Against Meidias*). To understand the scale of such an offence, one
can recall how many people were put to death in 415 during the famous Hermo-
kopidai scandal for simply acting out the Eleusinean mysteries before uninitiat-
ed eyes during a private party. ὕβρισεν is so vague that it is impossible to ascer-

257 Fisher 2005: 69–89; see also Fisher 1992, and 1998: 68–97
258 X. *Ath.* 3.5; MacDowell 1976:28–29; contrary Harris 2004: 63, n. 44.
259 See also the discussion in Lys. 4 above.
260 Din. 1.23; Lape 2001: 85–6.

tain what was exactly that Themistios did. Moreover, the case of Themistios is mentioned in a list of cases punished with unexpected severity, like that of a man who was put to death for having a free boy working in a mill, a job typically reserved for slaves and criminals, or that of Euthymachos who was put to death because he established in a brothel a free girl from Olynthos, no doubt at a time when the Athenians were very sympathetic to the Olynthians for their suffering in the hands of Philip.[261] So, Themistios need not have done something as gross as raping the flute-player during the festival, but whatever he did was perceived as offensive to the Two Goddesses, and this is why he was punished with extraordinary and perhaps undeserved severity.

The procedure itself needed not be a γραφὴ ὕβρεως, and in fact, since it would be difficult to imagine that any ordinary Athenian would risk a fine of 1000 drachmas to defend the honor of a foreign entertainer, this probably was not a *hybris* procedure.[262] A prosecution by the magistrates overseeing the mysteries, an *endeixis*, as in Andocides *On the Mysteries* for violations in the same festival, or maybe even an *eisangelia*, or a *probole*, as in D.21, would be more logical suggestions. Over all, the information available on this incident is insufficient to conclude that the *hybris* procedure, with all the risks that it entailed for the unsuccessful prosecutor, was used in the Athenian legal system to seek redress on behalf of a mere flute-player from Rhodes, or even that there was anything sexual in the misconduct of Themistios. His crime was to somehow offend the Two Goddesses, and that was definitely punishable by death, as several other incidents confirm.

There are specific references to the rape of male and female prostitutes where the term *hybris* has been employed in several sources. Neaira refers to the abusive behavior of Phrynion towards her, which included public sex in a party to show off to his friends, as *hybris*.[263] Aeschines refers repeatedly to the abuses upon the body of Timarchos by lovers as *hybris*,[264] and a passage of Lucian portrays an unwilling young woman trained by her mother to be a hetaira to be considering as *hybris* all sexual acts performed on her body for money.[265] The customer of the ancient prostitute bought immunity from prosecution when he

---

261 Din. *Dem.* 23.
262 About the viability of *hybris* prosecutions for any offence at all see the discussion in Ch. 4.1.
263 D. 59.38, and Omitowoju 1997: 1–24.
264 Aesch. 1.29, 55, 87, 116, 185, 188; see also Fisher 2005: 67–89, and the discussion above and also in Ch. 4.1.
265 E.g. Luc. *DMeretr.* 3.3 Phil. Τί οὖν; ἀνέχωμαι διὰ τοῦτο (sc. the money) ὑβριζομένη ὑπ' αὐτοῦ;

paid the fee. Society may have been willing to tolerate a certain amount of violence among young people, a few blows and black eyes over a hetaira, so long as it did not cause serious bodily harm or end up in court. Once the courts were involved the full force of the law applied, and Athenian law did not treat civil violence leniently.[266] The same applied to violence against prostitutes, male or

---

266 The speech *Against Konon* (D. 54.8–12), although it does not refer specifically to violence against prostitutes, draws attention to one aspect of violence which might help us understand better why societies so much accustomed to war and bloodshed still firmly discouraged civil violence, and viewed it as one step below murder. Perhaps the two were not as far apart in the ancient world as they might be nowadays, with the potential intervention of modern healthcare. In this speech Ariston, the prosecutor, was assaulted by Konon and his associates for reasons which appear to be rather trivial, nothing much more than posturing and naked aggression, if we believe the speaker. One day he got a severe beating by a whole gang led by Konon, was carried home injured, and a doctor was called in who appears as a witness in the subsequent trial. The speaker provides an invaluable step by step account of his recovery as well as the medical care which he received. We hear that the doctor was not worried about the cuts and bruises on Ariston's face, but became gravely concerned about the relentless fever and severe pain all over the body of the patient, and was worried that he might die of suppuration. The speaker says that a massive spontaneous hemorrhage offered relief and saved his life. The modern reader is left wondering how efficiently the ordinary Greek physician could deal with an infected cut, a blood-clot, a damaged artery or so many other hazardous conditions as a result of a violent assault, which in our times might only be a matter of a few hours in the emergency room, but for ancient medicine were insurmountable challenges. The law was clear: if the victim of the assault died immediately or a month later it did not matter at all. The attacker was liable for intentional homicide and faced the death penalty in either case.

Antiphon 2 suggests that substandard medical care resulting in death was no adequate defense against the charge of deliberate homicide, since the doctor was immune from prosecution and thus the responsibility for the death reverted entirely to the attacker. Drunkenness or laddish behavior would be no adequate defense either. Society might be willing to overlook drunken brawls of young men, so long as no serious injury was caused, but, beyond reasonable doubt, the Areopagos court would not acquit an obvious murderer because he was drunk when he committed the crime. Although modern legal systems do not treat leniently an assault which resulted in someone's death, they might define intent differently and also allow for a set of mitigating circumstances, like for example temporary insanity, or medical errors in the treatment of the victim of the assault, to affect the sentence. The Athenian legal system made no such allowances: the death of a victim of a premeditated assault was intentional homicide at all times and carried a death sentence. This is why the attacker, even if he never intended to cause any kind of serious injury, but only to assert his superiority over the victim with moderate use of violence, might end up paying for his aggression and lack of self-control with his life. The constant pleas for self-restraint, and the stress upon the need to defer such disputes to the authorities at all times, instead of taking violence into their own hands, everywhere in the Attic orators, as Gagarin has demonstrated, and elsewhere in Greek literature, probably were much

female. A certain amount of aggression by customers and lovers might be tolerated as part of the job. No one expected the aggressive soldier to be a gentle lover, and no prostitute expected to avoid completely fights and arguments involving jealous lovers and male competition and posturing. However, when the violent client bruised the prostitutes, the pimp might take him to court seeking compensation. The recourse that Battaros is seeking in Herodas 2 on behalf of the assaulted prostitutes is purely financial; something like "you broke it, you bought it." Retribution for the abuse and humiliation inflicted upon prostitutes is not widely reported in our sources, and it seems that the best defense a woman or man in prostitution had against abusive or insolent behavior, violence, bruises, beatings and injuries, physical or emotional, was their own value in the market place. The laws of Athens, as well as those of other Greek cities applied equally to prostitutes, at least in matters of physical assault, rape or *hybris*. At the same time, however, the limits of acceptable violence were higher in the case of hetairai, as young people sometimes might be rowdy and laddish about these matters, and customers expected a certain degree of immunity from prosecution for aggressive and abusive behavior against prostitutes. Considering that the rowdiness of young people around hetairai is a topos, but there are hardly any prosecutions for this, and the existing ones seem to be dictated by ulterior motives or particularly aggravating circumstances, it is safe to conclude that, as in our times, only a small percentage of assaults against or around prostitutes ever reached the courts.

4.4 Trials involving prostitutes in Athens

No trials or court-proceedings involving sex workers are attested in the 5th century, no doubt because such cases were not deemed significant enough to be mentioned in the high literature of the period. From the 4th century we have references to several notorious trials involving sex workers, partly because some of these hetairai became famous enough to attract public attention, and partly because the interest of later antiquity in the Attic Orators has contributed to the better preservation of 4th c. forensic oratory and information about court cases in that period. It is noteworthy that most of these trials are not directly related to any kind of sexual offence; usually they are introduced to court under different charges, mostly citizenship and immigration offences or religious

---

more concrete than some topos or empty moralizing. It may genuinely have been a matter of life and death.

transgressions. However, opposing litigants do not miss an opportunity to drag through the mud a sex worker for her/his lifestyle, and prostitution typically becomes a key point in such cases. Although often irrelevant from a legal point of view, references to prostitution were intended to evoke prejudice and damage the image of a litigant before the jury. This is why, although they are riddled with inaccuracies, rhetorical exaggerations, legal tricks and much factual distortion, these court-cases are very important for our understanding of prostitution in the classical period, as well as wider issues and perceptions of gender, sexuality and social dynamics.

In the *Corpus* of Lysias we find two speeches delivered before the Areopoagos in cases of deliberate wounding. The quarrel in both cases revolved around a prostitute, a young man named Theodotos in Lysias 3, and a female slave (or ex-slave, depending on which side of the story we are to believe) in Lysias 4.[267] Lysias 3 is a response to a man called Simon, who had accused the unknown speaker for deliberate wounding. Simon argued that he had contracted for three minae a young Plataian boy named Theodotos, who sounds around 15 or 16 years old at the time, to stay with him for a certain period of time. The speaker, who disputes the existence of such a contract, seemingly stole Theodotos away from Simon and this started a quarrel which led to a violent incident in front of the house of Simon. The latter argued that the speaker had gone to his house with the intent to injure him, while the speaker tries to minimize the events by saying that everyone gave as good as they got in the ensuing fight, and that he only went to the house of Simon in order to help Theodotos, who had been abducted and dragged there against his will. The speaker expresses embarrassment and emphatically states that it was regrettable for a man of his age to be fighting over a prostitute boy. The charges were serious and conviction would result in exile and confiscation of his property.

Throughout this affair Theodotos, although a citizen boy, is treated like nothing more than a pricy commodity, constantly changing hands, and suffering abuse and violent assaults as he is caught up in the middle of angry exchanges between the two men. The reader is left with the feeling that such mistreatment was to be expected in the life of a prostitute, and sometimes he/she had to put up with the insecurities, jealousy and violent outbursts of clients. However, there is no form of moral judgment against Theodotos, no insult or

---

[267] The topics of sexual violence and physical abuse, for which these speeches are important sources are discussed in greater detail in Ch. 4 iv. Here it will be sufficient to present a brief outline of the court-cases and explore how prostitution features in the argumentation and forensic strategy of each speech.

even a vaguely condescending remark. The speaker treats him with much courtesy and affection, and speaks respectfully of the youth, even though it might have been in his best interests to pin some of the blame upon Theodotos. It is clear that he loved the young man and did not want to implicate him in any way in his messy quarrel with Simon.

By contrast, the speaker in Lysias 4 refers to the woman who was in the center of the quarrel quite disparagingly. The speaker in Lysias 4, also accused of assaulting his opponent in a quarrel over a prostitute, is embarrassed too, but in this case he does not consider it worthy of a man in his position to be dragged to court over a slave whore (ἕνεκα πόρνης ἀνθρώπου).[268] The two sides disagreed over the status of the woman. The speaker treated her as a slave, while his opponent claimed that she had been set free. The two men, it seems, were sharing the woman at some point; they had bought her in common and were jointly sharing her affections.[269] However, this relationship did not end amicably, because, it seems, strong emotions and jealousy took over. The opponent of the speaker appears to have been the winner in love; he set the woman free and was keeping her as his concubine. The speaker acted like a sore loser, they started fighting, and he ended up with injuries and a nasty court battle before the Areopagos. The speaker, perhaps because he was the one who had lost in love, treats the woman as nothing more than a common slave whore, worth some money, but certainly not worth his affections and the trouble that he went through over her. It is noteworthy that in both cases mentioned above the charge of deliberate wounding (γραφὴ τραύματος ἐκ προνοίας), although risky for the prosecutor,[270] could have an immediate benefit, which provided a strong motive: with the convicted opponent permanently removed from Attica the successful litigant was by default the winner in love.

The two most important documents concerning prostitutes on trial from the classical period are two lengthy speeches, which have survived in their entirety. They concern a man who strongly denied that he had been a prostitute and a woman who admitted that she had been a notorious hetaira in her younger days. Both were delivered within a space of 4 or 5 years in the second half of the

---

268 Lys. 4.9.
269 For a similar arrangement see D. 59.29–30, where Eucrates and Timanoridas had bought Neaira together, and shared her affections over a long period of time, probably more than a year, until one of them was about to get married. However, Eucrates and Timanoridas ended this arrangement amicably. They accepted a reduced payment and set her free. Their case was different because, unlike the rivals in Lys. 4, they had not fallen in love with Neaira.
270 There is a long discussion about this procedure and the potential risks that came with it, which does not concern us here. See Phillips 2007: 74–105.

340's, and both were political trials motivated by animosities in public life related to the vexed question whether Athens should oppose Philip II of Macedon or seek an alliance with him, and in reality had nothing to do with sexual morality. However, a bombastic rhetoric of moralistic banalities dominates both texts, rhetoric which has generated much discussion about moral discourse in 4th century Athens, and needs to be treated with caution. Neither of these texts offers a systematic exploration or discussion of Athenian sexual morality; what we find in both is exploitation of largely untrue events in order to ruin the image and reputation of the opponent. In both cases prostitution falsely appears to be directly related to the main charge.

From the point of view of the prosecutor, the fact that Neaira had been a prostitute proves that she was alien and thus not the wife of a citizen man, but from the point of view of the defense it proves nothing at all.[271] The defense agreed that she had been a prostitute and that she never was the wife of Stephanos; she was his life-long concubine, and there was nothing unlawful in this. The prosecutor of Timarchos alleged that the defendant had been a prostitute and thus unsuitable to be a practicing politician, but the defense disagrees and demands evidence proving that Timarchos had been a prostitute, which was never provided because it did not exist. In both cases the inherent weakness of the prosecution is countered by a colorful narrative, with many hints and references to prostitutes of both sexes and their lifestyles. These memorable narratives are the main reason why both texts have remained very popular and have influenced the debate on sexual morality in the classical period to an extent that far exceeds their true merit as historical sources.

The prosecution of Neaira took place shortly before the war of Athens with Philip in 339. Philip's attack on Olynthus in the summer of 348 had sparked a long and twisted quarrel between two minor political players. Apollodoros, the son of the super-rich banker Pasion, was a supporter of Demosthenes and bitterly opposing Philip, while Stephanos, the son of Antidorides, was a supporter of Euboulos, and fervently advocated a policy of accommodation with Philip. There is no doubt that both were serving larger interests when they kept attacking each other with a number of lawsuits, one more vicious than the other, for almost a decade. Personal animosity, generated over time by the mutual assaults and battles between the two men in public life, may also have played a large part of this quarrel. The climax of this angry exchange was the prosecution

---

271 For a more thorough discussion of the rhetorical manipulation of the theme of prostitution in the speech see: Glazebrook 2005: 161–187; Patterson 1993: 199–216; Hamel 2003; Kapparis 1999 (esp. 28–42).

of Neaira, a completely innocent elderly woman who had nothing to do with the political squabbles of the two men or Athenian politics as a whole.[272] She was the life-long concubine of Stephanos, and had been a famous hetaira in her younger days, but had given up prostitution for more than 30 years before her trial. Apollodoros argued that she was living with Stephanos as his lawful wife, because their children were recognized as Athenian citizens, which would not have been permissible if she were simply an alien concubine. Stephanos argued that his citizen children were not from Neaira but from his first wife who had been an Athenian citizen.

In a society which kept detailed written records of all births it would have been a simple matter of checking the register, but since Athens, like most ancient societies, did not keep such records things became complicated. Athens only kept records of adult male citizens at the local deme registers, and no doubt all three boys of Stephanos, men in their 30's at the time of this trial, were registered with the deme of Eroiadai. Apollodoros knew that directly trying to cast doubt on their citizen status would be difficult and required serious proof. This is why he leaves the three boys alone. His strategy consists of a three-prong attack. First, he discusses in considerable detail Neaira's career as a prostitute, initially in Corinth, then in Athens and other parts of the Greek world. This part of his narrative is legally irrelevant, but for that reason significant. A seasoned orator and politician like Apollodoros, with 30 years of experience in the Athenian court system, would not have devoted one third of his speech to a meaningless quest, a point on which the defense agreed, unless he had something substantial to gain.[273] By recreating the image of a fickle hetaira, he wanted to

---

272 In all likelihood the timing of the prosecution of Neaira is not accidental. It follows the siege of Byzantium by Philip (343/2), which proved that he never sincerely meant an accommodation with Athens, and completely discredited the peace party. Now, as Athens was preparing for the final confrontation with Philip, which was going to come a few years later in the field of Chaironeia (338), there was significant political realignment, and even the old champion of the peace party, Euboulos, abandoned his former ally Stephanos and sided with Apollodoros in his bid to remove Stephanos from public life through an attack on his elderly concubine Neaira. If the attack succeeded, Stephanos would face financial ruin and a large debt to the state, which most likely he would not be able to pay, and consequently he would be disfranchised (ἄτιμος) and removed from the political stage; see Kapparis 28–42.

273 Six more of his speeches have survived in the *Corpus Demosthenicum*, mistaken for speeches of Demosthenes (D. 46, 47, 49, 50, 52, 53). Several more court-cases are known, where Apollodoros was involved, but his speech has not survived (e.g. the argument with Phormion [D.36], the trial for the *graphe paranomon* in 347/6 and a homicide trial probably in 346 [D. 59.3–11]).

tell the jury that the elderly woman sitting in front of them was more of a menace to society than her appearance suggested.

The second part of the attack is concentrated on the daughter of Stephanos, a woman called Phano. Apollodoros alleges that she actually was the daughter of Neaira from an unknown father born in Megara in the 370's, when Neaira temporarily lived there for a few years. Stephanos maintains that she was his own daughter from his first wife, and there is a whole series of events which if correctly interpreted confirm beyond reasonable doubt that this was the case. However, in the narrative of Apollodoros Phano is nothing more than an extension or alter ego of Neaira, alien, immoral, deceitful and ruthless, just like her. Through this stratagem the orator hopes to continue his attack on Neaira and at the same time assert his claim that Phano must have been her daughter, because she had the same traits and behaviors. He even alludes that Phano had been prostituted by her parents, while she was in between marriages, ironically in order to secure a dowry for her second marriage, but there can be no truth in this claim or the assertion of the prosecutor that the house of Stephanos was doubling as a brothel and its clients were forced to pay extortionate sums. The evidence he presents in support of these rather serious allegations, if any at all, is very weak and highly questionable, which allows the safe conclusion that this is just mud thrown at the opposing litigants.

The third part of the prosecutor's attack consists of a couple of long digressions which, again, are legally irrelevant, but no doubt significant in terms of emotional impact upon the jury. Apollodoros knew that he had a very weak case in his hands and tried to divert the attention of the jury towards matters where he stood on more solid grounds, even if they were not legally significant. He played with the fears and prejudices of the jury by telling them that if a prostitute as notorious as Neaira was allowed to transgress the boundaries and become an Athenian wife, the daughters of the jurors would be transgressing the boundaries in the opposite direction and becoming whores. If prostitutes could steal good Athenian men as their husbands, then decent Athenian girls would not be able to find a husband and might take up prostitution. In the final push, in the short argumentation of the speech, the stakes are raised and this case is presented as one concerning and threatening everyone.[274] The rhetoric employed at this point is strikingly dissimilar to that of later centuries where prostitution is presented as an inherent and absolute evil contaminating the whole of society with sin and moral decay. In the speech *Against Neaira*, it is not their

---

[274] The argumentation is included in sections 107–124, and represents less than 1/6 of the speech.

morals that the Athenians should be concerned about, but the boundaries between citizens and aliens or wives and whores. Prostitution is not seen as a
threat to someone's soul, but to much more specific things like the laws, the
institutions of the state, the continuation of the *oikos*, the legitimacy of children, the marriage of legitimate daughters and the honest conduct of citizens in
public life.

One might argue that it is precisely this rather nonchalant expediency
which makes the speech an important source for the life of prostitutes in three
cities, Corinth, Athens and Megara. Many a time, especially in the first third of
his speech, where he provides the details of Neaira's career as a prostitute,
Apollodoros simply states matters without even a single line of criticism or moralizing, as if the facts could speak for themselves, and mostly they do. The
heavy moralizing tones do not really come in until Phano enters the picture,
(who ironically was a properly born and twice married Athenian woman), and
peaks near the end with the passionate pleas of the orator to convict Neaira.
Thus, at least the first third of the speech can provide us with reliable and important information on issues like the trafficking of children for the purposes of
prostitution, a hetaira's education, career, working practices, liberation from
slavery, evolution from the high end of the market to concubinage and respectable anonymity, and numerous other topics.

Equally significant, but even less believable is the speech *Against Timarchos*, which was delivered in 346 during the trial of an Athenian politician under the law on the scrutiny of the orators (δοκιμασία: passage 5b).[275] Aeschines
had prosecuted Timarchos with an ἐπαγγελία alleging that he continued to
advise the assembly, even though the law forbade citizens who had been male
prostitutes in their adult life to do so. The background and ulterior motives of
this prosecution were political,[276] while this speech is the first known instance
where sexual moralizing is extensively employed as a smoke-screen to hide the
vicious political wrangling backstage. The heavy moralizing tones of Aeschines
right from the outset obscure the issues and inhibit our understanding. The
narrative of the speech begins with recitations of laws which were supposedly
relevant for this case, and proved that Solon, the quintessential Athenian law-

---

275 For a more thorough discussion of the numerous topics which this speech raises see Ch.
4.2. Here I only discuss the development of the argument and the impact which the charges of
prostitution had on it.
276 Aeschines was a supporter of an alliance with Phillip II, while Timarchos belonged to the
anti-Macedonian party. If Timarchos lost he was to be disfranchised. His permanent removal
from the Athenian political stage would make it easier for the supporters of the peace of Philocrates to sell it to the Assembly.

giver, had a very clear agenda regarding the sexual conduct of boys and men, and that he firmly discouraged male prostitution.[277] How effective this rhetorical device was can be amply demonstrated by the fact that in several modern studies of Greek homosexual relations this legal narrative is accepted unquestionably as a sound foundation for historical analysis. In reality, this odd assembly of laws and decrees covered a time-span of over 200 years and a wide variety of offences, and included several provisions which had been obsolete long before the time of Aeschines (see above Ch. 4.2.). Among them there were regulations about the function of schools, rules about athletic and musical competitions, two obsolete statutes, one about the order of the speakers in the assembly and one about procuring, and the two laws on male prostitutes speaking in the assembly (5a and 5b), all thrown together as if they were parts of a master-plan to control the sexual urges of Athenian males. Most of this part of the speech is legally irrelevant, but certainly very significant as part of a rhetorical narrative which suggested that the orator was well informed and that the lawgiver had taken great care to regulate the sexual conduct of boys and men.

After this unusual introduction to the case (in fact, unique in the surviving corpus of the Attic orators), the proper narrative begins with the young Timarchos allegedly using a doctor's practice as his own personal brothel. Aeschines suggests that Timarchos only pretended to be a doctor's apprentice in order to get in touch with potential clients.[278] The orator then tells the jury about an alleged relationship between Timarchos and Misgolas, an affluent, aristocratic and quite respectable Athenian man, widely known for his preference of boys, hired young musicians and entertainers.[279] A passage of from the comic poet Timocles makes a joke about Misgolas and his rent-boys:

You do not think that Misgolas is approaching
Excited by young men at their prime[280]

---

277 Aesch.1.9–38.
278 Aesch. 1.40. This claim is flatly contradicted by the numerous references to the fabulously good looks of Timarchos both in Aeschines and Demosthenes (see Ch. 3 i.). We do not need to give much thought to this allegation; a citizen boy of exceptional looks in the prime of youth and from an affluent family would not need to be fishing for clients in the dreary practice of an ancient physician. If he wanted to make himself available for hire, he would have been vigorously pursued by men willing to spend a fortune for his favors.
279 See also Ch. 5 iv.
280 Timocles fr. 32.

Two more comic passages make jokes about Misgolas' attentions to boy musicians, one by Amphis and one by Antiphanes.[281] The passage of Antiphanes is referring to prostitution: it is a joke about the unkempt private parts of the ageing hetaira Sinope, with the comment that Misgolas is not fond of that spot, because it is full of sharp thorns (undoubtedly an impolite reference to her pubic hair), and that he prefers cithara boys. The name of Misgolas is included in Libanios' list of men who preferred men. The testimony of Aeschines about Misgolas is in line with what we find in other contemporary sources. This is how he describes him:[282]

> Misgolas the son of Naukrates, men of Athens, from the deme of Kollytos, is a good man in every other respect, and no one could find blame with him, but when it comes to this act, he has studied it in great detail and has always been accustomed to have around him some singers and cithara players.[283]

It was certainly this reputation that brought Misgolas into the picture. Whether Timarchos ever had any kind of relationship with Misgolas, sexual or otherwise, is not easy to ascertain. Aeschines goes to great lengths trying to convince the jury that Timarchos was one of the rent-boys of Misgolas, but he can only get witnesses to testify that Timarchos visited the house of Misgolas for a short period of time, and this may have been sufficient, considering the reputation of the latter. One thing is certain: the relationship, as described by Aeschines, is seriously misrepresented. Aeschines presents the relationship as one where an older, more mature lover was earning the affection of the younger boy with gifts and substantial spending. In this pattern Misgolas is the rich, older man who spends a lot of money on the attractive, young Timarchos. However, Aeschines had to deal with a troubling issue of credibility at this point: Timarchos clearly looked older than Misgolas, because he truly was older, perhaps by quite a few years. Aeschines attributes this as much to the bad lifestyle of Timarchos as to the good heredity of Misgolas, who apparently was looking very handsome in his mid-forties. Misgolas was 45 years old in 346, when this trial came to court, and Timarchos was at the very least 45 too, if not a good bit older.[284] We can do

---

281 Antiph. fr. 27; Alex. fr. 3.
282 Lib. *Or.* 64.83; Aesch. 1.41–53.
283 Aesch. 1–41.
284 Aeschines says that around 346 Misgolas was the same age as him, that is, 45 years old (1.49). Timarchos was also middle-aged at that time and probably older that Aeschines and Misgolas. As he was a member of the Boule in 361, and its members had to be at least 30 years old, Timarchos was born before 391, which would make him at the very least 45 years old in

the math, but the Athenian jury did not have the time or opportunity to do so and potentially could have been deceived by the erroneous facts of the prosecutor at this point. If there ever was an erotic relationship between the two men, Timarchos probably was the older man in this short-lived affair, taking under his wing the young Misgolas, whose looks were also fantastic, by the admission of Aeschines himself.[285]

The next set of allegations is even more distorted. Aeschines suggests that Timarchos was so depraved that he hired his body to a man named Pittalakos, a public slave. How a slave could afford an expensive citizen prostitute, how he could bypass the law that forbade slaves to pursue citizens and how he could own a profitable gambling establishment, if he was property of the city himself, are some questions which would be very difficult to answer if we believed Aeschines at this point. However, we do need to worry about such impossibilities: Pittalakos was probably an affluent metic, and if he had ever been a slave in the past, certainly he had been freed long before this trial, long enough to amass substantial property, establish himself in social circles and be in the position to set his eyes upon a young citizen man from a good family. There is no question that many jurors would consider a libertine to be an unsuitable lover of a citizen, no matter what his financial standing was, and Aeschines builds his case precisely on this prejudice. He provides no evidence proving that Timarchos ever hired out his body to Pittalakos, or even that there was any sexual relationship between them. It may well be the case that the libertine was aiming higher than his social standing allowed, and through the pursuit of friendship with well-connected citizens, like Timarchos and Hegesandros, Pittalakos was trying to elevate his own position. In the final scene of this episode the property of Pittalakos and the man himself were attacked by a drunken crowd with Timarchos in their midst. Aeschines presents this event as a lover's vengeful quarrel, but since no formal prosecutions were made, nothing can be certain. The whole affair might have been nothing more than a drunken brawl in a disreputable gambling establishment, with no sex, male prostitutes or lovers in the picture.

The next person with whom Timarchos allegedly had an affair was Hegesandros, a prominent Athenian politician, offspring of a wealthy family and well-connected in the upper echelons of Athenian society. One can see the reasons why a young, ambitious politician like Timarchos sought the friendship of Hegesandros, but whether they were lovers or not remains to be proven. Aes-

---

346 (See Fisher 2001: 20), and this assuming that he joined the Council of the Five Hundred as soon as he was eligible. See also Fisher 2001: 20, and the discussion in Harris 1988: 211–214.
285 Aesch. 1.49.

chines assumes an improper relationship: Timarchos offered his prime youth to Hegesandros in exchange for a lifestyle of luxury and debauchery. However, no evidence is presented that the relationship between the two men was even sexual, apart from rumors and innuendos. All he can say was that the two of them had rowdy parties with hetairai and gourmet food, really nothing more than what many affluent young Athenians would be doing on a routine basis. And even if the relationship was sexual, this did not make it automatically improper, unless one could prove that Hegesandros had hired the services of Timarchos, which is never proven in this speech through any form of evidence. Aeschines tries to argue that they were corrupt even in public life, but he is so short of any concrete evidence that he has to resort to alleged crimes which Hegesandros and Timarchos were going to commit in the future, but never completed because they fell under suspicion and their plans were disrupted.

The alleged love-affair with Hegesandros comes as a climax: it is as if Timarchos moved from the lustful but generally respectable Misgolas, to the low-life libertine Pittalakos and finally to the worst man in town, Hegesandros, a man who was powerful, but also corrupt, lewd and deeply immoral. After this climactic narrative there is hardly anything worse that Aeschines could offer the jury in terms of sexual scandals, so he turns his attention to other character defects of Timarchos. First he alleges that Timarchos liquidated his parental estate to pay for his vices, but we must be very skeptical of this because Timarchos was not a poor man at the time of his trial.[286] Then he argues that Timarchos was mistreating his old mother and his blind uncle, but apart from a quarrel with his uncle, where Timarchos does not seem to be at fault, the justification for this charge is truly slim.[287] However, it is noteworthy that even though Timarchos was not at fault, the quarrel with his uncle may have been costly, as the blind old man appeared as a hostile witness during this trial.[288]

---

287 Very likely Timarchos, as a city man with a great interest in politics, did not have the time or disposition to run some of the smaller businesses which he had inherited from his father and liquidated them. Aeschines interprets this as squandering one's fortune.
287 Aeschines alleges that Timarchos mistreated his old mother because he sold a remote piece of land where she wanted to be buried, and that he mistreated his uncle because he allowed him to claim a disability benefit. However, one might not think the worst of Timarchos for selling a seemingly useless piece of land (ἐσχατιά), and his uncle was entitled to his disability benefits as a blind Athenian. If this is all the justification that Aeschines can put together for the charge that Timarchos had abused his relatives, we can be certain that the allegation is unfounded and that Timarchos had done his duty to his relatives.
288 Aesch. 1. 95–105; Arignotos, the uncle, was blind by birth and claiming disability benefit. In order to collect the benefit, he had to appear before the Council once a month. Arignotos

The next set of allegations concerns public life. Aeschines argues that Timarchos had accepted bribes and stolen a lot of money from the public purse through various schemes and tricks. One bribery charge was certainly true, because Timarchos had admitted to it and was fined; several others may be true considering that bribery and corruption were not uncommon in 4th century politics, but Aeschines is not in the position to present any evidence to substantiate any further allegations. In the last third of the speech Aeschines presents citations from poetry, especially the Iliad, where he contrasts the pure love of Achilles and Patroclus with the shameless and whorish ways of Timarchos and other indecent men of his time.[289] He also tries to anticipate the arguments of the defense and respond to them in advance, as he will not have another chance to answer any objections or counter-arguments.[290]

There is not a single part in this lengthy speech which makes a credible case against Timarchos, but this did not save him from disfranchisement. The reasons behind the jury's verdict can be many. First and foremost, there is no known instance of a large public trial where the jury voted against the current, namely contrary to the prevailing political sensibilities of the time.[291] In 346 BC, when this trial went to court, the political climate was favorable for Aeschines and those who advocated a peaceful accommodation with Philip, and unfavorable for Timarchos and Demosthenes who saw Philip as a great threat to the

---

missed a meeting at a time when his nephew was serving on the Council, and went back another day to plead with the Council to award him the missed payment. The Presidents of the Council understandably refused, but Arignotos was angry with his nephew because he felt that Timarchos had failed to support his claim. But Timarchos did not have the authority to award the benefit to his uncle, and even if he wanted to be supportive it is far from certain that the Council would have bent the rules. In retribution Arignotos appeared and testified against his nephew during the trial. This must have been a memorable moment, which potentially could weigh heavily in the minds of the jurors, especially older men who depended on their relatives for their maintenance.

289 For the recitations of Homer as part of Attic law-court speeches see Ford 1999: 231–256.

290 The only dedicated study on the anticipation of arguments in the Attic orators is still Dorjahn 1935: 274–295.

291 An Athenian jury convicted Alcibiades and inadvertently doomed to failure the Sicilian expedition, following public anger over the Hermocopid scandal in 415. Socrates was put to death, arguably for no good reason, because the political climate in 399 was seeking a scapegoat for the defeat in the Peloponnesian war. Kallistratos, for all his political acumen and great services to the Athenian state, was convicted to death for losing Oropos to Thebes in 361, at the time when the Thebans were perceived as a great threat by the Athenian state. Aeschines himself ironically lost the case against Ktesiphon in 330, although he was legally right, because the political climate had changed and history had vindicated the prediction of Demosthenes that Philip would overrun the whole of the Greek world.

interests of Athens. Around the same time Apollodoros, the political ally of Timarchos and Demosthenes, lost a *graphe paranomon* trial, even though he had carried the vote of the Assembly allowing the use of theoric monies for military purposes only a year ago, while Olynthus was under siege from Philip. He would take his revenge a few years later with the prosecution of Neaira, the concubine of his primary political opponent. We should have been surprised if Timarchos actually had won at that point, but we should not be surprised to find him losing even a non-existent case like this one. Unfortunately for him political sentiment was leaning towards his opponent, and the jury was more inclined to put faith in the words of the good Ambassador who had worked hard to forge the much-desired peace with Philip, rather than Timarchos and his party who had tried to sabotage it.[292] Other considerations need not be totally excluded and the power of Aeschinean rhetoric should not be underestimated, but this trial was born out of politics, not morals, and it stands to reason that it was judged on account of political sentiments and sensibilities, not moralistic platitudes, and produced an outcome perfectly aligned with contemporary political dynamics.

Several other speeches from Athenian court-cases involving sex workers are preserved in fragmentary form. Some of these fragments are quite lengthy, like the papyrus extract preserving a portion of the speech of Hypereides *Against Athenogenes*, while others amount to nothing more than short quotations in later lexicographers. The oldest of these cases appears to be a trial involving Lais. We have a few fragments from a speech attributed to Lysias from that trial, but both Harpocration and Athenaios express doubt about its authenticity.[293] Both authors use it as a source for the early days of high-class prostitution in Athens. Harpocration draws information about Lagiska, who eventually became the concubine of Isocrates, and Athenaios quotes a fragment mentioning a number of hetairai who flourished in the late 5th or early 4th century and gave up prostitution while still at their prime, seemingly to become concubines of wealthy lovers. These meager fragments suggest an early 4th century date, and at least in this respect do not preclude Lysianic authorship.

It is difficult to comprehend how Lais could have been involved in an Athenian court-case while living in Corinth. It is not unlikely that the case involved

---

292 The events surrounding the contentious embassy which forged the peace accord with Philip are discussed in the two great public speeches *On the False Embassy*, one from each side of the argument (D. 19, and Aesch. 2). For background and discussion the reader could consult the substantial commentary of D.M. MacDowell on the Demosthenic speech (OUP 2000).
293 Harp. s.v. Λαγίσκα; Athen. 13.51.

one of her copy-cats, some of whom were around during her lifetime. Alternatively the fact that the speech is a response to a case initiated by Lais (πρὸς Λαΐδα) allows for the possibility that she used the Athenian legal system (through a citizen patron) to take to court an Athenian man, perhaps a former client, and he is responding with this speech.[294] The orator seemingly devoted a part of his narrative to tales about other hetairai, as Apollodoros did in the narrative of *Against Neaira,* where he mentioned several other notorious women and related their stories to the early days of Neaira. A fictional case against Lais in one of the *Declamations* of Libanius may contain some traces from this case.[295] Another speech mentioned among the fragments of Lysias in defense of Nikomache (ὑπὲρ Νικομάχης) may also be referring to a sex worker, considering that respectable women in other titles are typically mentioned by the name of their father (e.g. Περὶ τῆς Ὀνοματοκλέους θυγατρός; Περὶ τῆς Φρυνίχου θυγατρός).[296]

Among the fragments of Hypereides there are at least four cases involving sex-workers, which suggests that by the middle of the 4th century in increasing numbers sex-workers were wealthier and prominent enough to be involved in high profile cases. The first, the case against Athenogenes, is not directly related to prostitution, but one of the villains, the woman who deceived the love-struck prosecutor into making a catastrophic business transaction, is a former hetaira, turned pimp in her older days, named Antigona.[297] The prosecutor does not miss the opportunity to mention her background as a notorious hetaira, and then a pimp, as he creates the portrait of a ruthless and deceitful woman, playing all the tricks that a prostitute would play in order to deceive someone and extract a large profit from the naïve victim. László Horváth has intriguingly suggested that Hypereides tried to compensate for the inherent weakness of the case through connections with contemporary comedy.[298] Hypereides consistently

---

294 Carey (2007: 429) has suggested that the title of the speech is To Lais, rather than Against Lais because as a woman she could not be prosecuted directly with a private lawsuit, and the case had to be tried through an agent, a citizen patron, who spoke in court on her behalf.
295 Lib. *Decl.* 25.2.40. For example there is a passage in Libanios with a reference to the Athenian hetairai of old days. However, the women mentioned there are different from those in the Lysianic fragment. In Libanios the women are the most prominent hetairai from the Athenian past (Aspasia, Phryne, Myrrine and Theodote), and there is little in that torrent of late antiquity moralistic stereotypes that one could use to reconstruct the early 4th century court case.
296 Fr. 257; 260–61; 303 Carey.
297 The Doric form of the name implies an alien woman, perhaps from Corinth, like her partner in crime Athenogenes, who was Egyptian.
298 Horváth 2007: 25–34

plays with the stereotypes of the alien sex-worker and the deceitful Egyptian to build a case which presents his client as the innocent victim of a conspiracy of expert con artists.

A few fragments of a speech of Hypereides against the hetaira Timandra survive in citations from grammarians and lexicographers.[299] We do not know the cause of the dispute which landed her in court, but it appears that Hypereides did something similar to what Apollodoros did in the speech Against Neaira. He started his narrative from the beginning, the early childhood of Timandra and her sister, and explained that they were orphaned with no one to look after them. After explaining how Timandra took up prostitution, he then went into her career as a hetaira providing some graphic details, which later rhetoricians found somewhat distasteful. Demetrios attests that Hypereides had mentioned silver plates, dildos and mattresses.[300] The silver plates should be understood as a reference to symposia and the licentious behavior of the participants, while the mattresses clearly imply sexual activities. Demetrios obviously thought that Hypereides had given too much detail, but if the phrase of Apollodoros that Neaira was having sex from three holes is authentic, and the information that Lysias said about the hetaira Antiope that she was having sex from two holes is correct, then perhaps distasteful references in speeches involving prostitutes, meant to shock and titillate the audience, were not as uncommon as the scholars of later antiquity would have wished them to be. In fact, Dionysios attests that he had collected a whole list of such rough and rude expressions from the spurious speeches of the Demosthenic Corpus in one of his studies, which appears to be lost.[301]

More numerous and even more difficult to arrange are the fragments from the two speeches against Aristagora, another case against a hetaira brought by Hypereides. This case is intriguing because Idomeneus, Hermippos and Plutarch attest that Aristagora was a concubine of Hypereides, established in his house in Piraeus, but here we find them on opposite sides.[302] Could it be the case that they fell out at some point and love turned into hatred and bitter court battles? Even if one were to assume that Hypereides was simply paid to write the speeches, he could not have written two prosecution speeches against his own concubine. If Aristagora had indeed been the concubine of Hypereides, these

---

299 Hyp. fr. 164–5 Jensen.
300 Demetr. *Eloc.* 302 Radermacher.
301 D.H. D. 57; see also the debate in Kapparis 1999: 402–404. Dionysios, however, might simply have been referring to syntax or vocabulary, not necessarily obscenity.
302 Idomeneus *FGrH* 338 F. 14; Hermippos fr. 68 Müller; Plu. 849 D.

prosecution speeches undoubtedly were written after a bad break up, and this is why it is not difficult to believe that he was personally involved in this case.

The other intriguing feature of this case is that, although it is a γραφὴ ἀπροστασίου, namely a prosecution of an alien for not having an Athenian sponsor (προστάτης), as the law required, two speeches Against Aristagora are attested, as a set.[303] There should be only one as this was a public prosecution, with only one long speech needed for the case. Fragment 20 may have the answer to this, when it says that the procedures for the bribery of a magistrate (δωροξενίας) are applicable to this case. If someone accused of immigration offences bribed a magistrate and avoided punishment, his/her accusers could reopen the case through a γραφὴ δωροξενίας, which was very untypical as Athenian law did not normally allow double jeopardy.[304] In this instance it appears that there was a first trial initiated through a γραφὴ ἀπροστασίου where Aristagora was acquitted, but then her accuser alleged that she did so through bribery and reopened the case through a γραφὴ δωροξενίας. Since the subject matter was the same the lexicographers and rhetoricians of later antiquity lumped the two cases together under the title of the original trial, as if the second speech from the δωροξενία case had been a mere deuterology. However, it appears that most of the references to prostitution and quotes of later times come from the second speech. One might think that Hypereides was trying to compensate for the failure of the first case by dragging Aristagora through the mud over her past in the second trial. This unusual process underlines the viciousness of the attack against Aristagora, and the use of strong language (κακολογεῖν).[305] Her accuser would not take "no" for an answer and was prepared to pursue the former mistress to the ends of the world. The scenario of a jilted lover using the Athenian legal system to get back at the one who had betrayed him makes perfect sense.

A reference to illegitimate children might partially explain the persistent attacks against Aristagora. If children had been born as a result of the love-affair, which of course would be illegitimate, they might be caught in the middle of this fight. A few more citations of legal terms allow us further insights into this case. At some point the ἀφαίρεσις εἰς ἐλευθερίαν (removal to freedom) is men-

---

303 About the *graphe aprostasiou* see Kapparis 2005: 71–113.
304 Sopater 8.268 Walz: δὶς περὶ τῶν αὐτῶν μὴ εἶναι κρίσιν (There can be no trial twice over the same case); Isoc. 2.42; Isae.6.52; And. 4.9; D. Ep. 2.23 al. About δωροξενία and the reasons why double jeopardy was allowed in this instance see Kapparis 2005: 97–98.
305 Hyp. fr. 25 Jensen.

tioned.[306] In the speech *Against Neaira* the freedom of the former prostitute was questioned and her partner Stephanos removed her to freedom. It appears that Aristagora was in a similar position; she was a former hetaira who had been freed by Hypereides, like his other concubines, Myrrine and Phila, probably for a lot of money. At some point it seems someone tried to hale her to slavery (perhaps Hypereides himself after the break up), but someone else was prepared to defend her freedom.

The reference to the metoikion, the special tax levied upon all resident aliens in Athens, certainly has to do with the main charge of trying to evade the immigration laws and lacking a sponsor.[307] The πωληταί were the auctioneers of the state, who dealt with confiscated property on behalf of the public treasury, and their mention suggests legal proceedings involving property belonging to the state, probably as a result of debts or fines. A reference to spiders (φαλάγγια)[308] is intriguing because a hetaira named Aristagora, mentioned together with two other 4th century hetairai, Thais and Lais, in a passage of Philostratos, was renowned, we are told, for her skill with *pharmaca* (poisons or magic potions).[309] If it is the same woman, maybe the accusation was that she used the poison of spiders for her potions.

Theon says that the second speech contained an attack against hetairai.[310] Athenaios quotes a passage mentioning Lais, Okimon and Metaneira. All three women flourished at the beginning of the 4th century (see index s.v.), which suggests that this passage comes from the narrative of the speech, and in particular a section reminiscing about the famous hetairai of the past. Aristagora could not have been their contemporary because Hypereides was not even born when they reached their floruit.[311] Two more women are mentioned in the

---

306 When someone haled a person to slavery arguing that he/she was a slave, any free person could remove the alleged slave to freedom (ἀφαίρεσις εἰς ἐλευθερίαν) by providing sureties that this person will appear for trial at a later date to decide his/her status. See Kapparis 1999: 248–250.

307 The *metoikion* was a fixed poll-tax of 1 drachma per month for a man, and half a drachma for an independent woman, plus a fee of three obols per annum payable to the secretary. Cf. Poll. 3.55, and Kapparis 2005: 108–110.

308 Hyp. fr. 19 Jensen.

309 Philostr. *Ep.* 1.22.

310 Theon *Prog.* 68 Spengel

311 Idomeneus *FGrH* 338 F. 14; Hermippos fr. 68 Müller; Plu. 849 D. Hypereides was born around 390, and the cases against Aristagora probably did not reach the courts before the middle of the 4th c.

speech, the so-called Aphyai (sardines),[312] who never appear in lists of the old hetairai, the women who flourished at the turn of the century, and this may be an indication that they were contemporaries of Aristagora. Like other prosecutions of sex workers in the 4th century, it seems that the past of Aristagora played a disproportionately large part in a prosecution that technically had nothing to do with prostitution, and seemingly was motivated by the relentless quest of a bitter former lover for vengeance.

Another famous prosecution of a prostitute in the 4th century appears to have been motivated by jealousy, and this time a few sources, albeit later, actually say so. One of the most famous cases of Hypereides was his defense of Phryne in a trial for impiety. Two modern paintings have perfectly encapsulated the popular mythology of the event. A painting by Genrich I. Semiradsky presents her disrobing at the seashore in Eleusis during a religious celebration. Phryne standing in the middle of the painting is taking off her garments assisted by several servants, while on both sides the stunned crowds are watching. According to some tradition this was the incident which landed her in court with accusations of impiety (ἀσεβείας). The other painting by Jean-Léon Gérome is representing the most famous scene from that trial. Hypereides has just removed her garment and a nude Phryne is standing in the middle of the room covering her face with embarrassment, while the jurors are gazing at her with amazement. This scene is following the version of the story as presented by Quintilian,[313] where Hypereides pulls the gown off Phryne and leaves her standing completely naked, and reflects a widespread tradition, best attested in Athenaios and Pseudo-Plutarch, according to which Hypereides in a bold move secured Phryne's acquittal with this stunt.[314] Poseidippos in his play *Ephesia*

---

312 These were two sisters of Athenian origin, named Anthis and Stagonion, who got their nickname from the fact that they had big eyes and pale skin (see App. I).

313 Quint. Inst. 2.15.9: Et Phrynen non Hyperidis actione quamquam admirabili, sed conspectu corporis, quod illa speciosissimum alioqui diducta nudauerat tunica, putant periculo liberatam. "They believe that Hyperides freed Phryne from danger not with his pleading, however admirable, but by the demonstration of her body. Because she had such a beautiful body, he stripped her naked by removing her gown." In the version of Athenaios Hypereides only bears her breasts (Athen. 13.59, γυμνά τε τὰ στέρνα ποιήσας) while pleading with the jurors to be merciful to the servant of Aphrodite. The version of Athenaios is repeated by Sextus Empiricus Adversus Mathematicos 2.4, the sophist Athanasius (14.173 Rabe) with a disparaging comment (τῶν ἐλεεινῶν μαστῶν μέρη παραδείξασα ἔπεισε), al. In the version of the anonymous scholiast of Hermogenes (7.335 Walz) Phryne herself tears off her garment and reveals her breasts in an act of mourning and desperation.

314 Athen.13.59; Plu. 849 D-E. For a more detailed presentation of the sources with commentary see Cooper 1995: 3030–318.

offers an alternative version of the events, according to which Phryne went around the jury, shook the hand of each juror, and tearful pleaded for her life. Thus, she secured her acquittal. There is no nudity or dramatic revelation in this version, and it has been argued that it represents a truer version of the events that took place during the trial.[315]

The prosecution and trial of Phryne for impiety are historical facts. Euthias, who according to some sources was a jilted lover, prosecuted Phryne,[316] while Hypereides, who boldly admitted that he was one of her lovers in the opening sections of the speech, defended her.[317] This much is certain from the scant fragments of the speech preserved mostly in the form of quotations by other authors.[318] A few brief references and citations in the rhetoricians are all that we have from this trial. Among these we find what appears to be the first three words from the Latin translation of the speech by Messala (*Bene fecit Euthia* "Euthias did the right thing").[319] The most significant of these fragments, is a quotation of the closing statement of Euthias, which provides us with the main points of the prosecution:

> Phryne is on trial for impiety, because she was carousing in the Lycaeum and introduced a new god, and put together groups (θίασοι) of men and women. "I have demonstrated to you that Phryne is impious, and that she was shamelessly carousing, and introduced a new deity, and gathered together illicit groups of men and women." At this point he is only providing the mere facts of the case.[320]

---

315 Poseidippos fr. 12; Casanova 1962. Casanova's argument is unlikely to be correct as it assumes a close personal interaction between the defendant and the jurors inside the courtroom which is not attested anywhere in classical sources.

316 Harp. s.v. Εὐθίας; Alciphr. 4.3–5, Hermippos fr. 50 Müller = Athen.13.60; Anaximenes *FGrH* 72 T 17a. According to some of these sources Euthias used a speech written by Anaximenes.

317 Plu. 849 E; Athen. 13.58; Poll. 5.93, 2.124; Moeris in *Anecd. Bek.* 195.8; Alciphr. 4.3 and 4.4.

318 fr. 171–180 Jensen.

319 Messala fr. 22: *Oratio Hyperidis Pro Phryne In Latinum Versa: Bene Fecit Euthia* "The Speech of Hypereides In Defense of Phryne, translated into Latin: Euthias did the right thing". The opening topos is familiar from Attic law-court speeches. See for example the opening of Lys. 24: Ὀλίγου δέω χάριν ἔχειν, ὦ βουλή, τῷ κατηγόρῳ, ὅτι μοι παρεσκεύασε τὸν ἀγῶνα τοῦτον ... (I almost owe a favor to my prosecutor, men of the Council, because he initiated this trial against me). Quintilian approves of the style of the translation, and says that Messala captured that subtlety which was most difficult for Romans (*illa Hyperidis pro Phryne difficillima Romanis subtilitate contenderet*).

320 Anonymus Seg. *Ars Rhet.* 215 Hammer.

A quotation from Harpocration reveals that the new god whom Phryne supposedly had introduced to Athens was Isodaites, a deity with a special appeal among prostitutes.[321] A few references in other sources suggest that this was a wild oriental deity related to vegetation and fertility,[322] and also connected to the sympotic space,[323] the sun,[324] and the underworld, like Dionysos.[325] Esther Eidinow has explained the trial of Phryne as part of a witch-hunt against magic and women who practiced it, and has offered an intriguing exploration of the true motives behind this trial, compared to a few other cases where women were prosecuted for similar reasons around the middle of the 4th c.[326] She convincingly argues that envy was the prime factor. Laura McClure correctly underlines that the prosecution of Phryne most likely had nothing to do with religious scruple.[327] Although the personal motives of revenge from a disappointed lover seem to have played a part in her prosecution, other factors like pushing the boundaries of what was and what was not acceptable for a woman of her time, and widespread envy for her wealth, beauty and fame probably played a big part. Eleonora Cavallini has insightfully pointed out that Phryne intentionally cultivated her own image with splendid dedications to Delphi and her native Thespiae, and posed for prominent artists like Praxiteles and Apelles (see Ch. 6.1.).[328] No doubt, the notorious hetaira sought fame, profit and empowerment through this self-promotion, but attracting too much attention upon oneself was always dangerous in the Greek city-states. After all, she would not be the first person that Athenian society would bring down a peg, when the common feeling was that this person had grown too big for their shoes.

Beyond this point the dramatic details of the trial which have captured public imagination are far less certain. C. Cooper has effectively highlighted the weaknesses of the traditional story and argued that the entire episode of her trial as told in Athenaios and Pseudo-Plutarch is a creation of later antiquity on the basis of the pleas read in the peroration of the speech *For Phryne*.[329] His main

321 Harp. s.v. Isodaites, repeated by Photios s.v. and Sud. i 648.
322 Plu. 389 A.
323 Luc. *Sat.* 32.20
324 *Lex. Seg.* 267.3 Bekker.
325 Hsch. s.v.
326 Eidinow 2010: 10–35, and 2015.
327 McClure (2003: 126–136) offers a very useful discussion of the true background behind the prosecution and trial of Phryne.
328 Cavallini 2010.
329 Cooper 1995: 303–318. See also Kowalski 1947: 50–62, and the previous bibliography discussed by Cooper.

argument in support of this view is that there is no contemporary source corroborating this story, and the entire episode has been generated from the misreading of phrases in the speech and tales about Phryne modeling nude for artists like Praxiteles and Apelles. From a legal standpoint too several of the details of this story raise questions; for example, impiety was not always punished by death. It was an ἀγὼν τιμητός, namely one of these procedures where if the person was found guilty, the jury would assess the penalty afterwards.[330] One wonders why in every version of this trial the death penalty is taken for granted, and this lack of attention to the legal formalities of the case perhaps undermines further the credibility of these stories. David Phillips has argued that the procedure was an εἰσαγγελία, but there is no evidence to support this in any of the sources, and the simplest explanation is that the legal irregularities are the result of invention and wild story-telling.[331] The trial of Phryne for impiety, the defense of Hypereides, who spoke as her advocate (συνήγορος), the acquittal of Phryne, and the apparent disfranchisement of Euthias, who reportedly never spoke in a case again, are relatively uncontroversial.[332] On the other hand, the colorful episodes which might or might not have secured her acquittal are impossible to verify or deny conclusively, and perhaps it is best if they are left in the sphere of the popular mythology surrounding this legendary figure.

Among the mimes of Herodas there is one traditionally given the title Πορνοβοσκός (pimp), named after the main speaker, a pimp named Battaros.[333]

---

330 For impiety as a legal procedure see MacDowell 1978: 197–200; Cooper 1995: 303–318. The *Apology* of Plato offers us valuable insights into the process in an ἀγὼν τιμητός. Once the defendant was found guilty, two short speeches followed, in which each side would propose a penalty (τίμημα). Naturally prosecutors would propose a severe penalty and defendants a more lenient one. Sometimes, the two sides talked it through and agreed upon a penalty (συγχωρεῖν). See also D. 59.6 and 53.26, where the prosecutor gives in to the pleas of the defense and agrees to a substantial fine as the penalty.

331 Phillips (2013: 458) comes to the conclusion that the trial of Phryne was initiated through an *eisangelia*, because the death penalty appears to be the only possibility in case of conviction in all sources. However, every source which mentions this famous case speaks about a trial for impiety (ἀσεβείας; e.g. Alciphron 4.3; Anon. Seg. *Ars Rhetorica* 215; Chorikios 29.2.45 and 76; Eustathios *Com. Il.* 4.579).

332 Hermippos (fr. 50 Müller = Athen.13.60) reports that Euthias never spoke in public again because he was furious with the verdict. In reality, if this tale is true, most likely he was disfranchised. If he lost with less than 1/5 of the votes, a fine of 1000 drachmas would be imposed, which would lead to his disfranchisement as a debtor to the state, if he could not pay. Moreover, there is some evidence which suggests that a speaker who lost a public lawsuit suffered partial disfranchisement and could not bring to court another lawsuit of this type.

333 Herodas 2. See Redondo 1994: 361–7 for a rhetorical analysis of the speech of Battaros.

The mime contains a fictional account of a trial before a jury for damages. Battaros, the pimp, has sued one of the clients of his brothel for assaulting and injuring one of the girls and damaging property in a brawl, which started because he did not want to pay the asked price for the girl, a slave prostitute named Myrtale. The problem of Battaros with Thales, a rich merchant whose coat alone, we are told, costs three minae, is not that he injured the girl, but rather that he refused to pay for the damage. The pimp argues that he needs to eat, so he needs to be paid, and if Thales is as madly in love with the girl as he claims, then he should pay the asking price and buy her off. "Then," Battaros says to Thales, "you can break your own things as much as you like", meaning that once the girl becomes his slave he could use any amount of violence upon her as he desires. This chilling presentation of the slave-girls of the brothel as nothing more than property which can be hired or bought for the right price, and then be used and abused at the master's wishes probably reflects quite accurately the conditions of lives of the numerous slave workers in the brothels of the ancient world. Although fictional, this account no doubt echoes disputes between brothel-keepers and pimps on the one hand, and rowdy customers on the other.

Such disputes probably were frequent, considering that carousing, property damage and physical violence are well-attested realities in the lives of sex workers in the ancient world (see Ch. 5.3.). This kind of quarrel did not often make it into the high literature because it would be too petty, too small to merit an expensive speech by a well-known orator, and too insignificant to attract the attention of philosophers and intellectuals. But there should be no doubt that such disputes did happen and often ended up before the magistrates, and in more serious cases before the courts. Few of those were particularly vicious and ended up in court with serious charges, as in Lysias 3 and 4, where the defendants were charged with deliberate wounding by their opponent and if convicted would be punished with exile. Some were motivated by politics, like the two most substantial speeches from the classical period, the speeches *Against Neaira* and *Against Timarchos*. A couple of those prominent cases involved famous hetairai and rich, powerful lovers, like the cases against Phryne and Lais. Finally a couple of these surviving cases seem to have been motivated by the wrath and determination of a jilted or betrayed lover, like the cases against Aristagora and Phryne.

All these cases have one important factor in common: with the questionable exception of the speech *Against Timarchos*, none of the rest is directly related to prostitution, simply because it was not illegal. They all concern other offences, but the sordid past of the prostitutes involved is invoked and vividly portrayed in an attempt to titillate the jurors, capture their attention and imagination, and use it to present the opposing litigants in an unfavorable light. The worst of the qualities associated with prostitutes, like deviousness, cunning, ruthlessness, shamelessness, and intent to take advantage of someone constitute recurring topics in these speeches, while the marginalization and social exclusion of prostitutes always hangs as a threat above the heads of society. Respectable citizens are frequently warned that unless they take a tough stance against the breaches of laws, customs and social rules, soon the entire city will be infected with such behaviors and the loose morals of those marginal groups will overrun civilized society. It is unfortunate that the surviving speeches are all prosecutions.[334] It would have been interesting to see how exactly the defense of a prostitute could be built in opposition to such prejudices and *topoi* commonly found in prosecution speeches. Perhaps, if we had the urbane speech in defense of Phryne in its entirety, our perception of the morals of the Athenians as surmised from their court documents would have been different.

---

334 This may be significant as a reflection of the choices of later antiquity, which enjoyed texts berating the embattled prostitute, but might have felt much more uncomfortable with a text defending pronounced sexuality and venal sex.

5 The Economics of Ancient Prostitution

5.1 Introduction

> Philoumene to Kriton: Why do you keep writing and tormenting yourself? I need fifty golden pieces, and I certainly do not need more letters. If you love me, pay up, but if you love your money more, stop harassing me. Bye.[1]

The world-wide net value of prostitution would be impossible to calculate, since its illegal status in many countries means that no reliable financial records exist. A recent estimate found that the world-wide worth of prostitution compared with other recreational activities is only second to that of alcohol and addictive drugs, about three times higher than that that of the world-wide film industry, sixteen times higher than the net value of the entire tourism industry and over 20 times the value of the music industry.[2] Even if one were to question the accuracy of these figures, the fact remains that there has been no society ever in history where prostitution did not exist in some form or shape, despite legal, social and religious sanctions. Countless people throughout history have been willing to serve the sexual needs of others for payment, either as prostitutes or as procurers, and even larger numbers were forced by someone other than the client to do so for profit. Economics have driven the industry of prostitution in every human society, often in defiance of strict laws, powerful social conventions or religious condemnation. When someone is willing to pay handsomely for a service, someone else will always be willing to provide this service, and this is why any and all attempts by individuals or groups to eradicate prostitution have failed without exception. The precise economic patterns of venal sex are complex, and correlated to legal, ideological, social, cultural, political and religious factors. Something illegal but desirable is more expensive than something legal and easily accessible, but on the other hand something socially and culturally acceptable may be widely available, which means that even if it costs less, the high turnover results in good profits. The ancient Greek world, because it allowed prostitution to take its own course without legal restrictions, and incorporated this trade into the finances of the city-state by means of taxation,

---

1 Alciphr. 4.15: fictional letter supposedly by a hetaira to one of her lovers. The current citation is the entire letter.
2 Data from Elliott Morss: "The Economics of the Global Entertainment Industry," 2008. URL: http://www.morssglobalfinance.com/the-economics-of-the-global-entertainment-industry/

DOI 10.1515/9783110557954-005

may be an excellent paradigm for the study of the economics of prostitution and their relation to the life of the host community.

5.2 Forms and Economics of Ancient Prostitution

From the early days of prostitution in the Greek world financial prosperity was tied to the development of a vigorous and multi-tiered sex market.[3] The two early centers of high-class prostitution Corinth and Naukratis were both affluent merchant cities in the archaic period. Naukratis, the hometown of Rhodopis, the first hetaira to be known by name, was a flourishing commercial center as for some time it was the only Greek settlement and harbor in Egypt.[4] Athenaios, a citizen of Naukratis himself, assures us that the city had beautiful and notorious hetairai in those early days.[5] The merchants who flocked into its harbor from every part of the Greek world were seeking the company of women, especially after a long voyage at sea, and were willing to spend good money on them. One such famous story tells us how the brother of Sappho, a man named Charaxos, went to Egypt to sell Lesbian wine, fell in love with Rhodopis and spent most of the profits on her; then an annoyed Sappho attacked Rhodopis with biting verses. The historical truth behind this narrative is difficult to ascertain and has been a hotly contested issue in the international bibliography (see the discussion in Ch. 1.1.). What seems certain is that the prosperity of the city as a commercial center brought together wealthy merchants from three continents and created very favorable conditions for the early development of vigorous prostitution markets.

Corinth was also a wealthy city throughout most of its long and illustrious history, and a commercial center which attracted merchants from all over the Mediterranean.[6] It was also the most prominent center for top of the range prostitution in the Greek world, and more famous for its hetairai than it was for its

---

3 This does not mean that prostitution was completely absent from less prosperous places; it only means that it was not worth a mention in literature.

4 About Rhodopis see Hdt. 2.135; Str. 17.1.33, and Ch. 1.1. A reference to a garland of Naukratis in Anacreon (fr. 89 Page) seems to be referring to a sympotic setting, and thus may be an allusion to the famous hetairai of Naukratis. Ancient scholars were intrigued by this reference and attempted to explain it (see Theopompos *FGrH* 115 F 106 b, and a vivid discussion in Athen. 13. 11 and 18). About the commercial importance of Naukratis and its wealth see Hdt. 2.179; Str. 17.1.33; Bresson 2005: 133–155, with previous bibliography.

5 Athen. 13.69.

6 For a comprehensive history of Corinth see Salmon 1984.

splendid buildings or its many accomplishments in the arts, commerce and engineering. Ancient authors keep repeating the proverb "Not every man can sail to Corinth" as a sign of the affluence of the city, due to prostitution.[7] Strabon links the proverb to the city's prostitutes as following:

> Because of them the city was a very popular destination and a rich place. Sailors were easily induced to spending a lot, and thus the proverb that "Not every man can sail to Corinth." [8]

Diogenian explains the proverb arguing that the hetairai "taxed" (ἐδασμολόγουν) travelers upon their arrival, and Zenobios adds that they did so in order to secure their own provisions (ἐφόδια). The use of ἐδασμολόγουν must be metaphorical: Diogenian meant that the hetairai extracted large sums of money from the travelers, in exchange for sexual services. This usage of ἐφόδια, on the other hand, is closer to its Modern Greek meaning, and simply means "provisions or living expenses" in a generic sense. A passage of Plautus may actually help us clarify how exactly the Corinthian hetairai "taxed" the visitors in the city:

> The hetairai have this custom:
> They send to the harbor their servants and maids
> To check whether some foreign ship has arrived;
> They make inquiries, who is he, what's his name,
> Then they immediately attach themselves, they glue themselves to him
> If they lure him in, they send him home penniless.[9]

This evidence echoes the widespread view that the Corinthian hetairai were a rich man's exclusive privilege, and only those with deep pockets should even attempt the journey. The same idea is conveyed in Aristophanes Wealth:

> They say that the Corinthian hetairai
> ignore a poor man trying to seduce them, but if he is rich
> they turn their ass to him right away.[10]

---

7 E.g. Ar. fr. 928; Str. 8.6.20, 12.3.36, Diogenian *Paroem. Gr.* 7.16; Sch. Luc. 70.27, al. Richard Janko (2007: 296–297) proposed that this phrase formed a couplet with another proverb "When you go by Maleas, you better forget your home," but there is no evidence linking the two together; each proverb is always quoted separately.
8 Str. 8.6.20.
9 Plaut. *Men.* 338–343.
10 Ar. *Plu.* 149–152.

The earliest reference to the Corinthian hetairai in our sources is a Pindaric *skolion*. The passage is very controversial as it has been interpreted as evidence of sacred prostitution in the city of Corinth. Although this interpretation is undoubtedly mistaken, the *skolion* still provides important evidence about the degree of integration of the hetairai into the upper strata of Corinthian society, and the perception of them as a significant resource in the economic and cultural life of the city.[11] This perception is also the underlying concept behind a passage of Theopompos, repeated by Chamaileon, Timaios and several other sources, that the hetairai participated in the sacrifices and subsequent festivities at the temple of Aphrodite. Theopompos relates this tradition to the years of the Persian wars, when the hetairai went en mass to pray to the goddess in the face of the imminent peril from the armies of Xerxes.[12] This story is probably an *aition* invented to explain the mass participation of the hetairai in the religious festivities at the temple of Aphrodite, but one does not need to resort to such means in order to understand why the hetairai would participate in large numbers in the festivities of their patron goddess. Even if one were to discount religious zeal, this would be the perfect occasion for them to be seen by large crowds and attract the attention of potential clients. Sophisticated and timocratic Corinth was the kind of city where such prolific creators of wealth as its many and famous hetairai would not be shunned during a communal occasion, and their open participation in large numbers must have been a sight which stunned the visitors to the city, especially those coming from more closed and conservative communities around the Greek world.

Important evidence about the workings and finances of one of those very exclusive Corinthian brothels is provided in the narrative of the speech of Apollodoros *Against Neaira*. Its clients were men of considerable means like the Athenian Phrynion, Lysias the orator, or the Cretan Sotadas, and high-born offspring of the best Greek families, like Simos the heir to the Aleuadai of Larisa, the noblest and most powerful family in central Greece. The brothel was run by the libertine Nikarete, who owned a small number of hetairai, probably one or two at a time, and presented them as her own daughters to clients (see below), for it seems this pretense of respectability made the girls more desirable and pricier. Clients were expected to pay large amounts of money for the girls, enough to maintain the entire household and still yield a profit in the end. Two men who bought Neaira, one of the girls, found the 30 minae which Nikarete asked in order to sell Neaira to be a good deal in the long run, as it seems that

---

11 Pi. fr. 122 Snell. For a more detailed discussion of this passage see Ch. 1.1.
12 Theopompos *FGrH* 115 F 285 a; Chamaileon fr. 31 Wehrli; Timaios *FGrH* 566 F 10.

they were spending even more on a day to day basis trying to satisfy the constant demands of Nikarete.[13] Considering that the price of a house in a good area of Athens was between 10 and 15 minae, only rich men could afford to spend two or three times that on a Corinthian hetaira. The proverb that Corinth was not for everyone's purse was after all true.

Athens itself provides ample evidence of the close link between economics and prostitution. Economically depressed Solonean Athens needed specific laws to define prostitution and protect the daughters and sons of the poor from exploitation (see Ch. 1.2.). The term ἑταίρα does not appear in the literature meaning "prostitute" until the middle of the 5th century.[14] There is a tradition that high class prostitution was introduced by Themistokles (for sources and debate see Ch. 3.1.), and this may be an *aition* to explain why there is no mention of hetairai anywhere before the first half of the 5th century, when high class prostitution seems to arrive in Athens. It seems clear that the upper end of prostitution did not develop until the city became prosperous in the years of the Athenian empire. The Solonean law trying to define prostitution recognizes the existence of brothels and organized prostitution as well as free-lance workers,[15] but undoubtedly there was a vast difference between the street-walkers of Solonean Athens and the top-end hetairai of the classical period. The 5th and 4th centuries, when Athens becomes the economic and cultural heartland of the Greek world, are the golden era of the hetaira, and they would be remembered as such in the plays of New Comedy and the literature of the second sophistic. The link between the economic strength of the city and the development of top-end prostitution is unmistakable. Athens had much to offer, and unlike the more exclusive Corinthian market, it catered for all tastes and purses. There was great variety in the numerous brothels of the Kerameikos and the harbor area in Piraeus (strangely, where most brothels can still be found in the modern city), and much more in terms of entertainers of all kinds and free-lance prostitution from low street earners to highly paid hetairai. The size of the Athenian market, its buying power and the cultural openness which the first democracy fostered created the ideal circumstances for the many faces of prostitution to thrive and leave their own unique mark upon history.

---

13 D. 59.29.
14 The first reference to the hetaira in the sense "paid companion, high-class prostitute" in Attic literature is in Herodotos 2.135, referring to the adorable (ἐπαφρόδιτοι) hetairai of Naukratis, of which the first to acquire fame was Rhodopis.
15 D.59.67.

Half way on the road between Athens and Corinth lies the prosperous commercial center of Megara. Its busy markets were frequented by merchants trading in livestock products, and the economic success of the city invited the envy of its big neighbor. In 432 an Athenian decree imposed a trade embargo upon Megara which contributed to the outbreak of the Peloponnesian war.[16] The last war in history between Athens and Sparta in 373–371 also suffocated the trade of Megara.[17] Apollodoros, who is narrating these events, describes in some detail the economic depression in the city, and the impact that it had upon the lives of prostitutes. He tells us that during the war no merchants would come into Megara from the outside, which meant that the numerous prostitutes in the city had to rely on local clientele. However, the hard-working farmers and shepherds of the Megarid were not keen on spending lavishly their earnings on luxurious hetairai. Things only improved after the defeat of Sparta at Leuctra and the end of the war, when the markets reopened and trade was restored.

The prostitutional market in Megara, as in Corinth and Athens, relied partly on local workers and partly on imports. For example, the famous and erudite Nikarete, the student and concubine of Stilpon, seems to be a local girl from a good family, but Neaira, who worked there for two years, was an immigrant who went to Megara for work.[18] A fragment of Strattis and a passage of Plautus suggest that there was a fair number of passing sex workers coming into Megara from neighboring Corinth and Athens, and then moving on again in pursuit of better profits.[19] The comic poet Kallias refers to a group of hetairai who were called Megarian Sphinxes (Μεγαρικαὶ Σφίγγες), but despite the popularity of the joke in later lexicography we still do not understand well this reference.[20] There is no doubt that as the animal products industry of Megara flourished, so did the sex industry, benefitting from the influx of traders and the affluence they brought into the city.

Several other prominent centers of prostitution in the Greek world, mostly coastal towns and harbors, seem to operate along similar lines. T.D. McClain and N.K. Rauh have argued that the area around the Sacred Lake at Delos was

---

16 Thucydides 1.139–40; MacDonald 1983: 385–410. A more comprehensive history of the city is provided by Legon 1981.
17 D. 59.36–37.
18 D. 59.36–7.
19 Strattis fr. 27; Pl. *Pers.* 139; cf. Kapparis 1999: 241.
20 Kallias 28; cf. Hsch. μ 486; Phot. s.v.; Sud. μ 385; Phot. s.v.; Diogenian 6.35; Apostol. 11.15. The joke may have something to do with σφίγγω "to squeeze," both in a physical and a financial sense.

something of a "red –light district." [21] They date the development of the district into a hub for male recreational pursuits to the 2nd c. BC, when Delos experienced explosive growth as a commercial center, and at any moment large numbers of men with money in their purse were walking the harbor areas looking for some fun in the form of a gym, a shop, a tavern or a brothel.

Prostitution certainly was not limited to coastal communities. Even in austere Sparta, the famous brothel of Kottina was going to be remembered for centuries, and the potential success of the coup of Pelopidas in Thebes, which expelled the Spartan garrison, was based upon the assumption that typically after dinner the guests were to be entertained by hetairai.[22] However, harbors had much higher numbers of transient men with a lot of spendable income, and thus created an ideal environment for the development of prostitution, in all forms and shapes. Market forces were simply taking advantage of the higher availability of clientele, and this is why, as in our times, harbors and commercial centers offered the ideal locations for sex workers. However, unlike modern "red-light districts," which can be a drain on the resources of a city, ancient states knew how to make a profit out of the demand and the availability, by taxing the earnings of prostitution. Large market towns like Piraeus, Corinth or Delos, ever aware of the economic benefits of prostitution, were quite happy to allow the trade to go on legally, economically regulate it, indirectly take advantage of the generous flow of income into the city and the benefit to local businesses, and directly claim a chunk of the profits for the public purse.

5.3 Taxation of the Earnings of Prostitution

The procedure followed in the collection of the prostitution tax is explained by Aeschines, and it is a rather standard method of collecting taxes in Athens.[23] The prostitution tax (πορνικὸν τέλος) was outsourced through an auction at the beginning of the year to the highest bidder. The winner had a year to recover the money which he had paid to the public treasury and additionally make a profit.

---

21 McClain-Rauh 2011: 147–171.

22 About the conspiracy and coup of Pelopidas and his companions see the narrative of Xenophon (*H.G.* 5.4) While normally prostitutes would be brought in to entertain the guests, as in other Greek symposia, in this case the entertainers were to come into the room veiled. Thus Pelopidas and his men, disguised as women, were able to get sufficiently close, kill the pro-Spartan *boeotarchs*, and put an end to the Spartan occupation of Thebes. The brothel of Kottina is described by Polemon Periegetes (fr. 18 Müller).

23 Aesch. 1.119.

Andocides describes in some detail one such auction, that of the *pentekoste*, namely the 2% tax on imports and exports.[24] In 402 a group of citizens led by the democratic leader Agyrrios paid 30 talents during the auction to acquire the right to collect the tax on all imports and exports. Since this sum would be too much money to pay individually, it was common to have a group of people pooling resources and sharing the profits. Andocides states that the sum of 30 talents paid by the group led by Agyrrios was far too low, and their profits were very substantial. That year alone they cleared a profit of 3 talents (= 10%). When they went back next year and offered the same sum Andocides outbid them offering 36 talents, and still he was able to make a modest profit, which means that had the group of Agyrrios not been outbidden the second year, they would have made more than 6 talents (= 20%) profit in one year. There is no doubt that there was good profit to be made from those taxes, and this is why, it seems, there was never any shortage of bidders.

Aristophanes in the *Wasps* mentions that numerous activities were taxed at a rate of 1 % (πολλὰς ἑκατοστάς), but does not specify which ones.[25] Along with other sources of income for the state such as court fees, proceeds from mines, markets and harbors, rents and sale of confiscated properties, they amounted to 2000 talents annually. The figure may be somewhat exaggerated as Bdelykleon is trying to make a point to his father that less than 10 % of that income actually goes to the remuneration of juries, but still we get the impression that there were numerous taxes at the rate of 1 %. It is very likely that those activities which were taxed at the rate of 1% in 422, were taxed at 2 % in the fourth century, and thus the *hekatostai* mentioned by Aristophanes are the same taxes as the *pentekostai* mentioned by 4th century authors. This suggestion would strengthen the position of D.M. Lewis that there were many taxes in the 4th century called *pentekostai*, of which the one on imports and exports mentioned by Andocides, and a separate one on the imported wheat, mentioned by Apollodoros, are two well-known examples.[26]

In this context it might be reasonable to suggest that the *pornikon telos* too was a typical *pentekoste*, namely a tax at a rate of 2 % auctioned to the highest bidder at the beginning of the year. We do not have any indication of the amount of income which the state expected to raise from this tax, but if the

---

24 And. 1.73 and 133–136; MacDowell 1962: 109–110 and 158–9. *Pentekoste* (literally "the fiftieth") meant 1 drachma of tax for every 50 drachmas, or 2 drachmas for every 100, namely 2 %.
25 Ar. *V.* 658–660. A *hekatoste* (literally "the hundredth") amounted to 1 drachma of tax for every 100 drachmas, namely 1 %.
26 D. 59.27; Lewis 1959: 243–244.

plural used by Aeschines when referring to the people who bought it is significant, then we may be talking about a hefty sum which would be above the financial capacity of a single individual and needed a pool of buyers.[27] Who was
eligible to pay this tax is not clear. The most logical suggestion would be that all
sex workers in identifiable establishments of prostitution, large and small, had
to pay. Street-walkers and other free-lancers might be able to operate under the
radar of tax collectors unless they had a well-known base of operations, which
could be targeted. Prominent hetairai might also escape if they maintained a
façade of "friendship" and "gifts," like Theodote in Xenophon's *Symposium*,
rather than direct payments. Passing workers, who came to Athens from Corinth, Megara or other neighboring centers of prostitution for a short period of
time, maybe for an event, or a short stay with a client, as Metaneira and Neaira
did while in the ownership of Nikarete, were outside the grasp of the tax collectors during their stay in Attica as they could not be easily tracked and targeted
without a fixed abode. However, it is reasonable to suggest that all men and
women who were known sex workers and had a fixed residence in the city,
which functioned as a brothel, either separate from their home in a workshop or
condominium, or as part of their regular home, had to pay this tax, and the
assertion of Aeschines that the tax collectors who bought it knew exactly who
owed it must be accurate.

Failure to pay could result in seizure of one's property as a passage of Demosthenes reveals.[28] Androtion is accused of harsh tactics in the collection of
tax arrears and public debts, and among others it is said that he seized as pawn
property from two prostitutes, Sinope and Phanostrate. Demosthenes alleges
that his actions were improper as the two women did not owe anything, and
accuses Androtion of lacking empathy and humanity. It is conceivable that
Sinope and Phanostrate, both wealthy hetairai, maintained a façade of "gifts"
and "favors" with their clients, and this is why they could claim that they did
not owe any tax, but considering that both had well-known establishments in
Athens, this explanation seems less likely. It is easier to believe that they had
already paid their taxes, and Androtion was simply trying to extort more money
out of them.

Allison Glazebrook sees the direct taxation of prostitutes as unique because
professions and trades were not routinely taxed in Athens.[29] However, prostitution may not be unique because, as mentioned above, we do know that certain

---

27 Aesch. 1.119 τοὺς πριαμένους τὸ τέλος (those buying the tax).
28 D. 22.56.
29 Glazebrook 2011: 46–49. For the taxation of prostitutes see also Fisher 2001: 258–9.

trades had direct taxation, especially in the services industry, even though we do not have a list of those. Apart from the various *pentekostai*, the *dekate*, a ten percent contribution to a temple, was standard in the case of spoils of war, and also mentioned as a regular tax by the lexicographers.[30] Moreover, many of the financial activities in the agora were liable to taxation, especially if they involved foreigners trading in the markets of Attica. Foreigners routinely had to pay tax (*xenika*) for trading, in addition to the tax that resident aliens had to pay while living in Attica (*metoikion*). Considering that most sex workers in the Athenian markets were not Athenian citizens, it is not surprising that they were asked to pay tax for trading in Attica, and this might explain the origin of the prostitution tax. Maybe it was initially established as a form of *xenikon telos*, a tax on the numerous alien sex workers trading in Attica, but later even Athenian sex workers were coerced to pay.[31] By the middle of the fourth century, when we have references to this tax in the Attic orators, no one would find anything unusual about the fact that the workers of this very profitable trade had to pay taxes. The orators do not consider the prostitution tax to be remarkable in any way, probably because by their time taxation of various trades was not uncommon.

The regulation of sex workers extended to the setting of a ceiling price for the numerous entertainers used for symposia and private parties around the city. By the time of Aristotle this seems to be a firmly established rule, but we do not know when it was introduced.[32] A clue as to the origins and purposes of this rule may be hidden in the fact that it was enforced by the astynomoi, the officers in charge of public order in the streets of the city. One can imagine that competition about flute players, dancers, singers and other entertainers in private parties and public occasions led to frequent quarrels and price gauging, which resulted in legislation capping the prices and even allowing for selection of entertainers by lot, if there were numerous contenders. The price in the time of Aristotle was set at two drachmas (roughly the buying power of 200 US dollars).[33] The state, meanwhile, wanted to make sure that this law will not become

---

30 Harp. s.v. δεκατεύειν and δεκατευτάς. Phot. δ. 151, 154, 156; Ps. Zonaras s.v. δεκατεύειν, al.
31 The narrative of Aeschines (1.119) makes clear that Athenian prostitutes were also liable. If Athenian prostitutes had been exempt Aeschines would not have failed to mention it as a substantial counter-argument to the assertion of Demosthenes that Timarchos could not have been a sex worker because he never had to pay the prostitution tax. It seems both Demosthenes and Aeschines agreed that, at least theoretically, Timarchos would have been eligible, if he had been a prostitute.
32 Arist. *Ath. Pol.* 50.2 and Rhodes 1981: 574.
33 I calculate this figure on the basis of what an unskilled worker earned for a day's work, and what an unskilled worker would earn nowadays on minimum wage. In Athens an unskilled

dead letter with sly pimps arm-twisting or blackmailing desperate party-goers, and to that effect it took the rather extraordinary step of allowing an *eisangelia*, namely a public prosecution without risk by any citizen, against unscrupulous pimps who charged more than they should.[34] The price of 2 drachmas only included the standard entertainment, namely playing the flute, dancing or singing. Sexual services were extra, and since there was no price control for these the tipsy guests could be induced to pay a lot for a night with the entertainer. Essentially, hiring an entertainer was a two-tier system, and in order to understand precisely how the finances of this rather complex system worked, we first need to understand how and why people decided to hire entertainers, who hired them, how often and what they expected from them.

5.4 Entertainers, Types and Economic Structures of Prostitution

One of the most powerful orthodoxies in secondary literature is that the symposion was an elitist institution, born out of the lifestyle of the aristocracy in the archaic period and continuing to reflect its ideals even in the classical period.[35] This may be true for the archaic period but it is absolutely certain that in the classical period the symposion was not limited to the upper strata of Athenian society, and there was no good reason why it should be. Unlike typical pursuits of the upper classes such as chariot racing or studying with sophists who charged exorbitant fees, the symposium was affordable for everyone. The fact that the price of entertainers was set to a mere two drachmas, a sum which even

---

worker would earn 3 obols (1/2 drachma) a day, while nowadays an unskilled worker on minimum wage would earn a bit over $ 50 a day. This sum in the present economics would be able to secure modest accommodation, and buy the most basic necessities of life, with some difficulty and not much to spare for even small luxuries. Likewise, the unskilled worker's wage in Athens would secure a roof over one's head, a meal and the most basic necessities. Keeping this in mind it is convenient to think of 1 drachma as having the buying power of $ 100. This equivalence could be extended to serve as a guide for other price estimates; for example, in the housing market 10 minae would buy a modest house in Athens, just as $ 100,000 would buy a modest house in many parts of the United States.

34 Hyp. *Eux.* 19.18. In a normal public case a prosecutor who failed to obtain 1/5 of the votes of the jury was liable to a hefty fine of 1000 drachmas. Sometimes, however, the state waved this rule, when it wanted to encourage citizens to come forth and prosecute offenders, as for example in the case of maltreatment of orphans and *epikleroi*.

35 E.g. Hartmann 2002: 135–149; Kurke 1997: 106–154; Murray 1990: 149–161; See Corner 2011: 60–85 for more recent bibliography.

poor Athenians could occasionally fork out, conclusively supports the argument that the symposion was not the bastion of elitism that it has been thought to be. Anyone could afford to pay for an entertainer, some food and some wine, and have a few friends around for a social evening.

Not all symposia needed to disintegrate into a the drunken brawl, like the fictional *Symposion* of Lucian, with broken bones, black eyes and bloody noses, and not all symposia needed to be lewd affairs with group sex on the couches and nude prostitutes satisfying the whims of drunken guests, as numerous vase paintings seem to suggest.[36] Many a time a social evening was just that, and in a place where having friends and connections among one's fellow citizens was of paramount importance, one could argue that the symposion, which offered ample opportunity for this kind of networking, was a necessity for the ordinary citizen, as much as was his participation in the religious festivals of the city and in traditional citizen bodies like the *gene* and phratries. We have the explicit testimony of Plato that the symposium could be for everyone, the poor and the rich alike, the low classes of the market place (φαῦλοι καὶ ἀγοραῖοι) and the men of good breeding and education (καλοὶ κἀγαθοὶ καὶ πεπαιδευμένοι), and depending on the company it could range from a civilized conversation to a wild and costly affair under the loud music of flutes:

> It seems to me that speaking about poetry much resembles the symposia of the vile men of the market place. Since they cannot socialize with each other while they are drunk using their own voice and their own words, because of their lack of an education, they turn flute-players into a precious commodity spending a lot of money on another voice, that of the flutes, and through that they socialize with each other. However, in symposia where the participants are gentlemen with a good education, you will not see flute-players, or dancers or psaltery-players. The participants are in the position to socialize with each other without the nonsense and this kind of games but through their own voice speaking and listening in turn, even if they drink a lot of wine.[37]

This passage of Plato is important because it describes an entire range of symposia for all social and economic classes, although it favors the refined and elitist symposion of the educated καλοὶ κἀγαθοί. In the Attic orators many a time we get to hear about parties and symposia of the variety that would not meet with the approval of Plato, events that went out of hand, like the unconventional parties of Pyrrhos and his wife which upset the neighbors and led them to believe that she could not be Athenian, because Athenian women did not be-

---

36 See the discussion in Ch. 6.2.
37 Pl. *Ptg.* 347 c-d.

have like this, the infamous dinner parties of Timarchos, or the brawls which landed in court Simon and his rival for the love of the Theodotos.[38] All these constitute a far cry from the idealized symposion of Plato, Xenophon or Athenaios, and confirm the thesis that the classical symposion was a widespread institution for every man's purse and taste. The provisions about the hiring of entertainers certainly support this argument: they do not make sense unless there were many symposia around the city throughout the year. Only vigorous business with a high turnover and healthy profits could justify such restrictive caps and regulations, and there would be no need to impose caps and provide for the selection of entertainers by lot, unless there was much demand for the service.

We are repeatedly told that for a fine party one needed good food and delicacies, garlands for the guests, wine, entertainers and prostitutes (πόρναι).[39] The last two groups were not mutually exclusive. Sometimes the entertainers were the *pornai*, but on other occasions in addition to the entertainers, like flute-players and dancers, expensive hetairai joined the guests not overtly as sex objects, but rather as company for the men. Sometimes authors want to differentiate between those high-cost hetairai and the regular entertainers by stressing that the hetairai were not performers (ἑταίρα πεζή). A passage of Theopompos, for example, lists psaltery-players, flute-players and *pezai hetairai* among the entourage of Chares, while he was on his military campaigns. A note of Hesychios clarifies that this is how they called hetairai who did not use an instrument. Prokopios uses this term to defame Theodora, when he says that she did not even have any kind of skill, but only gave away her body to anyone willing to pay for it, like a common whore. In reality, however, the ones who could get by without additional skills were those who did not need them, because they had other means to attract lovers, like youth, beauty, charm and fame.[40] Common prostitutes from brothels or the streets might also be hired for some of the rowdier parties, when hosts and guests wanted more than good company and conversation from the outset.

Hosts who did not want to spend a lot on the entertainers might just do with only one, but in more affluent households, when one was trying to impress his guests an entire host of entertainers might be invited, as for example in Xeno-

38 Is. 3.13–4; Aesch. 1.42, 75, 115; D. 54.14; 59. 24–30; Lys. 3.5–20 al.
39 Ar. *Ach.* 1089–1093; Amphis fr. 9; Antiphanes fr. 224, 233; Nikostratos fr. 27 al. See also Corner (2011: 60–85) about the presence of prostitutes in the ἀνδρών and the sympotic space; Blazeby 2011: 86–105; Coccagna 2011: 106–121, and Murray 1990.
40 See. Theopompos, *FGrH* 115 F 213; Hsch. s.v. πεζὰς μόσχους; Procopios *Anecd.* 9.12.

phon's *Symposion* where three have been hired from a ruthless Syracusan pimp, a female flute player, an acrobatic dancer and a boy, or in Aristophanes *Frogs*, where the inn-keeper promises Xanthias/Heracles a flute-player and three dancers, all freshly plucked.[41] The objective partly was to have variety in the entertainment of the evening, from loud flute-players to gentle psaltery players and singers, to performers and dancers. However, an additional motive might be at work: the mindful host would want to provide plenty of prostitutes, to prevent ugly fights between the guests over them, and to keep his guests happy in this respect too. There was no standard format for such matters; it all depended on the generosity of the host, his financial means and the purposes for which he was throwing the party. But there was one strong convention in the Greek world when it came to parties: respectable women typically stayed away.[42]

The primary role of the flute-players, dancers and other musicians was to entertain the guests, and this was included in the price of two drachmas per entertainer, which the host had to pay to hire them in the first place. And as with modern parties one might have a preference for loud party music, while someone else would rather have a gentle sing-along with the soft tones of a delicate instrument, the ancient host did have a choice too. The flute was loud and exuberant, and this is why it seems to be the dominant party instrument. References to flute-players outnumber those to other entertainers at a ratio of 3 to 1 or higher, which suggests that the flute was the primary instrument to be heard in symposia, and this is not surprising considering that a successful, fun and spirited party sooner or later was going to need some noise.[43] Moreover, flute players were frequently employed as companions to serenades and carousing in the streets or outside the house of the person with whom someone was in love.[44]

A play of the comic Theophilos entitled *Philaulos* (flute-lover) had as a main character someone addicted to prostitutes, as we can deduce from the few frag-

---

41 X. *Symp.* 2.1–2; Men. fr. 224; Ar. *Ra.* 512–516;

42 See e.g. D. 59.24 and Is. 3.14, Nepos *Praef.* 6–7, and my previous discussion of the topic in Kapparis 1999: 217–220.

43 I have obtained these data from the TLG. There are 376 references to flute-players but only 98 to *psaltriai* and 128 to dancers. There are more than 700 references to kithara players and singers, but admittedly only a small fraction of them can be safely placed into a prostitutional context. See also Starr 1978: 401–410, for a brief account on flute-players.

44 X. *Symp.* 2.1; Pl. *Tht.* 173 d; *Symp.* 212 c; Zeno fr. 3 von Arnim; Plu. *Pyr.* 13.7; Luc. *Vit. Auct.* 12, al.

ments of the work which have survived.[45] A passage of Metagenes which certainly refers to a sympotic context states that flute-players offer themselves to sailors right away for money.[46] In Aristophanes' *Wasps* the naughty old man Philokleon has stolen a slave flute-player from a symposion which he attended, and tries to seduce her with the promise to free and keep her as his concubine.[47] A fictional letter of Aelian returns to this traditional topic, and there the son tries to deceive his father by introducing a freed flute-player as a respectable bride. The indignant father complains that instead of a dove he brought into the house a wild pigeon, and vows to cast out the pseudo-bride and force his son to do some hard manual labor in the farm.[48] Aeschines repeatedly says that Timarchos spent his youth in the company of flute-players and hetairai, fancy dinners and a decadent lifestyle.[49] Several comedies are entitled *Flute-Player* (Αὐλητρίς), by Antiphanes, Menander, Diodoros and Phoenikides (Αὐλητρίδες, in the plural), and, on the whole, there are countless references to prostitute flute-players, hired by customers for parties or revelries, and offering extra services for additional payment.[50]

It is difficult to tell whether most flute-players habitually doubled as prostitutes, at least for as long as they were young and attractive enough to fetch a fair price. We know that many flute-players were prostitutes, and also that flute-players were frequently used on religious occasions, weddings and festivals without a sexual subtext. It is possible that the dividing lines between the first and the second type of flute-player were never very clear, since in most cases one would be talking about trained slaves serving the interests of a master who would hire them out to make money in any way he or she could. The question is whether customers would consider it appropriate to hire a well-known prostitute entertainer for a wedding or a religious occasion, if they were fully aware of

---

45 Theophilos, fr. 11–12.
46 Metagenes fr. 4.
47 Ar. *V.* 1335–1363.
48 Ael. *Ep.* 16. The proverb φάτταν ἀντὶ περιστερᾶς "a wild pigeon instead of a dove" was well known as it first appears in Plato (*Tht.* 199 b), and was included in the collection of the paroemiographer Arsenios (17.81b), there probably derived from Aelian.
49 Aesch. 1.42, 75.
50 E.g. Men. *Per.* 340; Demetr. *Eloq.* 240 Radermacher, mentions flute-players in the brothels of Piraeus together with common whores and revelers; Plu. *Pyr.* 13.6, where a flute-player is leading a group of revelers during a *komos*; Plu. 363 A, where we read that in the houses of the wasteful one can hear flute-players playing into the morning hours, and drunken guests hanging around the doors; Harp. s.v. Νεμεάς wonders how the name of a festival could have been given to a whore. See also Starr 1978: 401–410.

her background and other activities, and there is some evidence suggesting that this might be a problem, as on the occasion where the flute-player Bromias, mistress of Phayllos, wanted to play at the Pythian games using the influence of her powerful lover, but the crowd stopped her.[51]

The flute was the primary instrument to accompany dancers while they performed. In Xenophon's *Symposion*, which provides in some detail reliable information about the performance of two dancers, a girl and a boy, a man named Philippos is dancing under the sound of the flute, and when he wants to dance more vigorously he simply instructs the flute-player to pick up the pace.[52] A host who wanted to have dancers also needed to assume the cost of a flute-player to accompany them. The two dancers are very different in style. The girl is an acrobatics performer (τῶν τὰ θαύματα δυναμένων ποιεῖν), while the boy performs an elegant dance with delicate and gracious moves of the entire body, which inspires Socrates to praise the health benefits of such an exercise. The first show of the girl is juggling rings, at some point as many as 12 of them, and the second is bending and leaping over swords arranged in a circle. A similar masculine theme is the inspiration for the performance of a female dancer in Xenophon's *Anabasis*.[53] She is dressed in battle armor (holding a light shield, we are told) and dances the war dance (πυρρίχη). Aristotle mentions that it is customary for dancers to use their hands as feet and their feet as hands, implying acrobatic routines.[54] A passage of Krates mentions some dancers whose trademark was long hair all the way to their genital region, no doubt as part of some strip-show act, while Metagenes makes a clear reference to prostitute dancers (ὀρχηστρίδας ἑταίρας) ready to give themselves to sailors for a fee.[55] Aristophanes calls a dancer "little whore" (πορνίδιον) and alludes to a brothel where she was established, and the dancers in the *Frogs* are teenagers and have just removed their pubic hair.[56] Theopompos reports that Straton of Sidon invited from all over Greece two kinds of young slave prostitutes, singers (ὠδικάς) and dancers (ὀρχηστρικάς). Persaios provides important evidence about the infamous Thessalian dancers who danced wearing a simple girdle (and nothing else); this he considers as "dancing in the nude," and says that it excited the guests of a party

---

51 Theopompos *FGrH* 115 F 24 = Athen. 13.83.
52 X. *Symp.* 2.2–27; about the dance of Philip 2.21–23.
53 X. *Symp.* 2.1, 8, 10–11, 15–6; *An.* 6.1.12.
54 Arist. *EE* 1246 a 34–35.
55 Krates fr. 34; Metagenes fr. 4.
56 Ar. *Nu.* 996, *Ra.* 516. In the Byzantine period it seems that it was customary for strippers/dancers to perform for customers in brothels, which in some ways are similar to modern strip clubs (e.g. Nikephoros Gregoras *Historia Romana* 1.447).

so much that they started leaping from their couches.[57] This suggests that total nudity was not to be routinely expected from dancers; one would imagine that total nudity would cost extra. However, dancing in skimpy outfits was the trademark of many entertainers, and the difference between those Thessalian dancers and others probably was one of quantity, namely how much more they were prepared to reveal. A play of Alexis is entitled *The Dancer* (Ὀρχηστρίς), from which comes the famous quote that women are eternally content so long as there is unlimited flow of wine.[58] A fictional letter of Aristainetos is addressed to a dancer, but it does not contain any useful information other than endless, cliché flattery for the girl's appearance.[59]

In the Hellenistic period some dancers and entertainers reached high status and acquired much influence in the royal courts. The first to reach high status was Philinna of Larissa, concubine of Philip II and mother of his son Arridaios, the one who was elevated to the throne under the name Philip III, after Alexander's death.[60] Demetrios, one of his successors to the Macedonian throne, kept a flute-player and hetaira, the notorious Lamia, as his concubine.[61] Polybios mentions the flute-players Mnesis and Potheine who reached high status in the court of Ptolemy Philadelphos and possessed the finest houses in Alexandria.[62] Procopios knew a couple of dancers who reached prominence in the time of Justinian (6th c. AD). One was Macedonia of Antioch, who reached prominence by exploiting her relationship with the emperor, the other was a woman named Chrysomallo ("golden hair"), who for some time had even worked as a high-class hetaira and gained status as a friend and attendant of Empress Theodora.[63] Emperor Constantine VII Porphyrogennetos believed that the concubines in the harem of Astyages were also dancers and kithara players, and it is likely that he is echoing a source now lost.[64]

In a significant fragment from the comedy of Theophilos *Philaulos* (flute-lover) one of the characters confesses his undying love for a female kithara player:

---

57 Persaios fr. 451 von Arnim.

58 Alexis fr. 172.

59 Aristainetos, *Ep.* 26 "To a dancer" (πρὸς ὀρχηστρίδα).

60 Ptolemy Megalopolis *FGrH* 161 F 4 = Ath. 13.40.

61 For the love affair see Ch. 3.1., and Appendix I.

62 Pol. 14.11. The wording of Polybios is ambiguous; Potheine may not have been a flute-player.

63 Procop. *Anecd.* 9.28–32; 12.17, 32–37.

64 Constantine VII, *De Insidiis* 29.

> Who says that those in love have lost their minds?
> He must be someone stupid in his ways,
> For if one were to take pleasures away from life
> There would be nothing left but to die;
> Me too, I am in love with a kithara girl,
> A young slave-girl; by the gods, I have lost my mind.
> Beautiful in appearance, tall in height, and an expert in her art.[65]

Diogenes of Babylon believed that the music of the flute was not conducive to love, and that background listening music (τὴν ἐπ᾽ἀκουσμάτων) was much better for that, while Plato and Plutarch complain that the flute kills conversation, because it is too loud for the guests to hear their own voice.[66] The psaltery (ψαλτήριον), a triangular instrument similar to a harp, produced gentler sound and would be more suitable for somewhat restrained and low-key events, as would be the kithara, an instrument similar to the lyre. Both were traditional instruments played in a variety of events, public and private, and were often accompanied by song, either by the performer him/herself or a singer.[67] Aristotle attests that those musicians came from the lower social strata, and many of them, both men and women, were prostitutes hired to entertain guests in private parties.[68] A play of Anaxandrides was entitled *Kitharistria*, while the masculine *Kitharistes* was the title of plays by Antiphanes and Menander, which might also refer to male sex workers. Antiphanes, Klearchos, Alexis, Nikon, Anaxippos, Diphilos and Sophilos wrote plays entitled Κιθαρῳδός (kithara player and singer), where the gender could be either masculine or feminine. Moreover there are numerous specific references to psaltery and kithara players employed as prostitute entertainers. Aeschines, for example, attests that Misgolas, one of the alleged lovers of Timarchos, had a reputation for being very fond of kithara boys, while Antiphanes and Alexis confirm this with jokes about Misgolas and his kithara boys.[69] In Xenophon's *Symposion* the beautiful boy who

---

65 Theophilos fr. 12.
66 Diogenes of Babylon, fr. 79 von Arnim.
67 See e.g. Pl. *Alc.* 106 e, where Alcibiades, we are told, had learned how to play the kithara; *Euth.* 272 c, where Socrates admits that he is learning how to play the kithara; Pl. *Lg.* 812 d-813 a for a description of what a psaltery player does. A passage of Hippocrates explains the techniques of κιθαρῳδοί, namely persons who sing accompanied by the kithara (Hip. *Carn.* 18). Deinarchos (1.23) mentions the case of an Athenian man, Themistios of Aphidna, who was put to death because he insulted (or maybe assaulted) a Rhodian woman playing the kithara during the Eleusinian Mysteries. See also Haldane 1966: 98–107 for the use of musical instruments in worship.
68 Arist. *Pol.* 1339 b 7–10. See also X. *Symp.* 2.2.
69 Aesch. 1.41; Antiphanes fr. 26; Alexis fr. 3.

could play the kithara and dance aroused enthusiasm among the guests and made his master a lot of money.[70] A slave-boy belonging to the host of the party is brought out to play for the guests in the fictional narrative of Achilles Tatius.[71] The boy himself is a domestic slave, not a prostitute, but his song about the love of Apollo and Daphne inflames the love of Kleitophon for Leukippe, which offers us a glimpse into how this kind of acoustic, background song could be conducive to erotic encounters in parties, just as Diogenes suggests.

The host might try to control the mood of the party sometimes by requesting something more exuberant to lift the spirits, and then something more soothing to calm down a wild party. There is a story about Damon the musician, told by Poseidonios and repeated by Galen, that once he calmed down a party which was getting out of control by simply asking the flute player to change the song from a Phrygian to a more austere Doric tune.[72] The choice of the instrument might be just as effective for controlling the tone of the party. The flute would probably create a livelier atmosphere, but if someone preferred something gentler the psaltery or the lyre would be more appropriate. A generous host who could afford more than one entertainer might book a few for variety. For example, one could start with the soothing sounds of the psaltery, bring in the dancers to give the guests a good show, and then lift the mood of the party with the flute. There should be plenty of time for socializing and good conversation too, and near the end of the party there might be an auction for the entertainers.

Xenophon, who is telling us in the *Symposion* that the Syracusan pimp made most of his money during the party, above and beyond the standard fee paid to hire the entertainers for the evening, is not very clear as to how this happened. On the other hand, a passage of Persaios describes in some detail the auction of a flute-player near the end of the party; the highest bidder could spend the night with her:

> One of the philosophers was drinking with us, when a flute-player was brought in. Since there was plenty of room next to him, the girl tried to sit there, but he wouldn't let her, and appeared to be severe. However, later on, when the flute-player was auctioned, as is customary in drinking parties, he was very hasty in trying to buy her, and awkward to the one who was selling her. When someone else offered more money, he kept arguing with

---

70 X. *Symp.* 2.2–3.
71 Ach. Tat. 1.5.4.
72 Damon Testimonium 8 D-K = Poseidonios fr. 417 Theiler.

him that she had not been sold to him. Finally, he came to blows with him, that same stern philosopher who earlier would not even let the flute-player sit next to him.[73]

Under the influence of alcohol and the spirit of competition with other men, one can imagine that the bidding could be extravagant, and that altercations would not be uncommon. The entire process was designed to do two things: first, benefit most the owner of the entertainers, and then make sure that it was the people who would enjoy the sexual favors and not the host who carried most of the cost. The two drachmas which the host paid amount to an advance to call out the entertainer and cover the music, dance, or song, while significantly more was to be made in exchange for sexual services later in the evening. How much more depended on the looks and skill of the entertainers, the economic capacity of the guests, and the particular circumstances of the occasion, namely how much they had to drink and how strong their male ego was and their competitive spirit towards an antagonist in the room whom they were determined to outbid, whatever the cost. In this light, the regulations on the price and allotment of entertainers seem less benign. While keeping prices and tempers under control and protecting the customer from exploitation by unscrupulous pimps and owners were legitimate concerns, it seems that the main reason behind such regulations was to make sure that the cost for sexual favors was borne by the recipient and not the host of the party, and the allotment of entertainers was intended to make sure that the houses of the less well-off would not be shunned, because the entertainers did not expect to make much additional profit. The objectives of these regulations are financial, not moral and intended to ensure the smooth operation of the market and the ready availability of entertainers for everyone's party.

5.5 Brothels and other Establishments of Prostitution

Although, strictly speaking, entertainers did not need a brothel as a basis for their operations, since their work was routinely carried out in the houses of clients, there is some evidence suggesting that at least some of them were tied to brothels, taverns or inns, from where clients could hire them, or where they could visit them. In Aristophanes *Clouds*, for example, there is a reference to the brothel of a dancer, and the inn in the *Frogs* is fully equipped with an entire set of prostitute entertainers. Theopompos also speaks about flute-players, singers

---

73 Persaios fr. 451 von Arnim.

and dancers established in brothels in Piraeus.[74] The practice of inns and taverns routinely equipped with flute-players and prostitutes is well attested for the Roman period and continued unabated until the time of John Chrysostom and beyond. Furthermore, there is some evidence suggesting that some inns and taverns were access points for venal sex even in the classical period, and they were certainly used for such purposes in Roman times.[75] Horace's "meretrix tibicina" (hetaira flute-player) comes to mind, who was attached to a tavern and played there for the guests.[76] Archaeological evidence from houses Z and Y in Kerameikos, both suspected to be brothels for part of their life, suggests that parties may have been taking place there, in the large dining halls and *androues* of both buildings.[77] The difficulty of fully understanding how the market of hired entertainers functioned is tied to the more complex problem of understanding the Greek brothel. The wide range of forms, prices and practices in the prostitutional market of the ancient Greek world complicates the issue and renders a simple, comprehensive definition of the brothel very elusive.

Thomas McGinn defined which establishment should be considered to be a brothel rather broadly: "a brothel is an establishment where two or more prostitutes can work simultaneously and whose activity forms the main, or at least a major, part of the business as a whole."[78] This definition could be applied to most Greek brothels too, but it would not resolve all difficulties. First, it would leave out establishments like inns, taverns and other shops where prostitution may have been a marginal activity, but not the main part of the business. Second, it would leave out establishments like the house of Theodote,[79] where one prostitute, often a hetaira commanding large fees in the form of "gifts" and "donations" from her lovers, would be living and working on her own. Perhaps there is an argument to be made that such houses were not brothels, but rather exclusive homes where few "friends" were allowed in very selectively. This arrangement was not untypical in the Greek world, where many prominent hetairai had such living and working arrangements. Gnathaina, for example, was sharing a house with her daughter Gnathainion, and when she was older,

---

74 Ar. *Nu.* 996–7, *Ra.* 512–16; Theopompos *FGrH* 115 F 290.

75 Is. 6.20 (see also the discussion on this passage below); Philippides fr. 25; Palaiphatos *De Incredibilibus* 45, where Herakles meets a beautiful woman in a tavern, one of the staff, and decides to stay and spend some time with her; J. *AJ* 3.276; John Chrysostom *Adversus Judaeos* 48.915.44–5, Packer 1978: 5–53; McGinn 2004: 15–22.

76 Hor. *Epist.* 14.25.

77 Knigge 2005: passim; Glazebrook 2011, 42–45.

78 McGinn 2004: 9.

79 X. *Mem.* 3.11.

she was the procuress of her daughter. Theirs was a well-known residence in the circles of prostitution in Athens, a hybrid between a residential home and a brothel where parties, drink and sex with guests were routine activities, but it would not qualify as a brothel following McGinn's definition, because Gnatainion was the only hetaira working in this house.[80] We simply need to accept some grey areas in our terminology, perhaps to be expected of a market as diverse in its practices as that of classical Athens.

Archaeology is not very helpful in our attempts to understand better the Greek brothel. The widely-publicized arguments of Ursula Knigge that the famous Building Z in Kerameikos was a brothel offer a very alluring possibility but no certainty. The house has large dining halls, where guests could be entertained, numerous small rooms with direct access to the central court-yard (which could have been used for sex with clients), lavish consumption of water, and items of feminine toiletry in substantial numbers.[81] Archaeologists have sought support in literary sources, most notably the descriptions of brothels in Attic comedy, and the reference to the brothel of Euktemon, run by the former prostitute libertine Alke, mentioned in a speech of Isaios.[82] The most extensive of these sources is a passage from the *Pentathlos* of Xenarchos:

> Terrible, terrible and intolerable acts
> Are committed by the youth of today
> When there are very beautiful girls
> In the brothels, whom you can see
> Basking in the sun, topless,
> And one can choose whatever pleases him:
> Thin, fat, rounded, tall, shrivelled,
> Young, old, middle-aged, mature.
> There is no need to use a ladder to enter in secret,
> No need to go down through a hole in the roof,
> Nor to be brought in with some trick hidden in the hay:
> The girls are the ones who are forcing and pulling you in,
> The old men they call "papa,"
> The younger they call "brother,"
> And you can do each one of them without fear, cheaply,

---

80 See e.g. Eub. fr. 88, where someone says that he had dinner at the house of Gnathaina, and Machon fr. 16.258, where Diphilos, the poet and long-term lover of Gnathaina, was also invited for a dinner party. Such references suggest that this was a residence where select guests were invited for dinners and parties, and neither a typical Athenian residence, nor just a base for sex, but a hybrid of the two.
81 Knigge 2005; Glazebrook 2011, 42–45; Davidson.
82 Euboulos, fr. 67; Xenarchos fr. 4; Is. 6.18–21.

During the day, in the evening, in every possible way.
The other kind of women you can barely see, or look at properly,
You are always shaking with fear and terrified,
Afraid to hold your own life into your hands.[83]
O Holy Mistress Kypris, how can they fuck
When they remember the laws of Drakon
As they are thrusting back and forth?[84]

The same theme can be found in the play of Euboulos *Nannion*, named after the famous hetaira. The account of Euboulos although shorter is very similar to that of Xenarchos:

Whoever is secretly sleeping in dark beds
How is he not the most miserable among men?
When he could look at them in the sun
Lined up naked on both sides
Standing in thin, see-through nets,
Girls whom Eridanos moistens with its pure waters;
You can buy pleasure for a small coin,
Instead of chasing, stealthy sex, the worst of all sicknesses,
Not because of desire, but because of arrogance.[85]

The third comic poet of that period to exploit the same topic was Philemon in his play *Brothers*. Like Euboulos and Xenarchos, Philemon contrasts the dangerous chase of married women with the ready and irresponsible availability of those in brothels.

But you, Solon, founded it for all humans,
They say that you first saw that particular law
A popular, by Zeus, and terrific thing
(And it is fitting for me to say so, Solon)
Seeing that the city is full of young men,
Satisfying their physical needs
By committing crimes against those whom they shouldn't touch;
You bought and established women in certain locations,

---

83 The reference at this point is to the Drakonian law on justified homicide, which permitted the killing of an adulterer caught in the act without punishment (*IG* i³ 104; D. 23.22; Lys. 1.30, Kapparis 1995b: 105–110; Todd 2007: 126–134). Alternative punishments included bodily humiliations without the possibility of redress and substantial financial compensation. The speaker suggests that it is foolish for the young men of Athens to be chasing respectable women at great risk, when brothels provide a great variety at a low price.
84 Xenarchos fr. 4.
85 Euboulos fr. 67.

Common for everyone and available.
They stand naked; don't be deceived, inspect everything.
... The door is open,
It's only one obol; hop in, there is no
prudery, no mockery, she won't pull back;
but she will give in immediately, as you want and in whichever way you want,
You are done. You tell her to get lost; she is nothing but a stranger to you.[86]

All three passages are dealing with the same theme, namely brothels versus adultery, in very similar ways. In all three accounts brothels are by far the better choice, because one can have his desires satisfied without the mortal dangers of the adultery laws, the trouble that comes with the deception of the woman's *kyrios*, and the unethical behavior. The fragment of Philemon attributes to Solon the wisdom of devising an alternative for the sexual urges of young men and the actual establishment of brothels.[87] The other two, although they do not specifically relate this tradition, suggest in equally strong terms that the presence of brothels in the city is an excellent idea, because that way men can have their physical urges satisfied without the need to interfere with someone else's women, or commit criminal and immoral acts. All three mention that brothels offer hassle-free sex at a low price. Philemon says that the fee is only an obol and Euboulos says it's only a small coin. There is no good reason to conclude that the fee in all brothels was equally low or flat at a very low price, but this evidence certainly suggests that there were some brothels in Athens where, at least for some of the women, the fee could be as low as one obol.

All three passages mention an inspection of the women by the customer. Philemon suggests that the women are lined up naked, and Xenarchos says that they are standing topless. Although, again, we do not need to assume uniform practices in all brothels of Attica, the passage of Euboulos, which suggests that they are almost but not totally naked, wearing only thin, net-like clothing, is probably closer to common practice. All three suggest a line up for the benefit of the customer who is welcome to take a good look before choosing. Euboulos and Xenarchos mention a line up in the sun, one would think in an enclosed courtyard, just like the one in Building Z, and a couple of sources suggest easy access either through an open or half-open door.[88] All three passages suggest easy availability; the customer picks whom he wants, and there are none of the games, rejections or fake coyness typically associated with hetairai; the women

---

86 Philemon, fr. 3.
87 See Ch. 1.2. for the relevant discussion.
88 Philemon, fr. 3.12; Aesch. 1.74.

throw themselves at the potential customer. Xenarchos and Philemon add that, unlike the furtive and unsatisfactory meetings in the dark, typical of adulterous affairs, in the brothel one can ask for whatever sexual position or treat he wants, and he can have it, in the broad daylight and without the need to hide or be shy about it. Philemon concludes that the final advantage of the brothel is the lack of any kind of responsibility on behalf of the customer; one pays for sexual favors and when he is done he has no worries, as the woman is nothing to him. These three comic accounts of the Athenian brothel are certainly inter-dependent. The oldest is probably that of Euboulos, followed by Xenarchos and the latest is the one by Philemon.[89]

Outside Attic poetry the most extensive account of a brothel in a classical source is in the speech of Isaios, *On the Estate of Philoktemon.* Some modern scholars wanted to identify Building Z with the brothel of Euktemon, but there is no evidence to support such an identification, other than the location of Ker-ameikos. This is not much to go by considering that there were numerous broth-els in that part of the city, and besides it is by no means certain that the condo-minium of Euktemon in Kerameikos was a brothel. The text of Isaios certainly identifies a condominium (συνοικία) of his in Piraeus as a brothel, and mentions another condominium in Kerameikos, managed by the former prostitute Alke, which sold wine. We may infer that this too was a brothel from these facts, but there is no certainty as the text of Isaios does not explicitly identify this condo-minium as a brothel, and a *synoikia* could simply be an apartment complex which included a wine shop. Isaios provides this account of the brothel(s) of Euktemon:

> Euktemon lived 96 years, and for most of this time he was thought to be blessed, for he had plenty of property, a wife and children, and in every other respect he was doing well. However, in his old age a great misfortune befell him, which destroyed his entire house-hold and lost him a lot of money, and put him at odds with those closest to him. Why and how this happened I shall explain as briefly as I possibly can. He had a freedwoman who was managing his condominium in Piraeus and was keeping prostitutes. One of the wom-en she acquired was named Alke, who is well known to many of you, I believe. When Alke

---

89 Philemon, a contemporary and rival of Menander, is somewhat later and reached the height of his career closer to the end of the 4th century, so he should probably be placed last. Euboulos is older, just at the borderline between Old and Middle comedy and reached the peak of his career in the 360's, while Xenarchos is slightly younger. Between the two it seems more likely that the account of Euboulos is the original, as it is shorter and the themes are less developed, while Xenarchos appears to be expanding on these themes. Philemon adds the significant detail that having brothels around the city was the excellent idea of Solon, the wise founding father of the Athenian democracy.

was bought she was established for many years in the brothel, but when she got older she gave up prostitution. A freedman named Dion was living with her in the condominium where she was housed, from whom she said that she had those children, and he brought them up as his own. After some time Dion got into a bad deal and in fear for his life he fled to Sikyon. Euktemon then appointed that woman, Alke, to manage his condominium in Kerameikos, the one near the gate, where wine can be bought. When she took residence there, gentlemen, she became the cause of many ills. Every time Euktemon went up there for the rent, he stayed around for a long time, and sometimes he stayed over with the woman, leaving his wife and children and the family home. His wife and sons took it pretty badly, but instead of stopping he ended up living there permanently. He got into such a state of mind, either through drugs or old age or something like this, that he was persuaded to introduce the oldest of her children to the phratry as his own son.[90]

What is most remarkable in this extract from the speech delivered during an inheritance dispute over the estate of Philoktemon, the oldest son of Euktemon, is the rather dispassionate way in which the speaker describes Euktemon as a brothel-keeper. There is no judgment or inherent stigma attached to the fact that this respectable Athenian, a man once considered happy and fortunate, was a brothel-owner. Keeping prostitutes is presented simply as a business enterprise perfectly appropriate for a well-off Athenian family man, and could have continued without ill consequences if he had not crossed the line and put a retired prostitute ahead of his family, his property and the laws of the city. As a brothel owner, the "fortunate" Euktemon before his fall from grace is a far cry from the vile libertine Kerdon ("Profit") in *The Pimp* of Herodas or the ruthless mother of Theodora in the *Anecdota* of Prokopios. Things start going wrong and his actions are criticized only from the moment that he decides to set aside the best financial interests of his family, quarrel with his closest relatives and ignore the law, for the sake of Alke; surely he must have been affected by some illness, or potion, or magic that made him lose his mind.

Another sentence of the speaker which is certainly noteworthy, but not unique in the Attic Orators, is the statement that many of the jurors would know

90 Is. 6.18–21. Only legitimate children could be introduced to the phratry, and this action was the first step towards conferring full citizenship upon them. The process would be completed much later when they reached their 18th year of age and registered with the deme of their father. Introduction of a child to the phratry by his father amounted to public acknowledgment of his legitimate birth and entitlement to citizenship. If the father was not alive, other male relatives or the guardian would take this important, although not legally obligatory, step. The son of the freedwoman Alke was either the offspring of some unknown man or maybe the libertine Dion, who was bringing him up along with Alke, and certainly not entitled to citizenship. The speaker here assertively says that Euktemon must have been out of his mind to contemplate such deception. About the introduction to the phratry see Lambert 1993: 143–190.

who Alke was, no doubt because they had been customers in her establishment. Apollodoros makes the same assumption about the jurors in the speech Against Neaira, where the visits of the jurors to brothels and personal familiarity with famous hetairai are treated as routine facts of daily life bearing no stigma or moral judgment. The brothel of Euktemon in Piraeus seems to be quite non-descript. From the sound of it, this was just a regular condominium with the apartments used for venal sex, and it is remarkable that Alke resided there as a prostitute, and continued to do so after her retirement, along with Dion and their children. From a practical point of view, it certainly makes sense to use a building like that with its numerous small apartments for the purposes of a brothel. The condominium in Kerameikos again seems to be a non-descript *synoikia*, but this one in addition has a wine-selling facility, possibly an inn or tavern attached to it, which would not be unusual as taverns and inns often served as access points for prostitutes, and from the sound of it, this was a brothel too. Equally non-descript are the various brothels in the area of the Agora described by Aeschines in the speech *Against Timarchos*. In a significant passage he states that a brothel is indistinguishable from any other kind of workshop or warehouse in every respect except the nature of the work performed there:

> It is not the buildings or the dwellings that give the name to their inhabitants, but rather the inhabitants with their practices give the names to the places. Where many people pay for a place and live there after they divide it, we call this a condominium, but where one person lives, we call it a house. If a doctor moves into one of these workshops on the streets, it is called a doctor's practice; if he moves out and a copper-smith moves into the same workshop, then it is called a copper-smith's shop, if a fuller, a laundry, if a carpenter, a carpenter's shop; if a pimp and whores, then from this work it is called a brothel.[91]

Aeschines confirms what other sources are hinting, namely that we should not be looking for custom-made brothels in Athens. Any building, workshop or warehouse could be rented and converted into a brothel for a period of time, and then maybe returned to other uses when the prostitutes moved out. This is why one should probably expect a variety of settings. The brothel described by Euboulos, Xenarchos and Philemon, essentially a building centered around a courtyard where the women stood so that the client could make his choice, just like Building Z with its numerous little rooms around the yard, which could serve as the sex-rooms, may have been one possible format. The condominium of Euktemon in Piraeus, with numerous apartments where the girls could be

---

91 Aesch. 1.123–4.

living and waiting for clients, with the door half-open, as Aeschines suggests,[92] may have been an alternative format. A workshop or warehouse in a busy area like the market place or the harbor, with minor modifications, such as the addition of cubicles, to make it somewhat more appealing for sexual activity could have been another type of building used for such purposes.

The possibilities are endless, and there is no particular reason why all brothels should look the same. For the purposes of basic functionality several rooms would be needed where the prostitutes could live and work and a central room, or yard where the girls could be lined up for the customer or briefly socialize with him before he could make his choice. In some establishments, but maybe not all, there were wash-rooms, and dining rooms or facilities where wine and food was sold to customers, and entertainment in the form of flute-players or other entertainers was provided and could be hired out. Places varied and undoubtedly prices varied accordingly. The one obol attested by Philemon seems too low to be regular pricing; he is probably quoting the lowest possible price in a few low-grade establishments, and even there one might think that this price would only get the customer older and less attractive workers.

From the Roman period Juvenal's description of a common brothel, where the *meretrix Augusta* (Messalina) escaped at night to have her insatiable sexual appetites satisfied, must be the most memorable description of the sordid atmosphere in a low-class establishment in the entire classical literature. His description of the plain practical mats, the cubicles for sex on the spot, the stench of sweat and soiled sheets, and the images of the prostitute-empress wearing a blond wig, welcoming her customer, and taking his money with blandishments flash vivid images of the ancient brothel and its practices before our eyes. Although inspired by the Roman reality, these features are not particularly time or place specific and could safely be transported anytime, anywhere in the ancient world:

> Are you worried by Eppia's tricks, of a non-Imperial kind?
> Take a look at the rivals of the gods; hear how Claudius
> Suffered. When his wife, Messalina, knew he was asleep,
> She would go about with no more than a maid for escort.
> The Empress dared, at night, to wear the hood of a whore,
> And she preferred a mat to her bed in the Palatine Palace.
> Dressed in that way, with a blonde wig hiding her natural
> Hair, she'd enter a brothel that stank of old soiled sheets,
> And make an empty cubicle, her own; then sell herself,

---

92 Aesch. 1.74.

Her nipples gilded, naked, taking She-Wolf for a name,
Displaying the belly you came from, noble Britannicus,
She'd flatter her clients on entry, and take their money,
Then lie there obligingly, delighting in every stroke.
Later on, when the pimp dismissed his girls, she'd leave
Reluctantly, waiting to quit her cubicle there, till the last
Possible time, her taut sex still burning, inflamed with lust,
Then she'd leave, exhausted by man, but not yet sated,
A disgusting creature with filthy face, soiled by the lamp's
Black, taking her brothel-stench back to the Emperor's bed.
Shall I speak of spells and love-potions too, poisons brewed,
And stepsons murdered? The sex do worse things, driven on
By the urgings of power: their crimes of lust are the least of it.[93]

Definitions become blurrier when it comes to the establishments of free-lance prostitutes like the alleged shack of Thersandros, which he used for the purposes of receiving lovers, in the novel of Achilles Tatius *Kleitophon and Leukippe*.[94] We are told that this was a narrow, small space which Thersandros rented after he left home, in theory in order to better himself through education and association with worthy men, but in reality he used it as a brothel (οἴκημα) and received anyone who would be useful to his pursuits, engaging in every kind of debauchery. This establishment would not be a straight-forward brothel, because only one person worked there, and even then, all such activities took place under pretext, and does not present any of the primary features which one would typically associate with a brothel, like a fast turn-over of clients, a business-like approach to sex, a pimp and manager to oversee the workings of the establishment, and anonymous sex for a small fee. The entire presentation is slanderous and meant to present Thersandros in the worst possible light, and the portrait of the young Thersandros without a doubt is based upon the narrative of Aeschines *Against Timarchos*.[95] It is difficult to tell whether any addition-

---

93 Juv. 6.114–135; online translation by A.S. Kline, published 2011.
94 Ach. *Tat.* 8.9.2–4.
95 Cf. Aesch. 1.40. What is most intriguing about this is that Achilles Tatius fills in some of the details which in the narrative of Aeschines remain intentionally vague allusions, and hence the difficulty to tell whether he is doing so on the basis of lost sources, or he is simply making things up. The other interesting aspect in his narrative is that, unlike the sleazy characters parading through the pages of Aeschines supposedly being lovers and customers of Timarchos, the lovers of young Thersandros were very respectable men, and the association maintained the pretext of an educational encounter. While Aeschines sought to prove a point by presenting Timarchos as the associate of lustful, vile or arrogant men, Achilles Tatius choses to do the

al details are based upon other sources now lost to us, or are the product of the imagination of the novelist.

James Davidson has identified one particular type of brothel or establishment which would probably match quite well the shack of Thersandros. He has argued that the term *oikema* specifically indicated an independent room, which might or might not be part of a complex, but had direct access to the street; the prostitute established in it worked alone (but not necessarily independent of a pimp, who might be nearby), and the client entered directly, and more discreetly, without the parade, pomp and ceremony implied by Euboulos and his imitators. Knigge has identified several rooms in Building Z with direct access to the street, and Glazebrook is prepared to accept that these were *oikemata*. Tempting as this possibility may be, the evidence cited to support it is very tenuous. Davidson's main argument is derived from the speech *Against Timarchos*, where the term *oikemata* is used for some buildings in the Agora with direct access to the street and male prostitutes awaiting clients in them with a half-open door. However, this does not mean that the term *oikema* was specifically describing this particular type of brothel and no other; it could just as easily be the case that he simply calls them "brothels" and that the term *oikema* could be applied to all other brothel formats.

Further information about the establishments and homes of free-lance prostitutes is provided in several other classical sources, and more abundantly in Lucian's *Dialogues of Hetairai*. We are told that typically free-lance sex workers were living in ordinary houses, and often faced ordinary problems, like money difficulties, illness, worries about the future and personal insecurities, but at the same time some of the acts taking place in these houses would be unthinkable for an ordinary Athenian household, and such acts would single them out as the establishments of prostitutes. For example, Apollodoros goes into some detail over Neaira's financial and personal difficulties and tells us that her partner Stephanos was acting as her pimp, and that they were practicing prostitution from their family home to such an extent that an old lover of Neaira called their house a brothel, and commented that they were making a handsome living from this kind of work. None of this information is likely to be true in this instance, but the mere fact that Apollodoros could make such claims before an Athenian jury suggests that there was nothing unusual about free-lance prostitutes working from their homes, and that at least in appearances these homes

---

opposite, namely portray Thersandros as the most depraved man in contrast with his associates.

would be simply ordinary with no distinguishing features.[96] As Thomas McGinn correctly points out, the lack of moral concerns over prostitution before Christianization made zoning unnecessary, while increasingly negative attitudes towards prostitution in the Christian era created a moral imperative to segregate it from respectable society.[97]

Despite a façade of normality the neighbors and the community would be under no illusion about the nature of the work taking place in these seemingly ordinary homes. They would notice the strange comings and goings, men visiting all hours of the day and night, and possibly the parties and revelries, carousing and garlands left at the doorstep by infatuated lovers. A passage of Isaios indicates that such behavior marked out a hetaira's residence as no one would compromise the reputation of a respectable woman with such behavior outside her house; a κῶμος was something that happened outside disreputable houses, but it would be very inappropriate for an ordinary Athenian home.[98] Plato states that this is rather typical behavior which comes with love and infatuation, but Galen takes a very different approach and from a late antiquity moral point of view considers hetairai and carousing to be affectations of the soul.[99] In Lucian's sharp critique hetairai and carousing are taking away all shame.[100] In the literature of later antiquity hetairai and carousing usually come as a package of ill behavior.[101] The familiar dichotomy between the less judgmental language of the classical period and the moralistic and damning language of later antiquity is clearly visible in our sources in this instance too. In classical authors usually a *komos* at a hetaira's door was a fun-loving revelry of merry party-goers, with no ill-intentions and no bad consequences for anyone, except perhaps the unfortunate neighbors who might be trying to catch some sleep. In the uptight morality of later antiquity a *komos* always had ill connotations and consequences, from financial to social, and in the Christian era it was one of those activities that could condemn someone's soul to eternal damnation.

The precise definition of a *komos* is not clear, as it included a range of different activities. Some lines of ambiguous paternity in the Hesiodean *Scutum Herculis* suggest that it consisted of singing, dancing, and playing games under the sounds of a flute, while a rather important passage of Theognis considers

---

96 See D. 59.66–7, and Kapparis 1999: 308–313.
97 McGinn 2004: 78–111, and 2006: 161–176.
98 Is. 3.13.
99 Pl. *R.* 573 d; Gal. *De propriorum animi cuiuslibet affectuum diagnotione et curatione* 5.5 de Boer.
100 Luc. *Bis Acc.* 17.
101 E.g. Philostr. *VA* 1.13; Sopater 8.357 Walz; Lib. *Decl.* 34.2.30 al.

the *komos* to be a blessing concomitant of wealth and peace. In another passage of Theognis someone complains that he cannot speak at all, because his voice is gone after last night's revelry, and an Attic cup from the early 5th c. cites the beginning of this line as part of a sympotic theme.[102] In Pindar a *komos* is the celebration for a victory in the Panhellenic Games.[103] In Xenophon's *Symposion* the word is used for the indoors entertainment of the party, and the meaning is the same in *The Education of Cyrus*, where the Babylonians are said to be drinking and engaging in a *komos* for the whole night.[104] From an early time the *komos* becomes closely associated with drink, parties and prostitute-entertainers, such as flute-players and dancers, and from the 4th century it appears to be a standard feature at a hetaira's house, so much so that a speech of Isaios uses it as a dividing marker between houses of hetairai and respectable households; *komoi* are a regular feature of the former, but no one would dare to bring a *komos* into the presence of married women.[105] The *komos* included the festive part of the *symposion* and sometimes the after-party in the streets, or outside the house of a hetaira.

From the drinking songs of the *komos*, a subgenre seems to have emerged in the Hellenistic period, which centered around the sorrows of love, the plight of the unsuccessful lover locked out of the house of his beloved, and invective directed against the cruel mistress. The origins of the motif go back to Old Comedy. In Aristophanes *Ecclesiazousai* a choral song sung by a young man outside the house of a young girl with whom he is in love has all the marks of the *paraklausithyron* motif:

[Young Girl]: Come, come
My darling, come to me,
Come and sleep with me
The whole night long.
For love is shaking me badly
Of your lovely hair-locks,
And insufferable desire is burning me
And I have a yearning

---

102 Hes. *Sc.* 279–283; Thgn. 1.885–887, 1.939–40; 205174 = ARV[2] (1963), 437/128, 1653. = Munich, Antikensammlungen: J371.

103 E.g. Pi. *O.* 4.9; 6.18.

104 X. *Symp.* 2.1: "When the tables were taken away and the guests offered a libation and sang the paean, a Syracosian man came in for the *komos*, bringing with him a great flute player, and a dancer, one of those who can perform magic tricks, and a very beautiful boy". *Cyr.* 7.5.15.

105 Is. 3.13; Lys. 3.23; D. 47.19, 59.24, 33; Pl. *Tht.* 173 d; *R.* 573 d; Lys. 14.25; Theopomp. *FGrH* 115 F 162; Plu. *Pyr.* 13.7, al.

Love, I am begging you,
Make him come
To my bed.
[Young Man]: Come, Come
My love, come, run,
Open this door
And if you don't, I'll fall down and lie here,
But I want to be lying in your bosom
And smack your bottom.
Oh Kypris, why do you make me so mad over her?
Love, I am begging you,
Make her come
To my bed.[106]

A clearer form of the motif in Greek Literature can be traced in an epigram of Kallimachos, where a lover locked out and forced to sleep at the doorstep of his beloved is complaining about his treatment:

May you sleep, Konopion, as you make me sleep
At your cold doorstep,
May you sleep, unjust woman, the way you make your lover
Sleep, and you have no pity, not even in your dreams.
The neighbors feel sorry for me, while you don't even dream of pity.
However, the grey hairs will remind you of all this.[107]

Although the roots of the *paraklausithyron* are undoubtedly Greek, in the surviving literature we find it in its most developed form in Latin authors of the Golden Age. The primary study of the *paraklausithyron* is still that of Frank Copley, and according to recent scholarship the motif is well attested in Roman elegy, Horace, Catullus and Petronius. The term *paraklausithyron*, literally meaning "crying by the door," has prevailed in the bibliography despite the fact that there are only two instances of this term in the surviving Greek literature, and none in Latin. One of these instances is in the *Erotic Discourse* of Plutarch, where the *paraklausithyron* is a song sung by infatuated lovers. The second one is the title of a song otherwise known as the Alexandrian Erotic Fragment, a mutilated composition found on a 2nd c. BC papyrus, which is generally believed to be representative of this subgenre. If it is, then it may not be a typical one, as the speaker is female and she is pleading with a male lover who has locked her

---

106 Ar. *Ec.* 951–969.
107 Callim. fr. 63 Pfeiffer = *AG* 5.23. He means that when she gets old, and will no longer be desirable, she will remember how unjustly she has treated her lover in the past.

out to relent and give in to her love. Either this gender inversion of a theme supposedly sung by a man in love outside the doorstep of his beloved woman represents a modification of the traditional motif, or at least in one version of the motif the composition was symmetrically antiphonic, with a part of it sung by the woman and a part by the man, just like the Aristophanic choral song above. If so, the surviving part would represent the woman's section, while the missing end of the poem consisted of the man's response.

Aside from the possible gender inversion, the first 50 or so verses of the Alexandrian Erotic Fragment which have survived contain the themes that we would expect to find in the *paraklausithyron*: the jilted lover at the doorstep, jealousy, anger, intense infatuation, pleas for pity, reminders of past love-bonds and begging to be allowed back in. These we should probably recognize as the typical themes of the motif before it became fashionable in Roman lyric. But ever since Catullus gave voice to the closed door itself, a theme also exploited by Propertius in a poem which in the opinion of Copley is the best among the surviving representatives of this motif, Roman authors down to the time of Ovid adapted and subverted the *paraklausithyron* in many imaginative ways. Although in its original form the *paraklausithyron* was typically associated with hetairai and rejection in favor of a richer lover, in later times the motif was expanded to include a wider range of settings, themes and objectives.[108]

The revelries and garlands placed on the doors of hetairai, the parties of intoxicated admirers singing at the doorstep, the infatuated fools who stood outside the door begging for entry, occasionally the sound of flutes and other instruments, the noise coming from the outside and the inside of the woman's house, the dancing and singing and the voices of people going in and out at any hour, especially at night, were certainly not activities to be associated with respectable family homes, and thus they marked the houses of prostitutes as places of ill-repute. The question whether we should call brothels the homes of all free-lance prostitutes, or following McGinn we should only call brothels those establishments which housed clusters of sex-workers, two or more, is more than simply a question of definitions. A brothel in the traditional sense was essentially a public place, where the customer was granted access once he

---

108 I am very grateful to Professor Timothy S. Johnson for sharing with me unpublished work on the *paraklausithyron*, which pointed me in the right direction and probably saved me months of work. For the sources of the motif see Plu. 753 A; *Lyrica Adespota* fr. 1 Powell; Catullus 67; Propertius 1.16; Tibullus 1.2.85–86; Horace *C.* 1.25 and 3.26. See also Copley 1956; Burck 1932: 186–200; Henderson 1973: 51–67; Jones 1992: 303–309; Nappa 2007: 57–73; Schmeling 1971: 333–357; Johnson (forthcoming).

paid the fee, and no one was excluded who had the means to pay, perhaps with the rare exception of someone whose previous behavior got him barred from a certain establishment. By contrast the houses of free-lance prostitutes were more exclusive and perhaps stand in a grey area between the private home and the public space. Clients and lovers were given extensive access which would be well beyond the boundaries of propriety in an ordinary household, but the space was still private and guests could be admitted or excluded at the whim of a fickle mistress.

Two important classical sources provide substantial information about the operation of such houses at the top end of the market. Xenophon's description of the house of Theodote, with carefully worded allusions to the acts taking place there, offers important information about the way high class prostitution worked in the classical period in Athens. Although the house is a very comfortable and quite large mansion, the reader immediately knows that this is not a typical Athenian house, because the scene begins with direct access to the mistress of the house posing nude for a painter. Socrates and his entourage enter the house, sit quietly watching the nude Theodote being painted, and occasionally comment on the affluence of the household. When Theodote puts her clothes back on she is wearing luxurious outfits and expensive jewelry (πολυτελῶς κεκοσμημένην), and her mother is also wearing fancy clothes and is surrounded by many servants. Even the numerous female slaves of the household are well dressed, pretty and diligently made up. Whether this was an accurate picture of the household of the historical Theodote is immaterial. This description of an immaculate place where much attention has been paid to appearances, is an image of how the home of a high-end hetaira should be. The wealthy clients of these women paid for airs and graces and expected to be surrounded by images of affluence, luxury and beauty, not by poor furniture and scruffy slaves, and having the right image was extremely important for one's perceived value. The affluence of the household prompts Socrates to inquire about the sources of Theodote's wealth and sparks the legendary dialogue between the hetaira and the philosopher, which was going to prove influential in the literature of later antiquity.[109]

Another well-known household, where prostitution was the primary activity is described by Apollodoros in the speech Against Neaira, this time a top-notch Corinthian establishment. It was run by a libertine called Nikarete, who, we are told was a skillful procuress and very successful in her line of work. She bought little slave girls with promising looks, brought them up, trained them how to

---

109 See the discussion in Ch.3.3.

become exclusive and expensive companions, and carefully maintained a fa-çade of respectability in her house by pretending that the girls were her daugh-ters.[110] This is an interesting remark as we try to understand the practices and economics of the classical brothel, since it underlines how blurred the lines actually were between a notable establishment of prostitution and a family home. Reason suggests that one should not expect to find in this household tasteless images of copulation on the walls or graffiti with obscene lines and improper praise of the girls, but rather, as in the house of Theodote, a carefully maintained appearance of affluence and elegance. If we excavated this house today, we should not expect to find anything that singled it out as a brothel, for the entire economic philosophy of this establishment rested upon this ambigui-ty.

The practice of buying young slave girls years before they were marketable was a long-term and rather uncertain investment, because one would not know how these girls turned out as adults, if they reached adulthood altogether. However, little slave girls would be very cheap to buy, as they represented noth-ing more than a promise, while grown women bought for the purposes of prosti-tution would be much more expensive and more difficult to instruct on how to meet the expectations of procurers and customers. So, there was a clear logic in Nicarete's plan, and it seems that it paid off quite handsomely when seven of those girls reached adulthood and became famous and very expensive hetairai. Their names, as provided by Apollodoros in a rough chronological order, are Anteia, Stratola, Aristokleia, Metaneira, Phila, Isthmias and Neaira.[111]

I have argued elsewhere that the girls were not of equal age, but reached their peak at different times over a period of 30 years.[112] It seems that Nikarete bought them at intervals so that when one or two of them went past their prime, their replacements would be reaching their floruit. Apollodoros assures us that before they came to the end of their prime Nicarete sold them to infatuated lov-ers for large amounts of money. This information seems to be confirmed by other sources too. Lysias in the speech *Against Lais*[113] said that Anteia stopped prostitution while still in her floruit, and this should be interpreted as an indica-tion that an infatuated lover bought her. Christopher Carey, combining two different passages of Athenaios, adds Aristokleia to this Lysianic list of women

---

110 D.59.18–20.

111 D. 59.18.

112 Kapparis 1999: 206–210.

113 Or, *To Lais*: the exact title is disputed. See Carey 2007: 429.

who gave up prostitution while still in their prime, probably correctly.[114] The combined evidence of Idomeneus and Plutarch adds that a woman called Phila was set free by Hypereides for the sum of 20 minae, and became his mistress.[115] Neaira was initially sold for 30 minae to two infatuated lovers, Timanoridas of Corinth and Eucrates of Leukas, and after a couple of years she was set free when Phrynion, a rich Athenian, former lover of hers, was prepared to pay her masters 20 minae for her freedom. Thus, it seems that for four out of the seven girls in his list, there is verifiable information that they were sold for a high price by Nikarete while still at their prime, but not before she had already made considerable profit from each one of them. The timing of the sale had to be right; too early would mean less profit for Nikarete, and too late could result in rapid devaluation. The prices of 20–30 minae which these women fetched were certainly a lot of money for the average person, but rather typical for this kind of transaction, as a passage of Isocrates suggests and several other sources confirm.[116]

The very broad range of activities and forms which prostitution took in the classical period could be suitably accommodated in an equally broad range of settings. It may be fair to say that there is no such thing as a standard format for a Greek brothel, because there is no standard format for Greek prostitution. Tempting as it may be to consider Building Z as "one of the few remaining structures of prostitution from ancient Greece," [117] there are numerous other explanations for the structure and findings in it, and without conclusive proof that it was a brothel we need to be content with the alluring possibility but refrain from using evidence from this particular structure as a rule or norm for identifying and understanding Greek brothels. Further attempts by Davina McClain and Nicholas Rauh to identify brothels in the area around the Sacred Lake at Delos have also produced intriguing possibilities but no definite identification. There should be no doubt that in that part of Delos, as well as in the part of Kerameikos where Building Z can be found, there were brothels and chances are that

---

114 Lysias fr. 208 Carey; cf. Athen. 13.51, 13.62,

115 Idomeneus *FGrH* 338 F 14; Plu. 849 D. Plutarch says that the mistress of Hypereides was free-born from Thebes and he paid the 20 minae as ransom. Plutarch may be confused, but of course the possibility that he is talking about a different woman than the girl of Nikarete remains open.

116 Isoc. 19.288; cf. D. 53.7, where Nikostratos has just been set free from a group of slave-traders for the sum of 26 minae; D.L. 3.20, where Plato is ransomed from his captors by Annikeris of Cyrene for 20 (or 30) minae.

117 Glazebrook 2011: 39.

even if the suggested buildings were not brothels, other similar structures nearby were.

As we cannot rely with certainty on archaeological data, references to places of prostitution in literary sources remain our most reliable avenue for understanding such establishments and their operation and finances. These suggest that brothels would normally be indistinguishable from other establishments or individual houses in terms of architectural features, but the community would be well aware of their function. Some could be as sleazy as the one described by Juvenal, others could be as discreet and upmarket as the house of Theodote, most would be somewhere in between. Some could offer dining and drinking facilities, many would offer a bed for the night, and most would try to offer some variety to attract a broader range of customers. There should be no doubt that many had a mix of sexes, predominantly women, but boys too, and perhaps some transgender workers to accommodate all tastes. A mix of ages and price ranges probably could be found in the larger establishments, and at least some of them hired out sex workers and entertainers to private parties. Forced zoning on moral grounds did not take place before the Christian era, but market forces created higher concentrations of sex establishments in certain parts of cities, such as the agora or the harbor. Prostitution was a ubiquitous feature of Greek cities, and could be found anywhere, in workshops, large buildings, condominia, small shacks, villas or ordinary private houses. Diversity is the concept which dominates the Greek prostitutional markets, the forms which prostitution took, and the establishments where sex was up for sale.

5.6 Prices, Costs and Profits of Prostitution

The economy of a brothel like that of Nikarete was based on exclusive patronage, just as Aristophanes says was the rule with Corinthian hetairai.[118] Only one or two girls at a time were in action, and their work provided for the entire household.[119] We get a glimpse of how this arrangement could work out from the exaggerated description in Ballio's brothel in Plautus' Pseudolus. There the prostitutes are required to press their lovers to provide the finest materials in abundance for the birthday celebration of their vile procurer, but of course the

---

118 Ar. *Plu.* 149–152. This passage jokes that Corinthian hetairai would shun everyone except the wealthiest clients.
119 D. 59.29.

evil pimp gets what he deserves in the end.[120] More realistic perhaps is the account of Xenophon about Theodote's wealth. She claims that she does not demand payment, but that her many "friends" offer her numerous "gifts" as a token of their affection, which she graciously accepts.[121] But, of course, one could not pay for all the expenses and the operation of such an affluent household through gifts and tokens of affection. Real money was necessary, and there should be no doubt that the majority of the "gifts" were cash contributions. This is why Socrates proposes to her that she should be using an agent, a friend who would find rich admirers of beauty (πλουσίους καὶ φιλοκάλους) and cast them into her net. Harsh words such as "pimp" or "procurer" are nowhere to be seen in this account; the language is metaphorical, employing images of hunting and spider webs to describe the entrapment of clients in the high end of prostitution.

The practice of gift-giving is attested in a few other sources from the classical period, but features more prominently in the literature of later antiquity, especially Lucian's *Dialogues of Hetairai*, the fictional letters of Alciphron and Theophylaktos, and the tales of Athenaios.[122] Several scholars have read powerful symbolism into this exchange of gifts instead of cash payments. James Davidson theorized that the exchange of gifts was appropriate for the hetaira, as opposed to the more egalitarian exchange of cash, which is the mark of the *porne*. This dichotomy was essentially accepted and expanded upon by Leslie Kurke, who has added political and cultural dimensions to it.[123] Kurke sees the contrast between two monetary systems as the underlying cause of the dichotomy. The exchange of gifts was the way of the old aristocracy, while the introduction of money in the 6th century made the women accessible to everyone on a more egalitarian basis. Dean Hammer has raised substantial objections to Kurke's position, arguing that it is based on unsafe assumptions rather than substantial evidence.[124] One such assumption which I would consider insurmountable is that of the terminology, the definitions of *hetaira* and *porne*. The traditional view that these terms represent the polar opposites in the spectrum of ancient prostitution, one the top end, and the other the bottom end of the market, has been rightly called a "deceptively helpful taxonomy of prostitution." [125] In more recent studies a consensus is building up that this polarized

---

120 For an analysis of the references to the brothel of Ballio see Hallett 2011: 172–196.
121 X. *Mem*. 3.11.
122 E.g. D. 59.46; Theopompos *FGrH* 115 F 248; Luc. *DMeretr*. 5.4; 6.2; Alciphr. 4.17.5; Theophylaktos *Ep*. 42, and Ch. 6.1. about larger dedications and monuments.
123 Davidson 1997: 109–136 and 194–205; Kurke 1997: 106–154.
124 Hammer 2004: 479–512.
125 Glazebrook-Henry 2011: 4.

dichotomy between *hetaira* and *porne* is highly problematic, at best seriously questionable, and probably one that should be abandoned.[126]

As explained in greater detail in the Introduction, the ancient evidence suggests that there was no absolute distinction between the terms, that they are often interchangeable for a number of reasons, and that the status of women and men who worked in prostitution was fluid and subject to shifts and changes. Moreover, I have argued that the terms *hetaira* and *porne* are not mutually exclusive, but that the *hetaira* is only a subcategory of the *porne*. The dichotomy which modern scholars have created does not match unproblematically the socioeconomic realities of ancient prostitutes, and the explanation for the exchange of gifts should not be sought in some convenient anthropological scheme, but rather in the practicalities of ancient prostitution.

The exchange of gifts was not some fossilized ritual from the archaic period but rather an act with concrete and practical significance. In our attempt to fully understand it, one critically important passage from the speech *Against Neaira* should point us in the right direction. There we are told that Lysias the orator, by that stage of his life a rich old man who had already spent a lot of money on the Corinthian hetaira Metaneira, wanted to give her something other than money; he wished to offer her a personal favor (χάριν) which no one could take away from her.[127] The significant sums of money which he had spent on her went to Nikarete, her procuress, since Metaneira was a slave at that stage, while the expenses for her initiation into the Eleusinean Mysteries would be a personal and inalienable gift to the woman herself. This would appear to be a more pragmatic interpretation of the practice of gift-giving that does not need to rely upon problematic terminological definitions or archaic anthropological models. If one considers that throughout antiquity the majority of sex workers were slaves, personal gifts were significant gestures of affection, in a way that money, which went to the owner, could never be. But even in the case of free prostitutes, gifts of gold and silver, jewelry, servants, luxurious outfits, or travel retained this personal touch: they were thoughtful gifts to the woman or man, signifying attention and affection, while transactions in cash lacked this personal touch. It is noteworthy that references to gifts are rather sporadic compared to the numerous references of monetary exchanges, and nowhere is it suggested that gifts functioned as an alternative to monetary payment. After all,

---

126 For the more recent debate on this vexed question see McClure 2003a: 9–18; Glazebrook-Henry 2011: 4–8; Glazebrook 2011: 34–35; Corner 2011: 72–78; Sorkin-Rabinowitz 125–128; Kapparis 222–223.
127 D. 59.21–22.

Lysias' gift to Metaneira was an additional favor borne out of good will, not routine payment for her services. For those her procuress had been well compensated in cash.

Significant for our understanding of gift-giving, the contents of these gifts, their purposes, and their function as compensation for services is a fictional dialogue of Lucian, as gifts for services is its main theme and in all likelihood echoes references to gifts in classical sources, probably lost comic plays.[128] In the dialogue the sailor Dorion has just been locked out by the hetaira Myrtale. Apparently she has found a more generous and better-off lover, a merchant from Bithynia. Dorion is complaining that she has not shown sufficient gratitude for everything that he has offered her. At this point Myrtale challenges him to list his gifts to her, and of course we should expect a list of cheap and unsuitable offerings. More important for our understanding of the whole concept of gift-giving is the fact that Dorion translates each one of his gifts into monetary values, as it seems that their worth in cash is what made them valuable in the exchange for sexual favors. He reminds Myrtale that he offered her shoes from Sikyon worth 2 drachmas, which enabled him to sleep with her for two nights, an alabaster jar with perfume from Syria, also worth two drachmas, onions from Cyprus, fish from Bosporus, dried bread and figs from Karia, sandals from Patara, and cheese from Gythion, worth about 5 drachmas. During the festival of Aphrodite he offered one silver drachma to the goddess for his beloved, and also bought a pair of shoes worth two drachmas for the mother of Myrtale, while he tipped the maid, sometimes with two, and sometimes with four obols. Dorion then wants to know what kind of gifts her new rich lover had bought her, and here we should expect a list of stylish and precious gifts. She mentions a few such items, like a dress, a thick necklace with emeralds, earrings, and a rug. But these were just the gifts; the main payment, which is emphatically mentioned separately, consisted of a cash advance of two minae and payment of the rent, which Myrtale considers an appropriate compensation, while she sneers at the sandals and cheese which Dorion had offered her. Adding insult to injury she dismisses Dorion with the sarcastic remark that his future lover will be very fortunate if he offers her onions and cheese.

The dialogue clearly suggests that gifts, whether precious or not, were extras; they did not pay the bills or the rent. For these cash was needed, as another passage from the *Dialogues of Hetairai* cynically indicates:

---

128 Luc. DMeretr. 14.

MOTHER: So Mousarion, when we need shoes and the shoemaker asks for two drachmas, we'll tell him that we don't have any money, "but you may have a few of our hopes." We'll also tell the flour-seller the same, and when we are asked to pay the rent, we'll tell them "wait until Laches of Kollytos dies; I'll give it to you after the wedding." [129]

This passage underlines the day-to-day practicalities which necessitated cash transactions. Gifts would be welcome and appreciated as extras, when one's primary financial needs had been met, but gifts alone could not perform this function, and could not serve as the main form of payment. Many of the gifts mentioned in the sources could not be liquidated, and even when a golden necklace could be pawned for cash, still cash payment for services would have been easier from the start. It would be bad business to routinely accept payment in gifts or objects for services rendered, as one needed to find ways of liquidating them first before their value could be applied to payments for goods or other services, and we have no reason to believe the hetairai of the ancient world were bad businesswomen.

William T. Loomis offers a detailed list of prices mentioned in literary sources, starting from as low as a single obol, while he outlines the difficulties of trying to guess the value or denomination of coins in vase paintings.[130] His list is very helpful, as it is a quite inclusive collection of references to the remuneration of sex workers. At the bottom of the list we encounter some indefinite references to a small coin. In the play of Eupolis *Cities* an Athenian man is comically bragging about the low cost of prostitutes in Kyzikos: for a small coin one could get a woman, a young boy (or girl; the word παῖδα is ambiguous) and an old man.[131] In Athens a small amount of money (οὐ πολὺ ἀργύριον) would buy the sexual favors of Epichares, if we were to believe Andocides, but probably we should not; Epichares was a popular politician here slandered by his opponent in court. As MacDowell eloquently puts it, "to us Andocides' accusation of his accuser seems neither logical nor relevant; but such considerations never worried Greek orators, who were always ready to descend to personal abuse if they thought it would impress the jury." [132] Two more passages from the comic poet Euboulos suggest that a small coin could buy pleasure in the brothels of Athens.[133] Several sources mention a single obol as compensation for sexual services. One obol was the price which the well-known parasite Korydos allegedly

---

129 Luc. *DMeretr.* 7.2

130 Loomis 1998: 166–186; see especially 166. 1 and note 1.

131 Eupolis fr. 247.

132 Andoc. 1.100; MacDowell 1962: 137.

133 Euboulos 67.7 and 82.7.

charged in the days when he was a prostitute.[134] The famous passage of Philemon mentioned above, which contrasts the complicated and dangerous sexual activities with married women to the cheap and easy pleasure offered in brothels, mentions a fee of one obol, but here the author had a reason to deflate the price to the bare minimum.[135] A similar comment was reportedly made by the philosopher Antisthenes: when he saw a seducer on the run he said "poor man, he could have saved himself from so much trouble for a single obol." In the same spirit a self-deprecating epigram of Lollius Bassus (1st c. AD) echoing classical sources mentions two obols:

> I will never turn into golden rain, let someone else turn into an ox,
> And someone else could be the sweet-voiced swan on the shore.
> Let such games be reserved for Zeus; I will give Korinna
> Two obols, and I'm not going to be flying.[136]

The nature of these sources would not allow us to take their testimony at face value and reach the conclusion that brothels routinely charged as little as one or two obols, but this does not mean that we should exclude the possibility of special offers, where sometimes, especially when business was slow, customers could buy pleasure for a small coin or two.

Loomis considers more realistic the evidence of Antiphanes that three obols was a rather standard price for a prostitute in a brothel.[137] Loomis also gathers from the fact that the philosopher Polemon had hidden 3 obol coins in many places to pay for his pleasures that this was the average price.[138] Three obols is also the price which an ageing Lais could be persuaded to accept according to the comic poet Epicrates, but this is probably an exaggeration; the famous hetaira never needed to accept this kind of price.[139] She was free and wealthy, and never needed to work in a brothel for such a low fee. A fragment of Krates jokes that a talent must be paid to a prostitute and a mere 3 obols to a philosopher. This may be interpreted as a comic reversal: the philosopher, who would normally charge his students quite a lot, is only to be given what a lowly prostitute

---

134 DL 6.4; Athen. 6.40.
135 Philemon fr. 3.
136 *AG.* 5.125; the hints of turning into a golden shower, a bull and a swan refer to transformations of Zeus in mythology in pursuit of lovers: a golden shower for Danae, a swan for Leda and a bull for Europa.
137 Antiphanes 293.
138 Loomis 1988: 173 and n. 29; D.L. 4.16.
139 Epikrates fr. 3.

gets, namely 3 obols, while she should get his exorbitant fee of one talent.[140] A fragment of the comic poet Plato suggests that different prices might be charged for different sexual services. In the hierarchy which he presents the one with the woman on top arching her head backwards is the most expensive (*Lordon*: 1 drachma), the position with the man on top and coming from behind is cheaper (*Kybdasos*: 3 obols), while the "horse" with the woman riding the man is the cheapest (*Keles*).[141] A witty remark which Machon attributes to Gnathaina also confirms that "doggy-style" sex (*kybda*) routinely cost 3 obols. The story goes that one day, in her old age, she was shopping in the market-place and asked a witty young butcher how he weighs his meat. "Doggy-style for 3 obols" he replied.[142] An average price of 3 obols sounds reasonable: it would be equivalent to the daily salary of an unskilled worker, or the per diem remuneration of *dikasts*. To put it in today's terms, it would be the equivalent of someone working for 8 hours on minimum wage to make around $ 60, and the price of a visit to the brothel was $ 60.

One drachma is the lowest attested price for someone who appears to be a free-lance worker, an Athenian woman called Europe, according to an epigram of Antipater of Thessalonike (1st c. BC / 1st c. AD) from the *Greek Anthology*. However, even in the reality of the epigram this price seems to be unusually low: the lover is boasting that for a single drachma he can have Europe, without fuss or love quarrels. She has spotlessly clean bed-sheets and a charcoal fire when it is cold. These basic comforts are all a drachma can buy, and certainly the simple charms of Europe are decidedly beneath the airs and graces of the haughty hetairai of classical Greece. The price, if realistic is probably on the lowest end of the market for free-lance workers, and is presented as really nothing more than one step up from the uncomplicated and virtually anonymous sex in a brothel. Low is also the price of two drachmas which a woman called Leme or Parorama, "the eye-sore", was reported to charge.[143] Two drachmas is the price for a pretty boy-cupbearer in Lucian's *Symposium*.[144] The Athenian boy Diophantos, "the Orphan," was claiming 4 drachmas for the act from a foreigner, and when the latter refused to pay, Diophantos took him to the magistrate.[145] We are not ex-

---

140 Krates, fr. 13 Diehl.
141 Pl. Com. 204.17–18.
142 Machon 16.302–310; cf. Gow 1965: 114.
143 Athen. 13.70.
144 Luc. *Symp.* 15.
145 Aeschines (1.158) says that the magistrate was the archon, and Diophantos went to him because it was the responsibility of the archon to protect orphans. The actual case was heard

plicitly told whether this was the fee for a single sexual encounter or more pro-longed liaisons, but one would imagine that 4 drachmas would buy a rather short amount of time with a citizen boy in the prime of youth, if the pay of Dio-phantos is not seriously understated by Aeschines. One stater (= 4 drachmas) is also the upper end of the price which an ageing Lais allegedly commanded (the lower end being 3 obols). 5 drachmas is the price offered to Tryphaina by Char-mides.[146] Theopompos the comic poet in his play *Kallaischros* attests that the average price of hetairai was one stater, which Loomis considers to be an exag-geration.[147] However, this does not seem to be far off the truth; on several occa-sions we are told that one could buy a night or two for a couple of drachmas,[148] while the exorbitant prices that we hear about in the case of high class hetairai were rather exceptional, often exaggerated, and usually covered services for a prolonged period of time. For example, in Lucian's *Dialogues of Hetairai* the customary remuneration of Ampelis is just above average, set at 5–10 drachmas, but it sky-rockets into the exaggerated figure of 1 talent for a period of 8 months, when her lover becomes jealous. A possessive lover's generosity notwithstand-ing, the figure of one talent is inflated and covers exclusive services for a long period of time.

The expenses which an old woman has to pay for her young male lover in Aristophanes Wealth amount to 20 drachmas for a cloak and 8 drachmas for shoes.[149] No doubt these were exorbitant prices for a few items of clothing, in-tended to underline the foolishness of the old woman, and they clearly suggest that what she was really paying for was sexual favors. The price of the virgin Korinna is 1 mina, which Loomis considers just barely possible, but more likely an exaggeration.[150] 1 mina by a man named Antiphanes, and 2 by a farmer are offered to Mousarion, but she rejects them in favor of her young lover, who en-joys her favors for free. Loomis rightly points out that Mousarion is presented as foolish, turning down exorbitant offers for a good looking pauper, and thus these offers are exaggerated.[151] Athenaios quoting Lynkeus says that a young man who offered Gnathainion one mina expected unlimited service, but her mother and procuress Gnathaina, well known for her sharp humor, cut him off

---

by the archon's assessor, the experienced politician Aristophon of Azenia. Aeschines mentions this case among several examples of shameless behavior by indecent citizen boys.

146 Luc. *DMeretr.* 11.1.
147 Theopompos, the comic, fr. 22 οὔ φησιν εἶναι τῶν ἑταιρῶν τὰς μέσας / στατηριαίας.
148 E.g. Luc. *DMeretr.* 14; *AG* 5.109.
149 Ar. Plu. 980–983; 1018–1019.
150 Luc. *DMeretr.* 6.1–2; Loomis 1998: 181.
151 Luc. *DMeretr.* 7; Loomis 1998: 181.

while he was saying that he would not expect to stay forever a student at the school of Hippomachos, if he only paid a mina (and thus he should not expect that he would be forever enjoying the company of her daughter for this money).[152] According to Machon, Phryne at her prime asked for 1 mina (= 100 drachmas), and when the client complained that she had offered herself before to someone else for two gold coins (= 40 drachmas) she replied, "oh well then, wait until I'm horny again." [153]

Machon attests an even more exorbitant price, which Gnathaina once demanded, when she was acting as the pimp for her daughter Gnathainion. According to this tale, a 90 years old satrap came to Athens, saw Gnathainion and wanted to spend a night with her. Gnathaina asked for 1000 drachmas, but he offered her only 500 (which would be a preposterous amount of money for one night). She agreed, arguing that once he sleeps with her daughter he will be willing to offer twice as much.[154] At the top of the list we expectedly find Lais asking 10,000 drachmas (100 minae) from Demosthenes the orator for a single night. His response was that he was not going to pay all this money to buy regret.[155] This tale cannot have any truth in it, as Demosthenes was born in the 380's, by which time Lais, who we are told was a young child in the years of the Sicilian expedition (415–413), would be in her 40s, and by the time Demosthenes would be an adult and rich enough to be able to afford this kind of price she would have been in her 60's or 70's. The only way that the dates could work out would be to assume that it referred to a younger copycat of the famous hetaira, but then again only the famous Lais could be presented as insolent enough to command such a price. Very likely this story, attested only in much later sources, is a fabrication linking the famous hetaira to the notorious rich playboy orator (see Ch. 3.1.). Even a mina for a night is a stretch, and anything above that for a single night seems to be fictional, or unrealistic. When, for example, Krokale asks for 2 talents for an exclusive relationship with an Aetolian man, she only wants to discourage him and does not expect that he would come up with this kind of money.[156]

Beyond this point the hefty prices that we hear about cover an extended period of time. The 3 minae which Simon had supposedly paid to the Plataian boy Theodotos, in the speech of Lysias *To Simon on the Deliberate Wounding*, were

---

152 Athen. 13.47.
153 Machon 18.450–55.
154 Machon 17.333–348.
155 Aulus Gellius *Noctes Atticae* 1.8.5–6; Sch. Ar. *Plu.* 149d.
156 Luc. *DMeretr.* 15.2

the price for a long-term contract.[157] Since this account is not fictional, even if the actual details of this contract may be questionable, a 3 minae contract must have sounded plausible to be believed by an Athenian jury. Aeschines attests that Timarchos spent 20 minae to keep the hetaera Philoxena over a period of time.[158] In a fictional letter attributed to Aeschines a citizen man named Melanopos, companion and friend of Timarchos, commands a price of 30 minae for a long-term arrangement.[159] This figure is probably not realistic if one considers that this was the top-average price for the sale or manumission of high class hetairai, but perhaps it should not be dismissed outright if one were to consider that Melanopos was a citizen man of high birth, and if he had been a prostitute hiring out his services for a long term he might be charging as much as this. However, since the account is fictional and the historical Melanopos, son of Diophantos, of Sphettos is nowhere else reported as a prostitute, it may be safer to remain skeptical about this evidence. Another fictional account of an exorbitant sum is offered by Diogenes Laertios in the *Life of Speusippos* (quoting Timotheos).[160] When a rich man was in love with an ugly person,[161] Speusippos urged him to move on with the promise to bring him in touch with a much nicer woman for 10 talents. This comment seemingly was meant to be ironic, and thus it cannot be taken as reliable evidence. At the top of the list, the highest sum ever commanded by a hetaira must be the alleged 250 talents which Demetrios collected from taxing the Athenians to give to Lamia and her hetairai friends to buy perfumes.[162] While the heavy taxation of a disgruntled Athenian public and the wanton extravagance of Demetrios and Lamia may be facts, the suggestion that all this money went on soap and perfumes is simply ludicrous. One could probably buy the soap production of the entire world for that kind of money. It seems clear that payments exceeding 20 minae (maybe 30 with a push), even for

---

157 Lys. 3.22–25. For a more detailed discussion of this speech see Ch. 4.2 and 4.3.

158 Aesch. 1.115. The modern reader might find this remark strange as it comes in the same breath with allegations about an indecent, money-based relationship between Timarchos and Hegesandros, but the ancient Greek audience probably would not be puzzled by such a reference, as man to man courtship and simultaneously relationships with female prostitutes seem to be rather typical in the sympotic space.

159 Aesch. Ep. 7.3. This fictional Melanopos is probably based upon Melanopos, son of Diophantos, of Sphettos (D. 35.6), a historical personality mentioned by Demosthenes (D. 24.12, 13, 125) as a companion of Androtion (also accused by Demosthenes of prostitution: see Ch. 4.1.).

160 D.L. 4.4.

161 The gender is uncertain as the genitive ἀμόρφου could be masculine or feminine.

162 Plu. *Demetr.* 27; See also Ch. 3.1.

extended periods of time, are suspect and most if not all of them are exaggerations or wild tales.

In New Comedy and its Latin adaptations the prices mentioned are considerably higher, and it is difficult to judge whether this was the result of inflation in the early Hellenistic period, or dramatic economy and comic exaggeration. When, for example, in Menander's *Samia* Demeas threatens Chrysis that as a free-lance hetaira she would only fetch 10 drachmas a night we don't know whether he is joking or making a reference to a realistic price:

> Demeas: Unlike you, Chrysis, bought for a mere ten drachmas,
> they run to the parties
> and drink unmixed wine until they drop dead,
> or they starve if they do not do this
> readily and fast.[163]

The price of "only" 10 drachmas for a single night ought to be as much of a joke as the idea of being compelled to drink unmixed wine (a guilty pleasure and a favorite of women in the Greek comic tradition).[164] Even more exaggerated seems to be the fee of 12 drachmas per diem for Habrotonon, paid to her pimp. These prices would be two to three times higher than the price of 4 drachmas per diem attested in more reliable sources, and in this respect although not impossible they probably were exaggerated for comic effect. The prices for long term contracts range between 20 and 60 minae, and this also sounds like an exaggeration considering that 20 to 30 minae is the average price for buying a top of the range hetaira, or paying for her freedom.[165] William Loomis considers these prices to be exaggerated and explains them as part of the joke.[166] He also agrees with Gomme and Sandbach that a 3 minae per day price mentioned by Menander's *Colax* is unlikely to be realistic.[167] A price of one talent from a comic fragment also seems to be an exaggeration.[168] Likewise, the offer of 1 talent and

---

163 Men. *Sam.* 392–6.

164 E.g. Ar. *Ec.* 1123, Ar. fr. 364. A very similar joke is made in Ar. *Ach.* 73–5, where the Athenian ambassadors say that they were "forced" to drink sweet, unmixed wine while remaining at the palace of the Persian King.

165 E.g. 20 minae for exclusive access to the hetaira Philaenium for one year in *Asinaria* 229–231; 20 minae, reduced to 10, for Philematium in *Mostellaria* 294–298; 20 minae in *Pseudolus* 51, 20 minae for Phronesium in *Truculentus* 543; 30 minae in *Rudens* 45, 40 (30 plus 10) minae in *Curculio* 344; 60 minae in *Persa* 683; see also Loomis 1988: 175.

166 Loomis 1988: 176.

167 Gomme – Sandbach 1973: 430–1; Loomis 1988: 177–8.

168 Sextus Turpilius 35–6 Ribbeck.

the promise of another to Pannychis in Lucian's *Dialogues of Hetairai*, are exaggerations probably derived from comic sources.[169]

5.7 Conclusions

The complex economics of prostitution in the ancient world are strikingly proportionate to the type, quality and length of service offered to the client. With powerful market forces at work and substantial profits to be made sex workers were prepared to go to great lengths to offer their clients what they wanted. The ancient prostitutional market was very diverse because it was free to flourish without interference from the law, established religion or intense cultural opposition, and slave markets and poor homes provided plentiful human resources. At the bottom of the scale we find cheap brothels where even slaves or the poorest of people could have a sexual encounter with a slave woman, one would imagine not one in her prime, for a low fee, typically 3 obols, or a day's wages for an unskilled worker, and maybe from time to time for even less. Brothels could take many shapes or forms, and sometimes they were integrated into establishments which offered food, wine or shelter, like inns, taverns, or maybe even bakeries and other shops. From there one might be able to hire an entertainer, like a flute-player or dancer, or a girl for the night. In addition to this organized face of prostitution there was a very extensive market of free-lancers or individuals working for themselves or through an agent, a pimp who procured clients and took a large share of the profit, if not most of it. Within this subdivision undoubtedly there were wide variations. Slave street walkers working for a pimp were offering clients a quick sexual encounter for a small fee. Some individuals might be able to afford a small place, where they took clients for a higher fee. For the higher-end workers their home was often their place of work too, as it created the all-important façade of respectability in order to offer the client the illusion of erotic conquest. But even within this group there is substantial gradation. The Xenophontean model of Theodote's establishment, a super clean environment full of airs and graces, all intended to offer an illusion of "friendship" and upper-crust *charis*,[170] is an example of the very high end of the market, while the lower end brothel-homes in Lucian's *Dialogues of Hetairai*, with drunken revelers carousing outside, noisy parties upsetting the neigh-

---

169 Luc. *DMeretr.* 9.3–4.
170 For *charis* (grace) as a concept in erotic conquest cf. Ch. 4.2.

bors in the middle of the night, and rowdy youths or violent soldiers coming and going would represent the lower end of the hetaira market.

A corresponding gradation can be observed in the sympotic space too. The lowly flute-girl of Perseus (see above) is not even allowed to sit next to one of the guests, but on the other end of the scale the fabulous and haughty *pezai hetairai* of Machon and Athenaios would not hesitate to take on the guests, make fun of them and not infrequently treat them with sarcasm and disdain. In between the two ends one can find a broad hierarchy of entertainers prepared to offer sexual services for an additional fee, sometimes a very high one, like the musician girl in the Hippocratic work *On the Seed*, or the attractive and charming boy belonging to the Syracusan pimp in Xenophon's *Symposion*. One can also find hetairai who either came to the symposion with men, or came to meet men, often both, and these were usually younger women with exquisite looks and charming personality enchanting lovers and offering companionship and friendship in addition to sexual favors, and commanding considerably higher prices than the entertainers or the anonymous sex workers of the brothels and the streets.

Ancient city-states for the most part profited from this flourishing market directly through taxation and indirectly through increased economic activity. Profiting from the earnings of prostitution did not create legal complications or implications, as no Greek state penalized or prohibited prostitution. Whether they approved or not, to what extent, and for what reasons are complicated questions to answer, but ultimately irrelevant. The Greek city-states accepted as a fact of life the human condition where someone prepared to pay for sex, companionship or personal empowerment and affirmation will always find someone else willing to offer the service, and did not try to interfere with restrictive laws. The morality of profiting from the earnings of prostitution, which is a vexed issue in modern states, did not trouble the Greeks because they were prepared to accept the fact that some forms of economic activity would not be very respectable, but were nonetheless necessary as economic resources. The infamous biblical duo of the prostitute and the tax-collector concerns activities which might be distasteful for mainstream morality, and might even be outright sinful in the Christian era, but both were a fact of life about which the ancient states, from the Greek cities to imperial Rome, were prepared to be pragmatic.[171]

---

171 οἱ τελῶναι καὶ αἱ πόρναι: *Ev. Matt.* 21.31; 21.32; Catena Matt. 173; Catena Marc. 271 al.

6 Artistic Expressions and Representations of Prostitutes

6.1 Monuments and Dedications of Hetairai

The comic poet Philetairos joked in his *Korinthiastes* that there are many monuments to hetairai, but not a single monument to a lawful wife in the whole world.[1] Although, strictly speaking, this is not true,[2] it is indicative of the attention which monuments to hetairai have received. This attention grew in proportion to the gradual intensification of moralistic views in later antiquity. Honors and dedications for immodest women were increasingly seen as offensive. We often get the impression that these monuments represented a paradox: they honored those women whom society dishonored and marginalized, and yet they were prominently displayed in public places or religious buildings and sanctuaries. Diane Burton in a study of funerary monuments to respectable family women points out that these dedications emphasized domestic values consonant with city ideology.[3] Consequently we should not be surprised if monuments celebrating prostitutes were ostentatious and non-canonical, based on a different ideological platform and intended to impress, if not to shock. As such they deviated from accepted standards and violated convention for public buildings. For such reasons the authors of later antiquity often found these dedications fascinating and astoundingly bold, even if highly improper. Modern scholars too, under the influence of sources like Athenaios, Clement of Alexandria, Plutarch or Gregory Nazianzenos, often reach the conclusion that all monuments to prostitutes were deemed to be offensive norm-breakers by their contemporaries, with an inherent shock value. However, the simple dichotomy between prostitutes and other women is an insufficient premise in this investigation. The great span of time and place, as well as the diversity of purposes for which these dedications were made necessarily require subtler approaches, with an awareness of the period, the genre, the author, and his ideological convictions.

---

1 Philaiteros fr. 5. The title of the play *Korinthiastes* means "a man who goes to Corinth;" one would think referring to someone who loves hetairai and the fun time that he can have with them in the famous brothels of the city.
2 See e.g. Kiessling 2006: 75, n. 27, with references to previous articles and bibliography, and also the discussion of McClure (2003a: 137–165). See also R. Osborne (1997: 3–33) about women and the funerary monuments of Athens.
3 Burton 2003: 21–35.

DOI 10.1515/9783110557954-006

The oldest of these monuments attested in our sources was allegedly a community project sponsored by King Gyges of Lydia (early 7th c.), in honor of his dead mistress. Klearchos of Soli, as quoted by Athenaios, describes the project as following:

> Gyges, he says [sc. Klearchos], the king of Lydia, not only became the subject of much talk because of his mistress while she was alive, since he handed over to her his entire kingdom, but also when she died he brought everyone in Lydia together, and heaped up a mound which is still called to the present day "the tomb of the hetaira," raising it to such a height that every time he was on tour somewhere in the countryside within the region of Mt. Tmolus he could see the monument from whichever direction he turned his eyes, and that it would be visible to all inhabitants of Lydia.[4]

The monument may have been real, since the narrative of Klearchos suggests something concrete and still standing in his time. The fact that no differentiating features are mentioned other than a large mound, leads us to believe that he either had in mind a man-made elevation, or maybe even an unusual geological formation. The story surrounding it no doubt is an invention, perhaps an *aition* to explain the unusual site and its name. It is unlikely that high-class prostitution, as we recognize it in the stereotype of the hetaira-concubine of the Hellenistic despot, was around in Lydia as early as the 8th century. Moreover, the communal project to honor the dead hetaira mistress by distraught lovers is a theme that we recognize easily in other stories, like that of Rhodopis, in whose honor allegedly the pyramid of Mykerinus was built, or Pythionike, for whom Harpalos built three very expensive and prominent monuments.

According to a certain tradition the pyramid of Mycerinus was built in honor of Rhodopis of Naukratis (or Thrace, see Ch. 1.1.) by local magistrates who had been in love with her. Herodotos objects to that tradition emphasizing that a great deal of time had passed between the reign of Mycerinus (26th c.) and the reign of Amasis (6th c.), where he places the floruit of Rhodopis. He also draws attention to the immense expense for the construction of the pyramid, which would have been beyond the means of almost any individual, including Rhodopis herself.[5] At this point Herodotos feels the need to provide additional data about the wealth of Rhodopis. He acknowledges that she was highly sought after in her heyday (κάρτα ἐπαφρόδιτος) and that she amassed consider-

---

4 Klearchos fr. 314 Müller = Athen. 13.31.
5 Hecat. *FGrH* 264 F 25; Hdt. 2.134–5; Verner 2001: 242–253, for a detailed description of the pyramid of Mycerinus (Menkaure). Strabon (17.1.33) relates a modified version of the story, compensating for some of the objections of Herodotos, where Rhodopis became the queen of Psammetichos I and he built the pyramid as her grave.

able wealth, but even her resources would not have been sufficient to finance the pyramid. As evidence for that he mentions a dedication which Rhodopis made to Delphi, which was equal in monetary value to one tenth of her worth. This dedication, or at least part of it, was surviving in his time and he describes it as following:

> Rhodopis desired to leave her own monument in Greece, creating an artifact unlike any other found in a Greek sanctuary, and dedicated this to Delphi as a memorial to herself. Using one tenth of her wealth she made as many iron ox spits as the tithe could afford, and sent them to Delphi. These can be seen to the present day in a pile behind the altar dedicated by the Chians, opposite from the temple.[6]

Herodotos clearly was intrigued and considered this dedication to be unique. We can trust his testimony that the spits were still standing in a pile during his time, while the base of the monument with the inscription "Rhodopis dedicated" has survived to our times.[7] However, his interpretation of the monument may be less secure than it seems, and it has puzzled modern scholars too. The main issue appears to be the complete lack of functionality, cultic or otherwise, to the iron spits, which raises the question whether this monument truly was a cutting-edge artistic inspiration. Catherine Keesling agreed that no practical use for these spits can be detected, as the monument was constructed in such a manner that the spits could not be removed and used for anything else. She concludes that the monument uses functional cultic implements but converts them into non-functional pieces of a unique and quite subversive artistic composition.

Intriguing as this interpretation of the Rhodopis monument may be, the truth of the matter may be more pedestrian. Keesling mentions several other instances where accumulations of iron bars have been found in Greek sanctuaries. The most impressive of these finds consists of 96 bars found in a bundle at the temple of Hera in Argos. Charles Waldstein, the chief archaeologist in charge of the excavation of the Heraion, says describing the bundle, "if it had belonged to Roman times, one would have called it a huge iron rendering of the lictor's staffs," and concludes that "our finds ... furnish us with a most striking archaeological confirmation of the statements of ancient historical writers."[8]

---

6 Hdt. 2.135.
7 *GerKeram* 635; *SEG* 13.634; [τοὺς ὀβελοὺς ἀνέθε]κε Ῥοδ[ῶπις τἀπόλλονι δεκάταν]. Part of the dedication is a restoration by Mastrokostas (1953: 635–646); but see also C. Kiessling (2006: 61). The words that survive probably were part of a longer phrase in metric form.
8 Waldstein 1902: vol. 1, p. 61 and 62.

The statement he had in mind is primarily a story found in literary sources, which may explain how the spits were placed there in the first place. Waldstein, followed by Keesling, cites the *Etymologicum Magnum* as the only source for the relevant story, but, in fact, it is much older and better attested. As far as we know, it was first told by the student of Plato Herakleides of Pontos, repeated in the *Etymologicum* of Orion, and from there passed into the Byzantine dictionaries of the second millennium. It reads as following:

> In earlier times rough iron spits (ὀβελίσκοι) were used as currency. The Ionians call it obelos, while we call it obolos. Pheidon the Argive was the first who minted coins in Aigina, and then, when he put the coins in circulation, he collected the iron spits and dedicated them to the temple of Hera at Argos. Because at that time the spits would fill the hand, that is, as much as one can grasp (δράξ), we still call the currency drachma (δραχμή) from the verb "to grasp" (δράξασθαι), even though our own six obols (ὀβολοί) do not fill the hand.[9]

There is no positive identification of the bundle found in the Heraion with the dedication of Pheidon, but there is no particular reason why we should reject such an association either. A symbolic act of this kind, where the old currency was collected and dedicated to a temple to mark the passage into a new era of economic activity, is not something that should surprise us at the point of a transition as historically significant as this one. Whatever our take on it, the story confirms that the Greeks in the 4th c. were preserving the historical memory of currency bars as dedications to the temples. Waldstein notes that no silver or other coins were found at this level, and this is why he is certain that these bars and other metallic pins found in the place were primitive currency, and mentions other cultures who have used metallic bars, spits or pins for similar purposes.

More dedications like the one in the Argive Heraion were found in the temple of Hera in Perachora, but in this case there is positive identification leaving no room for doubt that at some point in history the dedicated iron bars were monetary standards. Three limestone stelai held spits (*obeloi / oboloi*) equal to the value of a drachma, with one of them still retaining the inscription "I am a drachma" (δραχμὰ ἐγώ).[10] Even in the face of such clear evidence attesting to

---

9 Heraclid. Pont. fr. 152 Wehrli = Orion o 118; EM s.v. ὀβελίσκος; Waldstein 1902: vol. 1, 61–62 (with an image of the iron spits bundle in p. 63). The word δραχμή from δράττεσθαι "to grasp" indicated not only currency but also a weight standard (equivalent to 4.3 grams), and in this sense it has survived in the English dram. Herakleides is aware of both meanings, and relates them back to the time when one used iron spits to pay for things, and also as a standard.
10 Keesing 2006: 62–3; Payne et al. 1940: 258–61; Courbin 1983: 149–156.

the economic significance of these dedications, some voices remain skeptical. L. H. Jeffery (and more recently Catherine Keesling) still insisted that these dedications were cultic, but this position was effectively countered by P. Courbin and H.W. Pleket.[11] The dates of Pheidon and his reforms, as well as the precise time when minted coins were adopted in various parts of the Greek world, feature prominently in the debate, perhaps with a degree of exaggeration. There is no need to assume that all parts of the Greek world adopted silver coins at once, nor that this was a linear and cleanly done procedure. If anything, the story of Plutarch about the death of Epameinondas may suggest otherwise: he says that the great general died leaving nothing behind except a single iron bar found in his house, which would suggest that iron bars might still be around in Thebes as late as in 362 BC.[12] The same conclusion could be drawn from the persistent tradition that the Spartans used iron spits as coinage throughout the classical period.

Recently Jaqueline Christien questioned this tradition arguing that there are no known cases of trading using iron spits, and concluded that the entire iron currency tale is yet another Spartan myth.[13] However, many sources provide strong support for the widespread use of iron bars or spits (*obelos/obeliskos/obolos*) as currency, at least in the archaic period (and considering the conservatism of Spartan institutions, such a practice could easily have carried on). Aristotle was well aware of the use of iron spits as currency in archaic Argos and, according to Pollux, he explicitly said in his now lost *Argive Constitution* that in the old days *obeloi* were used for payment (βουπόροις ὀβελοῖς ἐχρῶντο πρὸς τὰς ἀμοιβάς). Above all, the weighty testimony of Xenophon works against Christien's thesis, and confirms the tradition that iron spits were still in use as currency in classical Sparta. Although he does not mention *obeloi*, the use of iron bars is clearly implied when he says that if one tried to bring into the house a sum as modest as ten minae, he could not possibly do it without being noticed, for he would need a horse and a cart to carry it and a very large space to store it. Xenophon also mentions elsewhere that in his time the Spartans were hoarding precious metals, like gold, but this he takes to be a sign of departure from their traditional ways, and moral decline.[14]

Plutarch was adamant that the entire world used obeloi as currency in old times, and the Spartans continued their use until much later, because they were

---

11 Jeffery 1961: 122 ff.; Pleket 1964: 301–2; Courbin 1959: 209–233; Keesling 2006: 62–3.
12 Plu. *Fab.* 27.4.
13 Christien 2002: 171–190.
14 Arist. fr. 8.44.481 Rose = Poll. 9.77 and 10.179; X. *Lac.* 7.6 and 14.3.

difficult to hide or shift around, and thus suitable as a means of state control over the finances of households, and an effective way to discourage the un-Spartan vice of avarice. He provides significant details about these spits: they were not just like regular iron bars but were processed differently by being dipped into acidic dye while the metal was still hot, so that they would not rust and could not be recast. This confirms the aforementioned testimony of Heraclides that the currency obeloi were different and had a rough surface (although this might not be universal practice). Plutarch then adds the interesting comment that many of these bars were still around in his time, even though they had fallen into disuse, and it seems that he draws the information about their manufacturing method from his own inspection of a surviving sample.[15] This is perhaps the most substantial argument against the position of Christien: unlike other Spartan myths in Plutarch, this one does not seem to be based on arcane traditions or unreliable ancient sources, but on material evidence and his own testimony as an eyewitness.

This and other evidence, which is beyond our purposes to explore in full at this point, has led David Schaps to the following conclusion:

> He [sc. Herodotos] seems, however, to have believed that Rhodopis herself had been paid in some other medium, presumably coins, which she then exchanged for the spits she dedicated. Herodotus, who (unlike Plutarch) was not aware of the monetary use of spits, imagined them to be a purchase intentionally bizarre, but in view of what we have already seen, it would seem more likely that the spits themselves had been her accumulated treasure, whatever her particular tariff may have been.[16]

This conclusion of Schaps seems to be the easiest and most reasonable resolution to a long and vexed debate. In a move undoubtedly intended to secure her notoriety (οὕτω δή τι κλεινὴ ἐγένετο ὡς καὶ οἱ πάντες Ἕλληνες Ῥοδώπιος τὸ οὔνομα ἐξέμαθον), Rhodopis dedicated one tenth of her actual wealth, accumulated in iron spits, to the most centrally important sanctuary in the Greek world.

There is strong evidence to suggest that Rhodopis was a contemporary of Sappho and probably reached her floruit in the earlier part of the 6th century (see Ch. 1.1.). For this early age, even if electrum, silver or gold coins had already started to make their appearance in various parts of the Greek world and the Near East, in all likelihood iron or copper spits were still widely used as currency, and it is reasonable to assume that the famous hetaira would have amassed her wealth in that form of currency. There is no challenging artistic

---

15 Plu. *Lys.* 17.
16 Schaps 2004: 86.

concept involved; simply a tenth of the iron currency spits stored in her private treasury was removed and sent to Delphi, bundled together and fastened on a solid base, as in the cases of the finds in Argos and Perachora. Although such a motive cannot be proven, it might add an unexpected twist to the saga of this dedication if Rhodopis, like Pheidon, offered the iron bars at a time when they were losing their value as currency, as silver and gold coins were gradually being introduced in all parts of the Greek world. That would make the dedication less unselfish, since in that case Rhodopis would be offering to the Delphic god only what was no longer valuable and practically useful to her.

Around the middle of the 4th century another monument of a hetaira at Delphi caused sensation in the Greek world and was remembered as a very controversial piece of art long after the work itself was lost.[17] The artistic value of it was not in question. This was an exquisite work of Praxiteles, made of gilded bronze. It stood on a tall column in a prominent place near the entrance to the temple of Apollo, between the statues of two kings, Archidamos III of Sparta and Philip II of Macedon, and on the base there was a simple inscription: "Phryne, Daughter of Epikles, from Thespiai" (Φρύνη Ἐπικλέους Θεσπική). Sheila Dillon surmises from the prominence of its location that it was probably a public dedication, as Alketas (quoted by Athenaios) suggests, rather than a private offering, as Pausanias says.[18] Almost as soon as it was erected, it invited bitter criticism. The most enduring remark was that of the Cynic philosopher Krates, which was often repeated down to the late Byzantine dictionaries. It is reported that when he saw the dedication Krates said that it stood as a monument to the Greek lack of boundaries (ἀκρασία).

Keesling has argued that the monument was not as transgressive as generally thought because from the late classical period onwards dedications of statues of individuals become more common, and the findings of Dillon certainly confirm this.[19] However, the artistic value of the monument or whether it followed contemporary trends are not the issue here. If Phryne were a respectable priestess, a high-born member of a powerful family, or an individual who had performed extraordinary service to the community, some of her contemporaries might think of the dedication as somewhat ostentatious but no one would have found it offensive. Objections to Phryne's monument were raised by those who

---

17 Corso 1997: 123–150 provides a complete discussion of this work and interested readers should consult this study for further details.
18 Plu. 336 C; Paus. 10.15; D. Chr. 37.28; Alketas *FGrH* 405 F 1 = Athen. 13.59; Ael. *V.H.* 9.32; Lib. *Decl.* 25.2.40; Stob. 3.6.46; Dillon 2010: 48; Corso 1997: 123–150; Keesling 2006: 59–76.
19 See Keesling 2006: 59–76; Dillon 2010: 9–59.

thought that a whore's image does not belong in the most revered sanctuary of the Greeks, and in such a prominent place among kings. If an oration of Chorikios about a probably fictional statue of Aphrodite made for the Spartans and modeled on Phryne preserves the gist of those objections, then what seems to be the problem for the critics of later antiquity is the dedication to a hetaira in such a prominent place.[20] Other sources point in the same direction. Plutarch's critique draws an incomprehensible parallel with Sardanapallos, Aelian goes to great lengths to qualify the statement of Krates, saying that not all the Greeks but only the most incontinent among them (ἀκρατεστάτους) would make such a dedication, while one of the declamations of Libanius expresses astonishment with the ambiguous word θαυμαστόν.[21] However, it must be noted that all these sources are late, and the moral indignation they express bears the cultural marks of their own time. There is no evidence from the classical period to suggest that anyone else, other than an ever-critical Cynic philosopher whose opinion is probably not representative of the time, found the monument of Phryne disturbing, or even inappropriate as a dedication to the most holly place of the Greeks.

Two more dedications of Phryne are mentioned in the sources. The Eros of Thespiae, according to a story told by Pausanias, was among all Praxiteles' works the one the artist himself valued most:

> Phryne once upon a time was asking for the best of his (sc. Praxiteles) works. They say that he agreed to give it to her, as a lover would do, but he did not want to tell her which of his works he considered the best. So, a servant of Phryne rushed in and told Praxiteles that most of his works were gone in a fire which had destroyed his workshop, but a few pieces had not been destroyed. Praxiteles started running to the door saying that if the flames had consumed the Eros and the Satyr he had nothing left. Phryne told him to stay put, for there had been no accident, but he fell for her trick and confessed which of his works he considered to be the best. This is how she picked the Eros.[22]

---

20 Chorikios (or. 29) is generally reshuffling themes from classical sources to create his compositions, and sometimes he sticks so faithfully to his sources that we can use his text to restore corrupted text in his source. It is likely that the arguments he employs here come, at least partially, from a polemic against Phryne in his sources, along with banalities from late antiquity and the Christian era about the unsuitability of a prostitute as a representation for the divine.

21 Θαυμαστόν could mean both "admirable" and "weird" at the same time.

22 Paus. 1.20.1–2.

Athenaios gives the shorter version, saying only that Phryne chose the Eros over the Satyr, but adds that she dedicated the statue to her native city of Thespiai.[23] Kallistratos in his work *Ekphraseis* describes in some detail a bronze statue of Eros by Praxiteles portrayed as a winged boy with bow and arrows,[24] but this could not be the original Eros of Thespiae, which was made of marble and had been destroyed centuries before his time.[25] Cicero considered this famous statue to be the only attraction of Thespiae worth a visit, emphatically saying that other than the Eros there was nothing left to see. Everything else had been carried away to Rome, but the Eros was left untouched by L. Mummius because it was consecrated. Less than a century later the less scrupulous Caligula carried the statue to Rome; Claudius gave it back to the Thespians, but Nero took it to Rome for a second time, where it was destroyed by a fire during his reign. In a rare explosion of religious sentiment Pausanias adds that both Caligula and Nero deservedly suffered a terrible fate for their sins against the god.[26]

Whether the Eros of Thespiai was of the same type as the one described by Kallistratos has been the subject of some debate. Antonio Corso on the basis of literary sources has argued that the Eros Farnese of Centocelle type, where Eros is presented as a sad teenage boy, is more likely a copy of the Eros of Thespiai.[27] However, it must be noted that the evidence cited in support of this identification is very weak. Pausanias, a generally trustworthy source, Athenaios, who often had reliable sources in his hands, and Cicero, who may have seen the original statue or at least could have obtained first-hand accounts by people who had, do not describe the Eros. One is left with authors like Alciphron and some epigrams from the Greek Anthology, either of unknown dates or from much later times. All these sources are fictional and chronologically removed by several centuries and as such they should be used with extreme caution. At best these authors had seen a copy, and most likely they built their compositions on commonplace information about this famous work in the literature of later antiquity, rather than on an authoritative source.

The Eros which Pausanias saw standing in Thespiai was a copy by the Athenian artist Menodoros. Pausanias mentions that in the same location there

---

23 Athen. 13.59.
24 Callistr. Stat. 3.
25 Paus. 9.27.3; Cic. *Ver.* 2.4.4; Corso 1997–1998: 63–91; Keesling 2005: 70–71.
26 Cic. *Ver.* 2.4.4; Paus. 9.27.3. Strabo (9.2.25), followed by Eustathios (*Com. Il.* 1. 406), says that it was Glykera, of Thespiai, not Phryne, who dedicated the Eros of Praxiteles to her native city, and that the statue was a gift to her by the artist. Most likely Strabo is mistaken; he has mixed up Glykera with Phryne.
27 Corso 1997–1998: 63–91; for the opposite point of view Rizzo 1932: 20–24.

were also a marble statue of Phryne and a marble statue of Aphrodite, both made by Praxiteles. The three statues are known in modern scholarship as the triad of Thespiai. Alciphron adds that the statue of Phryne stood in the middle between the Eros and the Aphrodite, but this information may be derived from Pausanias and adapted to suit Alciphron's literary purposes, where Phryne is presented as the center of these honors. Corso has suggested that the two were added to the statue of Eros shortly after its dedication to Thespiai. The Aphrodite has been identified as a statue of the Aphrodite of Arles type, while Phryne's head has been recognized in a couple of representations of a hetaira's head which resemble those of Aphrodite of Arles, as they ought if Phryne had been used as the model for both herself and Aphrodite.[28]

It is also attested in the literature of later antiquity that Phryne was the model for the revered Knidian Aphrodite of Praxiteles and for the Anadyomene of Apelles, perhaps the most famous painting in the ancient world. Clement adds that painters and sculptors were coming in droves to use her as a model, with the unfortunate side-effect that believers in the temples were paying their respects to the image of a whore.[29] The aforementioned *dialexis* of Chorikios seems to be repeating the same complaint about prostitutes modeling for the statues of goddesses. The argument in Chorikios is based upon the premise that at some point Spartan women started giving birth to hideously ugly girls. The Spartans, who took great pride in the good looks of their women, sought the advice of the oracle at Delphi and were told that Aphrodite was angry with them and needed to be placated with a statue. They gave the order to Praxiteles, who used Phryne as a model. The Spartans were displeased because they did not want to honor the image of a prostitute, and in the *dialexis* they outline this position, while Praxiteles presenting the counter-argument tries to convince them to accept the statue. Curiously Corso and others accept this as a true story.[30] There is no doubt that this is a rhetorical composition, a fictional account based upon stereotypes and themes from classical literature with no historical basis. Neither do the moralizing tones of later antiquity which pervade this story befit the ideology of classical Sparta, nor is it likely that the Spartans would commission an Athenian artist around 350 BC. The impoverished state of Sparta

---

28 Paus. 9.27.5; Alciphr. 4.1; Corso 1997–8: 69–71, and plates 7, 11 and 12; Corso 2004: 257–280; Lauter 1988: 21–29.
29 Athen. 13.59; Clem. Al. *Protr.* 4.53.5–6. The information in Clement that the model of Praxiteles for the Knidian Aphrodite was the hetaira Kratine is either his own misreading of his source, or a textual mistake for Phryne. There is no reference of a hetaira named Kratine anywhere in the sources. See also Havelock 1995: 42–47 and 86–93; Seaman 2004: 531–594.
30 Chorikios Or. 29; Corso 1997–8: 74.

had much bigger concerns at that time than placing orders with outsiders for pricy works of art.

The mesmerizing effect of Phryne upon artists did not end with the ancient world. There are more than a dozen modern paintings and several films based on her; the prominent hetaira has continued to scandalize and titillate her audiences to the present day.[31] These works usually focus on themes from the popular mythology around Phryne in the authors of later antiquity, usually Athenaios, Pausanias and the Greek Anthology. Cavallini perceptively has suggested that this mythology was first cultivated by Phryne herself. She says:

> In fact, when examining ancient documents about Phryne, one gets the impression that the first forger of her 'myth' was not a biographer nor a poet, but the woman herself, with her skilful use of provocative statements that were bound to cause a sensation, especially among conformists, as well as a series of carefully contrived, spectacular public appearances. Moreover, the sources emphasize Phryne's tendency to 'celebrate' her own beauty by having expensive images of herself placed in 'strategic' places, such as Eros' temple in Thespiae, her hometown, or even the Delphic sanctuary, where a golden statue of Phryne made a fine show next to the simulacra of kings and queens.

Where Phryne differs from most contemporary hetairai is that she was prepared to push the boundaries further than any other woman of her time and keep testing how far she could go. Such actions as those emphasized by Cavallini were not just sensationalist stunts, common among the hetairai of the 4th century. For a woman of her time to be able to possess substantial personal wealth and spend it on dedications of personal aggrandizement, to advertise and celebrate her own beauty and to seek a place of fame and notoriety among kings, intellectuals, artists and other prominent men of her time, instead of the customary respectable anonymity, are radical steps which reset the limits of female empowerment. Perhaps this is Phryne's lasting appeal and the reason why her startling and captivating image, even though it started as a carefully cultivated and meticulously marketed product, eventually took on a life of its own and continued to mesmerize long after she herself and the artists whom she inspired were gone.

Phryne's great rival in the literature of later antiquity was Lais. The two women are often presented as exact contemporaries locked in an antagonistic relationship, when in reality they probably lived half a century apart and in different cities; Lais lived in Corinth, while Phryne was based in Athens. The Corinthians were claiming Lais as their own, even though most sources agree

---

31 See Cavallini 2010.

that she was from Hyblaia Hykkara in Sicily. Pausanias describes a cypress grove located before the entrance to Corinth, which contained a precinct of Bellerephontes, a temple of Aphrodite Melainis and a monumental grave of Lais. On top of it there was a statue of a lioness holding in her front paws a ram. The symbolism was unmistakable: the strong male is caught and subdued by the female predator. The location of the monument, in the company of the patron goddess of the city and the most revered Corinthian hero, can only suggest that by the time of Pausanias Lais had been elevated in the collective memory of the Corinthians to an iconic symbol of the city, worthy of dwelling among its gods and heroes.[32] Pausanias comments on the affection and adoration of the Corinthians for the woman whose beauty had surpassed that of all other hetairai in their city, and adds that they proudly claimed her as their own even though she was not, and according to an alternative tradition she was not even buried there.

Pausanias is aware of a claim made by the Thessalians that the grave of Lais was located there, and not in Corinth. In a story told by Timaios and repeated by Athenaios, Lais moved to Thessaly because she fell in love with a man called Pausanias (or Hippostratos, according to the traveler Pausanias).[33] There she incurred the jealousy of local women, who beat her to death with wooden footstools in the sanctuary of Aphrodite. Timaios also reports that the temple was since renamed as the precinct of the Unholy Aphrodite (ἀνοσίας Ἀφροδίτης), and the grave was situated at the banks of the river Peneios. The grave had an urn standing on top and the following inscription:

> Once upon a time the invincible Greece
> Was enslaved by the god-like beauty of Lais
> Who was the child of Eros and the ward of Corinth
> But she lies in the glorious fields of Thessaly.[34]

This cruel tale of jealousy and cold-blooded murder sounds like a local *aition* and is unlikely to be true. Lais is one of the most scrutinized women in history before the modern era, and there are numerous references from more reliable sources to her living into a grand old age as an independent woman, who still took lovers in her advanced years (see Appendix I). This would flatly contradict the story of Timaios where Lais while still young and attractive becomes the concubine of a man in Thessaly, and is still ravishing enough to evoke deadly

---

32 Paus. 2.2.4.
33 Timaios *FGrH* 566 fr. 24a; Athen. 13.55; Paus. 2.2.5.
34 Timaios *FGrH* 566 fr. 24a = Athen. 13.55; *AG* Appendix 155.

jealousy. Besides, a lynching in the temple of Aphrodite would be an end too ironic for a celebrity of her magnitude to escape the attention of almost everyone except for a Hellenistic historian with a taste for preposterous tales. Pausanias does not seem inclined to believe this story, even though he has heard of it, but he does not explicitly disprove it either. He is simply amazed by the fact that several Greek cities are competing for the resting place of the notorious hetaira. The question is whether, after we reject the lynching tale, we also need to reject the possibility that Lais was actually buried in Thessaly, and not in Corinth where one would normally have expected her to be buried considering that she lived there for most of her life.

There is a simple explanation for the discrepancy in this case. An epigram of the Byzantine scholar Agathias the Scholastic could hold the key for reconciling these two versions. According to Agathias the grave of Lais, with an epigram identifying it as such, was to be found in Ephyra. This was an ancient mythological name of Corinth, sometimes found in poetry, as for example in Propertius with specific reference to Lais,[35] but also the name of another three cities, according to Strabo and the scholiast of Pindar (who may be drawing his information from Strabo).[36] It seems that sometimes even ancient authors were confusing these cities.[37] It is not unlikely that Timaios misunderstood one of his sources, which was speaking of Corinth in poetic language, and took it to mean the Thessalian Ephyra. Beyond that the tale took a life of its own, and Timaios may have combined into a new narrative existing elements, including the epigram which he probably drew from Athenian literary sources as it bears a mark unique to the Attic dialect.[38] The possibility that the grave in Thessaly belonged to another Lais, one of the several copy-cats that sought to benefit from the notoriety of the famous hetaira in the late classical period and subsequent centuries, cannot be excluded but in the light of this evidence it seems less likely. The grave of Lais was indeed located in Ephyra, but not the Thessalian one at the banks of Peneios.

---

35 Prop. 2.6.1: Ephyraeae Laidos.
36 One of those, the most prominent was the Thesprotian Ephyra, the impressive remains of which have recently been excavated near modern Parga. Another Ephyra was located in Thessaly which Strabo and the scholiast of Pindar identify with Krannon, and the fourth was in Elis. See Str. 8.3.5; Paus. 2.1.1; Sch. Pind. *Py.* 85a and 85c.
37 E.g. Str. 7.7.10.
38 In line 3 Θετταλικοῖς is the telling sign that this was an epigram composed in the Attic dialect. One would expect some form of local dialect for an epigram composed in Thessaly, or at least a standardized form of Ionic Greek, customary in epigrams.

Around the middle of the 4th century (in or shortly after 340) another famous monument was erected in honor of a hetaira, this one in Chalcedon, on the Asiatic shore of Bosporus, south of Chrysopolis, which was still standing at least until the end of the first millennium. The monument was built in memory of the Athenian Boïdion (literally: heifer), one of the mistresses of the general Chares who had followed him during his campaign against Philip in Byzantium. She took ill and died, and Chares erected an altar and a monument consisting of a pillar and a statue of a cow carved in stone, with an inscription explaining its history and purpose. Three of the primary sources describing the monument consist of eye-witness accounts and expectedly there are no notable differences. The oldest of the sources is the local geographer Dionysios of Byzantium in his detailed study of the Bosporus area.[39] Dionysios placed the monument at Chalcedon, on the edge of the Asiatic shore and right across from Byzantium. He was aware of the inscription explaining the history and purpose of the monument, but did not cite it. However, he used the inscription as evidence to reject alternative explanations of the monument. The second source, the Byzantine scholar and chronicler Hesychios of Miletos, Illustrius, whose lifespan extended into the early years of the reign of Justinian (c. 530 AD), offered a very similar account of the location and description of the monument, but also cited the inscription in full:

> I am not a sculpture of the cow of Inachos,[40] nor have I
> given my name to the nearby sea of Bosporus.
> The heavy wrath of Hera chased her all the way
> to Alexandria. But I am of the Kekropian dead.
> I was the lover of Chares; I sailed with him
> when he sailed here to face the fleet of Philip;
> Boidion was my name, but now as the lover of Chares
> I have the pleasure of enjoying two continents.[41]

---

39 Dionysios *Per Bosporum Navigatio* 110.

40 This is a mythological reference to Io, the daughter of Inachos and lover of Zeus, who was transformed into a cow by Zeus to escape detection and the wrath of Hera.

41 Hesych. Mil. *Patria Constantinopoleos* 30. Hesychios of Miletos was the source for many of the entries of Suda, especially those about personal names. Interestingly in the brief entry of Suda (β 581), a citation of a single line from the epigram (Βοΐδιον ... Χάρητος), is not derived from Hesychios of Miletos, as a textual variation reveals, since where Hesychios gives "my name was Boidion" (Βοΐδιον οὔνομα δ' ἦεν ἐμοὶ τότε), the text of Suda (and *AG.* 7.169) has "Boidion I was then called" (Βοΐδιον δὲ καλεύμαν τότε ἐγώ). The entry of Suda in this instance is derived from Constantine VII Porphyrogennetos, who gives the same version. Page (1981:

The third of the sources is a reference in Emperor Constantine VII Porphyrogen-netos, no doubt an eyewitness too, as he was talking about a well-known local monument less than two miles away from the Great Palace of Constantinople, on the other side of the Bosporus. His account completely agrees with the ac-count of Hesychios except for a minor textual difference in the citation of the epigram, and thus confirms that the monument and the inscription had sur-vived intact all the way into the Macedonian era.[42]

A considerably different account of the monument is offered by Arrian, as cited by Eustathios in his commentaries on Dionysios Periegetes.[43] Arrian seem-ingly said that the cow was made of bronze, there was no reference to a column or to the epigram, and the cow was perceived to be a representation of Io. Denys L. Page considered Arrian to be of equal authority with the other three sources and thus concluded that the monument was "problematic." [44] However, the account of Arrian is not a source of equal authority with the other three in this instance. The information from Arrian is not a first-hand account but actually a citation of a citation of Arrian, and something could have gone wrong in this line of transmission. Second, even if the citations are accurate there is nothing to suggest that Arrian had actually seen the monument; he could be reporting something which he found in another source or a distorted traveler's tale. Against the basically unanimous testimony of three eyewitnesses Arrian's in-formation is useless. Dionysios of Byzantium, Hesychios and Emperor Constan-tine VII were all locals and without a doubt had seen the monument with their own eyes, their descriptions agree, Hesychios and Constantine cite the inscrip-tion while Dionysios is aware of it, and all three link it to Boidion the mistress of Chares. Without a doubt their accounts preserve the correct description and interpretation of the monument.

Comparable in prestige and ostentation but much pricier and on a larger scale were the monuments that Harpalos built for his mistresses in the later part of 4th century. Harpalos, who at some point had access to the entire treasury of the Achaemenids, and thus the wealth of Asia, surprised and shocked his con-temporaries with costly dedications to his mistresses, and in particular Pythi-

---

373) rightly points out that it is very difficult to decide which version in our sources is actually preserving the exact wording of the inscription.

42 Constantine VII Porphyrogennetos, *De Thematibus Europ.* 12. Constantine was emperor from 913 to 959, which suggests that the monument outlasted the first millennium of the Chris-tian era.

43 Arrian *Bithynicorum* fr. 36 = Eust. *Commentarii in Dionysii Periegetae Orbis Descriptionem* 140, p. 240.33.

44 Page 1981: 371–374.

onike, who seemingly died giving birth to the daughter of Harpalos. Distraught by her death he erected three monuments in her honor, as attested in literary sources. The monument which he erected in Babylon was too far away from the Greek world to receive much attention. It is simply mentioned by Theopompos with the note that it was completed. The second monument in Athens is much better described. All sources agree that it stood on the way to Eleusis. According to Dikaiarchos it was standing on the side of the Sacred Way at the western entrance into the plain of Athens, and dominated the landscape at the point where the visitor first got a glimpse of the Acropolis.[45] Thus the monument was strategically located to be the first large-scale structure visible to the visitor entering the basin of Athens from the west. Dikaiarchos and Pausanias say that the visitor would naturally think that such a splendid structure belonged to one of the illustrious men from the glorious past of Athens like Kimon, Miltiades or Pericles. Consequently it would not only be surprising but also demeaning for the city of Athens to discover that this was the monument of a whore. Plutarch attests a cost of 30 talents for its construction. This is not necessarily at odds with the information of Theopompos that this monument and the one in Babylon together cost more than 200 talents, because the monument in Babylon could have been the more extravagant of the two. However, it is very likely that Theopompos is inflating the cost in order to raise the alarm about the extravagance of Harpalos. None of these sources is actually describing the monument. A third monument, a sanctuary with a temple and an altar dedicated to Aphrodite Pythionike is attested by Theopompos.[46]

As Andreas Scholl points out, the literary evidence marks the site of the Pythionike monument in Athens so clearly that a search was launched by archaeologists to find it.[47] A recent publication by the historian of modern Chaidari Kostas Foteinakis outlines the thrilling search for the famous monument in the past two centuries.[48] While his findings, for the most part, independently agree with those of Scholl, Foteinakis was also intrigued by the hunt

---

45 His description suggests that the monument was standing in modern Chaidari close to the point where *Hiera Odos* veers off from *Leoforos Athinon*.

46 The main sources are Theopompos *FGrH* 115 F 253, Dikaiarchos fr. 29, Pausanias 1.37.5, and Plutarch *Phoc.* 21–22. Several modern studies discuss the buildings and their significance in greater detail: see Müller 2006: 71–106; Scholl 1994: 239–271; Eder 2000: 201–215.

47 Scholl 1994: 254–61.

48 I was able to find the report of Kostas Foteinakis online. The title of the report is Συμβολή στην έρευνα για την ανεύρεση του Μνημείου της Πυθιονίκης στην Ιερά Οδο, στο χώρο του Διομήδειου κήπου, and the date is March 2010. The URL is: http://www.scribd.com/full/29095607?access_key=key-89il2ywlty1zj9zmvng.

itself for the monument of Pythionike, which had begun even before the creation of the modern Greek state. At the turn of the 19th century the French diplomat, painter and antiquarian Louis Francois Sebastian Fauvel, then consul in Athens, was seemingly looking for the monument. Demetrios Kampouroglou, the prominent lawyer, antiquarian and poet of the late 19th century, commented with a hint of sarcasm that Fauvel was looking for the grave of a hetaira and found instead the monument of a priestess of Athena. Further searches by Chateaubriand, the French army major Elie Jean de Vassoigne, and the archaeologist fr. Lenormant failed to identify the monument. In 1892 Kampouroglou located the base of a large structure in modern Chaidari, to the southwest of the Sacred Way near *Nikomedeias Street*, in the area called the Garden of Diomedes (Διομήδειος Κῆπος), but did not associate it with the monument of Pythionike.

In 1936 a twenty-page monograph by the epigraphist and archaeologist A.A. Papagiannopoulos-Palaios made the connection of the structure which Kampouroglou had discovered in the Garden of Diomedes with the monument of Pythionike.[49] He suggested that the 30 m. long and 16 m. wide base might have hosted a monument similar in inspiration to the Pergamon Altar with two symmetrical buildings standing side by side at the façade of the structure.[50] An Ionian column found on the site was thought to be part of the building. Foteinakis mentions an on the spot geological survey by Michael Stamatakis, professor of industrial oryctology and Chair of the Department of Geology at the University of Athens, who concluded that the column was carved out of local "arouraios" stone, but did not find any evidence that it was part of that structure. The research of Papagiannopoulos – Palaios was somewhat forgotten, as the rare book itself was difficult to obtain, and the Greek Archaeological Institute has neither confirmed nor denied his identification of the structure in the Garden of Diomedes with the monument of Pythionike. In 2010 Foteinakis obtained a copy of the book, was able to confirm that the structure is exactly where Papagiannopoulos – Palaios said it was, and urged the Archaeological Institute to prove or disprove the identification with the Pythionike monument with further research.

The timeline of the building program to honor Pythionike is steeped in uncertainty. The monument in Babylon most likely was built shortly after the death of Pythionike, while Harpalos was still residing there. The monument in Athens is more problematic. Theopompos suggests that it was built while

---

49 Papagiannopoulos – Palaios 1936.
50 The Pergamon Altar itself was not built until much later in the early 2nd century. For a drawing of a possible reconstruction of the Pythionike monument see Scholl 1994: 254–61.

Harpalos was still in Asia. The letter of Theopompos to Alexander, where both monuments, as well as the temple of Aphrodite Pythionike, are mentioned as complete, was supposedly written while Harpalos was still in charge in the heartlands of the old Achaemenid empire and Alexander was in India (early 320s). Plutarch, on the other hand, suggests that the Athenian monument was built after the escape of Harpalos to Greece (324), and was commissioned to Charikles, the son in law of Phokion. The latter appears to be a personal friend of Harpalos, if we can judge by the fact that he became the guardian of the daughter of Harpalos and Pythionike after the death of her father. If one assumed that the letter of Theopompos was not a real letter, but a literary construct in epistolary format telescoping together events that took place over a long period of time, this would open the way for the version of Plurach, but this solution is not without its problems either, because it would assume that Harpalos built the second monument several years after the death of Pythionike, and after he had turned his affections to Glykera, in whose honor he erected a bronze image in Syria and demanded from the people that she be venerated along with him and be addressed as "queen" (βασίλισσα).[51] This is not unlikely, but if the entire building program of Harpalos was a public display of grief, as most sources seem to suggest, this strengthens the version of Theopompos that all these buildings were constructed within a short period of time after her death, when money was no object for a mourning Harpalos. It is possible that Harpalos was well acquainted with the family of Phokion before his escape to Athens, and thus the information of Plutarch that the monument was commissioned to Charikles may also be correct.

There appears to have been another magnificent monument inspired by that of Pythionike, this one dedicated by Ptolemy II Philadelphos in honor of his mistress Stratonike. Ptolemy VIII Euergetes II (Physkon) says that it stood on the coastline of Eleusis. Ptolemy Physkon mentions Stratonike among several mistresses of Ptolemy Philadelphos, among whom we can recognize Bilistiche of Argos, a hetaira of noble birth (see Appendix I). However, there may be a special reason behind this generosity towards Stratonike. The generally knowledgeable Scholiast of Lucian says that Stratonike was a wife and sister of Philadelphos, not a mere mistress.[52] The name Stratonike is certainly significant as it was a well-known mythological name, carried also by several Hellenistic queens and princesses in the various courts of the Diadochi, and does have a noble ring to

---

51 Theopompos *FGrH* 115 F 25; DS 17.108; Athen. 13.50.
52 Ptolemy *FGrH* 234 F 4 = Athen. 13.37; Sch. Luc. 24.15 Rabe.

it. Thus, it is possible that Stratonike had a splendid monument constructed in her honor because she held a higher status than a mere prostitute – mistress.

In any case, Philadelphos was very generous towards all his mistresses, according to the weighty testimony of Polybios. Among them the privileged position of the royal cupbearer belonged to a woman named Kleino. Polybios attests that there were many statues of her around Alexandria, representing her dressed in a single tunic and holding in her hands a drinking cup. In the same passage Polybios attests that the generosity of the king to his mistresses was not limited to public monuments. Three of them, the flute-players Mnesis and Potheine and the common whore Myrtion, had the nicest houses in Alexandria no doubt offered as gifts from the king.[53] Polybios may be harsh in his description of Myrtion as a common whore, as there are a few other references implying that she was a well-known hetaira. The same Myrtion is also mentioned by Ptolemy VIII in a manner which suggests a royal concubine of Philadelphos, while a hetaira named Myrtion from an unspecified point in the past was known to Lucian.[54] Moreover, in his *Dialogues of Hetairai* Lucian portrays a fictional hetaira named Myrtion who is pregnant by her lover Pamphilos.[55]

We need to be cautious when it comes to Hellenistic royalty with the definitions of what is a concubine and what is a prostitute, as these lines are often blurred; the hetaira-concubine is a standard feature of Hellenistic courts. We also need to be open-minded about the levels of sleaze and impropriety that would be permissible for a royal concubine, as these seem to be considerably higher compared to other monarchies of the ancient world (see Ch. 3.1. and 7).[56] Demetrios Poliorketes and his mistresses are a prime example of how traditional boundaries had been reshaped to accommodate their excesses. The flute-player Lamia became the most powerful royal concubine, and her improprieties with Demetrios became the stuff of legend (see Ch. 3.1.). At the height of the power of Demetrios, if any one wanted to flatter him they might try to do so by keeping on the good side of his capricious mistresses. The historian Demochares, nephew of Demosthenes, mentions two temples of Lamia Aphrodite and Leaina Aph-

---

53 Plb. 14.11; Ptolemy *FGrH* 161 F 3; Athen. 10.26.
54 Ptolemy *FGrH* 234 F 4 = Athen. 13.37; Luc. *DMort* 22.7.
55 E.g. Ar. *Lys.* 1004; Poll. 2.174
56 A comparison with the Achaemenid court might be informative. The women of the harem were sheltered away from the prying eyes and desires of other men, and only the king, his close relatives, the royal physicians and the palace eunuchs had access to these women. By contrast, the concubines in the Hellenistic courts, especially those who had started as prostitutes, were participating in the social life of the palace, and the parties sometimes included sleazy sexual encounters with men other than the king.

rodite, to honor the primary mistresses of Demetrios Lamia and Leaina. Moreover he mentions altars, precincts, libations and songs composed for the courtiers of Demetrios. The flattery became too sleazy and sickening even for Demetrios: he indignantly declared that there was no great or brave Athenian man left in his day.[57]

Polemon the traveler also mentions a temple of Lamia Aphrodite dedicated by the Thebans. It is perfectly possible that such temples were erected by both the Athenians and the Thebans to flatter the man who had the whole of Greece under his sway. These temples would be modeled on the precedent of the temple of Aphrodite Pythionike erected by Harpalos for his beloved mistress. Polemon mentions another dedication, this time by Lamia herself, to the city of Sikyon, where we are told that she built a painted portico.[58] The reason why Lamia, who was Athenian, decided to erect an elaborate, and no doubt costly, public building in Sikyon, and not in Athens, is not clear. Political expediency entwined with the schemes of Demetrios at first appears to be the most reasonable explanation, but admittedly it is not supported by the narrative of Polemon or Athenaios. This is why patronage for the arts may be a credible alternative explanation: Sikyon was famous for its painters, as the work of Polemon *On the Paintings of Sikyon* (Περὶ τῶν ἐν Σικυῶνι πινάκων) suggests, and conceivably Lamia was an admirer and certainly rich and powerful enough to be a patron.[59] Whatever the precise motive behind her choice of the location, the underlying reason why she built it is clear: like Phryne, Kotinna and other rich and powerful women of her time she wanted to leave a lasting monument, bearing witness to her wealth and prestige. A large and elaborate portico with a colonnade located on the south-side of the market place in Sikyon (105 x 16 meters) has been identified by some with the stoa of Lamia, but this identification is contested on the grounds that there would not be enough wall space for paintings in this building, and it seems that further research will be needed before a positive identification can be made.[60]

Another instance where literary evidence pinpoints exactly the location of a building, but modern research has not yet resulted in a conclusive identification is that of the brothel of the famous Spartan hetaira Kottina, and the exact location where she had placed a dedication. Polemon in his work *On the Dedications at Lacedaemon* identifies a house on the hill of Kolona next to the temple of

---

57 Demochares *FGrH* 75 F 1 = Athen. 6.62.
58 Polemon fr. 14–5 Müller = Athen. 6.62, 13.38.
59 See Bringmann – Von Steuben 1995: vol. 2, 118.
60 See Bringmann – Von Steuben 1995: vol. 2, 117–118.

Dionysos Kolonatas, on the central-east side of the city as the brothel (οἴκημα) of the notorious Kottina.[61] Polemon attests that this was a quite prominent building and its use as a brothel was widely known. He adds that Kottina had offered a dedication standing near the temple of Athena Chalcioikos, which consisted of two small bronze statues: one was a cow, the other was an image of herself. The district where her brothel was situated was within the boundaries of the village of Pitana, and thus Kottina dedicated the statues to the local temple of Athena. The purpose of the dedication as well as the meaning of it are not clear. Like Phryne, Kottina dedicated an image of herself, but unlike Phryne's dedication of a gilded masterpiece standing in a prominent place in the primary Panhellenic sanctuary, and undoubtedly aiming at personal aggrandizement and notoriety throughout the Greek world, Kottina's dedication was small in scale, placed in the vicinity of the local temple, and seemingly had a personal and/or cultic significance which eludes us.

Revision of history with hetairai being retrofitted into the picture was quite common especially during the second sophistic (see Ch. 3.1.). A process of rein-terpretation of famous works of art to link them to prominent hetairai took place in later antiquity, but the process had already started in the late classical peri-od. Several monuments, dedications and works of art around the Greek world were reinterpreted and associated with hetairai, and etiological myths and tales were invented to explain monuments or aspects of them from this angle. The reasons vary, but for the most part are either intended to make a rather dull traditional tale more racy for the tastes of audiences in the Roman Empire, or to remove or moderate homosexual references in traditional hero stories by inject-ing heterosexual content into them, to make them more palatable for the changed morals of later antiquity. While, for example, classical audiences found the love between the tyrannicides Harmodios and Aristogeiton noble and worthy of such men, audiences in the later Roman empire and the Christian era found it somewhat disturbing and incompatible with these almost mythical heroes. This is why later antiquity had some revisions to make to the ancient tale (see the discussion in Ch. 3.1.)

Revisionist interference can also be diagnosed in the story told by several late classical and Hellenistic authors about the alleged contribution of the Co-rinthian hetairai to the Persian wars. Plutarch chastises Herodotos in his study *On the Malice of Herodotos* for omitting the relevant story, while he had incorpo-rated so many other unworthy tales in his work.[62] Plutarch does not even con-

---

61 Polemon fr. 14 = Athen. 13.3.
62 Plu. 871 A–C.

sider the possibility that Herodotos might be unaware of a story, which in reality was a later invention, built on very thin foundations. In the temple of Aphrodite in Corinth, on the left side of the entrance, according to the Scholiast of Pindar, there was an inscription. Plutarch, Athenaios and the Scholiast of Pindar quote different versions of it.[63] The differences are not as substantial as C.B. Gulick thought, but rather the result of dialectic alterations.[64] The version of Plutarch in Doric Greek is probably the closest to the original. Athenaios has a couple of atticized forms, while the scholiast of Pindar has fewer Ionic/Attic features but three additional deviations which are essentially interpretations of difficult words or forms:[65]

> These women stood in prayer to the divine Kypris
> For the Greeks and the brave-fighting citizens,
> For Aphrodite willed it not that the citadel of the Greeks
> Should be betrayed to the bow-bearing Medes.

The tablet in all probability did exist; the Scholiast of Pindar describes its location with remarkable precision and Athenaios independently acknowledges that it was there in his time. However, its interpretation is another matter. The identity of the women mentioned in the inscription cannot be inferred from the tablet, and was certainly open to interpretation; one might say that it was like a challenge for the visitor to the temple to fill in the details. Among our sources Chamaileon of Herakleia is the first author to offer an explanation.[66] He says that during the Persian wars the hetairai of Corinth went to the temple of Aphrodite and prayed for the salvation of the Greeks. As a recognition a tablet was dedicated to the temple of Aphrodite, and in subsequent times when the city needed to pray to Aphrodite about something important the hetairai were always invited. The story is repeated by Theopompos and Timaios,[67] but it barely

---

63 Plu. 871 A-C, Athen. 13.32; Sch. Pi. O. 13.32.b.
64 Gulick 1937: 97, n. h.
65 Athenaios has Ἑλλήνων instead of Plutarch's Ἑλλάνων, and εὐθυμάχων instead of ἰθυμάχων. Athenaios also has ἐμήσατο instead of Plutarch's ἐμήδετο, but this may be correct and it is not easy to decide between the imperfect and the aorist. The scholiast of Pindar maintains the Doric form, but has altered the verb from ἔσταθεν to ἔστασαν, ἰθυμάχων (brave-fighting) to the less suitable ἀγχεμάχων (close-fighting), and ἐμήδετο to the interpretative ἐβούλετο. The epigram, like almost every other epigram from the Persian wars, was attributed to Simonides. Plutarch's reference to bronze statues to go with the inscription is not confirmed by the other sources, and this is why the veracity of this piece of information is questionable.
66 Chamaileon fr. 31 Wehrli = Athen. 13.32.
67 Theopompos *FGrH* 115 F 285; Timaios *FGrH* 566 F 10.

makes sense. Why in a time of imminent peril, when, let's say, Xerxes had already burned Athens and Corinth was next, the prayer of some of the women of Corinth, even if they were hetairai, would be a special and memorable event remains inexplicable. Then, even if we accepted that the hetairai of Corinth somehow managed to boost morale around the city with some spectacular and very public supplication to the goddess, which was recognized and remembered when the danger had passed, why would they need a special invitation to join the rest of the citizens in prayer in subsequent times of crisis? The strange rationale behind the explanation of Chamaileon exposes it as an invention of a much later time. Whoever these women were, who were mentioned in the inscription at the temple of Aphrodite, their identity was effaced in order to be replaced by the one group of its women for which Corinth was best known throughout history, the hetairai.

Athenaios quotes Alexis of Samos saying that the temple of Aphrodite in the Marsh was built by hetairai who were following Pericles during the siege of Samos (439 BC).[68] Alexis says that the women built the temple from their earnings from prostitution. This unlikely tale, which is not recorded anywhere until the time of Alexis (2nd c. BC), sounds very much like a foundation myth invented in the Hellenistic period to explain the establishment of the temple of Aphrodite. How it would be possible for the hetairai to work in the middle of a siege and in 9 months of a fierce war effort make enough money to build a temple in the besieged territory is a logical impossibility which suggests that there can be no truth to this story. Besides, as suggested elsewhere, the practice of hetairai following armies is not common until later times (see Ch. 3.4.).

The sources which provide information about the impact and socio-cultural context of the monuments dedicated either by hetairai or in their honor are almost exclusively from the period of the second sophistic (2nd c. AD), if not later, and include several Christian authors. This is why the information they provide is often questionable and may reflect their own moral standards, convictions and expectations, not those of a period that was, from their perspective, 600 or 700 years in the past. A society like classical or early Hellenistic Greece found nothing inherently offensive about nudity, or else some of their most revered festivals, games and competitions would not have been held in the nude. It also found nothing inherently inappropriate in celebrating sexuality through religious festivals (e.g. Thesmophoria, Haloa, Adonia, et al.), portrayed the divine in nude human form, accepted homosexual relationships as equal and interchangeable with heterosexual relationships, and had imagined its

---

68 Alexis fr. 1 = Athen. 13.31.

gods and heroes as omnisexual beings with unbridled desires. One wonders why a civilization which held such values would be offended if a beautiful hetaira served as a model for Aphrodite, or she made a dedication to the gods, or an infatuated lover did so on her behalf. We should be surprised if we actually had reliable evidence from the classical period attesting to that. But no such evidence exists before the second sophistic, and no doubt there is a good reason for it. The classical world might have found the hetaira a trap, a bad habit, a certain avenue towards financial ruin, but it did not find her offensive to the gods or the temples, never tried to exclude her from worship, and never tried to save her immortal soul through a path of redemption which included her abandoning her wicked ways.

From their perspective the prominent hetairai of the ancient world, if we believed for example a mere fraction of what Theodote says in her dialogue with Socrates, far from feeling marginalized and isolated, were well connected with high society and had friends and lovers, past and present, in high places among kings, generals, artists, philosophers and poets. In some aspects they were more privileged than high-born respectable women, who were usually excluded from such associations, and one would excuse in them some feeling of self-importance and grandiosity, if powerful and famous men like Alcibiades, Demosthenes or Hypereides would compete for their affections. Women like Lais, Phryne or Lamia were celebrities throughout the Greek world, each in her own different way. Lais it seems relied mostly on her raw sex appeal, Phryne on a carefully cultivated public persona, and Lamia on her association with the most powerful man in Greece, but all of them had more power, wealth and prestige than any woman in their time could possibly imagine. We can excuse and understand their desire to leave behind permanent monuments, and we can easily discern the motivation of Greek hetairai to test the boundaries, push the limits and reach as far as a woman could reach in their day. This they certainly did, and although their contribution in history as pioneers for women's empowerment is normally ignored, we cannot deny to some of these exceptional women their status as role-models for women's emancipation in the long centuries of silence that were about to follow classical liberalism.

6.2 Images of Prostitution in Vase Iconography

"In Greece the remarkable innovation of athletic male nudity, which surely originated in a ritual, religious context, developed special social and civic meaning. It became a costume, a uniform: exercising together in the gymnasia marked men's status as citizens of the polis and as Greeks. On the vases, this is how young men were shown. Female figures shown naked in public, on the other hand, were usually entertainers. Women represented as exposed were violated, stripped of their clothing, and in dreadful danger, as vulnerable and unprotected before a male attacker as Athenian law conceived them to be in life." [69]

This citation from Larissa Bonfante encapsulates the dominant view in the interpretation of nudity and sexuality on Greek vases, which only recently has been hesitantly questioned. This model has tried to link historical concepts about the role of women in Greek society, as this was understood in the literature of the later 20th century, with their representation in art. However, as many 20th century orthodoxies and certainties about men, women, gender and sexuality, are coming under closer scrutiny in recent years, and historical perceptions are changing, so are artistic interpretations. The two certainly go together. Scholars have sought to interpret iconography by placing it in its historical context, and iconography in turn has often been taken face value and used as a historical source, perhaps more extensively than it is prudent. Thus, since the 1970's a strong, mutual bond has been established between visual representations and social history, and many conclusions have been drawn about the social practices and historical realities of the Greeks in the Classical period on account of visual representations. Scholars in the 21st century have been more cautious about the historicity and interpretation of those images unsure about the boundaries between fantasy and reality, artistic convention and historical realism, or symbolism and decoration. ip.

The vexing question remains and still causes much controversy and scholarly debate. To what extent it is appropriate, sensible and necessary to use artistic representations as historical sources, for the social, religious and cultural practices of the Greeks, and how much reality we can find in these representations, are still hotly debated issues by art historians and classical scholars. The famous saying that "an image tells one thousand words" in this instance leaves us perplexed, because interpreting vase iconography is not a straight-forward process.[70] While it is beyond the scope of this study to fully engage in this controversy, and a thorough study of the vast corpus of Attic vase paintings which

---

69 Bonfante 1989: 569.
70 John Boardman (1991: 79–102; the citation comes from p. 81). Boardman emphasizes the "single tableau" preference of Greek painters, focusing on a single critical moment, a still from an action sequence. While describing the process of interpreting vase iconography he stresses that the ancient and the modern reader share "the ancient reader's ready identification of many figures by dress or attitude... Mood and action can be conveyed by gesture, from obvious belligerence to more subtle indications of, say, dismay, by a hand held to the forehead. Most gestures are obvious, some may puzzle us."

might be representing prostitutes would be more than one book in itself, it is still necessary to establish some methodological principles and try to answer two questions at this point: first whether visual representations can be safely used as historical sources for our understanding of prostitution in the ancient Mediterranean, and second, if they can, whether they tell us anything new, which we would not know from other sources. In order to be able to answer these questions we need to briefly examine the relevant iconography, and follow the main lines of the scholarly debate. Here I will present the most significant representations of prostitutional themes, then I will try to establish some clear rules about the use of this evidence as historical material, and finally I will address the issue whether what we learn from those representations enhances in any way our understanding of the historical facts and circumstances of prostitution in the ancient Mediterranean.

Much of the current bibliography interprets naked female figures as "hetairai," without taking notice of a rather substantial anachronism. The vases in question for the most part come from the late 6th or first half of the 5th century. However, the term "hetaira" with all its connotations, as we understand it from numerous references dating from the late 5th century and subsequent literature, such as Attic Comedy, historiography, oratory, philosophy, epigram, and the tales of Athenaios, is not attested in Greek before the middle of the 5th century. Its first appearance is in Herodotos, and this usage does not proliferate in written sources until the last quarter of the 5th century. So, strictly speaking, none of the women appearing in Attic red-figure vases produced before 450 BC can be called a "hetaira," without using the term anachronistically. Considering that almost all of the erotica on Attic red-figure vases precede 450, it would be fair to say that no hetairai were ever depicted on Attic red-figure vases. This does not mean that no prostitute was ever depicted in vase iconography; the implication is that our interpretations of images of prostitution need to be more precise, nuanced and chronologically sensitive.

Beyond terminology, the hetaira as a cultural construct is largely based upon exclusivity, limited availability, and long-term relations with one client at a time, qualities which would be antithetically opposite with group-sex in a party, drunken and indecent behavior, or excessive exposure of one's body for everyone present to see. This kind of behavior would be against every manual, every piece of advice of how to be a successful hetaira (cf. Ch. 2.1.), and numerous sources suggest that it ought to be avoided at all costs, as it would be very bad for business. Athenaios reports that it was very difficult to see Phryne naked because she wore at all times a vest under her garments and never used public baths. But what is more interesting is the reason why she made her body so unavailable. It was, we are told, because her "unseen parts" (τοῖς μὴ βλεπομένοις) were superbly attractive, reserved only for artists and clients who paid dearly to view and enjoy them.[71] Other hetairai might avoid showing their body for the exact opposite reason, like Philemation the elder in Lucian's fictional account.[72] Her pursuer Charmides has been induced into spending much money on her precisely because he is eager to see her naked, and she does not let him. Her rival Tryphaina reveals to Charmides that Philemation's entire body in the unseen parts, from the neck to the knees (ἀπὸ τοῦ αὐχένος εἰς τὰ γόνατα), looks like a leopard's skin, full of spots, and this is why she would not give in to his requests to see her naked. This account may be fictional, but perhaps not far removed from reality. We are told by Antiphanes that Nannion was nick-named "forestage" (προσκήνιον), because once she took off the jewelry and luxurious garments she was disgustingly ugly (αἰσχροτάτη), and Theophilos includes her in a list of hetairai whom pimps dress up in fancy linen, to hide the flaws of their appearance (see the discussion in Ch. 3.2. and 3.3.).[73]

Revealing one's body in a symposion before many, and even worse, actually engaging in sexual acts, would remove the mystique, the aura of unavailability and exclusivity, and would expose one's flaws to prying eyes. After that, playing coy and maintaining the pretense of a precious commodity only available to those willing to spend lavishly, would be impossible; one's value would have already dropped sharply. Our sources leave us in no doubt that the exclusive nature of a hetaira's company and group sex in a symposion were incompatible. The classical hetaira would not devalue herself with public nudity and lewd conduct in front of potential and present lovers. There is only one instance in literary sources where we are told that a hetaira (temporarily retired at the time) had sex in public, during a symposium. In an infamous scene from the speech *Against Neaira*,[74] Apollodoros says that she had sex with Phrynion in public, before the eyes of his friends. He was showing off the power which he had over her, and then as the night progressed and a drunken Phrynion fell asleep, she had sex with some of the other guests and even some of the servants. We should be in no doubt that the lewdness of Neaira in this instance is exaggerated.[75]

---

71 Athen. 13.59.
72 Luc. *DMeretr.* 11.3.
73 Athen. 13.51; Theophilos, fr. 11.
74 D. 59.33–35; for a closer reading of this episode see Kapparis 1999, ad loc.
75 The insatiable lust of Theodora, who sleeps with thirty men at once in a scene from the *Anecdota* of Prokopios (9.16–19) based upon the Apollodoran narrative, is even more excessive and exaggerated, while the narrative of Sophronios of Jerusalem in the *Life of St. Mary of Egypt*

However, regardless of the level of exaggeration, Neaira left Phrynion and ran away shortly afterwards, because of his abusive behavior. The famous hetaira was deeply insulted by a lover who had made her a public spectacle. It is not only a question of terminology, but also a matter of substance: the realistic representation of nudity and sex involving hetairai would virtually be a historical impossibility, and the usage of the term "hetaira" to describe prostitutes presented in vase paintings is anachronistic, inaccurate and euphemistic.

Numerous studies have stressed that a vase painting is not a photograph. As Mary Beard puts it: "the very process of selection and juxtaposition within the restricted frame of the pot necessarily converts the reality of everyday life into something very different: an image, a representation, an intellectual construct."[76] Beard also stresses the second issue at hand, namely the difficulty in distinguishing between the real world and the imaginary element, and concludes "that there is no one approach to recommend." This raises an important question. Did the artists of vase paintings intend to portray images of prostitution, and did they expect their viewing public to understand these images as such, or did they leave matters open to interpretation? The broad consensus is that they did intentionally portray images of prostitution, that artists have left clues for the viewer, including sometimes brief inscriptions, to guide the viewer's understanding. It is precisely around the interpretation of these clues that much of the controversy centers, and we need to discuss briefly those alleged symbols and indicators, if we are to establish a consistent method of reading these works.

The obvious starting point is whether nudity in itself can be read as an indication of prostitution. While most scholarship before the turn of the millennium considered nudity to be a definite indicator of a prostitute, more recent literature has effectively challenged this view, and suggested that women, like men, can be portrayed nude in a broad variety of settings, realistic or fantastical. The primary argument for considering every female nude to be a "hetaira" is fundamentally historical: respectable women would be violated, and made to look vulnerable and unprotected if stripped off their clothing. However, this line of thinking is flawed for a number of reasons, and this is why it has been intensely questioned in the 21st c. literature.

First, the central argument upon which it is based, namely that respectable women were strictly segregated away from prying eyes and that only the sexual-

---

(18–21) takes this familiar theme to surreal extremes, with Mary forcing entire boatloads of sailors to have sex with her, repeatedly and in every conceivable way.
76 In Rasmussen – Spivey 1991: 20.

ity of available female prostitutes could be celebrated in art, is no longer tenable. A wider consensus is building up in recent years, according to which Athenian women were not sequestered away; they left the house often to go to houses of relatives or friends, temples, shops, or public festivals, and did this even if they were not working. Many, however, were working, and thus had to be out in public places among strange men.[77] The whole myth of secluded female respectability was more of a reflection of twentieth century sensibilities, generated in the conservative environment of mid-20th century European and North-American Universities, rather than historical reality. Second, female sexuality was not a forbidden subject; far from that. It was celebrated in Attic Comedy and lower Historiography with countless jokes and tales presenting women as sexual beings,[78] it was condoned by contemporary medical theory, which considered sexual abstinence gravely harmful for a woman's health,[79] and was enshrined in Athenian law, which made it all but obligatory for a woman to have a husband, and compelled the guardians of orphaned girls (ἐπίκληροι) to find them a husband as soon as they reached sexual awareness at the age of 14. In the light of this, the assumption that women's sexuality should be suppressed and consequently nudity equals prostitution in Greek moral standards, artistic intentions and viewer perceptions is absurd.

Martin Kilmer and Sian Lewis were among the first to question this assumption and reached the conclusion that nudity should not be automatically perceived as evidence of prostitution, followed by almost every study published in the third millennium, with varying degrees of assertiveness. The most systematic discussion of the subject is that of Ulla Kreilinger, who has argued that nudity in itself is not an indication of prostitutional iconography. Kreilinger convincingly argued that representations of nude women on the laver could not be images of prostitutes, because no woman would be expected to take a bath dressed. Thus, if respectable women could be presented nude in the bath, where else could they be portrayed nude? Subsequently, in an attempt to clarify what makes a prostitute in vase iconography, Kreilinger formed a series of criteria, which mark a very clear, yet convincing departure from established interpretations of pottery images. I have accepted the core of these principles, with a few departures, and incorporated them into my methodological approach.

---

77 The primary studies which helped build this new consensus are Blundell 1995 and Schnurr-Redford 1996.
78 See e.g. Ar. *Lys.* passim, *Ec.* 227–228; Pl. Com. *Phaon* fr. 188, al.
79 Hip. *Nat.Mul.* 3 (cf. *Superf.* 34); *Mul.* 127; *Virg.* 1; King 2004.

Homosexual sex scenes are not typically interpreted as prostitutional, as it is impossible to tell whether a youth engaging in sex acts with a man is a prostitute or a lover.[80] However, such scenes have been extensively used to construct the social history of homosexual relations in classical Athens, ever since the pioneering work of Dover on Greek homosexuality. Dover has drawn some conclusions which border the irrational, such as the concept that the passive lover never enjoyed penetration, because the penis is typically presented as flaccid.[81] Using an image, which on top of everything else was probably adjusted to the tastes of the Etruscan buyer, to draw such broad conclusions about the ideology surrounding Greek homosexual relationships, and one for that matter which fits well into modern homophobic sensibilities, underlines the inherent and grave dangers of using these images to construct social history, and advises much caution in their interpretation. Dover constructed an entire edifice of sex and power relations between the *erastes* and the *eromenos* largely on the basis of vase iconography, which has profoundly influenced scholarship on these matters in the past 30 years. In this interpretation, sex *a tergo*, whether heterosexual or homosexual, was indicative of an uneven relationship, with a dominant and a dominated partner.

The centerpiece for Dover's interpretation is the famous Eurymedon vase, which was published by K. Schauenburg in 1975,[82] when Dover was writing his book on Greek homosexuality. The vase portrays an almost nude male figure holding his erect penis and advancing to penetrate another man dressed in a Scythian outfit. The man dressed as a Scythian is bending over as a willing participant to copulation, and happily raises both hands to the side of his face making a funny gesture of delight. Schauenburg interpreted the vase as an allegory

---

80 See for example Beazley 200414 = ARV[2] (1963), 51/204 and 356/56 = Paris, Musee du Louvre: G81; Beazley 200641 = ARV[2] (1963), 79/6 = Naples, Museo Archeologico Nazionale, 81326, Naples, Museo Archeologico Nazionale, H2614; Beazley 200977 = ARV[2] (1963), 115/2, 1626 = Berlin, Schloss Charlottenburg: F22792, Berlin, Antikensammlung: F2279, al.

81 Online forums in our times can offer plentiful, direct and reliable evidence on this matter, as well as the mechanics of previously forbidden sexualities as a whole, and in a sense can help to demystify an issue which in the 1970's was a major taboo, only imperfectly understood through rumor and innuendo. Dover clearly misunderstood the mechanics of man-to-man sex; a flaccid penis during penetration is very common, has mostly to do with the intensity and tempo of the thrusts, and is unrelated to pleasure. Pre-ejaculate fluid may be a more accurate indication of the level of pleasure which the penetrated partner experiences. During intercourse the penetrated partner's penis will often fluctuate between a flaccid state and a full, or almost full erection several times.

82 Beazley 1107 = Hamburg, Museum für Kunst und Gewerbe 1981.173; Schauenburg 1975: 97–121.

of the battle of Eurymedon, with the nude Greek man about to "bugger" the Persian, and Dover accepted this interpretation.[83] Subsequent studies by Amy Smith, Detlev Wannagat, and Margaret Miller have essentially accepted this interpretation of the Eurymedon vase, but not without raising some serious questions.[84]

On the other hand, two studies by Gloria Ferrari Pinney and David Braund have altogether rejected the interpretation of the Eurymedon vase as a historical allegory of the battle.[85] As Smith points out an allegory of the battle would be unique in Greek vase iconography, and Ferrari Pinney argues with good reason that an allegory with such content would sully the memory of the victorious battle. Both of these objections are very valid: important as the battle of Eurymedon was from a strategic point of view, it was fought on the edges of the Greek world and never captured public imagination to the same extent as other great battles fought on Greek soil. When far more glorious victories like Marathon, Thermopylae, Salamis or Plataia never became the object of allegorical vase paintings what is the chance that a battle fought in a remote corner of Asia Minor would do so? Moreover, the Greeks did not portray their battles as sexual acts, and the idea that the victory which permanently ended the Persian wars would be portrayed as such would be a cultural oddity, not least because, as James Davidson convincingly argues, the Greeks did not "screw" or "bugger" their enemies.[86]

Davidson has effectively challenged Dover's use of the Eurymedon vase to establish the rules and parameters of his model of Greek homosexual relations. Moreover, he has correctly rejected the notion that *kybda* penetration is in any way indicative of subjugation into a position of inferiority. In reality, the *kybda* position, as a passage of Machon clearly indicates, was one which allowed minimum bodily contact and, as Davidson rightly points out, was favored for outdoors sex, or quick and unemotional contact, and this is why it was the cheapest sexual position in brothels, typically costing only 3 obols.[87] This information may lead us to a very different interpretation of this playful image. David Braund did not relate it to the battle of Eurymedon, but to a man called Eurymedon the son of Speusippos, who was the founder of the Scythian archers.

---

83 The battle of Eurymedon took place in the early 360s, was a sound Greek victory and it was the last conflict between the Delian League and the Persians.

84 Smith 1999: 128–141; Wannagat 2001: 51–71; Miller 2010: 304–338.

85 Ferrari Pinney 1984: 181–183; Braund 2006: 109–113.

86 Davidson 1997: 169–182; see also Ch. 5.2. and 5.3.

87 Machon 17.349-375 = Athen. 13.44.

He interpreted the painting as a joke aimed at the police force of Athens and its founders. Gloria Ferrari Pinney also emphasized the comic aspect of the image, and saw in it a double entendre: Eurymedon means "wide smile" and a rude joke related to the comic "εὐρύπρωκτος" may indeed have been intended by the painter.

What in my mind should firmly deter us from interpreting this image as a sexual allegory of a victorious battle, besides historical or cultural factors, however powerful these may be, is the tone and spirit of the image itself. It is difficult to see in this playful, light-hearted image a violent representation of rape and domination. Building upon the interpretations of Braund and Pinney, and the sound reasoning of Davidson, I would be inclined to offer an alternative interpretation of the image as a comical and mischievous sex scene between a prostitute and his client. The prostitute in exotic attire, dressed up as a Scythian archer, like the numerous men who assisted the Eleven as the police force of Athens, is playfully inviting with "camp" gestures the client to penetrate him κύβδα, for a mere τριώβολον. There should be no doubt from the dotted body suit, the quiver, and the headgear that the outfit is not Persian but Scythian,[88] the one familiar to us from images of the Scythian archers of Athens. The beard and the empty quiver are both significant for the concept. The beard enhances the farcical theme and the empty quiver suggests that this is not a real archer, and that this entire action is part of a game, perhaps a dance routine[89], and a prelude to intercourse *a tergo,* with the "Scythian" very willingly offering his bottom to his partner. The name Eurymedon, is attested as a common name[90] and literally means "broad smile". Could this be a known prostitute's nickname, or should we read in it an obscene double-entendre (a broad opening)? We may want to consider the entire scene to be a jibe at the police of Athens and its founder, or perhaps as a sex-game where prostitute and client are dressed as "cop" and "criminal". We could also read this image as a farcical theme, a social commentary or an image of teasing ambiguity, none of which need to in-

---

88 There should be no doubt that 5th century Athenians knew the difference between a Persian and a Scythian. The Scythian archers were an everyday presence in Athens, while the Athenians fought the Persians many times in the first half of the century, and should know how the Persians dressed. If an Athenian artist wanted to portray a Persian, he should know how to dress him.

89 It would not be unusual for prostitute entertainers to dress up in military gear (shields, swords, tunics etc.), and perform sexy dance routines, including the war-dance (πυρρίχη). See the discussion in Ch. 5.4.

90 E.g. *IG* ii² 1627 b 209: Εὐρυμέδων Χαριδήμου; *Sup. Epigr. Gr.* 23: 124, 9: Εὐρυμέδων Ἡγεμάχου.

volve dark themes of violence, rape or domination.[91] The possibilities are endless, and it is quite possible that the artist was simply teasing his audience with all these entertaining options. What we can tell for sure is that the frivolous use of vase iconography as a historical source in this case has led to a feeble edifice about power and domination in sexual representations, which has established itself as a mighty orthodoxy in the international bibliography, despite the fact that as a concept it is fundamentally un-Greek.

Heterosexual erotic scenes have often been interpreted as images of venal sex, automatically and without qualification, on the grounds that respectable women could not be portrayed as objects of desire and raw sexuality. The study on the iconography of prostitution by Carola Reinberg, published in the late 1980's, is perhaps the most representative example of how the later 20th century viewed expressions of female sexuality. Every nude female, even on her own in a private setting or in an all-female environment, every female who is overtly sexual, and every female who exhibits any kind of eroticism, even something as innocent as an embrace, an affectionate look, or a conversation with a man is immediately designated as a hetaira.[92] Such assumptions are without a doubt based upon 20th c. prejudices and concepts of respectability, but they are not consonant with Athenian law, ancient medical theory or social perceptions.

While extramarital sex for women destined for family life was unacceptable, sex within marriage was seen as medically necessary for the woman's health, as it opened the pathways for the menstrual blood to flow, and thus prevented many of the severe complications caused by retained menstrual blood, such as depression, general ill health and gynecological complications.[93] The overt, proud and pronounced sexuality of women in Greek Comedy need not be a gender transgression, or role reversal; such interpretations are based precisely upon the same misplaced concept of respectability that turns all nude female figures in vase iconography into prostitutes. Images of heterosexual erotica, whether joyous and carefree or charged with tensions and dark emotions, can be just that, and need not be images of prostitution. Kreilinger and Lewis, among others in recent years, have raised objections to the traditional interpretation of all erotica as prostitution scenes, and are prepared to accept that vase iconography sometimes simply portrayed sex scenes without any particular subtext, pornographic representations for the pleasure of the users of

---

91 For example, we could read a theme making fun of the bond between a hoplite and his Scythian attendant, and presenting it as camp and comically sexual.

92 See Reinsberg 1989: 91–162

93 See Pinault 1992: 123–139; King 1998: 188–204.

those cups and vases in parties, or sometimes more nuanced mythological or cultic representations without a prostitutional element to them.

A fine example of an unmarked and open-ended image of heterosexual copulation, an Athenian kylix from the Tarquinia collection dated in the first half of the 5th century, simply portrays a man and a woman having sex on a recliner in the missionary position.[94] Apart from the staff and the couple's clothes neatly arranged, there is no other symbol or signal in this image, and the expression of the couple is one of simple satisfaction and pleasure. There is no reason why one would read anything more into this image except a couple merrily engaged in intercourse. A similar theme is found on a cup, also from the Tarquinia collection, another heterosexual love-making scene, only this time the man is considerably older and balding. Again, there is nothing to indicate anything except a love-scene.[95]

Playful images of women bathing together should not be construed as images of prostitution. As Kreilinger has pointed out, there is no reason why women bathing, either alone or in female company, should be understood as prostitutes. In fact, the voyeurism of the viewer might choose to see them as virginal or respectable, and thus normally unavailable women, instead of easily available prostitutes. The group of women bathing in the open sea on an amphora from Louvre, a naked woman lifting a laver on a cup from the British Museum, or two women playfully washing on a cup from Etruria now in the museum of Naples, just to give a small number of examples, are not prostitutes; the viewer has no reason to see anything else except women washing, just as in very similar scenes of men washing in or at the laver one would not need to see much more than the act of washing, voyeuristic as this may be.[96]

Scenes of solitary masturbation need not be interpreted in a prostitutional context either. Besides the obvious reasons, literary evidence links both prostitutes and sexually deprived married women to the use of dildos and masturbation, and several plays of Aristophanes make jokes about male masturbation involving ordinary men and slaves, while a passage of Aristotle goes into details about masturbation and pleasure in boys not yet fertile.[97] Such scenes portray

---

94 Beazley 203885 = Tarquinia, Museo Nazionale: XXXX0.3885.

95 Beazley 203886 = Tarquinia, Museo Nazionale Tarquiniese: XXXX0.3886.

96 Beazley 200013 = Paris, Musee du Louvre: F203; 200943 = London, British Museum: E34; 200173 = Naples, Museo Archeologico Nazionale: STG5. For very similar scenes of men washing see 14212 = Florence, Museo Archeologico Etrusco: 4222; 200799 = Boston (MA), Museum of Fine Arts: 10.214.

97 See for example Ar. *Lys.* 109–110 (cf. Sch. Ar. Lys. 158), where Lysistrata mentions a dildo covered in leather, approximately 20 cm. long, as a consolation for sexually deprived women;

women using dildos, one or more, and men masturbating in various positions.[98] Among the most interesting ones we could count a cup from the early 5th c. with a youth at the moment of ejaculation, with dots of semen spurting out of his penis, a naked woman using simultaneously two dildos, one for vaginal one for anal penetration, from a cup in the Hermitage Museum of St. Petersburg, and another female figure from a cup in the British Museum also using two dildos but this time for vaginal and oral penetration.[99] Considering that the majority of solitary masturbation scenes involve satyrs or other mythological beings with pronounced sexuality, these scenes should probably be read as a celebration of sexuality, sensuality and fertility, and sometimes as religious imagery, but not as snapshots of venal sex.[100] On the other hand scenes of masturbation in a group may sometimes be interpreted in a prostitutional context. An Athenian black-figure cup scene portrays two men reclining and masturbating.[101] We have no reason to interpret this scene as prostitutional; however, a sympotic scene from a Florentine cup portraying a group of women and men, some masturbating, should probably be interpreted in a venal sex context: these women taking part in an orgy could not be viewed as anything but prostitutes, and in this case the masturbation images are part of the sexual activities involving prostitutes.[102]

Jewelry or make-up are not signs of prostitution by default, as respectable Athenian women wore plenty of costly jewelry too, and often it was a sign of high social status, and was even calculated in the dowry. Moreover, there is plenty of evidence that they wore make up, like the young wife of Ischomachos

---

Sch. Ar. *Lys.* 110, where it is said that dildos were used by widowed women; in Herodas 6 a group of women are talking about the best dildo maker in town; Ar. *Eq* 24–29, involving two domestic slaves, with one of them reiterating the joke that masturbation makes one's skin fall off; *Pax* 290; Arist. *GA* 728 a 9–17. On the other hand, a dildo is mentioned among many other prostitute's accessories in a fragment of Aristophanes (332), and we are told that it was mentioned in the speech *Against Timandra*, attributed to Hypereides (fr. 165 Jensen), among many items used by prostitutes.

98 310515 = Beazley, J.D., Attic Black-Figure Vase-Painters (Oxford, 1956): 157. 86 = Boston, Museum of Fine Arts, 10.651.

99 200848 = Brussels, Musees Royaux: R260; 200587 = St. Petersburg, State Hermitage Museum: 14611; 201043 = London, British Museum: E815.

100 See for example, CAV 14933 = Kassel, Staatliche Museen Kassel, Antikensammlung: ALG214; 17675 = Pontecagnano, Museo Archeologico: T3955; 302839 = Berlin, Pergamonmuseum: F1671, a 6th c. black-figure amphora portraying a satyr touching his enormous penis; 302572 = Munich, Antikensammlungen: J335 has a Dionysiac theme and includes several satyrs with erect penises, while the central figure is a satyr masturbating.

101 200694 = ARV[2] (1963), 86/(α), 1578/16 = Paris, Musee du Louvre: G13.

102 CAV 200964, Florence, Museo Archeologico Etrusco: 1B58.

in Xenophon, or the women in the fragment of Euboulos making fun of cosmetic accidents and excesses.[103] All these trappings, like make-up, cosmetics, jewelry, costly dresses and materials were not the exclusive privilege of hetairai, and this is why representations of female figures with those accessories need not be understood as images of prostitutes. Moreover, mirrors, scenes of depilation, or other feminine toiletry do not indicate a hetaira. Looking beautiful by whatever means necessary was the prerogative of every woman in the ancient world, not only that of prostitutes (see Ch. 3.2. and 3.3.). However, numerous anthropological parallels suggest that prostitutes tend to wear jewelry and make up differently from ordinary women, more excessively, more abundantly, in order to attract attention, and perhaps this could be a differentiating mark. Ribbons or other headgear (such as the fashionable Lydian linos) are no indication of prostitution either, as such items followed fashion requirements, and at least ribbons were often used in a cultic context, while selling ribbons was a low-end job which even poor Athenian women would do. Ribbons, as well as wreaths and garlands, were typically worn at parties, religious occasions and other festivities by men and women, and this is why their exclusive association with prostitutes is absolutely untenable.[104]

Boots are not necessarily a sign of prostitution, according to Kreilinger, who considers them to be a sign of wealth, and this is probably the case as there is no indication in literary sources that boots were the exclusive privilege of prostitutes. Maybe at some point they were risqué, a provocative sex symbol like the famous boots of Daisy Duke in modern fiction, which only fashion conscious and affluent city women would wear in the winter months. But with fashion accessories what is cutting edge one year, could be main stream next year, and this is why identifying such items as signs of prostitution, just because they seem too provocative to be worn by ordinary women, is fundamentally flawed. As discussed in Ch. 3.3, while hetairai might have been renowned for their expensive and flashy tastes, and some excess in matters of outfits and appearance, there was no such thing as an exclusive hetaira uniform, or any kind of outfit worn only by hetairai, as this would very quickly become as unfashionable and undesirable as a prison uniform. Thus, to use garments or other personal apparel of this kind to identify female figures as hetairai is no more reliable

---

103 As for example in D. 41 *Against Spoudias* (see also my commentary on this speech in Wolpert – Kapparis 2011: 150–160); X. *Oec.* 7; Euboulos fr. 97. See also Ch. 2.3.

104 E.g. Empedocles 112.12 D-K; Ar. fr. 205; X. *Symp.* 5.9; Pl. *Symp.* 212 e (the famous scene where Alcibiades turns up with garlands, ribbons and an ivy-wreath on his head); D. 57.34, where allegedly a citizen woman had been a ταινιοπῶλις, Eupolis fr. 262 al.

than the myths about prostitutional uniforms found in the literature of later antiquity (see. Ch. 3.3), and needs to be abandoned as a methodological tool. The same applies to the serious misconception about cropped hair, which has been taken by some to be evidence of a slave woman, thus indicating a common prostitute. It is a simple matter of common sense: no one would want to pay to have sex with someone who looked like a downtrodden slave in a uniform. On the contrary, making the best of one's looks with fashionable accessories, and probably looking somewhat provocative and inviting, would be the desirable image for attracting customers and making them pay generously for the privilege.

καλή (beautiful) inscriptions are not an automatic sign of prostitution, according to Kreilinger, and this is probably the case considering how many times the *kalos/kale* inscription appears over men and women in so many different settings. In vase iconography there is a substantial number of inscriptions linked to both male and female figures usually giving a name and the adjective *kalos* (masculine) or *kale* (feminine). Such examples include the famous Λέαγρος καλός, Ἐπίλυκος καλός, for a youth in a *komos* (revelry) scene, Ἱππόκριτος κάλλιστος (the most handsome), Καλλισάνθη καλή, (Ἁρμονία) καλή, (Δήμητρα, the Goddess) καλή or more generally ὁ παῖς καλός (the boy is beautiful), and also Κολούρα "stump-tailed" kale, for a favorite horse on a vase with an equestrian theme.[105] The number of vase inscriptions involving men and the masculine *kalos* vastly outnumber those involving women and the feminine *kale*.[106] None of these persons can be safely identified as a sex worker through cross-referencing with other literary or epigraphic evidence. This may have to do with the fact that there is little relevant literature from that period. H. Jucker has tried to sort the names in order and draw some chronological data from them, however the entire enterprise is perilous, as it seems that real and fictional persons are mixed together, and the fact that we may recognize some names

---

105 See Beazley 187 = New York 1972.11.10; 352 = Basel Market (M.M.); 784. = Blatter (1971), 424; 5551 = Berger–Lullies (1979), 50–51, no. 18 (A, B); 74 = Boston 68.105; 5627 = New York 22.139.11; 6131 = Paris, Cab. Méd. 424. See also Ferri 1961: 174–180; Shapiro 2000: 12–32; Thomson 1971: 328–335; Francis - Vickers 1981: 97–136; Brenne 2000: 31–53.

106 See Henry Immerwahr's collection of Attic Vase Inscriptions for relevant data. A simple search found *kalos* on 1237 pages, but *kale* only on 55. Even allowing for the rather basic character of this search, there is no doubt that *kalos* inscriptions are much more numerous than *kale* ones.

and we are able to make the occasional connection here and there[107] does not make all the names real. Who was real and who was not becomes even more complex if we consider that what the modern reader thinks as fictional or mythical, was not necessarily fictional, mythical or unreal to the ancient artist and his public. It is difficult to reach firm conclusions without adequate supporting evidence in literary sources. Thus a cautious approach, leaving possibilities open but not trying to establish certainties on such a shaky grounds as these inscriptions, is imperative.

In addition to vase inscriptions, there is a number of inscriptions on stone and graffiti mostly from Attica praising beauty or insulting a certain individual. The standard way to praise the good looks of a boy or a girl in these inscriptions was basically the same as in vase iconography. However, between vase inscriptions and wall graffiti there are some substantial differences. First and foremost, while vase inscriptions could refer to real, imaginary or fantastical characters, wall graffiti almost always refer to real people, for praise or insult. Second, there is no image to support the text. The infatuated lover would simply write the person's name, followed by the adjective *kalos* / *kale* (beautiful), as in the example *Arisemos kalos*, or *Prososia kale*.[108] As with vase iconography, the number of references to boys vastly outnumbers the references to girls, but in this case there may be an additional reason why only a handful of female names are preserved: it would be compromising for a real, living girl or woman to have her name inscribed in graffiti on a public wall in Athens. It would indicate an existing relationship between the woman and her admirer, and would destroy her precious reputation. However, there was no such danger with dead women, and this is why several times we see funeral inscriptions praising their beauty (e.g. Δαμοῦ χαῖρε καλή "farewell, beautiful Damou," for a Spartan woman who lived 32 years).[109] The purpose of these graffiti was to express love, affection and adoration for beauty, not to insult a real, living woman, and this is why it was permissible to express love for boys or men by name, but inappropriate to name respectable girls or women.

When the purpose of the graffiti was the opposite, namely to insult someone, women are mentioned more often with an insult like καταπύγαινα or

---

107 Like for example the identification of Leagros appearing in several vases painted by Euphronios with the Athenian general Leagros, son of Glaukon, known to us from Thucydides (1.15.4) and Andocides (1.117–121).
108 E.g. *IG* i³ 1402; Agora, Graffiti XX1 C 31.
109 *IG* v¹, 1187;.

λαικάστρια next to their name.[110] Later lexicographers attest that both terms were used for "prostitute," but this should not be taken as evidence that every woman mentioned in these graffiti really was a prostitute. One then, as in our times, could insinuate that someone was a "whore" with the sole objective to insult that person, even if she had nothing to do with prostitution.[111] Sometimes a boy can be explicitly identified as beautiful and a "whore," as in one inscription from Thorikos dated between 400 and 350 BC, where we read Χάρης πόρνος καλός.[112] The sense we have is that in this case the objective was not to insult Chares, but simply to indicate the availability of his beauty. The masculine καταπύγων next to someone's name was often used when insult against a man or boy was intended.[113] Mika, a woman, mentioned in a vase from Anagyrous with the inscription "Dedicated by the beautiful Mika," may be the same person as the woman who was defended by Hypereides (Ὑπὲρ Μίκας), and very likely was a hetaira.[114] Chances are that several of the people mentioned in these inscriptions or graffiti were prostitutes, but it is not possible to ascertain from these brief inscriptions whether someone was a prostitute or not, and this is why these names have not been included in the index of sex-workers in Appendix I. Comparisons with Pompeian graffiti are generally hazardous, as the cultural backdrop is significantly different from Attica, and even in those instances where individuals are mentioned with prices for sexual services attached to their name, it is still difficult to decide whether they refer to actual prostitutes or are acts of defamation, humorous or malicious.[115]

While so many of the scenes which have been interpreted as images of prostitution in twentieth century scholarship in all likelihood would not be viewed as such by an ancient audience, some scenes should be interpreted in this context because the artist wanted his audience to read them as images of venal sex by leaving behind significant clues, which compel this interpretation. On the other hand, if the artist meant to leave us wondering, to leave the boundaries between prostitutes and respectable figures undefined or fluid, and let the viewer's imagination run free either by not specifying or by leaving behind confusing or contradictory tips, we should accept this choice too as a legitimate

---

110 See e.g. *IG* i³ 1402; Agora, Graffiti XX1 C 27, 33 and 34 al.; Milne –Bothmer 1953: 215–24.
111 E.g. Sud κ 738; Lex. Seg. κ 270; Hdn.Gr. 248.12.
112 *SEG* 34: 198.
113 E.g. Agora, Graffiti XX1 C 5, 18, 22, 24 al.
114 Μίκα καλή ἀνέθηκεν: See Lida Shaw King. 1903. "The Cave at Vari. IV. Vases, Terra-Cotta Statuettes, Bronzes, and Miscellaneous Objects". *AJA* 7: 325–327. For the speech of Hypereides in defense of Mika see Hyp. fr. 125 Jensen.
115 See e.g. *CIL* IV 1751; 5048; 5372; 5408; 8940.

artistic expression, and not try to force it to fit into one of our categories; many a time ambiguity is what makes a work of art intriguing. The methodology which I propose is that each representation should be examined and discussed on its own merits and only those images which have clear and identifiable marks should be considered as representations of prostitutes. In this process we need to abandon the convenient and all-encompassing, but inaccurately anachronistic term "hetaira" in favor of more precise terminology. The study of a representative selection of images might be sufficient to establish a consistent methodology and draw safe conclusions about the potential of these scenes as direct and reliable witnesses to historical realities.

In a cup from Cambridge portraying a sympotic scene a naked flute-player dominates the scene, while around her half-dressed men are reclining on sofas in various stages of drunkenness. While the nudity of the flute-player is probably a fantasy, because entertainers did not typically perform completely nude, we are meant to understand that she is a prostitute entertainer playing for a group of guests who are more interested in their drink than in her.[116] By contrast in a sympotic scene from a British Museum cup the flute player stands fully dressed and plays unabashed in the middle of a wild group copulating, dancing naked and drinking all around her, while a half-naked youth is just about to make advances to her. A second female figure engaging in copulation is invisible under her lover except her vulva facing us. We are meant to understand that these women are prostitutes, one of them an entertainer and the other a *porne* hired for sex.[117] Fully dressed is a young female flute player entertaining a reclining man in a cup from Louvre, and even though the scene is a tame image of relaxed gratification we are probably meant to understand that the woman is a hired entertainer.[118] In a similar scene where a reclining drinking man is enjoying the company of a modest youth playing the flute one wonders whether we could read a prostitutional sub-context.[119] The inscription above (οὐ δύναμαι οὐ) is a citation from Theognis: "I cannot sing like a nightingale, for I was partying last night." [120] This context of sympotic debauchery may steer the viewer towards considering the boy to be a prostitute entertainer, but, as usual with male representations, we cannot be certain.

---

116 204353 = ARV[2]: 402.12, 1651 = Cambridge, Corpus Christi College.

117 203927 = ARV[2]: 372.29 = London, British Museum: E71.

118 203728 = ARV[2] : 355/45 = Paris, Musee du Louvre: G135.

119 205274 = ARV[2] (1963), 437/128, 1653. = Munich, Antikensammlungen: J371.

120 Theogis, 1.939–40: Οὐ δύναμαι φωνῇι λίγ' ἀειδέμεν ὥσπερ ἀηδών· / καὶ γὰρ τὴν προτέρην νύκτ' ἐπὶ κῶμον ἔβην.

In a street-scene a flute-player is walking among a party of comasts, fully dressed, as realistically the scene is outdoors. This is another image of prostitution, as we know from literary sources (see Ch. 5.4.) that entertainers were regularly hired to accompany comasts through the streets on their way to carousing outside the house of a lover or potential lover, typically a hetaira.[121] Two young women, no doubt prostitute entertainers, are portrayed in a lekythos from Brussels, one playing the flute the other holding a lyre (or psaltery). Such combinations of entertainers, one to lift the mood with the loud music of the aulos, and the other to offer gentle background music for civilized company were often hired together, as attested in literary sources, to offer variety for the party (see Ch. 5.4.).

An all-female sympotic scene from the Hermitage, with a number of women reclining on sofas, drinking and one of them playing the flute is usually interpreted as a gathering of hetairai, but the scene should probably be interpreted as fantasy, as there is no evidence that in real life prostitutes gathered together to have naked symposia.[122] The only comparable scene to be found in literature is the highly eroticized sacrifice dinner of the hetairai in Alkiphron, which is also a fictional account.[123] We encounter a similar scene in the famous Madrid representation of two women reclining naked facing each other, one drinking and one playing with her cup, which Carola Reinsberg has interpreted as a scene with the ubiquitous hetairai.[124] Again there is no reason why they should be identified as prostitutes; on the contrary, a woman to woman erotic scene might be more appealing as a sexual fantasy if the viewer were to see them as non-prostitutes.[125]

The flute in vase iconography is played by both men and women of all ages, maenads, satyrs, and other mythological beings, in a wide variety of settings, realistic and fantastical, and in this respect the flute on its own is not a conclusive sign of prostitutes being present. For example, in one sympotic scene the flute-player is male, a seated, bearded figure who appears to be one of the guests, while a nude youth serves as the wine-bearer.[126] Likewise, one of the male comasts seems to be the flute-player in a *komos* scene from the British

---

121 205384 = ARV[2] (1963), 483/1, 1655.= Paris, Musee du Louvre: G336.

122 200078 = ARV[2]: 16/15, 1619 = St. Petersburg, State Hermitage Museum: 644.

123 Alciphr. 4.13. An all-male sympotic scene where everyone is dancing naked, is just another expression of this motif: possible in real life, but not realistic (ARV[2]: 431 = Boston 98.930).

124 Reinsberg 1989: 112–114.

125 200443 = ARV[2]: 58/53, 1574, 1622 = Madrid, Museo Arqueologico Nacional: L151.

126 4704 = Carpenter, T.H., with Mannack, T., and Mendonca, M., Beazley Addenda, 2nd edition (Oxford, 1989): 393 = Karlsruhe, Badisches Landesmuseum: 70.395.

Museum.[127] One of the participating youths is playing the flute in another *komos* scene from the British Museum.[128] Only in a sympotic context, where female entertainers play for the pleasure of male guests and their companions, we can be confident that we are seeing prostitute entertainers. Players of other instruments, such as the lyre or the kithara, can also be viewed as prostitutes in the context of a symposion or a *komos*. For the most part sympotic scenes with kithara or lyre players tend to be gentler than the exuberant and often lewd scenes involving the flute, just as we would expect them to be from descriptions in literary sources where the kithara and lyre create the background for civilized party banter. Such images include a rather polite proposition from a young man to a fully clothed woman playing the lyre, or a scene with a naked youth playing the lyre, possibly a prostitute entertainer given that the two guests sitting on the couch although fully clothed are mischievous.[129] More interesting is a mixed sympotic scene, with a flute-player and a lyre or psaltery player entertaining a group of guests. On one of the sofas a young man, above whom we can read the inscription "Demonikos," is sitting with a fully clothed woman. She is holding a large cup. Given that the date could be around 450, one wonders whether this is a rare representation of a true high-end hetaira painted at a time when the institution was becoming more common and an important feature of Athenian social life.[130]

Naked women dancing are typically interpreted as hetairai, but Kreilinger rightly objects. Naked dancers are not a historical reality. Even the infamous nude dancers from Thessaly were not dancing completely naked (see Ch. 5.4). They wore a girdle of some sort in the genital area, and they were famous because they revealed too much. Dancers typically wore more than a simple girdle, and this makes sense, as exhibiting all the goods before the customer paid would be unwise. In private parties and symposia, where dancers were invited to perform, the host only paid the standard two drachmas for the hiring of the entertainers. However, potential clients who wanted sexual services would need to negotiate with the procurer of the dancers, and these services came with a considerably higher price tag. It would make sense for the dancers to entice potential clients with provocative outfits, such as diaphanous or short tunics, sexy moves, and only partial nudity, and then charge them much more for the rest. Representations of completely nude dancers, male or female, are more

---

127 200191 = ARV[2]: 31/6, 1573 = London, British Museum: E767.
128 200444 = ARV[2]: 59/54, 1622. =London, British Museum: E40.
129 ARV[2] 86 = Paris G13; ARV[2]: 175, 1631 = New York 07.286.47.
130 203923 = ARV[2] 1574 = London E 68.

likely a fantasy, not standard and routine historical reality in the parties of the ancient world.

Dancing outside the *komos* or symposion environment should not be taken as a sign of prostitution, as dance from men and women was widely included in the state religion, festivals and other events and celebrations. Thus a lone female figure dancing with *krotala* fully clothed in a cup fragment now in Fayetteville, Ar., cannot be confidently identified as a prostitute, as dancing or the *krotala* are not sufficient to point the viewer in this direction.[131] The significance of the *krotala* in literary sources is typically cultic.[132] The only references clearly linking *krotala* with prostitutes are several epigrams from the *Greek Anthology* dating to the 1st c. and beyond.[133] While *krotala* were sometimes used by entertainers in classical symposia, their widespread use in a different context means that on their own they cannot be taken as a sign indicating a prostitute.

By contrast, female dancers presented as performing in symposia and *komoi* should be perceived as prostitute entertainers, since respectable women would not be dancing in the company of men in such settings. Nudity should not be an issue as some are portrayed as nude, some as clothed and some as semi-clothed. For example, we should interpret as prostitutional the setting of a cup from the Getty Museum, where a nude female figure is dancing with *krotala* between two men with erections. The surrounding scenes, with men and youths some vomiting and some holding drinking jugs suggest a *komos* passed the civilized stage. In a similar *komos* scene a naked woman is portrayed dancing while an older man next to her is playing the *diaulos* (double flute).[134] Interesting is a kantharos from Boston, where a woman is portrayed in the midst of sexually excited youths and is just about to engage in intercourse with one of them. She seems to be engaged in a provocative dance alluringly turning her behind towards the youth who is leaning forward with hands extended to grab her, while her hands are above her head performing what looks like a dance routine. The woman seems to be an exotic dancer, a hired prostitute entertainer in the end of a salacious routine which will result in intercourse.[135] As with other entertainers, we can only identify dancers as prostitutes in the symposion/*komos* erotic context.

The most difficult question to answer is whether we can identify with any degree of certainty upper end hetairai in Attic Vase iconography. This issue is

---

131 200568 = ARV[2] 66.130 = Fayetteville (AR), University of Arkansas Museum: 57.27.29.
132 E.g. E. *Cyc.* 215, *Hel.* 1308; Str. 10.3.15; used by Indian acrobats 15.1.22; Luc. *SyrD.* 44.
133 E.g. *AG.* 5.175; 5.271; 7.223.
134 ARV[2] 390 = Berlin VI3218.
135 ARV[2] 132 = Boston 95.61.

entangled with another difficult issue, whether the fact that the word "hetaira" does not signify a prostitute before 450 BC is simply a question of transmission or a more complex matter linked with cultural and socioeconomic circumstances. Overall, no conclusive answer can be given to his question.[136] However, when it comes to the Athenian market specifically, perhaps the appearance of the term "hetaira" in the middle of the 5th c., and not before or after, may be significant. High-end prostitution probably did not reach Athens before the city became sufficiently wealthy to support this kind of market in the years of the Athenian empire, and maybe this is why the term "hetaira" does not appear in Athenian sources before the middle of the 5th century. Vase iconography may be supporting this conclusion. The prostitutes appearing in it are for the most part lower end entertainers, such as flute-players, kithara or lyre players, dancers or singers hired out for the modest fee of two drachmas, and paid extra to offer sex to the drunken guests of the party later in the evening. The other group of women who can be identified as prostitutes seems to consist of low end, freelance workers or slave women from local brothels, hired out to readily shed their clothes before everyone and satisfy the sexual needs of the guests, without much pretense, coyness, or airs and graces.

Such behaviors were not to be expected from upper end hetairai. They would not readily strip in public or give themselves to a guest right away and thus shatter the illusion of unavailability, that mystique of something which is desirable because it has to be conquered with repeated petition, much expense and considerable trouble. We should not expect to find hetairai naked in the midst of a party copulating with two or three men at a time, or playing instruments and performing tasks associated with regular prostitutes and entertainers. One would imagine that true hetairai would have been portrayed in a symposion sitting side by side with their lovers, engaged in civilized conversation or adoringly staring a lover in the eyes, or accepting a precious gift or, to sum up, engaged in some of the activities which popular imagination associated with fabulously seductive women like Lais, Phryne, Bacchis or Pythionike in later centuries. The rather striking absence of such scenes may be taken as evidence confirming that the hetaira does not enter Athenian culture before the middle of

---

136 Although it is almost certain that high end prostitution had already existed in other places, such as Corinth or Naukratis, well before the middle of the 5th century, we cannot be sure that the term "hetaira" was ever used before for any of the women working in those markets. There is a very real possibility that the term was invented, or more precisely appropriated, by Herodotos and subsequently adopted and normalized by Athenian authors. We cannot tell for sure on the basis of the existing evidence.

the 5th century. Born out of financial affluence, a taste for luxury and the good things in life in a culturally open and tolerant society, where the democratic constitution safeguarded a citizen's right to do as he pleased in his private life and to feel just as entitled to fun and joy as everyone else, the classical hetaira is not present before the peak of the Athenian empire around 450. This conclusion seems to be the most obvious route, but still there is no certainty. The fact that these vases were painted to be exported to foreign markets, predominantly to Etruria, may be a reflection of preferences in those markets, and the absence of hetairai from vase iconography may simply be due to the possibility that the portrayal of the Attic hetaira could be culturally irrelevant and thus alien to the Etruscans, and as such not in demand.

Even more tantalizing is the possibility that some of our vase iconography actually portrays real hetairai from time to time, but that they are not as easily detectable as prostitute entertainers and low-end sex workers, because they appear in scenes which could be interpreted as domestic or cultic. The most obvious candidates for such an interpretation are scenes showing men offering women a purse. The women are sometimes portrayed as seated and sometimes as standing while men approach them and offer money.[137] One of them I find particularly interesting.[138] A youth is approaching a seated woman with a small purse, but she is turning away to watch an older man approaching a standing woman with a much bigger purse. One could easily interpret it as an image of prostitution in the context of literary references, like for example Lucian's *Dialogues of Hetairai*, where young men are often presented as freeloaders or at least as far less generous than older men, and the women are presented as money-grabbing and more interested in someone's big purse than his youth or good looks. Also intriguing is a scene where a man offers a purse to a seated youth.[139] Could this be one among few scenes where we are able to identify an image of male prostitution? It is difficult to tell. If we accepted that the scenes involving women represent hetairai being approached by potential lovers with offers of money, then we might be more inclined to see this youth too as a male prostitute negotiating with a potential client. But this assumption, although a distinct possibility is by no means certain. For all we know these images represent do-

137 See for example: 204627 = ARV[2] 421.82 = Oxford, Ashmolean Museum: 1966.491; 205338 = ARV[2] 449.4, 1653 = London, British Museum: E51; 212121 = ARV[2] 832.31 ,1672 = Altenburg, Staatliches Lindenau-Museum: 271; San Antonio 86.134.59, and Reeder 1995: 181; Davidson 1998: 86–87; Reinsberg 1989: 120–135.
138 ARV[2] 469 = Paris G 143 (Toledo 1972.55), and Reeder 183–185.
139 ARV[2] 437.1653 = New York 52.11.4.

mestic scenes, and the purse represents the economic power of the man as a provider, or maybe the purse has another meaning which has eluded us. Beyond the purse there is nothing in these images compelling us to interpret them as a prelude to venal sex. However, if the women represented truly are to be perceived as hetairai, it would be astonishing that of all the themes that ancient painters could have chosen to portray they picked the preliminary financial negotiations. It would seem utterly pedestrian, but then again this was perhaps the most significant feature in ancient perceptions of the hetaira as the money-grabber, the financial ruin to the household, or a luxury which only the big purse of a few could afford.

The third type of scene, which according to Ingeborg Peschel contains images of prostitution, is the erotic complex. As such she identifies scenes where two or more persons are presented engaging in sexual acts. Women appearing in sex scenes of any kind are often identified as hetairai indiscriminately. Although this view has been challenged in recent years, and I am inclined to accept routine heterosexual sex scenes as at least ambiguous, if not as perfectly domestic, it is difficult to interpret group sex scenes, especially the wilder ones, as anything except sex with prostitutes. For example, in a lustful scene of a wild orgy, with a woman aggressively penetrated by an older man and simultaneously fellating a younger man, while next to them a young man is forcibly pulling a woman towards his humungous erect penis, it is difficult to see respectable Athenian wives.[140] In most instances erotic complex scenes involving prostitutes have clearer markers. For example, in a hydria from Brussels two youths are portrayed in erotic embraces with two naked young women. There is nothing overtly lecherous or whorish in the conduct of the youths and the women in this instance. On the contrary the scene is one of tender and affectionate love making, and what appears to be a hanging flute-case behind them may be the only clue revealing that the women are prostitute-entertainers.[141] Such markers of venal sexuality include sympotic instruments, cups, skyphoi, kraters and other such implements, suspended flute cases or musical instruments. In a threesome scene, where an older woman is engaging in aggressive sex with two men, one older and one younger, the scene is marked as one of venal sex by the suspended skyphos over the woman's back and the wine-skin underneath her.[142] In an orgy scene from a Boston kantharos, where a woman is fellating one youth, while another is attempting to penetrate her with a giant dildo, the woman is

---

140 ARV[2] 86 = Paris G13.
141 200192 = ARV[2] 31/7 = Brussels, Musees Royaux: R351.
142 ARV[2] 326 = Basle BS 440.

marked as a prostitute entertainer by a flute-case suspended in the background.[143]

Such markings indicating a prostitute entertainer are not only found in wild orgy scenes but even in quite tame solitary or couple scenes. For example a nude woman on a psycter from Hermitage holding a cup, with a suspended flute case in the background, has all the markings to be identified as a prostitute entertainer enjoying thoroughly her drink.[144] A woman engaged in intercourse a tergo with a bearded man may be identified as a prostitute from a cup suspended above.[145] Likewise a woman who is about to be penetrated by an old man, under the sound of the flutes, played by a young man who could also be a prostitute entertainer, is identified as a prostitute by the kalyx krater suspended above her head. More explicit and intended to remove all ambiguity about the woman's profession is a cup from Munich, where a couple is presented having sex a tergo (κύβδα) and above them a purse is suspended. Could this be a representation of a common prostitute having sex in the kybda position for a mere 3 obols? [146] These instances, and many other similar cases, suggest a pattern: artists placed clues for their viewers referring them back to the sympotic space, where respectable women did not belong and only prostitutes inhabited it, usually entertainers, such as dancers, flute-players, kithara players or low-end prostitutes hired out to offer sexual favors to the guests late into the night for a modest price.

In conclusion, using vase iconography as a historical source has all the advantages and disadvantages of using any kind of material evidence for this purpose. While its authority and reliability are not in question, its interpretation is a complex and delicate process. Vase iconography is not a photographic reproduction of the past; it is art, and the elements of reality sometimes appear as they are but just as often they are resequenced. During the creative process, real life can be subverted, altered to convey a message, or sometimes simply to playfully confuse the viewer and provoke a response. So, when we use vase iconography as a historical source we are in danger of confusing fantasy with reality, taking the extraordinary for ordinary, considering the extreme to be routine, and mixing up fact with fiction. Our most reliable safeguard against such perils is to cross-reference iconographic representations with literary evidence, but here we encounter two major difficulties.

---

143 ARV[2] 132 = Boston 95.61.
144 ARV[2] 16.15, 1619 = St. Petersburg, Ermitage B 644.
145 ARV[2] 315.2 = London E 816.
146 ARV[2] 923.29 = (Once) Munich Arndt.

First, the erotica iconography which has reached us dates from a time when literary evidence is scarce, very fragmentary and scattered in space, some from Ionia, some from the Doric world, and hardly anything from Athens, the place of origin of most erotic paintings. Their production slows down to a virtual halt around the middle of the 5th century, just as we start having more abundant Athenian literature. The reason why the production of erotica stopped is disputed: some have read into this a conservative turn in social attitudes, but what we know from classical Athenian sources would not justify such a conclusion. The fact that the vases containing erotica were largely manufactured for the Etruscan market should point us in the right direction. Etruscan civilization starts declining in the first half of the 5th century, and after the decisive defeat of the Etruscans at the battle of Cumae in 474, their power and influence diminished sharply. This decline in Etruscan power and wealth coincides with diminishing demand for costly artistic erotica from abroad. When the Etruscan market dries up, so does the demand for explicit erotica, as it seems that pornographic vase iconography did not have a broad appeal in Athens or other Greek cities which bought Attic vases. Thus, Kilmer's explanation of the diminishing erotica as a matter of taste is probably not far off the truth, but it not the whole historical truth.[147]

Given this time-frame, it is difficult for us to correlate directly vase iconography to contemporary literary sources. Kilmer, who points out the chronological difficulties, makes a vivid comparison: he suggests that using late 5th and 4th century literature to provide context to 6th and early 5th century iconography would be comparable to using Victorian sources to explain pornographic material from our times.[148] In addition to the time differential, the interpretation of literary sources themselves is not always unproblematic or straight forward, and this has seriously affected the interpretation of vase iconography. Major misinterpretations of vase images, such the one considering any nude female figure to be a "hetaira," were born out of misconceptions of literary sources. The gloomy view of the Athenian woman as a joyless creature, locked away from the light of the sun, to serve and to obey, dominated later 20th century literature. It is no wonder that any woman who seemed to be having any kind of fun in vase iconography, like taking a bath, or having a nude swim at sea with her girlfriends, enjoying a drink or having sex with her husband ought to be indecent, and a paid prostitute at that. This is why it is very important that, when we try to establish links between vase iconography and literary evidence, we handle with

---

147 Kilmer 1993: 2.
148 Kilmer 1993: 4–5.

caution the literary evidence too. In recent years a better understanding of the freedoms and limitations of Athenian women has led to a gradual abandonment of the omni-present, blanket "hetaira" interpretation of any nude female, and has encouraged more nuanced and precise interpretations of Attic vase iconography.

Ultimately there is no golden rule, or easy standard to apply universally. Each image needs to be studied as a unique piece of art, with a creator, a message and an intended audience. In this complex pattern, there are some fixed points of reference. Ingeborg Peschel identifies three areas, the symposion, the *komos* and the "erotisches symplegma," as these fixed points of reference around which we should try to identify images of prostitution, and I believe that this is broadly correct.[149] Literary sources leave us in no doubt that at least in the Athenian reality of the classical period women present in symposia and komoi were perceived as prostitutes.[150] Thus, we can identify with some certainty female figures in symposion/*komos* themes as prostitutes. As mentioned above, there are no certain images of hetairai, but there are plentiful images of flute players, dancers, lyre players and kithara players in various stages of undress, from fully clothed while an orgy is erupting around them, to fully nude. There are also images of entertainers in copulation with one or more men, identified usually by a suspended flute case and frequently also by the presence of cups, wineskins, skyphoi or other wine containers, making a direct connection to the sympotic space and thus marking the women as prostitute entertainers. Other prostitutes engaging in sex with one or more persons are usually identified with some kind of sympotic instrument, while on some occasions there is no identifying mark, allowing at least for some ambiguity, and inviting the viewer to fantasize a scene of wild sexuality, which might actually be domestic. Once we move away from the sympotic space, it is impossible to identify anyone as a prostitute with any degree of certainty, for even in those intriguing images where a man is offering a woman money, there can always be an alternative explanation, sufficient to introduce an element of reasonable doubt.

There is no new information on ancient prostitution obtained from vase iconography alone, which we would not know from literary sources, but this does not diminish the significance of vase iconography as a historical source. The images bring to life what we read in literary sources, and moreover tempt us with some interesting suggestions. The fact that sex scenes dominate the sympotic imagery does not mean that all ancient symposia were an excuse for an

---

149 Peschel 1987: 11.
150 See e.g. Is. 3.14; D.59.24 and my note in Kapparis 1999: 217–221.

orgy. There is a substantial amount of fantasy element in this portrayal of the symposion, as well as an imbalanced focus upon the unruly part of it, since the civilized parts would be less exciting as art subjects. There was no specific format for a symposium, nor did all symposia have the same type of guest. As Plato suggests, there were numerous symposia around the city, some among the elite (καλοὶ κἀγαθοὶ καὶ πεπαιδευμένοι), more among those he considers as the lower, working classes (φαῦλοι καὶ ἀγοραῖοι), and not all were the same.[151] Some evolved around civilized company, others started as civilized affairs and got wild later at night, and surely some were meant to be wild parties from the outset. Like modern parties, which range from the polite dinner with one's co-workers or relatives to the drugs- and alcohol-infused wild rave, where the guests arrive intent on getting "hammered," ancient symposia varied widely too. However, while literary sources seem to be recording more of the civilized symposion in the works of Plato, Xenophon, Athenaios or Aulus Gellius, vase iconography seems to stress the wild side of it. If we could bridge this disparity somewhere in between, it would suggest that venal sex and bad behavior were more prominent than what literary sources imply, but probably things did not escalate until late at night, just as Apollodoros and Aristophanes imply.[152]

Another interesting notion which vase iconography suggests is that common prostitutes (*pornai*) ready for sex on demand, without all the complications of courtship, pursuit, failure, competition or long-term romance with a hetaira, might be part of the retinue of some symposia, just as Dikaiopolis says in Aristophanes' Acharnians, when he enlists all the things necessary for a party:

Everything else is prepared,
Couches, tables, cushions, mattresses,
Garlands, perfume, dainties, the prostitutes (*pornai*) are standing by,
Cakes, flat breads, sesame loaves, honey buns
And dancers.[153]

---

151 Pl. *Ptg.* 347 c-d; for a discussion of this passage see Ch. 6.4.
152 In D. 59.33–4 as the party goes on into the night Phrynion falls asleep and a drunk Neaira, by then a free woman and his concubine rather than a working hetaira, ends up having sex with some of the other guests. The setting is a spacious mansion of the rich Chabrias at the cape Colias, by the seaside. One would think that such a house had a number of rooms, where the guests could sleep, and perhaps it was in these rooms that Neaira ended up having sex with other guests. In Aristophanes' *Wasps* (1326–87) Philokleon steals the flute-player from his sympotai in the end of the night, with promises of manumission and keeping her as his concubine.
153 Ar. *Ach.* 1089–1093.

It is interesting that Dikaiopolis speaks of two different types of prostitutes, common whores ready to have sex with the guests (*pornai*), and entertainers (*orchestrides*), just as vase iconography suggests. A third, even more exciting suggestion is that same sex lovers often shared a woman, who had sex with both men simultaneously. This is only vaguely hinted in some literary sources, but it is a motif too frequent to ignore in vase iconography.[154] In this case iconography may hold the key towards resolving one of the most troublesome issues which have plagued our understanding of homosexual relations in classical Athens, namely how predominantly heterosexual men and boys routinely engaged in relations with each other. The answer suggested by vase erotica is that there was much more of a heterosexual component to these relationships than thought before, as the two lovers would share women as well as each other's affections. If anything, the fluidity of Greek sexuality and a more honest, spontaneous and capricious approach to sexual desire, one still unaffected by the strict rules and norms of the Judeo-Christian tradition, are nowhere portrayed more vividly than they are in the Attic vase erotica.

Using details of the iconography, such as facial expressions, to reconstruct social attitudes and write history is a perilous exercise, as Kilmer has rightly pointed out. Dover's interpretation of the "flaccid penis" of boys being penetrated by their male lover as a sign that they were not supposed to enjoy the encounter, but only grudgingly give in, is only one example of how far wrong one can go when using images to write history. The use of vase iconography may not be sufficient to write the history of prostitution, the information we draw from it may be too little and too confusing to form the basis of our study, but the immediacy of these images, the direct glimpses into the past which they offer, when read in conjunction with carefully selected and interpreted literary sources, amount to a potency which even the most detailed literary account does not have. They can bring to life, right in front of our eyes, a snapshot from the past and capture our attention and imagination, even if that snapshot is mostly or entirely a fantasy.

---

154 E.g. D. 59.28–9; Lys. 4 passim; Aesch. 1.42. A more detailed discussion of this fascinating aspect of vase erotica and their use as historical sources is forthcoming in an independent article.

7 Epilogue: Profiling Prostitution

7.1 Prostitution, Religion and the Polis

For centuries before the advent of feminism religion was the most significant factor in the formation of attitudes towards prostitution, and perhaps it still plays a key role. Almost certainly the prohibition of prostitution in 49 out of the 50 US states is not motivated by feminist sentiments but rather conservative and traditional moral values inspired by religion. On the other hand the fact that in Shintoism prostitution was never a taboo has resulted in relatively liberal attitudes towards prostitution in Japan over the centuries. Greek religion was a significant factor in the formation of an environment which allowed the hetaira to become an iconic cultural symbol of the classical period. Greek religion generally did not have the same fear of sexuality and the body as Christianity and other off-shoots of ancient Judaism; on the contrary, in many ways it celebrated sexuality. It was enshrined in the ritual, especially in the women-only festivals, like the Haloa and the Thesmophoria, which celebrated human sexuality and had their origins in ancient Mediterranean fertility rites. The cycle of life, the renewal of nature, the abundance of the crops, and the enhancement of fertility were concepts central to both festivals. However, while the Thesmophoria was limited to respectable women, the Haloa was open to all women, and hetairai along with citizen matrons had the opportunity to get together in the sanctuary at Eleusis and celebrate the festival, with an all-night feast. Two more festivals which seemingly embraced prostitutes were the Adonia, and the festival of Poseidon on the island of Aegina, which attracted many visitors from all over the Greek world. The key fact in the entire debate about prostitutes and ancient Graeco-Roman religion may simply be that, unlike many other religions past and present, it did not oppose prostitution. Hetairai could enter without any hindrance into the temples to participate in the rituals, sacrifice and pray. It seems that this only changes in the Christian era, where the prostitute becomes persona non grata in the church, unless she is prepared to repent and set aside her ways. The delightful narrative of Sophronios of Jerusalem in the *Life of St. Mary of Egypt* comes to mind. Mary while still practicing as a prostitute is prevented from entering the church during the festival of the Holly Cross by an invisible force-field, stopping her inexplicably at the doorstep of the church.[1]

---

[1] Sophronios, Vita Mariae Egypitae, quae ex meretrice asceta facta est in Solitudine Jordanis, 22.

DOI 10.1515/9783110557954-007

In Athens, the festival of the Haloa, celebrated in late December, most likely as a winter solstice festival, was the primary religious event which attracted hetairai.[2] The nine archons were present outside the sanctuary, as no man was allowed to enter, and on behalf of the city offered a sumptuous buffet feast for the large crowd of women from all over Attica gathering at Eleusis for the *pannychis*. The women sat around fires inside the Great Hall (as an inscription with an order of large amounts of wood attests)[3] feasting, eating and drinking. The learned scholiast of Lucian probably misunderstood the light atmosphere and sexual jokes about men and men's parts told by the women around the fire as some kind of ritual.[4] What made the festival a major event in a hetaira's calendar were the private parties held during the festival in Eleusis and throughout Attica as part of the festivities. Men on the occasion might invite their friends, hetairai and other entertainment for a party, and hetairai threw parties of their own as a means of self-promotion and meeting new clients. The celebration was such a major event and a time for big business that the hetaira Sinope risked the substantial consequences of the law in an attempt to gain notoriety by means of a sacrifice at the yard of the temple in Eleusis, even though sacrifices were not permitted in the temple itself during that day. The person who broke the rules to perform her sacrifice, the Hierophant Archias, was actually punished for his indiscretion.[5]

Equally big business seemingly was the festival of Poseidonia in Aegina, which attracted people from all over the Greek world. The festival, which in later times lasted for a whole two months, attracted men from everywhere, and, expectedly, numerous prostitutes. The Adonia, a festival of overt sexuality, also attracted sex workers, but this was smaller in scale and a rather private celebration in people's homes.[6] Phyrne appears to have been trying to introduce into Attica another cult, that of Isodaites, a sympotic deity favorite among prostitutes, which, among others, provided the excuse for her prosecution for impiety under the pretext she was trying to introduce new deities (see also Ch. 4.4.).

Festivals were public occasions and offered opportunities for business as large crowds of people were gathering from all walks of life. Any prostitute who wanted to be seen and to create opportunities for new affairs and new clients, had a precious opportunity to orchestrate some ostentatious event, like the

---

2 For further discussion and bibliography see my note in Kapparis 1999: 413–417.
3 *IG* ii² 1672; the most significant account of the festival is Brumfield 1981.
4 Sch. Luc. 279.24 Rabe; see the discussion in Sfameni-Gasparo 1986: 287–293.
5 D. 59.115–116.
6 The classic study for the Adonia is the book of M. Detienne (1977).

sacrifice of Sinope at the sanctuary of Eleusis, or make a stunning appearance engineered to attract attention. Pagan religious festivals, by sharp contrast to the religious gatherings of the Christian era, allowed sex-workers to be present and be integrated into the life of the community without danger of persecution or expulsion, and moreover offered great opportunities for self-advertisement and networking. Because the fear of sexuality was absent, and paying for sex, although imprudent for some, was not considered directly immoral or destructive for someone's relationship with the Divine, ancient religions were able to accommodate and tolerate prostitution without difficulty. The extent of acceptance of prostitutes in the public religion of the Greeks is perhaps nowhere more clearly summarized than in a 4th century sacred inscription from Ephesos imposing two days purification after sex with one's wife, and three after sex with a hetaira. The impurity accrued after intercourse with a prostitute is only marginally greater than that with one's wife, and on the whole insignificant.[7]

Whatever anyone's private feelings may have been about paying for sex, when it came to large communal events there is no evidence of overt hostility towards the presence of sex workers in any public occasion in Athens, or anywhere else in the Greek world. However, one forgotten factor in the debates about Athenian sexual morality and the role of the hetaira is the fact that Athens was a democracy where things happened in accordance to the rule of law, not the will of the individual magistrates, potentates, kings, princes or religious leaders. Many a time in history sex workers have been routed, tortured, persecuted or executed by the acts of individuals, or have been forced to serve the desires of a specific ruling class. Classical Athens and other Greek states which had a similar politically open outlook allowed prostitution to exist safely, because there was no individual who had the power to route them, and no law of the city forbade their trade and activities. And when Androtion harassed two prominent prostitutes in the city, apparently illegally, he got a lot of flak for it from his opponent Demosthenes in court.[8]

7.2 The aftermath: Hellenistic and Roman Period

During the Hellenistic period prominent hetairai often turned to mistresses and concubines of the strong men of the day, kings, princes and courtiers associated with Hellenistic royalty, simply because these were the men who had the most

7 *LSA* 29.5–7.
8 D. 22.56–7.

power and wealth to attract and keep these high-maintenance mistresses. The dividing lines between prostitutes, hetairai, entertainers, concubines and even wives become hazy, as Daniel Ogden has amply demonstrated, and the difficulties in our sources are not simply a matter of definitions; many a time such boundaries were fluid in real life too.[9] When we compare the lives of those Hellenistic mistresses with that of the classical hetaira, we can appreciate how much the political freedom of the classical polis had contributed to the liberalism and diversity of the prostitutional markets. The free hetaira of the classical period lived in a democracy, and did not have to obey anyone, except the laws of the city. She could be in charge of her own property and dispose of it in any way she wished, unlike wealthy citizen women who were restricted by family considerations, and there is good evidence suggesting that some of those hetairai were actually very wealthy women. When Phyrne, for example, in an attempt to gain notoriety, decided to dedicate some splendid, and no doubt pricy, sculptures to her native city of Thespiae or to Delphi, she was very much at liberty to spend her own money in any way she wished.

The dominance of the independent hetaira who went from party to party, and from lover to lover, but in the end of the day remained mistress of her own fate and had a degree of independence unparalleled among women in the ancient world, came to an end in the Hellenistic period. Enormous changes in the political and socio-economic landscape of the Greek world hastened the end of the Greek polis, and the merging of the Mediterranean world into the monarchies of the Hellenistic period and ultimately into a single unit under Rome. In the Hellenistic world of the Diadochi, the monarchies of the Ptolemies, the Seleucids and the Antigonids, and eventually in the palaces of the Roman emperors, power and wealth became centralized around the monarch, his court and the favorites of the time, however fleeting such favors might be, especially in unstable times. The ideal of the democratic polis, where wealth and privileges were shared among the citizens, even if in unequal proportions, and opportunity for advancement was open to all with a sharp business instinct, occasionally even to persons who started life as slaves like the banker Pasion and his successor Phormion,[10] was to be forgotten for millennia only to be resurrected in an-

---

9 See Ogden 1999: 215–272.
10 Pasion started his career as a lowly slave working for a banker. His master eventually set him free and after his death made him his heir. Pasion's sharp instincts for business allowed him to accumulate vast wealth and buy his way into citizenship, through generous donations to the Athenian state. Pasion then freed his capable slave Phormion and put him in charge of his bank. When he died, he gave his much younger wife Archippe to Phormion, to be his wife. Phormion was thus able to repeat the success story of Pasion and eventually buy his own way

other continent in the modern period. In the Hellenistic courts much of the privilege would be inherited or acquired through favor from the monarch, and, since hetairai tend to be attracted to privilege and money, without a doubt the courts of the Hellenistic period became the primary stage of the hetaira. The Hellenistic and post-Hellenistic Hetairai, or at least the most prominent of them that we hear about, tend to be not independent agents moving from one man to the next, as they did in the classical period, but rather concubines attached to the various strong men of the Hellenistic world.

Lamia, perhaps the most famous of all prostitute concubines, became the exclusive *eromene* of Demetrios Poliorcetes once they met and fell in love, and as far as we know there was no other man in her life after that. Perhaps the fact that she met him just as she was coming out of her prime may also have something to do with this, but one wonders how much room she would really have in her life for any other man once she became the privileged companion of the king, and even more powerful and influential than the noble-born queen Phila. However, Lamia may not be the stereotypical paradigm of a Hellenistic prostitute-concubine. Not all affairs of Hellenistic monarchs would be quite as enduring as hers was with Demetrios for the simple reason that the monarchs themselves might not maintain a lifelong interest in a favorite concubine, and once they moved on to the next favorite, their previous affair could be passed on to one of the king's strong men as a favor, or she might be free to pursue her own opportunities away from the court. The example of Flora of Osci, a famous beauty and favorite concubine of Pompey, who was passed on to one of his officers once he tired of her, comes to mind.[11] We are told that Flora was deeply saddened by this treatment, fell ill and never got over it down to her old age. If another historical parallel may be appropriate at this point, besides the unique position and power of Hürrem Sultan as the queen consort of Suleiman II, the Magnificent, there were countless women in the Ottoman harems who were far less important: the favors bestowed upon them were temporary, and a night at the side of the Sultan a rare and exceptional event. Likewise, in the Hellenistic courts, there may have been a few influential women like Lamia, but also many other hetaira-concubines, who enjoyed favor and prosperity for the short period of time only to be easily replaced by new favorites at the whims of the king and his courtiers. The time when the hetaira was calling the shots was irrevocably gone from history.

---

to citizenship through the same avenue used by Pasion. For the affairs of the family see Trevett 1992 and D. 36, 45 and 46.

11 See the discussion in Ch. 3.1. and also App. I.

The Hellenistic hetaira should not be viewed as a victim of circumstances, virtu-ally enslaved or locked up in the palace of some Hellenistic monarch, in the manner that concubines would be locked into harems in the ancient orient or in the Ottoman Empire in later centuries. In the relationships between the hetairai and the strong men with whom they associated there was still a certain degree of mobility and choice, and such connections were more often than not volun-tary, temporary and rather fleeting. The symposia of the Hellenistic Period that we get to hear about were either thrown by various potentates, kings and princ-es or were centered around them, and in those the hetairai continued to play an important role, while prostitute-entertainers continued to perform just as they had done for centuries. If anything, these symposia would be much more elabo-rate, lavish and ornate affairs than an ordinary Athenian symposium, because their hosts had much more money to spend and stronger motivation to impress. The symposia of Lamia and Demetrius were legendary for their extravagance, as were the symposia of the Ptolemies, and entertainers certainly continued to play an important part in such events.

Unlike the typical symposion of the classical period where the host only provided part of the food and entertainment, while the rest was contributed by the guests, the patronage and often the cost for the Hellenistic aristocratic sym-posia was borne by the rich man, and in this respect he was by right at the cen-ter of the event. The large image of Trimalchio dominates the famous dinner in the *Satyricon* of Petronius. The other necessary participant of the later antiquity dinner party, the ubiquitous parasite, who feasts much better than his economic circumstances would permit by securing invitations for the lavish symposia of the rich, becomes a literary *topos*. With fewer people holding in their hands much of the privilege and wealth and being able to throw the legendary and fabulous parties with the entertainers and the hetairai, freeloaders participating in the symposia, sometimes offering sexual favors themselves in exchange for the meal and the entertainment, seems to be getting a feature more and more common from the Hellenistic period, while the couplet of the hetaira and the parasite becomes a familiar literary theme.[12]

In the Hellenistic Courts the Hetaira competes with high-born women for the affections of her lover, to the extent that sometimes it is really difficult to tell the difference between the prostitute concubine, and other mistresses.[13] The

---

12 See e.g. Luc. *Tim.* 12; Athen. 13.48; Alciphr. 2.32.1 σπαθήσας τὴν οὐσίαν εἰς ἡμᾶς τοὺς παρασίτους καὶ τὰς ἑταίρας.

13 A good example of such confusion may be the case of Agathokleia (see App. I), who seems to be a high-born woman, but still confused with a hetaira-mistress.

hetaira in the end loses this contest to some degree because gradually she will be pushed off center stage in the sympotic space, as respectable matrons come to occupy the position of honor in the Roman period. When a Roman gentleman was throwing a party he might invite entertainers and hetairai, but his wife and other respectable women could also be invited, and their presence alone would detract from the attention paid to the hetairai and inspire some restraint. As the Roman practice of mixing the sexes in the symposium and accepting high born women in the company of men spread throughout the Empire, the hetaira lost her privileged position in the sympotic space and her role gradually declined. When Athenaios is writing in the imperial era about the famous hetairai of the classical period he romanticizes and idolizes them as we would idolize film stars.

The classical hetaira of Athenaios is idealized, but also distant and alien, a relic from a past long gone and not a familiar figure in a typical Roman symposium of the 2nd century AD, where the hetaira is no longer at the spotlight. When attitudes towards prostitution undergo a very radical change at the beginning of the 1st century of the Christian era, as eastern influences gradually change the landscape of sexual morality, the hetaira has already lost her luster. Prostitution of course has continued unabated in a wide variety of forms throughout the harbors and cities of the empire, like Delos, Ephesos, Alexandria Ostia, Pompeii, and even in Rome venal sex finds fertile grounds to flourish, as Thomas McGinn has demonstrated. In this new order of things certainly we can find expensive prostitutes and a high-end market, but the hetaira as a cultural icon, a symbol of feminine independence, wit, spirit, intelligence and charm is an image from the past. Gradually the icon of the hetaira as a companion with whom once could share a good conversation and intellectual pleasures, and as someone who would stimulate a lover's mind as much as his body and sexual appetites fades away, and the term ἑταίρα gradually becomes a mere synonym of πόρνη for a few centuries before its disappearance from the language in the Byzantine period.

The landscape of prostitution was already undergoing changes in the earlier part of the Roman period, even though prostitution was still prevalent throughout the Roman world.[14] The major change, a historic shift in cultural attitudes towards prostitution, does not really come before the 1st century of the Christian era. Many a time this dramatic shift has been identified with Christianity, but in the 1st century the new religion was not influential enough, or widespread enough, to effect major changes in social attitudes throughout the empire. Rea-

---

14 See the important studies of McGinn 1998 and 2004; Stumpp 1998, Edwards 1993.

son and historical occasion point towards the East of the empire as the source of new cultural influences upon mainstream Roman thought, which gradually generate a shift in attitudes. The Jewish historian Josephus would argue around that time that the Jews have a better claim than the Greeks to intellectual purity, because they have been meticulous in their preservation of their sacred heritage.[15] Indeed, in no area are such influences more evident than religion. The peoples of the empire are now looking much further to the east than the shores of the Aegean for their spiritual needs. In eastern cults and religions, such as the cults of Isis or Cybele, Mithraism and eventually Christianity, they will find new forms of emotional fulfillment and new certainties to anchor them in an increasingly uncertain and unsafe world.

As eastern religions start to exert considerable influence upon European hearts and minds, their cultural influence also increases just as dramatically and gradually changes the world-view of the peoples of the Empire. Along with these cultural influences changes in social attitudes to issues like virginity, monogamy, abortion and prostitution become noticeable. Soranos, for example, will stand up against a 500 year old medical orthodoxy and argue that virginity is not harmful for the body, while Musonius Rufus will openly condemn abortion and contraception as unlawful practices, going against centuries of more tolerant attitudes to these matters, and Philo, a Jew himself, will have a hard task trying to convince men in the Graeco-Roman world to accept monogamy within marriage, as in Jewish law and custom.[16] In relation to prostitution the intolerant views of Judaism towards prostitutes, well attested in the texts which the Septuagint translation had brought to a Greek-reading audience in previous centuries, begin to spread westwards after the 1st c. A.D. and with the consolidation of Christianity in the coming centuries will eventually dominate western social, legal, political and religious views.

Michel Foucault described that critical junction in the history of sexuality as following:

> For example, the meaning of the sexual act itself: it will be said that Christianity associated it with evil, sin, the Fall, and death, whereas antiquity invested it with positive symbolic values. On the definition of the legitimate partner: it would appear that, in contrast to what occurred in the Greek and Roman societies, Christianity drew the line at monogamous marriage and laid down the principles of exclusively procreative ends within that conjugal relationship. Or the disallowance of relations between individuals of the same

---

15 Josephus *AJ* 1, 1–17.
16 See Soranos *Gyn.* 1.30 and Pinault 1992: 123–139; Musonius Rufus *Diss.* 15; Kapparis 2002: 149–150; Philo *De Josepho* 43.

sex: it would seem that Christianity strictly excluded such relationships, while Greece exalted them and Rome accepted them, at least between men.

Foucault did not accept a sharp divide between pagan and Christian morality and this is how he explains his thesis:

> One would only have to point out the direct borrowing and strict continuities between the first Christian doctrines and the moral philosophy of antiquity. The first great Christian text devoted to sexual practice in married life – Chapter XX of Book II of *The Pedagogue* by Clement of Alexandria - is supported by a number of scriptural references, but it also grows on a set of principles and precepts borrowed directly from pagan philosophy."[17]

Both of these principles are correct, even if they appear at first to be contradictory. The transition from the pagan Graeco-Roman world to Christianity was earth-shattering and changed the shape of western civilization, but at the same time it was a continuum, a process which became ever more entangled, and the two worlds became permanently inseparable when Christian authors made the deliberate and conscious decision to adopt vast and significant parts of Graeco-Roman culture into Christian dogma. This process lasted for centuries and by the end of it Christianity had been transformed into a monumental edifice which far exceeded its humble biblical origins.

Hostile attitudes to prostitution as a moral evil for society are well-attested before the 3rd century, when Christianity starts having widespread influence upon the culture of the Roman world. In Jewish documents such as the *Tanakh* (or the *Old Testament* as it is known in the Greco-Roman world through the translation of the Septuagint) and in authors like Philo, and Josephus to some degree, and also in the *Testaments of the Twelve Patriarchs*, or the authors of the *New Testament* and most vehemently Paul, we find vocal condemnation of prostitution as a practice which erodes the morals of society, and can lead someone's soul to eternal damnation. From these documents, some of which eventually acquired canonical status among Christians with the consolidation of the Biblical Canon from the 4th century onwards, intensely hostile attitudes to prostitution passed into the whole of Christian literature, and subsequent European and American legal documents, social contracts, and academic literature. When William M. Sanger, M.D. wrote his marvelously flawed history of prostitution in 1895, treating it as a medical condition that required a physician's attention, he inadvertently encapsulated in his work many centuries of western hostility towards "the oldest profession." Intriguingly, more than a century later a report

---

17 Foucault 1990 (trsl.): 14–15.

prepared for the European Parliament, introduced by Maria Carlshamre, independently reiterated some of Sanger's views treating prostitution as a health issue, and at some points as a health hazard, but the language of this document took care to avoid the moral undertones commonly found in Sanger's work.[18]

The curious and surprising connection between prostitution and idolatry from the 1st century onwards further proves that intensely hostile attitudes originated in eastern monotheism. This connection is attested for the first time in Philo and the contemporary *Testaments of the 12 Patriarchs*, and subsequently encountered countless times in the Christian literature of later centuries.[19] Although prostitution is ever present in uniformly Christian Byzantium as well as the Christian West, still its association with idolatry persisted for many centuries after the complete Christianization of the European continent. It is not accidental that this motif is first noticed in a pre-Christian author but from the same socio-cultural and geographical background as the authors of the *New Testament*, who consolidate the connection between prostitution and idolatry as alien to the Christian way of life. It is fair to say that first century Jews identified prostitution with idolatry with good reason, because in their eyes it was a practice befitting idolatrous societies, but not the people of Yahweh. This identification from Jewish sources eventually spreads into the mainstream of Graeco-Roman thought along with Christianization and becomes a frequent topos in sources of the late empire and medieval period, even though such an association no longer made sense.

The famous references to homosexuality in the *New Testament*, especially in Paul, thus must be viewed not as references to consensual homosexual relations in the traditional Graeco-Roman model, because if this were the case and these references were made with this very strong cultural stereotype in mind, one would have expected that they would have been more numerous, more explicit, and more specifically addressing this dominant feature of the Greek way of life in particular. The fact that the few passages which seem to be alluding to man-to-man sexual relations invariably appear in a context which discusses prostitution, points to a reading of these passages as references to male prostitution, not same sex relationships in their entirety. Moreover, it seems that they refer to

---

18 See Sanger 1895; Carlshamre, Proposal for the European Parliament 2007/2263 (INI) dated at 03/19/2008.

19 Philo *De Decalogo*, 8 Cohn. I was able to count 373 instances in a *TLG* search for the combination of πορν- and ειδωλ-, and the number would probably be much higher if one were to add synonym search terms; see for example: *Testamenta XII Patriarcharum* 1.4.6, Justin *Dialogus cum Tryphone* 132.1; Gregory of Nyssa *In Canticum Canticorum Homilia* 15, 6.318 al. Petersen 1986: 187–191; Wright 1984: 125–153, and 1987: 396–398; Kapparis 2011: 222–255.

very specific forms of male prostitution as it was practiced in the brothels of the ancient world around the time of Paul, where pretty boys from a young age were groomed to cater for the needs of customers.[20] For as long as they worked in those brothels they were feminized and deliberately retained an ambiguous sexual identity, imposed upon them by pimps and the desires of customers, and it appears that these are the practices which Paul is condemning in his famous references in the *New Testament*.

I am convinced that eastern, predominantly Jewish, and eventually Judeo-Christian influences are what establishes the link between prostitution and moral decay into mainstream Greco-Roman thought and its descendants in the western hemisphere all the way to the modern era. To a large degree, our own views of prostitution have their origins in that critical historical period. Before this major shift prostitution was often linked with joy and pleasure in Graeco-Roman sources. The prostitute added to the quality of life of her or his customers, by offering physical pleasure, companionship and many a time even emotional fulfillment. The hetaira, the lover-boy, and even the cheap and degraded prostitute of the brothel who had to offer her/himself to a number of customers every day, are mentioned in a positive way as instruments of joy, as one of the things which made life better, easier and worthwhile in a world where everyday reality many a time was hard and marked by adversity, difficulty, ill-health, wars, ravages and plagues, uncertainty, and for many individuals a relentless struggle for survival.

The most pronounced criticism of prostitution in classical Greek authors was that it caused financial ruin, that men spent the family fortune on such illicit pleasures, fickle hetairai, and greedy pimps. Moral decline or corruption were not significant factors in discussions of prostitution. This is why in the pagan Greco-Roman world it brought no shame or stigma for iconic figures like Harmodios and Aristogeiton or prominent men like Pericles, Aristotle, Ptolemy, Sulla or Pompey to be associating with prostitutes. Almost every notable man in the ancient world, including those who seem to be of primarily homosexual orientation, were associated with some famous hetaira or another. Far from attaching any kind of disgrace or stigma, such associations were deliberately

---

20 The four canonical Gospels completely ignore the issue. That the three much-publicized references in the Pauline letters refer to prostitution and not same-sex relations in general should be very clear from the fact that one refers to the fee (ἀντιμισθία) paid in return for man to man sexual services (*Ro.* 1.26–7), and in the other two the critical word ἀρσενοκοίτης, a term with no history, created by Paul, is always found in conjunction with terms directly and recognizably meaning "male prostitute" such as πόρνος (*1 Ep. Ti.* 1.9) or μαλακός (*1 Ep. Cor.* 6.9). The general distaste of Judaism for prostitutes is well attested (see the discussion in Ch. 4.1.1.).

cultivated as image enhancers of those men. The fact that they could attract and retain the interest, attention and the affections of renowned hetairai spoke in their favor rather than against them, as it projected an image of power and prestige

As a famous saying of Apollodoros suggests, in the classical period a citizen had choices provided that he had the means to support them.[21] He could take a lawful wife, and also visit prostitutes at will, co-habit with a prostitute, or take a former prostitute as his concubine, to the great displeasure of wives and much quarreling in the family. Sometimes a man might even take a boy in the family home, as Demosthenes does repeatedly, according to several rather reliable sources from the classical period. However, this probably was not typical behavior: Demosthenes and Alcibiades, who dared to take their lovers into the family home, are the quintessential rogues in classical Athens, and their behavior was seen as an effrontery to their wives. Generally, it was not socially acceptable to compel a lawful wife to share her distinct place and privilege with another lover of the husband in the family home. However, if the husband was sufficiently tactful and kept these affairs away from the family home, in the houses of bachelor friends, social acquaintances, or assuming that he was rich enough, in other houses which he owned or rented, society would not look down on him and would not consider his behavior immoral. It took centuries before Christian authors could persuade men to abandon these practices.[22] The struggle of John Chrysostom to convince Christian men to adhere to monogamy very clearly proves that even as late as the 4th century that battle had not yet been won for the Church, if it was ever won. As the prominent Byzantine scholar Hans-Georg Beck puts it, monogamy was always an illusion, not a real state, something which Christianity came to espouse as an afterthought, a cause born out of practical considerations rather than some deep dogmatic conviction, and even then it was never about the union of a true pair of equals, as the woman was pushed into the inferior position of a decidedly uneven contract.[23] Moreover it is noteworthy that even after monogamy for both men and women was firmly established as a moral command in mainstream Christian thought, never in history has it been observed to the full extent.

---

21 D. 59.122.
22 See for example Tertullian *De Monogamia*; Clem. Al. Str. 3.1.4.3; Origen *In Jeremiam Homiliae* 12–20.20; John Chrysostom *Homilia de capto Eutropio* 52.410.
23 Beck 1984: 38–9.

7.3 The timeless appeal of hired pleasure

The reasons why prostitution was frequently presented in a positive light in the ancient world are complex, and have something to do with the fact that prostitutes, male and female, provided physical pleasure but also emotional outlets for companionship, friendship and occasionally even love. And while it is true that wives and non-prostitute lovers, whom the Greeks called *eromenos/e*, also provided similar outlets, our sources typically present such relationships as quite complicated, and much more difficult than the relationships with sex workers. Premarital sexual affairs with women who were not prostitutes were not only morally unacceptable in Greek society, but they were also criminal and on a rare occasion could even result in death for a man caught with someone's unmarried daughter. The same law applied to extramarital affairs with someone else's wife, mother, sister or concubine. Thus, relationships with other women, except those who were available for money, and were explicitly excluded from the force of the adultery laws by a Solonean statute,[24] were dangerous, complicated and criminal. Relationships with male lovers, although legal, had their own complications, too, and if we believe Plato's accounts of such relationships or some of Aeschines' comments in the speech *Against Timarchos*, there was a lot of pursuit, competition, gifts and a considerable amount of persuasion before one could win the heart of his beloved. This is why straight-forward sex and uncomplicated affairs with prostitutes are recommended as a better alternative to the difficulties of human relationships in 4th century comedy. Other than the financial burden that this temporary situation created for the man, there was no other obligation.

In the Christian era there was a fundamental shift in the culture of the body. Pleasing oneself and giving in to desires were not priorities in a culture which increasingly would stress a culture of denial of the flesh, and as the centuries went by even advocated the punishment of the flesh in order to enhance spiritual qualities. The financial factor, which is so dominant in pre-Christian criticisms of prostitution, is not significant among Christian authors, for the simple reason that in a religion which advocated poverty and, in fact, considered finances and money a burden that might lead to someone's exclusion from Heaven, the drive to safeguard the family property would be unimportant. On the other hand, the defilement of body and soul through the practice of prostitution or encounters with prostitutes would be presented as equally detrimental to the prostitute as to her client, as they threatened one's immortal soul with eternal

---

24 D. 59.67; see the discussion in Ch. 1.2

damnation. For many Christian authors starting with Paul, celibacy was the ideal state of affairs. If one could completely abstain from all forms of sexual activity that would be ideal, but if one had to give in to sexual urges this should only happen for the purposes of procreation. Any sexual activity beyond pro-creative intercourse would eventually be viewed as defilement, and thus as unacceptable and improper.

Ideology hostile to the body never gathered sufficient force to limit inter-course to procreational purposes, or stop extra-marital sexual activities, at any point in history. On the contrary, even this most glorious defender of Christiani-ty, Constantine himself, is accredited with the creation of a brothel in his shin-ing new capital city of Constantinople. Thomas McGinn rightly disputes this as a fable, but nonetheless considers it significant as it suggests that zoning prosti-tution, something that had never happened before in the Greco-Roman world, was a solution favored by many Christians.[25] The tale about Constantine zoning prostitution is also significant for another reason: it implies that in the city of Constantine itself, the symbol of a Christian Empire to rise out of the wreckage of the pagan Graeco-Roman world, prostitution does have its place, so long as it is kept quarantined.

Whether legal or not, and tolerated or not, prostitution continued to exist and often flourish in Christian Europe, and almost every human society, regard-less of restrictions, laws, disapproving social attitudes, religious sanctions, or the sure promise of an eternity in hell. Prostitution has proved to be irrepressi-ble, and every time one tried to oppress, repress or suppress it, the result was to push it underground; if authorities chased prostitutes away from one area of the city, almost certainly they moved into another area. If one were to expel the brothels out of the city center they would go into the periphery. The laws of supply and demand have ensured the continuing existence of the sex industry throughout history, and even Christianity, with all its serious sanctions, the heavy rhetoric and the fiery opposition, has failed to eradicate it. If one tried to understand why prostitution is a universal feature in human societies, a deeper look into its causes would be necessary.

In the ancient world, as respectable women were out of reach, the sexual needs of men were expected to be fulfilled by prostitutes. Euboulos, Philemon, Xenarchos and several other sources suggest that this was the purpose of prosti-tution, and considered it an excellent idea, as it provided outlets for the physi-cal needs of young men, but at the same time safeguarded the purity and good reputation of women destined for marriage and childbirth, and by doing so

---

25 McGinn 2004: 79–111.

reassured society about the legitimacy and proper birth of children born within marriage.[26] Since the purity of the citizen stock was a core concern for most Greek city states, and as a result adultery was perceived to be a heinous crime, while prostitution was believed to be the remedy and an effective preventative measure safeguarding against adultery, it was only reasonable that attitudes to prostitution would be tolerant. The comic passages mentioned above praise the insight of Solon when he allowed brothels, because by doing so he made sure that one did not need to break the law or put his own life at risk in order to have a sexual encounter. While the rich could be striving for the favors of some capricious mistress, the poor would be content with a visit to the local brothel, or some sex with an entertainer at a local party, and there were many shades in between. The ancient prostitutional market had developed such diversity that it could accommodate almost everyone's wallet, age, sexual orientation, desires and sexual fantasies.

Prostitution proved willing to serve every socioeconomic strata, all the way down to the numerous slaves in Greek and Roman cities, who could not have families unless their master permitted it, but still needed outlets for their sexual urges, to be found in the low cost brothels of the city. We can imagine that the visit to the brothel would be one of the few things that made a slave's life enjoyable for the short period of time that he spent there. Xanthias, the slave of Philokleon in the *Wasps* of Aristophanes, is joking about a prostitute refusing intercourse a tergo (κελητίσαι) during one of his routine visits to the brothel.[27] Considering that this was the least involved and cheapest position (see Ch. 5.6.), this is a joke combined with a word-play involving horses and sexual positions. Delighted with the promise of several prostitute entertainers in the brothel of the underworld is Xanthias disguised as Herakles in the *Frogs*.[28]

Asking for unusual positions and forms of sexual activity which would be beyond the tastes of a modest wife, has always been one of the reasons for which men visited prostitutes. The hetaira *Dodecamechanos* apparently was thus nick-named because she offered her customers a choice of twelve different positions.[29] Apollodoros made the sensational revelation that Naeara in her younger days was having sex from three holes, while Lysias had said about Antiope that she was offering sex from two holes.[30] Sex workers through time

---

26 See the discussion in Ch. 1.2.

27 Ar. *V.* 500–502.

28 Ar. *Ra.* 512–6.

29 See entry in App. I.

30 See the discussion in Kapparis 1999: 402–405.

have offered their customers the choice to satisfy darker impulses and secretive desires. When someone walked into a brothel in the ancient world he often had the choice of a woman, a boy, or a man, and any position or contraption that would satisfy his desires. Once the price was right, every dark fantasy could be fulfilled. We get to hear about transvestite prostitutes, men or women from every corner of the earth, black, Indian, North-African, red-headed men and women form the Euxine, Egyptians, Lydians, and Greeks from every shore of the Mediterranean.[31] Prostitution has also been a popular choice among sailors throughout history. In Piraeus as well as other harbor cities and trading outposts of the Mediterranean travelers and merchants on their way to business trips, far away from families and from female companionship for months at a time, were easy clientele for the numerous brothels, taverns and other disreputable establishments set up to cater precisely to the needs of sexually deprived seamen.[32]

Prostitution provided to its customers an escape from the responsibilities of daily routine. A man had to provide for the household, conduct business, manage the farm, fulfill his duties as a citizen and soldier, serve in the juries of the democracy, attend the assembly, vote, and sometimes assume office himself, and moreover provide for everyone in the household, and be prepared to lay down his life in the battlefield in order to defend them. The expectations were high, and this is why the break from responsibility in the arms of an attractive partner who made no further demands once the right fee had been paid should come as a relief from a life of duty. In this respect, it seems that prostitution to some degree was a byproduct of the ideology of the male conqueror.

Marriage throughout history has often been about finances, children, family life, and household management. Apollodoros in a famous quote from the speech *Against Neaira* recognizes the birth of legitimate children and good household management as the primary purposes of a typical Athenian marriage.[33] By contrast, the relationships of men with hetairai or other sex workers were about carefree enjoyment, away from such worries. The client paid for a certain service agreed in advance, and the sex worker was expected to provide this service for the agreed price. The client did not need to be attractive, young, thin, muscular, interesting, intellectually bright, or socially adept. These complications of real life courtship were not a significant factor in such exchanges. On the contrary, we are told repeatedly that the less attractive and the old make

---

31 *AG* 5.105, Appendix 2; Ch. 2.2.
32 See the discussion in Ch. 1.1.
33 D. 59.122.

the most suitable clients because they pay more. As Philemon puts it, the girls in the brothel, when the customer walked in, did not care if he is young or old; everyone was just as welcome.

When the encounter with a prostitute was over, there was no additional obligation, even if children were born as a result. The man owed no obligation to a prostitute who conceived his child, and it was entirely her decision to abort it, with great risk to her own health, or keep it, and bear the difficulties of single parenthood. Sometimes we hear that men provided for their children with prostitutes, but this was entirely their choice; neither the law nor custom expected of them to do so, unless they voluntarily chose to acknowledge these children as their own and care for them.[34] In a traditional marriage caring for the children was legally required and expected by one's family and society, and to that end if one added the cost of keeping the entire family happy and healthy, married life created just as many financial obligations in the ancient world as it would in our times. In a prostitutional setting someone's financial obligations ended with the payment of the fee, unless, of course, the object of his desires was some haughty hetaira with endless demands, only for deep pockets. One could argue that precisely this no-obligation dynamic has been one of the most forceful reasons for which men and women throughout history have chosen to pay for sex.

The reasons mentioned above are compelling; prostitution has been a universal feature in human societies because traditional social structures create fertile grounds for it. These reasons are not just casual or superficial; they generate powerful dynamics in interpersonal relationships which have rendered prostitution stronger than the fires of Hell, which Christian churches have threatened for the last two thousand years, stronger than stern laws, prison sentences, career endangerment, very public embarrassment for men charged in courts of law for affairs with prostitutes, and stronger than an endless series of naïve social imperatives and initiatives trying to eradicate it from some social setting or other. The attraction of prostitution has been that it provided for some of the deepest physical and emotional needs of men and women throughout history, but without the complications that make such transactions and encounters vexed and complicated personal and communal affairs, and chances are that as long as human relations and expectations remain complex and exacting, prostitution will always find fertile ground to grow as the uncomplicated alternative outlet.

---

34 See for example D.59 passim; Plautus *Truculentus* passim; D. 54.26; Is. 6.21 al.

Appendix I

Collections of Ancient Sex Workers

Attempts to create catalogues of known hetairai and other sex workers from the classical past had already started in the Hellenistic period. Athenaios (13.21) attests that the first collection listing Attic hetairai was compiled by Aristophanes Byzantios in his work Περὶ τῶν ἐν Ἀθήνῃσι ἑταιρῶν *(On the Hetairai living in Athens)*. The fact that Aristophanes limited himself to the hetairai of Athens, leaving out the numerous hetairai of Corinth and other cities, suggests that his primary interest in them may have been literary rather than historical. The total number of sex workers in classical and early Hellenistic Athens must have been substantial, but the high-end of the market was only a small fraction of it. Aristophanes was able to name 132 women in approximately 200 years of history. No doubt these were not only the most prominent, but moreover women probably known through literary works, as Aristophanes was not generally interested in trivia, but rather in the literary and cultural legacy of classical Athens, which he wanted to preserve and transmit. Athenaios attests that Aristophanes had missed a fair amount of women, some of them quite prominent like Gnathaina and her daughter.[1] The grammarian Apollodoros added more names in his own collection, while the historian Gorgias expanded even further the collections of his predecessors. Ammonius and Antiphanes are also mentioned as compilers of such collections.

In the modern period the first person to attempt such a feat was K. Schneider in his monumental article in the *Real Encyclopaedie*. His list includes many of the famous hetairai, but there are many omissions too. Even as it is, the list is crude in that it does not make any attempt to separate fact from fiction, does not contain any other sex worker, except some of the most prominent hetairai, and does not make any attempt at providing sources or other information about the women. McClure's list in her book on Athenaios was more carefully crafted but limited in scope as she has only included names found in Athenaios. This list is meant to be the most comprehensive thus far. I have collected the names found primarily in sources written in Greek. Sex workers from Latin sources have been included selectively, like for example the hetairai mentioned in the plays of Latin Comedy, in this case because they often come from Greek originals. In this list I have also included sex workers who appear in fictional literature.

---

1 Athen. 13.46, 50–51.

DOI 10.1515/9783110557954-008

I have not included names found in vase iconography under the *kalos/kale* inscription, as many of the names in such inscriptions are decidedly not prostitutes, like for example Leagros, an Athenian youth from a noble family, whose name appears on several vases with the inscription Λέαγρος καλός ("Leagros is beautiful"), or a horse named Koloura ("stump-tail") mentioned on a vase with an equestrian theme and the inscription Κολούρα καλή. The consensus building up in the literature in recent years is that καλός/καλή is not an automatic indication of prostitution, and this is why I do not think that these names belong in a list of sex-workers (see the discussion in Ch. 6.2.). I have also excluded people like the politician Timarchos, because I do not believe that he had ever practiced prostitution, and thus I do not think that he belongs to this list. When it is known precisely what form of prostitution this person practiced (e.g. a flute player or a dancer), I indicate this next to the name. Persons who were erroneously identified as prostitutes by some ancient source may be included if there is a chance that some of the allegations were true, or omitted altogether, if the allegations seem completely unfounded (as, for example, in the case of queen Semiramis of Assyria, who was called a "whore" by Stabrobates, the king of the Indians, in the narrative of Ktesias [FGrH 688 F 1b], and the allegation stuck in later authors). Interpretations have been provided only for nicknames obviously referring to a prostitutional context, but not for true proper names or regular names which hetairai could be sharing with other women. As Greek names usually meant something, it would obscure the picture and confuse our understanding of the nicknames which hetairai chose, if we interpreted regular names. Persons known with more than one name are cited by all names, but only one primary entry is given. Fictional characters are identified as such, although the reader needs to keep in mind that some of them may have been based on real persons.

Catalogue of Known Sex Workers

Acca Larentia: (8th c. fictional). According to a tradition first related by Dionysios Halicarnasseus (1.84.4) she was a former prostitute (Lat. *lupa*) and brought up Romulus and Remus. Dionysios says that the myth of the She-wolf arose from a misunderstanding of the word "lupa", which had both meanings (literally "she-wolf" and metaphorically "prostitute"), but Servius says that the myth was invented to disguise the shame of the founders of Rome (Servius *Com. Verg. Aen.* 1.273). This legend is also attested in later authors (e.g. Plu. *Rom.* 4,4; Zonaras *Epit.Hist.* 2,88; Eust. *Com. Od.* 2,275, 323).

Acroteleutium "sloppy seconds": Fictional hetaira in Plautus *Miles Gloriosus*.

Adelphasium "little sister": One of the reluctant hetairai in Plautus *Poenulus*.

Aerope: (probably early 4ᵗʰ c.). A fragment of the comic poet Nikostratos (fr. 20) mentions a woman named Aerope in conjunction with the well-known hetaira Okimon (s.v.), which suggests that Aerope was a hetaira too, carrying the mythological name of the mother of Agamemnon (Tzetz. *Sch. Il.* 1.122, E. *Hel.* 391; *Or.* 18. Sch. Ar. Ra. 849).

Agallis "pleasure": According to Athenaios (13.46), she was one of the women missed by Aristophanes Byzantios, Apollodoros and Gorgias in their collections of Attic hetairai.

Agathokleia: (late 3ʳᵈ c.; died 203/2). Daughter of Oinanthe and sister of Agathocles. She was an influential lover of Ptolemy IV Philopator, and probably not a prostitute. After the assassination of her brother by an angry mob she was dragged naked through the streets, along with her mother and sisters, and lynched (Plb. 11.14.5; 15.25–33; Ptolemy Euergetes *FGrH* 234 F 4; Strabo 17.1.11, Plu. 753 D, *Agis* 54.3; Athen. 13.37). See also Pomeroy 1984: 49–51; 54–55.

Aglais "pleasing", **daughter of Megalokles** (Poll. 4.89)**, or Megakles** (Athen. 10.7; Ael. *VH* 1.26): (3ʳᵈ c.). She was a well-known, professional trumpet-player in Alexandria, but no source explicitly names her as a sex-worker. One might extrapolate from the fact that she played the trumpet on a public procession wearing a wig and a helmet that she may have been a sex worker at some point in her career, but perhaps not in her latter days, when we are told, probably with a degree of exaggeration, that she ate 12 pounds of meat and 4 daily portions of bread, and drank a whole pitcher of wine. It is possible that Aristainetos (1.19) was aware of a real-life sex worker from the past named Aglais, whom he makes the mother (and implicitly, pimp) of his fictional musician sex-worker Melissarion.

Agonis "game": (4ᵗʰ c.). Athenaios (8.22) quotes a passage of Alexis (fr. 3) from a play entitled *Agonis*, where someone, perhaps a hetaira, is begging her mother not to threaten her with Misgolas (the notorious boy-lover; see Ch. 4.2.), for she is not a cithara boy. A passage from *Suda* (α 335) also confirms that there was a hetaira under that name.

Aedonion "nightingale": Hot-tempered fictional hetaira in Alciphron (3.2).

Alco: Clearchos (or Dikaiarchos) attests that Pythagoras during one of his reincarnations took the form of an attractive hetaira named Alco. It is difficult to
ascertain whether there was a real person with that name somehow connected
to the Pythagorean school (Aulus Gellius *Noctes Atticae* 4.11).

Alexander of Abonoteichus: (2nd c. AD). The primary source for his life is Lucian's *Alexander*, which offers some support to archaeological evidence about this
prominent cultic figure of the 2nd c., sometimes referred to in modern literature
as 'the false prophet'. Lucian is a hostile source, and this is why the charge that
Alexander was a very handsome boy, who prostituted himself indiscriminately,
then became the lover of a magician until adulthood (*Alex.* 5), although not
impossible, cannot be taken at face value either.

Alexo: Fictional hetaira mentioned in an epigram of the *Greek Anthology* (5.200)
for leaving behind her sweet scent and perfumes after a night of passion.

Ampelis "vine-tree": Fictional hetaira in Lucian (*DMeretr.* 8) advising her friend
Chrysis that a jealous and violent lover is the perfect subject for exploitation. A
fictional woman named Ampelis is the recipient of a letter from an old jilted
lover in Aristainetos (2.9). Another fictional hetaira ominously named Ampelis
is an old drunk in an epigram of Ariston (2nd c.) from the *Greek Anthology* (7.457).

Ampelisca "vineyard": Friend and companion of Palaestra, a citizen-born
pseudo-hetaira in Plautus *Rudens*, which was based upon a play of Diphilos.
She belonged to the violent pimp Labrax, but in the course of the play she escapes his control, together with Palaestra.

Anterastylis "rival lover": One of the reluctant-hetairai in Plautus *Poenulus*.

Anthis: See n. Aphyai.

Anthrakion "Little charcoal": Fictional hetaira mentioned in Alciphron (4.14.2).
If based on a real person, the name might have been generated from the dark
skin or hair color of the woman.

Anteia (or Antheia, or Antia, or Anthia: late 5th – early 4th c.).: There is some
confusion as to the correct form of the name, probably due to the fact that all
four forms are well attested in various sources for several individuals, fictional

or real. Although different sources give preference to different forms (e.g. the *Lexica Segueriana* s.v. *Antheia* prefers *Antheia* and acknowledges *Anteia* as an alternative), there is substantial evidence that *Anteia* was the correct form of the name for the famous hetaira. First, we have the weighty testimony of Harpocration that *Anteia* was the form he found in Lysias. Second, as Athenaios reports (3.101 and 13.51), the correct form should be "Anteia" because in several plays by Eunikos (or Philyllios; Athenaios is uncertain about the author in this instance) Antiphanes and Alexis were named *Anteia*. Third, "Anteia" is the form given by Anaxandrides (fr. 9). The manuscripts of the speech *Against Neaira* (D. 59.18) do not help as we have a split tradition. She was a contemporary of Lais and Lagiska, and flourished around the turn of the 4ᵗʰ century. According to Apollodoros she was one of the seven girls owned by the notorious pimp Nikarete and gave up prostitution while still at her prime (Lys. fr. 208 Carey), liberated by an infatuated lover (D. 59.18). See also Breitenbach 1908: 119–127; Kapparis 1999: 208–9.

Antigona of Pella: (4ᵗʰ c.). One of the prostitutes in the army of Alexander. She had been captured by the Persians at sea, and then taken by the Macedonians when they took Damascus. She caught the eye of Philotas, the son of Parmenion, and for a while she was asked to spy on Philotas on behalf of Alexander (Plu. 339 D-F).

Antigona, the libertine: (4ᵗʰ c.). Our main source for her activities is the speech of Hypereides *Against Athenogenes*. A hetaira at her prime, she turned pimp when she became older, and is presented as the partner of Athenogenes in the deception of a man probably named Epikrates (Hyp. *Athen.* 11). She is portrayed as a ruthless woman responsible while at her prime for the ruin of an unknown man from the deme of Cholleidai, and certainly the source of much distress for Epikrates.

Antikleia: Fictional hetaira with big eyes and a great smile in an epigram of Meleagros (*AG* 5.198), owner of a beautiful hand-fan in an epigram of Antipatros (*AG* 6.206). In an epigram of Archias closely related to that of Antipatros she is blond (*AG* 6.207).

Antikyra, aka Oia (or Nais, s.v.): (Later 4ᵗʰ c.). A contemporary of Lamia and one of the lovers of Demetrios, according to Plutarch (*Dem.* 24). She is also mentioned in a fragment of Menander (fr. 4), and possibly in an obscure reference in Diphilos (fr. 125). Aristophanes Byzantios in his work *On the Athenian Hetairai* mentions that her proper name was Oia, and that Antikyra was a nickname (Ar.Byz. fr. 5.2.2. Nauck; Athen. 13.51). Harpocration offers competing interpretations as to why she was called by that name, both related to the town of Antikyra (on the Corinthian gulf, at the coast of Phocis). The town was famous for its production of hellebore, which was used to treat mental illness. Thus, according to one interpretation she was nicknamed Antikyra because she associated with mentally disturbed and crazy men. The alternative interpretation was that one of her lovers, the physician Nikostratos, left her in his will a large quantity of hellebore, but nothing else (Harp. s.v. Athen. 13.51; Ar.Byz. fr. 5.2.2. Nauck). The note of Athenaios (13.51) identifying her with the hetaira Nais (see note s.v) must be a mistake. While Antikyra clearly is a contemporary of Demetrios (c. 350–280) and Menander, and lived in the later part of the 4th century, Nais, who is mentioned by Lysias and Aristophanes, certainly lived at the beginning of the 4th c. (see n. Nais for the relevant sources). The only way to reconcile the evidence is to accept that Athenaios was mistaken, and that the two women lived half a century apart.

Antiphila: (Possibly 4th c.). She is mentioned in a passage of Sextus Turpilius (*Palliatae* 188), along with several other Attic hetairai like Thais, Erótium (Erotion), Lais and Pythias.

Aphyai "sardines": Two sisters, **Anthis** and **Stagonion** were nicknamed Aphyai (sardines), because they were skinny and pale with big eyes (Athen. 13.50 = Apollod. *FGrH* 244 F 210). Athenaios, quoting Antiphanes *On Hetairai*, mentions that another hetaira named **Nikostratis** was also nick-named *Aphye* for the same reason.

Aphye: see n. Nikostratis.

Apopharsis: Mentioned by Hegesandros of Delphi (fr. 29a), according to a note in Hesychios (s.v.).

Archias: (Early 4th century). Pimp and *kyrios* of the hetaira Nais, who probably brought the lawsuit against Philonides for violence (*dike biaion*: Lysias fr. 140 Carey, Harp. s.v. *Nais*, Athen. 13.51).

Archeanassa of Colophon: (Early 4th c.). According to a later and probably fabricated story (Athen. 13.56; cf. D.L. 3.31) she was the lover of Plato. The story appears to have been generated from an epigram of Asclepiades (*AG.* 7.217), where it is said that Archeanassa in her youth set many men on fire, and she looked lovely even in her old age. There is no specific reference to Plato in this epigram, but Athenaios and Diogenes Laertios understood that in it there was some connection to the philosopher, which eludes us.

Archidike, of Naukratis: (6ᵗʰ c.). Herodotos (2.135) reports that she was a junior of Rhodopis, and although famous in her own right, not quite so much of a household name as her illustrious predecessor.

Archippe: (End of 5ᵗʰ c.). Lover of Sophocles before his death, according to Hegesandros (fr. 27 Müller = Athen. 13.61). When her former lover Smicrines was asked how Archippe was doing he replied "she is sitting on the grave like owls do".

Argeia: Psaltery-player, whose statue was made by Herodotos of Olynthos (Tat. *Orat.* 33.4).

Aristagora, of Corinth: (4ᵗʰ c.). According to Hermippos (fr. 68a1 Wehrli = Athen. 13.58) she was a lover and concubine of Hypereides established in his house in Piraeus. It appears as if the love-affair, which may have produced off-spring, turned sour, and Hypereides prosecuted Aristagora for an immigration-related technicality, namely for not having a sponsor (Hyp. fr. 13–26 Jensen). There is some evidence to suggest that she was acquitted, but then her embittered former lover reopened the case under the process of *doroxenia*, namely by alleging that Aristagora had been acquitted in the first trial because she bribed some members of the jury. Most of the quotes in the grammarians and lexicographers appear to be from the speech delivered in that second trial, and it seems that her past as a prostitute was brought up quite a lot, in an effort to discredit her.

Aristagora, of Corinth: (3ʳᵈ / 2ⁿᵈ c.). Lover of Demetrios, the thesmothetes, a descendant of Demetrios Phalereus. He erected for her sake a scaffold higher than the pillars of Hermes during the Panathenaic festival, and a throne near the Anaktoron in Eleusis, challenging anyone who would dare to try and stop him (Hegesandros fr. 8 Müller = Athen. 4.64).

Aristion, son of Aristoboulos the Pharmacist, of Plataia: (4ᵗʰ c). A youth of exceptionally good looks, with whom Demosthenes had a long-term relation-ship, and had him living in his house. Aeschines alleges that Demosthenes used him to get close to Alexander, who was unaware of the boy's unsavory past, in order to convey secret pleas of reconciliation (Aesch. 3.162). Diyllos (*FGrH* 73 F 2) repeats the story, but citing evidence from the speech of Hypereides *Against Demosthenes* he suggests that alternatively Aristion may have been from Samos, not Plataia (which would also make him an Athenian citizen), and that he was sent not to Alexander but to Hephaistion. Although neither source clearly states that the youth was a prostitute, it is unmistakably implied by Aeschines with his customary fake modesty.

Aristion: Female dancer appearing in an epigram of Thyillos (1st c.). mourning her death (*AG* 7.223).

Aristokleia: (early 4th c.). She is mentioned in a fragment of Lysias among women who gave up prostitution while still at their prime, probably to become concubines (Lys. fr. 208 Carey = Athen. 13.62). Apollodoros (D. 59.19) confirms this information. He mentions that Aristokleia was one of the seven girls whom Nikarete of Elis bought, brought up and educated to become prominent hetairai, and states that all the girls were eventually sold to infatuated lovers, who set them free.

Aristomache: (late 5th – early 4th c.). It appears that she was a prostitute based in the area of Marathon (Ar. *Th.* 806, and Sch. Ar. *Th.* 806: πόρνης ὄνομα).

Aristonika: Mentioned by Plutarch as one of the flute-players or dancers from Samos who gained favor as mistresses of Hellenistic monarchs (Plu. 753 D).

Arsinoe: Fictional flute-player, lover of Knemon in the *Aithiopika* of Heliodoros (1.15.5–7).

Aspasia of Megara (False): Herakleides (fr. 59 Wehrli), with some confusion generated from the famous Aristophanic passage from the *Acharnians* (524–529) about Aspasia and the Megarian decree (see below), reached the conclusion that a hetaira named Aspasia from Megara was the lover of Pericles. This is inaccurate and the woman he had in mind is Aspasia of Miletos the concubine of Pericles.

Aspasia of Miletos: (middle 5th c.). The concubine of Pericles, and mother of his son Pericles the younger. Since she was born in Miletos, she could not be the lawful wife of Pericles, and their son could not be legitimate after 451, when a law introduced by Pericles himself required Athenian parentage from both sides as a precondition for citizenship. However, their relationship was a life-long commitment, often admired and just as often reviled in the sources (see e.g. Kratinos fr. 259; Ar. *Ach.* 523–40; Antisthenes, fr. 35 Caizzi; Duris *FGrH* 76 F65). Several contemporary sources (e.g. Kratinos fr. 259; Ar. *Ach.* 523–40; Aeschin. Socr. fr. 26 Dittmar; Heraclid. Pont. fr. 59 Wehrli), and a number of later sources (e.g. Lucian *Gallus* 19–20; *De Saltatione* 25) attest that she was a hetaira before she became the partner of the most powerful man in Athens, and Aristophanes suggests that she maintained a brothel while living with Pericles. The reliability of this information has been questioned in recent scholarship, and it is possible that it amounts to nothing more than malicious gossip and biting jokes directed against a powerful woman and a remarkable intellectual, whose only transgression was to be a prominent woman of letters (see e.g. the composition of an *Epitaphios* attributed to her in Pl. *Mx.* 235 e -249 e and the modern scholarship in Heitsch 2009: 229–236; Trivigno, 2009: 29–58, Bell 1994; Glenn 1997: 19–41, and also Aeschin. Socr. *Aspasia*, fr. 15–33 Dittmar; Ehlers 1966). However, it may be unwise to dismiss out of hand the testimony of so many contemporary sources that she had been a sex worker, at least for some part of her life, especially since she is mentioned by name, even in friendly sources, which is not customary for respectable women, Athenian or metic, and the expressions of her public persona are not dissimilar to those of other prominent hetairai of the classical and early Hellenistic Periods, like Phryne, Nikarete of Megara or Danae the Epicurean. While in the case of Aspasia it is very difficult to separate fact from fiction, the patterns of her life resemble those of prominent hetairai in the ancient world starting life as sex-workers, but achieving personal power, reputation, wealth, education, intellect, and a degree of independence from established social norms that would typically be beyond the reach of respectable women. It may be fair to say that the ambiguity in our sources, where one cannot see the line between the agent provocateur and the wise advisor, or the hell-raiser and the intellectual, is responsible for the popularity of this remarkable woman and generated a personal mythology around her which has endured through the centuries. (For further information see the excellent monograph of Henry 1995, Loraux 1993: 123–154 and Reinsberg 1989: 80–5).

Aspasia, aka Milto of Phocaea: (late 5th – early 4th c.). She is probably the same person with "Aspasia the Younger" in Athenaios (13.56). Athenaios (citing Zenophanes) says that she was a hetaira from Phocaea named Milto, but when she became the lover of Cyrus he renamed her Aspasia. Athenaios adds that she was a woman of exceptional beauty and wisdom (13.37). Plutarch agrees about these attributes, but further to the point establishes a deliberate link between this woman and the famous Aspasia, saying that this one was renamed Aspasia after her renowned and glorious (ὀνομαστὴ καὶ κλεινή) predecessor. In Plutarch's version she was not a hetaira but the favorite concubine of Cyrus (Plu. *Per.* 24.11–12). Plutarch adds that her father's name was Hermotimos, and after the death of Cyrus she was taken to the court of Artaxerxes II, where eventually she acquired great power.

Astaphium "dried grapes": Maid and protégé of the ruthless hetaira Phronesium in Plautus *Truculentus*.

Astra "star": According to Athenaios (13.46), she is one of the hetairai missed by Aristophanes Byzantios, Apollodoros and Gorgias in their collections of the Attic hetairai.

Atherine "smelt": Flute-player, possibly fictional, mentioned in the comedy of Archippos *Fish* (fr. 27), evidently because of the significance of her nickname.

Atthis: Fictional hetaira mentioned in an epigram falsely attributed to Lucian (Ps.Luc. *Epigr.* 6.17), specializing in oral sex.

Bacchis, the Flute-Player: (4th century). According to Theopompos (*FGrH* 115 F 253), she had been a slave of the famous hetaira Sinope, and in turn she became the owner of Pythionike, the mistress of Harpalos. According to the historian Menetor (Athen. 13.66), she was exquisitely attractive, but also good-natured and free of jealousy. When a youth from Kolophon, a regular lover of Bacchis, was asked by Plangon of Miletos to bring the famous necklace of Bacchis as payment for her services, Bacchis agreed to the pleas of the youth and offered her necklace. Plangon moved by her selflessness returned it, accepted the advances of the youth, and shared him with Bacchis. There is a possibility that a play of Epigenes (4th c.). was named after her (see Athen. 11.99 and Breitenbach 1908: 169–170). Athenaios also mentions a parody by Sopatros of Phakos entitled *Bacchis* (4.48 and 78); elsewhere Athenaios gives this play the title *The Suitors of Bacchis* (4.50 and 14.51) or *The Wedding of Bacchis* (14.74). A brief fragment of the play allows us to understand that in the plot several men are travelling to Athens to meet Bacchis. A fictional Bacchis apparently based upon the 4th century hetaira features heavily in the letters of Alciphron. There is one letter addressed to her by Glycera, concerning Menander (4.2), one by Bacchis to Hypereides congratulating him for his victory in the defense of Phryne (4.3), one to Phryne herself (4.4), one to Myrinne scolding her for her indiscretion to take as a lover Euthias, the prosecutor of Phryne, (4.5), and one addressed to Bacchis by the wicked hetaira Megara scolding her for genuinely loving her *erastes*. Finally there is a letter by her heartbroken *erastes* Menekleides mourning her death and extolling her virtues to high heavens. Bacchis is presented as the rare exception of the good-natured, kind, faithful and well-intentioned hetaira, and this is her reputation and stereotypical portrayal in the fictional literature of later antiquity. Very likely this tradition is drawing from classical sources, maybe the lost play of Sopatros, which seemingly was quite popular. O. Knorr (1995: 221–235) examining the character of Bacchis, as presented in Terence *Heautontimorumenos* concludes that she has all the features of a good hetaira, as these are described in Plutarch's *Quaestiones Convivales* (712 C). Without a doubt the Terentian portrait draws from the same tradition where Bacchis is consistently portrayed as the stereotypical *chreste hetaira* reciprocating the love of her admirers (Plu. 712 C 8–9: χρησταῖς καὶ ἀντερώσαις). Since Terence's Bacchis in both the *Hecyra* and the *Heautontimorumenos* is modelled on Greek originals, it is not surprising that her character bears some of the marks of this tradition.

Bacchis, of Samos: Fictional charater in Plautus *Bacchides* (the two Bacchis), with whom the Athenian youth Mnesilochus is in love. The play was based upon Menander's *The Double Deceiver*.

Bacchis, of Athens: Fictional charater in Plautus *Bacchides* (the two Bacchis), with whom the Athenian youth Pistoclerus is in love.

Ballio: Fictional brothel-keeper, pimp of Phoenicium, in Plautus *Pseudolus*.

Barathron "pit": (4th c.). She is mentioned in a fragment of the comic Theophilos (fr. 11) among women whom pimps dress up in linen, in order to charge lovers a lot more than their worth.

Batrachos "frog": Possibly fictional pimp mentioned in Plutarch *How the Young Must Listen to Poetry* (18 C) and presented as an easily recognizable but distasteful literary figure. This is why there is a good possibility that Batrachos is a textual corruption and that the correct reading at this point is Battaros, referring the notoriously infamous pimp in Herodas 2.

Battaros, the son of Sisymbrides, son of Sisymbras: Fictional pimp in Herodas *Mimiambi* 2.

Bilistiche, of Argos: (3rd c.). Noble-born hetaira who supposedly derived her origins from the Atreidai, mistress of Ptolemy II Philadelphos (Ptolemy *FGrH* 234 F 4 = Athen. 13.37).

Bitinna: Fictional hetaira wearing beautiful sandals in an epigram of Antipatros (*AG* 6.206), and one of Archias (*AG* 6.207).

Bromias "the follower of Bromius": Flute-player, 4th c. According to Theopompos (*FGrH* 115 F 24 = Athen. 13.83) Phayllos, the brother of the Phocian leader Onomarchos, gave her out of the treasures of the Delphic oracle a golden cup, which had been dedicated by the Phocians, and a golden ivy-wreath dedicated by the citizens of Peparethos. No doubt thanks to the influence of her powerful patron she was to play the flute at the Pythian games, but the audience found it distasteful, reacted badly and put a stop to it.

Boa, the Paphlagonian: (4th c.). Flute player, mother of Philaiteros of Pergamon, according to the historian Karystios (fr. 12 Müller = Athen. 13.38).

Boïdion: Athenian hetaira, mistress of the general Chares. She followed him on his campaign at the Bosporus area, got sick and died there. In her memory Chares erected a monument, a cow on a white-stone pillar, in Chalcedon (see Ch. 6.1.). The monument had survived well into the Macedonian era and is described by the geographer Dionysios of Byzantium (110), the Byzantine chronicler Hesychios of Miletos, Illustrius (30), Emperor Constantine VII Porphyrogennetus (*De Thematibus* Europ. 12), and inaccurately by Arrian (*Bithynicorum* fr. 36). The Athenian Boïdion may well be the inspiration for the Boïdion mentioned in an epigram of Hedylos (3rd c.)., along with Euphro and Thais, as one of the there ageing prostitutes under the authority of the pimp Diomedes (*AG* 5.161).

Boïdion: Fictional flute-player mentioned in an epigram of the *Greek Anthology* wrongly attributed to Simonides (*AG* 5.159) together with a woman called Pythias. Both women are presented as high-class prostitutes exploiting wealthy lovers.

Boïdion, the Epicurean: (Late 4th – early 3rd c.). Some sources consider her, along with the other women in the Gardens of Epicurus, to be hetairai, but this is not certain. Although sexual morality in the Gardens was different from the outside world, it is difficult to believe that all the women frequenting the place were paid sex workers, especially since some of them were genuine students of the great philosopher, and others, like Themista, were married (see Poseidonios fr. 290a. 495–506; Plu. 1089 C, 1097 D; D.L. 10.7.and the discussion in Ch. 3.3.).

Chares: A beautiful male prostitute whose name appears in an inscription from Thorikos dated between 400 and 350 with the comment that he is a male prostitute and very attractive (*SEG* 34:192, Χάρης πόρνος καλός).

Chariklo: Fictional hetaira in two epigrams of Paul Silentiarius (*AG* 5.259 and 5.288), possibly inspired by the mythological figure responsible for the blindness of Teiresias (e.g. Apollod. *Bibl.* 3.69–70).

Charito: Fictional hetaira in an epigram of Philodemos (*AG* 5.13) maintaining her shining beauty even in her sixties.

Charixene: (5th c.). Flute player, composer of tunes for wind instruments, and poet, writer of erotic songs. Some Byzantine sources speak of her artistic skills quite respectfully. Eustathios (*Com. Il.* 1.590), for example, includes her in a list of women poets and composers highly praised for their ability, like Sappho, Erinna and Praxilla (cf. also *EM* and Hsch. s.v. ἐπὶ Χαριξένης). However, much of the press she had was negative. She is often reviled for stupidity and naivety (εὐήθης καὶ μωρά: Sch. Ar. Ec. 943; Sud. χ 116), while "at Charixene's" was a proverbial expression for stupidity (*epi Charixenes*: Hsch. s.v. and *Appendix Proverbiorum* 2.82), and she was on the receiving end of jokes by comic poets (Cratin. fr. 153; Ar. *Ec.* 943; Theopompos fr. 51). Suda calls her a hetaira, but probably she was more of a flute-player, composer and entertainer, and in the expression "at Charixene's", we may be able to read an establishment, some kind of tavern or house which offered the clientele entertainment and venal sex.

Chelidonis "swallow": According to Cicero, she was an influential hetaira, lover of governor Verres (Cic. *Ver.* 2.5.34).

Chelidonion "little swallow": Fictional hetaira in Lucian's *Dialogues of Hetairai* (*DMeretr.* 10).

Chelidonion: A fictional transgender individual, probably a prostitute, who annoys a stern Stoic philosopher by sitting next to him (*Merc.Cond.* 33).

Chelidonion: Fictional hetaira in love with Philonides in Aristainetos (2.13).

Chimaira "chimera": According to Athenaios (13.46), she is one of the hetairai missed by Aristophanes Byzantios, Apollodoros and Gorgias in their collections of the Attic hetairai.

Choregis: (late 5th – early 4th c.). Lover and concubine of Aristophon of Azenia, the politician. Karystios (fr. 11 Müller) mentions that they had a son together, who was rendered illegitimate when Aristophon revived the Periclean law on citizenship in 403. However, the decree of Aristophon, which re-established Athenian parentage from both sides as a requirement for citizenship, explicitly covered only those born after the archonship of Eucleides, but did not interfere with those born before that date (D. 57.32). This means that a child of Aristophon and Choregis already born when the decree was introduced would not be affected, and this tale is probably a rehashing of an older literary theme where Pericles rendered his own son from Aspasia illegitimate when he introduced his citizenship law in 451. There is also a play of Alexis entitled *Choregis* (Athen. 7.28). It would be reasonable to suggest that it was a comic attack on the concubine of Aristophon, as Aspasia was reviled on the comic stage at the height of the power of Pericles (see note and Ch. 3.1.). The strong woman at the side of the leading man was seen as a legitimate target for some comic slander and vilification, in the typically Athenian spirit of cutting down to size powerful figures.

Chrysogone "Gold-bearer": Fictional flute-player in Theophylaktos (Ep. 12.2).

Chrysomallo "Goldilocks": (6th c. AD). Dancer, then turned hetaira, friend and court-attendant of Theodora the Empress. Marriage with her unchaste daughter was forced upon a nobleman named Satorninos (Procop. *Anecd.* 17.33–37; cf. Sud. χ 577).

Chrysis "Golden": (4th c.). She is mentioned as an old woman in a passage from the *Kerkopes* of Timokles (fr. 27), probably with a degree of exaggeration, and also a fragment from Menander's *Colax* (fr. 5) among several other Attic hetairai of the time, like Antikyra and Korone. A play of Antiphanes entitled *Chrysis* (fr. 223–4), the surviving fragments of which make reference to flute-players, rich foreign lovers and a lifestyle of luxury, probably was based on her. The fictional mistress of Demeas and main character in Menander's *Samia* may also have been based on the real-life Chrysis. The Menandrian Chrysis clearly provided the inspiration for Lucian's Chrysis in his work *Philopseudes* "the lover of lies" (14–15). Chrysis is also a character in Terence *Andria*.

Cleareta: Fictional procuress owner of Philaenium in Plautus *Asinaria*.

Cluvia Facula: (Late 3rd c.). Campanian hetaira who lived around the time of the second Punic war (Val. Max. 5.2.1).

Cyrene: see s.v. Dodekamechanos.

Damasandra "The one who tames men": (late 5th c.). She was the mother of Lais the Younger (Athen. 13.34), and one of two hetairai who constantly accompanied Alcibiades down to the time of his death (cf. Ch. 3.1.).

Danae, Daughter of Leontion, the Epicurean: (c. 300 -240). We do not have any information about her life, but her death is described in some detail by Phylarchos (*FGrH* 81 F 24). In her final days we find her in a position of power in the Seleucid court of Antiochus II, Theos, no longer a hetaira but the trusted confidante of Laodice and privy to important information which allowed her to save the life of Sophron, a former lover. Danae was thrown off a cliff at the orders of Laodice, as soon as she discovered that her confidante had betrayed her plans. Before her death Danae exclaimed 'no wonder that most people treat the gods contemptuously; this is my reward from god for saving my own man, while Laodice who killed hers is enjoying such honors" (a reference to the widespread rumor that Laodice had poisoned her husband).

Daphnis: Fictional character in one of the letters of Aristainetos, portraying the tough and savage hetaira (1.17).

Dardanis "Trojan": (5th c.). Flute-player mentioned in Aristophanes *Wasps* (1373; cf. Sch. Ar. *V.* 1373a). In the plot Philokleon steals her from his symposiasts; the character may be based on a real, well-known flute player from the region of Troy.

Delphis "Delphic" (gen. Delphidos): Fictional hetaira mentioned in Lucian's *Dialogues of Hetairai* as a cheaper alternative to Myrtale, the former mistress of Dorion (*DMeretr.* 14.4).

Delphis: Fictional hetaira, lover of Habrakomes in Aristainetos (2.21), praised by her lover for her natural charms.

Demarion: Fictional hetaira in an epigram of Meleager praised for her perfumed doorstep (*AG* 5.198).

Demo "of the people": (late 4rd- early 3rd c). Prominent hetaira, perhaps aptly named after the mythological daughter of King Keleos (*h. Cer.* 109); her name has connotations of openness and accessibility. There is some confusion in the sources as to whether she should be identified with Mania, the witty mistress of Demetrios Poliorketes. According to Athenaios (13.40), Ptolemy, the son of Agesarchos, considers her separate from Mania, and reports that Demo was the mistress of Antigonos the father of Demetrios, while Mania was the mistress of Demetrios. On the other hand, Plutarch (*Dem.* 27.1) considers her to be the same person as Mania, and disapprovingly adds that she resided on the Acropolis, along with the other mistresses of Demetrios, when the Athenians slavishly offered him "hospitality" in the temple of Athena (*Dem.* 24.1). Herakleides Lembos (fr. 4 Müller) attests that she was the mistress of Demetrios Poliorketes, and that his father Antigonos in a rage had a man named Oxythemis, a friend of Demetrios, put to death because Oxythemis had tortured to death some servant girls of Demo. It is noteworthy that if we accept the version of Ptolemy, that Demo was the mistress of Antigonos, and a different person from Mania, the mistress of his son, then this story of Herakleides makes better sense. See also n. Mania.

Demo "of the people" (fictional): The connotations of the name, and maybe the popularity of the historical Demo provided the inspiration for several fictional characters featured in the epigrams of the *Greek Anthology* (*AG* 5.115, 160, 172, 173, 197, 244; 6.174; 7.711; 12.173).

Dexithea: (4th c.). Friend and contemporary of Gnathaina (Machon 16.295–299 = Athen. 13.43), perhaps the same woman as Dexithea of Phlious, who allegedly had been a student of Plato (Anonymus *De Philosophia Platonica* 4).

Didyme "twin": (3rd c.). She was a lover of Ptolemy II Philadelphos, a local African woman of fabulous beauty (Ptolemy VIII Euergetes *FGrH* 234 F 4 = Athen. 13.37). A fictional black hetaira named Didyme in the *Greek Anthology* (*AG* 5.210) may be drawing inspiration from the historical Didyme of Egypt.

Diokleia: A very skinny fictional hetaira (*AG* 5.102).

Diomedes: A possibly fictional pimp in charge of three ageing hetairai, Boïdion, Euphro and Thais, in an epigram of Hedylos or Asclepiades (*AG* 5.161). It is difficult to tell whether the epigram referred to a real person. At least two of the women mentioned have the same names as well-known real hetairai, which may imply that the epigram was based upon real people.

Diophantos, the orphan: Well-known citizen prostitute, who in an episode narrated by Aeschines (1.158) took a foreigner to the magistrate (archon) for failing to pay him the agreed fee of 4 drachmas, seemingly for a single encounter. The fact that Diophantos asked the assistance of the *archon*, who was responsible for the well-being of widows and orphans around the city, suggests that he was still under 18, and not yet legally independent. The fact that Diophantos seemingly had no family to look after him may explain why he had taken up prostitution at such a young age. Aeschines speaks disdainfully about the entire episode, and we may infer from his tone that Diophantos was "cheap", in a literal and metaphorical sense.

Diopeithes: (4th c.). Probably the procurer of Telesis; the wording of Philaiteros (fr. 9) is unclear, and he could be her father.

Dodekamechanos "twelve positions", **aka Kyrene:** (late 5th c.). This was a nickname given to the hetaira Kyrene because she allegedly had intercourse in twelve different positions (Ar. *Ra.* 1327–8; Hsch. κ 4670; Phot. δ 868; Sud. δ 1442; Sch. Ar. Ra. 1328). The information of Suda (ε 3266) that she was Corinthian cannot be trusted, as in the same sentence it is said that Rhodopis (s.v.) was also Corinthian from Thrace (sic). Sch. Ar. Plu. 149 includes her in a list of Corinthian hetairai. Eustathios (*Com. Il.* 2.326) attests that she is mentioned in comedy, and Michael Apostolios (*Paroem.* 6.41) understood the expression "Kyrene Dodekamechanos" as proverbial for those who loved variety in their "customs" (ἔθεσιν).

Dordalus: Fictional pimp in Plautus *Persa*.
Doricha (Rodopis): Herodotos disputes a story which linked her to the building of the pyramids, aware of the great antiquity of these monuments (Hdt. 2.134–135). He reports that she flourished during the reign of Amasis (570 - 526 BC). Originally a slave from Thrace, she was brought to Egypt by Xanthos of Samos, and set free for a lot of money by Charaxos of Mytilene, the brother of Sappho. Upset by this, Sappho attacked her with caustic verses. Rodopis erected a monument in Delphi with part of her proceeds as a hetaira. This story is repeated by

Athenaios (13.69). Lidov (2002: 203–237), Kurke (1997: 106–150), and Henry (2011: 14–33) question the actual involvement of Sappho. Rodopis is accredited with the start of high-class prostitution in the Naukratis of Egypt, and was followed by another famous hetaira, a native of Naukratis called Archidike. For more detailed discussion see Ch. 1.1. and 6.1.

Dorio: Fictional procurer in Terence *Phormio*.

Doris "Dorian": Fictional hetaira featured in epigrams of Dioscorides (*AG* 5.55) and Paul Silentarios (*AG* 5.230).

Dorothea: Fictional hetaira in an epigram of Meleager praised for the garlands at her doorstep (*AG* 5.198).

Drosis "dew" or "refreshment": Fictional hetaira, lover of the young Kleinias, in Luc. *DMeretr.* 10.

Eirene: (3rd c.). Lover of Ptolemy, son of Ptolemy II Philadelphus. She followed Ptolemy to the temple of Artemis, where he took refuge, when he was pursued by his father's troops, and she was killed there along with him (Athen. 13.64).

Eirenis: (4th c.). She was the lover of Leocrates and, according to Lycurgus, accompanied him when he sailed away from Athens after the battle of Chaironea (Lycurg. *Leoc.* 17).

Epicharis "graceful": According to Polyainos (8.62.1), she was a hetaira belonging to Melas, a brother of Seneca. She was aware of a conspiracy against Nero by Piso and Seneca, but refused to reveal anything when she was tortured for information, and hanged herself in order to avoid betraying them under more torture. The story as told by Tacitus (*Ann.* 15.51–57) is more detailed, although not significantly different in the main points. He mentions that Epicharis was a libertine and dryly comments that she was a woman who never cared about anything worthwhile before (*neque illi ante ulla rerum honestarum cura fuerat*), but goes on to contrast her brave and determined stand against Nero with the lame attempts of the men who were supposed to lead the Pisonian conspiracy.

Eriphyle of Argos (False): Clement of Alexandria calls the mythical Eriphyle of Argos a hetaira because of her fabulous love of jewelry, which he considers irreconcilable with the values of Christianity (Clem. *Paed.* 109.4; for the myth of Eriphyle see Hom. *Od.* 11.326; Pl. *R.* 590 a, al.).

Erotion, the Epicurean: (Late 4th – early 3rd c.). One of the hetairai who frequented the Gardens of Epicurus, maintained sexual relations with Epicurus and Metrodoros and studied philosophy (Epicurus Ep. 101 = D.L. 10.7). Erotium is also the name of a fictional hetaira in Plautus *Menaechmi.*

Euardis, the Fat: (Late 4th – early 3rd c). According to Machon (18.457 = Athen. 13.45) she was a contemporary of Niko "the Goat", whom we can firmly place in the reign of Ptolemy II, Philadelphos. The two women were rivals, competing for the affections of a man named Python. Gow (1965: 136) treats the form of the name with suspicion because "it is not plain what it should mean", and would prefer the form Eualdis ("well-grown"). However, an individual's name need not signify a quality which this person acquired in adulthood.

Euboule: (late 5th – early 4th century). The scholiast of Aristophanes (Sch. Ar. Th. 808) was not sure who she was but she appears side by side with several well-known prostitutes of the time, which probably suggests that she was a prostitute too.

Eueteris: Fictional psaltery-player in Herodas (7.99–104). The shoemaker Kerdon claims that she visits his shop every day trying to buy some shoes for five staters, but he won't sell for less than four darics, because she once insulted his wife.

Eukleia: According to Athenaios (13.46), she is one of the hetairai missed by Aristophanes Byzantios, Apollodoros and Gorgias in their collections of the Attic hetairai.

Euphro: Fictional hetaira mentioned in an epigram falsely attributed to Lucian (Ps.Luc. *Epigr.* 6.17), specializing in anal sex. There is a chance that the character in this epigram is based upon the hetaira Euphro, who is mentioned along with Thais and Boïdion in an epigram of Hedylos (3rd c.). as one of the ageing prostitutes under the authority of the pimp Diomedes, and may have been a real person, like Thais and Boïdion, both 4th c. Athenian hetairai (*AG* 5.161).

Euphronion: Fictional flute-player in Aristainetos (1.19).

Euphrosyne: She was the daughter of a fuller. According to Athenaios (13.46), she is one of the hetairai missed by Aristophanes Byzantios, but included by Apollodoros and Gorgias in their collections of the Attic hetairai.

Europe of Attica: A fictional, cheap prostitute who always charged one drachma for a night, a clean bed and a warm room (*AG* 5.109).

Eurynome: An epigram from the collection of Agathias (6th c. AD) extols the skills of a hetaira named Eurynome in taming men, like a Bacchant taming a bull (*AG* 6.74). Without a doubt the epigram draws inspiration from a myth, first appearing in our sources in John Malalas (*Chronographia* 39–40), a senior contemporary of Agathias. According to this myth, Eurynome was one of six daughters of Kadmos. The Suda (β 141) was also aware of this epigram and uses it as evidence to interpret the term "bassaris" as "hetaira, porne".

Euxippe: Fictional hetaira in Alciphron (4.6), rival of Thais for the love of the young Pamphilos.

Flora, of the Osci: (1st c.). Italian hetaira of exceptional beauty born in the first quarter of the 1st c. BC. She was the lover of Pompey, and like other hetairai of Roman statesmen, she is reported to have been deeply in love with him, while he was fully in control of the entire relationship. Plutarch, our main source, reports that Geminius, one of Pompey's trusted men, desired her, but she refused his advances because she loved Pompey. Then Geminius secured permission from Pompey to have sex with her, but Pompey never touched Flora again. Plutarch says that she did not react like the typical hetaira, but took it to heart, fell ill from her sadness and continued to speak fondly of Pompey in her old age (Plu. *Pomp.* 2). An epigram of Philodemos, one of her contemporaries, immortalizes her outlandish beauty, referring to every part of her body, her movement and voice, and is pleading with the reader to excuse her barbaric origin and inability to sing Sappho, on the grounds that even Perseus fell in love with the Indian Andromeda (*AG* 5.132; cf. Sider 1997 ad loc.; and Ch. 3.1.).

Galateia: (4th c.?; probably not a real person). According to Phainias (fr. 13 Wehrli = Athen. 1.11), she was a flute-player, and lover of Dionysios of Syracuse. When the poet Philoxenos of Kythera, a guest of Dionysios, seduced her the Tyrant cast him into the infamous quarries of Syracuse. There Philoxenos composed a poem entitled *Cyclops*, where he parodied Dionysios presenting him as the one-eyed Cyclops in love with the Nereid Galateia. A few fragments from the poem still survive (fr. 1–20 Page). The poem and the myth of Cyclops and Galateia were very popular in subsequent centuries (see e.g. Timaios *FGrH* 566 F 69; Moschos *Epitaphius Bionis*, where the theme is running through the poem; Luc. *DMar.* 1, a parody of the theme, al.). A fictional hetaira with this name, who kissed very softly, is probably modeled on this favorite tale of the "beauty and the beast" (*AG* 5.244). Duris gives a different version of the story, saying that Philoxenos invented the myth because he could not understand why there was a sanctuary of the sea-goddess Galateia on mount Aetna (*FGrH* 76 F 58). In his version there is no real person named Galateia, which should confirm our suspicions that the story of Phainias about a mistress of Dionysios named Galateia is nothing more than a tale built around the genesis of Philoxenos' masterpiece.

Galene "calm": A brief note in the Lexicon of Photios (γ 20) says that there was a hetaira named Galene, mentioned by Theopompos.

Galla "Gaul": Fictional ageing prostitute in Martial (10.75).

Glykera "sweetie", **of Thespiae, daughter of Thalassis, aka Glykera of Attica,** or affectionately **Glykerion:** (Later 4th c.). Athenaios (13.50) expresses some doubt whether Glykera, the daughter of Thalassis (s.v.), from Thespiai, mentioned by Hypereides (fr. 28 Blass) is the same woman as Glykera of Attica, who lived with Harpalos. While it is possible that they are two different women, one perhaps slightly older than the other, it is not inevitable as many Thespians were living in Athens in the 4th century, after the subjugation of their city by Thebes in 373, and like Phryne, another famous Thespian, Glykera could be of Thespian origin but born and brought up in Athens. Considering that only two later sources (D.S. 17.108; Constantine VII Porphyrogennetus *De virtutibus et vitiis* 1.247) explicitly state that Glykera was Athenian, it is likely that the two women are one and the same person. Her love-affair with Harpalos is well attested (Theopompos *FGrH* 115 F 254a = Athen. 13.50, 68; Python fr. 1. Snell; D.S. 17.108). Glykera became his mistress after the death of Pythionike. According to Theopompos, Harpalos demanded that she be honored at his side, erected a statue of her in Syria (perhaps the one made by Herodotos of Olynthos, according to Tatian, *Oratio ad Graecos* 33.4), and required that the people of Tarsus address her as queen, which caused some indignation. Moreover, she was believed to be the mistress of Menander in later antiquity (Athen. 13.66; Alciphr. 4.2, 14, 18, 19.). Alfred Körte (1919: 87–93) discusses in some detail the evidence on Glykera and concludes that Menander's Glykera and the one of Harpalos were the same person, but he is rightly skeptical about many of the reported details of the affair between the hetaira and the poet. Two more recent studies concur that this evidence is later and consequently weak, and if one considers the fact that Glykera is the main character of *Perikeiromene*, a favorite Menandrian play in later centuries, the possibility that the entire affair is a fabrication of later antiquity with no historical basis cannot be excluded (see the debate in Ch. 3.2.). Glykera was famous for her wit, and several jokes and humorous remarks are attributed to her in the sympotic literature of later antiquity (Machon 18.411 -21 = Athen. 13.45; Satyros fr. 23 Müller = Athen. 13.46; 13.49; Alciphr. 4.18 and 19). One of her most famous sayings, according to Klearchos (fr. 23 Wehrli = Athen. 13.84) was that boys are only attractive for as long as they look like women. The famous hetaira was probably the inspiration for the fictional Glykera (or Glykerion) in one of Lucian's *Dialogues* (*DMeretr.* 1), and a fictional person appearing several times in Horace (*Carmina* 1.19.5; 1.30.3; 1.33.2; 3.19.28). The Latinized form Glycerium is a fictional character in Terence *Andria*.

Gnathaina: (4th c.). According to Athenaios (13.46), she is one of the hetairai missed by Aristophanes Byzantios, Apollodoros and Gorgias in their collections of the Attic hetairai, which is curious as she was one of the best known hetairai of the 4th century, immortalized for her wit by Machon (14.212–217; 16.258– 17.401; 18.433–438), Lynkeus of Samos in his *Memorabilia* (apud Athen. 13.46, 47), Aristodemos in the second book of his *Memorabilia of Jokes* (fr. 9 Müller = Athen. 13.48) and Athenaios (9.33; 13.6, 22, 39, 41, 43, 46, 47, 48). Curiously, she seems to have slipped through the cracks in Schneider's list in *RE* too, where she is the only prominent hetaira without an entry, as Gow observed (1965: 7, n. 2). The first reference to her career is in Anaxilas (fr. 22), where she is presented as an old woman, and a similar joke about her being an old woman is reiterated by Timocles (fr. 27). Gow (1965: 7–11) finds these jokes perplexing as he places her floruit around 310, on account of her association with the poet Diphilos and her friendship with Mania, one of the mistresses of Demetrios Poliorcetes. However, a hetaira in her 30's could be considered an old woman in this line of work, thus when Gnathaina became the subject of jokes by Anaxilas and Timocles she was probably only that old. Then, she did not need to be very young when she had the famous affair with Diphilos; on the contrary, since this relationship seems to be long-term and rather more committed than a superficial affair with a hetaira, we need not assume that she was at her prime when she was the lover of Diphilos (more information about the affair can be found in Ch. 3.2.). Her friendship with Mania could have happened when Gnathaina was middle-aged or even old. Thus there is nothing in these associations which precludes a dating for her floruit closer to the middle of the 4th century and her birth before 350, which can reconcile all these sources. Additional support to this dating may be provided by an inscription dated to 340 or shortly after (*IG* ii/iii² 1517, face B, 180), where Gnathaina's name is mentioned. If she is the same person, this would support the dating of her birth to the 360's rather than later, but the evidence is insufficient to draw definite conclusions. Numerous jokes and witty responses attributed to Gnathaina in her dealings with lovers, merchants at the market place, women friends of hers, or clients of her daughter Gnathainion are preserved by several authors (see Appendix 3 for some of them). In her old age she became the procuress of her daughter Gnathainion. Athenaios reports that she had even composed a 323 lines long document of rules and bylaws for lovers about to be admitted to symposia with her and her daughter, in the model of similar documents composed by philosophers. Athenaios quotes the beginning of it: "This law was written equal and alike" (see Ch. 2.1.).

Gnathainion "little Gnathaina": (Later 4ᵗʰ c.). According to Athenaios (13.46), she was one of the hetairai missed by Aristophanes Byzantios, Apollodoros and Gorgias in their collections of the Attic hetairai. Her relationship with Gnathaina puzzled Gow (1965: 9), because Athenaios twice calls her the granddaughter (θυγατριδῆ) of Gnathaina (13.44, 46), but his sources Machon (17.350 = Athen.13.44, and 17.381 = Athen.13.44) and Aristodemos (fr. 9 Müller = Athen.13.48) consider Gnathainion to be her daughter. Of course, the sources are not of equal value; no doubt Athenaios is the one who is mistaken. The earliest source to mention a hetaira named Gnathainion is Euboulos in the *Pornoboskos* (fr. 88 = Athen. 9.13). Since it is unlikely that Gnathainion was ready to be procured before the last quarter of the 4ᵗʰ century, it would be a great stretch to extend the life and work of Euboulos so late into the 4ᵗʰ century, and for that reason it would be easier to assume that he is using the diminutive for Gnathaina herself, not her daughter, at a time when the daughter was either not born, or still too young, and there was no danger of confusion between the two women. Gnathainion had a long-term affair with the actor Andronikos, and a baby-boy from him (Machon 17. 349–375 = Athen. 13.44). When Andronikos was away, she had a short affair with a coppersmith for a lot of money, and apparently she had sex with him five times *a tergo* (probably anal intercourse). When Andronikos found out he was upset not because she took another lover in his absence, as this probably would not be untypical with hetairai, but because she had sex with the coppersmith in a position which she had always refused him. She replied that she studied the matter and concluded that this was the best position to achieve minimal contact with the body of the coppersmith. It seems that the love affair turned sour later on, because Andronikos was not paying (Machon 17.376–386 = Athen. 13.44). Gnathainion fetched the very high price of 500 drachmas for a single night from a 90–year-old, rich, foreign satrap, according to Machon (17.333–348 = Athen. 13.44). The deal was closed by Gnathaina, who had initially asked for 1000 drachmas, and was confident that the satrap will be happy to pay the difference once he goes to bed with her daughter. The specifics of the story have all the signs of an exaggerated anecdote, but the core of it, namely that Attic hetairai extracted exorbitant sums from rich old men, is certainly truthful.

Gnome "Opinion": (4th c.). Her association with the infamous parasite Korydos would place her in the second half of the 4th century (Athen. 6.47; Gow 1965: 59).

Gomer, the daughter of Diblaim, wife of Hosea: She was a prostitute whom Hosea was ordered by God to marry (*Ho.* 1). She bore him two sons, Jezreel and Lo-ammi, and a daughter Lo-ruhamah. The passage is pervaded by intense hatred towards the prostitute and her offspring.

Gorgona: Fictional hetaira appearing in Lucian. (*DMeretr.* 1)

Grymea: According to Athenaios (13.46), she is one of the hetairai missed by Aristophanes Byzantios, Apollodoros and Gorgias in their collections of the Attic hetairai.

Habrotonon "soft tune", **of Thrace:** (early 5th c.). The alleged mother of Themistokles. The story is probably a fabrication of later antiquity (See Ch. 3.1.).

Habrotonon: Psaltery-player, fictional character in Menander's *Epitrepontes*. Lucian's Habrotonon is probably based on the Menandrian character (*DMeretr.*1).

Harmonia: Euhemerus (apud Athen. 14.77) in his *Sacred History* reinterpreted the myth of Kadmos and Harmonia, saying that Kadmos was a cook of the king of Sidon and Harmonia was a flute-player of the king, and the two of them ran away together.

Hedeia "sweet", **the Epicurean:** (Late 4th – early 3rd c.). One of the attractive hetairai who frequented the Gardens of Epicurus, maintained sexual relations with Epicurus and Metrodoros and studied philosophy (Epicurus Ep. 101 = D.L.

10.7; Plu. 1089 C; 1097 D; 1129 B). She is one of the Epicurean women mentioned in a 4th c. inscription from the Asclepeion in Athens (*IG* ii² 1534). See also Castner 1982: 51–57.

Heliodora: Fictional hetaira in an epigram of Meleager praised for her sandal (*AG* 5.198).

Hedylion "sweetie": Fictional hetaira in an epigram of Quintus Maecius (*AG* 5.132).

Hermione: Fictional hetaira in an epigram of Asclepiades (*AG* 5.158).

Hermonassa: Fictional hetaira in an epigram of Paul Silentarios (*AG* 5.281).

Herpyllis: (4th c.). Life-long companion of Aristotle, mother of his son Niko-machos. There is disagreement in the sources about the precise status of Herpyl-lis. Timaios (*FGrH* 566 f 157) says that she was a servant girl, and the philoso-pher's concubine after the death of his wife. Diogenes Laertios (5.1) and Suda (α 3929) only say that she was his concubine. Hermippos thought that she was a hetaira, turned concubine (fr. 46 Wehrli = Athen. 13.56). Aristocles the peripatet-ic (fr. 2.90–92 Heiland = Eusebios *Praeparatio Evangelica* 15.2.15) thought that Herpyllis was a citizen woman from Stageira (Σταγειρῖτιν), and the second wife of Aristotle. He thus considered Aristotle's son Nikomachos to be legitimate. However, the terms of the will of Aristotle as cited by Diogenes Laertios (5.12–16), leave no room for doubt that Herpyllis was a concubine, not a wife, and her son Nikomachos was not legitimate, for otherwise there would be no reason for Aristotle to adopt his nephew and intended son-in-law Nicanor (for a more de-tailed discussion of the will of Aristotle see Ch. 3.3.). Whether she had been a humble servant, whom the philosopher elevated by choosing her as his concu-bine, as Timaios says, or a hetaira, as Hermippos attests, is difficult to tell, as both sources are roughly contemporary and neither is inherently superior. On grounds of probability, it is somewhat more likely that a wealthy and influential older man, as Aristotle was at the time when he chose Herpyllis as his concu-bine, would rather fall for the charms of a hetaira than a humble servant girl.

Hierokleia: (4th c.). One of the ageing hetairai mentioned in the *Orestau-tokleides* of Timokles (fr. 27 = Athen. 13.22).

Hippaphesis "letting the horses go": (Late 5th – early 4th c.). According to Lysias, she gave up prostitution while still at her prime, probably to become the concubine of a wealthy lover (fr. 208 Carey = Athen. 13.62).

Hipparchia: (4th – early 3rd c.). Lover of Krates, the philosopher, and mother of his son (D.L. 6.89).

Hippe "horse": (3rd c.). She was named after a mythological figure (e.g. Call. *Aet.* 66, Eratosth. *Cat.* 1.18). Machon says that after she had consumed all the money of Theodotos, the man in charge of the royal hay stores (ὁ ἐπὶ τοῦ χόρτου) in Alexandria, she arrived late at a dinner party and asked for a large drink. King Ptolemy told her that she truly needed one after all the hay (χόρτον) that she had devoured (Machon fr. 18.439–449 = Athen. 13.45). Eustathios commenting on this passage says that Ptolemy was making fun of her drunkenness and greed (*Sch. Il.* 4.461).

Hispala Faecenia: Spanish hetaira (quite likely from Hispalis, modern Seville), according to Livy (*Periochae*, ex POxy 668: 39.37).

Horpyllis of Kyzikos: She is mentioned by Photios (*Bibl.* 190. 151b. 15), but no further information is provided.

Ioessa: Fictional hetaira, lover of a young man named Lysias in Lucian (*DMeretr.* 12).

Ischas "dried fig": (later 4th c.). She is mentioned in a fragment from the *Kolax* of Menander as a contemporary of Korone and Antikyra (fr. 256).

Ismenodora: Fictional flute-player in Lucian (*DMeretr.* 5.4).

Isthmias: (4th c.). She is one of the seven girls who, according to Apollodoros (59.18), were bought by Nikarete of Elis, brought up and educated to become glamorous hetairai. A passage of Philetairos (fr. 9), which mentions three of Nikarete's girls in the same verse seems to confirm the narrative of Apollodoros, and suggests that the three women were roughly contemporaries (see Kapparis 1999: 206–210). A double entendre in a comedy of Plato probably refers to Isthmias too, as at first level it alludes to the Isthmian games, but there is a secondary level joking about a game of *kottabos* with Isthmias (fr. 46).

Kallikoite "good lay": Fictional character of a typical hetaira in Aristainetos (1.18).

Kallistion, the daughter of Korone, aka **Hys** "the Sow", or **Ptochelene** "Poor Helen":** (4th c.). She was a contemporary and friend of Gnathaina (Machon 18.433 = Athen. 13.45), and thus could not have provided the inspiration for the play of Kephisodoros *Hys* "the Sow" (Poll. 4.173; Athen. 3.89), since he was a contemporary of Aristophanes. Of course, a case of mistaken identity would not be untypical, as we only have Machon's word for this identification, and it would be unusual to have two nick-names for the same woman (the Sow and Poor Helen), and moreover, when Eustathios (*Com. Il.* 4.587) mentioned her, he only recognized two names, Kallistion and Ptochelene. This evidence, although not conclusive, may suggest that Kallistion, the contemporary of Gnathaina, was never nick-named "the Sow". A story of Athenaios (13.49) about a lover with whip-marks on his back is remarkably close to a story told about Gnathaina (Machon 16.285 = Athen. 13.43); it seems that Athenaios was confused at this point. Several references to fictional hetairai named Kallistion may be drawing inspiration from the famous hetaira (Poseidippos, *AG* 12.131; Hedylos 5.192, Meleager 5.192).

Kallistrate of Lesbos: An obscure reference in Athenaios (5.63) states that she had paid much attention to the methods of attracting of lovers, probably in a written work, as the connection with Philainis of Samos, a well-known poet of erotica, may suggest. See Ch. 2.1.

Kallixeina of Thessaly: (4th c.). She was hired by Olympias to have sex with Alexander, as his parents were uncertain about his sexual preferences and ability to perform with women. Olympias made Kallixeina recline next to the prince, but despite repeated attempts at seduction Alexander showed no interest in her (Hieronymos fr. 38; Athen. 10.45; Eust. *Com. Od.* 1.409).

Kalyke "bud": Fictional hetaira in Aristainetos (2.1).

Kephisodoros, the so called son of Molon: (4th c.). Athenian male prostitute who, according to Aeschines (1.158), destroyed his exquisite looks with his bad lifestyle (καλλίστην ὥραν ὄψεως ἀκλεέστατα διεφθαρκότα).

Kerkope "cock-faced": (4th c.). Philaiteros (fr. 9) joked that she had already lived for 3000 years. An entry in the *Lexica Segueriana* (s.v.) says that she was thus nicknamed because she was deceptive (cf. Sud. κ 1410; Ps-Zon. s.v. Kerkopes).

Kerkourion of Samos: Fictional prostitute established at the harbor of Samos and preying on young sailors, like a pirate (*AG* 5.44).

Kinnaros, aka **Konnaros,** or **Konnidas,** of Selinous: According to Timaios (*FGrH* 566 F 148) Kinnaros was a Sicilian pimp, who had become very wealthy from the business. While alive he was promising that his property was going to be left to Aphrodite, but his final wish was that everything was to be plundered, which generated the expression "the plundering of Kinnaros" (cf. Zen. *Epit.* 1.31). Hesychios (s.v. ἁρπαγὴ τὰ Κόννιδα) gives the name as Konnidas, while the Scholiast of Callimachos gives the form as Konnaros, with the note that it should actually be Konnidas (Sch. in Diegeseis in Iambos 201, col. 9).

Kirke: There is a tradition from later antiquity interpreting the traditional myth of Circe in a prostitutional context. The earliest confirmed reference to it is in Heraclitus, the Paradoxographer (*Incred.* 16), whose entry on Circe reads as following: *"The myth says that she transformed humans with a potion. But she was a hetaira, and first she charmed the visitors with every possible allurement and gained their favor. Then, when they were under her spell and irrationally driven towards sexual pleasure, she possessed them. Odysseus defeated her too."* See also Clem. Al. *Protr.* 12.118.2 and Sch. Clem. Al. Protr. 318; Palladas *AG* 10.50. In this light a reference in Herodian (*Epim.* 65) that *Kirke* is the name of a *porne*, may well refer to this tradition rather than an individual prostitute.

Kleino: (3rd c.). Flute-player and the wine-bearer of Ptolemy II Philadelphos. Polybios mentions numerous statues of her around Alexandria holding a tunic and a drinking horn (Plb. 14.11.2; Ptolemy Megalopolis *FGrH* 161 F 3 = Athen. 10.26).

Kleio: Fictional hetaira mentioned in an epigram falsely attributed to Lucian (Ps.Luc. *Epigr.* 6.17), specializing in vaginal sex, as opposed to Euphro, who specializes in anal sex, and Atthis who specializes in oral sex.

Klepsydra "Water-clock" or "Timer", aka **Metiche:** (4th c.). A play of Euboulos was named after her. Her real name was Metiche, according to Asclepiades, son of Areios, in his work on Demetrios Palereus, but she was nicknamed "water-clock" because she timed the length of sexual intercourse with clients (Athen. 13.21).

Klonarion "little branch": Fictional hetaira in Lucian (*DMeretr*. 5).

Klymene "famous": Fictional hetaira in Alciphron (3.5).

Klyte, daughter of Eurypylos "famous": She was a noble woman who took up prostitution, along with her sister Morphe, out of preference (Hdn. 3.2.1).

Knosion: (4th c.). Possibly a male prostitute, lover of Demosthenes, and also, at the same time, the wife of Demosthenes with the consent of the orator, according to Aeschines and Idomeneus (Aesch. 2. 149; Idomeneus *FGrH* 338 F 12 = Athen. 13.63; Sch. Aesch. 2.149). Hypereides implies a close personal and professional relationship (3.13), not unlike the familiar Roman pattern of the client/patron.

Kochlis "Snail": Fictional flute Player, the victim of violence of a drunk soldier in Luc. *DMeretr*. 15. A notoriously unstable hetaira in Aristainetos, deliberately modeled on Medea (1.28) and probably an anagram for Kolchis, the birth-place of Medea.

Konalis: (4th c.). A fragment of Timocles (fr. 27 = Athen. 13.22) jokes about her being an old woman.

Konon: Fictional prostitute in the Letters of Phalaris (*Ep*. 93.1; 121.1)

Konopion "Mosquito": Fictional hetaira in an epigram of Kallimachos which is reminiscent of a paraklausithyron theme (63 Pfeiffer = *AG* 5.23).

Korianno: A popular play of Pherecrates, possibly drawing inspiration from a real person, is named *Korianno* (fr. 73–84). Prostitutional themes and settings probably run through the play as the few remaining fragments indicate, where we encounter references to gourmet eating, bath houses and women drinking to excess.

Korinna: Young fictional hetaira in Lucian (*DMeretr*. 6), undergoing instruction by her mother on how to become successful in her trade.

Korinna: A very cheap fictional prostitute costing only two obols (*AG* 5.1250).

Korone "Crow", aka **Theokleia** (?), **the daughter of Nannion, the elder** (no. 234): Athenaios believed that Theokleia was her proper name while Korone "Crow" was a nickname, and that Aristophanes Byzantios, Apollodoros and Gorgias had missed her in their lists of Attic hetairai. This evidence is problematic because Theokleia is mentioned among several hetairai who gave up prostitution while still young in the speech of Lysias *To Lais* (Πρὸς Λαΐδα, fr. 208 Carey = Athen. 13.62), which would place her floruit in the late 5th or early 4th c. (see also the discussion ad loc.). However, the famous Korone was a contemporary of Gnathaina and reached her floruit approximately half a century later (Ephippos fr. 15 = Athen. 8.58; Men. fr. 256; Machon 18.433–438 = Athen. 13.45).

Korythia: A monolectic entry in Hesychios (s.v.) says that she was a fluteplayer.

Korydos, the "Lark": (4th c.). Famous parasite, renowned for his wit (see e.g. Athen. 6.38–9 with a long list of citations from classical authors, mostly Middle Comedy poets, and Athen. 6.40, where Athenaios cites Lynkeus citing a whole array of witticisms and jokes by Korydos). He was believed to have been a male prostitute in his younger days and was the object of a joke by Philoxenos the Pternokopis "ham-cleaver", who said that he remembered the days when the Lark went for a single obol (Athen. 6.40).

Kotinna, of Sparta: Famous Spartan hetaira, owner of a prominent brothel on the hill of Kolona, near the temple of Dionysos Kolonatas. Polemon Periegetes (fr. 18 Müller), who mentions her brothel and its location, says that she had dedicated to her local temple of Athena Chalkioikos a bronze statuette of hers and a bronze statuete of a cow (see Ch. 6.1.).

Krobyle: Pimp in Lucian (*DMeretr.* 6), no doubt named after the proverbial Krobylos (below), procuring her daugher Korinna.
Krobylos (4th c.).: Supremely attractive Corinthian prostitute, whom Hagnon, one of the extravagant courtiers of Alexander, offered to buy as a present for the King. Alexander flatly refused. (Plu. *Alex.* 22)

Krobylos "hair-knot" or more rarely "pubic hair" (Hsch. s.v.): Proverbial pimp, who owned two prostitutes. The expression "the pair of Krobylos" was used for deceitful and rapacious people (Diogenian. *Paroem.* 5.65; Zen. *Paroem.* 4.69; Pausan.Gr. κ 49; Hsch. s.v. al.).

Krokale "beach": Fictional hetaira in Lucian (*DMeretr.* 15).

Krousmation or Kroumation "Beat": Flute-Player (Alciphr. 4.13). The precise form of the name is questionable, as the text is uncertain, but in either case it seems to be a made-up name from the beat of music.

Kydilla: Fictional hetaira in the *Greek Anthology* (5.25).

Kymbalion "little cymbal": Rather unattractive, fictional flute-player in Lucian (*DMeretr.* 12.1). It appears that she is mentioned again (14.1), as one of the cheaper alternatives of Dorion, as he quarrels with Myrtale about her high fees.

Kynna: (5th c.). Prostitute mentioned in Aristophanes (*Eq.* 765; *V.* 1032). Later grammarians and the scholia of Aristophanes do not seem to have any useful additional information (see. e.g. Hsch s.v.; Sch. Ar. Eq. 765 and V. 1032).

Kyrene: See Dodekamechanos.

Kythereia "the one from Kythera": Fictional hetaira named after Aphrodite and willing to accept all currencies (*AG* 5.31).

Labrax "sea bass": Violent pimp in Plautus *Rudens*, which is based on a play of Diphilos.

Lagiska, or Ionic Lagiske, "the little hare": (early 4th c.). According to Anaxandrides *Gerontomania* (fr. 9), she was a contemporary of Lais and Anteia, which would place her floruit at the beginning of the 4th century. It is likely that she came from Corinth, if we can judge from the fact that in all sources except Plutarch (839 B) her name appears in the Doric dialect. Strattis (fr. 3 = Athen. 13.26) makes an obscene joke about Lagiska in his *Atalantos*, which makes clear that by that time she had already given up prostitution to become the concubine of Isocrates. Lysias in the speech *Against Lais* (fr. 208 Carey) mentions that Lagiska gave up prostitution while still young. If the speech is authentic (cf. Athen. 13.62 where doubt is expressed), this must have happened well before 380. Hermippos (fr. 65 Wehrli = Athen. 13.62) and Plutarch attest that Lagiska had a daughter with Isocrates, who died at the age of 12. Plutarch (839 B-C) mentions a wife, whom Isocrates married after the death of his daughter from Lagiska. Her name was Plathane and she had been the wife of Hippias the sophist before that, from whom she had three children. Isocrates adopted the youngest of the three, a boy named Aphareus. There are several issues with the details of this story. First, we are not told what happened to Lagiska after the marriage of Isocrates, and then we are not told how Isocrates was allowed to adopt the son of Hippias, when the latter was not an Athenian citizen. Hippias was from Elis, which means that his sons would be citizens of Elis too. These inconsistencies cast doubt upon the details of this marriage, if not the entire notion of it. Photios, in a comment which is reminiscent of the narrative of Apollodoros regarding the children of Neaira (D. 59.36–7), says that Lagiska had three children from another man when Isocrates met her (*Bibl.* 260 488a). Lagiska (diminuitive) is probably the same person as Lagis, who according to Athenaios (13.62), was a lover of Lysias and Kephalos the orator wrote her encomium.

Lais, the daughter of Megakles, from Hykkara, Sicily (more widely, but inaccurately known as **Lais of Corinth**), aka **Axine** "hoe" or "pickaxe": (Late 5th c. – early 4th c.). One of the most notorious hetairai of the ancient world. Several authors firmly assert that she was born in Sicily and brought to mainland Greece as a slave during the Sicilian expedition. At least the fact that she was born in Hykkara, a small town on the east coast of Sicily should not be in question, as it is very widely attested (Philistos *FGrH* 556 F 4; Nymphodoros *FGrH* 572 F 1; Timaios *FGrH* 566 F. 24; Paus. 2.2.5; Polemon Perieg. fr. 44a Müller; Plu. *Nic.* 15.4; Athen. 13.54–5; Gregory Nazianzenos 743; Synesius Ep. 3; Sch. Ar. Plu. 179). Apion disagreed with Timaios and believed that Polemon alone considered Lais to be Corinthian (*FGrH* 616 F 30). A few other sources also attest that she was Corinthian (Strattis fr. 27; Gell. *NA* 1.8). The Scholiast of Aristophanes is well aware that she was from Hykkara (sch. Plu. 179), but still calls her "Corinthian" (sch. Plu. 149). These references can be easily explained on account of the fact that Lais lived the whole of her life and worked in Corinth, and thus she could be rightly considered Corinthian, even though she was not born there. The fragment of Strattis implies that she was traveling from Corinth to Megara and then to Athens, which if we compare with Neaira's travels (D. 59.18–40), seems rather typical for contemporary working patterns. Equally easy to explain is the information of Philistos in his *History of Sicily* (*FGrH* 556 F 44) that she was from Krastos, a Sicilian city very near her native Hykkara. The information about her alleged love-affair with the rich Athenian Philonides (Ar. *Plu.* 179) may be false, as there is a good chance that *Nais* should be read instead of *Lais* at this point in the manuscripts (See the discussion in Ch. 4.4.). Her outlandishly good looks are often mentioned in contemporary sources. A fragment of Hypereides (fr. 13 Jensen) states that she was the most beautiful woman of her time. Timaios (*FGrH* 566 F. 24b) and Plutarch (767 F) agreed that her beauty was renowned, Anaxandrides calls her a "toy" (fr. 9), and Aristainetos in the 5th century AD composed a detailed portrait of her appearance, which may contain some features from literary sources or artistic representations now lost to us, but more likely is an expression of an aesthetic ideal (see the discussion in Ch. 2.2.). Her fame and beauty are standard themes in Roman literature too (e.g. Prop. 2.6.1–2; Ov. *Am.* 1.5.12; Fronto *De Eloq.* 5.5). Equally famous was her fall from grace in her old age, if we accept as historical the dirt which the comic poet Epicrates piles upon her in his *Antilais*, accusing her of alcoholism, sloth and gluttony (Epicrates fr. 2–3). He also says that while at her prime it was easier to see Pharnabazos than Lais, in her older days she accepted small coins for services and took the money in person. Philaiteros in a passage where, with visible exaggeration he mentions several hetairai who continued to work well past their prime, says that Lais died copulating (fr. 9). Athough these sources are undoubtedly hostile and should be treated with much skepticism, they seem to imply that Lais continued to work past her prime, while her splendid looks continued to decline partly through bad life-style choices. Beyond this point the mythology about this fabulous figure is mixed with historical facts and it is not always easy to tell truth from fiction. Her long-term affair with Aristippos of Kyrene is probably historical, but her association with Diogenes is more questionable (see the discussions in Ch. 3.3.), and her famous negotiation with Demosthenes, where she asked 100 minae for one night, is only attested in Roman sources, it is chronologically impossible and without a doubt not historical (see Ch. 6.6.). The tale of Timaios that she was lynched while still at her prime inside the temple of Aphrodite in Thessaly and was buried there is a misunderstanding, probably generated from the confusion of the Thessalian Ephyra with a mythological name of Corinth (also Ephyra; see the discussion in Ch. 6.1.). Lais almost certainly died at an old age in Corinth, where in later centuries she acquired an almost heroic status, and in Roman times her grave was a tourist attraction, along with other monuments to mythical heroes of the city (see Ch. 6.1.). Despite hundreds of references in classical authors, what we actually know about this most renowned of Greek hetairai from reliable contemporary sources is surprisingly little. While Lais without a doubt rivals Phryne in her skill for self-promotion, she does not seem to share the grandiose aspirations of the latter for immortality through ambitious artistic dedications or public statements of her fame. Perhaps Lais did not have to try as hard to gain a place in history, as this was guaranteed by her splendid looks and the impact she had upon her contemporaries through her charm and strong personality.

Lais the Younger, of Athens: (First half of the 4th c.). According to Athenaios (13.34) she was the daughter of Damasandra (s.v.), a favorite of Alcibiades, which would place her peak in the 380's (see also Ch. 3.1.). If so, she was only slightly junior to the famous Lais, by twenty years or so, which makes perfect sense, as we should not expect to find imitators of Lais many years after she had fallen out of the picture, but rather within a time frame where her reputation was still alive and at its highest. Unlike the original Lais, who was based primarily in Corinth, the field of operations of the younger Lais seems to be centered in Athens. This is why there is a good possibility that she is the woman involved in a lawsuit in an Athenian court very likely in the 380's, from which some fragments can be found among those of Lysias (fr. 208 Carey). Beyond that it is very difficult to separate the details of her life and actions from those of her more famous model, or any other copy-cats that subsequently tried to capitalize on the famous name, and it is possible that some of the mythology which is typically associated with Lais of Hykkara might have its roots in the life and actions of her younger contemporary, who happened to live in the city from which we have most of the evidence.

Lambito, of Samos: (late 4th – early 3rd c.). She was born around 330 and was a lover of Demetrios Phalereus. Demetrios liked to be called Lambito himself (Diyllos *FGrH* 73 F 4 = Athen. 13.65; D.L. 7.76 [citing the *Symposiaka* of Didymos as his source], Sud. δ 429).

Lamia: (late 6th – early 5th c., probably false). According to a story told by later authors she was one of the four original hetairai whom Themistocles introduced to Athens yoked to a chariot (Idomeneus *FGrH* 338 F 4a and 4b = Athen. 12.45 and 13.37). The story is an invention of later centuries, an *aition* to explain the introduction of high-class prostitution to Athens shortly after the Persian wars, when prosperity in the city was rising. This means that Lamia too is probably an invented character, with the name borrowed from one of the hetairai of later times, perhaps the renowned lover of Demetrios Poliorketes.
Lamia, daughter of Kleanor, of Athens: (late 4th - early 3rd c.). Athenian hetaira, daughter of Kleanor (Polemon fr. 14 Müller; Ael. *VH* 13.9 making a joke about Lysander). She was born around 330, if we can judge from the fact that when she met king Demetrios Poliorketes after the naval battle of Salamis (306), she was coming to the end of her prime (Plu. *Demetr.* 16: λήγουσα τῆς ὥρας). The

name is probably a pseudonym, after the mythological monster which took children (Duris *FGrH* 76 F 17; D.S. 20.41.3; Luc. *Philops.* 2; Str. 1.2.8). The name generated a joke by the father of Demetrios, Antigonos Monophthalmos "the one-eyed", that his son is sleeping with Lamia (the monster: Plu. *Demetr.* 19. Cf. Plu. *Comp. Dem. Ant.* 3). She started her career as a skilled flute player (Phylarchos *FGrH* 81 F. 12; Plu. *Demetr.* 16, Athen. 13.39, 14.3), and while she would continue from time to time to entertain her guests with the flute, she became a famous hetaira. She was accompanying the fleet of Ptolemy during the naval battle of Salamis (Plu. *Demetr.* 16), and after the overwhelming victory of Demetrios Poliorketes, she was taken to his camp along with the spoils. Seemingly it was instant attraction, and she ended up in a long-term relationship with him, one which raised many eyebrows for its excesses and legendary lewdness (Machon fr. 13; Athen. 13.39. Clem. Al. *Protr.* 4.54.6). Several sources comment on the fact that she was already past her prime when the relationship started, and in subsequent years Demetrios got some flak for sleeping with an "old" woman (in reality in her 30s or early 40s by that time), but it appears that to some degree the attraction extended beyond her good looks and was largely based upon her captivating personality and sharp wit (Plu. *Demetr.* 27). She acquired great influence, which caused the envy of his courtiers and other women of the royal circle (Plu. *Demetr.* 27). However, the information of Athenaios (13.38) that Lamia had a daughter from Demetrios named Phila must be a mistake, because Phila was the name of the queen, the wife of Demetrios, and such an effrontery as to name the daughter of the favorite mistress after the queen would probably be even beyond Lamia and Demetrios. Machon has included several of her witticisms (see App. II). Athenaios compares her wit to that of Gnathaina with the comment that Lamia was very sharp and intelligent in her answers (Athen. 13.39; Plu. *Demetr.* 27 where Lamia expresses her dissatisfaction about the judgment of Bochoris; see Ch. 4.1.13.). The dinners which she put together for Demetrios and his friends were legendary (Plu. *Demetr.* 27; Athen. 4.1), as was her extravagance. In one of the stories Demetrios collects the sum of 250 talents from the Athenians and orders them to hand it over to Lamia and the other hetairai of his court for perfumes (Plu. *Demetr.* 27). She acquired the nickname *helepolis* (taker of cities), because she often financed her costly dinners through involuntary contributions from the citizens (Plu. *Demetr.* 27; see the discussion in Ch. 6.1.). There are several reports of questionable authority suggesting that the Athenians (in one of the sources, the Thebans) erected a sanctuary of Aphrodite Lamia in order to honor the mistress of Demetrios (Athen. 6.62). Ancient authors are shocked that he used the Parthenon as his residence, bringing Lamia and his other hetairai into the temple of the virgin goddess Athena (e.g. Clem. Al. *Protr.* 4.54.6). A fictional letter of Alciphron (4.16) from Lamia to Demetrios contains surprisingly little factual information about her life or relationship with the king. It appears the only substantial information which the author had from other sources was about the dinners of Lamia; otherwise the love-struck, meek woman of Alciphron bears little resemblance to the haughty and capricious mistress who, at the height of the power of Demetrios, had the whole of Greece do her bidding.

Lampas: According to Athenaios (13.46), she is one of the hetairai missed by Aristophanes Byzantios, Apollodoros and Gorgias in their collections of Attic hetairai.

Lampyris "shining": According to Athenaios (13.46), she is one of the hetairai missed by Aristophanes Byzantios, but included by Apollodoros or Gorgias in their collections of the Attic hetairai.

Lastheneia of Arcadia: (4th c.). She was a student of Plato, along with Axiothea of Phleious, who dressed in men's clothes (Dikaiarchos fr. 44 Wehrli = D.L. 3.46 and 4.2; Athen. 12.66; Clem. Al. *Str.* 4.19.122.2). She was also said to be a student of Speusippos (Athen. 7.10, 12.66; *Socraticorum Epistulae* 36.1), and even Pythagoras (Iamb. *VP* 36.267.73; Pythagoristae a1.49 D-K.). Athenaios (7.10) confirms that she was a hetaira.

Leaina "lioness": According to tradition, she was the hetaira of Aristogeiton or Armodios, the tyrannicides. According to Plutarch (505 D-E), while she was being tortured by Hippias for information on the death of Hipparchos, she bit off her tongue and spat it on his face in order to avoid a confession. He tortured her to death, and later the Athenians dedicated a bronze lioness on the Acropolis which did not have a tongue. Pausanias (1.23.2.) confirms the existence of the statue, and so does Athenaios (13.70). Most likely this tale is an etiological myth intended to explain the statue of the lioness without a tongue (see the discussion in Ch. 3.1.).

Leaina of Athens: (Early 3rd c.). Lover of Demetrius Poliorketes and rival of Lamia for his affections (Machon 12.168 = Athen. 13.39; Polemon Perieg. fr. 15 Müller = Athen. 6.62), in whose honor he erected a temple of Leaina Aphrodite (Demochares *FGrH* 75 F 1 = Athen. 6.62; see also Ch. 6.1.) Two fictional hetairai, one in Lucian (*DMeretr.* 5) and one in Alciphron (4.12), may be inspired by the famous mistress of Demetrios. A note in Suda and the scholiast of Aristophanes

(Sch. Ar. Plu. 149) stating that there was a Corinthian hetaira named Leaina is probably a mistake of place and time. There seems to be only one historical Leaina, the woman who was the lover of Demetrios Poliorketes.

Leimone "field": Fictitious character in one of the letters of Aristainetos (1.3), where a young man has sex with a hetaira in a field under a tree.

Lembion "the Boat", **of Samos:** Fictional prostitute established at the harbor of Samos and preying on young sailors, like a pirate (*AG* 5.44).

Leme "eye-sore", **aka Parorama** "oversight": (4th c.). Lover of the Athenian orator and politician Stratocles (Gorgias *FGrH* 351 F 1 = Athen. 13.70).

Lemniselene "Lemnian moon": Fictional hetaira, lover of Toxilus, in Plautus *Persa*.

Lenaitokystos: According to Athenaios (13.46), she is one of the hetairai missed by Aristophanes Byzantios, Apollodoros and Gorgias in their collections of the Attic hetairai.

Leontion, of Attica "little lioness": (Late 4th – early 3rd c.). A hetaira named Leontion is reported to be the lover of the poet Hermesianax, who seemingly dedicated a long poem to her (Athen. 13.71). Leontion was also reported to be the lover and student of Epicurus, the mother of a hetaira called Danae, who was put to death by the Seleucid leader Laodice, and an Athenian hetaira in rivalry with Glykera. Conceivably the same woman could be the protagonist of all these stories. Hermesianax was a senior contemporary of Epicurus, while an ageing Danae was put to death by Laodice I during her sole rule after the death (or poisoning) of her husband between 246 and 236. If Leontion was born around 330 she could have reached her peak around 310, when she met Hermesianax, then spent the next 10 years or so working as a high-class hetaira. When she was approaching the end of her prime, around 300, she became the concubine and student of Epicurus. Danae was probably born shortly before that time, as she was not the daughter of Epicurus, which means that she was in her late 50's or 60's when we find her in a position of responsibility in the court of Laodice. Whether Leontion first decided to study philosophy and then become the lover of Epicurus, or the reverse, is not clear, but our sources leave us in no doubt that she was both (Hermarchos fr. 41 Longo Auricchio; Theon Progymn. 112.1 ff. Spengel; Athen. 13.53, 64, Alciphr. 4.17; D.L. 10.23). Hermar-

chos attests that she had been a notorious hetaira before she joined the Epicureans (Hermarchos fr. 41). Athenaios relates a story where she was jealous of
Glykera because the lover who took her to a symposium was paying more attention to her rival (13.49). A fictional letter of Alciphron (4.17), allegedly written by
Leontion to Lamia, the lover of Demetrios Poliorketes, may contain information
from sources lost to us, but very likely also contains numerous fictional elements and thus cannot be trusted. It suggests that a young Leontion at her
prime was planning to leave the jealous 80–year-old Epicurus for another lover,
the man who had taken her virginity, a handsome Athenian youth named Aeschines. Letters from Epicurus to Leontion with philosophical content are attested, from which Diogenes Laertios preserves a colorful phrase: "*In the name of
Paian, my sweet Leontarion, how alarmed I was when I read your little letter*"
(D.L. 10.5.4–5).

Leontis "lioness": Fictional hetaira in an epigram by an unknown author (*AG*
5.201).

Lesbia: Fictional hetaira in Lucian (*DMeretr.* 2).

Lopadion "oyster": (4th c.). One of the ageing hetairai mentioned by Timocles
(fr. 27 = Athen. 13.22).

Lychnos "oil-lamp", aka **Synoris:** See n. Synoris.

Lycus "wolf": Fictional pimp in Plautus *Poenulus*.

Lyde "Lydian": (Late 5th – early 4th c.; possibly fictional). She was mistress (or
wife, according to Plutarch) of the poet Antimachos, to whom he dedicated a
collection of elegies entitled *Lyde* after her death, the theme of which was unhappy love in myths (Hermesianax fr. 7.41–6; Plu. 106 B-C).

Lyde: Hetaira, mistress of the poet Lamynthios of Miletos, to whom he dedicated a collection of poems entitled *Lyde* (Klearchos fr. 34 Wehrli = Athen. 13.70).
Lyde: Fictional barbarian hetaira in *AG* 5.49. Lyde serves 3 men simultaneously
for speed, one on top of her, one underneath and one behind.

Lyka "she-wolf": (4th c.). Wealthy hetaira, whom Amphis calls a "trap" for one's
fortune (fr. 23 = Athen. 13.22).

Lykainis "she-wolf": Fictional hetairai in two different epigrams of the *Greek Anthology* (*AG* 5.187, 13.327).

Lykinos: Fictional male prostitute in one of the Letters of Phalaris (4.1), where Lykinos allegedly was, among others, a prostitute as a boy, lustful as a young man, an adulterer with women and licentious with his pleasures. Since the name is very common, it is impossible to determine which historical figure may have provided the inspiration for this character.

Lyra "lyre", daugther of Daphnis: Fictional hetaira in Lucian (*DMeretr.* 6).

Lysidike: Fictional hetaira with very revealing outfits (*AG* 5.104).

Macedonia: 6th century AD, dancer from Antioch. According to Prokopios (*Anecd.* 12.28–32), she gained prominence and power by exploiting her relationship with Justinian to get rid of her enemies and seize their confiscated properties. We are told that when the future empress Theodora passed through Antioch on her way to Constantinople, while still a prostitute working her way through the whole of North Africa and the Middle East, Macedonia encouraged her with the promise that soon she will marry the king of the demons (sc. Justinian) and have the wealth of the whole world. Since the passage is strongly reminiscent of the narrative of Apollodoros about Neaira's work as a prostitute all over the known world (D. 59.108), it sounds like a literary composition based on the passage of Apollodoros, with limited historical value.

Malthake "soft": (4th c.). The comic poet Theophilos (fr. 11 = Athen. 13.52) lists her among several women whose appearance was enhanced with fine linen. A fictional character in Menander's *Sikyonios* is also named Malthake, perhaps inspired, like several other Menandrian characters, from real life hetairai. Lucian's reference (*Rh.Pr.* 12), where Malthake is listed together with several other hetairai is probably derived from Menander. Clement (*Paed.* 3.2.7.2) mentions a play of Antiphanes entitled *Malthake*, and adds that the poet made fun of the ways of the hetairai in it. Modern editors stress the final syllable, understanding it as a generic reference to feminine softness and luxury, but it is equally possible that it should be stressed in the penultime and understood as a reference to Malthake the hetaira.

Mammarion "mamma", **the Epicurean:** (Late 4th – early 3rd c.). One of the hetairai who frequented the Gardens of Epicurus, maintained sexual relations with

Epicurus and Metrodoros and studied philosophy (Epicurus Ep. 101 = D.L. 10.7). According to Hermarchos (fr. 3 Longo Auricchio), she was the mistress of Leonteus.

Mania "madness", aka **Melitta** "honey-bee": (late 4th – early 3rd c.). The most significant source about her life is Machon (13.174 – 15.257 = Athen. 13.41–42). She was Athenian by birth and this is why Machon seems greatly surprised that she bore a Phrygian name, suitable for a slave (cf. Sch. Ar. Th. 728 ὄνομα κύριον δούλης τὸ Μανία, and X. HG 3.1, where Mania is the name of a noble local woman in the Hellespontine regions, appointed satrap by Pharnabazos). Machon adds that her real name was Melitta "honey-bee", which sounds very suspicious, as it is the direct opposite of her nickname "mania, madness", and thus seemingly invented to underline the contrast. The name Mania need not be foreign in origin, since it makes good sense as a Greek noun, and can be explained as a joke or an insult (see the detailed, but inconclusive debate in Gow 1965: 96–106). Machon describes her as rather small, with a stunningly pretty face, a charming voice and sharp wit, and asserts that with these qualities she was very successful and took many lovers, including Demetrios Poliorketes (Ptolemy Megalopolis FGrH 161 F 4 = Athen. 13.40). Plutarch (*Dem.* 27.9) seems to have confused her with Demo, the mistress of Antigonos, father of Demetrios, and conflated the two women into one person. Two other prominent lovers of hers were Leontiskos and Antenor, both career pankratiasts, and it seems that she was the exclusive companion of Leontiskos for some time.

Manilia: Aulus Gellius (*NA* 4.14.3–6) tells the story where an aedile called Aulus Hostilius Mancinus attempted to gain entry by force into the house of the meretrix Manilia. She repelled him with stones, and when he tried to sue her showing the injury from the stone, the tribunes did not allow the lawsuit. The reference to Manilia as unduly interfering in legal affairs in Juvenal (6.242–245), most likely has this story in mind.

Medontis of Abydos: (Late 5th c.). According to a fragment attributed to Lysias, Alcibiades and Axiochos shared the hetaira Medontis, had a daughter from her, and neither knew who the father was, and had relations with the daughter as well, when she came of age (fr. 8 Carey = Athen. 12.48; cf. 13.34). See also the discussion in Ch. 3.1.

Medousa: Heraclitus the Paradoxographer (1), reinterprets the myth of Medousa and Perseus, making her a ruthless hetaira falling in love with the hero and spending all her fortune on him.

Megara: Fictional hetaira featured heavily in the letters of Alciphron (4.6, 7, 11, 13, 14).

Megiste: According to Athenaios (13.46), she is one of the hetairai missed by Aristophanes Byzantios, Apollodoros and Gorgias in their collections of the Attic hetairai.

Melaenis "black": Fictional prostitute/pimp (*meretrix*) in Plautus *Cistellaria*.

Melissarion, the daughter of Aglais. Fictional hetaira and entertainer in Aristainetos (1.19). In this letter Aristainetos adapts the famous abortion scene involving an unknown musician in the Hippocratic Study *On the Seed* (*Sem* 13; see also Kapparis 2002: 111–112), but he gives the woman the name Melissarion, suitable for a musician (from *melos*), and is quite uptight about the messy details of the abortion, which the medical record provides. Moreover, in a happy ending scenario reminiscent of New Comedy, his Melissarion later meets a nice young man, they fall in love, have a baby-boy, get married and then she changes her name to Pythias, and becomes very respectable.

Meirakiophile "lover of young men": Ominously named, fictional character of a hetaira who only sleeps with young and attractive men in Aristainetos (1.18).

Mekonis "Opium": She is mentioned in a fragment from the *Flute-Lover* of Theophilos (fr. 11 = Athen. 13.52.), among several women whose looks are enhanced through artificial devices.

Melissa: Actress and hetaira of some renowned making a brief appearance at the banquet of the Deipnosophists (4.45), which may have provided the inspiration for a fictional hetaira in several epigrams of the *Greek Anthology* (e.g. *AG* 5.27, 32). The Attic form Melitta, which supposedly was the real name of the hetaira Mania (see n. s.v.), is used for a fictional hetaira in Lucian (*DMeretr.* 4). **Melite:** Fictional hetaira in several epigrams of the *Greek Anthology* (*AG* 5.15, 36, 94, 242 al.).

Melitta: See n. *Mania*.

Menophila/Menophilas/Menophilos: A fictional transgender prostitute in several epigrams of Marcus Argentarius (*AG* 5.105, 113). Most intriguing is 5.116, where Menophila can be easily switched to Menophilos, to satisfy all tastes.

Metaneira: (early 4th c.). The most significant source about her life and career is the speech of Apollodoros *Against Neaira* (D. 59.19–23). She was one of the seven slave-girls bought and brought up by Nikarete of Elis, and became the lover of Lysias the orator in the 380's, when he was in his sixties. Apollodoros describes one of the visits of Metaneira to Athens, accompanied by Nikarete and an underage girl, who was later going to become the prominent hetaira Neaira. The purpose of the visit was Metaneira's initiation to the Eleusinean Mysteries, the cost of which Lysias was happy to pay as a personal favor for her. A letter of Lysias addressed to Metaneira attested in a number of later sources is probably fictitious (fr. 453–456 Carey; Poll. 7.130; Sud. o 292; Sch. Pl. Gor.g. 469d). Athenaios (13.62) citing this letter as his source says that Metaneira was also the lover of Isocrates. Athenaios may have been confused as such an affair is not attested anywhere else. A fragment from the second speech of Hypereides *Against Aristagora* (13 Jensen) suggests that her looks were almost as legendary as those of Lais, talked about half a century after her prime, while Hegesandros speaks of her wit (fr. 28–29 Müller).

Metiche: see n. Klespydra.

Mika: (4th c.). Although there is no specific reference to her as a prostitute in literary sources, an Agora graffiti saying "Mika is beautiful" (*Mika kale*), combined with the title of a speech of Hyperides *For Mika* (fr. 125 Jensen), probably suggests that she was a prostitute, as respectable women neither had their names inscribed on graffiti (see Ch. 6.2) nor were named with their personal name when involved in lawsuits, but rather as "the daughter of x" (cf. Ch. 4.4.).

Milto "red dye", **aka Aspasia, of Phocaea:** See n. s.v. Aspasia (no. 41).

Mnesis "memorable": (Later 3rd c.). Flute-player employed and favored by Ptolemy Philopator (Plb. 14.11 = Athen. 13.37).
Mnesitheos, the so-called son of the cook. (4th c.). Athenian male prostitute (Aesch. 1.158).

Morphe "Face", **daughter of Eurypylos:** She was a noble woman who took up prostitution, along with her sister Klyte, out of preference (Hdn. 3.2.1).

Moscharion "little calf": Fictional hetaira in Alciphron (4.14).

Mousarion "young Muse": Name given to a fictional hetaira in Lucian (*DMeretr.* 7) and to an actress/hetaira in Aristainetos (1.24). The *Etymologicum Magnum* confirms that the name is derived from the comic tradition (*EM* s.v. ὑποκοριστικόν), while the Scholiast of Lucian (80.2.1 Rabe) asserts that the name is found in Attic authors.t

Myia "Fly" **of Athens:** Although Lucian (*Musc.Enc.* 10) assures us that this was not a popular name among parents, several prominent women are known by this name, including an Attic hetaira. He also preserves a single line from an unnamed comic poet written about her saying "the Fly bit him all the way to his heart".

Myrinna: (5ᵗʰ c.). It was mentioned in the second *Autolykos* of Eupolis that a man threw away his fortune for her sake (Sch. Ar. Nub. 109 d).

Myrrine: (4ᵗʰ c.). Very expensive (πολυτελεστάτη) hetaira, lover and concubine of Hypereides, whom he took to live with him in his primary residence in Athens, when he threw his son Glaukippos out of the house (Hermippos fr. 68 Wehrli; Plu.849 D; Athen. 13.58). She appears in the list of ageing hetairai cited by Timocles in his *Orestautokleides* (fr. 27 = Athen. 13.22). If there is any truth in this joke, then clearly her relationship with Hypereides came to an end while she was still young enough to resume her activities as a hetaira. Several Menandrian characters are named Myrrine (in *Dyskolos*, *Georgos*, *Heros* and *Perikeiromene*), and this probably provided the inspiration for several fictional hetairai with this name in Alciphron (4.5, 10, 14). It seems that she was famous enough in later antiquity to make it into a list of Attic hetairai cited by Libanios (*Decl.* 25.2.40), along with major names like Lais, Aspasia, Theodote and Phryne. The note of the scholiast of Aristophanes (Sch. Ar. Plu. 149) that she was Corinthian is of no historical value.

Myrinne, of Samos: (Late 4ᵗʰ-early 3ʳᵈ c.). Influential lover of Demetrius Poliorketes (Nicolaus of Damascus *FGrH* 90 F 90 = Athen. 13.64).

Myrtale "Myrtle": Fictional common prostitute, the girl with whom the fierce Thales was in love in Herodas 2.79.

Myrtale: Fictional hetaira in Lucian (*DMeretr.* 14), commanding a fee of two minae from a rich, older merchant. In addition he offers her expensive gifts, which arouse the jealousy of her previous, stingy lover Dorion.

Myrtion "little Myrtle": (later 3rd c.). The name is a diminutive of *myrtos* "myrtle-berry", commonly used as a slang word for female genitalia (e.g. Ar. *Lys.* 1004; Poll. 2.174). According to Polybios (14.11) she was a common prostitute employed and favored by Ptolemy Philopator. Ptolemy VIII (*FGrH* 234 F 4) says that she was a mistress of Philadelphos. She owned one of the finest houses in Alexandria, no doubt a gift from the king (Plb. 14.11). Lucian (*DMort* 22.7) seems to be aware of a hetaira named Myrtion, which might be the same person as the famous mistress of Philadelphos.

Myrtion: Fictional hetaira in Lucian, eight months pregnant with the child of her lover Pamphilos (*DMeretr.* 2).

Mysta: (3rd c.). According to Phylarchos and Ptolemy she was a lover of Seleucus II (Phylarchos *FGrH* 81 F 30 = Athen. 13.64; Ptolemy Megalopolis *FGrH* 234 F 4 = Athen. 13.40). Polyainos says that she was the wife of Seleukos (8.61) and his queen (52.9), but this is incorrect, as the queen of Seleucus II was Laodice II. All sources agree that after the defeat of Seleucus at the hands of the Gauls (the battle of Ancyra in 240), Mysta sensing the danger cast off the royal outfits and dressed as a servant. She was captured and sold as a slave in Rhodes, along with her maids. When she identified herself to the Rhodians, they paid the ransom and sent her with splendor back to Seleucus.

Nais, mistakenly identified with **Oia / Antikyra:** (Early 4th c.). The scant fragments from the speech of Lysias *Against Philonides* suggest that Philonides of Melite, one of the richest and most extravagant men in Athens, was prosecuted for the rape/sexual assault of Nais by her pimp and agent (*kyrios*) Archias (Lys. fr. 140 Carey, Athen. 13.51; Harp. s.v. Nais; see also the relevant discussion about the entire case in Ch. 4.4.). The bitter love-affair between Philonides and Nais is also mentioned in Aristophanes (*Plu.* 179), if we accept the suggestion of Harpocration (s.v. Nais, cf. Sud. v 16) that Nais should be read instead of Lais in this place. Nais is also mentioned in Aristophanes *Gerytades* (Harp. s.v. Nais) and as a toothless old woman in Philetairos (fr. 9.7), while Alcidamas of Elea composed her encomium (Athen. 13.62). Since all these sources place her firmly in the early 4th century, she must be a different woman from Antikyra (aka Oia), with whom she was confused by Athenaios (see n. s.v. Antikyra).

Nannarion: It may be an affectionate name for Nannion the younger (no. 247). Several references to her can be dated to the middle of the 4th century, and as such fit the life-span of Nannion, but the possibility of another hetaira or a copy-cat with a similar name cannot be excluded. According to Theophilos, she was one of those hetairai whom pimps dress up in fancy linen (fr. 11), which reminds us of the joke of Antiphanes that Nannion was called *Proskenion* "forestage", because once she took off the fancy dresses she was very ugly (Athen. 13.51). A fragment from the *Kolax* of Menander (fr. 256 = Athen. 13.52) mentions her together with Korone. This might speak for her identification with Nannion; in this senario mother and daughter would be working together.

Nannion: (Early 5th century, if she was a real person). According to a tale from later antiquity she was one of the four hetairai whom Themistokles yoked on a chariot and drove through the Kerameikos, when he introduced hetairai to Athens (Idomeneus *FGrH* 338 F 4a, Athen. 13.37; see Ch. 3.1.). It is highly doubtful that she was a historical person.

Nannion (the elder, the mother of Korone): She must have flourished in the late fifth or early fourth century and became the founder of a dynasty of hetairai (Athen. 13.51). Her daughter Korone and granddaughter Nannion were also famous. There is a possibility that some of the biographical data traditionally attributed to her better-known granddaughter ought to be attributed to the elder Nannion, but there is no way to verify who did what.

Nannion, the younger, the daughter of Korone, aka Aix "The Goat": She probably flourished in the middle of the 4th century, since she was mentioned in the speech of Hyperides *Against Patrokles for Procurement* (Κατὰ Πατροκλέους προαγωγείας: fr. 141 Jensen = Athen. 13.51), and in several Attic comedies from that period. She was the daughter of the famous hetaira Korone, and the granddaughter of Nannion the elder (no. 245), after whom she was named. This is why she was sometimes sarcastically called "third level whore" (τρίπορνος: Athen.13.51). The information that she acquired the nickname Aix "the Goat" when she 'ate through' a lover called Thallos "the green branch" (Apollodoros *FGrH* 244 F 211b = Athen. 13.51; Harp. s.v. Nannion; Suda ν 25) is problematic because, according to Athenaios, both Machon and Lynkeus of Samos told the same story about Niko (see the discussion under Niko). Antiphanes called her *Proskenion* "forestage", because she was all a façade, a pretty face with nice clothes and jewelry, but very ugly when she undressed (Athen. 13.51). Both, Amphis and Anaxilas, speak of her ruthlessness and mercenary attitude which had allowed her to amass substantial wealth (Amphis fr. 23 = Athen.13.22; Anaxilas fr. 22.15 = Athen. 13.6). Amphis calls her a "trap" (παγίς), while Anaxilas compares her to the mythological Skylla, who, as soon as she has "drowned" (ἀποπνίξασα) two of her lovers, is hunting for the third. A fragment of Alexis mocks her for drunkenness (fr. 225 = Athen. 13.51). She was already well past her prime in the time of Timocles (3rd quarter of the 4th c.). who calls her an old woman, along with Phryne, Gnathaina, Pythionike and several others (fr. 27 = Athen. 13.22). Athenaios ascribes a play entitled *Nannion* either to Eubulos or to Philip, the son of Aristophanes, and quotes 11 lines from it, which constitute a well-known account of a brothel scene. Just a few lines above, Athenaios attests that a modified quotation of this fragment comes from the *Pannychis* of Euboulos (Eub. fr. 67, fr. 82; Athen. 13.24). The woman called *Niko* "the Goat" in Machon (fr. 18.423 = Athen. 13.45) is undoubtedly Nannion, as the aforementioned story about Thallos and her mother's name are given here too. Thus Niko, if it not a textual mistake, is a blunder of Machon, instead of Nanno. An epigram of Asclepiades, which jokingly disapproves of the lesbian sexuality of two women from Samos named Bitto and Nannion, probably does not refer to this Nannion or any of her predecessors with that name, since all hetairai with this name seem to be Athenian (*AG* 5.207).

Nanno: (born in the first half of the 7th century, probably not a real person). Flute-player and lover of Mimnermus, according to Athenaios (13.70) and Hermesianax (fr. 7.37 = Athen. 13.71), also appearing with Mimnermos in an epigram of Poseidippos (*AG* 12.168). One of the collections of Mimnermos is entitled *Nanno*, which may have generated the story about the love-affair in later antiquity, however, we cannot be absolutely certain that there is no truth to such an affair.

Nape: Fictional hetaira in the *Greek Anthology* (*AG* 5.5) perhaps named after a town of Lesbos.

Nausimache: (late 5th – early 4th century). A prostitute mentioned in Aristophanes *Thesmophoriazousai* (804; cf. Sch. Ar. Th. 804).

Nausion: False reading in Athenaios (13.52), for Nannarion in the fragment of Theophilos which he is citing (fr. 11).

Neaira: (4th c.). The details of her life and career over a period of 60 years are reported in the famous prosecution speech of Apollodoros (D. 59), delivered around 342. Neaira stood accused of breaching the law which forbade foreigners to pretend lawful marriage with a citizen, but the whole prosecution was motivated by politics and was directed more at her life-long partner Stephanos, son of Antidorides, of Eroiadai, than the woman herself. Nonetheless, it was Neaira personally who was brought to court and faced enslavement in her old age. We are told that she started life as a slave girl owned by Nikarete of Elis. She was brought up to become a prominent hetaira and was initiated into prostitution in the mid 380's. However, she did not reach her floruit until 380, and for the next five years or so she would become one of the most renowned Corinthian hetairai in the whole of Greece. She became the mistress of rich men, poets, actors, athletes, and members of some of the most prominent families in the Greek world, while traveling on both sides of the Aegean with her lovers. Her procuress commanded huge fees, and eventually sold her for the high price of 30 minae to two men, who shared her as their exclusive mistress for a couple of years. When they had enough of her and decided to settle down and have families, they accepted a reduced price of 20 minae, and set her free. Phrynion, the man who paid for her freedom, a rich and dissolute Athenian from a well-known family, a cousin of Demosthenes, brought her with him to Athens in 374, and naturally assumed that he had certain rights over her. He treated her abusively, and in order to escape him she fled to the neighboring city of Megara, where she stayed for two years and tried to make a living as a hetaira in difficult circumstances, since the last war in history between Athens and Sparta had closed the trading routes and there were no foreigners or merchants in the city. When the war was over she met a young Athenian man, named Stephanos, who was in Megara for business. He fell in love with her, and was willing to risk a conflict with Phrynion in order to take her with him to Athens. Phrynion indeed tried to take her back by force, Stephanos sued him and in the end all parties reconciled on condition that the two men would share Neaira. At this point Phrynion drops out of the picture. Probably he was persuaded by Neaira to let her be with Stephanos. For the next forty or so years of her life she would live as the concubine of Stephanos and help bring up his four small children from his previous marriage to an unknown Athenian woman. Around 342 Apollodoros, probably acting on behalf of a wider political alliance which pursued the agenda of a confrontation with Philip II, decided to attack Stephanos, and it seemed more efficient to carry this attach through the prosecution of Neaira. An attack against an ageing prostitute might seem an easier target to succeed than a direct assault on a politician with personal appeal to the demos and strong connections. If they succeeded, then Stephanos would be facing a huge fine for having illegally married an alien woman, and moreover he would have to pay a large ransom to buy back the freedom of Neaira. Beyond financial ruin, if he was unable to pay the fine in its entirety, he would lose his civil rights (*atimos*) and no longer pose a threat to his political enemies. The case against Neaira was inherently weak, but the tactics that her skilled prosecutor used, which included a lengthy narrative about her career as a hetaira, were brutal, and there is a good possibility that he succeeded in a case literally built on thin air and a lot of prejudice and slander. (See the discussion in Ch. 4.4., Kapparis 1999 and Hamel 2003).

Nemeas, or Nemea: (4th c.). Flute-player, mentioned by Hyperides in the speech *Against Patrocles* (fr. 142 Jensen = Athen. 13.51). Harpocration (s.v. *Nemeas auletridos*) implies that the name was Nemea, which may be supported by the proverbial expression *Nemeas auletridos* ("for skilled flute-players", according to the Appendix Proverbiorum 4.5). The entries in Suda and Photios are based on Harpocration, and thus are of no independent value (about the controversy on naming a hetaira after a Panhellenic festival see Ch. 4.1.14.).

Nikarete, of Megara: (Early 3rd c.). According to Athenaios a woman of noble birth (οὐκ ἀγεννής), student and lover of the Megarian philosopher Stilpon. Athenaios attests that her learning was admirable, and includes her in a list of very distinguished women, who were also hetairai (13.70). Diogenes Laertios attests that Nikarete was the concubine of Stilpon, who also had a wife and a daughter at the same time (2.114). An epigram of her contemporary Asklepiades, which may be referring to this Nikarete, extols her beautiful face and sparkling eyes (*AG* 5.153).

Nikarete, of Elis, the wife of Hippias: (4th c.). Her activities as a procuress are described in some detail by Apollodoros in the speech *Against Neaira* (D. 59.18– 31). She was a freedwoman, who initially belonged to a man named Charisios, and once freed she had married the cook of Charisios. At some point she moved to Corinth and set up shop as the procuress of one or two girls at a time. She maintained a façade of respectability in her home, and called the girls her daughters, even though they were slaves whom she had bought while they were still children with promising looks. She expected the lovers of the girls to provide for the entire household, commanded huge fees, and sold them while still at their prime to infatuated lovers for a lot of money. Neaira was sold for 30 minae, and Apollodoros tells us that all seven girls whom she owned were eventually sold and freed by infatuated lovers. We can certainly confirm this information about Anteia and Neaira, and possibly about Phila (see the discussion s.v.). Nikarete clearly ran a tight ship, and when Lysias, who was at the time a lover of Metaneira, invited her to Athens to be initiated into the Eleusinean Mysteries, Nikarete went along. Apollodoros presents her as a successful businesswoman with a keen eye for potential in the little girls she bought, savvy in the way she educated the girls to become prominent hetairai, but also protective of her investment and ruthless. If the list of the seven girls provided by Apollodoros is accurate, then he was right to think that she knew how to make a living out of this business, since at least four of them are known from other sources, and Neaira, Anteia and Metaneira were truly famous.

Nikidion, the Epicurean: (Late 4ᵗʰ – early 3ʳᵈ c.). One of the hetairai who frequented the Gardens of Epicurus, maintained sexual relations with Epicurus and Metrodoros and studied philosophy (Epicurus Ep. 101 = D.L. 10.7; Plu. 1097 E). According to Hermarchos (fr. 3), she was the lover of Idomeneus.

Nikion: (2ⁿᵈ c. AD). Renown hetaira making a brief appearance at the banquet of the Deipnosophists to tease the guests about eating lentils instead of the more luxurious fish (Athen. 4.45). She was also known to Eusthathios (*Com. Il.* 3.662), possibly from Athenaios.

Nikippe: Fictional hetaira in Alkiphron (4.10).

Niko "victory", **aka Aix** "the Goat": (4ᵗʰ c.). Athenaios drawing from two different sources, Machon (18.423–430 = Athen. 13.45 and 18.456 = Athen. 13.45) and Lynkeus (apud Athen. 13.47), says that she was nick-named Aix "Goat", because she devoured (κατέφαγεν) the wealth of a foreign merchant named Thallos "green branch" visiting Attica to buy the famous Attic honey and black figs (cf. Gow 1965: 132–3). The lexicographers (Harp. s.v. Nannion; Suda v 25) explain that goats love to eat green branches. The same story about Thallos is linked to Nanno by Apollodoros (*FGrH* 244 F 211b = Athen. 13.51). Gow thinks that between the two women Niko has the better claim (1965: 131–2). We are told by Machon that she had a very attractive behind, while an epigram of Asclepiades (*AG* 5.150), which may be based on this Niko, says that she was renowned (ἐπιβόητος). A reference in Athenaios (5.63) may help explain her notoriety, if we accept that she is the same woman as Niko of Samos, the writer of a manual of erotica. The theme of an epigram from the *Greek Anthology* (5.205), a spell to bring back someone's lover, may be alluding to some part of this manual, and if so, the manual of Niko, with magic spells and other advice on how to win a lover, could be a popular reading.

Niko of Samos: An obscure reference in Athenaios (5.63) suggests that she had paid much attention to the means of attraction of lovers, perhaps in a written work.

Nicopolis: (2nd c.). Roman hetaira (perhaps of Greek origin if the name is any indication), born around 150 BC. She was the lover of the young Cornelius Sulla. Plutarch attests that she was quite well-off at the time when they met, and at her death she left her property to Sulla (Plu. *Sul.* 2).

Nikostratis, aka **Aphye** "sardine": According to Athenaios (13.50), Antiphanes in his work *On Hetairai* said that she was nick-named "sardine" because she was slim and pale with big eyes.

Nysia of Halicarnassos: (5th c.). According to Photios, Plesirrhoos, a lover of Herodotos, fell in love with a hetaira from Halicarnassos named Nysia. When she rejected him, he hanged himself, and this is why Herodotos did not mention her name (*Bibl.* 190, 150b 27). The whole story probably is a later antiquity aetion.

Nysa: (Dancer, 3rd c.). Concubine of Seleucus II, the younger, according to Ptolemy Megalopolis (*FGrH* 161 F 4 = Athen. 13.40).

Nitarios: A naïve pimp (Sch. Ar. Plu. 1011).

Oia: See notes *Antikyra* and *Nais*.

Oinanthe: (3rd c.,probably false). According to Plutarch (753 D; *Agis* 54.3) she was an entertainer (flute-player or dancer), and a pimp, mother of Agathokleia (s.v.), the influential hetaira and concubine of Ptolemy IV Philopator, and Agathokles, the powerful advisor of Ptolemy IV and regent to his son. Probably the accusation that she had been a lowly prostitute and a pimp should be attributed to a hostile tradition, as in reality Oinanthe was a powerful woman of noble birth. Polybius describes in chilling detail how a mob, enraged by the excesses of her family, removed Oinanthe from an altar where she had taken refuge after the assassination of her son, dragged her naked through the streets of Alexandria and tore her limb from limb along with Agathokleia and her other daughters.

Okimon "Basil": (early 4th c.). The author of the *Lexica Segueriana* (o 318) wasn't sure whether this was her proper name or a nickname. A fragment of Hypereides (13 Jensen = Athen. 13.52) attests that she was one of the most beautiful women of her time, and this is confirmed by a fragment from the *Geronto-mania* of Anaxandrides (fr. 9 = Athen. 13.26). She is also mentioned in the *Pandrosos* of Nikostratos (fr. 20 = Athen. 13.52). She may have been based in Corinth, as a double entendre from the *Kerkopes* of Euboulos (fr. 53 = Athen. 13.21) suggests, where the speaker jokes that he was ruined in Corinth eating basil (ὤκιμον), and lost even his tunic.

Oholah and Oholibah: Iconic sisters and prostitutes, standing as metaphors for Samaria and Jerusalem, practicing prostitution in Egypt and offering themselves to wealthy Assyrians and Chaldeans (*Ez.* 23).

Olympia, of Laconia: (early 3rd c.). Athenaios (13.61) citing Nicias of Nicaea, attests that she was the mother of the philosopher Bion of Borysthena. Diogenes Laertios (4.46) relates a story, where Bion is speaking to Antigonos Gonatas, and admits in his own words that his mother was a common prostitute in a brothel before his father, a libertine, married her.

Orsilochos: (5th c.). Mentioned in the Lysistrata of Aristophanes as a desperate alternative for the sexually deprived women (725). The scholiast says that Orsilochos was effeminate, a pimp, and an adulterer, which suggests that he probably did not know who this person was (Sch. Ar. Lys. 725). The joke might work better if Orsilochos was an effeminate, male prostitute and the last man in town a woman would go for sex.

Pagis "trap": See n. Philemation, the elder.

Palaestra "wrestling grounds": Citizen-born hetaira in Plautus *Rudens*, which was modeled on a play of Diphilos. During the course of the play she escapes from the control of the violent pimp Labrax and ends up marrying her sweetheart Plesidippus with the blessing of her long-lost father Daemones.

Panarete "all-virtuous": Dancer. Fictitious character in Aristainetos (1.25).

Pannychis "all-nighter": Given that it is the title of several old and middle-comedy plays (Pherecrates, Alexis, Kallippos and Hipparchos), the possibility that there was a classical hetaira under this name remains open. In our sources a fictional hetaira in Lucian is called Pannychis (*DMeretr.* 9).

Parmenis: Fictional hetaira in the *Greek Anthology* (*AG* 5.247; 6.290).

Paroinos "drunkard": According to Athenaios (13.46), she is one of the hetairai missed by Aristophanes Byzantios, but included by Apollodoros or Gorgias in their collections of the Attic hetairai.

Parorama: See n. Leme.

Parthenis "virginal": Fictional flute-Player (Luc. *DMeretr.* 15.1). Perhaps based on the same person as Parthenion, the infamous flute-player who has mesmerized old Koriskos in Alciphron (2.31), to the dismay of Anthylla, his wife of 30 years.

Pasiphila/Pasiphile: See n. Plangon.

Pausanias, pornos "the whore": Mentioned in a ficticious letter of Demosthenes (4.11), also cited by Libanios (*Ep.* 506.4). The inspiration for the character may have been provided by the person of Pausanias the pornographer, a famous painter of erotica (Polemon fr. 16 Müller = Athen. 13.21, where the form of the name is probably incorrectly transmitted in our manuscripts as Παυσίαν, but the epitome gives Παυσανίαν).

Peitho: (late 3ʳᵈ c.). According to Eumachos (*FGrH* 178 F 1 = Athen. 13.37), she started as a common prostitute established in a brothel, but ended up wife of Hieronymos, the teenage tyrant of Syracuse (216–5 BC), and queen.

Pellana: The name of a hetaira according to the Scholiast of Aristophanes (Sch. Ar. Lys. 996; the text of Aristophanes on which the scholion is based is disputed).

Petale: (Possibly 5ᵗʰ c.). Several fictional hetairai in Alciphron (4.8, 9, 14) and Aristainetos (1.25). If a well-know play of Pherecrates entitled *Petale* was named after a hetaira, it may have provided the inspiration for Alciphron and Aristainetos.

Phanion: (4ᵗʰ c.). A hetaira who provided the inspiration for the play of Menander *Phanion* (Athen. 13.21).

Phanostrate, aka: Phtheiropyle "Flee-gate": (4th c.). She is mentioned in the speech of Demosthenes *Against Androtion* (D. 22.56), as one of two women who had their property seized because they were accused of tax evasion. Demosthenes states that this seizure was illegal. Apollodoros in his study on Athenian hetairai, mentions that she was nick-named Phtheiropyle because she stood at the door step to de-lice herself (Apollodoros *FGrH* 244 F 209. Cf. Athen. 13.50; Harp. s.v.; Phot. s.v.; Suda φ 78 al.). She was certainly a well-known hetaira, famous enough to have a play of Menander named after her (fr. 106.190 Austin).

Pharsalia: Dancer, (4th c). Theopompos (115 F 24 = Athen. 13.83) narrates an unlikely story about her. He says that Onomarchos, the Phocian general, gave her a golden bay wreath, which had been dedicated to Delphi by the city of Lampsakos. When she entered the market at Metapontium, some oracles, alerted by a voice coming from a bronze statue of a bay tree standing in the market place, fell on her in a manic state and killed her. Thus, the stolen bay-wreath became the cause of her undoing. Plutarch (397 F) provides a rationalized version of the story, still taking place in Metapontium. A group of young men went after the golden wreath which Pharsalia was wearing, and as they were fighting with each other with over it, she was inadvertently killed.

Phila, of Thebes (or Corinth): (4th c.). Lover and concubine of Hypereides. Idomeneus (*FGrH* F 14 = Athen. 13.58) says that he paid a lot of money to set her free and kept her in his house in Eleusis. This information would be consonant with the comment of Apollodoros that the lovers of the girls of Nikarete paid a lot of money to buy their freedom. Phila is mentioned in the list which he provides (D.18–19; cf. Kapparis 1999: 209). Plutarch (849 D) says that the lover of Hypereides was from Thebes, while Nikarete's girl was a slave from Corinth. Besides the good possibility that Plutarch is mistaken, there is no strong reason why Phila could not be originally from Thebes. Although it was not customary for free-born girls to end up as slaves in the hands of pimps, it is not inconceivable either. This comment of Plutarch might be the only information preventing us from identifying the mistress of Hypereides with Nikarete's girl, but it should not be sufficient grounds to think that we are dealing with two different women. Nikarete's girl is probably the same woman as the mistress of Hypereides, and almost certainly the person mentioned in a fragment of Philaiteros (fr. 9), along with two more of the women from Nikarete's set, Isthmias and Neaira.

Phila, of Elis: (First half of the 4th c.). Lover of Aristippos, along with Theodote of Elis. Diogenes Laertios (4.40) seems to suggest that Aristippos was living with both women simultaneously.

Philainis, of Samos, the daughter of Okymenes, aka affectionately **Philainion:** (4th c.). Athenaios (5.63) includes her in a list of four writers of erotica manuals, along with Kallistrate of Lesbos, Niko of Samos and Pythonikos of Athens, and mistakenly thinks that she was from Leukas. There is no doubt that she was actually from Samos, as she gives her full name and demotic in the first line of her work, a few fragments of which have been preserved (POxy. 2891), and there is plentiful additional evidence to link her with Samos (e.g. Athen. 8.13; *AG* 7.450). While the other three writers are nothing but names to us, the work of Philainis was famous throughout antiquity (see the more detailed presentation in Ch. 2 i. and Tsantsanoglou 1973: 183–195). Since her manual was known to Klearchos of Soli, Timaios, Chrysippos and possibly Aristotle (Klearchos fr. 63,1 Wehrli; Timaios *FGrH* 566 f 35 b; Chrysippos fr. 5 and 6 von Arnim; Arist. *Div.Somn.* 464 b 2), we can place her in the second half of the 4th century. Poseidonios (fr. 290 a 500 Theiler) attests that she was one of the women frequenting the Gardens of Epicurus. The fame of her manual, especially the part about sexual positions, is probably responsible for numerous references to a hetaira named Philainis in fictional literature (e.g. Asklepiades *AG* 5.162, 202; Poseidippos 5.186; Luc. *DMeretr.* 6.1; Aristaenet. 1.25; Philodemos *AG* 4.1; Maecius *AG* 5.130 al.). Philaenium is also a hetaira-character in Plautus *Asinaria*.

Philemation "Little kiss", the elder, aka **Pagis** "trap": Fictional hetaira pretending that she is half the age she actually is in Lucian (*DMeretr.* 11.2). Philematium is also the name of a fictional hetaira in Plautus *Mostellaria*, set free by Philochares.

Philemation "Little kiss", the younger: Fictional young hetaira, who has just lost her virginity in Lucian (*DMeretr.* 11.2).

Philinna, of Thessaly (Larisa): Dancer (4th c.). Lover of Philip II, and mother of his son Arrhidaios, who assumed the throne as Philip III, after Alexander's death, as joint king with Alexander's infant son from Roxanne (Ptolemy Megalopolis *FGrH* 161 F 4 = Athen. 13.40; Porphyry *Chronica* 3.1, 4.1, 7.1).

Philip of Carthage: (early 2nd c. BC). Famous male prostitute, lover of Lucius Quintius Flamininus when the latter was governor of Gaul. Flamininus (the brother of Titus) was removed from office because at the behest of Philip he ordered the execution of a Gaul (Liv. *Periochae* 39, 8–16).

Philistion: Fictional hetaira in the *Greek Anthology* (*AG* 5.114).

Philostratos: An otherwise unkown Athenian, reviled as a pimp by the Scholiast of Aristophanes (Sch. Ar. Lys. 957 and Eq. 1069).

Philotis: Fictional hetaira in Terence *Hekyra*.

Philoumene "beloved": (Probably 4th c.). A woman mentioned in a fragment of Krobylos (fr. 5), may be a hetaira. A fictional hetaira named Philoumene in Alciphron (4.14) put her husband to sleep and sneaked out to meet her hetaira friends and go together to the Adonia, shortly after her marriage, and another hetaira named Philoumene cynically asks for money (4.15).

Philoxene: (4th c.). Aeschines alleges that Timarchos spent 20 minae from a bribe on the hetaira Philoxene, over a short period of time.

Philyra: (Late 5th – early 4th c.). According to Lysias, she gave up prostitution while still in her prime, probably to become the concubine of a wealthy lover (fr. 208 Carey = Athen. 13.62). She may have provided inspiration for a play of Ephippos entitled *Philyra* (21–23).

Phoenicium: Fictional hetaira in Plautus *Pseudolus*.

Phronesium: Fictional character of the ruthless, manipulative and money-grabbing hetaira in Plautus *Truculectus*.

Phryne, daughter of Epicles, from Thespiai, aka **Mnesarete:** Born c. 370. The most famous hetaira in the ancient world next to her senior contemporary Lais. Her true name was Mnesarete, but apparently she was nick-named Phryne "the toad", because of her pale complexion (Diod. Ath. fr. 5 = Athen. 13.60; Plu. 401 A). Timokles joked that before she reached her prime she was making a living as a capers-gatherer (fr. 25 = Athen. 13.22). An anecdote told by Galen suggests that unlike most hetairai who relied heavily upon artificial cosmetics, her beauty was natural and truly exquisite (Gal. 10.42). She was a citizen of Thespiai, a small city approximately 20 km. away from Thebes, 80 km. (equivalent to a day's journey) away from Athens, and a similar distance from Corinth, but it is not certain whether she was born there as many Thespians were living in Athens in the 4th c., after the subjugation of their city by Thebes in 373. The details of her life suggest that she spent most of it in Athens, although she retained ties with her homeland, if we can judge by the fact that she made dedications to the city of Thespiai (Athen. 13.79), like the famous Eros of Praxiteles. According to one version of the story, her native city with great pride for the greatest celebrity ever to come out of Thespiai returned the favor supposedly by dedicating the famous and controversial statue of Phryne at Delphi (see Ch. 4 i. for the relevant debate). A story from the work of Kallistratos *On Hetairai* as transmitted by Athenaios (13.60) intends to provide evidence of the substantial wealth of Phryne. We are told that like a good citizen of Thespiae, Phryne apparently did not miss the opportunity to take a dig at Thebes, when Alexander destroyed the city. In a statement, which was no doubt full of irony, she offered to restore the walls of Thebes, if only the Thebans agreed to add the inscription "Alexander destroyed, but Phryne the hetaira restored". Thebes had destroyed the walls of Thespiai twice in the past, and this bitter joke would be her way of getting back at the old enemy. She reached her prime around the middle of the 4th century, a time when the economic and social climate was particularly conducive for high-class prostitution in Athens. The prosperity of the Euboulos years and the cultural openness of the city had created the golden era of the Attic hetaira. Phryne succeeded in acquiring great wealth and fame and became an iconic figure for the independent-minded Greek hetaira of the classical period in subsequent literature and art. Unlike many famous hetairai of her time, Phryne was never a slave or some alien of low birth. She was a free-born Greek woman, citizen of a small city which despite adversity was fiercely proud of its independence and identity, and had earned its own glorious place in history at the battle of Thermopylae. This endowed her with a certain pride and air of superiority which becomes apparent through her sharp wit, as this was remembered in the sympotic literature of later antiquity (see App. II). The fact that she did not have to share her considerable earnings with an owner or procurer allowed her to accumulate a large fortune (Athen. 13.60). Undoubtedly a keen businesswoman, she was aware of the effectiveness of good marketing and self-promotion. Even when she got older, she was still very pricy and used to joke that she sells the left-overs of the wine for more money than she sold the wine itself, because of her reputation (Plu. 125 A). Although, as we are told, she might give a discount to the odd client, she was generally very demanding. According to one of the stories of Machon, Moirichos, a very wealthy and money-conscious Corinthian (cf. Luc. *DMort.* 21.1), was seeking her company. She asked for a mina, but he wanted her to settle for two gold coins, as she had done with a foreigner a few days before. She answered "wait then until I get horny again" (Machon fr. 18.450 = Athen. 13.45). Anaxilas (fr. 22 = Athen. 13.6) is joking that she was like Charybdis, for she "swallowed" the entire ship of one of her clients. Pollux mentions that she took great pleasure from spinning a coin on the tip of her finger as a game (χαλκισμός: 9.118). The most famous incident of her life, however, was her trial for impiety, which E. Cavalini has dated to 335 (Cavalini 2004: 231–238). Hypereides, one of her lovers, delivered the defense speech, of which a few fragments still survive (see the more detailed discussion in Ch. 4.4.). A rhetorical study preserves what appears to be the summary of the charges against Phryne from the speech of Euthias, her prosecutor: *"Phryne is prosecuted for impiety, because she was carousing at the Lycaeum, and introduced a new god, and formed illicit religious groups (θιάσους) of men and women"* (Anon. Seg. *Ars Rhetorica* 215 Hammer). If these references retain something from the truth of the matter, then one might assume that Phryne was prosecuted by an angry former lover under some pretext which included some religious transgressions and the introduction of foreign rituals to Athens. How flimsy the real grounds for such prosecutions could be is well attested in two well-known parallels, the prosecution of Timarchos and that of Neaira. However, at least in one of these cases (Timarchos), the mud thrown by the prosecution in the form of vague and unfounded allegations for male prostitution, corruption and extravagance stuck. Unlike Timarchos Phryne was acquitted, but just barely. We are told the only thing that saved her from sure conviction was a trick of Hypereides: he removed her garment and implored the jury not to put to death such a divine beauty, and it worked. Craig Cooper (1995: 303–318) has rightly argued that much of the tradition about the trial of Phryne is fabricated. C. Havelock (1995: 3–4 and 42–47) has suggested that Phryne is a largely fictional character, but this blanket statement is not historically sensitive, does not take into account the nature and reliability of the sources, and fails to separate the factual from the fictional with consistent criteria, difficult as this may be for a figure surrounded by personal mythology, so much of which was intentional and generated by Phryne herself. Phryne was probably prosecuted because she was unconventional, she pushed boundaries, acquired personal fame and wealth which would be unimaginable for contemporary Athenian women, and invited envy. She is the quintessential Athenian hetaira, spirited, independent, intelligent, and in some ways worlds apart from her contemporary women, and this is why she has had such a mesmerizing effect upon future generations.

Phylakion "guardian": (Late 3rd –early 2nd c.). Hetaira, concubine of Stratokles, an influential demagogue under Demetrios Poliorketes. (Plu. *Demetr.* 11.3)

Phyllis: Fictional psaltery-player, in Alciphron (3.9).

Placentina "pleasing": (Early 2nd c.). Hetaira, mistress of lover of Lucius Quintius Flamininus when the latter was governor of Gaul. Flamininus (the brother of Titus) was removed from office because, among others, at the behest of Placentina he had a convicted man beheaded with an axe (Liv. *Periochae* 39, 8–16).

Plangon of Athens, the daughter of Pamphilos: (4th c.). Although it is not certain that the mistress of Mantias, in the two speeches of the Demosthenic Corpus *Against Boeotus* (39 and 40) was a hetaira at some point, it surely seems to be the case. The speaker does not hesitate to use her first name in front of the jury and speak quite disrespectfully of her; this would be uncustomary for Athenian litigants, when they referred to female kin. First Mantitheos, the speaker, alleges that she had extramarital relations with his father as his mistress while his mother was still alive, but refuses to get into the details of how they met and suggests that it would be inappropriate for him to mention such matters before the jury (40.8; since it is likely that Plangon was the first wife of Mantias, it is not in the best interests of Mantitheos to explain properly the early years of their relationship). Then he says that Plangon was exceedingly attractive (40.27), and lived extravagantly surrounded by maids and luxury (40.51), even though her family was dirt-poor and her father died owing the state five talents. And finally, he says that his father was too ashamed to bring her into his home as his wife, even after the mother of Mantitheos, had died (40.8). The two children of Plangon and Mantias were treated as illegitimate and lived with their mother, while the speaker, the one recognized legitimate son, was living with his father, until the father was persuaded (or, compelled according to the speaker) to recognize and legitimize his sons from Plangon, which he was able to do since their mother was Athenian after all. All this could easily suggest to a jury a hetaira's lifestyle, without the speaker saying the word. The image of Plangon which he portrays is that of a woman of splendid appearance from a good, but impoverished family, who capitalized on her looks and took lovers in order to provide for herself and her children, and like a typical hetaira, ruthlessly deceived her long-term lover to have her brood legitimized. How much truth there is in this remains uncertain, but that Mantitheos wants the jury to think of Plangon as a hetaira without actually saying the word is clear. Maximus of Ephesos (14.438 Rabe) also read the Demosthenic text in this manner, and interpreted the facts of the case under the assumption that Plangon was a hetaira.

Plangon, of Miletos, aka Pasiphila / Pasiphile "Lover of Everyone": (4th c.). A passage of Anaxilas (fr. 22 = Athen. 13.6) suggests that she was very popular among the barbarians, possibly because she started her career in her native Miletos, a cosmopolitan city with many non-Greeks around. She seems to be a well-known hetaira in Athens, which probably should be interpreted as evidence that she moved there at some point. Anaxilas, who is comparing her with Chimera, is also telling us that a single knight (ἱππεύς) took her entire fortune, even the furniture of the house. Even if this refers to a real incident, there is no doubt that Plangon remained one of the most prominent hetairai of her time. Timocles (fr. 27 = Athen. 13.22) lists her among several ageing hetairai. Athenaios, quoting Menetor (fr. 1 Müller = Athen. 13.66) tells the unlikely story of how she was overcome by the generosity of Bacchis and after that she was nicknamed Pasiphila. In fictional literature Plangon has provided inspiration for a play of Euboulos which was named after her (Harp. s.v. *metoikion*), and maybe for several Menandrian characters (in *Dyskolos*, *Heros* and *Samia*), a character in Chariton's novel *Chaireas and Kallirhoe*, a hetaira in Alciphron (4.13), and an epigram of Asclepiades (5.202).

Poikile: Fictional flute-player (Phot. *Bibl.* 190.152 b 25).

Porphyra "purple": (Possibly 4th c.). A number of comic plays by Timocles or Xenarthos (Athenaios [7.108] was not sure; cf. Suda τ 624) and Augeas (Suda α 4410) are possibly named after a hetaira, but this is not certain, and the title might simply allude to luxury and royalty.

Potheine: (later 3rd c.): A flute-player employed and favored by Ptolemy Philopator (Plb. 14.11.5).

Prodike: A fictional ageing hetaira (*AG* 5.103).

Psamathe: (Late 5th – early 4th c.). According to Lysias, she gave up prostitution while still at her prime, probably to become the concubine of a wealthy lover (fr. 208 Carey = Athen. 13.62).

Ptochelene: See n. Kalliston

Pyrallis "dove": Fictional hetaira, enemy of Ioessa, the lover of Lysias, in Lucian (*DMeretr.* 12.1). In a classic sympotic scene when Lysias wants to make Ioessa jealous, because he thinks that she is sleeping with someone else, he bites an apple and throws it to Pyrallis. She picks it up and places it in her breasts.

Pyrrhine "fiery red": Mentioned in Suda (ε 3266) among several supposedly Corinthian hetairai, several of whom we can recognize as certainly non-Corinthan. The nickname suggests a woman of foreign origin.

Pythias, the daughter of Niko: (Possibly early 3ʳᵈ c.). An epigram of Asclepiades, assuming it refers to a real person, gives the name of her mother as Niko, the well-known hetaira. If so, then she was following her mother's trade. She is described in it as deceitful for locking her lover outside all night. Pythias is also mentioned in an epigram of Poseidippos, and is the character with whom a fellow-hetaira converses in a fragment from an unknown play of the poet Phoinikides of Megara. Although these references come from fictional literature, they are anchored in the 3ʳᵈ c, and suggest that they are drawing from a real person who lived in the first half of the 3ʳᵈ c. Further references in the fictional literature of later antiquity (Luc. *DMeretr.* 12; Aristainet. 1.12, 19, 2.2; *AG* 5.159, 164, 213) are probably drawing from this Hellenistic tradition.

Pythionike: A woman of humble origins, who received great honors after her death. According to Theopompos she was initially a slave of the flute player Bacchis, who had been a slave of the hetaira Sinope, and this is why he calls her "a third-generation slave and a third-generation whore" (τρίδουλος καὶ τρίπορνος). Her affair with the extravagant Harpalos, the treasurer of Alexander the Great, catapulted her to fame. Plutarch mentions a daughter of Harpalos and Pythionike, who was looked after by Phokion and his son in law Charikles after the death of both her parents (Plu. *Phoc.* 22). The information of Pausanias that Pythionike was the wife of Harpalos (1.37.5: ἔγημε) is probably mistaken, since something as shocking as a marriage to a prostitute would not have been left out by hostile contemporary sources. Theopompos who offers much of the available information about her life is a hostile source (*FGrH* 115 f 253; D.S. 17.108.5). When he mentions the honors and splendid monuments which Harpalos dedicated to his dead mistress, he adds that before that Pythionike was just a cheap whore available to anyone who wanted her for a small fee. Two plays, one by Antiphanes and one by Timokles, make jokes to the same end (Antiphanes fr. 27, Timokles fr. 16). Timokles calls her greedy (ἄπληστος) and elsewhere he includes her in a list of ageing hetairai. Harpalos and Pythionike were mentioned in a satyric play by Python. Pausanias mentions that she had been a hetaira in Corinth and Athens. After her premature death a distraught Harpalos dedicated monuments in her honor in Athens and Babylon. Authors who had seen the monument in Athens, such as the travelers Dikaiarchos (fr. 29) and Pausanias (1.37.5), and the historians Theopompos and Plutarch (*Phoc.* 22), seem rather annoyed by the fact that such a splendid structure was built for a prostitute (see the discussion in Ch. 6.1.).

Rahab (Greek *Raab*): According to the book of *Joshua* (2) she was a prostitute in Jericho, who welcomed and hid the spies of Joshua. When the city fell, Rahab and her family were spared from the massacre and then integrated into the Jewish population. The term *porne* in relation to Rahab appears in the Septuagint translation but is not explicitly used in Hebrew sources. In Josephus (*AJ* 5.8), for example, she is simply the inn-keeper, but the word he uses for inn (καταγώγιον) implies a brothel. Christian authors read the Septuagint version and took it for granted that Rahab was a prostitute. They were fond of the story of Rahab, because to them it symbolized penitence and faith. In Christian interpretations Rahab saved herself and her family, despite her disreputable profession, because she had faith in God and assisted his people (see e.g. *Ep. Hebr.* 11.31; Clement of Rome *Epistula I ad Corinthios* 12.1: διὰ πίστιν καὶ φιλοξενίαν ἐσώθη Ῥαάβ ἡ πόρνη "Rahab the whore was spared because of faith and hospitality"; Origenes *Com. Ev. Mat.* 12.4.52; Hippolytus *Com. Dan.* 2.19.5 al.).

Rhodanthe "rose-bud": Fictional hetaira in the *Greek Anthology* (5.218, 237).

Rhodokleia "name of the rose": Fictional hetaira in the letters of Theophylaktos (51, 66) and the *Greek Anthology* (5.36, 73, 74, 16.283).

Rhodope "rose-face": Fictional hetaira in the *Greek Anthology* (5.36, 92, 219, 228, 249).

Salabaccho, or, probably mistakenly, Salabaccha in Sch. Ar. Eq 765: (late 5th – early 4th century). She makes a couple of appearances in the plays of Aristophanes (*Eq.* 765, *Th.* 805), which suggests that she was quite notorious and Aristophanes expected his audience to know who she was. Later lexicographers and scholiasts did not have any additional information, beyond what they could extract from the Aristophanic text.

Sannio "zany /clown": Fictional procurer in Terence *Adelpoi*.

Sappho of Eressos: Probably fictitious, made up to explain the tradition according to which Sappho was a hetaira. Later antiquity could not reconcile the image of the beloved and revered poet with the Attic comic tradition which had turned her into a hetaira, and invented another hetaira to take this role (Ael. *VH* 12.19; Phot. S.f. Leukates, seemingly referring to Athen. 13.70; see the discussion in Ch. 1.1.).

Satyra "Satyr-woman": Fictional hetaira; according to Idomeneus, one of the four original hetairai introduced by Themistokles in Athens (*FGrH* 338 F 4a; see the discussion in Ch. 3.1.). Suetonius in his study *On Insults* mentions this word as a generic term for prostitute (see Kapparis 2011: 241).

Sige "silence": According to Athenaios (13.46), she is one of the hetairai missed by Aristophanes Byzantios, Apollodoros and Gorgias in their collections of Attic hetairai.

Silenium: Citizen girl brought up to be a hetaira in Plautus *Cistellaria*.

Simaitha of Megara: (5th c.). Megarian prostitute mentioned by Aristophanes (*Ach.* 524). Suda (σ 428) and the Scholiast of Aristophanes (Sch. Ar. Ach. 524) preserve an alternative tradition where Alcibiades fell in love with her and instigated her seizure by a group of Athenian youths. The name is also used by Theocritos for one of his most famous characters, that of the Pharmakeutria in Idyll 2.

Simiche: Fictional hetaira in Lucian (*DMeretr.* 4).

Sindis: Otherwise unknown prostitute mentioned by Hesychios (s.v. Sindis).

Sinope, of Thrace, aka **Abydos:** (4th c.). Sch. Ar. Plu. 149 erroneously includes her in a list of Corinthian hetairai. In reality she was from Thrace, according to Theopompos (*FGrH* 115 F 253), or perhaps more precisely from Sinope on the Black sea, hence the nickname. Theopompos also reports that she first worked as a hetaira in Aigina and then moved to Athens where she set up business for many years, until her old age as several references suggest (Anaxilas, fr. 22 = Athen 13.6; Harp. s.v. *Sinope*). Herodikos Kratetios (fr. 1; Harp. s.v. *Sinope*; Athen. 13.50) reports that she was nicknamed Abydos because she was old (this city on the Asiatic coast of the Hellespont had a reputation of being run down). Amphis (fr. 23) calls her "a trap", and states that she was very wealthy. Androtion is accused of inhumanity by Demosthenes because as a tax collector he tried to forcibly extract from Sinope taxes which she did not owe (D. 22.56). Apollodoros (D. 59.116), attests that Sinope in an attempt to gain notoriety persuaded Archias the Hierophant to perform a sacrifice for her at the yard of the Sanctuary at Eleusis during the festival of the Haloa. This was prohibited by the ritual of the festival and Archias was punished (see Kapparis 1999: 410–413). Her fame was such that Athenaios (13.50) was able to provide a list of plays where she was mentioned: Antiphanes in the *Arkas* (fr. 43), the *Gardener* (fr. 114), the *Sempstress* (fr. 23), the *Sea-Woman* (Ἁλιευομένη, fr. 27), and the *Chick* (Νεοττίς, fr. 168), Alexis in *Kleobouline* (fr. 109), and Kallikrates in *Moschion* (fr. 1). Apostolios (*Paroemiogr.* 15.50) even reports a proverbial expression originating from her: σινωπίζειν meant "to behave lecherously".

Sisymbras: Fictional pimp, grandfather of Battaros in Herodas (2.76).

Sisymbrion "bergamot-mint/ornament": (4ᵗʰ c.). One of the women whose appearance pimps enhance with linen in a fragment of Theophilos (fr. 11).

Sisymbriskos: Fictional pimp, father of Battaros in Herodas (2.76).

Skylla: Herakleitos the Paradoxographer (2) interpreted the myth of the Skylla in a prostitutional context, where Skylla was a beautiful island-girl who preyed upon sailors and swallowed their fortune, but Odysseus was able to resist her because he was the only prudent man among his crew.

Skione: (Late 5ᵗʰ – early 4ᵗʰ c.). Sch. Ar. Plu. 149 includes her in a list of Corinthian hetairai. However, the fact that she had the name of the city of Skione may suggest that in reality she came from that part of the world, like several other hetairai nick-named after their native cities (e.g. Sinope). According to Lysias, she gave up prostitution while still at her prime, probably to become the concubine of a wealthy lover (fr. 208 Carey = Athen. 13.62). The fictional hetaira named Skione, who was one of the four original hetairai introduced to Athens by Themistokles, according to a later tale, may have drawn some inspiration from the real Skione.

Stagonion: See n. Aphyai.

Stephanium "little garland": Fictional hetaira in Plautus *Stichus*.

Stratola: (4th c.). One of the girls of Nikarete of Elis, according to Apollodoros (D. 59.19).

Stratonike: (late 5th – early 4th century) Mentioned among other prostitutes in Ar. *Th.* 807.

Stratonike: (3rd c.). Wife and sister of Ptolemy II Philadelphos according to the scholiast of Lucian (Sch. Luc. 24.15 Rabe), but a prostitute and his mistress according to his descendant Ptolemy VIII Euergetes II (*FGrH* 234 F 4 = Athen. 13.37). See also the discussion about the monument of Stratonike in Ch. 6.1.

Strongyle "round": A hetaira nicknamed, we are told, after her ability to turn a sober man into a drunk and to sober up a drunk man (*AG* 5.135).

Synoris, aka **Lychnos** "the Lamp": According to Athenaios (13.46), she is one of the hetairai missed by Aristophanes Byzantios, Apollodoros and Gorgias in their collections of Attic hetairai.

Syra: Fictional procuress in the play of Apollodoros *Hekyra* "the mother-in-law", (fr. 8), and its Latin adaptation by Terence.

Telesippa (4th c.**).:** One of the free women following the army of Alexander, lover of Antigenes, a warrior in the army of Alexander. When Telesippa decided to go back to Greece, Antigenes pretended to be wounded in order to be able to follow her, but Alexander, who saw through the pretense, advised him instead that he should try to persuade Telesippa to stay with gifts and promises (Plu. 339 D).

Telesis, the daughter or protégé of Diopeithes: (4th c.). A fragment of Philaiteros (fr. 9 = Athen. 13.52) says that she was 13,000 years old, and looked disgusting.

Thaïs, of Athens: (4th c.). She is best known for her alleged role in the burning of the palace of Persepolis (see the discussion in Ch. 3.4.). She was a mistress of Ptolemy and followed him all the way as Alexander's army was fighting its way into Persia. As several authors say (e.g. Athen. 13.37; D.S. 17.72.2; Curtius 5.7.3–8; Plu. *Alex.* 38), on that fateful night after a drunken party Thais was the first to throw the torch on the splendid monument, in retribution for the burning of Athens by Xerxes. The story sounds very suspicious as it bears the marks of a later antiquity literary composition, and Arrian (4.10–14) was not convinced that it was true; this is why he did not accept it. She is also mentioned in an *adespoton* from an unknown poet (Luc. dial. mer. 3,2), where she receives a passionate kiss by a lover. Athenaios (13.49) citing Lynkeus praises her wit, and Eustathios (*Com. Od.* 1.348) upon reading these stories in Athenaios calls her "the wise hetaira Thais" (ἡ σοφὴ ἑταίρα Θαΐς). In fictional literature the fame of Thais was such that she provided inspiration to numerous authors, as we encounter the name in use, with reference to Attic hetairai, for hundreds of years. In her own time, or shortly afterwards, Menander gave the title *Thais* to one of his plays (Harp. s.v. *metaulos*; Athen 13.21), and so did Hipparchos (fr. 3). Thais is also a hetaira-character in Terence *Eunuchus* and in an epigram of Asclepiades (or Hedylos: *AG*. 5.151). Fictional hetairai in Lucian (*DMeretr.* 3), Alciphron (4.6, 7, 14) and Aristainetos (2.16) were named Thais, most likely on account of the popular play of Menander. A wax-based rouge for the face (*keroton Thaidos*: Paulus Med. *Epitome* 3.25.7) and the golden anklets of Thais mentioned by Philostratos (*Ep.* 1.22) might have some tenuous connection with the famous hetaira.

Thalatta "sea": A hetaira who gave her name to a play of Diocles, according to Athenaios (13.21).

Thalassis "sea": (early to mid 4th c.). Mother of the hetaira Glykera, and probably a hetaira herself, if we judge by the fact that Hypereides (fr. 28 Blass = Athen. 13.50) identified Glykera by the name of her mother, presumably because she was notorious enough to be known by his audience.

Thallousa "blooming": The comic poet Theophilos (fr. 11 = Athen. 13.52) lists her among several women whose appearance was enhanced with fine linen.

Thamar, the pseudo-prostitute: In a strange tale from *Genesis* (38), Thamar, twice widowed from sons of Judah, disguises herself as a prostitute and lures Judah into sleeping with her, in order to provide an heir for his line. Then she returns to her state of widowhood, but when she is accused of prostitution and faces the death penalty, as she was pregnant without a living husband, she sends Judah his staff and seal. These objects she had asked as security when she agreed to sleep with him for the price of a goat, and returned them to Judah with the message that the man who gave her those was the father of her child. Thus, Judah recognized himself as the father and commuted the death-sentence of Thamar (see also the narrative of John Chrysostom *In Genesim Homilia* 54.533–

34). Christian authors were ambivalent about this story: Eusebius (*Quaestiones evangelicae ad Stephanum* 22.897 and 905) seems quite annoyed that Matthew (1.3) chose to mention Thamar in the genealogy of Jesus, and praises Luke for not doing so. Likewise, the author of the *Catena in Matthaeum* (6) has difficulty with this passage but interprets it as an act of humility from God to be associated with the dregs of society, and as a symbolism that the message of Christianity was for all, including lowly and unworthy gentiles. Theodoretus, on the other hand, (*Quaestiones in Octateuchum* 83–84) completely absolves Thamar and considers her actions proper and moral, as her objective was not lust but child-bearing, and thus consonant with the will of God for the line of Judah.

Thaumarion: According to Athenaios (13.46), she is one of the hetairai missed by Aristophanes Byzantios, Apollodoros and Gorgias in their collections of Attic hetairai.

Theano: (4th c.). A very thin hetaira mocked for being skiny in contemporary comedy. A passage of Anaxilas (fr. 22.20) compares her with a plucked Siren having the glance and voice of a woman and the legs of a blackbird. Antiphanes (fr. 27) jokes that one could balance a few small fish and a turtle-dove against her entire weight.

Thelxinoe: "Pleasing the mind": Fictional character in Aristainetos (1.19 and 1.25).

Theodoros: (4th c.). A procurer from southern Italy. He approached Philoxenos, one of the admirals of Alexander with the proposition to sell to the king two exquisitely attractive slave boys. A furious Alexander curtly turned down the proposal. (Plu. *Alex.* 22).

Theodote, of Athens: (5th c.). Athenian hetaira featured in Xenophon's *Memorabilia* as a conversation partner of Socrates. In Xenophon's account Socrates visits Theodote's house, which is described in some detail as a clean, affluent and gracious environment, and discusses with her high-end prostitution, economics, culture and friendship. The famous dialogue has influenced later antiquity literature, with a notable example in Lucian's *Dialogues of Hetairai* (6). See also the discussions in Ch. 3.1., and 7.

Theodote, of Elis: (First half of the 4th c.). Lover of Aristippos, along with Phila of Elis. Diogenes Laertios (4.40) seems to suggest that Aristippos was living with the two women in an erotic triangle.

Theodotos, of Plataia: (early 4th c.). Male prostitute around whom a quarrel erupted that landed the litigants in court in Lysias 3. A man named Simon, who is described as young and virile, hired Theodotos on a long-term contract. The speaker, who sounds older and probably more affluent, tried to lure Theodotos away from Simon. We should be in no doubt that the speaker offered Theodotos much more, in order to induce him to leave his current lover and follow the speaker on a trip. The two stayed away from Athens for months but when they returned Simon was waiting for them. In the scuffles that ensued Simon was injured and sued the speaker for deliberate wounding before the Areopagos, which carried permanent exile as the penalty. We do not know the outcome of the case, but in the trial the speaker explains the affair and, in doing so, offers us some valuable insights into the circles of male prostitution in the early 4th c. (see the discussion in Ch. 5.3. and 4.).

Theokleia, aka **Korone** "the Crow": (late 5th – early 4th c.). According to Athenaios (13.46), she is one of the hetairai missed by Aristophanes Byzantios, Apollodoros and Gorgias in their collections of Attic hetairai. The same passage states that she was alternatively called Korone. However, Theokleia, who according to a fragment from the speech of Lysias *Pros Laida* fr. 208 Carey = Athen. 13.62) gave up prostitution while still young, probably to become the concubine of a wealthy lover, must be differentiated from the famous hetaira named Korone, who was a contemporary of Antikyra and Gnataina and thus flourished in the second half of the 4th century (see n. above). It is likely that Athenaios or one of his sources was confused and Theokleia was not nicknamed Korone, but it is not impossible that the two women, separated by more than half a century, were both nick-named Korone.

Theolyte: (Late 5th – early 4th c.). Anaxandrides in his *Gerontomania* (fr. 9 = Athen. 13.26) mentions that Theolyte had a very beautiful face and was very attractive, and flourished at the same time as Anteia and Lagiska, which would place her around the turn of the century. Philaiteros (fr. 9 = Athen. 13.52) seems to confirm this information when he jokes a number of years later that no one could remember the time when Theolyte was born. A character named Theolyte, who appears to be an old slave enticed to sleep with a fellow slave, in the *Nemea* of Theopompos (fr. 33) may have been modeled on the famous hetaira.

Theoris, of Sikyon: (5th c.). Lover of Sophocles in his later years, and mother of his son Ariston (Hermesianax 7.59–60; Athen. 13.61, 118; Hsch. s.v. Theoris, Sch. Ar. Ra. 78, *Vita Sophoclis* 48).

Thettále: Fictional hetaira in Alciphron (4.10 and 14) possibly inspired from the Menandrian tradition. We have a few fragments from a play of Menander entitled *Thettále* (with the accent on the penultima, unlike the geographic Thettalé "from Thessaly" stressed on the ultima: Hdn *Prosod.* 321; Stephanus *Ethnica* [epitome] 311, and Sch. Ar. Nu. 749 b).

Thisbe: Psaltery-player. Fictional character in Heliodoros *Aethiopica* (2.8.2).

Thonis: According to Plutarch (*Dem.* 27.12–13), she was the hetaira involved in the judgment of Bocchoris (see Ch. 4.1.13.; cf. Hdt. 2.114).

Thryallis "candle": According to Athenaios (13.46), she is one of the hetairai missed by Aristophanes Byzantios, Apollodoros and Gorgias in their collections of Attic hetairai.

Timandra: Born probably around 420, if a later biographical tradition that she accompanied Alcibiades in his last days, and picked up his dead body after his assassination, is correct (Plu. *Alc.* 39; Athen. 12.48). Another later tradition, which seems less likely to be accurate, makes her the mother of the famous Lais (Athen. 12.48; Sch. Ar. Plu. 179). This tradition essentially would come in conflict with the version of events where Lais was captured in Sicily and brought to Greece as a small child during the Sicilian campaign, because of her promising looks. The scholiast of Aristophanes tries to bridge these versions by suggesting that Timandra too was from Hykkara. We need to examine this story in combination with another passage of Athenaios (13.34), where Damasandra, the other hetaira that accompanied Alcibiades in his last days, was the mother of Lais the younger. The whole edifice where the two hetairai of Alcibiades were supposedly the mothers of the two Laides is too artificial to be true. Either it is a complete invention, or Timandra was said to be the mother of the original Lais in analogy with Damasandra, who was truly the mother of the younger Lais. The evidence is insufficient to reach a firm conclusion. Dio Chrysostom attests that her beauty was famous (6.4.2), and includes her in a list of glorious women from the past (ἐνδόξους γυναῖκας), which includes Sappho, Semiramis and the wise Cypriot politician and lawgiver Demonassa. From a speech of Hypereides "Against Timandra" only a few fragments survive, too scant to give us any idea about the case, but enough to allow us to understand that the defendant had been a hetaira. Demetrios of Phaleron (*Eloc.* 302 Radermacher) referring to this case says that many distasteful references to her previous career were made in the courtroom.

Timarion "little precious": Fictional hetaira in several epigrams of Meleager (*AG* 5. 96, 204, 12.109, 113).

Timo "precious": Fictional hetaira in two epigrams of Meleager (*AG* 5. 197, 198).

Tryphaina "luxury": Fictional hetaira in Lucian (*DMeretr.* 11).

Tryphéra "tender": Fictional hetaira in epigrams of Asclepiades and Meleager (*AG* 5.154, 185).

Xanthippe: A fictional psaltria (singer), with dangerous charms (*AG* 5.131).

Xantho "blondie": Fictional hetaira in the *Greek Anthology* (*AG* 5.4, 9.570).

Zenophila: Fictional hetaira praised for her lovely singing and charms in several epigrams of Meleager, reminiscent of the themes of a *paraklausithyron* (*AG* 5.139, 140, 144, 149. 151, 152, 171, 174, 177, 178, 195, 196).

Appendix II

Bawdy Humor

Humor plays a very important role in interpersonal interactions, as an expression of physiological, psychological, and social drives. Studies on the complex personal and social factors surrounding humor, a detailed discussion of which is beyond our purposes here, have concluded that its primary functions can be summarized as following:[1] Humor responds to physiological and kinesiological needs as a mechanism of tension release, and contributes to physical and emotional health. At a psychological level it contributes to ego assertion, inhibition release, a safer expression of aggression and also a mechanism for diffusing aggression, and a safe mechanism for the discovery and exploration of violations to rationally learned patterns. This is why it plays a very important social role in conflict control and displacement, and also in uniting communicators under common recognizable patterns of though and value systems. Its importance as an avenue and format of effective communication was not missed by the trainers of upper-end hetairai in the ancient world and, it seems, much effort went into the systematic cultivation of that all-important wit and sense of humor which would enable the women and men to shine and attract lovers in social settings like the symposion, and also effectively diffuse tense situations. The humor and witticisms attributed to Attic hetairai have been studied by Laura McClure and James Davidson as part of the sympotic banter in their literary and cultural context, and the reader should refer to their work for a more thorough literary appraisal of these topics.[2] In this appendix I prefer to keep things light and I hope that the reader will find this subjective selection of jokes as amusing as I did. In order to be able to convey some of the humor, I have been somewhat more liberal with the translations, but still I have tried not to violate the meaning of the original.

Wait until I get horny again

Moirichos was propositioning Phryne, the Thespian.
When she asked him for a mina

---

1 See e.g. Meyer 2000: 310–331; Stephenson 1951: 569–574.
2 McClure 2003a: 79–105 and 2003b: 259–294; Davidson 1997.

DOI 10.1515/9783110557954–009

Moirichos said "Too much! Did you not
do that foreigner the other day for a couple of gold coins?"
"Then you wait," she replied, "until I get horny again,
and you can have me for the same price"
>> Machon 18.450–455

From behind to get ahead

Eukrates, the Lark (Korydos), said to a young man who seemed to have abused his youth to get rich from his good looks, "young man, I can see that from behind you got ahead".
>> *Gnomologium Vaticanum* 292 (s.v. Εὐκράτης)

Too much pork

It is said that Niko, the Goat, once was abandoned by a certain Python
Who then took as a lover Euardis the Fat,
But then at some point,
He asked Niko back. "It looks like," she said,
"He had enough pork,
and he is craving kid again".
>> Machon 18.456–461

In love with his personality? Seriously?

What are you saying? Are you really trying to tell me
That someone in love with a pretty boy
Is enamored with his personality, and not his looks?
He must be really stupid. And I don't believe it.
It would be like a poor man who keeps bothering
rich people but does not want their money.
>> Amphis *Dithyrambos* fr. 15

Corrupting the young

Stilpon once accused Glykera during a party that she was corrupting the young,
as Satyros says in his *Lives*. Glykera replied: "We are accused of the same
things, Stilpon. They say that you corrupt those who associate with you with
useless erotic sophistries, and I do the same. So, there is no difference for our
long-suffering companions whether they stay with a philosopher or a whore."

      (Satyros Biogr. fr. 19 Müller)

Delicious testicles

Then someone came in bringing a platter full of testicles;
The other women were utterly disgusted
But the man-killer Gnathaina said laughing:
"the kidneys are really lovely,"[3] by Demeter our friend,
and snatching two of them she gulped them down
and everyone fell on the floor laughing.

      Philippides *Ananeousa* fr. 5.

Who's frigid?

They say that Diphilos was once invited for dinner
At the house of Gnathaina, for the festival of Aphrodite.
Of all her lovers he was the one she preferred the most
And loved him deeply.
He arrived bringing two jugs of Chian wine, and four jugs of Thasian.[4]
He also brought perfume, garlands, delicacies, a goat, ribbons,
A fish, a cook, and to top all that, a flute-player.[5]
At the same time, one of her lovers, a foreigner from Syria

---

3 Eustathios, the irreverent bishop of Thessalonica, was very amused, and tried to explain the
joke as a metaphor used by Gnathaina as a way of dealing with the embarrassment of the other
women. In reality, it is still a standing joke in Modern Greece, where animal testicles (known as
ameleteta "the unspoken") are considered a delicacy, for unaware dinners to be tricked into
tasting the *ameleteta* under the pretense that they are kidneys.

4 Both were select, famous wines.

5 His generosity here is presented as exceptional, since he provided for everything in the
symposium.

Sent her snow and a fish. She did not want anyone to find out
About these presents, especially Diphilos,
Lest she would be punished for it, becoming the butt
Of jokes on the comic stage. She ordered the servant
To take the fish right away to some people who really needed sea-food
And to throw the snow into the unmixed wine without being noticed.
Then she ordered the boy to fill a cup with almost a whole pint
And bring it to Diphilos. He was delighted to drink the cup, and surprised
By such an unexpected thing Diphilos said:
"By Athena and the gods, your pot is frigid, Gnathaina."
She replied: "It is because we keep putting into it
The prologues of your plays."[6]
        Machon 16.262–284.

How much for the meat, boy?

When Gnathaina was advanced in years
And practically a corpse,
They say that she went to the marketplace
And was inspecting the goods, and haggling over
The price of everything. Then she saw accidentally
A butcher standing at his stall. He was very witty
And very young. "By the gods, young man,
You, the pretty one, tell me how much do you charge?"[7]
He smiled and said "A mere three obols from behind."
She replied "My dear boy, who is going to let you
Use Carian standards in Athens?"[8]
        Machon, 16.300–310

---

6 H.A. Khan (1967: 273–278) discusses further this passage. The joke is that he called her a frigid woman and she called him a frigid poet.

7 Gnathaina's question at a first level is innocent, and concerns the price of the meat, but at a secondary level is inquiring about the price of sexual services. He picks on it, and responds that the charge is the standard fee paid in brothels for sex from behind (3 obols).

8 A Carian posture, according to Hesychios (s.v.) was a perverse sexual position (we don't know exactly what, but one might guess from this reference that it was heterosexual anal intercourse). Thus, Gnathaina's joke was that since they are in Athens, he will not be allowed to use the Carian sexual position. Part of the joke rests upon the double meaning of σταθμόν "monetary standard", but also "place of standing, platform, position".

Silence is gold

When some yapper was going on and on that he had just arrived from the Hellespont, she asked him, *"and how did you miss the first city in that region?"* *"Which one?"* he asked. "Sigeion (Silence)," she replied.[9]

Athen. 13.47 (= Ael. *VH* 12.13)

There is no such thing as a free lunch

Someone went to Gnathaina's house and saw some eggs in a plate. "Are these raw or boiled?" he asked. "Copper" she replied.[10]

Athen. 13.47

The poor lovers

Some poor lovers were carousing outside the house for Gnathaina's daughter, and were threatening to bring down the house, if they were not allowed in; for they said that they had brought with them forks and spades. *"If you had such things,"* Gnathaina said, *"you would pawn them and have the money to pay"*.

Athen. 13.47

A bad wrestler

One day Gnathainion was going to Piraeus to meet a new, rich lover with an entourage of three servant girls, a nurse, and three donkeys, while she was riding a mule. Along the way they met a bad wrestler, and as it was difficult for him to go by he got frustrated and started yelling at the women, threatening to throw them and the donkeys to the ground. Gnathainion answered:
Poor man, please don't.
You have never done such a thing before.[11]

Machon (17.387–401 = Athen. 13.46)

---

9 Σίγειον, from σιγή, namely "Silence".
10 Meaning that he had to pay for them.
11 The joke is that he had never managed to wrestle an opponent to the ground before. Here I have shortened the text.

Now, you may

When once king Demetrios
was begging for Mania's ass
she requested something in return.
When he gave it to her
She came back after a while saying:
"Son of Agamemnon, now you may go there"[12]
>   Machon 15.226–230

I am not jealous

They say that once king Demetrios
Rode Lamia really well (*keletisai*),
And gave her a lot of praise; she replied
"Well, now if you wish, you can ride Leaina, too."[13]
>   Machon 12.170–173

From the neck down she is like a leopard

Tryphaina: It is obvious that you don't love me any more, but whom do you love? I might even be able to help you with the conquest, because I know how these things work....
Charmides: Philemation, dear Tryphaina
Tryphaina: Which one? There are two of them. The young one, who has just lost her virginity, and Damylos, the son of the general, is in love with her, or the other one, whom they call the Trap?
Charmides: The latter. ...
Tryphaina: And did you cry for her?
Charmides: A lot.
Tryphaina: Did you see the whole of her, or just the face and only those parts which are visible, as you should with a woman who is already 45 years old?

---

12 A quote from Sophocles *Electra* 2; cf. Gow 1965: 103.
13 A paraphrase of Euripides *Medea* 1358 "now, if you wish, you may call the lioness (λέαινα) too". Porson preferred "call" (κάλει), instead of "ride" (κράτει), in the text of Machon too, but the sexual joke works better with Lamia's adaptation of the verse (see Gow 1965: 93–94).

Charmides: But she is swearing that that next April she will be 22.

Tryphaina: And whom are you going to believe, her or your own eyes? Pay close attention to her temples, which is the only place where you can see her own hair. The rest is a dark wig, but near the temples, when the dye which she uses weakens, she turns really grey. And then, did you ever make her appear naked in front of you?

Charmides: She has never agreed to this.

Tryphaina: Naturally, for she knew that you will be disgusted by her spots and lesions. She looks like a leopard all the way from the neck to her knees... Ask your mother, if she has ever used the baths with her. As for her years, your grandfather too will tell you, if he's still alive.

> Luc. *DMeretr.* 11

How do you like your hetairai?

Grandpa, tell me, how do you take your hetairai, like ripened olives
Or kind-of virginal, like bitter olives?

> Aristophanes fr. 147

A transsexual universe

The universe of Menophila is not like that of other prostitutes;
It is different because it tastes of all kinds of licentiousness.
Chaldaean astronomers, you must run to her right away, for her sky
Has the Dog and the Gemini.[14]

> *AG* 5.105.

Man-raiders

The Boat (*Lembion*) and the other one, the Craft (*Kerkourion*),

---

14 Dog (Κύνα, nom. Κύων) is a reference to the constellation of Canis Major, but is also a medical term for part of the penis (see Kapparis 2011: 236), and thus a slang term for the male member. The Gemini (δίδυμοι) is both the constellation, but also a common slang term for the testicles. The joke is that Menophila, unlike other women prostitutes, actually has a penis and testicles. See also *AG* 5.116.

Both always raid the harbor of Samos.
Young men, watch the piracy of Aphrodite
Anyone sleeping with them is swallowed whole.

     AG 5.44

The game of the three holes

Three hetairai made me play these games.
Blessed Aphrodite, each one of them doing a different job
Euphro from the ass, then Kleio going the normal way
And Atthis, the third one from the mouth,
Mistress, pay to the first one the fee for a boy, to the second
The fee for a woman, but to the third give nothing.

     AG 6.17

Abbreviations

Abbreviations to Greek authors are as in the *LSJ*, and abbreviations to Roman authors are as in the *Lewis-Short*. Later antiquity and Byzantine authors, or more obscure works not included in the *LSJ* are citied in full. Following the *TLG*, all references to Athenaios are by book and chapter of the edition of Kaibel, rather than the common but awkward numbering of Casaubon. A similar principle has been applied to other authors: I tend to follow the numbering system of the *TLG* in order to make it easier for the reader to check references, as electronic databases are increasingly becoming the dominant form. All references to Galen are by volume and page of the edition of Kühn, unless otherwise stated. References to the fragments of Attic Comedy follow the edition of Kassel and Austin *Poetae Comici Graeci* (*PCG*), and references to the fragments of the Greek Historicans follow the edition of Jacoby *Die Fragmente der griechischen Historiker* (*FGrH*), unless otherwise stated. The fragments of presocratic philosophers typically follow the edition of Diehls-Kranz *Die Fragmente der Vorsocratiker* (D-K). For the fragments of other authors I indicate the editor. I am not fond of Latinizing the names of Greek authors, and I tend to keep them as close to their original form as possible, but for some commonly used names in English (like for example Plato, or Epicurus) one must keep the Latinized spelling. Inevitably this creates an inconsistency, but since it is not likely to cause any confusion, I find it acceptable. Bibliographical references follow the Chicago style, and all abbreviations of journals are as in *L'Année philologique*.

For the vase iconography I found the online searchable databases of the Classical Art Research Center and the Beazley archive particularly useful. In addition to a brief description of the painting, each record provides information about inscriptions and bibliographical resources. In order to facilitate access to this database, whenever available, I cite each vase with three numbers, first the reference number of the online database, then the number in Beazley and finally the collection where the work can be seen. Easy access to these databases removed the need to add to the book expensive plates of the iconography under discussion, especially in section 6.2.

Dates in the Christian era are typically marked (e.g. 14 AD, or 14 CE), while dates before the Christian era are not marked (e.g. 479), unless there is potential for confusion which necessitates additional clarification (e.g. 31 BC, or 31 BCE).

Select Bibliography

Adams, J.N. 1983. "Words for prostitute in Latin". RhM 126: 321–58

Adeleye, G. 1983. "The purpose of the *dokimasia*" GRBS 24, 295–306.

Alden, Maureen. 1999. 'The beguilement of Zeus – In all the better Shops' *Costume* 33: 68–73.

Ambrosio, A. 2001. *Women and Beauty in Pompeii*. Los Angeles: J. Paul Getty Museum.

Anderson, Carl Arne. 2008. "Archilochus, his lost shield, and the heroic ideal." *Phoenix* 62: 255–260.

Andrews, A. C. 1951. "Alkanet and borage in the classical period." *The Classical World* 44: 165–166.

Annas, Julia E. 2003. "Epicurus on pleasure and happiness." In, Yu, Jiyuan and Gracia, Jorge J. E. *Rationality and happiness: from the ancients to the early medieval*. Rochester (N.Y.): University of Rochester Press, 75–90.

Apostolakis, Kostas. 2006. "The Rhetoric of an Antidosis: [D.] 42 Against Phaenippus". Ariadne 12: 93–112.

----------. 2009. Πρὸς Φαίνιππον περὶ ἀντιδόσεως. Athens: Stigme.

Arenson, Kelly E. 2009. Pleasure and the absence of pain : reading Epicurus' hedonism through Plato's « Philebus ». Diss. Emory University.

Arnott, Geoffrey W. 1988. "New Evidence for the Opening of Menander's Perikeiromene?" *ZPE* 71: 11–15

----------. 1996. *Alexis: the fragments. A commentary*. Cambridge: Cambridge University Press.

Asquith, Helen. 2005. "From genealogy to « Catalogue »: the Hellenistic adaptation of the Hesiodic catalogue form." In, Hunter, Richard (ed.). *The Hesiodic Catalogue of Women: Constructions and Reconstructions*. Cambridge: Cambridge University Press, 266–286.

Assante, Julia. 2007. "What makes a 'prostitute' a prostitute? Modern definitions and ancient meanings". *Historiae* 4: 117–132.

Åström, Paul, and E. Gullberg. 1970. The thread of Ariadne. A study of ancient Greek dress, Studies in Mediterranean archaeology; XXI. Göteborg: Åström.

Auanger, Lisa – Rabinowitz, Nancy Sorkin. (eds.) 2009. *Among Women*. University of Texas Press.

Bakewell, Geoffrey W. 2008. "Forbidding marriage: Neaira 16 and metic spouses at Athens." *The Classical Journal* 104: 97–109.

Baldwin, M. A. 1992. "Split at the root: prostitution and feminist discourses of law reform." *Yale Journal of Law and Feminism*, 5, 47–120.

Bano, Shadab. 2012. "Women performers and prostitutes in Medieval India." *Studies in History* 27 (1) : 41–53.

Barry, K. 1995. The Prostitution of Sexuality. New York University Press.

Bartman, Elizabeth. 2001. "Hair and the artifice of Roman female adornment." *American Journal of Archaeology* 105: 1–25.

Beck, Hans-Georg. 1984. *Byzantinisches Erotikon*. Munich: Verlag der Bayerischen Akademie der Wissenschaften.

Bell, Shannon. 1994. *Reading, writing, and rewriting the prostitute body*. Bloomington: Indiana University Press.

Bertrand, Jean-Marie (ed.). 2005: La violence dans les mondes grec et romain: actes du colloque international (Paris, 2–4 mai 2002). Paris: Publications de la Sorbonne.

Biffi, Nicola. 1997. "Le storie diverse della cortigiana Rhodopis." *Giornale italiano di filologia* 49 1: 51–60.

Bing, Peter. 1993. "The bios-tradition and poets' lives in Hellenistic poetry." In, Ostwald, M.,Rosen, R.M. and Farrell. J. 1993. *Nomodeiktes: Greek Studies in Honor of Martin Ostwald*. Ann Arbor: University of Michigan Press, 619–631.

Binnicker, C. M. 1967. *Didactic qualities of Ovid's Ars Amatoria*: Diss. Univ. of North Carolina.

Bird, Phyllis A. 2006. "Prostitution in the social world and the religious rhetoric of ancient Israel". In Faraone – McClure 2006, 40–58.

Blazeby, Clare Kelly. 2011. "Woman + wine = prostitute in classical Athens?". In Glazebrook – Henry 2011: 86–105.

Blok, Josine H. - Lardinois André P.M.H. (eds). 2006. *Solon of Athens: New Historical and Philological Approaches*. Leiden: Brill.

Blok, Josine H. 2009. "Perikles' Citizenship Law: A New Perspective." *Historia* 58: 141–170. doi: 10.2307/25598460.

Blundell, Sue. 1995. *Women in Ancient Greece*. Harvard University Press.

Blundell, Sue - Llewellyn-Jones, Lloyd (eds.). 2002. *Women's dress in the ancient Greek world*. Swansea: Classical Press of Wales.

Bollansée J. 1999. Hermippos of Smyrna and his biographical writings: a reappraisal. Leuven: Peeters.

Bonnet, Corinne. 2009. "De la prostitution sacrée dans l'Antiquité, et du bon usage de la démonstration en histoire : (en écho à Stéphanie Lynn Budin, « The myth of sacred prostitution in antiquity », Cambridge, University Press, 2008)." *Les Études Classiques* 77 ((2)2):171–177.

Boudouris, Konstantine, J. 1989. *Ionian philosophy*. Studies in Greek philosophy; 1. Athens: Kardamitsa Press.

Breitenberger, Barbara. 2007. Aphrodite and Eros: the development of erotic mythology in early Greek poetry and cult. New York: Routledge

Brenne, Stefan. 2000. "Indices zu Kalos-Namen." *Tyche* 15: 31–53.

Brents, B.G. – Hausbeck, K. 2005. "Violence and Legalized Brothel Prostitution in Nevada. Examining Safety, Risk, and Prostitution Policy". *Journal of Interpersonal Violence*, 20: 270–295.

Bresson, Alain. 2005. "Naucratis : de l'« emporion » à la cité." *Topoi* (Lyon) 12–13 (1): 133–155.

Bringmann, Klaus - Von Steuben, Hans. 1995. Schenkungen hellenistischer Herrscher an griechische Städte und Heiligtümer. Akademie Verlag: Berlin.

Brown, C. 1983. "From Rags to Riches: Anacreon's Artemon". *Phoenix* 37: 1–15

Brown, G. McC. Peter. 2004."Soldiers in New Comedy: Insiders and outsiders" *Leeds International Classical Studies* 3.08: 1–16.

Brumfield, Allaire C. 1981. The Attic Festivals of Demeter and their relation to the agricultural year. Salem, N.H.: Ayer.

Budin, Stephanie L. 2006. "Sacred prostitution in the first person". In Faraone – McClure 2006, 77–94.

----------. 2008. *The myth of sacred prostitution in antiquity*. Cambridge - New York: Cambridge University Press.

Bundy, Elroy L. 1962. *Studia Pindarica*. Berkeley: University of California Press. (Digital Version, Berkeley 2006).

Burck, E. 1932. "Das Paraklausithyron: Die Entwicklungsgeschichte eines Motives der antiken Liebesdichtung." *Hum. Gymn.* 43: 186–200.

Burton, Diana. 2003. "Public memorials, private virtues: women on classical Athenian grave monuments." *Mortality* 8: 20–35.

Cairns, D. 1996. "*Hybris*, Dishonour, and Thinking Big." *JHS* 116: 1–32.

----------. 2005. "Bullish looks and sidelong glances : social interaction and the eyes in ancient Greek culture." In, Douglas L. Cairns (ed.) *Body language in the Greek and Roman worlds*. Swansea : *Classical Press of Wales*: 123–155.

Calame, C. 1989. "Entre rap ports de parenté et relations civiques: Aphrodite l'hétaïre au banquet politique des hétairoi," in *Aux sources de la puissance: sociabilité et parenté* Rouen: Presses Universitaires de Rouen.

Kalouche, Fouad. 2003. "The Cynic way of living." *Ancient philosophy* 23: 181–194.

Cambiano, Giuseppe. 1977. "Il problema dell'esistenza di una scuola Megarica", in: G. Giannantoni (ed.). *Scuole socratiche minori e filosofia ellenistica*. Bologna: Il Mulino, pp. 25–53.

Campbell, M. 1973. "Anacr. fr. 358 P." *Museum criticum* 8–9: 168–169.

Cantarella, Eva. 1992. *Bisexuality in the ancient Word*. New Haven: Yale University Press. (English Translation by Cormac Ó Cuilleanáin).

Canter, H. V. 1920. "The Paraclausithyron As a Literary Theme." *AJP* 41: 355–368.

Carawan, Edwin. 2007– 2008. "Pericles the Younger and the citizenship law." *CJ* 103: 383–406.

----------. 1998. *Rhetoric and the law of Draco*. New York: Oxford University Press.

Carbone, Gabriella. 1993. "Le donne di Lesbo nel lessico svetoniano delle ingiurie : (a proposito di Anacr. fr. 13 Gent.)." *Quaderni Urbinati di Cultura Classica* 44: 71–76.

Carey, C. 1995. "Rape and adultery in Athenian law" *CQ* 45: 407–17.

----------. 2007. *Lysiae Orationes cum Fragmentis*. Oxford: Oxford University Press.

----------. 1986. "Archilochus and Lycambes." *The Classical Quarterly (New Series)* 36: 60–67.

Casanova A. 1962. "Nel mondo delle etere. Il processo di Frine". *Diadosis, Voci di presenza classica*: Tortona.

Caspers, Christiaan L. 2006. "The loves of the poets : allusions in Hermesianax fr. 7 Powell." In, *Beyond the canon*. Edited by M. Annette Harder, Remco F. Regtuit and Gerrigje Catharina Wakker, *Hellenistica Groningana ; 11*. Leuven; Dudley (Mass.): Peeters, 21–42.

Castner, Catherine J. 1982. "Epicurean Hetairai as Dedicants to Healing Deities?" *GRBS* 23: 51–57.

Cavallini, Eleonora. 1988. "Erotima e la madre (Anac. fr. 1 P. = 60 Gent.)." *Giornale Italiano di Filologia* 40: 213–15.

----------. 2004. "Il processo contro Frine : l'accusa e la difesa". *Labeo* 50: 231–238.

----------. c. 2010. "Phryne in Modern Art, Cinema and Cartoon". Online Publication: http://www.mythimedia.org/doc/Phryne%20in%20Modern%20Art.pdf

Cheng, Sealing. 2011. On the move for love: Migrant entertainers and the US military in South Korea: University of Pennsylvania Press.

Church, S., Henderson, M., Barnard, M., Hart, G. 2001. "Violence by clients towards female prostitutes in different work settings: questionnaire survey". *BMJ* 322: 524–525

Churchill, L. J. 1985. *Heroic erotics. The anatomy of misogyny in the Ars Amatoria*. Diss. Univ. of California, Santa Cruz.

Christien, Jacqueline. 2002. "Iron money in Sparta : myth and history". In Powell, Anton – Hodkinson, Stephen. (eds.). *Sparta: beyond the mirage*. London: Classical Press of Wales and Duckworth, 171–190.

Cioccoloni, Francesca. 2006. "Per un' interpretazione dei « Medicamina faciei femineae » :
l'ironica polemica di Ovidio rispetto al motivo propagandistico augusteo della « restitu-
tio » dell'età dell'oro." *Latomus* 65: 97–107.
Cleland, Liza et al. (eds.) 2005. *The clothed body in the ancient world.* Oxford: Oxbow Books.
Coccagna, Helen A. 2011. "Embodying sympotic pleasure : a visual pun on the body of an
Aulētris". In Glazebrook – Henry 2011: 106–121.
Cohen, David. 1987. "Law, Society and Homosexuality in Classical Athens", *Past and
Present* 117: 3–21
----------. 1991. Reply to Hindley 1991. *Past and Present* 133: 184–194.
Cohen, Edward. E. 2006. "Free and unfree sexual work: an economic analysis of Athenian
prostitution". In Faraone - McClure (eds.) 2006: 95–124.
----------. 2000. " 'Whoring under Contract': The Legal Context of Prostitution in 4th c. Athens".
In Hunter, Virginia – Edmondson, Jonathan (edds.), *Law and Social Status in Classical
Athens.* Oxford: Oxford University Press, pp. 113–148.
----------. 2000b "Written Contracts of Prostitution in Fourth-Century Athens." In *Timai Iohan-
nou Triantaphyllopoulou*, 109–22. Athens: Sakkoula.
----------. 2003. "Athenian Prostitution as a Liberal Profession." In G. W. Bakewell and J. P.
Sickinger, eds., *Gestures: Essays in Ancient History, Literature, and Philosophy Presented
to Alan L. Boegehold*, 214–36. Oxford: Oxbow.
----------. 2005. "Work Ethics and the Practice of Prostitution at Athens." *Mediterraneo Antico*
8.1: 39–62.
----------. 2007. "Laws Affecting Prostitution at Athens." In E. Cantarella, ed., *Symposion 2005:
Vorträge zur griechischen und hellenistischen Rechtsgeschichte*, 201–24. Vienna: Verlag
der österreichischen Akademie der Wissenschaften.
----------. 2015. *Athenian Prostitution: The Business of Sex.* New York: Oxford University Press.
Conover, Kellam. 2010. *Bribery in classical Athens.* Diss. Princeton University.
Conzelmann, H. 1967. "Korinth und die Mädchen der Aphrodite: Zur Religionsgeschichte der
Stadt Korinth," *Nachrichten der Akademie der Wissenschaften in Göttingen*, Phil.-Hist. KL,
No. 8: 247–61.
Cooper, Graig. 1995. "Hyperides and the Trial of Phryne." *Phoenix* 49: 303–318.
Copley, Frank O. 1956. *Exclusus Amator: A Study in Latin Love Poetry.* New York: American
Philological Association.
Corner, Sean. 2011. "Bringing the outside in : the Andrōn as brothel and the Symposium's civic
sexuality". In Glazebrook – Henry 2011: 60–85.
Corso, Antonio. 1997–1998. "Love as suffering: the Eros of Thespiae of Praxiteles." *BICS* 42 :
63–91.
----------. 1997. "The monument of Phryne at Delphi." *NAC* 1997: 123–150.
Courbin P. 1983. "Obéloi d'Argolide et d'ailleurs". In Hägg R. (ed.). The Greek renaissance of
the eighth century B.C. Tradition and innovation. Proceedings of the 2nd international
Symposium at the Swedish Institute in Athens, 1–5 June 1981. Stockholm: Åström, 149–
156.
----------. 1959. "Dans la Grèce archaïque. Valeur comparée du fer et de l'argent lors de l'introduction du monnayage". *Annales: Economies Sociétés Civilisations* 14: 209–233.
Croom, A.T. 2002. *Roman Clothing and Fashion.* Stroud, Glos, and Charleston, S.C.: Tempus
Publishing.
Crowther, Nigel B. 1985. "Male beauty contests in Greece. The euandria and euexia." *L'Antiquité classique* 54:285–291.

Cusick, L., Martin, A., May, T. 2003. Vulnerability and Involvement in Drug Use and Sex Work, Home Office Research Study 268. London: Home Office.

Dalby, Andrew. 2002. "Levels of concealment : the dress of hetairai and pornai in Greek texts." In, Blundell and Llewellyn-Jones *Women's dress in the ancient Greek world*, 111–124.

Daniel-Hughes, Carly. 2010. Dressing for the Resurrection : modest dress as embodied theology in Tertullian of Carthage. Diss. Harvard Divinity School, 2007.

Dayagi-Mendeles, S M. 1989. *Perfumes and Cosmetics in the ancient world*. Jerusalem: Israel Museum.

Davidson, James. 1997. Courtesans & Fishcakes The Consuming Passions of Classical Athens. London: Harper Collins Publishers.

----------. 2001. "Dover, Foucault and Greek Homosexuality: Penetration and the Truth of Sex". *Past and Present* 170: 3–51

----------. 2006. "Making a Spectacle of Her(self): The Greek Courtesan and the Art of the Present", in Feldman – Gordon 2006: 29–51.

----------. 2007. The Greeks and Greek Love: A Radical Reappraisal of Homosexuality in Ancient Greece. London: Weidenfeld and Nicolson.

Davidson, John Frederick. 1987. "Anacreon, Homer and the young woman from Lesbos." *Mnemosyne* XL:132–137.

Davidson, P. F., and H. Hoffmann. 1965. *Greek gold. Jewelry from the age of Alexander*. Brooklyn Museum.

Davies David, Oliver. 1989. *The education of Socrates in Xenophon's Oeconomicus*: Diss. State University of New York at Buffalo.

Davies, M. 1981. "Artemon transvestitus ? A query." *Mnemosyne* 34: 288–299.

----------. 1980. "The eyes of love and the hunting-net in Ibycus 287 P." *Maia* 32: 255–257.

Deacy, Susan – Pierce, Karen, F. (Editors). and Karen F. Pierce. 1997. *Rape in Antiquity*. London: Duckworth.

----------. 1997. "The vulnerability of Athena: Parthenoi and rape in Greek Myth". In Deacy – Pierce (eds.) *Rape in antiquity*, 43–64.

Degener, Michael J. 1998. *Pothos and Blank Eyes of Stone: Longing and Absence in Ancient Greece*. Diss. University of Massachusetts at Amherst, 1998.

Delatte, Armand. 1933. *Le troisieme livre des Souvenirs Socratiques de Xenophon*, Bibliothèque de la Faculté de Philosophie et Lettres de l'Université de Liège 58. Paris: E. Droz

Delivorrias, Angelos. 1995. "Polykleitos and the allure of feminine beauty." In, Moon, Warren, G. (ed.) *Polykleitos, the Doryphoros, and tradition*. Madison: University of Wisconsin Press. 200–217.

Depew, D.J. (ed.). 981. The Greeks and the good life. Proceedings of the ninth annual philosophy symposium, California State University, Fullerton. Fullerton: California State Univ.

De Temmerman, T. 2007. "Blushing Beauty. Characterizing Blushes in Chariton's Callirhoe". *Mnemosyne* 60: 235–252

Detienne, M., 1977. *The gardens of Adonis: Spices in Greek mythology*. Princeton University Press. (Trsl. by Janet Lloyd).

Dierichs, Angelika. 1997. *Erotik in der Kunst Griechenlands*. Mainz am Rhein: Ph. von Zabern.

Dillon, Matthew 2003. Girls and women in classical Greek religion. London: Routledge.

Dillon, Sheila. 2010. *The Female Portrait Statue in the Greek World*. Cambridge Cambridge University Press.

Doblhofer, Georg. 1994. *Vergewaltigung in der Antike*. Stuttgart: Teubner

Doezema, J. 1998. "Forced to Choose: Beyond the Voluntary vs Forced Prostitution Dichotomy" in Kempadoo, K. - Doezema, J. (eds.), Global Sex Workers: Rights, Resistance, and Redefinition. New York: Routledge.

Dorjahn, Alfred Paul. 1935. "Anticipation of Arguments in Athenian Courts." *Transactions and Proceedings of the American Philological Association* 66: 274–295.

Dover, K.J. 1978. *Greek Homosexuality*. Cambridge, MS: Harvard University Press.

----------. 1980. *Plato: Symposium*. Cambridge: Cambridge University Press.

Duncan, Anne. 2006. "Infamous performers : comic actors and female prostitutes in Rome". In Faraone – McClure 2006: 252–273.

Eaverly, Mary Ann. 2013. Tan Men/Pale Women: Color and Gender in Archaic Greece and Egypt. A Comparative Approach. The University of Michigan Press, Ann Arbor.

Eder, Walter. 2000. Die Harpalos-Affäre. In *Grosse Prozesse im antiken Athen*. Ed. Leonhard A. Burckhardt - Jürgen von Ungern-Sternberg. Munich: Beck, 201–215

Edwards, Catherine. 1993. *The Politics of Immorality in Ancient Rome*. Cambridge: Cambridge University Press.

----------. 1997. "Unspeakable Professions: Public Performance and Prostitution in Ancient Rome." In *Roman Sexualities*. Ed. Judith P. Hallett and Marilyn B. Skinner. Princeton: Princeton University Press: 67–80.

Efstathiou, Ath. 2014. "Το Ιδιωτικό και το Δημόσιο στην δοκιμασία των ρητόρων στην Αθήνα των κλασικών χρόνων." in Athanassaki, L., Nikolaides, T. & D. Spatharas (eds) *Ιδιωτικός βίος και δημόσιος λόγος στην ελληνική αρχαιότητα και στον Διαφωτισμό. Μελέτες αφιερωμένες στην Ιωάννα Γιατρομανωλάκη*. University of Crete Press: Herakleio 231–54.

Ehlers, Barbara. 1966. Eine vorplatonische Deutung des sokratischen Eros: der Dialog Aspasia des Sokratikers Aischines. (Zetemata, 41.) Munich: Beck.

Ehrenberg, Victor. 1968. From Solon to Socrates: Greek history and civilization during the sixth and fifth centuries B.C. London: Methuen.

Ehrhardt, Christopher T. H. R. 1971. "Hair in ancient Greece." *Échos du monde classique = Classical Views* 15: 14–19.

Eidinow, Esther. 2010. "Patterns of persecution: 'Witchcraft' trials in Classical Athens". *Past and Present* 208: 10–35.

----------. 2015. Envy, poison, and death: women on trial in classical Athens. Oxford: Oxford University Press.

Ellis, Walter M. 2014. *Alcibiades (Routledge Revivals)*: Routledge. (First published in 1989).

Evans, E.C. 1935. "The Study of Physiognomy in the Second Century A.D." *TAPhA* 72: 96–108.

----------. 1969. "Physiognomics in the Ancient World". *TAPhS* 59.5: 5–101

Fantham Elaine. 1986. "ΖΗΛΟΤΥΠΙΑ. A brief excursus into sex, violence, and literary history." *Phoenix* 40 : 45–57.

----------. 1975, "Sex, Status and Survival in Hellenistic Athens: A Study of Women in New Comedy," *Phoenix* 29: 44–74.

Faraone, Christopher A. - McClure, Laura K. (eds.). 2006. *Prostitutes and Courtesans in the Ancient World*. Madison, Wisconsin: The University of Wisconsin Press.

Farley M - Barkan H. 1998. "Prostitution, violence, and post-traumatic stress disorder". *Women & Health* 27:37–49.

Farley, M. (ed.). 2003. *Prostitution, Trafficking and Traumatic Stress*, Binghamton, New York: Haworth Press.

Feldman, F. – Gordon, B. (eds.). 2006. *The Courtesan's Arts: Cross-Cultural Perspectives*. Oxford: Oxford University Press.

Ferri S. 1961. "Leagros kalos, Glaukon kalos". *PP* 16: 174–180.

Fine, Kit. 2011. "Aristotle's Megarian manœuvres." *Mind* 120: 993–1034.

Finnegan, Frances. 2007. Poverty and Prostitution; A Study of Victorian Prostitutes in York. Cambridge University Press.

Fisher, Nick. 2005. "Body-abuse: the rhetoric of « hybris » in Aeschines' « Against Timarchos »."". In Bertrand (ed.): La violence dans les mondes grec et romain: 67–89.

----------. 2001. *Aeschines Against Timarchos*. Oxford: Oxford University Press.

----------. 1998. "Violence, masculinity and the law in classical Athens. " In Foxhall – Salmon (ed.). *Masculinity, power and identity in classical antiquity:* 68–97

----------. 1992. Hybris: A Study in the Values of Honour and Shame in Ancient Greece. Warminster: Aris and Phillips.

Ford, Andrew. 1999. "Reading Homer from the rostrum : poems and laws in Aeschines' « Against Timarchus »." In, Osborne, Robin – Goldhill, Simon D. (eds.) *Performance culture and Athenian democracy*. Cambridge - New York (N. Y.): Cambridge University Press, 231–256.

Forde, S. 1989. The ambition to rule : Alcibiades and the politics of imperialism in Thucydides. Ithaca : Cornell University Press.

Fornara Ch. W. 1968, "The « tradition » about the murder of Hipparchus." *Historia* 17: 400–424.

Fortenbaugh W. W. 1974. "Menander's Perikeiromene. Misfortune, vehemence, and Polemon." *Phoenix* 28 : 430–443.

Forstenpointner, Gerhard. 2007. "Purple-dye production in Lycia: results of an archaeozoological field survey in Andriake (south-west Turkey)." *Oxford Journal of Archaeology* 26: 201–214.

Foucault, Michael. 1984. *History of Sexuality*. Vol. 2. *The Use of Pleasure*. New York: Vintage Books. (Trsl. Robert Hurley, 1990).

Foxhall, Lin – Salmon, John (editors). 1998. When men were men: masculinity, power and identity in classical antiquity. London : Routledge.

Fraenkel, E. *Elementi Plautini in Plauto* Florence 1960

Francis E. D. - Vickers M. 1981. "Leagros kalos". *PCPHS* 27: 97–136.

Frayser, Susanne G., Whitby, Thomas J. 1995 (2nd ed.). *Studies in Human sexuality: a selected guide.*Englewood, Co.: Libraries Unlimited.

Frost, Frank J. 2002. "Solon pornoboskos and Aphrodite Pandemos". *Syllecta Classica* 13 : 34–46.

Gabba, E. 1976 'The Origins of the Professional Army at Rome'. In *Republican Rome: The Army and the Allies*. Berkeley: University of California Press, 1976, 1–19. (Reprint from 1949 article).

Gärtner, Thomas. 2012. "Der Erotikerkatalog in der Elegie « Leontion » des Hermesianax von Kolophon : Überlegungen zu Aufbau und Überlieferung." *ZPE* 180:77–103.

Gagarin, Michael. 1981. Drakon and early Athenian homicide law, Yale Class. Monogr.; III. New Haven, CT: Yale Univ. Press.

----------. 2005. "La violence dans les plaidoyers attiques". In Bertrand (ed.): La violence dans les mondes grec et romain, 365–376.

Gagliardi, L. 2005. "The Athenian Procedure of *dokimasia* of Orators: A Response to Douglas M. MacDowell." In M. Gagarin and R. W. Wallace, eds. *Symposion 2001: Vorträge zur griechischen und hellenistischen Rechtsgeschichte*, 89–97. Vienna: Verlag der österreichischen Akademie der Wissenschaften.

García González, Jesús María. 2009. "Teano." In, Pérez, Andrés Pociña, and Jesús María García González. (eds.). 2009. *En Grecia y Roma III: mujeres reales y ficticias*: Editorial Universidad de Granada:115–134.

Garland. Rorbert. 1995. *The Eye of the beholder.* Ithaca, N.Y. : Cornell University Press.

Gentili, Bruno. 1973. "La ragazza di Lesbo." *Quaderni Urbinati di Cultura Classica* N° (1616): 124–128.

Gerber Douglas, E. 1989. "Archilochus f 34 West." *Acta classica* 32: 99–103.

Gernet, Louis. 1955. *Droit et société dans la Grèce ancienne.* Paris: Recueil Sirey.

Giangrande, Giuseppe. 1973. "Anacreon and the Lesbian girl." *Quaderni Urbinati di Cultura Classica* N° (1616):129–133.

----------. 1981. "Anacreon and the fellatrix from Lesbos." *Museum Philologum Londiniense* IV:15–18.

----------. 1995. "Anacreon's pubic hair." *Habis* 26:9–12.

Gibson, Roy K. 1998. "Meretrix or matrona ? : stereotypes in Ovid Ars amatoria 3." In, *Papers of the Leeds Latin Seminar 10*: 295–312.

Gibson, R – Green, Stephen – Sharrock Alison (eds.) 2006. *The Art of Love: Bimillennial Essays on Ovid's Ars Amatoria and Remedia Amoris.* Oxford: Oxford University Press.

----------. 2007. Excess and restraint : Propertius, Horace, and Ovid's « Ars amatoria », Bulletin of the Institute of Classical Studies. Supplement ; 89. London: Institute of Classical Studies, University of London

Glancy, Jennifer A, and Stephen D Moore. 2011. "How Typical a Roman Prostitute Is Revelation's" Great Whore"?" *Journal of Biblical Literature* 130 (3): 551–569.

Glidden, David K. 1981. "Epicurus and the pleasure principle." In, Depew (ed.). *The Greeks and the Good Life,* 177–197.

Gini, Anthony. 1992. "The manly intellect of his wife: Xenophon, Oeconomicus ch. 7." *The Classical World* 86: 483–486.

Glazebrook, Allison. 2006a. "Prostituting Female Kin (Plut. Sol. 23.1–2)", *Dike* 8: 33–53.

----------. 2006b. "The bad girls of Athens : the image and function of Hetairai in judicial oratory". In Faraone – McClure 2006, 125–138.

----------. 2009. "Cosmetics and *Sôphrosynê*: Ischomachos Wife in Xenophon's Oikonomikos." *Classical World* 102: 233–248.

----------. 2011. "Porneion : prostitution in Athenian civic space". In Glazebrook – Henry 2011: 34–59.

----------. 2005. "The making of a prostitute: Apollodoros' portrait of Neaira." *Arethusa* 38: 161–187.

Glazebrook, Allison – Henry, Madeleine M. (eds.). 2011. *Greek Prostitutes in the Ancient Mediterranean, 800 BCE–200 CE.* Madison, Wisconsin: University of Wisconsin Press.

Gilhuly, Kate. 2006. "The phallic lesbian : philosophy, comedy, and social inversion in Lucian's Dialogues of the courtesans". In Faraone – McClure 2006: 274–291.

Glenn, Cheryl. 1997. "Locating Aspasia on the Rhetorical Map". In Wertheimer (ed.) 1997: 19–41.

Golden, Mark. 1984. "Slavery and Homosexuality at Athens". *Phoenix* 38: 308–324.

Golden, Paul. 2002. *Culture of Sex in Ancient China.* Honolulu: University of Hawaii Press.

Goldhill, Simon. 1998. "The seductions of the gaze: Socrates and his girlfriends". In Cartledge, P.- Millett, P. - Von Reden, S. (eds), *Essays in order, conflict and community in classical Athens.* Cambridge - New York: Cambridge University Press, 105–124.

----------. 2001. "The erotic eye: visual stimulation and cultural conflict." In Simon Goldhill (ed.) *The erotic eye: visual stimulation and cultural conflict.* Cambridge: Cambridge University Press: 154–194.

Goldsworthy, A.K. 1996. *The Roman Army at War 100 BC – AD 200.* London: Thames and Hudson.

Gomme, Arnold Wycombe – Sandbach, F. H. 1973. *Menander: a commentary.* Oxford: Oxford University Press.

González Almenara, Guillermina. 2005. "Honor sin seducción : alternativa masculina para la castidad femenina." In *Plutarc a la seva època : paideia i societat : actas del VIII simposio español sobre Plutarco* ed. Montserrat Jufresa [et al.]. Barcelona: Departament de Filologia Grega Universitat de Barcelona, 587–594.

Gordon, Jill. 2003 "Eros and philosophical seduction in « Alcibiades 1 »". *AncPhil* 23: 11–30

Gordon, Pamela. 2012. *The invention and gendering of Epicurus.* Ann Arbor: University of Michigan Press.

Gow, A.S.F. 1965. *Machon.* Cambridge: Cambridge University Press

Green, Carin M. C. 1996. "Terms of venery : Ars amatoria I." *Transactions of the American Philological Association* 126: 221–263.

Grenfel, Bernard B. 1896. An Alexandrian erotic fragment and other Greek papyri chiefly Ptolemaic. Oxford : Clarendon Press, 1896.

Gribble, D. 1999. Alcibiades and Athens : a study in literary presentation. Oxford - New York : Clarendon Press.

Grillet. B. 1975. *Les Femmes et les fards dans l' antiquité greque.* Lyon: Centre national de la recherche scientifique.

Gulick. C.B. 1937. *Athenaeus, The Deipnosophists.* Harvard University Press: Cambridge, Massachusetts.

Guzzo, Augusto. 1957. ""Ἔχω, οὐκ ἔχομαι." Rendiconti della Classe di Scienze morali, storiche e filologiche dell'Accademia dei Lincei XII (Ser. 8a): 31–38.

Haldane, J. A. 1966. "Musical Instruments in Greek Worship" *Greece & Rome* 13: 98–107.

Haley, Shelley P. 2009. "Lucian's "Leaena and Clonarium": Voyeurism or a Challenge to Assumptions". In Auanger – Rabinowitz (eds.). *Among Women*: 286–303.

Hallett, Judith P. 2011. "Ballio's brothel, Phoenicium's letter, and the literary education of Graeco-Roman prostitutes", in Glazebrook – Henry 2011: 172–196.

Halperin, D. 1990. One Hundred Years of Homosexuality and Other Essays on Greek Love. New York and London: Routledge

Hamel, Debra. 2003. Trying Neaira: The True Story of a Courtesan's Scandalous Life in Ancient Greece. New Haven: Yale University Press.

Hammer, Dean C. 2004. "Ideology, the symposium, and archaic politics. " *AJPh* 125: 479–512.

Hammond, N.G.L. 1968: Review of Ruschenbusch, E. 1966. *Solōnos Nomoi. CR* 18: 36–38

Harding, Phillip E. 1976. "Androtion's political career." *Historia* 25: 186–200.

Harris, E.M. 2004. "Did rape exist in classical Athens ?: further reflections on the laws about sexual violence. " *Dike* 7 : 41–83.

----------. 1990. "Did the Athenians regard. seduction as a worse crime than rape?," *CQ* 40: 370–377.

----------. 1985. "The date of the trial of Timarchus." *Hermes* 113: 376–380.

----------. 1988. "When Was Aeschines Born?" *Classical Philology* 83: 211–214.

Harrison, A.R.W., 1968 (vol. 1); 1971 (vol.2). *The Law of Athens.* Oxford University Press: Oxford.

Hartmann, Elke. Heirat, Hetärentum und Konkubinat im klassischen Athen. Vol. 30. Campus Verlag, 2002.

----------. 2000, "Hetären im klassischen Athen." In Späth, Thomas - Wagner-Hasel, Beate (eds.) Frauenwelten in der Antike. Verlag J.B. Metzler: Stuttgart-Weimar. 377–394.

Hartney, Aideen. 2002. "Dedicated followers of fashion : John Chrysostom on female dress." In, Blundell and Llewellyn-Jones Women's dress in the ancient Greek world, 243–25.

Harvey, F. D. 1984. "The wicked wife of Ischomachos." Échos du monde classique = Classical Views 28: 68–70.

----------. 1985. "Dona ferentes. Some aspects of bribery in Greek politics." HPTH 6: 76–117.

Hashiba, Yuzuru. 2006. "Athenian bribery reconsidered: some legal aspects." Proceedings of the Cambridge Philological Society 52: 62–80.

----------. 1988. "Dokimasia (scrutiny) in Athens. The purpose and its significance for democracy." Journal of Classical Studies 36: 23–32.

----------. 1997. "« Dokimasia » reconsidered: what was its purpose." Kodai 8/9: 1–10.

Havelock Mitchell, Christine. 1995. The Aphrodite of Knidos and her successors: a historical review of the female nude in Greek art. Ann Arbor: University of Michigan Press.

Hawley, Richard. 1998. "The dynamics of beauty in classical Greece". In Montserrat, D. (ed.) Changing bodies, changing meanings: studies on the human body in antiquity. London - New York: Routledge, 37–54.

Hawley, Richard – Levick, Barbara. (eds.). 1995. Women in Antiquity: New Assessments. London: Routledge.

Hay, Jennifer. 2000. "Functions of humor in the conversations of men and women". Journal of Pragmatics 32, 709–742.

Haynes, K. 2001. "Power of the Prude: Configurations of the Feminine in the Greek Novel". Ancient Narrative 1: 73–92

Heitsch, Ernst. 2009. "Thukydides, Aspasia und Platons « Menexenos »." Philologus 153: 229–236.

Held, Dirk T. D. 2009. "Eros, beauty, and the divine in Plato." New England classical journal 36:155–167.

Henderson, W. J. 1973. "The Paraklausithyron Motif in Horace's Odes." AClass 16: 51–67.

Henry, Madeleine, M. 1985. Menander's Courtesans and the Greek Comic Tradition. Studien zur klassischen Philologie, vol. 20. Frankfurt am Main; New York : Peter Lang.

----------. 1995. Prisoner of history : Aspasia of Miletus and her biographical tradition. Oxford - New York : Oxford University Press.

----------. 2011. Traffic in women : from Homer to Hipponax, from war to commerce. In Glazebrook – Henry 2011: 14–33.

Herman, Gabriel. 2006. Morality and Behaviour in Democratic Athens: A Social History. Cambridge: Cambridge University Press.

Hicks, George. 1997. The Comfort Women: Japan's brutal regime of enforced prostitution in the Second World War: WW Norton & Company.

Higate, Paul. 2003. "Revealing the Soldier: Peacekeeping and Prostitution." American Sexuality Magazine, Volume 1, Issue 5: 1–3.

Hignett, Charles, 1962. A history of the Athenian Constitution to the end of the fifth century B.C. Oxford, Clarendon Press.

Hillgruber, M. 1988. Die Zehnte Rede des Lysias. Einleitung, Text und Kommentar mit einem Anhang uber die Gesetzesinterpretationen bei den AttischenRednern. Berlin: Walter de Gruyter.

Hindley, Clifford. 1991. Reply to Cohen 1987. *Past and Present* 1991: 167–183.

Horváth, László. 2007. "Hypereides' Rede gegen Athenogenes und die zeitgenössische Komödie." *Wiener Studien* 120: 25–34.

Hourcade, Annie. 2008. "Aristippe de Cyrène, la sagesse, le plaisir et l'argent." In, Rosetti, L. – Stavrou A.S.. (eds.). *Socratica 2005*. Bari: Levante, 215–233.

Hubbard, T. K. 1998. "Popular Perceptions of Elite Homosexuality in Classical Athens." *Arion* 6: 48–78.

----------- 2000. *Greek love reconsidered* (ed.). New York: Hamilton Press.

Hunter, R.L. 1983. *Eubulus: The fragments*. Cambridge: Cambridge University Press.

Huizenga, Annette Bourland. 2010. Philosophers of the household: moral education for women in the Pastoral and Pythagorean letters. Diss. University of Chicago.

Hyland, Drew A. 2008. *Plato and the question of beauty, Studies in Continental thought*. Bloomington (Ind.): Indiana University Press.

Immerwahr, Henry, R. 2009. *Corpus of Attic Vase Inscriptions*. Published online by the author (URL: http://www.unc.edu/~hri/Inscriptions.pdf).

Irwin, Elizabeth. 2005. *Solon and Early Greek Poetry: The Politics of Exhortation*. Cambridge: Cambridge University Press.

James, S. 2003. Learned Girls and Male Persuasion: Gender and Reading in Roman Love Elegy. Berkeley.

-------------. 2005. "A Courtesan's Choreography: Female Liberty and Male Anxiety at the Roman Dinner Party." In *Defining Genre and Gender in Latin Literature: Essays Presented to William S. Anderson on His Seventy-Fifth Birthday*, ed. by W. W. Batstone and G. Tissol. New York: 269–299.

Janko, Richard. 2007. "Pity the poor traveller: a new comic trimeter (Aristophanes ?)." *CQ* 57: 296–297.

Jax, K. 1933. Die weibliche Schönheit in der griechischen Dichtung, Innsbruck: Wagner.

Jeffery, L. H. 1961. *The Local Scripts of Archaic Greece*. Oxford: Clarendon Press.

Jones, H. 1992. "The Death of the Paraklausithyron: Propertius 1.16." In *The Two Worlds of the Poet: New Perspectives on Vergil*, ed. by R. M. Wilhelm and H. Jones. Detroit: 303–309.

Johnson, David Martel. 2009. "Aristippus at the crossroads : the politics of pleasure in Xenophon's « Memorabilia »." *Polis: the journal of ancient Greek political thought* 26: 204–222.

Johnson, T.S. "Horace's Elegiac Criticism and The Open-Ended Door (*C*. III.10)" (Forthcoming).

Johnstone, S. 2002. "Apology for the Manuscript of Demosthenes 59.67". *AJP* 123: 229–256.

Joyal, M. - J.C Yardley, J.C . – McDougall, I. 2008. *Greek and Roman Education A Sourcebook*. Milton Park, Abingdon, Oxon; New York, NY : Routledge.

Jucker H. 1975. "Einige Beispiele der Verklammerung von Kalos-Namen und Vasen-Malern, 550–450 v. Chr." *HASB* 1: 45–48.

Just, Roger. 1989. *Women in Athenian Law and Life*. London: Routledge

Kahn, Charles H. 1994. "Aeschines on Socratic Eros". In Paul A. Vander Werdt (ed.) *The Socratic Movement*. Cornell University Press: Ithaca and London. 87–106.

-----------. 2001. Pythagoras and the Pythagoreans : a brief history. Indianapolis: Hackett.

Kalouche, Fouad. 2003. "The Cynic way of living." *Ancient philosophy* 23: 181–194.

Kapitanffy, István. 1994. "Chorikios und die Hetäre Phryne." *AAntHung* 35: 159–166.

Kapparis, K. 1999. Apollodoros 'Against Neaira' [D. 59]: Edited with introduction, translation and Commentary. Berlin: Walter de Gruyter.

476 —— Select Bibliography

----------. 1995. "When were the Athenian adultery laws introduced? " *RIDA* 42: 97–122.
----------. 1996. "Humiliating the Adulterer: The Law and the Practice in Classical Athens." *RIDA* 43: 63–77.
----------. 1997. "Hare hunting without a dog (A critical note on Aristophanes Lysistrata 791)'. *Philologus* 141: 154–156.
----------. 1998. "The law on the age of the speakers in the Athenian assembly."
----------. 2011. 'Suetonius and the Terminology of Prostitution in Ancient and Medieval Greek" In, Henry – Glazebrook 2006: 222–255.
----------. 1995. "The Athenian decree for the naturalisation of the Plataeans." *Greek, Roman and Byzantine Studies* 36: 359–378.
----------- (with Andrew Wolpert). 2011. *Legal Speeches of Democratic Athens*. Indianapolis: Hackett Publishers.
RhM 141: 255–259.
Karlen, Arno, 1988. *Threesomes: studies in sex, power, and intimacy*. New York: Beech Tree Books.
Katsonopoulou, D, Petropoulos, I and Katsarou, S. (eds.). 2008. *Ο Αρχίλοχος και η εποχή του = Archilochos and his Age*. Athens: Diktynna.
Keuls, Eva. 1983. "The hetaera and the housewife. The splitting of the female psyche in Greek art." *Mededelingen van het Nederlands Instituut te Rome = Papers of the Netherlands In-stitute in Rome. Antiquity* 44–45 :23–40.
---------- 1985. The reign of the phallus. Sexual politics in ancient Athens. New York: Harper & Row.
Keesling, Catherine. 2006. "Heavenly bodies : monuments to prostitutes in Greek sanctuar-ies". In Faraone – McClure 2006, 59–76.
Keppie, Lawrence. 1984. 1998 The Making of the Roman Army: from Republic to Empire. Lon-don: BT Batsford. Reprinted Norman: University of Oklahoma Press.
Khan H. A. 1967. "Machon fr. XVI, 258–261 and 285–294." *Mnemosyne* 20: 273–278.
Khan, Mohsin Saeed, Eva Johansson, Shakila Zaman, Magnus Unemo, Naveed I Rahat, and Cecilia Stålsby Lundborg. 2010. "Poverty of opportunity forcing women into prostitution— a qualitative study in Pakistan." *Health care for women international* 31 (4): 365–383.
Kilmer, M. F. 1982. "Genital phobia and depilation." *Journal of Hellenic Studies* 102: 104–112.
----------. 1993. Greek erotica on Attic red-figure vases. London: Duckworth.
King, Helen. 1998. Hippocrates' Woman: Reading the Female Body in Ancient Greece. London: Routledge.
----------. 2004. *The Disease of Virgins: Green Sickness, Chlorosis and the Problems of Puberty*. London: Routledge.
Knigge, Ursula. 2005. *Der Bau Z*. Munich: Hirmer Verlag (Series *Kerameikos*, vol. 17).
Knorr, Ortwin. 1995. "The character of Bacchis in Terence's Heautontimorumenos." *AJPh* 116: 221–235.
Konstan, David. 1987. "Between Courtesan and Wife: Menander's 'Perikeiromene'". *Phoenix* 41: 122–139
Konstantakos, Ioannis M. 2006. "The lady and the loser : Aristodemos and Lynkeus on love-affairs of New Comedy poets." *Hermes* 134: 150–158.
Körte, Alfred. 1919. "Glykera und Menander". *Hermes* 54: 87–93.
Kosman, Aryeh. 2010. "Beauty and the good : situating the « kalon »." *Classical Philology* 105:341–357.
Kowalski G. 1947. "De Phrynes pectore nudato." *Eos* 1: 50–62.

Krasilnikoff, Jens A. 1992. "Aegean mercenaries in the fourth to second centuries BC : a study in payment, plunder and logistics of ancient Greek armies." *C&M* 43: 23–26.

----------. 1993. "The regular payment of Aegean mercenaries in the classical period." *Classica et mediaevalia* 44: 77–95.

Krenkel, Werner. 1988. "Prostitution," In M. Grant & R. Kitzinger eds., *Civilization of the Ancient Mediterranean: Greece & Rome*, vol. 2, New York : Scribner's, pp. 1291–7.

Krueger, Derek. 1996. "The bawdy and society: the shamelessness of Diogenes in Roman imperial culture." In, Branham, B. – Goulet-Cazé, M.O. (eds.) *The cynics. The cynic movement in antiquity and its legacy.* Berkeley: University of California Press, 222–239.

Kostoglou, Maria. 2003. "Iron and Steel Currency Bars in Ancient Greece." *Mediterranean Archaeology and Archaeometry* 3: 63–68

(Online Journal; URL: http://www.rhodes.aegean.gr/maa_journal/issues.html)

Kreilinger, Ulla. 2007. Anständige Nacktheit: Körperpflege, Reinigungsriten und das Phänomen weiblicher Nacktheit im archaisch-klassischen Athen, Rahden, Westf. Verlag Marie Leidorf.

Kueppers, E. 1981. "Ovids Ars amatoria und Remedia amoris als Lehrdichtungen." *Aufsteig und Niedergang der römischen Welt* II (N° 31.4): 2507–2551.

Kurke, Lesley. 1996. "Pindar and the Prostitutes, or Reading Ancient "Pornography"". *Arion* 4: 49–75.

----------. 1997. "Inventing the Hetaira: Sex, Politics, and Discursive Conflict in Archaic Greece". *ClAnt* 16: 106–154.

----------. 1989. "Counterfeit friends. Alcaean invective and the origin of coinage." *AAPhA*:156–156.

Kyrkos, Basileios A. 1980. "Aristoteles und die Megariker. Erkenntnisontologische Gegensätze." *Philosophia* 10–11: 346–362.

Lambert, S.D. 1993. *The Phratries of Attica.* Ann Arbor: University of Michigan Press.

Lambropoulou, Voula. 1995. "Some Pythagorean female virtues." In, Hawley – Levick: 122–134.

Lampe, Kurt Walter. 2007. *Cyrenaic philosophy : arguments, contexts and lifestyles.* Diss. Univ. of California, Berkeley.

Lanni, Adriaan. 2010. "The Expressive Effect of the Athenian Prostitution Laws". Classical Antiquity 29: 45–67.

Lape, Susan. 2001. "Democratic ideology and the poetics of rape in Menandrian comedy." ClAnt 20: 79–119

----------. 2006. "The psychology of prostitution in Aeschines' speech against Timarchus". In Faraone – McClure 2006: 139–160.

Lateiner, D. 1998. "Blushes and Pallor in Ancient Fictions". *Helios* 25: 163–89

Lauter. H. 1988. "Der Praxitelische Kopf Athen. Nationalmuseum 1762". *Antike Plastik* 19: 21–29

Λάζος, Γ. 2002. Πορνεία και διεθνική σωματεμπορία στη σύγχρονη Ελλάδα: Η εκδιδόμενη. Αθήνα: Εκδόσεις Καστανιώτη

Leach, Eleanor Winsor. 1979. "The soldier and society ; Plautus' Miles gloriosus as popular drama." *Rivista di Studi Classici* 27: 185–209.

Lefkowitz M.R. – Fant, M.B. (eds.). 2005. *Women's life in Greece and Rome: a source book in translation.* (3rd edition) Baltimore: Johns Hopkins University Press (first edition 1982).

Legon, R.P. 1981. Megara; *the Political Hisiory of a Greek City-State to 336 BC.* Ithaca- London: Cornell University Press.

Leão, Delfim F. 2011. "Paidotrophia et gerotrophia dans les lois de Solon." *Revue historique de droit français et étranger*): 457–472.

Leão, Delfim, - Rhodes, Peter. 2015. The Laws of Solon. A New Edition with Introduction, Translation and Commentary. London: IB Tauris.

Lesky, Albin. 1966. *A history of Greek literature*. Translated by James Willis and Cornelis de Heer. New York: Crowell.

Lewis, D.M. 1959. "Law on the Lesser Panathenaia". *Hesperia* 28: 239–247.

----------. 1983. "Themistocles' mother." *Historia* 1983: 245.

Lewis, Sian. 2002. The Athenian Woman: An Iconographic Handbook. London: Routledge

----------. 2003. Representation and reception: Athenian pottery in its Italian context. In Wilkins, J. B. & Herring, E. (eds.). *Inhabiting Symbols: symbol and image in the ancient Mediterranean*. Accordia Research Institute. University of London , p. 175–92.

Lidov, Joel B. 2002. "Sappho, Herodotus, and the hetaira". *CPh* 97: 203–237

Long, A. 1985. "Pleasure and social utility. The virtues of being epicurean." In, Gigon, Olof - Flashar, Hellmut (eds.) *Aspects de la philos. Hellénistique*. Vandœuvres-Genève: Fondation Hardt ,283–324.

Loraux, Nicole. 1993. "Aspasia : la straniera, l'intellettuale". In Nicole Loraux (ed.) *Grecia al femminile* Nicole Loraux. Rome: Laterza, pp. 123–154.

Llewellyn-Jones, Lloyd. 2002. "A woman's view ? : dress, eroticism, and the ideal female body in Athenian art." In Blundell and Llewellyn-Jones *Women's dress in the ancient Greek world*, 171–202.

Loomis, William T. 1998. *Wages, welfare and inflation in classical Athens*. Ann Arbor: University of Michigan Press.

Lowman J - Fraser L. 1995. Violence against persons who prostitute: the experience in British Columbia. Vancouver: Simon Fraser University.

Lu, Houliang. 2015. *Xenophon's Theory of Moral Education*, Cambridge Scholars Publishing.

Luppe, Wolfgang. 1974. "Nochmals zu Philainis, Pap. Oxy. 2891." *Zeitschrift für Papyrologie und Epigraphik* 13: 281–282.

----------. 1998. "Zum Philainis-Papyrus : (P. Oxy. 2891)." *Zeitschrift für Papyrologie und Epigraphik* N° 123: 87–88.

Lynn, John Albert, and John, A. 2008. *Women, armies, and warfare in early modern Europe*: Cambridge University Press Cambridge.

Lyons, Claire L. - and Koloski-Ostrow, Ann Olga (Eds.). 1997. *Naked truths: women, sexuality, and gender in classical art and archaeology*. New York: Routledge.

MacCary, W. Thomas. 1972. "Menander's Soldiers: Their Names, Roles and Masks". *AJP* 93: 279–298.

MacDonald B. R. 1983. "The Megarian Decree." *Historia* 32: 385–410.

McDonnell, Myles. 2006. *Roman Manliness:" Virtus" and the Roman Republic*: Cambridge University Press.

MacDowell, Douglas M. 2000. "Athenian Laws about homosexuality" *RIDA* 47: 13–27.

----------. 1990. *Demosthenes against Meidias (Orations 21)*. Oxford: Clarendon Press.

----------. 1983. "Athenian laws about bribery." *Revue internationale des droits de l'Antiquité* 30: 57–78.

----------. 1978. *The Law in Classical Athens*. London: Thames and Hudson.

----------. 1976. "*Hybris* in Athens." *G&R* 23: 14–31.

----------. 1963. *Athenian Homicide Law in the Age of the Orators*. Manchester: Manchester University Press.

----------. 1962. *Andocides, On the mysteries*. Oxford: Clarendon Press.

----------. 2005. "The Athenian procedure of *dokimasia* of orators" in *Symposion 2001*, 79–87. (with a reply by L. Gagliardi).

Mackenzie, D. C. 1985. "The wicked wife of Ischomachus ... again." *Échos du monde classique = Classical Views* 29: 95–96.

MacLachlan, Bonnie. 1992. "Sacred prostitution and Aphrodite." *Studies in religion = Sciences religieuses* 21: 145–162.

Makei, Vladimir. 2013. Human Trafficking in the Post-Cold War Period: Towards a Comprehensive Approach. *Journal of Interantional Affairs*. Online Publication: URL http://jia.sipa.columbia.edu/online-articles/human-trafficking-post-cold-war/

Makepeace, Clare. 2012. "Male Heterosexuality and Prostitution during the Great War: British Soldiers' Encounters with Maisons Tolérées." *Cultural and Social History* 9: 65–83.

----------. 2011. 'Punters and their prostitutes: British soldiers, masculinity and maisons tolérées in the First World War'. In *What is Masculinity? Historical Dynamics from Antiquity to the Contemporary World,* by John H. Arnold and Sean Brady (eds). Palgrave Macmillan: pp.413–430.

Mann, Wolfgang-Rainer. 1996. "The life of Aristippus". *AGPh* 78: 97–119.

Marcovic, Miroslav. 1983. "Anacreon, 358 PMG (ap. Athen. XIII. 599 C)." *American Journal of Philology* 104: 372–383.

Massey, Preston T. 2006. The veil and the voice : a study of female beauty and male attraction in ancient Greece. (Diss. Indiana University).

Mastrokostas, E. 1953. "*Latypê Delphikê*", in *Geras Antoniou Keramopoulou*, Etaireia Makedonikôn Spoudôn: Athens.

Matthews, Roger. 2008. *Prostitution, politics and policy*. Abingdon, - New York: Routledge-Cavendish.

Matthews, Victor Harold, Bernard M. Levinson, and Tikva Simone Frymer-Kensky. 1998. *Gender and law in the Hebrew Bible and the ancient Near East, Journal for the study of the Old Testament Supplement series*. Sheffield, England: Sheffield Academic Press.

----------. Matthews, Victor J. 1996. "Aphrodite's hair : Colluthus and hair-styles in the epic tradition." *Eranos* 94 ((1)1):37–39.

May, Regine. 2005. "« The rape of the locks » : cutting hair in Menander's « Perikeiromene »." Harwardt, Sabine et al. (eds.). *Festschrift für Hans-Otto Kröner zum 75. Geburtstag*. Hildesheim ; New York : G. Olms, 275–289.

McClain, Davina – Rauh, Nicholas, K. 2011. " Brothels at Delos : the evidence for prostitution in the maritime world". In Glazebrook – Henry 2011: 147–171.

McClure, Laura K. 2003a. *Courtesans at Table*. New York – London: Routledge.

----------. 2003b. "Subversive Laughter: The Sayings of Courtesans in Book 13 of Athenaeus' Deipnosophistae" *AJP* 124: 259–294.

McGinn, Thomas. 1998. Prostitution, Sexuality, and the Law in Ancient Rome. New York: Oxford University Press.

----------. 2004. The economy of prostitution in the Roman world : a study of social history & the brothel. Ann Arbor: University of Michigan Press.

----------. 2006. "Zoning shame in the Roman city". In Faraone – McClure 2006: 161–176.

----------. 2013. "Prostitution: Controversies and New Approaches." In Hubbard, Thomas K. (ed). *A Companion to Greek and Roman Sexualities*: Wiley 83–101.

McKechnie, Paul. 1994. "Greek mercenary troops and their equipment." *Historia* 43: 297–305.

Meyer, Elizabeth Anne. 2008. "Thucydides on Harmodius and Aristogeiton, tyranny, and history." *Classical Quarterly* 58: 13–34.

Meyer, John C. 2000. "Humor as a Double-Edged Sword: Four Functions of Humor in Communication". *Communication Theory* 3: 310–331.

Miles, Sarah. 2009. *Strattis, Tragedy, and Comedy.* PhD Thesis: University of Nottingham.

Miller, H. F. 1984. "The practical and economic background to the Greek mercenary explosion." *Greece and Rome* 31: 153–160.

Miller, Margaret Christina. 2010. "I am Eurymedon : tensions and ambiguities in Athenian war imagery." In, Pritchard, David M. (ed.) *War, democracy and culture in classical Athens.* Cambridge ; New York: Cambridge University Press, 304–338.

Milne, M.J. – Bothmer, D. 1953: "ΚΑΤΑΠΥΓΩΝ ΚΑΤΑΠΥΓΑΙΝΑ". *Hesperia*, 22: 215–224.

Miner, Jess, and Michael De Brauw. 2004. "Androtion's alleged prostitution contract : Aes. 1.165 and Dem. 22.23 in light of P. Oxy. VII 1012." *Zeitschrift der Savigny-Stiftung für Rechtsgeschichte. Romanistische Abteilung* 121: 301–313.

Mirus, Christopher V. 2012. "Aristotle on beauty and goodness in nature." *International Philosophical Quarterly* 52:79–97.

Mitsis, Phillip. 1988. Epicurus' ethical theory. The pleasures of invulnerability, Cornell studies. in classical philology; 48. Ithaca: Cornell University Press.

Monoson, S. Sara. 2000. "The allure of Harmodius and Aristogeiton." In Hubbard 2000 (ed.): 42–51.

Montserrat, Dominic (ed.) 1998. Changing bodies, changing meanings : studies on the human body in antiquity. London - New York: Routledge.

Morris, I. 1996 "The Strong Principle of Equality and the archaic origins of Greek Democracy" in J. Ober – C. Hedrick (ed.) *Demokratia: A Conversation on Democracies, Ancient and Modern*, Princeton: Princeton University Press.

Moysey, Robert A. 1985. "Chares and Athenian foreign policy." *CJ* 40: 221–227.

Müller, Sabine. 2006. "Alexander, Harpalos und die Ehren für Pythionike und Glykera : Überlegungen zu den Repräsentationsformen des Schatzmeisters in Babylon und Tarsos." In *ΦΙΛΙΑ: Festschrift für Gerhard Wirth zum 80. Geburtstag.* Ed. Vasile Lica . Galatz : Academica: 71–106.

Murnaghan, Sheila. 1988. "How a woman can be more like a man. The dialogue between Ischomachus and his wife in Xenophon's Oeconomicus." *Helios* 15: 9–22.

Murray, Oswyn (ed.). 1990. *Sympotica: A symposium on the symposion.* Oxford: Clarendon Press.

Myerowitz Levine, Molly. 1981. "The women of Ovid's Ars amatoria. Nature or culture?" *Scripta classica Israelica* 6: 30–56.

Nails, Debra. 1989. "The Pythagorean women philosophers. Ethics of the household." In, Boudouris (ed.). *Ionian Philosophy*: 291–297.

Nall, Gregory. 2001. Forms of classical Athenian homosexuality in transhistorical, crosscultural, biosocial and demographic perspective : a response to Dover, Foucault and Halperin. Diss., State University of New York at Albany.

Nehamas, Alexander. 2007. *Only a promise of happiness : the place of beauty in a world of art.* Princeton (N.J.): Princeton University Press.

Nappa, C. 2007. "Elegy on the Threshold: Generic Self-Consciousness and the Reader in Propertius 1.16." *CW* 100: 57–73.

Nee, Laurence D. 2009. "The city on trial : Socrates' indictment of the gentleman in Xenophon's « Oeconomicus »." *Polis: the journal of ancient Greek political thought* 26 (2): 246–270.

Nikolaidis, Anastasios G. 1994. "On a supposed contradiction in Ovid : (Medicamina faciei 18–22 vs. Ars amatoria 3.129–32)." *American Journal of Philology* 115: 97–103.

Nikolsky, Boris. 2001. "Epicurus on pleasure." *Phronesis* 46: 440–465.

Nowak, Maria. 2010. "Defining prostitution in Athenian Legal Rhetorics". *Tijdschrift voor Rechtsgeschiedenis/The Legal History Review* 78: 183–197.

Nussbaum Martha, C. 1991. "Epicurus' ethical theory : the pleasures of vulnerability." *Philosophy and Phenomenological Research* 60: 677–687.

Ober, J. 1989. Mass and Elite in Democratic Athens: Rhetoric, Ideology, and the Power of the People. Princeton: Princeton University Press.

Obdrzalek, Suzanne. 2010. "Moral transformation and the love of beauty in Plato's « Symposium »." *Journal of the History of Philosophy* 48:415–444.

O'Connor David, K. 1989. "The invulnerable pleasures of Epicurean friendship." *GRBS* 30: 165–186.

Ogden, D. 1996. *Greek bastardy in the classical and Hellenistic periods.* Oxford : Clarendon Press; New York : Oxford University Press.

----------. 1997. "Rape, adultery and the protection of bloodlines in classical Athens," In Deacy – Pierce (eds.) *Rape in antiquity*, 25–41

----------. 1999. Polygamy, Prostitutes and Death: The Hellenistic Dynasties. London: Duckworth.

----------. 2007. "Two studies in the reception and representation of Alexander's sexuality." In, Heckel, Waldemar, Lawrence Tritle, and Pat Wheatley. 2007. *Alexander's empire: formulation to decay*: 75–108.

----------. 2011. *Alexander the Great: myth, genesis and sexuality.* Exeter: University of Exeter Press.

Ogden, Jack - Williams, Dyfri (eds). 1994. *Jewellery of the classical word.* London: British Museum Press.

O'Keefe, Timothy. 2002. "The Cyrenaics on pleasure, happiness, and future-concern." *Phronesis* 47: 395–416.

Olson. K. 2008. Dress and the Roman Woman: Self-Presentation and Society. New York: Routledge.

----------. 2009. "Cosmetics in Roman Antiquity: Substance, Remedy, Poison".

Classical World 102: 291–310.

Omitowoju, Rosanna. 2002. *Rape and the Politics of Consent in Classical Athens.* Cambridge: Cambridge University Press.

----------. 1997. "Regulating Rape: soap operas and self interet in the Athenian Courts," in Deacy – Pierce (eds.) *Rape in antiquity*, 1–24.

Onfray, Michael. (ed.). 2002. *L' invention du plaisir : suivi de Fragments cyrénaïques.* Paris: Librairie générale française.

Osborne, Robin. 1997. "Law, the Democratic Citizen and the Representation of Women in Classical Athens." *Past and Present*, 155: 3–33.

O'Sullivan, Lara. 2009. "History from Comic Hypotheses: Stratocles, Lachares, and P.Oxy. 1235". *GRBS* 49 (2009) 53–79.

Outshoorn, J. 2004. The Politics of Prostitution: Women's Movements, Democratic States and the Globalisation of Sex Commerce. Cambridge University Press.

Owens, Ron. 2010. Solon of Athens: Poet, Philosopher, Soldier, Statesman. Eastbourne: Sussex Academic Press.

Packer. J.E. 1978. "Inns at Pompeii" *Cronache Pompeiane* 4: 5–53.

Pace, Cristina. 1996. "Anacreonte e la palla di Nausicaa : (Anacr. fr. 13 G. = 358 PMG, 1–4)."
Eikasmos 7: 81–86.

Page, D.L. 1981. *Further Greek Epigrams*. Cambridge: Cambridge University Press

Παπαγιαννόπουλος – Παλαιός Α.Α. 1936. Πυθιονίκη: Τὸ ἐν τῇ ἱερᾷ ὁδῷ μνῆμα τῆς ἑταίρας
Πυθιονίκης. Athens.

Patterson, C. 1981. *Pericles' Citizenship Law of 451–50 BC*. Salem N.H.: Arno Press.

----------. 1993. "The case against Neaira and the public ideology of the Athenian family." In,
Boegehold, Alan L, and Adele C Scafuro. (eds.) 2002. *Athenian identity and civic ideology*:
JHU Press, 199–216.

Patzer, Harald. 1982. *Die griechische Knabenliebe*. Sitzungsberichte der wissenschaftlichen
Gesellschaft der Johann-Wolfgang-Goethe-Universität Frankfurt am Main, Vol. 19, No. 1:
Wiesbaden.

Parca, Maryline G. 2002. «Violence by and against women in documentary papyri from Ptolemaic and Roman Egypt.» In Melaerts, H. – Mooren, L. *Le rôle et le statut de la femme en
Égypte hellénistique, romaine et byzantine*. Leuven: Peeters, 283–296.

Payne H. G. G., Bagenal H., Jenkins R. J. H., May J. M. F., Dunbabin T. J.& Wade-Gery H. T. 1940.
*Perachora. The sanctuaries of Hera Akraia and Limenia. Excavations of the British School
of Archaeology at Athens, 1930–1933*. Oxford : Clarendon Press.

Pelliccia, Hayden. 1991. "Anacreon 13 (358 PMG)." *Classical Philology* 86: 30–36.

Percy, William Armstrong, III. 1996. *Pederasty and Pedagogy in Archaic Greece*. Champaign, IL:
University of Illinois Press.

Peschel, Ingeborg, 1987. Die Hetäre bei Symposion und Komos in der attisch-rotfigurigen
Vasenmalerei des 6.-4. Jahrh. v. Chr. Frankfurt am Main - New York: P. Lang.

Petersen, William, L. 1986. "Can ἀρσενοκοῖται Be Translated by 'Homosexuals'?", *VChr*, 40:
187–91.

Phang, Sara Elise. 2001. The marriage of Roman soldiers, 13 B.C.-A.D. 235 : law and family in
the imperial army. Leiden; Boston: Brill.

Phillips, David Daniel. 2008. Avengers of blood : homicide in Athenian law and custom from
Draco to Demosthenes, Historia. Einzelschriften ; 202. Stuttgart: Steiner.

----------. 2013. *The Law of Ancient Athens*, University of Michigan Press: Ann Arbor.

----------. 2007. "Trauma ek pronoias in Athenian Law". *The Journal of Hellenic Studies* 127: 74–
105

Pierce, Karen F. 1997. «The portrayal of rape in New Comedy». In Deacy – Pierce (eds.) *Rape in
antiquity*, 163–184.

Pinault, Jody Rubin. 1992. "The medical case for virginity in the early second century C.E. :
Soranus of Ephesus, Gynecology" 1.32. *Helios* 19: 123–139

Ferrari Pinney, Gloria. 1984. "For the Heroes are at Hand," *JHS* 104: 181–183.

Plant, Ian Michael. (ed.) 2004. *Women writers of ancient Greece and Rome: an anthology*.
Norman : University of Oklahoma Press.

Pleket, H.W. 1964. Review of Jeffery 1961. *Mnemosyne* 17: 300–303.

Pomeroy, Sarah B. 1975. Goddesses, whores, wives, and slaves: Women in classical antiquity.
New York: Schocken.

----------. 1984. Women in Hellenistic Egypt : from Alexander to Cleopatra. New York: Schocken
Books.

----------. 1994. *Xenophon, Oeconomicus*: A Social and Historical Commentary. Oxford: Clarendon Press.

----------. 1996. Families in classical and Hellenistic Greece : representations and realities. New York : Clarendon Press.

Popov, Nadejda Vladimir. 2008. Soldier speech acts in Greek and Roman literature and society. Diss. Princeton University.

Porter, James I. 2003. " Epicurean attachments : life, pleasure, beauty, friendship, and piety." *Cronache ercolanesi* 33: 205–227.

----------. 1999. (ed.). *Constructions of the Classical Body.* Ann Arbor: University of Michigan Press

Poulakos, T. – Depew, D. (eds). 2004. *Isocrates and Civic Education.* University of Texas Press: Austin.

Pradeau, Jean-François - Marbœuf, Chantal (eds.). 1999. *Alcibiade.* Paris: Flammarion.

Pyclik, Jennifer M. 2006. The "Natasha" networks: sex trafficking in post cold-war Europe. Diss. University of NC, Chapel Hill.

Raaflaub, K.A. 2004. *The Discovery of Freedom in Ancient Greece*, Chicago: The University of Chicago Press

Rabinowitz, Nancy. 2011. " Sex for sale? Interpreting erotica in the Havana collection". In Glazebrook – Henry 2011: 122–146.

----------. 2009. " Excavating Female Homoeroticism in Ancient Greece: The Evidence from Attic Vase Painting. " In Auanger – Rabinowitz (eds.). *Among Women*: 106–160.

Rankin, H.D. 1977. *Archilochus of Paros.* Noyess Press: New Jersey.

Rasmussen, Tom – Spivey, Nigel (eds.). 1991. *Looking at Greek Vases.* Cambridge: Cambridge University Press.

Rauh, Nicholas K. 2011. " Prostitutes, pimps, and political conspiracies during the Late Roman Republic". In Glazebrook – Henry 2011: 197–221.

Redondo Moyano, Elena. 1994. "Bátaro, un ante los tribunales : (Mimo II de Herodas)." In, *Actas del VIII congreso español de estudios clásicos, vol. 2*, 361–367.

Reeder, Ellen D (with essays by Sally C. Humphreys, Mary R. Lefkowitz et al.). 1995. *Pandora: Women in Classical Greece.* Baltimore, Md. : Trustees of the Walters Art Gallery ; Princeton, N.J.: In association with Princeton University Press, 1995.

Reinhold, Meyer. 1970. History of purple as a status symbol in antiquity. Brussels: Latomus 96.

Reinsberg, Carola, 1989. Ehe, Hetärentum und Knabenliebe im antiken Griechenland. Munich: CH Beck.

Renehan, Robert F. 1984. " Anacreon fragment 13 Page." *Classical Philology* 79: 28–32

Resinski, Rebecca. 1998. Cosmos and cosmetics: constituting an adorned female body in ancient Greek literature. Diss. University of California, Los Angeles, 1998.

Rhodes, P.J. 1981. *A Commentary on the Aristotelian Athenaion Politeia*, Oxford: Oxford University Press.

----------. 2011. *Alcibiades.* Barnsley: Pen and Sword Military.

Richlin, Amy. 1993. "Not before Homosexuality: The Materiality of the Cinaedus and the Roman Law against Love between Men". *Journal of the History of Sexuality*, 3: 523–573.

----------.1995. "Making Up a Woman: the Face of Roman Gender," in W. Doniger and H. Eilberg-Schwartz, eds., *Off with Her Head: The Denial of Women's Identity in Myth, Religion, and Culture*. Berkeley: University of California Press.

Riess, Werner. 2012. Performing interpersonal violence: court, curse, and comedy in fourth-century BCE Athens. Berlin - New York: de Gruyter.

Riedweg, Christoph. 2005. *Pythagoras: his life, teaching, and influence.* Ithaca (N.Y.): Cornell University Press.

Rizzo, Giulio Emanuele.1932. *Prassitele*. Milan and Rome: Treves-Treccani-Tumminelli.

Riu, Xavier. 2012. "On the reception of Archilochus and of invective poetry in antiquity." In, 249–278.

Robertson, Noel. 1984. "Poseidon's festival at the winter solstice" *CQ* 34: 1–16

Roisman, Joseph. 2005. *The rhetoric of manhood: Masculinity in the attic orators*: Berkeley: University of California Press.

Rosati, G. 1985. *Ovidio: I cosmetici delle donne*. Venice: Marsilio.

Rosenmeyer, Patricia A. 2004. "Girls at play in early Greek poetry." *American Journal of Philology* 125: 163–178.

Rosivach, Vincent J. 1998. When a young man falls in love: the sexual exploitation of women in new comedy. Routledge: London-New York.

----------. 1995. «Solon's brothels.» *LCM* 20 (1–2) : 2–3.

Rossiaud, Jacques. 1988. *Medieval Prostitution*. English translation by Lydia G. Cochrane. New York: Basil Blackwell. (Italian original *La Prostituzione nel medioevo*, published in 1984).

Roth, Martha. 2006. "Marriage, Divorce and the Prostitute in Ancient Mesopotamia". In Faraone – McClure 2006, 21–39.

Ruan, Fang Fu. 2013. *Sex in China: Studies in sexology in Chinese culture*: Springer Science & Business Media.

Ruschenbusch, E. 1966. Solōnos Nomoi: die Fragmente des solonischen Gesetzeswerkes mit einer Text-und Überlieferungsgeschichte. Wiesbaden: F. Steiner.

Saiko, M. 2005. Cura dabit faciem. Kosmetik im Altertum. Literarische, kulturhistorische und medizinische Aspekte. Series: Bochumer Altertumswissenschaftliches Colloquium 66. Trier: Wissenschaftlicher Verlag.

Salmon, J. B. 1984. Wealthy Corinth: a history of the city to 338 BC. Oxford: Clarendon Press.

Salmond, Paul D. 1996. "Sympathy for the devil : Chares and Athenian politics." *Greece and Rome* 43: 43–53.

Sanger, W.W. 1937. *The History of Prostitution*, Ganis and Harris: New York.

Scaife, Allen Ross. 1994. "Ritual and persuasion in the house of Ischomachus." *The Classical Journal* 90: 225–232.

Scafuro, A.C. 1997. The Forensic Stage. *Settling Disputes in Graeco-Roman New Comedy*. Cambridge: Cambridge University Press.

Schaps, David M. 1979. *Economic rights of women in ancient Greece*. Edinburgh: Edinburgh University Press.

----------. 2004. The invention of coinage and the monetization of Ancient Greece. Ann Arbor: University of Michigan Press.

Schenk, Ronald. 1992. The soul of beauty : a psychological investigation of appearance. Lewisburg: Bucknell University Press.

Schepers, M.A. 1926. "De Glycera Menandri amoribus" *Mnemosyne* 54: 258–262.

Schmeling, Gareth. 2005. "Callirhoe: God-like Beauty and the Making of a Celebrity". In Harrison, S., Paschalis, M., Frangoulidis, S. (eds.). *Metaphor and the Ancient Novel*. Groningen: Barkhuis Publishing & Groningen University Library, (*Ancient Narrative Supplementum* 4): 36–49.

----------. 1971. "The Exclusus Amator Motif in Petronius." In Fons Perennis: Saggi critici di Filologia Classica raccolti in onore del Prof. Vittorio D' Agostino. Torino: 333–357.

Schmid, Stephan G. 1999. "Decline or prosperity at Roman Eretria ?: industry, purple dye works, public buildings, and gravestones." *Journal of Roman archaeology* 12:273–293.

Schniebs, Alicia. 2001. "Pacto sexual y pacto social en el « Ars Amatoria » : de la exclusión a la inclusión." In, Caballero de del Sastre – Schniebs, Alicia (2001) (eds.) *La fides en Roma: Aproximaciones*. Buenos Aires: Facultad de Filosofía y Letras, 49–76.

Schnurr-Redford, Christine. 1996. Frauen im klassischen Athen: sozialer Raum und reale Bewegungsfreiheit. Berlin: Akademie Verlag.

Scholl, Andreas. 1994. "POLUTALANTA MNEMEIA : zur literarischen und monumentalen Über-lieferung aufwendiger Grabmäler im spätklassischen Athen." *JDAI* 109 : 239–271.

Scott, Dominic. 2000. "Socrates and Alcibiades in the « Symposium »". *Hermathena* 168 : 25–37

Seaman, Kristen. 2004. "Retrieving the original Aphrodite of Knidos." *RAL* 15: 531–594.

Sedley, David N. 2002. "Diogenes of Oenoanda on Cyrenaic hedonism." *PCPhS* 48: 159–174.

Semenov A. 1935. "Hypereides und Phryne." *Klio* 1935: 271–279.

Serrao, G. 1968. "L'ode di Erotima: Da timida fanciulla a donna pubblica (Anacr. fr. 346, 1 P. = 60 Gent.)." *QUCC* 6: 36–51.

Sfameni Gasparro, Giulia. 1986. *Misteri e culti mistici di Demetra*. (Storia delle religioni, 3.) Rome: 'L'Erma' di Bretschneider.

Shackleton Bailey, David R. 1975. *Homosexuality and the western Christian tradition*. Hamden, CT: Archon Books.

Shapiro, Harvey Alan. 2000. "Leagros and Euphronios : painting pederasty in Athens." In Hubbard (ed.) *Greek love reconsidered*: 12–32.

Shaw, J. Clerk. 2007. *Plato and Epicurus on pleasure, perception and value*. Diss. Washington University in St. Louis.

Shear, L. 1936. "Psimythion," in E. Capps, J. T. Allen, and S. E. Bassett, eds., *Classical Studies Presented to Edward Capps on his Seventieth Birthday*. Princeton: Princeton University Press, 314–17

Shefton B. B. 1960. "Some iconographic remarks on the Tyrannicides." *AJA* 64: 173–179

Sider, David. 1997. *The Epigrams Of Philodemos: Introduction, Text, And Commentary*. New York - Oxford: Oxford University Press.

Simic, Olivera. 2009. "Rethinking 'sexual exploitation' in UN peacekeeping operations". *Women's Studies International Forum* 32.4: 288–295.

Sissa, Giulia. 2008. *Sex and Sensuality in the Ancient World*. (Translated by G. Staunton.) New Haven and London: Yale University Press.

----------. 1999. "Sexual bodybuilding : Aeschines against Timarchus." In, Porter 1999 (ed.): 147–168.

Skinner, M. 2005. *Sexuality in Greek and Roman culture*. Malden, MA: Blackwell.

Slater, William J. 1978. "Artemon and Anacreon. No text without context." *The Phoenix* 32: 185–194.

Smith, Tyler Jo. 2002. "Transvestism or travesty ? : dance, dress, and gender in Greek vase painting." In, In Blundell and Llewellyn-Jones *Women's dress in the ancient Greek world*, 33–53.

Solodow, Joseph B. 1977. "Ovid's Ars Amatoria. The lover as cultural ideal." *Wiener Studien* 11: 106–127.

Sommerstein, A.H - Atherton. C. (eds). 1996. *Education in Greek fiction*. Bari : Levante.

Spatharas, Dimos. 2011. "Kinky stories from the rostrum: storytelling in Apollodorus' Against Neaira". *Ancient Narrative* 9: 99–120.

----------. 2012. "Liaisons Dangereuses: Procopius, Lysias and Apollodorus" *Classical Quarterly* 62: 846–858.

Starr, Chester G. 1978. "An evening with the flute-girls." *La Parola del passato* 33: 401–410.

Stroud, Ronald S. 1979. The axones and kyrbeis of Drakon and Solon, Univ. of California Publ. Class. Stud.; XIX. Berkeley: University of California Press.

Stecchini, L. C. 1955. "Rhodopis." *American Journal of Archaeology* 59: 177–177.

Stephens, Janet. 2008. "Ancient Roman hairdressing : on (hair)pins and needles." *Journal of Roman archaeology* 21: 110–132.

Stephenson, Richard M. 1951. "Conflict and Control Functions of Humor". *American Journal of Sociology* 56: 569–574.

Stewart, Susan. 2007. Cosmetics and perfumes in the Roman world. Stroud: Tempus.

Stowasser, Martin. 1997. "Homosexualität und Bibel: exegetische und Hermeneutische Überlegungen zu einem schwirigen Thema." *NTS* 43: 503–526.

Strauss, Barry S. 1985. "The cultural significance of bribery and embezzlement in Athenian politics. The evidence of the period 403–386 B.C." *The Ancient world* 6: 67–74.

Stumpp, Bettina Eva. 1998. *Prostitution in der römischen Antike*. Berlin: Akademie Verlag.

Swain, Simon. 2007. Seeing the Face, Seeing the Soul. Polemon's Physiognomy from Classical Antiquity to Medieval Islam. Oxford: Oxford University Press.

Tanaka, Toshiyuki. 2002. Japan's comfort women: sexual slavery and prostitution during World War II and the US occupation: Psychology Press.

Taylor, Claire. 2001. "Bribery in Athenian politics. 1, : Accusations, allegations, and slander." *Greece and Rome* 48: 53–66.

----------. 2001b. Taylor, Claire. 2001. "Bribery in Athenian politics. 2, : Ancient reaction and perceptions." *Greece and Rome* 48: 154–172.

Thomas, B. 2002. "Constraints and Contradictions: Whiteness and Femininity in Ancient Greece" in Llewellyn-Jones, L. (ed.): 1–16.

Thompson W. E. 1971. "Leagros". *Athenaeum* 59: 328–335.

Thorp, John. 1992. "The social construction of homosexuality" *Phoenix* 46: 54–65.

Trundle, Matthew F. 1999. "Identity and community among Greek mercenaries in the classical world : 700–322 BCE." *The Ancient History Bulletin* 13: 28–38.

----------. 2004. Greek mercenaries : from the late archaic period to Alexander. London - New York: Routledge.

Tilg, Stefan. 2004. "Die naive Hetäre und die grosse Politik (Xenophon, « Memorabilia » 3, 11)". *MH* 61: 193–206.

Todd, S.C. 2007. *A Commentary on Lysias: Speeches 1–11*. Oxford: Oxford University Press.

----------. 2006. "Some notes on the regulation of sexuality in Athenian Law". In Rupprecht, H. A. (ed.) Symposion 2003, Vorträge zur griechischen und hellenistischen Rechtsgeschichte (Akten der Gesellschaft fur griechische und hellenistische Rechtsgeschichte). Vienna: Austrian Academy of Sciences.

----------. 2010. "The Athenian procedure(s) of *dokimasia*" in Thür, G. (ed) *Symposion 2009. Vorträge zur griechischen und hellenistischen Rechtsgeschichte* (Seggau, 25.-30. August 2009), 73–108, Wien. (with a response by L. Gagliardi).

Toohey, Peter. 1997. "Eros and eloquence : modes of amatory persuasion in Ovid's « Ars amatoria »." In, Dominik, William, J. *Roman Eloquence: Rhetoric in Society and Literature*. New York: Routledge: 198–211.

Trivigno, Franco V. 2009. "The rhetoric of parody in Plato's « Menexenus »." *Ph&Rh* 42: 29–58.

Tronson, Adrian. 1984. "Satyrus the Peripatetic and the Marriages of Philip II." *JHS* 104: 116–126.

Tsantsanoglou, K. 1973. "The memoirs of a lady from Samos". *ZPE* 12: 183–195.

Tsouyopoulos, Nelly. 1994. "Oikos, Oikonomia und die Stellung der Frau in der griechischen Antike bei Xenophon und Aristoteles." In, Richarz Irmintraut (Ed.). 1994. *Haushalten in Geschichte und Gegenwart : Beiträge eines internationalen disziplinübergreifenden Symposions an der Universität Münster vom 6.-8. Oktober 1993*. Göttingen: Vandenhoeck und Ruprecht.41–49.

Tyrrell, Wm. Blake. 2006. *The Suda's life of Sophocles (Sigma 815): Translation and Commentary with Sources*. Electronic Antiquity 9: 1–189 (URL: http://scholar.lib.vt.edu/ejournals/ElAnt/V9N1/TyrrellSuda.pdf).

Upson-Saia, Kristi. 2011. Early Christian dress: gender, virtue, and authority. Routledge studies in ancient history 3. London: Routledge

Urios-Aparisi, Eduardo. 1993. "Anacreon : love and poetry : on 358 PMG, 13 Gent." *QUCC* 44 : 51–70.

Urstad Kristian. 2009. "Pathos, Pleasure and the Ethical Life in Aristippus". *Journal of Ancient Philosophy* 3: 1–22.

----------. 2008. "Aristippus and Freedom in Xenophon's *Memorabilia*" *Praxis* 1: 41–55.

Valtz, Elisabetta. 2000. "Cosmetic containers from Seleucia on the Tigris." *Münstersche Beiträge zur antiken Handelsgeschichte* 19: 59–69.

Van den Toorn, Karen. 1989. "Female prostitution in payment of vows in ancient Israel" *JBL* 108: 193–205.

Van Elslande, Elsa, - Guérineau, Vincent, et al. 2008. "Analysis of ancient Greco–Roman cosmetic materials using laser desorption ionization and electrospray ionization mass spectrometry". *Analytical and Bioanalytical Chemistry* 390:1873–1879.

Vanoyeke, Violaine. 1990. *La prostitution en Grèce et à Rome*. Les Belles Lettres, collection *Realia*. Paris, 1990.

Verdegem, Simon. 2010. Plutarch's « Life of Alcibiades »: story, text and moralism. Leuven: Leuven University Press.

Verner, Miroslav. 2001. *The Pyramids: The Mystery, Culture, and Science of Egypt's Great Monuments* (English translation by S. Randal). New York: Grove press

Vickers, Michael J. 2000. "Alcibiades and Aspasia: notes on the « Hippolytus »". *DHA* 26: 7–17.

Volk, Katharina. 2006. "« Ars amatoria Romana » : Ovid on love as a cultural construct." In, Gibson et al. *The Art of Love: Bimillennial Essays on Ovid's Ars Amatoria and Remedia Amoris*: 235–251.

Von Albrecht, Michael, et al. (eds.) 2002. Περι τοῦ Πυθαγορείου βίου = Pythagoras : Legende, Lehre, Lebensgestaltung. Darmstadt: Wissenschaftliche Buchgesellschaft.

Waldstein, Charles. (ed.). 1902. *The Argive Heraeum*. (2 vols.). The Riverside Press: Boston.

Walker, Andrew. 1992. "Eros and the eye in the Love-letters of Philostratus." *Proceedings of the Cambridge Philological Society* 38: 132–148.

Wallace, R. 1997. "On Not Legislating Sexual Conduct in Fourth-Century Athens.' In Thür, G. - and Vélissaropoulous-Karakostas, J. (eds.), *Symposion 1995: Vorträge zur griechischen und hellenistischen Rechsgeschichte*, 151–66. Cologne.

Walle B, van de. 1934. "La quatrième pyramide de Giseh et la légende de Rhodopis." *L'Antiquité classique*: 303–312.

Walters, Jonathan. 1997. "Soldiers and whores in a pseudo-Quintilian declamation." In, *Accordia Specialist Studies on Italy* 6: 109–114.

Walters, K. R. 1983 "Perikles' Citizenship Law. " *CA* 2: 314–36..

Warren, James. 2009. "Aristotle on Speusippus on Eudoxus on pleasure." *OSAPh* 36: 249–281.

----------. 2001. "Epicurus and the pleasures of the future." *OSAPh* 21: 135–179.

----------. 2011. "Pleasure, Plutarch's « Non posse » and Plato's « Republic »." 61: 278–293.

Watson, Patricia A. 2001. "Parody and subversion in Ovid's « Medicamina faciei femineae »." *Mnemosyne* 54: 457–471.

Weißenberger, M. 1987. *Die Dokimasiereden des Lysias* orr. 16, 25, 26, Frankfurt. (Beiträge zur klassische Philologie 31).

Wertheimer, Molly Meijer (ed.). 1997. *Listening to their voices : the rhetorical activities of historical women.* Columbia : University of South Carolina Press.

Wigodsky, Michael. 1962. "Anacreon and the girl from Lesbos." *Classical Philology* 57: 109–109.

White, F.C. 1989. "Love and Beauty in Plato's Symposium". *JHS* 109: 149–157

Wheatley, Patrick V. 2003. "Lamia and the besieger: an Athenian hetaera and a Macedonian king." In The Macedonians in Athens, 322–229 B.C.: proceedings of an international conference held at the University of Athens, May 24–26, 2001. Ed. Olga Palagia - Stephen V. Tracy. Oakville (Conn.): David Brown Book Co.: 30–36.

Wheeler, Samuel C. 1983. "Megarian paradoxes as Eleatic arguments." *American Philosophical Quarterly* 20: 287–295.

Willard, P. 2001. Secrets of Saffron: The Vagabond Life of the World's Most Seductive Spice. Boston: Beacon Press.

Winkler, John J., 1990. The Constraints of Desire. New York: Routledge.

Wohl, Victoria. 1999. "The eros of Alcibiades." *ClAnt* 18 (2): 349–385.

----------. 2012. "The eye of the beloved : « opsis » and « eros » in Socratic pedagogy." In, Marguerite Johnson - Harold Tarrant (ed.), *Alcibiades and the Socratic Lover-Educator.* London: Bristol Classical Press, 45–60.

Wolpert, Andrew – Kapparis, Konstantinos. 2011. *Legal Speeches of Democratic Athens: Sources for Athenian History.* Indianapolis: Hackett Publishing.

Woodbury, Leonard E. 1979. "Gold hair and grey, or the game of love. Anacreon fr. 13.358 PMG, 13 Gentili." *Transactions of the American Philological Association* 109: 277–287.

Woodhouse, W. J. 1938, Solon the Liberator: A Study of the Agrarian Problem in Attica in the Seventh Century. Oxford University Press: Oxford.

Wright, D. F. 1984. "Homosexuals or Prostitutes? The Meaning of ἀρσενοκοῖται (I Cor., 6, 9; I Tim., 1, 10)", *VChr*, 38: 125–153.

----------. 1987. "Translating ἀρσενοκοῖται (I Cor. 6, 9; I Tim. 1, 10)", *VChr*, 41: 396–398.

Wyke, M. 1994. "Woman in the Mirror: the Rhetoric of Adornment in the Roman World," in Archer, L.J., Fischler, S. and Wyke, M. eds., *Women in Ancient Societies: An Illusion of the Night.* New York : Routledge.

Hashiba, Yuzuru. 1988. "Dokimasia (scrutiny) in Athens. The purpose and its significance for democracy." *JCS* 36: 23–32.

----------. 1997. "« Dokimasia » reconsidered : what was its purpose." *Kodai* 8/9: 1–10.

Zhou, Yiqun. 2010. Festivals, Feasts, and Gender Relations in Ancient China and Greece. Cambridge: Cambridge University Press.

Zimmermann, S. 1996. Making a living from disgrace. The politics of prostitution, female poverty and urban gender codes in Budapest and Vienna. 1860–1920; Budapest.

Zilioli, Ugo. 2012. *The Cyrenaics.* Durham: Acumen.

Zivie-Coche, Christiane. 1972. "Nitocris, Rhodopis et la troisiéme pyramide de Giza." *Bulletin de l'Institut français d'archéologie orientale* 72: 115–138.

Index of Ancient Authors

General Index

DOI 10.1515/9783110557954-011

CPSIA information can be obtained
at www.ICGtesting.com
Printed in the USA
BVHW030153081219
565571BV00005B/225/P

9 783110 658989